40

CHAMPION OF WOMEN
AND THE UNBORN

Facing page: Medal of Horatio R. Storer struck by R. Tait McKenzie in 1913.
Photo from the Storer Family Papers.

CHAMPION OF WOMEN AND THE UNBORN

HORATIO ROBINSON STORER, M.D.

Frederick N. Dyer

Science History Publications, USA

1999

First published in the United States of America
by Science History Publications/USA
a division of Watson Publishing International
Post Office Box 493, Canton, MA 02021

© 1999 Frederick N. Dyer

Library of Congress Cataloging-in-Publication Data

Dyer, Frederick N.
    Champion of women and the unborn : Horatio Robinson Storer, M.D. /
Frederick N. Dyer.
        p.   cm.
    Includes bibliographic references.
    ISBN 0-88135-266-7 (alk. paper)
    1. Storer, Horatio Robinson, 1830-1922.   2. Physicians—United
States—Biography.   3. Abortion—United States—History—19th
century.   4. Pro-life movement—United States—History—19th
century.   I. Title.
R154.S852D94   1999
610′.92—dc21
[b]   99-19740
                                                                        CIP

Manufactured in the U.S.A.

For Jean,

and in memory of two other remarkable women:

my mother, Lillie Minnie Dyer,
and Jean's, Caroline Esther Royer.

CONTENTS

ACKNOWLEDGEMENT

Completion of this project depended upon the assistance of a great many people and institutions. Certainly most important were Richard J. Wolfe, former Curator of Rare Books and Manuscripts at the Francis A. Countway Library of Medicine of the Harvard Medical Library and three of Horatio Storer's great-grandchildren. Mr. Wolfe edited the manuscript and repeatedly located documents such as the original Suffolk District Medical Society Report on Criminal Abortion and the two versions of the Buckingham-Barnard case which would otherwise have never been obtained. Ethel Storer and Robert Treat Paine Storer, Jr. loaned the extensive Storer Family Papers and Edith Overly provided the fine pictures of Horatio and his family.

The kind assistance of curators and reading-room personnel at the Massachusetts Historical Society is also acknowledged. They guided me to the Warner Diaries, Agnes Storer's Autograph Collection, the Dall Papers, and to other key manuscripts which might otherwise have been overlooked. Harvard University Archives personnel, particularly Patrice Donoghue, gave excellent suggestions that enabled documentation of early and late episodes of the Harvard Class of 1850. Several 1850 Class letters are included courtesy of the Harvard University Archives. The Library of Congress' atypical efforts that provided copies of letters to Joseph Toner are appreciated, as is the assistance of personnel at the Office of Smithsonian Archives who provided copies of letters to Spencer F. Baird.

Almost all of Horatio Robinson Storer's medical and scientific publications were located in the fine collections of journals and books at the Countway Library, Cleveland Health Sciences Library, the University of South Carolina, the University of Michigan, Vanderbilt University, Emory University, Auburn University, and the University of Louisville. I am also grateful to the late Dr. Joseph Stanton and to Dr. E. Stewart Taylor who reviewed an initial draft of the book and provided encouragement and excellent suggestions. Fr. Douglas K. Clark kindly helped me with Latin translations. Dr. Mary Beatrice Schulte at the Fordham Press was most helpful with recommendations related to publication of the book. Last, but not least, I thank my wife, Dr. Jean Royer Dyer, who provided moral and financial support and whose suggestions helped make the book publishable.

FOREWORD

> I was at once challenged and given the lie by Dr. Jacob Bigelow, who
> I have always supposed brought me into the world.

So wrote Dr. Horatio Robinson Storer in an autobiographical letter he sent to his son, Dr. Malcolm Storer, in 1901.[1] This reference to Jacob Bigelow's challenge is a good way to introduce Dr. Storer's biography. On the one hand, it indicates that Horatio Storer was proud that his delivery into the world on February 27, 1830 had been at the hands of Boston's most important physician and the statement also shows that Dr. Bigelow's influence on Horatio's life did not stop with delivery, as it surely did not. This particular objection of Dr. Bigelow was to Horatio's 1857 claim that induced abortion was frequent among the married Protestant women of New England. If one were to single out one area of achievement in the life of Horatio Storer, it would be his extensive research, writing, and speaking out on the highly taboo topic of induced abortion.

This challenge in February 1857 reflected just one of several conflicts Horatio had with Dr. Jacob Bigelow, with Jacob's son, Dr. Henry J. Bigelow, and with perhaps a dozen other powerful physicians and surgeons in Boston and elsewhere. Some of these conflicts, like Horatio's advocacy of chloroform as an anaesthetic in the city where "etherization" was discovered and virtually worshipped, are primarily of interest to medical historians. Others, like Horatio's unpopular and derided campaign for women's health, are highly relevant to current medical and social issues. Of most current relevance was Horatio's intense pioneering opposition to induced abortion which, as pointed out by the historian who most extensively documented abortion in America,[2] was to have a major influence on American law and attitudes related to abortion, and also on the frequency of abortion itself. Horatio's effective opposition to abortion was the initial reason for the research that led to this biography and no doubt will account for the bulk of any audience it may receive.

The key role Dr. Storer played in the successful "physicians' crusade against abortion," as it was termed by Mohr, is not well known, but there is even less awareness that Horatio was also a pioneer in the medical examination of women and in the study and rational treatment of women's diseases. When Horatio began medical practice in 1853, most physicians refused to examine the bodies of patients reporting "women's problems." They rarely prescribed any other treatment than medication, solely on the basis of the symptoms the women reported. As a result, women frequently suffered for decades or died from problems that could have been alleviated or cured by simple medical or surgical procedures, if the problems had been properly diagnosed.

However, it was not just Horatio's discussion of the taboo subject of criminal abortion, his pioneering study and practice of yet-to-be-named "gynaecology," and his advocacy of chloroform which were unpopular with many of his physician colleagues. Horatio began practice when almost every physician was a general practitioner who did everything that was medically and surgically called for. Specialization in *anything* was distinctly frowned upon. Specialization in the diseases of women was particularly suspect, however, given the existence of "quacks" who pandered to women's sexual appetites, and Horatio's decision to dedicate himself to women's diseases a few years after he began his own general practice was viewed by many as the ultimate insult to the medical profession. To the credit of Dr. Horatio Storer, he was undeterred by intense opposition from powerful medical quarters in his crusade to legitimize specialization in this controversial area. Horatio, however, grew up in a climate of intellectual controversy and was surrounded with attractive models of men engaged in conflict. These included his father, Dr. David Humphreys Storer; his uncle, Thomas Mayo Brewer; his Edinburgh mentor, Dr. (later Sir) James Young Simpson; and even the former President, John Quincy Adams.

What was the nature of this man who had an uncanny knack for recognizing important but unpopular causes and who was willing to vigorously espouse them, despite the strong opposition of powerful conservative physicians like the Drs. Bigelow who ruled over the profession in Boston and controlled the Harvard Medical School professorship that was Horatio's dearest dream? What were the forces that created this remarkable individual of large and numerous accomplishments and with relatively few actions that can be viewed as inappropriate, by yesterday's or today's standards? The answers to these questions constitute a remarkable story. Thanks to Horatio's prolific pen (nearly 200 published articles, seven books, and hundreds of extant letters) and to the prolific pens of others, such as his daughter, Agnes Storer, and his Harvard classmate and friend, Hermann Jackson Warner, and thanks to the families and institutions who preserved many of the unpublished manuscripts, much of this remarkable story is available to be told. It will often be told using the same words which inspired and motivated the members of Horatio's favorite medical societies and which so angered his enemies that Jacob Bigelow's son apparently purchased and destroyed the plates of Horatio's medical journal to prevent their further reproduction.

CHAPTER 1
EARLY YEARS

My Dear Abby,

Should you like to hear from dear little Horace this morning? He has been perfectly well ever since he left home, & as joyous & happy as a little fellow can be—perfectly contented—has not once expressed the slightest anxiety about home. He talks about Father & Mother but has never cried for them since his father left him, which is certainly very remarkable. We feared he would the first night. He had seen so little of us before. But we never have had any difficulty in getting him to sleep. He has delightful naps in the forenoon, & sleeps like a nabob all night, excepting twice, regularly he asks for water & then falls asleep. He has walked as far as the Dr's with me this morning & delighted them all with his *profound* knowledge of conchology! He returned in fine spirits drank his milk & after playing not a few pranks on the bed & saying many queer things, he has fallen into a peaceful sleep.[1]

Thus began a letter which Horatio's Aunt Margaret Susannah Storer wrote to Horatio's mother as the visiting Horatio napped. Unfortunately, Aunt Margaret did not date her letter, but August or September 1835 is the best guess as to the month it was written. Horatio's sister, Abby Matilda, was born on September 3, 1835 and Aunt Margaret appears to have been taking care of "Horace" during the confinement of his mother. Aunt Margaret mentions the "heat" which fits with late summer and an age of five-and-a-half years fits well with a Horatio who takes morning naps, drinks milk, plays "pranks on his bed" and says "many queer things" before sleeping peacefully. What is more, if Horatio had been six, he might have contributed to Aunt Margaret's letter to his mother. A letter to Horatio from his Grandmother Brewer in January 1836 began "I was very much gratified last evening in receiving your very neat, pretty letter." She continued, "I was quite astonished, for I did not know my dear Horatio could write."[2]

Five years of age, even five-and-one-half, may seem too young for a "*profound* knowledge of conchology," but Horatio's father, David Humphreys Storer, published a translation of the initial chapters of L.C. Kiener's *Species General et Iconographie des Coquilles Vivantes*, a French treatise on shells, in 1837,[3] and conchology no doubt was at maximum significance in the Storer household in 1835. "Conchology," the study of shells and mollusks, was only one of David Humphreys Storer's strong natural history interests. We learn more of these interests from a letter written in June 1892[4] by Horatio's brother providing data for Dr. Samuel H. Scudder's obituary of David Humphreys Storer. Francis Humphreys Storer wrote: "I doubt if [my father's] interest in conchology came in so early as that for minerals and insects but it was long retained. It was the immediate precursor of his study of fishes. I can myself well remember the time that he was still collecting shells, of which he had accumulated no inconsiderable number."

Natural science and natural scientists, particularly his natural-scientist father, were extremely important in Horatio's life. A twenty-year-old Horatio wrote in his first published scientific paper, "In the double capacity of naturalist and son do I dedicate this, my first species, to Dr. D. Humphreys Storer. On the one hand, for his extensive contributions to American Ichthyology; on the other, in slight token of remembrance and gratitude for the very many pleasant hours we have spent together in the study of nature."[5] This was only one of many dedications and tributes that Horatio made to David Humphreys Storer in his publications over the years. They show an immense bonding between Horatio and his father who obviously was more than willing to share with his sons the pleasures of his investigations which contributed greatly to the identification and description of the animals and plants of New England. These nature studies produced rapid development of a young mind and there probably was little exaggeration in proud Aunt Margaret's description of Horatio's "*profound* knowledge of conchology." What is more, had the subject been fish or birds instead of shells, Horatio's audience probably would have been similarly "delighted."

David Humphreys Storer not only motivated his sons Horatio and Frank to the study of natural science, but he did the same for his brother-in-law, Thomas Mayo Brewer, who was fifteen when David Humphreys Storer married Abby Jane Brewer. Francis Humphreys Storer also wrote in 1892 that his father "was interested in birds also, at one time, and he had a large collection of bird's eggs. It was through his example and interest that his young brother-in-law, T. M. Brewer, became a student of oology[6] and ornithology." David Humphreys Storer also was the person who introduced Thomas Mayo Brewer to John James Audubon. Brewer was a newspaper editor and publisher, but, like David Humphreys Storer, is best remembered for his natural science contributions.[7] Audubon dedicated at least one of the bird species which he discovered to his "valued friend," Thomas Mayo Brewer. Although there is no "Storer's Blackbird," David Humphreys Storer and Audubon were close friends, and Audubon, like many other famous natural scientists in the 1830s and 1840s, was a house guest of David Humphreys Storer.

Horatio was to pattern a trip to Labrador in 1849 on the trip which Audubon made to Labrador in 1833, and Horatio's Labrador journal frequently refers to Audubon's descriptions of Labrador. Years later, Horatio indicated that he learned of Audubon's Labrador exploits from Audubon himself. He wrote: "I have mentioned my personal interest in the Labrador. In my early days, now nearly a century ago, it was practically a terra incognita, save to a few scientists, among others my father's intimate friend, the great Audubon, whose tales of Labrador's treasures of bird life fired my boyish ambition to follow in his footsteps. This I did in 1849, as a Harvard student."[8] This opportunity to hear Audubon talk about Labrador may have occurred when Horatio was six years old. Audubon's diary indicates a visit to the Storer home on September 21, 1836. The entry begins: "Called on Dr. Storer and heard that our learned friend Thomas Nuttall had just returned from California. I sent Mr. Brewer after him, and waited with impatience for a sight of the great traveller, whom we admired so much when we were in this fine city."[9] At least one large opportunity thus existed for Horatio to hear Audubon's personal accounts of his exploits in Labrador and probably also the personal accounts of the adventures of Thomas Nuttall.

Another quote from Francis' 1892 letter sheds light on the development of the natural science interest and knowledge of Horatio and his brother, and also on Horatio's exposure to controversies, even battles, between scientists.[10]

It was a great pleasure to my father to have Agassiz call upon him on his arrival in Boston with the remark "My first visit was necessarily to Mr. Lowell who helped to call me hither, but I have come to *you* directly from Mr. Lowell's house." During Agassiz' residence in Boston and East Boston, hardly a day passed but someone of the "military family"—Agassiz, Desor, Pourtalès, Girard, etc.—was to be found in my father's house. They dined and tead with us habitually, and we children grew up among them on as familiar terms as if they had been our own relations. All this was broken up by the row with Desor in which my father acted as Desor's friend, though he finally acquiesced in the verdict of "not proven."

The most famous of these natural-scientist guests at the Storer home on 14 Winter Street in Boston probably was Louis Rodolphe Agassiz who moved to Boston and Harvard from Switzerland in 1846. However, the most able of these natural-scientist guests may have been Dr. Jeffries Wyman who appears to have played a sort of Lou-Gehrig role to the "Babe-Ruth" Agassiz. Both scientists strongly influenced Horatio, imparting, among other things, a state-of-the-science knowledge of embryology. Dr. Wyman also joined Horatio, Horatio's brother Francis, and Captain Nathaniel Atwood of Provincetown on the trip to Labrador in Atwood's thirty-three-ton sloop, *J. Sawyer*.

Schools, of course, also figured in the education of Horatio. The letter from his grandmother praising Horatio's "very neat, pretty letter" also included: "Will you tell Frank, I hope he will go to school and learn to write too, that his grandmother wants a letter from *him*." The school she credited for Horatio's writing skill was the Chauncy-Hall School of Boston. In April 1837, a report card with that date indicates that Horatio's lessons were "good," his deportment "improved," and his absences a remarkable twenty-three.[11] This number may be an error, or the marking period may have been for more than the stated month. However, it is a fact that Horatio's life was marked by frequent illness, and many trips were made during his youth and even later to improve his health, including his Labrador journey. These trips were generally successful, but this may have been because they got Horatio away from Boston allergens and also away from the dangerous medicines of the day which his physician father might have been too willing to administer.

In the summers from 1838 through 1840, Horatio attended a Quaker boarding school in Sandwich, near the north shore of Cape Cod. Much of these summers' correspondence to and from the eight-, nine-, and ten-year-old Horatio has been preserved. It provides fascinating glimpses of a well-adjusted, able youngster and also a great deal of discussion of his health, suggesting that Horatio's physical well-being was a factor in sending him to this school. The following is Horatio's first letter home and an accompanying note from Mrs. Mercy Wing, superintendent of the Quaker school.[12]

Sandwich July 14th 1838

Dear Mother

As I have not wrote to you before I hope you will excuse my not writing sooner. I hope you are all well. I do not wish for any more books at present than I can get down here. As you sent word yesterday for me to send word by Mr. Quincy for whatever I wanted I could not refrain from writing you a letter. I shall send down my journal with my books. I had a very pleasant ride down. and hope you will be able to come down soon. I have not seen Dr. Forsyth yet. and hope father will come down soon. We are about 1 mile from the shore. I do not wish for any thing in particular.

And believe me your
Affectionate and loving boy
Horatio

P.S. I have just come home from the sea shore and as I have leisure I will add a few words. I like the school and scholars very much. I go to the quaker meeting. I have not been home-sick in the least since I came down.

Dear Friend,

I forward by Quincy, H's journal and he will now commence on a single sheet and we will forward them when finished. Your son is very amiable and we all feel much attached to him, and I think we have not a boy in school more happy or contented. ...

Ever Thine   M K Wing

Horatio's "journal" was a printed paragraph per day documenting the rising, studying, playing, eating, and sleeping routine of the Sandwich students. It was the forerunner of at least three journals by Horatio documenting trips abroad and his life at Harvard College and in medical school.

Not all was smooth sailing for Horatio at his regular school, Chauncy-Hall in Boston. This is indicated by the following letter from the principal to Horatio's mother during Horatio's last year before going to the Latin School:[13]

Chauncy Hall
January 6, 1840

Dear Madam,

I reply to your note of Saturday, requesting that Horatio might sit in Miss Healey's room. I would say, that it is an indulgence extended to those boys only, of the upper school, who have evinced such a degree of self-control, as to render it probable that Miss Healey would have no trouble in the way of discipline, in case of their occupying desks in her apartment. And as your son had not yet arrived at that point, I think the experiment would be a dangerous one, because Miss· H. is particularly requested to notify me of the slightest infraction of order in any one enjoying the privilege, that he may be removed.

Without, as I presume, intending any disrespect, he is extremely apt to manifest impatience, when I speak to him, by a jerk on top of the head, or by a sudden protrusion of the lips. Now, this is very common in some *families*, but I scarcely know of another instance in this *school*; and it will be necessary for the habit to be corrected before any special favor can be expected. The faults for which I speak to him, are usually slight, but still infractions of order, which demand some notice, such as idling in his place, drawing the head down towards another boy, and either communicating with him or appearing to do so, etc.—and if I remind him of the fact, he looks as I had *wronged* him.

Very respectfully & truly,
Your friend & servant,
G.F. Thayer

Mrs. Storer,
Winter Street.

Although Horatio's problem at the Chauncy-Hall School sounds like it could really be Mr. Thayer's, Horatio sometimes upset his teachers at his school at Sandwich. Horatio wrote in May 1840, "I think that Uncle Joseph is pretty cross now as he will not let me go to town at all." In the same letter he mentioned, "I have to set 3 or 4 hours if I only miss 2 or 3 words."[14] One problem for Horatio at Sandwich was associated with his classmate, Forman Wilkinson, who was from Syracuse, New York. A letter from Horatio to his mother included an imperfectly crossed out sentence that can be deciphered as, "I do not like Forman Wilkinson because he calls me names."[15]   Abby Jane Brewer Storer no doubt had little trouble deciphering it as well. However, this was temporary, since in less than a month another letter from Horatio reported "I lent the paper from Syracuse to Forman Wilkinson and he seemed pleased with it." Horatio himself must have forgotten that he had crossed out the "calls me names" sentence, since he also wrote, "He and I are good friends again."[16]

Forman and Horatio even shared an interest in birds' eggs as indicated by a May 31, 1840 letter which included, "I go halves in eggs with Forman Wilkinson and Gustavus Fuller. We have got nine so far, they are catbirds, robins, blackbirds, and night-hawks."[17]   "Halves" with three partners is not explained, but it is probable and fitting that Horatio got half and Forman and Gustavus each got quarters, given that the idea for the collection surely originated with the partner whose uncle was the country's foremost oologist.

Plants captured Horatio's interest as well as animals and the grounds must have been spacious at the boarding school in Sandwich, since, in June 1839, Horatio reported somewhat contradictorily, "My garden gets along well there are so many weeds that I cannot tell them from the young plants."[18]   A year later it was "I have a garden with 2 other boys but there is not a great variety of seeds there being Muskmelons, Cucumbers, Radishes, and Sweet-peas."[19] Horatio's aunt, Catherine Brewer, was a key factor in developing the interest in botany which persisted throughout Horatio's life. Horatio noted in another 1840 letter, "I am very sorry that Aunt Katy has gone to Uncle Gardner's as when she was here she fixed the plants and made them grow."[20]

This letter to his Aunt Elizabeth also included, "On one of Mr. Nuttall's lectures he gave me the leaf of a Cape of Good Hope plant, which he said when put into some moist earth and covered with a glass would grow to be a perfect plant. I have tried the experiment and so far it succeeds very well." This ten-year-old who attended lectures on natural science pitched for adults and who returned from one lecture with a gift from the famous botanist, must have been both precocious and outgoing.

The particular visit of Aunt Katy that "fixed the plants and made them grow" apparently had been to take care of the Winter Street household while Horatio's mother recovered from the birth of the last of David Humphreys' and Abby Jane's five children. These children were Horatio (b. 1830), Francis Humphreys (b. 1832), Abby Matilda (b. 1835), Mary Goddard (b. 1837), and Robert Woodbury Storer (b. 1840). The salutations of the young Horatio's letters home often include mushy commands to bestow his affection on each of these siblings. If sibling rivalry existed in this highly affectionate family, it was well disguised.

Horatio's botanical interests undoubtedly were strengthened two years later by the arrival at Harvard of Asa Gray to take the Fisher Professorship of Natural Science. Gray would soon be recognized as the foremost botanist in America. Like Agassiz, Gray was a close friend of Horatio's father and both

Agassiz and Gray were later described by Horatio as his personal tutors. This relationship with Asa Gray continued into medical school. In May 1851, Horatio was "out botanizing" with Asa Gray and again a year later, according to the journal of Horatio's classmate and friend, Hermann Jackson Warner.[21] Horatio's medical school dissertation, not surprisingly, was botanical. It was entitled *Florula Cantabrigiensis medica*.[22]

David Humphreys Storer and his brother-in-law, Thomas Mayo Brewer, were key members of the Boston Society of Natural History which had been founded in 1830 by David Humphreys Storer's preceptor, John Collins Warren. Dr. Jeffries Wyman was the choice of this Society for the Fisher Professorship of Natural Science at Harvard College that went to Asa Gray. However, because a member of the Society made an unauthorized recommendation of Asa Gray, it was Gray instead of Wyman who got the post. A letter from David Humphreys Storer to Wyman,[23] who was studying in Paris, describes the mix-up and does not even attempt to conceal the rage of its author. "I have suffered a mortification I cannot get over," David Humphreys wrote, "it makes me sick of those about me." The twelve-year-old Horatio surely was aware of the controversy, given that it was such an emotional issue for his father and involved the close family friend, Wyman. Expectations that life would include villains, as well as heroes, no doubt were being generated by such incidents in the mind of the young Horatio.

If there was a branch of natural science that could be considered an "underdog" in the 1830s, it was ichthyology, the study of fishes. Dr. David Humphreys Storer carefully examined the "Catalogue of the Marine and Fresh Water Fishes of Massachusetts" prepared by fellow physician, Jerome Van Crowningshield Smith,[24] and concluded that it was greatly lacking. Fish were included that should not have been and others were missing. In a paper read to the Boston Society of Natural History in March 1836, David Humphreys said: "While the other departments of Natural Science among us, are yearly enlisting the aid of zealous and devoted students, who capture, with enthusiasm, the minutest insect—and carefully separate from collected sand, the microscopic shell—and arrange both, with scientific knowledge, Ichthyology, if not despised, is utterly neglected."[25] Two months later, David Humphreys Storer was appointed a Commissioner by the State of Massachusetts to provide a new survey of the state's fishes and reptiles. The resultant "Report on the Fishes of Massachusetts," published in August 1839,[26] received immense acclaim, here and abroad. It was followed a few years later by the less-heralded *A Synopsis of the Fishes of North America*.[27]

It is probable that Horatio learned a pair of lessons from his father's successful ichthyological work. The first is that valid criticism can lead to a worthwhile opportunity to correct the criticized problem. The second, perhaps of more importance, is that one can achieve fame by research and study of a subject that, "if not despised is utterly neglected." The almost universally

despised and more universally neglected branch of natural science that Horatio
would select for himself, slightly more than a decade after his father's success
with fishes, was "diseases of women." Horatio himself, due to a strange set of
circumstances, would refer to "diseases of women" as a branch of "natural
history" in 1854 in his first conversation with Dr. James Young Simpson, the
most famous physician in Scotland, and possibly in all of Great Britain. As will
be seen, this somewhat peculiar reference to the yet unnamed science of
"gynaecology" was well taken by Simpson, and Horatio's year of "intimacy"
with Simpson began that very day. Horatio judged it ever after as the most
important period of his life.

Unlike Horatio's experiences at Sandwich, which were well documented
by the letters to and from his parents, Horatio's years from 1840 to 1846, when
he lived at home and attended the Boston Latin School, are less well represented
by correspondence. The following initial paragraph from a letter from his Uncle
John, a Unitarian minister in Syracuse, provides some key information about
Horatio:[28]

Syracuse 24 Ap[ril]. [18]41

Dear Horatio,

Two months ago you wrote me by Mr. Brewer, I think, your first
letter to me, since your entrance into the Latin School. I was much
gratified to learn that in a class of sixteen you were *seventh* in rank.
You allude to the others being older than yourself. Think not much
of this: If the race is not always to the swift, be assured that distinction & honor are not the prerogative of age alone. All success
depends on your exertion—your *constant, steady, daily efforts*. If the
habit of *patient and careful attention* is once formed, & like all habits
it will be vastly quickened and strengthened by exercise, you will take
the foremost rank in your class. And, the particular book, or study
on which you are engaged, can have your clear and undivided
thought—it will cease to be difficult.

These strict and burdensome admonitions to "*constant, steady, daily efforts*" and
similar pleas for hard work, careful reading, good penmanship, etc., in the rest
of his uncle's long letter might have led some eleven-year-olds to burn such a
letter. Horatio preserved it, and his scholastic and professional prizes, his
dozens of scientific articles, his seven books, and his numerous medical,
surgical, and humanitarian achievements indicate that "the *habit* of *patient and
careful attention*" was indeed formed.

Four letters from Horatio to his parents in the summer of 1844 have been
saved. Horatio was visiting for an extended period at Concord at the home of
Mr. and Mrs. "B." which included a grist mill and saw mill on the Concord
River. These letters further demonstrate Horatio's strong interest in natural
science and natural scientists plus a love of fishing that transcended any

scientific interest in the catch. They show the closeness of the five Storer children and the last of these four letters also indicates a telling wish on the part of his parents, presumably his father, that Horatio become a medical doctor:[29]

Tuesday August 21st 1844

My dear Parents,

I should have written on Sunday but thought I would wait till I got your letter but did not receive it last night and therefore shall not wait any longer. Is Robert any better? How many and what sort of fish did you catch when you went to the rocks. How is Aunt Elizabeth? You say Dr. Reynolds has left the Medical School—what is that for?—and you say that I shall like it when I study medicine—if I dont change my opinion *that* moment is far off, for I dont much think I shall like to be cooped up studying medicine. Tell Frank that the big Pickerel we had in our Fish Pond got away, as the pond overflowed during a heavy rain—and that Mr Coleman killed a bat in one of his rooms and brought it to me—that I should have sent it down to him but it would not keep. There are not many kinds of fish to be taken here but I will send you a catalogue of them as furnished by Mr B. They are the Pickerel, Perch, Brook Trout, Shiner, Bream, Chub sucker, Common Sucker, L. Pulchellus, Horn Pout, Eel, and several kinds of minnows. ... Shad and Alewives also ascend the river to some distance above Lowell but do not come as far as here. When is Aunt Margaret coming? Tell Uncle Thomas that wild ducks and pigeons are plenty here—all sorts of hawks also—and that a fish hawk made us a visit on Monday. Frank must write me a letter—tell Abby and Mary that I have not forgotten them.

Good bye and believe me ever to be
yr loving son
Horatio

The reference to Dr. Reynolds leaving the Medical School was a reference to the Tremont Street Medical School, which was an adjunct to the Harvard Medical School. It was started in 1838 by Dr. Jacob Bigelow, Dr. Oliver Wendell Holmes, Dr. Edward Reynolds, and Horatio's father. The term of the Harvard Medical School was only four months, and the Tremont Street Medical School provided a supplementary course of instruction during the remainder of the year. In a sketch of David Humphreys Storer, Horatio's son, Malcolm Storer, wrote: "As a result of the great success of the Tremont Street School, before long Harvard found itself forced to take it over bodily, and its corps of teachers became highly honored Harvard professors."[30] Horatio placed a somewhat different slant on the Tremont-Harvard connection in the letter he wrote to Malcolm in 1901:[31] "The Tremont St. School, though nominally for quizzing, seems mainly to have been founded for the purpose, by its opposition, in a pseudo-friendly way, of securing the appointment of my father, H.J. Bigelow, J.B.S. Jackson, and Holmes, as professors at Harvard. In this it was successful, and shortly after, the school was closed. Bowditch was similarly taken from the Boylston School, and subsequently Buckingham, when that school came to an end also."

Horatio erred if he was including Dr. Henry J. Bigelow and Dr. J.B.S. Jackson among the founders of the Tremont Street Medical School, since they joined it later. Still it is intriguing that Horatio's father and Oliver Wendell Holmes may have already been angling for their future Harvard professorships in 1838. Jacob Bigelow already was Professor of Materia Medica at the Harvard Medical School and may have helped start the Tremont Street Medical School for the purpose of getting his co-founder friends onto the Harvard medical faculty. Jacob Bigelow may have also seen the Tremont Street Medical School as a way station to the Harvard Medical School for his son. If so, it worked, since Dr. Henry J. Bigelow joined the Tremont Street Medical School in 1845 and moved on to Harvard as Professor of Surgery in 1849.

No letters from or to Horatio have been located for 1845. However, Hermann Jackson Warner, Horatio's classmate at the Latin School, makes note in his diary of his intention to write for a prize on the subject of the ancient Etruscans. The date was October 17, 1845 and he recorded:[32]

> I have determined to try for the one, "A Dissertation upon Etrurian Antiquities." This seems to be the best most fit one for me although I have hardly the remotest expectation of getting it. Yet I am re-solved to try, as I have never written for any prize, yet, but if I do not succeed in obtaining it, I shall be consoled by the reflection that I have left no fair means, for securing it, untried, and I pray to the Almighty God that he will enable me to witness the success of my companions without the least pang of jealousy, but that at the sight of their achievements be stimulated on in the path of true glory.

Horatio was to write for this prize as well, and, several months later, won second place in the English Dissertation category with his dissertation upon Etrurian Antiquities. First place did not go to Hermann, but to Frederic Winsor. Hermann's diary entries show that he frequently lost in his competi-tions with Horatio, and, as will be seen, Hermann was not very successful in avoiding "the least pang of jealousy."

Early in January 1846, Hermann Jackson Warner provided a list of his classmates at the Latin School in his journal, with the order determined by their class standing. Warner himself was seventh. After describing the six ahead of himself, Hermann wrote, "8th Horatio Storer, son of Dr. Storer of this city, not generally in very good health, about 16."[33] This was the first reference of Warner to Storer in the Journal which Warner began in November 1844 and religiously maintained for decades. A Warner entry relating to Horatio for February 9, 1846 read:[34]

> Dixwell [Epes Sargent Dixwell—Head Master of the Latin School] was in a perfect passion today with me because on Sat. he told me to oil the desk I occupied last month in order to efface the scratches &c and today Storer who occupies the desk the present month acquainted him that it had not been done. D. broke out in a perfect fury and said that he did not waste his breath for nothing and that if it was not done soon he would know why, and all such stuff. Well let him bluster, it will not make me any better, though it may give satisfaction to him. Pedagogues must have something to talk about, and this will just suit him. The reason which I did not oil the desk was because I forgot it.

One can jump to conclusions about Storer. He complained to Mr. Dixwell about the scratched desk in the first place and complained again when corrective oiling had not occurred. Warner does not blame Storer in this journal entry, only Headmaster Dixwell. However, Warner *is* critical of Storer in his next journal reference to him on March 24, 1846, although it is another student named Dexter who bears the primary brunt of Warner's wrath:[35] "This afternoon while walking round the Common, Parker, Isaac, met me & asked me if I had written a piece on Genius [for the High School and Latin School student newspaper the *Bedford Street Budget*], with peculiar sneer at that word, said that he had heard something about it from Storer. Now how came this Storer, to know anything of the matter, but if Dexter has let loose the affair, he shall know to his case whom he has injured."

One can conclude from this that Horatio was part of some Latin School network and certainly not a social isolate, as seems to have been much the case with Warner. Horatio's willingness to gossip is confirmed by Warner's next Storer reference on April 7, 1846:[36] "Took a walk with Storer, whom I happened to meet at the head of Winter St., round the Common, got a talking about school, says he entered in 1840, told many anecdotes about his classmates of whom he and they are the only ones remaining. As I am much fatigued I can say no more." This may have been the first time that Warner and Storer walked together. It was only the first of dozens, perhaps hundreds of such walks. However, Gustavus Hay, Storer's roommate for all four years at Harvard, appears to have held the distinction of being the most common walking partner of Storer. Unfortunately, no diary of "Gus" has been located.[37]

Near the end of Horatio's stay at the Latin School and one day after the Exhibition where Horatio's dissertation on the ancient Etrurians was acclaimed and perhaps read, Horatio departed for a vacation in Provincetown, at the very tip of Cape Cod. Upon arrival, he wrote the following letter which reveals much about the young natural scientist:[38]

Provincetown, Sunday afternoon

Dear Father,

I did not sail before 1/2 past 8 last night as the vessel had to wait for a passenger. After we had started a fog came up and we had to anchor in the narrows, inside of Boston light from 10 o'clock all night. I turned in for a little which but the study of entomology did not suit me as well as the study of me did the insects, so I sat up, in a cabin not more than 5 foot high and 10 long, it raining and thundering and lightening all the time. We started again at 1/2 past 5 this morning with a smart breeze S.E. by E. and put her through, every stitch of canvass set. The boat went like a bird and arrived here before 12 this morning, getting in half an hour before the packet which sailed at 1/2 past 11 yesterday morning and beating her by a good 12 hours as she was sailing in the night while we were anchored. I never was out in such rough weather in my life, on deck nearly all the time, and yet was not so sick as I was at Nahant the other day. Captain Attwood [sic] would have me stay with him, and so here I am, duly installed. He was very much pleased with the *'Synopsis.'* I was very much pleased with him and his wife; they have 5 or 6 young children, all as talkative as can be. He has run a smack up to Boston ever since the Torpedo went, going some 14 times or so, he left off last week and now goes out every night except Saturday night catching mackerel in a drag net. On the promontory where he lives, which at high tide is entirely surrounded by water, are some 30 houses whose owners are employed nightly in this business. Hundreds of fish are strewed on the shore among which I notice menhaden, herring, goosefish, smooth and prickly skates, flounders, sculpin, old whiting, and old dogfish; the dogfish begin to come this week. I saw two great shark's heads with smooth teeth, and shall perform the duty of a dentist towards them. There is the skeleton of a whale lying on the beach, which was caught last Wednesday within half a mile of shore, and yielded 50 barrels of oil. Mr. Attwood spoke to me about a species of *Prionotus* [sea robin] which they take in their nets and which I am going to see. There is a Dr. Robinson in the town who is making a collection for some western museum, and upon whom I shall call; he has many skins of fishes, among which is an *entire Bone Shark.* I shall take a description of it. Tell Uncle Thomas that I made a great mistake in not bringing a gun, as the Captain says I can't find one any wheres down here, and there are birds without number, Plover, Loons, Ring necks, Terns and *Gulls,* ... I do not know whether to advise Frank's coming down or not as Mrs. Attwood is rather feeble. I spoke to the Captain about it; he wanted him to come here; I told him of course not; and he says he will inquire of the neighbours and let me know with the price tomorrow; I will write you then; if he comes send a gun. You will probably receive some "vara piscis" by the case of some marketman.

Monday Morning. Mr. Attwood has just got in with 70 or 80 mackerel and as many dog-fish—the first of the season—I must close to send by the smack.

love to all

yr's in a hurry

Horatio

The important friendship of the Storers with Captain Nathaniel Atwood had begun in 1842,[39] and he regularly sent fish specimens to the Boston Society of Natural History. He was to become a Corresponding Member of that Society in November 1847. Horatio, his brother Frank, and Jeffries Wyman would spend July and August of 1849 with the Captain on the voyage to Labrador that combined scientific discovery with the manufacture of cod-liver-oil.

Persons today may assume that the mail was slow in 1846, but two days after Horatio wrote his letter, both he and his parents are writing letters asking where the others' letters were. The "delay" in this case was a terrible storm, the beginnings of which had blown Horatio so swiftly to Provincetown. Horatio's letter[40] was again full of his natural history explorations and primarily those ichthyological. He also again decried the absence of a gun and discussed his newfound skills as a sailor. He signed his letter with the same Latin phrase *Stat nominis umbra* that he had used to anonymously sign his English Dissertation on the Ancient Etrurians.[41] It is the publication of this dissertation (or perhaps some other writing of Horatio's), plus the anxiety over two days of waiting for a letter that are themes of the following letter from his mother and father addressed to "Horatio R Storer, Care of Capt. Nat. E. Atwood, Provincetown, Mass."[42]

Boston Wednesday

My Dear Horatio

If you could hear the enquiries in regard to a letter from you, you might think yourself of some importance in the world and for myself I feel somewhat as you *imagined* I should in regard to Robie—not that I send to the office every 5 minutes, but I should like to, I will confess. How do you enjoy this delightful weather. The wind has been east here *all the time* since you left. We feel afraid you may wish yourself here, if you have such weather. You have appeared in print and I have been congratulated on having *such a son.* What do you think of that!!! Abbot recollected seeing you with a work on Etruria, and your father said you was amusing yrself. He thought afterwards it was the *most* wonderful precocity he ever knew. ...

yr's truly

Abby J. Storer

P.S. Grandfather, grandmother, Aunts Kate and Lizzy were *very much* surprised and delighted. I had to go over in the rain Saturday and tell the news. I think I never saw Grandfather appear more pleased.

Horatio's father added his concerns on the next page of the same letter:

Thursday Morn. My dear boy—Why have you not written us—we feel not a little anxious. Like to have heard yesterday. The weather has been very unpleasant, and we think you must have often wished yourself, at home. But if you do not get sick, I have no doubt that the change will be of service to you. Uncle Thomas goes to Nantucket about the 10th of June, and will take Frank with him. Another letter from Lorana, Robert doing as well as he did.

I was engaged all day yesterday with the M[assachusetts]. M[edical]. S[ociet]y and shall be again today, and have only time [to] say I hope you will enjoy yourself and feel back in health when you return.

yours

most affectionately

David.

With the Latin School behind them, Horatio and most, if not all, of his classmates began preparations to enter Harvard College. However, a natural history trip with his father intervened, since David Humphreys Storer reported at a meeting of the Boston Society of Natural History on August 19, 1846 "that a recent visit to Martha's Vineyard had enabled him to collect numerous ichthyological facts of considerable interest."[43] Horatio's presence is confirmed by Warner's journal entry for the same day: "Met Lang. Williams in Washington St. He says that Storer has been 'down East' with Mr. Dix[well]. who he says is a complete boy down there as regards fishing, bathing &c. It needs a great metamorphosis to make him a boy I should think."[44]

Warner included another comment in this August 19 entry which tells a great deal about Storer, particularly if Langdon Williams was somewhat average in diligence. He wrote, "Williams I find has studied very little. Storer he says has studied 6 hours a day on an average!!" Harvard required entrants to pass an examination, hence the discussion of studying. One suspects that the admonition of his late Uncle John Parker Boyd Storer in 1841 that "All success depends on your exertion, your *constant*, *steady*, *daily efforts*" was not wasted![45] His uncle's death in 1844 may have somehow reinforced in Horatio the work ethic that his uncle had recommended.

CHAPTER 2
HARVARD COLLEGE, RUSSIA AND LABRADOR

> I do hereby promise to abstain from all intoxicating drinks, except in case of sickness, and then only by absolute necessity, whilst I belong to Harvard College.
>
> H.R. Storer[1]

This pledge on a single sheet found among the papers preserved by Horatio's descendants actually indicates *two* commitments, one which was not totally kept and another which surely was. Throughout Horatio's life he showed the strong commitment implied by "whilst I belong to Harvard College." As we will see, Horatio never stopped "belonging" to Harvard.

School commenced in late August and Horatio's roommate at Mrs. Bradford's rooming house was his Latin-School classmate, Gustavus Hay. A letter from the sixteen-year-old Horatio to his fourteen-year-old brother Frank tells much about Harvard, hazing, and Horatio's relative, and perhaps, absolute bravery.[2]

Sunday Sept. 13th [1846]

Dear Frank,

I suppose you would like to hear how College goes on. I have to study very hard, but shall get used to it before long I hope. Gus Hay got back last week after being sick a fortnight. For 9 days we had the hottest weather there has been, and last Tuesday night there was a most tremendous thunder storm, the most severe Father says he ever knew; last night it rained very hard too. I got hazed night before last by a lot of Sophomore's. (I want you never to tell anyone about this because it wouldn't do to have it get round); I thought they might perhaps come so I had chained the blinds too with a strong chain—well, about 7 o'clock along they came, tried the door and found it fastened, and then climbed out and attacked the window, with an axe or crowbar—they smashed off the blinds and then came the tug of war; Gus Hay was very much frightened and I had to do all the defending, but after smashing in the window, they pried up the sash and in they came. There were about 20 of them. Jenks Otis was one of the leaders. Among them were George Shaw, Jos. Crane, Jo. Keyes of Concord, and George Gardner. They seated themselves very coolly and made us do all sort of anticks. Gus Hay did all they told him too right off, but I didn't till I was made too. They staid about 1/2 an hour and then went off. The other night one of the Freshmen had his room burst open, and they tried to get him on to his knees to pray for them but they couldn't; another had assafoetida and gunpowder through his keyhole etc. Yesterday morning there was stuck up on the bulletin board of the College where they put advertisements of different lectures, and meetings of Societies etc., the following notice:

Notice to All Classes.

The following Freshmen are hereby pro-
claimed as trustworthy in no respect, and the
public are cautioned against having anything
to do with them.

Then followed a list of names among whom were Ned. Everett and Lang Williams. I wish that you would write oftener.

Good Bye
Horatio

What is probably the most famous event in Boston medicine occurred on October 16, 1846. This was the first public demonstration of the use of ether as an anaesthetic during surgery. Prior to anaesthesia, surgery was performed in only the most drastic circumstances. Surgeons had to complete major surgery, such as amputation of a leg, as quickly as they could in order to make the time of pain as short as possible and thereby prevent the patient's death from shock. Horatio wrote in later life that he attended many of the operations at the Massachusetts General Hospital while he was still an undergraduate and saw many of the early operations using ether. However, he indicated that he was not present for the first of these operations, at which Dr. John Collins Warren removed a tumor from a man's neck. The ether was administered by W.T.G. Morton, a Boston dentist who was to become involved in long and bitter disputes related to his claim as being the inventor of ether anaesthesia. Hermann Jackson Warner wrote in his journal on December 1, 1846, "Heard today that there is a Doctor or rather Dentist in Boston who by the application of a peculiar kind of gas can so stupefy one as to perform the most painful Dental operations. Dr. Warren also tried it in the amputation of a leg. I think I will try it and have one or two teeth out."[3] One suspects that by December 1, 1846, Horatio had watched an operation in which ether anaesthesia was used and had communicated this information to Warner.

Two entries in Hermann's journal indicate that he regularly accompanied Horatio on Saturday visits to the Boston Athenaeum library where they continued the week's studies at Cambridge. However, it was not "all work and no play" for the studious Horatio and Hermann, given Warner's journal entry on March 30: "Took a long walk with Storer and ["Augustus" crossed out] Gus. Hay this evening which was much enlivened by many grand jokes."[4] A few weeks later, Hermann described a large upcoming event in Storer's life and the delicate health of Horatio who, despite this, was to outlive all of his sixty-six classmates and for his last two-and-one-half years to be the oldest living Harvard graduate. On May 5, near the end of the college year, Hermann recorded that "Storer, I learn, intends to leave College for a few months and to take a voyage to St. Petersburgh accompanied by his younger brother, in order to regain his health if possible wh. I should be inclined to think he never would be able to do. He sails I suppose in one of his uncle's vessels."[5]

The uncle of "his uncle's vessels" was David Humphreys Storer's older brother, Robert Boyd Storer. As a young supercargo and later captain he was involved in trade with Russia and for one year was United States Consul in Archangel, a northern seaport of Russia which in a few years was eclipsed as a port by St. Petersburgh. Robert Boyd Storer abandoned sailing, but remained involved in Boston shipping and also became the Russian Vice Consul. As such, he legalized Horatio's Passport which was issued, not by the State Department of the United States, but by the Commonwealth of Massachusetts. It described Horatio as seventeen years old, five-feet-seven-and-one-fourth inches tall, and having a light complexion, light blue eyes, and light brown hair.[6]

"May 18th, Tuesday—Left home today with Frank for Russia." So begins the journal of Horatio which not only covers their journey to St. Petersburgh and their return to Boston on September 24, but which continued to cover the day-to-day life at Harvard until January 1849, including a summer vacation in the White Mountains in 1848.[7] Horatio and Frank sailed on the Bark *Chusan* under a Captain Jenkins. Horatio made brief entries in his journal for a week, but most dealt with the seasickness that plagued both him and Frank and which prevented entries for nearly three weeks. On June 13, when they had crossed the Atlantic, Horatio resumed: "I have been rather worse off than Frank, having vomited daily the first eighteen days of the voyage and even now the twenty seventh day I do not feel right yet. I have had what the Captain calls the ery-sipelas very badly on my hands for 10 or 12 days, but it is now drying up. Frank has also had a slight eruption. We have both for a fortnight or more been exceedingly troubled with excessive pain in our feet both day and night; it is much worse than chilblains or anything else I ever had, and nothing seems to relieve it."[8] It would seem that Horatio's health could not have been too impaired *prior* to the trip, otherwise he might have succumbed on the voyage itself!

It is not clear whether "Elsineur,"[9] Denmark was the paradise that Horatio and Frank experienced or whether any port after five weeks on a sailing ship would have been thus perceived. In any case, the architecture, people, statues, food, and all else in Elsineur were described by Horatio in the most positive terms. In concluding these descriptions, Horatio wrote:[10]

> I never was so delighted with a place, or enjoyed myself so much in so short a time, as I did at Elsineur, and I came near acceding to Frank's proposition of staying there and not going to St Petersburg. When we reached the Chusan, the Captain said that he felt more homesick if possible at leaving Elsineur than he did at leaving home. I perfectly agreed with him. Here we took a pilot through the sound, and as the wind was fair had to relinquish our project of going to Copenhagen. Beautiful views again till night.

In a few days they reached their destination of St. Petersburgh. Horatio's and Frank's activities consisted of sightseeing, visiting with friends of his Uncle Robert, and exploration of the fine museums and botanical greenhouses. However, problems such as frequent requirements to bribe customs officials and other bureaucrats caused a negative impression of St. Petersburgh. Horatio's first attempt to visit the Hermitage art museum also was frustrated. "I went to the Hermitage in the Imperial Winter Palace," he wrote, "but was not admitted as I had a frock, and not a dress coat on." Horatio's most positive experience in St. Petersburgh appears to have been a steam bath, the complex mechanics of which and their resulting sensations, he described in his journal, along with his regrets that he put off the bath until the end of his visit.[11]

Armed with Russian vegetable seeds for Asa Gray and other Boston botanists, a collection of fossils provided by Charles Cramer for himself, and scientific works from Cramer to be delivered to various scientists at home, Horatio began the trip home with another delightful one-day stop in Elsineur. On the other hand, the long sail back across the ocean was even worse than the trip over. Seasickness again prevented entries in the log. A storm that must have led to terrible doubts about survival appears to have been the main reason for resumption of writing:[12]

> Sept. 1st Yesterday is the first day that has been pleasant enough to do any thing since I wrote last. Since then I have been seasick about every day, and we have had nothing but head winds all the time. At the outset we had a gale of wind and had to go nearly to Iceland having passed within sight of the Faroe Islands. One day last week, the 26th, we had another tremendous gale of wind and hurricane which lasted all night. It blew so hard that we had to lay to all the time and the fore topsail was split to pieces. We shipped several heavy seas and Frank and I had to go down below into the cook's apartments, as it was not safe to remain in our berths. In the course of the night I had a very severe nose bleed whilst trying to vomit. We however escaped, with the exception of a hen and a duck that

were drowned, as the water was often on a level with the top of the
rail on deck. At one time the mate was missing and they were afraid
he was overboard, but he proved to be down below. We are not far
from the Western Islands, much to the southward of our course. Off
the Nare of Norway the Captain caught a mackerel and at another
time a "Prionotus," both of which I have preserved.

Three more weeks were to pass before the following entry marked the return to
Boston:[13]

24th Took a good breeze in the night, and passed Boston Light at an
early hour in the morning. Anchored off Rowe's Wharf about 1/2
past 7 o'clock, and we were soon on shore again; and in a very short
time we were at home once more—at *home*, and I hope never again
to be so long away from it. I found Mother and Robert very low
with the dysentery. I think I never saw Robert look so sick before.
After we had seen Father and Mother, we went to see Uncle John
Brewer and Grandfather. Grandmother at first did not recognize us,
but was glad enough when she did. ... This week has been the session
of the Association of American Geologists and Naturalists. I went
into the meeting, and met, among others, Agassiz, Desor, Pourtalès,
Drs Wyman, Gould, Cabot, Abbott, Messrs Teschemacher, Zadock
Thompson, Ayres and Olmstead.

The first day home and Horatio celebrated with natural science! Perhaps more
correctly, the sociable Horatio celebrated with natural scientists!

A few days after his return from Russia, Horatio visited President Everett
of Harvard to determine his status in class, given the fact that he had left school
for Russia before the end of the school year. The faculty that day voted "that
Storer who had leave of absence in May last, be allowed to rejoin the
Sophomore class."[14] A few days later on October 9, 1847, Horatio reported
in his journal:[15] "Walked in with Gus and Hermann Warner. The Chusan
sailed today for the Azores. I walked over to East Boston with Frank to see
Messrs Agassiz and Desor and got a box of eggs containing 52 spec. which I did
not have before that came in the last steamer from Neufchatel, Switzerland."
"Walked in" means they walked the three-and-one-half miles east from Harvard
in Cambridge to Boston where his family and the families of Gustavus Hay and
Hermann Warner lived. The large shipment of eggs from Switzerland tells us
much about the famous Agassiz's willingness to help the young naturalist and
to please his influential father. Hermann Warner's account of this same
Saturday read:[16]

Walked into town immediately after this last recitation in company

> with classmates Storer and Hay. The former has lately returned from a trip to St. Petersburgh taken to recruit his health wh. I should judge to have been much improved. He is something of a naturalist and has already a very large collection of birds' eggs to which he is constantly receiving addition from every part of the country & also from Europe. From Switzerland he received a few days since a box containing 90 specimens found upon the Alps.

The discrepancy between ninety and fifty-two specimens, probably indicates that thirty-eight of the eggs from Switzerland were already in Horatio's large collection.

Louis Agassiz, after Humboldt, was perhaps the most renowned natural scientist in Europe. He had arrived in Boston in the Fall of 1846 from Neufchatel, Switzerland, where for many years he and his scientific colleagues had made enormous contributions, particularly their elucidation of existing glaciers and confirmation of the then controversial existence of an "Ice Age" when glaciers had covered much of the Northern Hemisphere.[17] Agassiz' lecture tour of America turned into a permanent stay when Agassiz became Professor of Natural History at the new Lawrence Scientific School at Harvard, and for more than a decade he would be the leader of natural history in America.

More that a dozen members of Agassiz' Swiss research team were to eventually follow him to the U.S. One can envision the scientists and technicians who Agassiz temporarily left behind scurrying over the Alps in search of prizes for Horatio's egg collection. Edward Desor and Count Francois Pourtalès were among the earliest to follow their master to America. Although many members of Agassiz' group "dined and tead" "habitually" with the Storers,[18] Desor appears to have been a particular favorite of the family. However, this friendship may have been somewhat muted when Desor's charges against Agassiz in 1848 of plagiarism and immorality were shown to be "totally false" early in 1849. Horatio's father was selected by Desor for the three-member panel that examined Desor's charges and whose "outcome firmly established Agassiz's personal and professional character as entirely blameless and beyond reproach."[19]

The months in the Storer home, where Desor first was no doubt seen as Agassiz' victim in the dispute and then was transformed into at least a semi-culprit, must have produced notable effects on the Storer family. None the less, there are strong indications that the Storers retained suspicions of Agassiz. Frank Storer was to write that his father "finally acquiesced in the verdict of 'not proven.'"[20] Further doubts about Agassiz's "innocence," if not about Desor's "guilt," arise from Warner's journal entry of May 2, 1849, several months after the "verdict." It included: "Storer says that the infamous reports circulated of Agassiz, of his keeping mistresses &c &c when young are no doubt true, his quarrel with Desor gave rise to them."[21] As will be seen, Horatio continued a close association with Desor, inviting him to Harvard Natural History Society meetings as late as April 27, 1849.[22]

Almost every day in the Fall of 1847, Horatio included a "walked with Gus" entry in his journal, and not infrequently this was the only entry for the day. On November 4, Horatio wrote, "Tonight Gus went home sick. Walked to Somerville with Hermann J."[23] It would be weeks before Gus was well enough to return to Harvard and regular walks with Hermann began which Hermann was to refer to frequently and fondly in his journal. Almost every day for the next few weeks, Horatio's journal included mention of a walk with Hermann or a walk with Hermann and Hermann's roommate, Joseph Henry Thayer. The effect of these regular walks with Storer on Hermann was almost immediate. He wrote in his journal on November 15th, "Storer has lent me today two works on Conchology one by Edgar A. Poe and the other by Say. Query: Is this Poe the one who has written those diabolical stories[?] I have resolved to cultivate Conchology as a Science, but good night."[24] "Yes" is the answer to Hermann's query about the Poe who wrote about Conchology.[25] However, Hermann's interest in shells was not to persist and this probably is because on November 23, Gus is back at Harvard and it is Gus and not Hermann who walks with Storer. In fact, no more walks by Horatio with Hermann are noted by either for nearly a year.

On November 19, Horatio wrote in his journal, "Have been chosen into the Nat. Hist Society. Went to its meeting this evening. Chase, the President, read a lecture on Conchology. Frank Emerson, Junior was chosen in."[26] This was the Harvard Natural History Society which was formed in May 1837 by students from the Classes of 1837 and 1838.[27] It had elected David Humphreys Storer an Honorary Member in 1840 when he delivered their annual address,[28] and it may have been inevitable that Horatio would become strongly involved with the Society. Horatio's election to membership as a Sophomore appears to have been a considerable honor, since he was the only Sophomore elected. Horatio's influence on the Society was swift and large. After the next meeting, Horatio wrote in his journal:[29] "17th [December 1847] Spent part of the evening at Dr Plympton's, dancing &c. Then went to a meeting of the Nat. Hist. Society where I read a lecture on Oology, on which a new department was formed of this branch and I was chosen curator. I then presented specimens of our Syngnathus Peckianus Storer, of the S[yngnathus]. typhle Lin[naeus]. from England and [of] the S[yngnathus]. lumbriciformis of Jenyns [types of pipefish] that I procured in the Baltic Sea this summer, and read a paper on them." Horatio was a most diligent worker for the Harvard Natural History Society and would be elected President of the Society in his Senior year.

Horatio's journal continued in 1848 and the following January entries[30] describe the wide range of Horatio's natural history interests, his experiences with hypnotism and ether, his spelling-match competitiveness, and his forgetfulness about the need for a gun at Provincetown.

13th Examined in Latin. Walked in town with Gibbs. Here ends this term. Went this evening with Abby and Mary [Horatio's two sisters] to see a Dr Sunderland perform mesmeric experiments—&c—a most blasphemous humbug. ... Toll 1c. G. paid. Lecture 12 1/2c Father p'd.

15th Finished packing the box of eggs for Switzerland. Etherized a mouse so that I carried it about the house in my hand before it came to. Went to Dr Sunderland's mesmeric lecture again this evening with Captain Atwood and saw various antics performed that I did not see before. Made an agreement to go to Provincetown tomorrow morning. Lecture 12 1/2 c. Father Pd.

Jan. 16 S Early in the morning embarked on board the smack *J. Sawyer* bound for the Cape, and arrived late in the afternoon; was not sea-sick.

17th It was so windy and boisterous that the fishermen were unable to go out today. Looked over Cod's stomachs on the beach and found some Nuculas [small marine bivalve shells]. With the Captain I found some little fish. Examined the entrails of several goose-fish.

20th Rough again today. Went to a spelling match at the school room tonight with the Captain and got chose in on one of the sides. Beat them all. Got a specimen of Motella candacuta [fish of some type] from Mr Herman Smith.

25th Skeletonized the head of a Snuffer, Phoecoena globiceps, and some sea gulls. Came home in the afternoon in a schooner, whose skipper I came home with when down here before, one Capt. Smith. Started about 4 o'clock P.M; got home about 1 at night. Saw a hump backed whale. I have had a very pleasant time all things considered; it is true the weather was so boisterous that I was unable to go out fishing with Capt. Atwood which was the chief object of my expedition, and that I was sorry that I had not carried a gun with me as I found shore birds and sea fowl so plenty. Fare 75c.

Although the Mexican War had ended February 2, 1848 with the signing of the Peace treaty at Guadalupe Hidalgo, news apparently had not reached Horatio by March 2 when his journal reflected his views (and Daniel Webster's and John Quincy Adams' views) on that war.[31] Nine days later, Horatio included in his journal, "I handed in a theme this morning; 'Give instances of weakness in the Characters of Great Men.' Took John Hunter for my subject."[32] John Hunter (1728-1793) was a remarkable English surgeon and scientist whose "investigation extended over every branch of natural history, particularly pathology, comparative anatomy, and physiology" who created a huge personal museum with some 10,000 specimens.[33] This was maintained after his death and was visited by Dr. Jeffries Wyman in 1842 and probably by Horatio in 1854. Horatio's awareness of and interest in Hunter, may indicate that the eighteen-year-old Horatio had some similar life plan in mind which would combine medicine and natural history. Decades later in a presentation on Edward Jenner, of smallpox vaccination fame, Horatio discussed the close relationship that Jenner had with John Hunter and how this led to Jenner's important skills of dissection and observation.[34] In that article, Horatio also pointed out the strong similarities between Hunter and Agassiz and the implication was that Hunter's beneficial effect on Jenner had a parallel in Agassiz' beneficial effect on Horatio Storer.

This Agassiz-Storer, mentor-student relationship is well illustrated by a journal entry on the following day:[35] "S[unday] 12th [March] Went over to East Boston in the morning to see Agassiz and Desor. Examined the development of the eggs of star-fishes through the microscope and attended divine service in his house, a Swiss clergyman officiating. Went to Church in the afternoon and heard Dr Francis preach." Embryology was a major interest of Agassiz and Jeffries Wyman and the lessons of the early development of individual animals were well learned by Horatio by this discovery process. The entry also shows that Agassiz and Desor had apparently not had their major split by March 12, 1848. It also shows that Horatio spent most of that Sunday, as he did almost every Sunday, at church. Like many of Boston's elite, Horatio's family was Unitarian.

Another major event of 1848 was the death of John Quincy Adams, sixth president from 1825 to 1829 and after that a member of Congress for several terms. The Storer family had a number of ties to John Quincy Adams. In 1829, David Humphreys was involved in keeping quiet an illicit affair of Adams' oldest son, George Washington Adams.[36] Earlier, Horatio's Uncle Bellamy Storer of Cincinnati had been actively involved in the election of Adams to the Presidency, and David Humphreys Storer no doubt was a supporter, as well, given the strong Whig Party affiliation of ten-year-old Horatio and which surely came from Whig parents, uncles, etc.[37] Adams had been treated harshly during his Presidency by Congressmen and he used the opportunity during his subsequent terms in Congress to get back at these persecutors. One sketch indicated:[38]

he soon grew to be designated "The old man eloquent." Although not naturally an orator, doubtless his severe experience had given him a certain force which enabled him to command an audience. Moreover, he had possibly, and certainly not without reason, become embittered against the few who had persistently stung him like so many gnats, and, now, finding himself in a position to retort upon them he became merciless.

The model of the pugnacious Adams probably was not lost on David Humphreys Storer or on Horatio, both of whom were involved in numerous controversies.

The Boston funeral of John Quincy Adams took place nearly two weeks after his death. Horatio noted in his journal for March 10, 1848: "Funeral procession of John Quincy Adams today but I could not go in town on account of a recitation." On April 15, Horatio wrote: "Mr Everett delivered his Eulogy on John Quincy Adams. I walked in the procession and after engaging in a slight row, in which all the students took part at the doors of Faneuil Hall, I made out to get in and hear him." The *Boston Atlas* the next day reported no "row" and in fact reported: "Although the crowd of spectators was very great, yet so admirably were the arrangements of the Police Department executed, that there was not the least disturbance or disorder to be seen or heard at any time, every one seeming desirous of paying due respect to the constituted authorities and properly observing the solemnities of the occasion." Unlike a month earlier, no recitation prevented Horatio from attending this tribute to the former President, nor did angry words, nor, despite the *Atlas* report, angry deeds.[39] Everett's inspiring eulogy surely did not provide Horatio his first acquaintance with John Quincy Adams' diligence and courage, but Horatio also was devoted to the eulogizer,[40] and this must have doubly imprinted these attributes of Adams as personal ideals for Horatio.

Horatio's journal entry for April 22, 1848 included: "22d I declaimed this morning from Henry V. Act IV. Scene III."[41] It is not clear whether this Shakespeare passage was chosen by Horatio or by one of his teachers. In any case, the passage's glorification of honor and fame ("But if it be a sin to covet honor,/I am the most offending soul alive.") no doubt vibrated with and reinforced Horatio's own "high aspirations," as he was to describe his own goals as a Harvard college youth when writing the obituary of his last surviving classmate, Thomas Jefferson Coolidge, in 1921 (discussed in Chapter 23). Shortly afterwards, the following entry was made that may have been Horatio's first experience with chloroform, the anaesthetic that was to become so highly significant in his own medical career: "31st Last day of Spring. Walked with Gus. Went with Gibbs to see him have a tooth out under the influence of chloroform administered by Dr Wyman [probably Jeffries' brother, Morrill]. It affected him rather severely and he did not get over it for some time."[42]

The anesthetic properties of chloroform had been discovered by James Young Simpson only seven months earlier. Simpson had administered ether during childbirth on January 19, 1847, this being the first use of anesthesia in obstetrics. However, Simpson was not totally satisfied with ether and on November 4, 1847, he and his assistants, George Keith and Matthews Duncan, inhaled chloroform and became intoxicated, then unconscious. They all survived this dangerous experiment confirming chloroform's anesthetic power, and

Simpson used the new anesthetic in his subsequent obstetric cases with good results. The use of anesthesia of any kind during childbirth upset some of Simpson's British colleagues who believed for various reasons that women were supposed to suffer during childbirth. However, when Queen Victoria used chloroform during the births of her later children, Simpson was largely freed from such criticism in his own country.[43] Boston physicians' criticism of Simpson was much more prolonged. Simpson published articles in medical journals and in the *Encyclopedia Britannica*[44] claiming that chloroform was a superior anesthetic to ether and this did not sit well with Boston's medical men who worshipped the anesthetic that was "discovered" in their city.

At the last meeting of the Harvard Natural History Society held that term, Horatio was elected Secretary and Treasurer and reelected Curator of Ichthyology and Herpetology. Horatio provided his curator's report and donated a specimen of Ranatra (a long legged bug from Fresh Pond) to the Society.[45] A day later, Warner announced an upcoming trip to the White Mountains by Horatio and indicated that Horatio asked Warner to accompany him.[46] However, the only companion of Horatio for the trip was Gus Hay. Entries in Horatio's journal between July 17 and August 17[47] describe several days of hiking from Centre Harbor, New Hampshire to the White Mountains, and describe sleeping at farmers' homes, having "country fare and good hard cider," and successfully fishing for trout along the way.

Their ascent of Mt. Washington was on horseback. Although the day was clear, previous rains had generated mud "up to the saddle-girths." Horatio also reported the "faithful creatures bore us in safety up rocky ascents that I should not have believed any creature could surmount." Horatio was greatly moved by the ascent. He recorded:

> The views had been growing grander and more sublime as we advanced and when we at last stood on the top of the highest peak east of the Rocky Mts the effects on my mind were not to be described. We were above everything—we could see the far ocean and the great Mts. seemed but little hills—The rivers dwindled into insignificance—and Winnipissegee, that vast inland sea, lay stretched below like a mill pond—not a sound was to be heard and we were in truth alone—far above the limits of vegetation and surrounded only by mighty fragments of black and storm beaten rock. ... I had been nearer heaven than I ever had before and been struck by the majesty and power of him who holdeth the mountains in the hollow of his hand.

Natural history was not neglected on the trip. "I have ... secured several species of snails," Horatio wrote to his father, "you may judge how hard pushed I have been from this." Other items were "several species of small fish, new to *me*, for you, and a beautiful snake for *'our'* society—all of which are contained within the precincts of a lemon syrup bottle."[48]

Vacation over, Horatio returned to Harvard. One of the few indications that Horatio violated his 1846 "promise to abstain from all intoxicating drinks, except in case of sickness," is reported in his journal for November 1.[49]

> Meeting of the Rumford [Chemical] Society. Met in our room, decided on the name, chose in members &c. After which adjourned to the Oyster room, where we celebrated our birth night over draught ale, "stewed" and "done in crumbs", at Carr's expense—after cracking jokes for an hour or so and seeing which could tell the greatest story we marched off as we came in single file to the sound of Fearn's flute. Studied oology a little while.

The oology study apparently *followed* the spree, and this is strong testament to Horatio's love of natural science.

The next day's entry included: "Handed in a Theme, 'Of leaving Memoirs or Correspondence to be published after perhaps many years after the writer's death.'"[50] The topic of the theme was not selected by Horatio, but by his teacher, Edward Tyrrell Channing, Boylston Professor of Rhetoric and Oratory at Harvard from 1819-1851. Hermann wrote a theme on the identical topic and probably every other member of the Class of 1850 did too. No copy of Horatio's version has survived, but it is possible that exposition and reflection on this topic was a factor in Horatio's preservation of much correspondence, several journals, and some of his other themes.

Although only a Junior, Horatio probably was the dominant force at the Harvard Natural History Society. Horatio's journal entry for October 20 included:[51]

> Meeting of the H.N.H. Society. As the President was absent, I as V.P. presided. I carried with me Lieut. Davis and Mr Desor, who gave us a beautiful lecture on the distribution of marine animal-life, and presented the Soc. with specimens to illustrate his remarks. He was followed by Dr Wyman who deposited some human crania and exhibited drawings of a new "distoma" [parasitic nematode worm with two suckers] from the peritoneum of a frog—also ova of a frog to exhibit the development. Next came Oliver, Senior, who gave a new theory of the laws and formation of crystals. I handed over the rest of Cooke's fossils and exhibited a specimen of Gasterosteus quadracus [stickleback] with 5 dorsal spines. After the election of members we adjourned.

Horatio's major role in the Society also is reflected in his diary entry for

November 3 where he "Proposed Desor and Davis as Honorary Members and had them elected,"[52] and in the entry in the Records of the Curator of Ornithology (not Horatio) for the November 17 meeting which reads: "In place of Mr. Howland, the regular lecturer for the evening, Mr. Storer delivered an interesting lecturer [sic] on the Dodo."[53] It also is reflected in Horatio's journal entry describing the meeting of December 8 where Horatio indicated he "gave a lecture on the comparative anatomy of Reptiles, without notes, as Herpetological Curator."[54]

The following December entries in Horatio's journal mentioned attendance at both Agassiz' and Desor's lectures during the height of their feud and described other "walked-in" activities of Horatio:[55]

12th Walked in and heard Agassiz' first lecture before the Lowell Institute on Comparative Embryology. He intends this course shall disclose a new and natural system of the Animal Kingdom.

13th Walked in alone and went with Mother and Mary Johnson to Faneuil Hall—intending to be present at what the newspapers called a promenade concert, but which, to my slight disappointment proved a second rate dancing party. Were rather amused, nevertheless. Walked out alone. Toll 2c. Tickets 75c.

14th Walked in alone and went to Mr Desor's lecture with Maria and Harriet Sayles. Walked out alone. Toll 2c.

15th Walked in with Gus. and went to Agassiz' lecture. Described with Father a new species of Hake. Toll 2c.

16th Walked in with Gus. Went down to the wharf and saw Capt. Jenkins [of the *Chusan*]. Called on Aunt Sarah and Louisa Merriam. Went with Mother and Aunt Margaret to the concert of the Philharmonic Society. Madam Anna Bishop sung; Richard Hoffman played on the piano; Josef Gung'l and his newly arrived German band did finely; and Herr Siede, one of them, did superfinely with his flute. Toll 1c. Concert 50c.

S[unday] 17th Mr Frothingham preached an anti-California-Gold sermon and a dismal man preached a "train-up-your-child-in-the-way-he-should-go" sermon. Walked out with Gus. Called on Agassiz. Toll 1c.

Horatio's undergraduate journal ends on January 19, 1849 without explanation and with dozens of blank pages remaining in the book. *Warner's* journal continued and it increasingly referred to Horatio. The following three entries are noteworthy:

Tuesday 13th [March] Had a long talk with Storer after supper on the progressive development of animals. He thinks man is the

Head of the animal creation, but sinks so insensibly into the class of brute that it is impossible to draw line of demarcation. Some of the New Hollanders approach the ouran-outang so nearly that one can hardly discern the difference.[56]

Mon 9th [April] Took another long walk with Storer after supper. We talked of various things, but more particularly of the superiority of the intellect of man above that of women and of the original nature of all intellect.[57]

Sat 14th [April] Boston. Storer brought me a blank book he had procured for the Treasurer of the Rum. Chem. Soc. this afternoon to copy in the account of my financial reign. I left them in perfect confusion as I was disgusted with the whole affair, but when appointed my successor he very good naturedly cleared them all up, but as my name's to be signed to them its a pity he wont get the credit of the work. *However, if it'll do him any good, I will give to him here the whole praise of disentangling them.*[58]

We learn of Horatio's plans for a Labrador trip and of his election as President of the Harvard Natural History Society from the following entries in Warner's journal:

> Fri. 25th [May] Took an extensive walk with Storer after supper, ... He proposes getting a company of *ten*, gentlemen of Boston, as Dr. Cabot the companion of Stephens in his travels in Yucatan, &c and chartering a vessel ... to carry us direct to the Moravian settlements of Labrador ... I hope 'twill succeed.[59]
>
> Sat 16th [June] Storer came rushing down to our house this afternoon—and wanted me to go with him to Labrador—as there's a prospect of his being able to charter a vessel—provided he can get a company of six or more. ... I've determined to go—if everything favors. Some day I'll tell why.[60]
>
> Fri. 29th [June] Played a game at chess with Storer after supper nearly two hours long. I lost my queen by negligence—got disgusted and let him beat. At meeting of the Nat. His. Soc. nothing done but choose members and elect officers. Storer, President. He deserves it.[61]
>
> Mon 2nd [July] Storer's sick, and is going to Labrador I understand on Fri. night. Cutting examinations &c. I'm sorry he leaves before the end of the term, for I like his company. The walks we used to take together were some of the most delightful I ever enjoyed. But [crossed out] The *past* is gone, but the *influences* of the past remain forever to animate and console.[62]

The weeks of planning of the Labrador trip make the following letter from

Horatio's father to the Harvard Corporation appear a little disingenuous. However, Horatio's illness may have been essential for the trip to occur.[63]

Dear Sir

I have visited Cambridge twice during the week past to speak to you of my son. After flagging for several weeks, he came home on the last day of June completely prostrated, and kept his bed for a day or two, after that he was able to move about a little, but had a severe cough with pain in his chest, and a recurrence of hemorrhage from the nose which continued nearly a day in spite of all remedies which were used. I felt exceedingly anxious respecting him, and was desirous of advising each of you upon the subject of a short voyage—he having been so much benefitted by a voyage to Europe a year and a half since. Not being able to see you, I put him on board a fishing smack, with his brother, and he sailed on Saturday night last for Labrador—to be absent from six to eight weeks.

He had prepared himself for all his examinations and was ready to meet them—but I was unwilling that he should make the effort. I trust a few weeks will restore his health, and enable him to return to duties at Cambridge. Under the urgent necessity which has compelled him to leave his post, I trust he will [be] excused by his Faculty and allowed to retain his rank in his Class.

Most respectfully
your obt svt
D. Humphreys Storer

"We commenced our voyage at about 1/2 past 10 o'clock on Saturday evening 7 July 1849—bound for Labrador."[64] So began Horatio's hundred-page journal of his Labrador trip. He continued:

This is a voyage that I had long wished to undertake—the descriptions by Audubon of the hardships to be borne and the perils perhaps to be encountered—the strange scenery, both grand and desolate—and the treasures awaiting the naturalist of every kind—all these had combined to excite my curiosity, but I had hitherto looked upon such a voyage as to me impossible. To say nothing of the expense thereof. It would consume under ordinary circumstances altogether too much time. I had been to Russia—had lost six months of my College course and ought to be preparing for the world and life, for very soon I should be called upon to work for, to take care of myself. So I had tried to forget Labrador.

Forgetting Labrador obviously wasn't a very important goal, since Horatio listed the various alternatives he explored over several weeks to make the trip which finally culminated in the journey with Captain Atwood on the *J. Sawyer*. The following paragraphs from Atwood's autobiography give his description of the Labrador trip:[65]

> During the spring of 1849 I was in Boston selling codfish. We were accustomed to take our livers to Boston, and we sold them for 25 cents a bucket. Some parties came and offered us 37 cents. I made inquiry and found they wanted them for medicine, but I thought it was pretty coarse medicine. I was acquainted with doctors, physicians, and chemists, and I inquired about cod-liver oil, and they told me that it had been used in France for some years and was getting more common every day. Afterward I made a little oil and they said at Boston it was just as good as they ever saw.
>
> I conceived the idea of going to Labrador to get cod livers, and Prof. Jeffries Wyman, Horatio R. Storer, and Frank H. Storer went with me. We started in pursuit of objects of natural history and the manufacture of medicinal cod-liver oil. It was late in the season, and most of the cod-fishing was over. I carried two dories. I got 300 gallons of cod-liver oil. We then returned home, and resorted to setting mackerel nets through the fall. My wife died while I was absent that voyage. This was the commencement of my manufacture of cod-liver oil, and I have been engaged in it ever since.

Atwood's sloop was small and there was not room for many passengers. Horatio's brother Frank convinced his parents that he should go, and, at the last minute, Dr. Jeffries Wyman decided to make the trip. Another significant passenger was Tiger, the Storers' Labrador retriever.[66] The party first sailed from Boston to Provincetown, where the Captain made last minute preparations and concluded that his sick wife and children were not so sick that he could not leave them. They then headed north to Nova Scotia, through the Gut of Canso, past the Magdalen Islands, visited numerous islands on the Labrador coast, and finally on July 25th "arrived at Bras d'Or—from which town I suppose Labrador took its name." Birds, fish, beached whales, seals, shellfish, plants, all were fair game for the three natural history collectors as they explored the waters, islands, and mainland of Labrador. As will be seen, Horatio would obtain previously unidentified species of fish and would extend the known range northward of more than a dozen others.

One interesting feature of the trip was observation of the "eggers," motley ships and their motley crews who collected thousands of eggs from the numerous sea birds that inhabited the many islands along the Labrador coast. These they sold as food in various cities in Canada. The party on the *J. Sawyer* collected them as well, and attested to their tastiness. They also observed the huge cod-processing operations by the summer inhabitants of villages such as

Bras d'Or and Horatio was amazed at the hard work of the women who processed their husbands' catch. Horatio wrote:

> The American women, grumble as they may, lead a dreadful easy life in comparison with these Newfound^ld ladies—and yet these fish wives when condoled with on their hard lot laugh at it and consider it as no more than their duty to do as much as the men in as much as they were taken as helpmates and are besides allowed to be the better half—so they work all summer long and then go home and there forget that they ever saw a codfish.

Horatio found several occasions to rig up primitive fish poles and lines and catch the most magnificent trout of his life. These typically would be broiled immediately over a camp fire providing more pleasure for the fisherman and for Frank and Dr. Wyman as well. Other incidents during the trip included a fire that the Captain set which threatened a Newfoundland village, near drownings in the sloop and its dories, and injuries and epidemics among the local population for which Dr. Wyman (out-of-practice and without medical instruments or medicines) could provide only small aid. There also were hob-nobs with residents, including the Mr. Jones whom Audubon had visited in 1833, with the crews and passengers of other sailing vessels, with the Lord Bishop of the region, with Indians, and with the ghosts of an old French graveyard. It certainly was the greatest adventure of Horatio's nineteen years and probably of his entire life. The anticipated six to eight weeks became more than two months, due largely to an absence of wind on the return trip. The Captain discovered on his return to Provincetown that he was not only a widower but had also lost his oldest son and his in-laws to an epidemic of dysentery. Fortunately, no such bad news greeted the Storers or Dr. Wyman who was most anxious to again greet his fiance.

The last entries in Horatio's Labrador journal deal with events after the trip and preparations for the next year at Harvard. The major event was the death and funeral of Dr. Horatio Robinson, an Andover physician who had been a close friend of David Humphreys Storer.[67] Horatio described his sadness at the loss of the "kind friend" whom he had loved. He also described his reluctance to approach "another years hard work with its attending headaches, dyspepsia and blues," and bemoaned his uncertainties about choice of career, noting that he was "almost as much in doubt as ever—inclination versus conscience, ambition versus the stillness of private life, which to choose I know not."

In this struggle over the decision about his own future profession, he was fortunate in that his father and uncles provided models that fairly well covered the range of professions of that period. His father, of course, was a physician. His late Uncle John Parker Boyd Storer had been a minister. Uncle Robert Boyd Storer was a successful businessman in Boston. His Uncles, Woodbury and Bellamy Storer, rounded out the professions, practicing law in Portland, Maine and in Cincinnati, Ohio, respectively. Horatio's quandary about his future profession and the drawbacks of medicine appear to have been major themes of a letter to his Uncle Woodbury. We only have his uncle's reply from Portland, dated December 20, 1849, from which the following passages have been excerpted:

> From your remarks as to the profession you ought to select, I feel quite clear (& your Aunt concurs in opinion with me.) that the medical profession is the one you seem to be peculiarly fitted for.
>
> I think you may be very useful in that profession, it is one fitted I think to your taste & sympathies & one in which I trust you will excel. Your father's position will tend to introduce you very speedily into practice, & the attainments you have already made in the theory & practice of medicine, will be of great service to you in your preparatory course of study.
>
> The *objections* you hint at, to the profession, have some weight, to be sure; but what situation in life is free from trials? Where is there to be found perfect rest?[68]

No journal by Horatio has been found that continues from the September remarks at the end of his Labrador journal. However, Hermann's included many references to Horatio after Horatio's return from Labrador. The following excerpts give us insight into both men and their friendship:

> Fri 14th A meeting of the Nat. His. Soc. came off this eve[g] ... Storer gave quite a description of some parts of his late tour—of the birds who throng the Gannet rocks in such numbers that thousands or thousands of dozens of eggs are annually taken from them, of the various kinds of eggs &c &c besides several pleasing anecdotes.[69]
>
> Fri. 28th Have been to a meeting of the Nat. His. this eve[g]. A set of snobs there pretend to regulate everything. Storer's the only decent man among 'em. He gave rather a long lecture tonight on herpetology. 'Twas slightly dull, however.[70]

Two weeks later, Horatio's classmate, Charles Hale, wrote his brother, Edward Everett Hale, that he was going to compete for the Bowdoin Prize, noting that one dissertation topic was the "History and Resources of the Mississippi Valley."[71] Horatio and Hermann Jackson Warner also were to enter this competition. Hales' disappointment at not winning may have gone unrecorded. As will be seen, Hermann's did not.

Horatio continued to be a major subject in Hermann's "useless logbook" as is indicated by the following entries which help pinpoint the "bombastic"

Horatio's decision to study medicine, refer to hospital operations that Horatio was observing prior to medical school, describe Horatio's Phi Beta Kappa selection, and document his winning of the Bowdoin Prize:

Fri 14th [December] Have been all the eve^g at a meeting of the Nat. His. Soc. They're getting to be interesting. Storer has given them an impulse which have literally made them attractive.[72]

Wed. 9th [January] ... went to a meeting of the Rum. Chem. Soc. with Storer—that present inseparable—a good fellow, though—some wit, considerable *bombast*, built on sound sense however and various information—a combination of qualities which is all a man want to enable him to pass creditably through the world...[73]

Sat 26th [January] ... at 1/4 to 11 called on Storer to go with him to the Hospital, which he's been pressing me to do these last two or three months—met Thayer & Hay there, a worthy posse of us, certainly—but d__n such snobs—The Operating Room of the Hospital is in one of the domes—semicircularly surrounded with raised seats for the Medical Students. Dr. Henry J. Bigelow performed most of the operations—splendid surgeon—but unfeeling—they extracted a tumor from a baby's face, a polypus from a d__d pretty woman's nose, a bone from a boy's arm & part of the same from a man's. What a situation for a woman—encompassed with men, &c &c verily I felt compassion for her. Stood the whole scene like a hero—no quemish fits came over *me*—it seemed as though I'd been inured to it for years. Walked along home with these snobs.[74]

Mon 18th [February] [Storer] came at 9 and we discussed a variety of things, among others a trip to Cincinnati next summer—seems inclined to go—he'd make a good traveling companion—though his knowledge of the world practically, experiencially as one might say, is not remarkably extensive.[75]

Thurs 21st [February] Loafed around the Common twice with Storer—met Miss Adams the pretty girl who sits before us in Church—she looked remarkably grave however ... Storer's a deuced good fellow—yet the rascal thinks of going to Labrador in May—leaving me destitute for my glorious Western Journey...[76]

Sat 2nd [March] ... Went into the operating room of the Hospital with Storer ... first a man had a finger amputated—the ether affected him singularly—he squirmed about and yelled so vehemently that all my philosophy was put to the test ... presently in came a good looking man with his testicles out of order—a beam had struck him near the parts some time since and completely disorganized one of them—which had grown to such an inconvenient size that no course was left but to extract it .. old Dr Warren—a cadaverous, lean, bony, skeleton like object—manipulated dexterously upon it—& semi-castrated the poor man—next came a woman with a cancer in the breast ... the knife was applied the blood streamed—and the woman woke with one of her nipples & half of her breast gone—a singular operation wound up the programme—an old fellow, 64 yrs of age, had dislocated his left shoulder—the only way in which it could be restored was by the application of mechanical force—an infernal set of pulleys was contrived and put into operation—but the poor cus nearly died under the torture—his face became ghastly white—his heart stopped its beatings—& he tumbled back stiff—apparently dead, but means were found to revive him ... such hellish sport was too much for my nerves ... rushed out into the open air in a sort of agony...[77]

Friday April 12th 1850 ... Storer's decided on Medicine ... of course... the very air of his house is impregnated with obstetrics & Diseases of Women...[78]

Wednesday May 1st Have just returned from a meeting of the Phi Beta Kappa—called at eight o'clock—Noble Secretary—went up exactly at eight to Noble's room 24 Holworthy—the Library of the Phi Beta Kappa ... Fred. Williams & Noble & Carter soon afterwards dropt in ... when followed the business of choosing the second eight members from our class—each man took a bit of paper and wrote down *eight* names—5 of which were on each bit—their admission was of course decided—vis: Borden, Stone, Storer, Chase, Hale—after considerable discussion Frost and Carr were added ...[79]

Tuesday May 7th Exhibition Day this—one of those days I hate—tedious, disagreeable, head-achy, direful, hungry &c &c ... Rushed down to the cars with Jan and Mary at 10—Storer's pretty sister came out—she *looks sensible*, clever, witty—above all good ... loafed about—now and then hearing the part[s]—weak—very weak mostly—Storer didn't do himself justice[80]—devilish slim play—stumbled—& so did others following his example—Noble was tolerable—Hersey better—Frost good—faith the talent of our class is not remarkable...[81]

Thursday May 16th Little has occurred today—and that little hardly worth noting—the only thing that does claim notice, though of things the least susceptible of description, is a long walk with *Storer*—in fact a two hours' stroll—left the supper table, despite the ominous look of the weather—proceeded towards Porter's—passed that venerable seat of vice & dissipation & strolled onward—the Lord only knows how far—a long way into West Cambridge—discoursing of various topics—principally of *women* that favorite theme of ours, wherein my friend has a chance to detail his experiences...

I've often mentioned Storer in these pages. Wherein indeed he probably occupies a larger space than any other individual, self excluded. Could I only transcribe a detail of our walks in the spirit in which they are made, this useless logbook of mine would be invaluable—but the fugitive thoughts and words—breathing friend-ship—show no sentiment. The twinkle of the eye, the smile, laugh, joke, sober reflections, &c, &c, pass the powers of language. God grant our friendship may not languish in after years.[82]

Tues—4th [June] 9 3/4 PM—Misfortunes never come alone—two dire calamities have befallen me this fourth day of June which have given me a disgust for almost everything—the which are that the first Bowdoin Prize has been assigned to H.R. Storer, 2nd to John Noble—and a negative reply to my venturous epistle to Greely of the New York Tribune. "its paid writers being [already] as numerous as they are able to have them". Well so goes the world—I wont say but that I *am* disappointed as to that d__d Bowdoin—& the more angry because of the pains I took with it. ... Storer got my d__d Disser. in the aft. made two or three *physical* alterations—away from my thoughts then thou shade of the past—dark as night—black as Hell![83]

Thursday June 6th Snoozed—rushed over to Harvard Hall to hear Storer read his Dissertation—good, but bless me if I could see the *remarkable* in it—a motley assemblage of topics—now one thing, now another—several fine passages—much general knowledge—a little speculation, and considerable logic here & there—historical part meagre. So the world goes.[84]

Sunday June 9th Storer loafed in just before six—went round the Common—talking   nonsense—and   criticizing   lecherous   per-sons—devilish fine loaf, however. Storer is a clever fellow—but damnit he has too much of the independent about him. My friendship with him I once though would be lasting—indeed some of the best of the few pleasant reminiscences I have of college life are connected with him—but as it doesn't seem to have been fully reciprocated by him—as our paths will hereafter be different—there being no similarity in our pursuits—it must sooner or later really, though not nominally I trust, break off. I accuse him of no fault—perhaps it is myself alone who am wrong. I would not embitter the few days I have left of college life by any saddening reflections. We shall hereafter meet—and I hope always with kindliness—but that commu-nity of feelings which I once flattered myself existed is gone—forever. So it is in this world. What such other other [sic] friendships will these pages record—begun at school—matured and ended at college? Alas, none probably in which I shall be so disinterested—in reality so earnest—so ardent.

I have entered into this little explanation to save myself the trouble of referring to the matter again. Such friendships fill a large space in the history of the soul—they are among its most treasured remembrances. Let me think of this as if a pleasant dream—wherein no alloy of bitterness shall enter and thank God that I have not been wholly unblest. Should these pages by any chance ever meet *his* eye, let him think of me *without* regret—pardon my infirmities—and believe me when I say that his friendship has really been—love.[85]

Warner's disappointment on Tuesday that Storer had won the coveted Bowdoin Prize and Warner's very negative reaction to Horatio's criticism of Warner's prize dissertation on Thursday are followed on Sunday by this touching admission of love for Horatio. The friendship did "languish," though probably as much because of Hermann's as Horatio's withdrawal. This no doubt was because of the different paths and lack of "similarity in pursuits" that Hermann noted, but perhaps also because Horatio's successes, like the Bowdoin Prize, too closely approached Hermann's hoped-for, but rarely-realized high achievements. Hermann spent much of his life in Europe and died there in 1916 and there is no possibility that Hermann's diary did "ever meet *his* eye," so Horatio never learned of the great importance Hermann placed on their college friendship, although, as will be seen, a pair of touching exchanges of letters was to occur between the two men, one a year later and one in the last decade of their lives.

Harvard has preserved Horatio's dissertation on "The History and Resources of the Valley of the Mississippi" in its Archives[86] and it sheds much light on the United States at the middle of the 19th Century. It also gives Horatio's views on a number of important issues, such as: "For Slavery even in those early days had begun to weave its network of guilt about the South, that has not yet been torn off—God grant it soon may be, though not in blood." About native Americans, Horatio wrote:

> That the Indians are a doomed race, there can be now but little doubt. Though Elliott's course has been often and nobly pursued—though Government has on the whole evinced a loving and forgiving spirit—though attempts have been made in Alabama to civilize them and in Kentucky to fashion them into scholars, it is all comparatively in vain. The White Man's fire water and his licentiousness have counteracted every good influence—their ways are not his ways, neither will they walk in the same path with him. We are now banishing the last of the Seminoles to beyond the Miss.; shortly they will all have vanished from before that fate which has driven them from the graves of their fathers towards the setting sun—will have been taken by the Great Spirit to the hunting grounds of the brave.

Horatio's views on manifest destiny follow:

Ere long will be banished by civilization those causes of sickness, peculiar to the West—miasmata, noxious vapors from marshy alluvions, which only need the treatment already applied so successfully to "the American bottom" by spade and plough. Steam will continue its hearty labors, and within the next 32 years will probably work as great a change upon the West again, as has come over it since the first steam boat was baptized by its waters in 1818. And the railroad must bind us to the Pacific—for those fertile plains beyond the Rocky Mts. were meant to be ours—the star of our westward extending empire can set but in the ocean, which at the West as at the East was placed by Nature as our boundary. The whaling vessels of those seas would be spared the dangers of Cape Horn—a new and fruitful field would be opened to that enterprize which now toils on the "banks" of Newfoundland—and the Anglo American, now Californian, under the stars and stripes would there show forth in still brighter light his "industrial feudalism" as an example to the World.

And Horatio had not changed his opinion of the Mexican War: "We might perhaps, geologically defining our limits, include also the late Mexican War—but we shall not—even were it for no other reason than that it would be for the interest and credit of our country always to pass that over as now, in silence." Contrary to Hermann's assessment, Horatio's essay really does show much of "the remarkable," at least by current standards.

June 14, 1850 was the date of the last meeting of the Harvard Natural History Society. Warner's journal for that date included: "last Nat. His Soc. in the evng ... lecture from Girard—*thinks that the study of the embryo is to work great revolutions in practical medicine.*"[87] Charles Frederic Girard had accompanied Agassiz to America. He no doubt was a guest lecturer at that Society meeting and probably described how "study of the embryo" was making people aware that developing human beings often were being destroyed by medical men when they did such things as restore menstruation. Horatio was present at the meeting, since Hermann also wrote: "Storer gave up his office with not so much feeling as he ought." It is possible that Girard, at this last meeting of the Society, planted the seed in Horatio's mind that grew into the "physicians' crusade against abortion."

On July 9, 1850, Warner wrote in his journal "Storer writing Nat His—describing fish he found at Labrador. ... good youth."[88] Horatio's paper, "Observations on the Fishes of Nova Scotia and Labrador, with Descriptions of New Species," was finished by September 4, when Horatio wrote in his "Medical School Journal," "Dr Wyman read my paper on the fishes of Labrador before the [Boston] Nat. Hist. Soc."[89] Horatio's paper was published in that distinguished Society's *Boston Journal of Natural History.*[90] Horatio discussed some twenty-nine different species of fish that he and his shipmates collected or observed on their trip to Labrador. The bulk of the paper consisted of Horatio's scientific descriptions of five species which he claimed previously had not been known. As already mentioned, one of these new species was dedicated to his father "in slight token of remembrance and gratitude for the very many pleasant hours we have spent together in the study of nature." This particular fish was *Acanthocottus Patris H.R. Storer* and is the lower of the three in the figure included in the photograph section of the book. In addition to identifying and describing new fish species, Horatio's paper also was a valuable scientific contribution in that it extended northward the known range of many of the other twenty-four species of fish.

CHAPTER 3
MEDICAL SCHOOLS, BOYLSTON MEDICAL SOCIETY

2 Sept. [1850] Monday—Began my studies in the Tremont St. Medical School—among the pupils of which I enrolled my name last Saturday night at Dr Bigelow's house. The old Dr. received me most graciously and imparted some good advice concerning the future—wh. shall endeavor to bear in mind.[1]

Thus commenced Horatio's new personal journal which covered the first ten months of Horatio's three years of medical study at the Tremont Street and Harvard Medical Schools. "The old Dr." Jacob Bigelow was on the faculty of both schools, the latter of which did not begin its term until November. Unfortunately, the journal entry does not describe Jacob's "good advice concerning the future."

Horatio's first month of medical school was spent in hospital rounds with Drs. David Humphreys Storer, George Cheyne Shattuck, Solomon Townsend, and Henry Ingersoll Bowditch. Surgical demonstrations occurred at the Massachusetts General Hospital on Saturdays, and Horatio and his fellow students watched surgeons, Henry J. Bigelow, Samuel Parkman, Townsend, John Collins Warren, and Jonathan Mason Warren as they operated. Recitations and quizzes were given by Jacob Bigelow, Henry J. Bigelow, J.B.S. Jackson, and David Humphreys Storer. Dissection began a few weeks after the school opened in late September and Horatio and four other students would share a cadaver. Horatio typically requested and obtained an arm or a leg.[2] An earlier and less official dissection of a human heart was to take place at the end of his first week of medical study. Horatio wrote:[3]

After the operations of today [7 Sept] we attended the autopsy of Groze—No 5 in Fathers ward. It was performed by J.B.S.J. The different parts were pretty thoroughly demonstrated to our great satisfaction—I obtained possession of the heart—& upon our departure had the misfortune to fall down in the yard—hurt myself badly & got wet—for it was raining *heart* (I meant to say hard)—& worst of all the paper burst & out flew the heart—to Jackson's horror. Went back again to the dead house & put it in my pocket safely. Spent the afternoon at home dissecting said heart with Nat. Hayward, who took tea with me.

This sounds like the story of the incident as Horatio told it to entertain his friends, but is not at all typical of Horatio's factual journal entries. More typical is the following which could have used some embellishment or at least expansion: "22 Sept. Sunday—Went to church—two very excellent sermons from Mr Briggs of Plymouth. Was attacked while walking through Temple St. with Father at about 8 in the evening, by two Irishmen—both of whom escaped with contusions & left a hat behind. Father was rather severely bruised."[4]

Horatio's entry a week and a half later also deserves note:[5]

2 Oct. Wednesday. Dissected. operations at the Hospital were for
    1. Hydrocele—left side—by J.M.W.
    2. Anchylosis of right knee joint by J.M.W.

"J.M.W." was Jonathan Mason Warren whose father, John Collins Warren, had been the dominant surgeon of Boston for decades and performed the first operation using ether as an anesthetic. Jonathan Mason Warren was considered to be one of the two best surgeons in Boston, the other being Henry J. Bigelow. Mason Warren became a close friend and supporter of Horatio and will be referred to frequently. However, the major reason for noting this particular journal entry of Horatio's was the second operation which Warren performed on "Anchylosis of right knee joint." Horatio himself in 1872 would have an ankylosed knee joint and repeated surgery failed to correct the problem. If Warren's surgery of October 2, 1850 was successful, Horatio may have regretted for all of his five decades on crutches that Jonathan Mason Warren died prematurely in 1867, and was not available to operate on his own knee.

Hermann Jackson Warner's friendship with Storer continued past graduation, despite Warner going on to the Harvard Law School in Cambridge and Horatio to medical school in Boston. The friendship had its ups and downs, however, at least for Hermann, who sometimes reported that Horatio "cut" him. On one occasion Warner wrote, "loafed down to Storer's—found him and Hay occupied—chatted awhile—the d__d jack is getting pompous and insolent—faith I must complain of something—he's one of those *acquaintances* whom 'twill be best to let slide—so he's gone."[6] Several weeks later, however, Warner wrote that Storer had visited him and noted that he was "Still the same enthusiastic genius that he was in college ... his eye flashes with the same wit, the same good humor, the same sincerity—his time is constantly occupied—in the dissecting room in the college and at private operations."[7] Despite Horatio's busy schedule, Warner proposed that they study German together and Horatio agreed. The following entry of Warner's journal shows the competition that he perceived between himself and Horatio:[8]

Monday November 18th Go up to Storer's at 7 1/2 ... mount into the
top loft—find him poring over medicine & in a d__d dark, sniveling,

miserable little room, however, it's to his credit than otherwise—he gives me a report of the results of his fishing exploits in Labrador &c—published in the Boston Soc. Nat Hist Journal—he's getting ahead of me ... But I hope to astonish the world by & by—it is merely scientific ...

Although there frequently are entries by both men in their respective journals for the same day, Horatio rarely makes specific reference to Warner. Typically, when Warner reports they are together, Horatio simply states "Spent the evening abroad." Warner invariably wrote more each day than Horatio, but it is probably not this alone that accounts for the difference. Their friendship was obviously more important for Warner who had many fewer social contacts and friends than Horatio. Warner himself more than once reported his envy of Horatio in this respect. However, even Storer was sometimes "left out." Warner wrote on December 3, 1850: "Storer spoke of Charly Hale's assemblage with some bitterness—neither himself nor Thayer were summoned—thus do college dislikes survive college life."[9]

Classes began at the *Harvard* Medical School on November 6 and Dr. John Ware gave the Introductory Lecture which traditionally marked commencement of the term and which was a public event attended by many physicians. Horatio noted the subject in his journal: "Causes of the physician's success in life."[10] Five years later, Horatio's father would give the Introductory Lecture that was a major impetus for Horatio's efforts in opposition to criminal abortion.

An event occurred early in the term, which showed most of the Harvard Medical School students to strongly oppose the admittance of women and blacks to the school. Horatio echoed his classmates' objection to women (only one student dissented from this resolution), but opposed the resolution objecting to blacks which was supported by about sixty-five students.[11] However, unlike a minority of twenty-six students who stated their strong support of their three black classmates, he joined with another twenty-two students who signed the following brief and ambiguous protest on December 11, 1850: "The undersigned not fully agreeing in the foregoing [majority resolution] do from motives of their own protest against the proceedings of yesterday therein alluded to."[12] Although Horatio apparently played some considerable role in the discussions, Horatio's journal makes only the following brief mentions of the controversy:[13]

9 Dec. Monday. Two teeth at Dr Harwoods—one filled, the other filed—At Holmes' quiz. Meeting of students after it to consider the conduct of Medical Faculty in admitting blacks & a woman (who did not appear) to lectures.

10 Dec. Tuesday. At lectures—Anoth student meeting. Resolutions read—Concerning women, which I favored—& blacks, against wh. I protested for various reasons. Adjourned to afternoon &

resolutions adopted. At Shakespeare Club in evening at Patterson's.

11 Dec. Wednesday. At lecture—Signed protest already mentioned. Snow storm—At Johnsons in evening.

The faculty decision was mentioned in Horatio's journal on 14 December. He wrote, "The woman is not to attend lectures & the blacks are to remain."[14] This was not the end of it for Horatio, however. Several days later he wrote:[15]

26 Dec. Thursday. Hospital with Bowditch. At lecture. Copied the following from the New York Evening Post of a few evenings since—with reference to my part in our student proceedings.

"Prof. Agassiz on the Negro.

"I see that one of your speakers at New York told Mr Foote that if the South only knew the sentiments of the North, they would find them to agree entirely with their own. I think the speaker must have had in view a certain portion of our own citizens—we Athenians put these Southern sentiments upon a sounder basis than mere constitutional right—namely upon Science.

"noris nos. docti sumus.

"Prof. Agassiz, whose special study it is to trace man in the animals & the animals in man, giving it as his decided opinion that the negro is of an inferior race & the Creator intended him to be a slave. The learning youth are already deeply imbued c their teacher's doctrine, as appears from certain proceedings which took place in our Medical College. Several students of color have joined it—& a short time ago, when one of them entered the lecture room, he was hissed at. Subsequently a meeting of some students was held, at which, particularly one of them, a Mr. S., the son of a well known physician here, declaimed most vehemently, & stated that a negro was a mere beast of burden, & intended to be such by the Creator & that Prof. Agassiz had proved it. The southerners will do well to send their young men to us to be educated, that they may learn to prove the divine institution of slavery, not only by the Bible but by Science also."

This purports to be from the Boston correspondent of the paper, & as far as concerning my ideas of Slavery & I presume those of Agassiz also—it is utterly false.

Horatio does not deny that he spoke before the group, only that his and Agassiz' views on slavery were "utterly" misrepresented. Agassiz had published a long article, "The Diversity of Origin of the Human Races," a year earlier. Agassiz saw the different races of man being created separately, even as he believed different animal species were created separately. He hedged, however, on the question of whether different races were different species. His treatment of the Negro is typified by statements such as: "And does not this [failure to mimic the civilizations of adjacent peoples] indicate in this race a peculiar apathy, a peculiar indifference to the advantages afforded by civilized society? We speak, of course, of this race in its primitive condition at home, and not of the position of those who have been transported into other parts of the world to live there under new circumstances."[16] One suspects that Horatio may have espoused his mentor Agassiz' following conclusions, if not words, in the "vehement declamation" described by the Boston correspondent of the *New York Evening Post*:[17]

> we entertain not the slightest doubt that human affairs with reference to the colored races would be far more judiciously conducted, if, in our intercourse with them, we were guided by a full consciousness of the real difference existing between us and them, and a desire to foster those dispositions that are eminently marked in them, rather than by treating them on terms of equality. We conceive it to be our duty to study these peculiarities, and to do all that is in our power to develop them to the greatest advantage of all parties. And the more we become acquainted with these dispositions, the better, doubtless, will be our course with reference to our own improvement, and with reference to the advance of the colored races.

Horatio's interest in the opposite sex from a non-medical view was sometimes described better in Hermann Warner's journal than in Horatio's. Horatio's typical entry in his "medical journal" was "evening with ladies." At the end of the year, however, Horatio was somewhat more specific and provided the following pair of intriguing entries:[18]

> 27 Dec. Friday. At lecture. To sleigh ride with Messrs Weld, Sam Johnson, May, Grant & Habersham—with Misses Weld, Morse, May, Merriam, Lizzie Reynolds & Mary J. Home at 1 A.M. Fine time.
> 28 Dec. Saturday. ... Called on Miss Elizabeth Reynolds—*my spouse*. Anat. Museum with Jackson. Hosp. in afternoon with Bowditch. Called on Mary J. In evening to Abbè's with ovum given me by Jackson.

There is no explanation of the "my spouse" comment related to Lizzie Reynolds, although this comment makes the visit the same day to "Mary J." seem somewhat adulterous. Horatio's real future spouse was to be Emily Elvira Gilmore, but her name never does appear in Horatio's journal which ended in June 1851, probably a half year before she came into the picture.

A pair of entries early in 1851 indicate Horatio's awareness of a local infanticide problem:

> 7 Jan. Tuesday. At lecture—In evening to see Gundry demon-
> strate a foetus wh. John Hathaway delivered in Ann St. last Wednes-
> day—& wh. died by being crammed by neighbors with ginger-
> bread—& wh. the parents, who were much pleased thereat, though
> they were Americans, gave readily to John to dissect.[19]
> 11 Feb. Tuesday. Got full grown foetus to dissect through Dr
> Reynolds. Infanticide.[20]

The "though they were Americans" comment reflected the prevalent differentia-
tion between early and late emigrants to New England and the much higher
expectations for the former by the former.[21] Dissection of the second fetus
occupied much of Horatio's time. His journal for February 15 indicated that he
demonstrated its circulation, etc. "at the Museum" and on the 17th he "Prepared
foetal stomach and intestines for Dr Jackson."[22]

Horatio undoubtedly took great pleasure from an event described in his
journal on January 10: "Wrote letter to Girard at Washington & sent to him a
package of my paper on Labrador fishes—whose contents are to be distributed
under the seal of the Smithsonian Institution."[23] Charles Frederic Girard
parted with Agassiz in 1850 and moved to Washington to work with Spencer
Francis Baird. His interests included ichthyology, and a portion of Horatio's
"Observations on the Fishes of Nova Scotia and Labrador" consisted of the
transcript of a letter Girard wrote to Horatio related to Labrador fishes that
Horatio had provided to Girard.

During this period the friendship with Hermann Warner was on again. A
pair of January entries in Warner's journal tells much about both men:

> Saturday January 25th round Common—luckily meet Storer—got
> headache & cold—tells the news—Coolidge is engaged to Nathan
> Appleton's daughter, i.e. to Five hundred thousand—clever dog...
> Geo Lowell is engaged &c &c. devilish fools these fellows, to
> shackle themselves this early—they'll repent it, I'll be sworn. As for
> me, why I don't even *know* a female ... Tells of his invitations to
> Newport, Baltimore ... chat pleasantly, delightfully—but desultorily,
> ... pity he's so d__d egotistic.[24]
> Tuesday January 28th Storer calls—I loaf out with him ... I bring
> up my old and favorite idea of meetings of members of professions
> who communicate what they think will be useful to each other,
> conducted in a liberal, literary, refined spirit, it might be made
> subservient to some of the highest ends of which our nation is capa-
> ble—refreshing, gratifying—a sort of Platonic, philosophic, associa-

tion. He enters heartily into the scheme. We two are the *nucleus*—we shall fashion it—kindred spirits *only* are to be united—a divine to check immoral propensities—an artist to injurn the ideal—a man of business & of the world to leaven us with the *practical*—doctors and lawyers ex necessitate—think of such an assemblage growing up from youth to age—mutually aiding each other in the great work of life—cultivating that reason which allies us with divinity—harmonizing those social affections which liken us unto angels—developing that strength of purpose which is to open the storehouse of success—& enable us to leave the scene of our labors prepared for higher spheres—I've used glowing language—but *associations* like souls, want inspiration—with a lofty, pure, ennobling end we have something to strive for, something to guide, something to console, us ... My friend has at heart much of the same purity of intent which I bless God still lingers about *me*. We sympathize—we *fraternize* ... nous verrons ["We shall see"] ...[25]

Horatio was elected a Resident Member of the prestigious Boston Society of Natural History on February 19, 1851[26] and two days later his journal includes: "Letter from Lieut Davis—offering me situation in South American Exploring Expedition."[27] There is no more reference to this Expedition in his journal or letters. Horatio's father had just convinced Horatio to abandon his plan to start a popular magazine with Hermann Warner and Charles Hale[28] because this would sidetrack Horatio's study of medicine, and it is possible that the same parental damper prevented Horatio from joining the ongoing U.S. Naval Astronomical Expedition to the Southern Hemisphere.[29]

Hermann's journal for once captured the topics discussed on one of his walks with Horatio. His entry for the first day of March included:[30]

[we] talked of various grave and merry things—how liquor is bad even in tinctures—how his brother Frank cogitates chemicyzing in Germany for some six years—how himself proposes to visit Paris some three years hence—& how we devoutly wish that we may go there together ... how he wrote a dialogue last night between the Sun & the Moon to show a damsel what might be made out of common subjects ... how we die—and how we live &c &c memory loves to linger over those few and fleeting moments which disclose what a blessing *life* may be.

On March 3, 1851, Horatio wrote in his journal: "Received eggs from Jardine. Got first prize of Boylston Soc. on 'Pelvis'—Gundry the second."[31] "Jardine" was Sir William Jardine, perhaps the foremost ornithologist of Great

Britain. Horatio would visit him in 1854. The Boylston Medical Society was a society of Harvard medical students and graduates which met to discuss medical issues and which awarded yearly the Boylston Prizes for medical dissertations. Horatio's father had become a member in 1822 when he became a student at the Harvard Medical School and in 1826 David Humphreys Storer won the Boylston Prize.[32] This must have made Horatio all the prouder to gain this same distinction in 1851. The minutes for the Boylston Society meeting of March 3 indicated that Storer's and Gundry's essays "were not of so high a character as those of the last few years, but still they judged them worthy of the prizes." "Thus ended a term of this Society," the Minutes ended, "which was never before equaled in the slight attendance of its members & want of interest, on their part."[33] Attendance soared the next year, and it may be no coincidence that this was after Horatio became a member and officer.

It is interesting that Horatio's Boylston Prize was not disclosed to Hermann by Horatio but by the newspaper. Hermann wrote: "Friday March 7th 1851 eve^g paper says Storer has taken 1st Prize of Boylston Medical School—glad of it—he deserves a thousand—only he's devilish still about it all."[34] Horatio may have been "devilish still" because he expected that Hermann would be jealous. And Hermann's entry for the next day read: "Saturday March 8th I'm going to write for the *Law Prize*, actually have come to that conclusion—my friend mustn't beat me too extravagantly. ... His prize by the way came from the Boylston Med. Soc.—not School."[35]

Hermann's error, appropriately corrected, may have occurred because there was a Boylston Medical *School* which was not connected with the Boylston Medical Society. Like the Tremont Street Medical School, the Boylston Medical School provided instruction for medical students during the long portion of the year when the Harvard Medical School was not in session. According to Dr. Zabdiel ("Zab") Adams, the Boylston School was founded "in opposition to the Tremont Medical School."[36] Its founders and early teachers included Drs. Edward H. Clarke, Henry W. Williams, Henry Ingersoll Bowditch, and Charles Edward Buckingham.[37] As we will note, there was much ill feeling between Horatio's father and Buckingham and later between Horatio and Buckingham, and this may have had its origins in the rivalry between the Boylston and Tremont Street Medical Schools.

On March 15, Warner described another walk with Storer "down to his Dissecting Room at Hospital—four dead bodies stretched on planks—one, a woman—runs a poker up her—&c—extremely disgusting—smell, fetid—& the associations nauseous—chat generally and homewards proceed ... offer him my microscope again—hope he'll take it."[38] Critics of Horatio Storer will undoubtedly castigate the twenty-one-year-old medical student for this act which this author also finds "extremely disgusting." It undoubtedly was a bad-taste toast to future marital pleasures. We can be nearly certain that neither man had ever gone beyond contemplation of the act of sexual intercourse that the thrust with the poker symbolized. It certainly did not destroy the highly moral

Hermann's opinion of Horatio, given that a few minutes later he offered Horatio the microscope of his beloved late half-brother, Charles Yates. Several physicians have reassured me that such behavior in the absence of a professor in the dissecting room is hardly remarkable and certainly not indicative of pathology.

Warner frequently in their walks had talked of the advantages of marrying a woman with money and Horatio had apparently agreed. Warner's entry for March 16 mentioned a refreshingly contrasting Storer view on the matter, particularly in light of the fact that two-and-a-half years later Horatio did marry a woman with considerable money: "Call at Storer's and pedestrinate at length—chat of marriage & kindred topics—says he's looking out for a partner of life—strong affections—just as like to pick up a girl without a shilling as not & thereby make a damn fool of himself—strong in the faith of Christ—and is thereby unmoved by religious doubts—wish I could cast anchor in the same blind haven."[39]

Hermann's entry the next Saturday discussed another long walk with Horatio, and ended with: "Lend Horatio my microscope, formerly Charles'—His natural history predilections are breaking out afresh—read a paper on Fishes on Wed before the Nat. His. Soc. of Boston—which is to be published. Hope he'll prosper in the path wherein he's setting his faculties to work."[40]

Horatio's entry two Saturdays later read: "Walked to Quincy & its quarries with Warner. Came near being killed on railroad bridge at Neponset—between two trains of cars—Tiger damaging his tail."[41] This certainly sounds like an interesting day, and this is confirmed by Warner's version written, because of fatigue, late the following day:[42]

> Storer interrupts my avocations—and proposes a walk—for the day—agree to it—though with considerable querying as to the place most proper for pedestrinating—come up stairs—plaster a dilapidated little toe—& sally forth—Stop at his house—procure his dog—and make for the Old Colony rail-road—the morning is muggy with an East wind—but soon clears high and warm—stroll across the rail road bridge to South Boston—opposed therein by an obstreperous paddy whom we succeed in passifying—and then along the road by Savin Hill—near which we encounter quite a thrilling accident—the bridge which passes along just here is laden with two tracks, with very narrow interval between them—& still less between each track and the side of the bridge—we are just upon the middle of the bridge & a whistle is heard a-head of us—ditto one behind—Storer grabs his dog by the neck and the tail—as both trains come tearing along—we have about half a minute to decide what to do—S anchors himself on his dog—I grasp his arm—& we put ourselves directly, as near as possible, in the middle of the interval which separates the tracks—and

the engines thunder by us—there being perhaps *two* feet between the trains & we located on this narrow space—the danger attendant upon the adventure is quite apparent—one of the trains was a long *dirt* one—and such trains are liable to have boards or other interesting things protruding from their sides—luckily this train was free, one is liable to be dizzy as he stands within half a foot of a track and faces an engine & train coming at *dreadful* speed upon him—the slightest loss of equilibrium instant death—of the most horrid kind too—however, we survived & I thank God for his mercy—lose a cane in the disturbance which is exceedingly annoying, it not being mine—it occasions some delay—proceed along this track, meeting little other incident ...

Several of Horatio's journal entries for April deal with a problem that was to bother him repeatedly during his surgical career. He wrote:[43]

6 April Sunday. Begin to feel the effects of a dissecting wound. Apply poultice. Cannot write journal easily.

14 April. Monday. Using for several days Sulph. of Zinc on dissecting wound—which will not heal—Under Dr J.M. Warrens care. Walked through Roxbury & Dorchester.

15 April. Tuesday. Use alum curd for hand—without avail—Bad whitlow on other hand. Stormy.

17 April. Thursday. Minot's ledge lighthouse swept away last night, with its keeper. Stormy—use "black wash" on hand. Op. for Cancer—Temple St. J.M.W.

19 April. Saturday. Apply Iod. of Potass. to hand ... With Warner ... to East Cambridge, Somerville & Charlestown.

The treatment with "Iod. of Potass." apparently was successful, since he does not mention the hand problem again.

Horatio's entry for April 29 read: "Parents left for Charleston S.C. I am in charge of the house."[44] The Charleston trip was to the Fourth Annual Meeting of the American Medical Association. This was the second annual meeting which David Humphreys Storer had attended and he presented a long review of literature on obstetrics and diseases of women.[45] Horatio's father remained an active member in the Association and was elected President in 1866, the year after the Association met in Boston.[46] Other Boston physicians involved with the Association in its initial years were Henry Ingersoll Bowditch, John Collins Warren, and Oliver Wendell Holmes. However, as will be shown, the organization came to be viewed as superfluous by some powerful Boston physicians, particularly Henry J. Bigelow, who may have regarded anything medical that originated outside of the "Hub" of Boston in this way.

A month later, Horatio mentioned some of the rare clinical instruction in gynecology he received as a student: "24 May. ... In afternoon with Hayward & Abbè to Deer Island Hospital where were well received & entertained by Dr Moriarty."[47] Horatio amplified this entry about Deer Island visits fifty years later in the following from his 1901 letter to his son Malcolm:[48]

At that time the only clinical gynaecological instruction available in Boston was that which a very few of us obtained by regularly going down to Deer Island in the City Boat, and seeing its superintendent, the very stout Dr. Moriarty, ... apply nitrate of silver in stick to chancred prostitutes, and in solution to their gonorrhoeal urethrae. I recollect there were iron clamps which seized their knees when the girls were in the tilting chairs and held them quiet despite their constant struggles.

One of Warner's angriest reactions to Horatio appeared in his journal on May 19, 1851:[49]

Storer has been here—this eve—spent half an hour or so—I have given him up as a friend!—he'll do for an *acquaintance*—so goes the world... leave a note for Storer asking if he knows anything of early officers of the society [Harvard Rumford Society]. ... S. knows nothing of matter aforesaid—chat indifferently—not worth noting—one of Gus Hay's sisters is said to be dying—&c &c. S has cut my acquaintance, the devil only knows why—let him go—my philosophy can stand it. ... I am sorry for S. I liked him once—but as time has gone by, he has turned away—I wont say I dislike him—wont let my feeling bring me so far—but I must say that all sympathy has gone ... If he lives, & preserves his health he will do well—prosper—gain considerable eminence—& perhaps wealth—will marry probably soon—& a rich girl if possible—happiness will await domestic & external—I rejoice for his success—I should lament his failure—at same time I dislike him—it's out—& I shall continue so to do.

Horatio's journal for the same day that produced Hermann's tirade contains only, "Walk with Hayes & Hayward."[50] On the other hand, that may have been what angered Hermann. Horatio may have been aware of Warner's anger, since he returned the microscope Hermann had provided him a month earlier. Hermann must not have been home when Horatio delivered it, since Hermann took it back to Horatio with this note:[51]

/No. 12 Franklin Place/ Boston
Tuesday 27 May 1851

My dear Storer:
    It was not my intention that my brother's little microscope should

be returned, if you found it to be of any service. It will [become] rusty and dusty in my room: I shall never use it. Will you receive it from your friend, if not for his sake as a slight memorial of early and I trust lasting friendship, at least for the sake of science in general, in however small degree it may contribute to aid you in those interesting pursuits to which you have begun to devote yourself; and

believe me ever truly your friend

Hermann J. Warner

If you write home during your trip, let me know of your luck.

Hermann's journal entry for the next day gives an explanation of the above note.[52]

Tuesday May 27th 1851 Storer brings my microscope back—return it to him with a note of gift in eve^g—don't want the thing—shan't ever use it—I began college with this individual's friendship which has continued til this time—in fact I do really cherish a strong—very strong regard for him—whether it is reciprocal in whole or in part I am not prepared to say—at least I have adopted him as a friend—& whatever may be my failings in other respects it shall not be said of me that I ever deserted such an adoption—It isn't often I make a *friend*—The world generally I care devilish little about—humanity in the concrete I reverence—I shall labor to serve—it is one of the strongest desires of my heart—perhaps the strongest—to do something—whatever lies within the compass of my poor abilities—to advance the great interests of my race ...

Hermann's journal entry for the next day gives Horatio's written response.[53]

Wed—28th Found a note from Storer on my desk on returning from Cam[bridge] this morning—*I copy it that I may have a double chance of preserving it*—I'm curious to know how this 'friendship' will turn out in after days—such memorials of early professions are interesting to the philosopher—However, I've not a particle of my friend's sincerity—God forbid I should have such a thought—he means well—our different professions will of course carry us widely apart—we may meet but seldom—but whenever that meeting does take place I trust it will be with the same warm feelings, mellowed but not lessened by time with which I now transcribe his note:

"27 May 1851—Winter St

"My dear Hermann:

"There was need of no microscope to show me your good

points, I trust I have know them long and well—our friendship required no such clasp.

"It was consecrated to toil—by one too early lost—scholar, man of genius, lover of nature—lamented by all his acquaintances—by the world—It should have passed into hands more worthy than mine. But his memory shall cling to it still—Nor as I use it, shall I forget you, my friend—nor your kind heart.

"Thus doubly endeared to me, will it disclose new beauty in my favorite studies—the works of God—&, let me hope, exalt, strengthen my faith in him—I thank you again—
"truly—H.R. Storer"

Immediately following his copy of Horatio's letter, Hermann added: "So goes the world." This time, for a change, Hermann meant the world was going well.

Horatio's medical school journal ends on June 9, 1851 and there are many blank pages following the last entry in the notebook, suggesting that it was not continued elsewhere. A possible factor in the demise of the journal was that the Tremont Street and Harvard Medical Schools did not change their curricula from year to year with both beginning and advanced students attending the same lectures. Continuing the journal may have been viewed as unnecessarily repetitive. Another factor in the abandonment of the journal may have been Horatio's extensive duties as the new Curator of Herpetology at the Boston Society of Natural History. Horatio's Curator's Report indicated that during this period he "devoted much labor" to saving deteriorating specimens, "arranged an almost complete series of the reptiles of Massachusetts," systematically arranged all the Chelonians [turtles and tortoises], and added many specimens through "the donation of Sir William Jardine, Drs. Cragin, Burnett, Durkee, and Storer, Messrs. Stimpson, Browne, Habersham, and Cary, and of the Curator himself."[54]

Although Horatio's journal stopped, we obtain views and activities of Horatio from Hermann's journal, the *Proceedings of the Boston Society of Natural History*, occasional letters, and also a published obituary of the first two members of the Class of 1850 to die. The obituary was only signed "S," but many of the same words and thoughts found their way into a letter from Horatio to Hermann. Horatio's claim about Ephraim Ball in the obituary: "To those of his classmates of similar tastes he became early endeared," indicates that many of the qualities Horatio attributed to Ball in the obituary and in the letter to Hermann, were the qualities Horatio perceived, at least somewhat accurately, in himself. The obituary included:[55]

Our companions were each men of worth, of good principles, of character. They were both of them good scholars, had attained high college honor, and had won the respect and esteem of their associates. The first [Benjamin S.H. Brown] was prevented by his retiring disposition and poor health, from engaging in many of the varied scenes of student life. But Ball was ever foremost—actively undertaking a thing, he resolutely pursued it to the end. To great natural talents and a fondness for study, were joined a clear judgment and the most indomitable energy; and to these a frank and fearless spirit, that brooked no control. He evinced an ardent love of nature, a decided leaning towards scientific pursuits; yet he wasted not his time—he stored his mind with treasures, and he knew their use. To those of his classmates of similar tastes he became early endeared; to them his original mind was often of aid, his affection cheering, his society pleasant converse, uninterrupted till his death. In the fervent study of His works he learned to see the Creator, and laid the foundation of a sincere Christian faith, which became of late more fully developed and perfected his character.

Horatio provided the following reflections on the deceased Ball to Hermann:[56]

> Winter Street: /Boston/
> /Friday/ 11 July 1851
>
> My dear friend:
> I receive your good letter last evening: for it, thanks. You have then heard of our classmate's death: equally sudden and terrible: which affected me more perhaps than has ever [any] event of the kind. When I last saw him, the night before I left for the Provinces, he was full of life, sanguine, vigorous, confident: apparently never anticipating for a moment any derangement of his plans, any check to his course. He was then about going to sea for some days with my old Provincetown skipper. I saw no more of him, but heard at various times and from various friends, of his movements and intentions.
> ... The first thing that struck my eyes on Monday morning upon taking up the newspaper was, that he was dead: and you may judge how I was shocked, how utterly overwhelmed for the time. I immediately informed those of us who were at hand, in the hope that they would attend his funeral, but in vain. I was the only one of his class who followed him to the grave. My chum's [Gus. Hay's] sister was buried on the same afternoon, but my thoughts were with Ball.
> ...
> I regret exceedingly that I was not informed of his illness, for I should have taken at least a melancholy pleasure in trying to soothe the last dread moments of an intimate friend. And such Ball has ever been to me, despite his roughness, his forbidding, even unpleasant

manners, his at times almost ill-breeding; traits that were owing to circumstances over which he had no control: a country life, a hard father, a forced seclusion from refined society. We had many tastes in common: we had studied together: we had travelled together and we had perhaps seen in each other's hearts a little that savored of independence, of self reliance, of disgust and contempt at the too common sycophant and "toad", that bound us by a still stronger tie: some might call the feeling "pugnacity" let them if they will: but I call it, as evinced in Ball, a noble trait of character: and wish to God that a spark of the same might be kindled in the breast of every man.

... In my home he came and went like one of the family: my father and mother were both pleased with him; the one with his frank and hearty manliness, the other with that naive, or rather rustic, brusqueness, which with us he never carried too far. I feel, and with sincerity I say it, that in him our Class has lost one who would one day have honoured us all, who had talent and energy, who aimed at a lofty mark, and who would have reached it, with the help of God: for despite his apparent carelessness of thought, he had principles, and good ones too.

But the poor fellow belied his looks and has gone before, to meet Brown, to await us. And as one by one we follow his footsteps through the dark valley, may we be as prepared, as universally mourned as he:

truly your friend
/Horatio Robinson/ Storer

Hermann J. Warner
at Mr Wilson's
Lenox: Massachusetts

Although not the Class Secretary, Horatio took it upon himself to compose the obituary of Brown and Ball and to write his longest letter ever to Hermann on the subject of Ball's death. A few months later, Hermann recorded in his diary that Horatio also spoke on the subject of death to his Sunday School class. Horatio's preoccupation with death, may have been because of his own fragile health and because of his frequent encounters with the dead and dying as a medical student and companion on his father's medical rounds.

In late September, Hermann included: "Sunday September 28th Storer went to Church with me—walked round common with him ... Storer is much after my mind in many respects—there is a great deal of genuine *modesty* about him—If I ever liked anybody—he is certainly the man."[57] Hermann usually complained of Horatio's egotism and pomposity and the above reference to "genuine *modesty*" is a bit of a shock. Hermann and Horatio may never have been on better terms as the above and the following entry of Hermann shows:[58]

Saturday October 11 ... call on Storer's—& take a musher of a walk
to Roxbury over Parker Hill—by a big old house—half way up the
Skie's—round of the Punch Bowl—homeward over the Mill
Dam—pleasant chat—of the gross absurdity—not to say the great
wickedness of advocating a dissolution of the Union—pretty girls &c
&c ... The more I see of this early friend, the more I like him—there
is a sympathy between us which fills up the great void in man ... we
know each other perfectly—consequently we enjoy ourselves together
without a particle of restraint, ceremonial or otherwise—landscapes
& houses—girls & apple trees, we contemplate as if with a sort of
intuitive perception of what is passing in the other's mind—we both
are ardent in hopes of the future—& we both have outwardly at least
the same past to look back upon—What a perfect Damon to Pythias
we are, though!

At least one rift in Hermann's friendship with Storer and one reconciliation
occurred before Hermann reported:[59]

Monday November 24th   Storer calls in eve[g]—stays fifteen minutes—says Thayer has been injured by a fall from a horse—says he
(self) is very busy—is Dr Bigelow's surgical assistant—dissects
much—wants to remedy the objects of the Medical Library to which
students have access—talk about law—& medicine & slavery—how
slavery is a great & desperate problem—how the Union depends upon
Compromise &c & how the colonization & civilization of Africa &
the black race is finally to be worked out—

It is significant that Horatio served as Dr. Henry J. Bigelow's assistant.
"Assailant" will be more the relationship two decades later and one wonders
whether bad feeling between the two men had its origins as early as this initial
relationship while Horatio was in medical school.

Friendly relations between Hermann and Horatio continued for at least the
next four days when the following indicates they met again:[60]

Friday November 28th ... go down to Lee Thayers Meet Storer
there—talk of matters in general—of Storer's big black dog which he
has with him—of habits of cats—of deer which are to be found at
Sandwich—of the great hunting that can be indulged in *down East*—of
classmates—how Joel Seavers is now engaged—how Frank Foster,
after one betrothed is dead has come into the condition again with an
individual of thirty five or six &c &c Of politics—Webster &
Clay—of the extraordinary feats of Webster—among wh is to be
enumerated his great powers of physical endurance &c &c ... came
away with Storer talking medicine—how hard words abound more in

his profession than in mine—home...

"[H]ard words abound in his profession" no doubt specifically applied to the Boston medical profession. Some of the incidents that Horatio was generalizing from surely involved his father who was noted for his pugnacity,[61] and some of these may have involved David Humphreys' rival, Dr. Charles E. Buckingham, of the Boylston Medical School. Horatio himself may have already been the recipient of "hard words," given Horatio's and Hermann's discussion of the topic and given that Hermann may not have been the only one who found Horatio pompous, bombastic, and egotistical. It also may not have been a coincidence that Horatio was now Henry J. Bigelow's surgical assistant.

Horatio's goal "to remedy the ... Medical Library" was undertaken via the Boylston Medical Society. Horatio had been elected Secretary of the Boylston Medical Society at the first meeting in November. Horatio's minutes for the Meeting of December 1, 1851, included: "Mr. Storer then called the attention of the Society to the present condition of the library of the Society and to that of the Medical College, both deficient in modern standard works, & urged the adoption of some means by which they might be increased."[62] The result was that Horatio "was directed to take such measures for the office, as shall seem to him the best."

The minutes of the next meeting included a discussion of Horatio's correspondence with Boylston Society Trustees and the University Librarian which identified a large number of medical books at Cambridge. The minutes concluded: "Upon motion of Mr Abbè, the Secretary was directed to lay before the Corporation of the University, the request of the Society that this collection of books be removed to the Library of the Medical College in Boston."[63]

Horatio's long letter to the Harvard University Corporation identified many of his own goals that demanded an excellent medical library.[64] He first described the inadequacy of the Medical Library, noting that it possessed only 1,200 volumes compared to 3,400 at "the little starveling at Brunswick." He contrasted the inferior status of the Harvard medical student compared to Harvard law and theological students who had "opportunities for reference unrivalled." These library deficiencies prevented the medical student from providing a "well digested and creditable inaugural thesis." They also hampered the student wishing "to distinguish himself in any special branch of medicine." He continued: "Is he called upon in any emergency to decide an important scientific or practical quest... involving perhaps his reputation as an observing scholar, as a judicious practitioner, or as a reliable witness in the Court of Justice, whither is he to turn? Medical authors may, and often do disagree, & need to be extensively, as well as faithfully compared."

Horatio then pointed out that the medical books at Cambridge were located too far from the Boston medical campus to provide much help, given that the students' medical lectures occupied most of their day. He called on the Corporation to arrange for these Cambridge books, including the 1,000 in the

Boylston Medical Library which had been earmarked for Cambridge, to be moved to the medical school. The letter concluded:

> If however, this our request cannot be granted, if these many books, almost equalling in number those we now have, are really cut off from us, there are yet others in the Cambridge library, bound there by no such stern resolutions, many of them duplicates of works in the Boylston Library, and now to all intents & purposes, utterly useless, to the student, to the college, and concerning these, we make the same request.
>
> By such changes, the Library of the university would be but little impaired and the Library of the Medical College would be greatly benefitted. Therefor do we suggest its propriety, not to say, its receptivity to the Corporation.
>
> For the Society
Horatio R. Storer, Sec.
>
> 14 Winter St.
>   3 Jan, 1852
>
> Whatever may appear imperfect, ill-advised or culpable in the above petition, is wholly owing to the youth and inexperience of the writer. He would have shrunk from the task imposed upon him by his comrades, had he not been emboldened to it by love for his Alma Mater & devotion to his chosen profession.
>
> But he hopes that the appeal he has offered may be successful. That the Society may not have labored in vain to increase the advantages of the College, and thus to exalt again the revered names of Boylston & Harvard.

Despite this impassioned plea, Horatio and the Boylston Medical Society were to learn a few months later that the request was turned down.[65] Horatio would try again in 1866 and 1900.

CHAPTER 4

EMILY ELVIRA, SIMPSON, THE LYING-IN HOSPITAL

The new session of the Boylston Medical Society included debates on medical issues with two members assigned to defend and two to oppose a proposition. The first of these took place on December 12, 1851 with the question being: "The induction of Premature Labor—is it ever justifiable?" Hathaway and Storer were in the affirmative and Z.B. Adams and Robertson in the negative. Horatio did not indicate in the minutes whether one side or the other was judged the winner, only that the negative deserved special praise since they had "the weight of evidence against them & labored therefore under greater difficulties than did their opponents."[1] The rights of the fetus, or the lack of same, probably were discussed by both sides and it is unfortunate that Horatio was so brief in his discussion of the debate.

The scheduled essayist did not show up at the next meeting of the Boylston Medical Society and Horatio filled in by describing a difficult case of labor *which he attended* where an impacted head did not advance for sixteen hours. Horatio's father and another physician were called in and forceps were tried but without success. Craniotomy, the crushing of the infant's skull, was recommended, but not allowed by the family. The child was eventually born, but died shortly after birth. Although the woman survived, Horatio's minutes included: "Mr Storer related the case for the purpose of showing the wisdom of using craniotomy in such an emergency, as advised him by Dr Cabot—the chances being that the child, if born alive, after further delay, would die, and probably the mother also."[2] Horatio's willingness to fill in in the absence of a programmed speaker, had been foreshadowed by his frequent similar behavior at meetings of the Harvard Natural History Society. More remarkable, however, was the apparent total initial responsibility of Horatio, a second-year-medical student, for this obstetric case. As will be seen, Horatio would eventually change his mind about "the wisdom of using craniotomy," following firsthand advice from the Edinburgh obstetrician and gynecologist, James Young Simpson.

At the same meeting, Horatio filled in for an absent debater with the debate subject being "Do the statistics of Ovariotomy justify the operation?" Horatio argued for the negative, but following a "spirited" contest, it was judged that the affirmative was the winner. Ovariotomy, the removal of diseased ovaries, was rarely done in 1851. Antiseptic surgery had not yet been introduced and opening the abdominal cavity frequently caused peritonitis or other problems that led to death of the patient. No successful ovariotomy was to be performed in the near vicinity of Boston until Horatio accomplished the feat after his return from Europe, and it is somewhat surprising that these members of the Society in 1851 decided that statistics justified the operation.

The question selected for debate at the next meeting was "The Comparative Merits of Sulphuric Ether & Chloroform," and Horatio was designated as one of the two arguing for chloroform. The Minutes of that meeting indicated that Horatio's side lost again.[3] We have mentioned Boston's commitment to sulphuric ether, and Boston medical men were already sensitive to any attempt to substitute another anesthetic in ether's place. Advocacy of chloroform may have been a risky endeavor, even in the context of a debate.

Hermann's rivalry with Horatio dominated in Hermann's journal entry for December 2, 1851 where he noted that their relationship was "changing." "So be it," Hermann continued, "let us see which will beat in the long run—I am not afraid of the trial."[4] Hermann probably anticipated that it would be in a Daniel-Webster-type role in which he would "beat in the long run." Hermann's journal is replete with positive references to Webster and his very selection of the law may have indicated that a similar outstanding political career was his life goal. However, if Hermann did not have enough problems with Horatio out-achieving him in the tangential domains of science and medicine, the following day's entry in his journal must have marked a very dark day indeed. "Talk with Suter—says the Whigs have nominated him as Clerk of the Ward—an honor which he did not expect—Storer is made Inspector—done last night. Hurrah for Politics—Wonder what *my* career in this line will be!"[5]

A few weeks later Hermann wrote:[6]

> Sunday—21st December ... Call at Storer's, not at home. This fellow seems to have entirely cut me, well so be it. He is in a different circle—a different sphere—our paths are separate—but it is as well we should separate—yet I honestly confess it is hard to bring myself to this conclusion. If I ever thought anybody was my friend, it is that fellow. ... If I ever thought of growing up and growing old in a friendship of close and kindly nature with anybody, it was with him. He goes & all my hopes of friendship go with him, blighted, disappointed ... my original skepticism of human nature returns. I shall relapse into my original moroseness.

Horatio's relationship with Emily Elvira Gilmore appears to have begun during this period.[7] It is too bad that Horatio did not mention Emily Elvira to Hermann. It might have given Hermann an understanding and tolerance of the behavior of Horatio that caused Hermann to write: "This fellow seems to have entirely cut me." However, Warner's break was not complete. His journal on Saturday January 10, 1852 included:[8]

> go round Common with Storer—who by the by has come in many re-spects to be d___d disagreeable. His manners are pompous, his

personal observations show as great a want of good breeding as of genuine politeness—nothing worth noting was elicited during the conversation, except that he remarked rumor had been free with his name in the matrimonial line, & that perhaps in six months he might be in for an engagement. Well from the way he talked I suppose the woman had money—& so goes the world ... Have pretty much determined to let him drop.

Botany also became important to Horatio at this time. The Minutes of the meeting of the Boylston Medical Society for February 6, 1852 included: "Mr. Storer read a paper upon 'The Claims of Botany upon the Physician.'"[9] At about the same time he "read a paper giving a botanical description and an account of the medical properties of *Cimicifuga racemosa*, Black Snakeroot of New England" at the Boston Society of Natural History.[10] For months afterward, Horatio regularly read papers on Medical Botany at this Society. Warner gives us a possible explanation of the botany emphasis. He noted in his journal for April 12, 1852, "he goes out every morning to study with Grey [sic] the botanist, seems to be preparing himself to become a professor of materia medica."[11] It will be recalled that when Horatio began his study of medicine, Dr. Jacob Bigelow, Harvard Medical School Professor of Materia Medica, "imparted some good advice concerning the future—wh. shall endeavor to bear in mind." It is possible that the aging Jacob was suggesting that Horatio might someday replace him as Professor of Materia Medica. Horatio's good relationship with "Old" Bigelow certainly continued at least until 1853 when Horatio provided to Dr. Bigelow a bound book of notes from Bigelow's 1852-1853 lectures on Materia Medica.[12] Horatio added this inscription: "To the honored Professor, faithful instructor & kind friend, these notes."

Each Medical Student was required to provide a written dissertation and, as noted earlier, Horatio's was entitled *Florula Cantabrigiensis medica*.[13] This probably was a compilation of Horatio's researches with Dr. Gray on the medical properties of various plants in Asa Gray's extensive Cambridge "garden," which included species from all over the country. Horatio's dissertation, like his Boylston-Prize-winning, "The Pelvis," apparently has not survived.

Horatio read a paper entitled "Remarks on the Use of Alcohol for the Preparation of Medicines" at the February 13 meeting of the Boylston Society.[14] This paper has not survived either, but Horatio's concerns about medicines with alcohol leading to alcoholism and his comment to Hermann about "how liquor is bad even in tinctures"[15] suggest that Horatio was arguing that all the alcohol be *eliminated* from any medicine which used it in its preparation.

Homeopathy was the subject of the debate at that Society meeting and the related minutes read:[16]

The Debate upon the question, "Are the doctrines of Homeopathy founded on Truth, or supported by Fact?" was opened by Mr.

Wood—who read a lengthy & very scientific dissertation in their favor. He was opposed successively by Messrs Blake, Robertson, Browne, Rice, Noyes & Storer. Although the Affirmative of the question was supported by Mr Wood alone, the debate was conducted with great spirit, and at times waxed hot. At its close the President remarked upon the arguments & put the question, which resulted in the negative.

The major premise of Homeopathy was that the symptoms of a disease are evidence of the curative process of the body as it responds to the disease. The homeopathic physician tried to increase these symptoms in order to help the body cure itself. Homeopathy originated in Europe and had attracted many practitioners in the U.S., including some who had been trained in medicine at Harvard. In not prescribing the typical medicines of the day, homeopaths probably did less harm than many of the "regular" physicians, i.e., physicians with medical degrees from Harvard and other "scientific" medical schools. However, most of the "regular" physicians viewed homeopathy as quackery and Mr. Wood may not have been arguing in support of his own views in defending it. The practice may have been such a tempting target that "Blake, Robertson, Browne, Rice, Noyes & Storer" all rose to shoot at it. Horatio never altered his opposition, and, as will be seen, eighteen years later he incurred the wrath of many members of the Massachusetts Medical Society who were embarrassed by Horatio's success in ridding that Society of its Harvard graduates who had switched to homeopathy.

In a pair of March entries, Hermann recorded momentous news:[17]

Thursday 18 March 1852 Met Amos Johnson, chatted on things indifferent, when suddenly he breaks out "Heard the news about your friend"?—"No what is it—dead or married"—"He's tied himself"—go while you're young is the motto of some people, engaged to a Miss Gilmore, who she is doesn't appear except that a part of the story is she's worth some fifty thousand dollars, which the Lord grant may turn out true. Amos says he did this thing up sly, acquainted nobody till the last moment. So goes the world—So go folks ahead of me. Well, I wish him joy if the girl be pretty, pure, sensible and has a comfortable property. Perhaps nothing could be better under these circumstances than to get married. Storer will succeed, I predict, in his profession, he has energy & ability, is already known in a large circle in Boston, belongs to clubs &c & moves in good society. What fairer prospect could be wanted. ... My future, I confess, is lamentably bleak, however, I don't propose to fret myself upon that score.

Saturday March 20th 1852 Walked round Common, met Hay,

says its a fact that Storer is engaged, that he told him, he hardly intends to be married for a year or two, that he has seen the girl, Hay thinks her pretty, he says she has got money. So goes the world.

Horatio would marry Emily Elvira Gilmore in July 1853, so Amos' and Gus' intelligence appears to have been correct. She was the daughter of the late Addison Gilmore who died in 1851 and of Emily Spaulding Patten Gilmore who was to survive until 1899. Addison "was builder and president of the Western Railroad, treasurer of the Old Colony Railroad and of the Hamilton Woolen Mills."[18] Addison's will provided an immediate $10,000 and the income of $30,000 to each of his daughters,[19] and, in 1852, this sum meant that Horatio did indeed have a wealthy fiancee.

Early April marked a break in medical school lectures and Horatio wrote the following to his old friend, Captain Atwood:[20]

> Boston, 10 April 1852
> 14 Winter St.
>
> My dear Sir,
>   My health has failed me—and I wish very much a week or two's medical treatment under your care—having in times past found the benefit of such. I think a little sea sickness would do me good. If you are now in the "Golden Eagle" and engaged in fishing for Halibut—& if you can stow away for a little while in a corner so troublesome a fellow as myself, I wish you would write me word. Frank enjoyed himself very much when he was with you on like business & I would gladly follow his example. You know me of old, I believe.
>
> very truly
> Horatio R. Storer
>
> Capt N.E. Atwood

If Horatio went for this "medical treatment" he did not go before Monday April 12, 1852 when Hermann wrote:[21]

> Called on Storer's house before eight, wanted to walk out with him, to chat over past matters, ... his ambition is great, & so far as I can see I should judge it noble, trust he'll prosper, already he goes with the best society, & is becoming known, & his opportunities are great, but it will give him a hard pull to beat me. ... Said he should study as long as he had originally intended, not four years more, which I doubt—told him that I didn't mean ever to get married, which I suppose he doubts, though I was never more serious than when I asserted it.

Hermann found Storer "not at home"[22] on March 17 and it is possible that Horatio had joined Atwood "fishing for halibut on Nantucket Shoals" in the new 80-ton *Golden Eagle*.[23] If so, Horatio had returned by March 21 when he presented another paper on medical botany at the Boston Society of Natural History.[24] Hermann saw Horatio at Sunday school the next week and reported:[25]

Sunday May 9th 1852 Storer opened the school & made a very brief address upon the spring time, quite good for a beginner. Told him I was going [west]. Says he shall go soon into the Boston Dispensary, & on 1st Sep spend a couple of months at Deer Island, asked him to accompany me. Says he must "stay dumb"—well, who doesn't work in this world. S. is cursed disagreeable in many things, doesn't possess the faculty of accommodating himself, his pomposity & miserable ambition after fashion peeps out in every word he utters. But perhaps I am too severe.

A month-and-a-half later we obtain a third-hand view via Hermann of the romance between Horatio and Emily: "Thursday July 15 At Boston. Met Mrs. Storer there [Earle's] fixing up her family—thought I was pretty much browned up—says Horace stays at *her* home at Rye Beach, while his affianced love stays at the Hotel—seemed to intimate that the aforesaid youth was devilishly infatuated."[26]

Hermann made his trip west to Cincinnati, the Great Lakes, Cleveland, etc.[27] Horatio's decline of Hermann's invitation to join him on the trip may account for Hermann's ill disposition when he returned to Boston. Hermann noted in his journal:[28]

Friday, 3rd September, 1852. Have just had a visit of an hour or more from Storer and devilishly ill disposed I was to see him. Am only afraid my aversion showed itself, it was certainly very ill disguised. Don't know from what cause, but the fact is certain that the fellow had become very distasteful in my sight, his egotism & bombast & conceit to begin with are disgusting. His talk is always of his own elevation and to the throwing other people into the shade. His expected possession of property has also tended to make him cursedly disgusting, wanted to know if I should like to sell my share in the Boston Athenaeum. He had been investing in other funds & didn't know but that he should like to make something of an investment in that institution. Said his health was not good. That he had been at Rye all Summer—that he proposed to spend the next month at Hingham &c &c talked of the Liquor Tax &c—and absurdly expressed himself in favor of its enforcement—& that people should be made to yield to it ... Didn't give me anything new, it was a relief to have him depart.

The famous experimental physiologist, Dr. Charles Brown-Séquard, came to Boston and provided a series of lectures in November and December "connected with physiology, and especially with that of the nervous system" which Horatio almost surely attended, since three of Horatio's Medical School classmates published a letter thanking the physiologist.[29] This visit of Brown-Séquard probably marked the beginning of the friendship between Horatio and the physiologist to which Horatio would proudly refer over the years.

Horatio was to occupy a good portion of the December 15 meeting of the Boston Society of Natural History expressing his concern for the Provincetown fishery. If he did not make the therapeutic fishing trip in April, he certainly was in touch with Captain Atwood and aware of Atwood's plight. The *Proceedings* indicate that Horatio blamed the bluefish for serious injury to the coastal fishery, noting that the normally large catch of mackerel at Provincetown "was now almost entirely stopped by the presence of these voracious marauders." The *Proceedings* continued by noting that Horatio proposed the Society "memorialize the Legislature on the subject." He proposed that Massachusetts place a bounty on the bluefish to induce fisherman "to make active exertions to exterminate such an injurious race."[30] Horatio also discussed the local prejudices that led to failure of Massachusetts to utilize fish which were considered delicacies elsewhere such as the bluefish and the pollack. As a result of the discussion it was "*Voted*, That a Committee of three be appointed to take into consideration the subject of the Preservation and Economic Value of our own Fish, and the Introduction of Foreign species into our waters. Mr. W. O. Ayres, Dr. D. H. Storer, and Mr. H. R. Storer were chosen a Committee for this purpose."[31]

When the Boylston Medical Society resumed its meetings, Horatio was elected Vice President. The first debate on December 3 dealt with the topic: "Is a surgeon justified in rendering a boy impotent, or a girl barren, who may labor under imperfect development of the sexual organs, in order to prevent the mental or physical misery of their maturity?" Horatio argued in the affirmative and the minutes indicate another loss for Horatio's side.[32] Horatio was absent from the December 31 meeting of the Boylston Medical Society, despite being one of the appointed debaters. One suspects that he was ill, since the debate topic, "Is mechanical dilation of the os uteri ever useful?", would have been one of much interest to Horatio, who Hermann had suggested was already committed to study and treatment of the diseases of women. What is more, Horatio was scheduled to speak in the affirmative.[33]

Warner's references to Storer dropped sharply in 1853, but one read: "Sunday 27 March 1853 Went to Church—hear that Storer has gone South for his health—hope 'twill do him good—he runs himself out during the winter & is obliged to rush off to recoup—but it will be a drawback upon him when he gets into practice."[34] "South" apparently was just to the adjacent state of

Connecticut since Hermann wrote nearly a month later:

> Saturday 21 May   Thayer dropped in and I am sorry to hear from
> him that Storer is in a poor way (to use his words) owing to the ardor
> with which he has pursued his studies. His restless disposition is
> proving too much for his physical power. He has gone to Hartford
> —lives upon a farm—and outdoor exercise—and is striving to im-
> prove. If this continued ill health does not alter somewhat I don't see
> how he can pursue the active duties of his profession—which I regret
> excessively for no man of his age & experience would be more
> competent to discharge them. I always thought him even something
> of a genius—strong affections—great determination to do his duty
> —fond of labor to excess—a fund of knowledge—& an open liberal
> Christian disposition—God grant that my early friend may recover.[35]

A week later Hermann wrote:[36]

> Monday 30 May 1853   Mother says Father had a talk the other day
> with old Brewer, Storer's grandfather, in which B. spoke of Hora-
> tio—& said if he didn't recover he (B) should have to send him to
> Europe—that his (S's) father had written that he should be at home
> by Fri or Sat—& that when the disaster at Norwalk occurred which
> was a Friday he was greatly disturbed & immediately proceeded
> thither &c—& that the excitement consequent upon it threw him quite
> back—that he was in a poor way—am devilish sorry to hear it.

The "disaster at Norwalk" had occurred on May 6, 1853. According to
the *Boston Daily Evening Traveller* it was "the most awful railroad accident
which it has been our duty to record."[37]   The engine and several cars of a
passenger train traveling north from New York City plunged through an open
drawbridge into the Norwalk River. Fifty-four passengers died in the accident,
including a number of physicians who were returning from the annual meeting
of the American Medical Association which had been held in New York City.
Among the survivors were Dr. Jonathan Mason Warren and his family who
were in the back half of the third passenger car which "parted in the centre."
We have noted that Warren was one of the principal Boston surgeons whose
operations Horatio routinely viewed and later assisted at the Massachusetts
General Hospital.

Horatio apparently was not too ill, for shortly after the Norwalk disaster
he "walked a week" with his Harvard classmate, Joseph Henry Thayer, who had
been Hermann's college roommate. Hermann gives us the following details that
seem to indicate Horatio became as enthusiastic about his fiancee as he ever had
been about birds' eggs:[38]

Saturday 18 June 1853 Took a ride with Thayer this afternoon ... & had a very pleasant time of it—It seems that when he went up to the White Mountains, or the Franconia Mountains rather, he had Storer for a companion. He says Storer & his family have been a little at East—S will get his degree he says by favor—His father says he had done no studying for a year & a half—Ever since his falling in with his girl—whom T describes as intelligent, but lacking in force of character. T thinks S has been a little out of his mind all the while—writes long letters to the girl, & since March when he went to Hartford has written hardly half a dozen lines to his family. S says people don't understand him. T met him at Conway or there-abouts & walked a week with him. He is now at Centre Harbor—is to be married in the early part of July—& spend the remainder of the summer there.—T says *he* himself is going to Europe in August.

Horatio and Emily Elvira Gilmore were married on Tuesday, July 12, 1853. The certificate indicates that Emily was 19 and Horatio was a physician. The ceremony was performed by Rev. Ezra Stiles Gannett, D.D., presumably at Gannett's Unitarian church in Boston.[39] For some reason, Hermann planned *not* to go to Horatio's wedding reception. Six days before the wedding he noted in his journal: "Wednesday 6 July 1853 Received a wedding card from Storer that he is *at home next Tues between 12 & 2*—well what of it, I shan't call within such imprudent limits as that—I hope he don't mean to *perform* on that occasion—so goes the world."[40] Two weeks after his marriage, Horatio received his M.D. The newlyweds' stay at Centre Harbor, New Hampshire apparently continued at least until mid-November when Horatio wrote the following to congratulate another medical school classmate, Edward Hitchcock, on Hitchcock's nuptials:[41]

> Centre Harbor, N. H.
> 16 Nov: 1853
>
> My Dear fellow,
>   Your good news, so very unexpected, has given me great joy. My prayers are with you.
>   The same mail brought tidings of my brother Frank's dangerous illness at the Cape of Good Hope—acute phthisis, we fear. Since marriage I have been too happy, perhaps—& needed this fearful blow from God.
>   To your wife give warm congratulations from *us*—& sometimes recollect
>
> Horatio R. Storer

Francis Humphreys Storer was on an expedition to the Bering Straits. He survived his "dangerous illness" which proved not to be tuberculosis.
    Horatio's next known letter was his resignation from the Herpetology

Curatorship of the Boston Society of Natural History. This December 19 letter indicated that he was sailing "this week for Europe."[42] Horatio's passport gives us another physical description of him: Stature—5 Feet 10 Inches; Forehead—broad; Eyes—grey; Nose—common; Mouth—small; Chin—round; Complexion—sandy; Hair—light; Face—oval.[43] Horatio must have been somewhat late maturing, given that he grew three inches after he was seventeen. Although steamships were available, Horatio, Emily Elvira, and Charles Gilmore, Emily's brother, sailed on the barque, *Sultana*, for Malta.[44] The ship sailed on December 24 with "wind WNW good breeze."[45]

Hermann noted Horatio's departure to Europe, and the ingrate who refused to visit Horatio on his wedding day, dared to say in the following that Horatio "acted shabbily & mean" in not visiting Hermann before departing:[46]

> Friday 23 December 1853   I hear that Storer has gone to Malagh—Hasn't even paid me the compliment of a talk—He has acted shabbily & mean—hope he feels the better for it—I once thought he had a character formed to admit a liberal friendship, but I was mistaken—my disappointment has been keen—but the subject is disagreeable—I shall drop it forever.

It is regrettable that someone more sympathetic than Hermann is not available as a source on this important and happy period of Horatio's life. The "long letters to the girl" that Horatio wrote during his engagement apparently were not saved. One can guess that they were masterpieces. The mental illness and early death of Emily Elvira may have caused Horatio to destroy such letters and other reminders of the great unpleasantness and grief that followed these early periods of their relationship when Horatio described himself to Edward Hitchcock as "too happy."

A decade later, Horatio noted: "Immediately on entering practice, it became evident to me that the great field for advance in obstetric therapeutics was *the interior* of the uterus,—an opinion that was daily strengthened during the intimate relations to which I was admitted by Prof. Simpson in 1854-55."[47] Thus we have one indication that Horatio practiced medicine even before leaving for Europe in December 1853. If so, it apparently occurred while he was in New Hampshire during the months immediately following his marriage. And here we thought that Horatio was just enjoying a long honeymoon!

> In Oct. [Dec.] 1853,[48] I went abroad with your mother, intending to spend two years in Vienna, and possibly have a passing glimpse at Simpson, whom Channing used constantly to praise in his lectures, and to whom he had given me a letter as interested in "natural history," on my way home.   John P. Reynolds, Ellis, Hodges, and C[harles]. D. Homans had just gone to V., and as I knew them all intimately, though a little older than myself, I had agreed to meet and

stay with them there.[49]

Thus Horatio described the trip to Europe in the letter to Malcolm nearly fifty years later. "Ellis" was Dr. Calvin Ellis, "Hodges" was Dr. Richard Manning Hodges, and these four Vienna-bound physicians would play key roles in Horatio's later professional career, particularly Ellis and Hodges.

The first entry in Horatio's Passport is by the "Superintendent of Police—Malta" on January 27, 1854, indicating a passage of about 34 days. On February 8, Horatio's passport was "legalized for the departure from Malta for Sicily and Naples." The passport indicates that February and March were spent moving slowly northward through Italy with stops at Naples, Rome, Venice, Milan, and other cities.[50] "Your mother's fall on a stairway in Venice when four months gone with Jessie," Horatio wrote in 1901, "disarranged all my plans, and sent me by stages [stagecoaches] ... to Switzerland, Germany, Paris, London, and Edinburgh, whence I expected, after your mother should be confined, to go back to Vienna."[51]

Paris captured Horatio from about April 4 to May 8, despite Emily's delicate condition. While there he watched operations on vesicovaginal fistula by Jobert de Lamballe. Horatio wrote in 1901: "These were all published the next day in the Gazette des Hopitaux as 'guérisons' [cures], and immediately thereafter the fistulae were as large as ever." Marion Sims already had achieved *bona-fide* cures for vesicovaginal fistulae by this time, but his techniques had not yet reached Paris. Although Sims had published on his successful technique in 1853, it is doubtful that Horatio was aware of it either, given his infatuation with Emily. This was not all that Horatio reported he did in Paris: "In Paris I attended the wards, obstetrical and puerperal, of Paul Dubois, and at the Lourcine, by special permission, studied venereal with Gosselin, I think it was,—and the same with Ricord, I think at Hotel Dieu. R. used to advise us to treat gleet with the hair of the dog that bit. I repeatedly saw Jobert apply the 'fer rouge' [cauterizing iron] to carcinomatous or merely hypertrophied cervices."

"In London I found nothing of especial interest," his 1901 letter continued, "Clay of Manchester was removing ovaries, and Baker Brown hypertrophied clitorides, but they were both under professional ban, which afterward proved unjustifiable." Horatio's interests in natural history probably had vent in London at John Hunter's museum, and surely did when he reached Edinburgh where he was the guest of Sir William Jardine. Horatio had corresponded with Jardine as early as 1850, received a box of eggs from him in 1851, and herpetology specimens after that. Horatio mentioned this visit in a May 24 letter to Dr. John Collins Warren,[52] President of the Boston Society of Natural History. It included a pamphlet picked up in Paris dealing with Warren's "favorite study," almost certainly mastodons. It also included a geological report written by Jardine and described Jardine's willingness to exchange more specimens with the Boston Society.

Hermann helps keep us in touch with Horatio and his brother Frank:[53]

Saturday 17 June 1854 Saw Miss Storer only—& she looked as pretty as she can & will look. Had quite a long & very pleasant chat—she says her brother Horatio is coming home in Oct—left Italy in April—went to Paris—& is now at Edinburgh, studying. Her brother Frank has resigned his situation on board the U.S. Expedition to Behring's Straits—& is in Canton waiting for a vessel in which to return home.

The key role that James Young Simpson played in Horatio's life has already been stressed and it is not surprising that this predicted October return of Horatio did not occur, since this would have allowed only about five months of work with the physician to whom he became as devoted as he was to his own father. In 1911, Horatio provided a highly autobiographical account of his time with Simpson in a letter to Sir Alexander R. Simpson, M.D., a nephew of Sir James.[54] It also included interesting details about the ether controversy in Boston, the later ether-chloroform controversy involving Boston and Edinburgh, and a related interpretation of the Harvard Medical School's long neglect of gynecology. The minor errors made by Horatio in the following excerpts are corrected immediately afterward in brackets:

Hotel Brighton, Atlantic City, N. J.
22nd May 1911

My Dear Doctor Simpson,—

Yours of the 6th inst. has reached me here on my way home to Newport from several months in Florida. As with many other kind letters I have had from you during nearly half a century, it has again reminded me of the happy period that I spent as almost a member of your uncle's household. A reminder as to how this came about may still interest you.

In 1846 surgical anaesthesia was realized in Boston, at the Massachusetts General Hospital, where it was rendered effective, being then, as ever subsequently, a virtual appendage of Harvard University, at which in 1847 [actually 1846] I matriculated as a student. My father was at the time one of the physicians of the hospital. For this reason I was permitted prematurely to attend the operations thereat in advance of my graduation in medicine in 1853. Though I was not present at the very first ether cases, I saw a great many of the early later ones, and was privileged to be present, as assistant, during 1851 to 1853, at perhaps most of the private surgical work of two of the most prominent surgeons at the hospital, Doctors Henry J. Bigelow and J. Mason Warren. Therefore from the outset I was trained to believe in the superexcellence of sulphuric ether.

Upon leaving for Europe in October [December] 1853 it was my intention to spend a couple of years at Vienna, then the Mecca of most young American Physicians.   For a very curious reason, however, I did not reach that city till twenty years later—in 1873. In the fifties Professor Simpson was at the head of living gynaecologists; indeed he may be truly said to have created this department, as distinguished from parturition and its few peculiar diseases. Appreciating this fact, and even then intending to make gynaecology my eventual specialty, I did not dare hope for more than a mere glimpse of so great a man.   Just before sailing, my preceptor in obstetrics, Dr. Walter Channing, who had visited Professor Simpson, and had written a large work upon *Etherisation in Childbirth*, asked if I would not like a letter of introduction to him. You can conceive my elation at this, and my subsequent chagrin upon finding that the letter commended me as "an enthusiastic student in natural history." Channing knew my real wish, but even then the intense jealousies of the ether-chloroform controversy were having their effect upon the Boston mind. My first impulse, fortunately not yielded to, was to destroy the letter, in utter disbelief in its possible usefulness. Having progressed toward Vienna as far as Venice, an accident of my traveling companion induced me to change my route, and after visiting hospitals in Paris and London, and finding myself so near to Edinburgh, I went thither, as I supposed, for merely a day or two. Bethinking of the Channing letter, I called at 52 Queen Street, with very little anticipation of what was there to occur.

Passing a great staircase, which many grand ladies were ascending, and through a hall filled with poor women, I was shown into a spacious library, around which were waiting a number of anxious husbands and physicians who had brought patients. At a desk in the centre sat a most attractive young secretary, the future Sir William Overend Priestley, a relative of the famous chemist, and who himself was to become so distinguished a gynaecologist in London. This gentleman received me most cordially, and the friendship, soon to become so close, remained unbroken until his death. Presently the professor came down from above, hastened from one to another, and then opening Channing's letter, said, "My friend mentions that Dr. Storer is greatly interested in natural history. Now, there is but little of that sort of thing in Edinburgh. My time is very limited, but for the next day or two I will try to show you what there is.   What branch do you care most for?" I replied, "the diseases of women." "Oh, ho!" he said, "that's wholly a different affair. Come upstairs."

He then took me into a little chamber adjoining his own central consulting-room. A lady was lying upon a couch. "She is the wife," he said, "of a very prominent clergyman in New York. Examine her. I will return in fifteen minutes, and you shall tell me her disease." I was greatly embarrassed, and so was the lady, but she said that in that house all must do as the professor commanded. He returned, and I acknowledged my utter ignorance. He replied that I was so far right, for he had himself seen but one similar case. Taking me into another chamber, I thought that the lesion here might probably be so and so. "Wrong, but very near the truth." Regarding a third patient I ventured a positive diagnosis, was this time right, and invited to breakfast next morning. Thence I gradually advanced day by day, through the professor's great kindness and patience, until he admitted me to full assistantship with Priestley, in charge of his private cases, even of the greatest importance, and his house became to me a second home.

I have spoken at length of this episode as showing how greatly a mere word, in season, may change a man's whole life.

Of Dr. Simpson himself, his leonine personality, his goodness to the poor, his tenaciousness of views that his experience had proved correct, his courage, his hatred of wrong, his deep religious belief, the world knows of all these. I could instance, from my own personal knowledge, a thousand examples. Better, however, that I, an old man, in my eighty-second year, should speak of matters of more general and important bearing.

Upon my leaving Edinburgh at the close of 1855 [May or June 1855] Dr. Simpson urged me to settle permanently in Glasgow, thinking, of course, that I might be of aid in the care of his even then very large number of American patients. I decided, however, to return to Boston. ...

From the beginning of the ether-chloroform controversy in 1848, and even now, the name of Simpson has been anathema in Boston. Immediately after 1846 the profession was in a ferment regarding the rival claims of Morton and Jackson—the one a seeker for an agent for surgical insensibility to pain, and the other the suggestor of sulphuric ether—both subsequently quarreling, and each claiming exclusive merit. No one who was not upon the spot can have the slightest idea of the professional rancour and virulence that prevailed. Into this turbulent camp, like a bomb, came the announcement of chloroform, and not unnaturally, and in self-relief as it were, even if we eliminate the national features of the case, the adherents of both great contending factions turned, as one man, against Simpson. Their sons and their sons' sons have inherited the unkind feeling, just as occurred in the Harvey and Jenner, and a great many other colossal professional controversies.   ...

Aside from the chloroform controversy, Simpson's fame as a gynaecologist was secure. ... At almost every one of the American colleges Simpson's teachings, as such, are perpetuated. There is, however, one great and marked exception. The Medical School of Harvard University has been, and is still prominent in its neglect of everything pertaining to gynaecology. In every other department there are professors, assistant professors, and instructors, almost without number. Here gynaecology is practically placed at the bottom of the list. It will be said that disapproval of chloroform has had nothing to do with this virtual boycott. The coincidence, however, is not undeserving comment.* [Footnote in the original: *Possibly my remarks regarding the Harvard Medical School, with its present immense resources, may be somewhat overdrawn, for I am not familiar with its latest curriculum, but they are certainly true of the neglect of gynaecology at its great hospital, at which both myself and my son were educated.]

Horatio concluded by describing his editorship with Priestley of Simpson's *Obstetric Memoirs,* his own illness in 1872 that led to his leaving Boston for Europe, and his return to Rhode Island where "Chloroform is not ... a chimaera dire, and Simpson's memory is beloved."

Horatio's 1901 letter to Malcolm, included some additional facts about the time with Simpson:[55]

At Edinburgh I was taught in the very first place to forget everything that I had previously learned, and to begin entirely anew,—not to employ the speculum in diagnosis, and to rely upon the touch and sound.[56] Every day for a year was one constant succession of real revelations,—and, above all, Priestley and I were made to form our own conclusions, aided by the suggestions, but never, aside from the lecture room, by the "I say so," of our great master.

In 1867, Horatio told the New York Medical Society the following about his Edinburgh year: "Being entered in the directory of that city as a regularly licensed practitioner, chosen into its several medical societies, and becoming the father of a Scotch lassie, I felt myself almost a Scotchman."[57]

The "Scotch lassie" was born on September 2 and they named her Jessie Simpson Storer. The middle name came from Horatio's mentor and her first name from his mentor's spouse. Horatio's pleasure with "the little chick" is not at all restrained in this letter to his sister Mary:[58]

Edinburgh
20 Oct. 1854

My Dear Mary,
    After writing Abby the other day, this fairly belongs to you. I

hope it will find a welcome.

Emily and Jessie both are doing nicely, & if you find additional attractions in babes who grow "sweeter & sweeter" each day of their lives, I think you would be satisfied with her. Mind by the way, that the epithet used above is none of mine, that is to say, it didn't use to be, but to tell the truth I can't help repeating it sometimes after hearing it applied by every friend who comes to see us. The little chick continues besides just as good in behavior as good can be which I consider the more praiseworthy, in as much as just at present she is suffering from a severe cold in the head. I am sure she does not inherit this tendency toward propriety from her father, for under similar circumstances he would certainly have kicked up a great row, especially at nights.

She is just beginning to know one from another to stretch her arms out towards persons or things. She takes greatest satisfaction in this aspect if & at such times to gather her face up into just the funniest little laugh of approval I ever did see.

I suppose you'll laugh at reading these my ecstacies in paper. I'm sure you would if you could see the real ones I go into at many & diverse times through each day, but I can fool myself with the reflection that Uncle Thomas & Uncle John[59] are, just about these times, each affording the same pleasant spectacles of

THE HAPPY MAN!

which so far as entertainment & a few other conducives to domestic enjoyment go, is a look of animal of which I had not the slightest previous conception.

. . .

Tell father I sent him *the rest* of those medical papers next Saturday, by Mr. Bartol & he should then have a complete series of 128 pages, besides several more independently numbered, that I sent by mother. In a trunk from Miss Kuhn to her mother there also is a roll of "Tables" for Professor S. My head has borne the effort much better than I could have expected. Seems *no worse*, & though my eyes were pretty severely tried by the night work, yet I trust their discomfort will be but temporary. I wanted the notes to be all in his hands before he began his course, & if they are of any help to him, then will not a whit of my debt of gratitude have been repaid. God bless him & all of you my Darlings, in Brotherly love. H.

This is the only letter that has been located from Horatio to his family during this trip abroad in 1854-1855. Of most importance, we learn of the immensely proud and happy young father of Jessie Simpson Storer. We also learn that in addition to his own study with Simpson, Horatio was taking great labors to help his father prepare for his new Professorship of Obstetrics and

Medical Jurisprudence at the Harvard Medical School. We have already noted how Horatio believed that the Tremont Street Medical School was founded as a means for the founding professors to be appointed to the Harvard Medical School. If so, the process of making the leap from Tremont Street to Harvard took fifteen years for David Humphreys Storer, probably because the distinguished Dr. Walter Channing so ably held the chair of obstetrics that best fit David Humphreys Storer. Channing was sixty-eight in 1854. As will be seen, he remained active in medical societies and medical publication after retiring and continued to be important in Horatio's life.

Horatio and William Overend Priestley, Simpson's other assistant, edited a collection of Simpson's articles on obstetrics and gynecology in 1854-1855. An editorial in the *Boston Medical and Surgical Journal* for March 29, 1855 made mention of this and praised the American editor:[60]

> The editing of these valuable papers is committed to the competent care of Dr. Horatio R. Storer, assisted by Dr. Priestley, of Edinburgh. Dr. Storer's abilities are well known to the profession here, and both he and his coadjutor have had the great advantage of close personal intercourse with Dr. Simpson, and of seeing a very large number of cases in his practice, many of which have been entrusted to their care.

This editorial indicated that Horatio was assisted by Priestley, and Horatio's 1901 letter to Malcolm indicated that the idea to collect and publish Simpson's papers was his own. However, Horatio signed himself "The Junior Editor" in his dedication of the American Edition of the two-volume work entitled, *The Obstetric Memoirs and Contributions of Sir James Y. Simpson, Professor of Midwifery in the University of Edinburgh.*[61]

Horatio wrote a separate and controversial "Preface to the American Edition." In it, he discussed generally acknowledged advances in gynecology made by Simpson, such as use of the uterine sound for diagnosis and use of sponge tents to dilate the cervix. Horatio also discussed other Simpson contributions, such as treatment of uterine displacements by intra-uterine pessaries, which Horatio admitted some medical men disagreed were advances. Horatio then proceeded to attack the credibility of the physician who most strongly disagreed about the utility of pessaries. This was Dr. Robert Lee of London and Horatio indicated that Lee had been Simpson's critic "since 1840,—the date of their competing together for the chair Dr. Simpson now holds in the University of Edinburgh." Horatio wrote: "I think no one can systematically follow out the details of this warfare, as I have done, and still consider Dr. Lee an earnest physician laboring only for truth's sake." He then noted some of Lee's science which Horatio viewed as flawed and concluded: "Objections to the intra-uterine pessary coming from such a source as this, and probably based on not a single truthful observation, should certainly gain no credence."[62]   The following concluding paragraph of Horatio's Preface shows his extreme devotion to Simpson, indicating that it paralleled the enormous devotion we have seen that Horatio held for his father:

> In conclusion, we omitted these matters [criticism of Lee, etc.], as I have said, in the Edinburgh edition, and I have referred to them here, because in the one case they seem needed.   In doing so, I have perhaps overstepped my bounds, and exchanged the coldness of an editor for the warmth—I trust still impartial—of a friend. If such is the case, I shall look for excuse to the peculiar relations in which I have stood to Dr. Simpson. For one year I was admitted to close intimacy with him—to his home. I learned to love him as my father; he treated me as a son. I am proud to call him master.

When the editors of the *Boston Medical and Surgical Journal* had the opportunity to view the published first volume they referred again, on June 28, 1855, most positively to the editorial effort:[63]

> We have already referred to the great care and industry bestowed by the editors Drs. Priestley and Storer, upon this valuable work. To unremitting labor they have evidently added that strong interest in their undertaking which has omitted nothing of value, and which has often induced them to make a digest of papers previously reported to Societies, &c.; much of this work having been done, of necessity, at late hours of the night, and through many months. We think that the profession, everywhere owe to these gentlemen a large debt of obligation, and we are sure they will acknowledge this, on the appearance of the book.

Almost a year later, the *New Orleans Medical and Surgical Journal* was much less kind to the American editor in a long scathing review of the "Memoirs and Contributions." It included:[64]

> The warlike attitude, offensive and defensive, assumed by the Boston editor, is altogether *con amore*, free-fighting, being "entirely without Dr. Simpson's permission, which is utterly refused." This protector-ship over Dr. Simpson, together with Dr. Storer's filibusterism against Dr. Simpson's enemies of the French Academy, and, more than all, against "the inveterate" Dr. Robert Lee, of London, as the sequel will show, is not only gratuitous and self-imposed, but altogether unwarrantable, and the more so because the reader is assured that "it will be painful to Dr. Simpson," as it is sure to be to all right-thinking readers of this volume. It is said by the editor that

"Dr. Simpson had replied at length to several attacks. The remainder he has probably considered beneath his notice;"—"he is desirous that by-gones should be past and wrongs forgotten." Alas! had he been saved from his friends!

The editor of the *New Orleans Medical and Surgical Journal* and author of the critical review was Dr. Bennett Dowler who was well known for his experiments on the nervous system of alligators.[65] He not only criticized Horatio's excessive praise of Simpson and Horatio's excessive criticism of Simpson's enemies, he denounced Simpson's intra-uterine pessary, denied that Simpson invented the uterine sound, and criticized Horatio's and Priestley's selection and organization of Simpson's works. Horatio was certainly vulnerable to criticism for his treatment of Dr. Lee, and the fact that the *Boston Medical and Surgical Journal* only praised his editorial actions, indicates that Horatio in these early days of his Boston practice was being protected by at least some of the Boston medical establishment. He would eventually receive quite different treatment from the *Boston Medical and Surgical Journal*.

In the *New Orleans Medical and Surgical Journal* review, Dowler also criticized Simpson's exploring needle used to "diagnosticate 'tumors about the cervix uteri, cases of extra-uterine pregnancy,' &c." and also Simpson's contention that such could be "inserted with 'impunity into even the viscera of the living body.'" "It is well known," wrote Dowler, "that the criminal abortion-procurers, who, not possessing Dr. Simpson's skill, (it may be,) insert needles into the os tincae, cervix uteri, &c., are apt to cause either two deaths or one, or dangerous inflammations of the uterus and its annexes."[66] We know that Horatio read Dowler's paper, since Horatio referred to Dowler's criticism of pessaries a few months later.[67] Dowler's reference to criminal abortion in March 1856, five months after Horatio's father's claim that induced abortion caused much uterine disease (discussed in Chapter 5), may have been one factor that influenced Horatio to commence his own research on criminal abortion, or at least to begin a tabulation of the instances where his married patients admitted to the induced abortions in their past.

While editing the "Memoirs and Contributions," Horatio also found time to take up the cause of his teacher and friend, Dr. Jonathan Mason Warren, and of the Boston Society for Medical Improvement. Warren was an outstanding surgeon, but Dr. James D. Gillespie, Assistant Surgeon at the Edinburgh Royal Infirmary, criticized Warren's "malpractice" of amputating an arm rather than resecting an elbow. A key paragraph of Gillespie's paper stated:[68]

We have given this case entire, not from any peculiarly interesting features it contains, but for the purpose of showing that a society, instituted for medical improvement, as it did not challenge the recorded malpractice, appears to be unacquainted with one of the most successful modern improvements in surgery, viz: Resection of the elbow-joint, evidently the proper procedure in the case in question.

Gillespie's attack appeared in the *Edinburgh Medical and Surgical Journal* in January 1855 and, at the time, Horatio was working with Simpson in Edinburgh. Horatio wrote and published a rebuttal of Gillespie's attack on Warren showing why amputation was appropriate, although it was not published until May 19, 1855 and then not in the Edinburgh journal, but in the *London Medical Times and Gazette*.[69] Horatio's rebuttal appears to have been mailed to Dr. Warren in America before it was published, since Warren praised Horatio for coming to the defense of "American Surgery" at an April 9, 1855 meeting of the Boston Society for Medical Improvement.[70]

Hermann Jackson Warner noted in his journal that Horatio returned to Boston on June 7, 1855.[71] Five days later, the first patient was admitted to the new Boston Lying-in Hospital where Horatio held the high honor of being one of three attending physicians.[72] David Humphreys Storer, as the Harvard Medical School Professor of Obstetrics, undoubtedly had a large influence on the new obstetric hospital and was to become one of its Consulting Physicians. Thus it is not too surprising that the relatively inexperienced Horatio was on the hospital's staff. One suspects that his father had been setting up the appointment while Horatio was in Edinburgh and Horatio hurried home to accept it before the first patient was admitted. As will be seen, a critic was later to note that there were more attending physicians for the Lying-in Hospital than was necessary for its clientele.

Horatio left for Centre Harbor, New Hampshire around the end of June where he spent the summer. Obviously, there were not so many patients at the new Lying-in Hospital that all three attending physicians needed to remain in the city. The Harvard alumnus who in 1851 wrote the Class Secretary, Charles Hale, that he would attend every class reunion "unless prevented by absence or by serious indisposition" wrote Hale from Centre Harbor on July 13 that Boston was too hot to make the trip.[73] Horatio was involved in medical affairs during his Summer in New Hampshire. We learn this from a record of the Boston Society for Medical Improvement. Dr. Calvin Ellis exhibited an unusual ten-pound diseased liver "sent by Dr. H. R. Storer, who saw the patient in Aug. 1855, in consultation with Dr. McIntire, of Goshen, N.H." The liver had been provided to Horatio by Dr. McIntire following the March-1856 death and autopsy of its owner.[74]

"Uterine tents" were mentioned in Horatio's "Preface to the American Edition" of Simpson's *Obstetric Memoirs* as one of the important gynaecological tools invented by his mentor. These were small pieces of dry sponge inserted into the small opening at the base of the uterus (cervix). As they absorbed moisture the tents expanded and thereby enlarged this opening. This made it possible "to expose intrauterine polypi."[75] However, Horatio himself had objections to Simpson's sponge tent. According to Horatio, the problems with sponge included its too-rapid expansion which led to irritation, inflammation, and even lacerations in some instances. There also was the its tendency to decomposition and to unpleasant odor when sponge was subjected to various uterine secretions. Horatio recommended that tents be made from the bark of the elm tree. He first made this proposal while still in Edinburgh in a paper presented to their Medico-Chirurgical Society in May 1855.[76] After returning to the U.S. and "being frequently questioned upon the subject," he prepared a long paper on "elm tents" which he signed on October 29, 1855 and which was published a week later in the *Boston Medical and Surgical Journal.*[77]

Horatio mentioned in his new paper that there were physicians who were unwilling to use sponge tents or any other form of expansible uterine tent. Horatio suspected in some non-users the problem was "lack of skill in their application," in others, "utter ignorance that tents have ever been proposed." However, Horatio found their rejection by "certain gentlemen" with neither of these excuses "quite unaccountable." He then all but named one "in the foremost rank of surgeons in this city, alike regarding age, position, and respect of all, and as the possessor of a most enviable European reputation in one branch of obstetric surgery." Horatio even more unwisely continued:

> This gentleman, in conversation not long since, informed me of his utter disbelief in the advantages of any form of uterine tent. I can only think that he is mistaken. Perhaps like another gentleman, of whom and whose reputation we are all justly proud, and who for many years is said to have doubted the existence at any time or under any circumstances, of a distinctly marked hymen, although he has now, I believe, changed his mind on this subject, my friend has probably been singularly unfortunate in the cases that have come under his notice.

Thus, with a single paragraph of his first major medical publication, Horatio made a pair of enemies, not counting the friends of these men with "enviable reputations." One suspects that some animosity already existed between Horatio or his father and these two physicians of high "rank" and "reputation" whom Horatio singled out for such cavalier treatment. After this foolhardy attempt at humor or even injury, Horatio went on to discuss the two major advantages of elm bark tents, namely their slower rate of expansion and the "abundant mucilage poured forth from the cells of the elm" that prevented the irritation frequently associated with sponge. However, one suspects most of his readers did not get beyond the paragraph discussing a prominent Boston physician's unfortunate lack of experience with "a distinctly marked hymen."

CHAPTER 5
FATHER'S LECTURE, MEDICAL PAPERS, MEDICAL SOCIETIES

The *Boston Medical and Surgical Journal* for November 1, 1855 printed the following invitation:[1]

Medical Lectures of Harvard University.—The Introductory Lecture will be delivered at the Massachusetts Medical College, on Wednesday, Nov. 7th, at 12 o'clock, by Professor Storer. Physicians, and gentlemen interested in Medical Science, are respectfully invited to attend.

The Introductory Lecture marked the beginning of the new term of the Harvard Medical School and was a major event attended by many physicians in addition to the students. David Humphreys Storer's lecture was entitled "Duties, Trials and Rewards of the Student of Midwifery," and one non-controversial portion was published immediately[2] and the "suppressed" remainder seventeen years later.[3] The non-controversial bulk of the address dealt with the unique requirements for treating the diseases of women and stressed the important role that the attending physician played in childbirth, even when all he did was patiently wait for nature to take its usual course, but particularly when it did not. Before launching into these two themes of diseases of women and midwifery, he cautioned the new students that only the truly committed should continue in medical studies. He wrote:[4]

If, however, you have unwillingly, or without having seriously considered the importance of the step, commenced your journey—if, as you advance, you are dissatisfied—your studies are irksome—for them you not only feel no enthusiasm, but an utter disgust—I would urge you to proceed no farther: relinquish the idea of entering our profession—engage in some more congenial pursuit. Ours is a calling requiring all a man's concentrated energies—worth all a man's undying devotion.

He went on to claim that the sacrifices and trials of the "accoucheur," i.e., the obstetrician, required the strongest commitment of all.[5]

No more trying duty can befall a member of our profession, than to be called upon to treat such cases as are often witnessed by the accoucheur. When life is suspended by a thread—the heart hesitates to throb—the next moment may remove the breathless suspense of agonized friends, or leave a household irrevocably desolate.

The practitioner in this department must be prepared to make great sacrifices. None are compelled to toil more incessantly nor more arduously. None pass so large a portion of their time in the chamber of the sick—none are called upon to observe more intense suffering—to administer aid in case of more heart-rending distress. None are obliged to relinquish so many of the social enjoyments of life.

General and specific advice pertaining to treating women patients and delivering babies followed and these made up a thirty-two-page pamphlet when the lecture was published.

The portion of David Humphreys' lecture which was "suppressed" was his claim that there had been a recent sharp increase in uterine disease and that this was the result of a similar increase in the frequency of criminal abortion. Dr. Hugh L. Hodge had made some of the same points in 1839 in an Introductory Lecture to the new students at his University of Pennsylvania Medical School and it was "by them printed." He apparently presented the Lecture again in 1854, and it was republished "in an amended condition."[6] However, David Humphreys Storer made no reference to Hodge's lectures and he may not have been aware of them. Hodge's and David Humphreys' views apparently were not known by some members of the Harvard medical faculty, since David Humphreys' claim that forced abortion was common was received with "astonishment and doubt."[7] However, as will be seen, others of that faculty, perhaps more correctly, one powerful other, did not doubt David Humphreys Storer's contention that forced abortion was common, but believed that publication of this fact would be "injudicious" and his view prevailed.

Although this was David Humphreys Storer's first public mention of the subject of forced abortion, he indicated in his Introductory Lecture that he had been aware of the problem "long ere" November 1855. David Humphreys not only described the problem as he discerned it, he pleaded for the medical profession to do everything possible to reduce the crime. He regretted that no strong "trumpet-tongued" man of the profession had come forth to take up this cause. His plea almost certainly led Horatio to attempt this role, and, within a year, Horatio had commenced his decades-long anti-abortion campaign.

The suppressed portion of David Humphreys Storer's lecture certainly sounded like the start of the "physicians' campaign against abortion." It began:[8]

I should feel that I had been guilty of an unpardonable neglect were I to omit to glance at a subject the importance of which, each succeeding year, has been more forcibly impressed upon my mind.

I had hoped that, long ere this, some one of the strong men of the profession,—strong in the affections of the community, strong in the confidence of his brethren,—would have spoken, trumpet-tongued, against an existing, and universally acknowledged evil. I have waited in vain. The lecturer is silent, the press is silent, and the enormity, unrebuked, stalks at midday throughout the length and breadth of the land. It is time that this silence should be broken. It is time that men should speak. It is no presumption in the humblest individual to point out a much-needed reformation, however others may doubt the expediency of his course, if he thinks by thus doing he shall awaken in any mind the slightest attention to the subject; particularly if he sincerely believes that anything which can be found to be wrong can be rectified, that anything which ought to be done *can be* done sooner or later, whether it affects an individual, a community, or a race.

David Humphreys then pointed out how there had been a great increase in uterine disease, that the major reason was criminal abortion, and that physicians were unwilling "to dwell upon, or even to refer to" this cause. A key passage read:[9]

Why should we shrink from the performance of any duty, however unpleasant or ungrateful to our feelings it may be, if we think that it is demanded of us? If we know it is clearly a duty, it should be performed. We may, it is too true, be misunderstood; we may be misinterpreted. But this should not prevent us from the full, free expression of our convictions. A true man fears, can fear, nothing.

David Humphreys next discussed the great reduction of the size of families. One reason was the "fashionable young bride" who was unwilling to give up the "excitement of society" and who terminated her pregnancy "apparently unconscious that she is not only committing a crime in the sight of the law, but also a sin in the sight of her Maker." Another was the mother who looked upon her children as her most valuable possessions, but who was unwilling to continue another pregnancy because she felt that it would reduce the family's standard of living, because she had learned "that woman was born for higher and nobler purposes than the propagation of her species," or because some remark by her physician had led her to believe that her good health precluded birth of another child. He then turned his guns on these women and their accomplices:[10]

I do not presume to stand here as a moralist. I would attempt only to point out a few of the duties obligatory upon the physician, as such. I should, however, be faithless to the noble profession which occupies my every thought; I should be unworthy the confidence or esteem of my brethren did I refrain, while referring to this subject, to enter my solemn protest against the existing vice; to express, emphatically, the universal sentiment of horror and indignation entertained among the upright men of the profession in this community. Of *horror*, that the female can so completely unsex herself, that her sensibilities can be so entirely blunted, that any conceivable circumstances can compel her to welcome such degradation! Of *indignation*, that men can be found so regardless of their own characters, so perfectly indifferent respecting those of their cotemporaries [sic], as to lend their services in such unholy transactions.

David Humphreys then moved from moral objections to forced abortion to its serious health consequences for the woman.

A law of the organ of which we have been speaking, requires that a certain specified time shall be occupied in perfecting its most important work; this period is fixed, uniform, universal. ... When the entire limit is reached, when the foetus has become perfectly developed, the system of the mother, gradually being prepared for the approaching event, is able to bear the momentous change unimpaired. ... When, however, from any accidental cause the organ is called upon to perform a duty for which it is unprepared, a greater or less degree of injury must be produced; and when any rude attempt is deliberately made to effect this object, infinitely greater is the probability of there being increased detriment and irretrievable harm; for in addition to the ... unpreparedness of the organ for the attempted change, are the unavoidable local lesions; and that cause, even more important than these (say what men may to the contrary), the deep, heart-felt depression which must weigh upon the spirit of the evil-doer. Hundreds of lives are unquestionably yearly lost by the innumerable methods which are resorted to to produce premature delivery, and thousands of females who escape the grave may date, from these operations, the origin of many exhausting, painful, incurable diseases.

Next came his advice on how physicians could change the situation that he viewed to be so undesirable and which he, unlike a subsequent Horatio, considered largely uninfluenced by laws against abortion.[11]

The laws of the land, with all their penalties annexed, can do but little to abolish the crime. ... in order to produce an effect co-extensive with the transgression, that course should be pursued, the lenity of which proves its sincerity. Reason should be dealt with; moral suasion should be used, and no one can exert a greater influence than the physician; for no one is compelled like him to witness the misery, to see the distress which is acknowledged by the sufferer to have been thus produced, to hear the disclosures as they reluctantly fall from the lips of the dying penitent. We can do much—we can do all. If our profession will feel and act as one man; if they cannot all regard the subject in the same light as I have, as respects its morality, but will look at it merely as a cause of physical suffering to the mother; if they will upon all proper occasions freely express their convictions of its injurious effects, of its present danger, of its detrimental conse-quences,—a triumphant result must follow. Years, a half century perhaps, may elapse before such a reaction shall have been produced, but, slow although it would be, it would be certain. Like all other crimes it might be occasionally perpetrated. To preserve a previously unsullied character, to prevent a deep and damning stain upon a family's reputation, it would be clandestinely resorted to, but the virtuous mother would no longer be found sacrificing her offspring.

There was another implication of the dangers of interrupting physiological processes before their natural completion. This was that contraception was a potential producer of disease. David Humphreys described his belief that repeated "repetition of the unnatural intercourse" would lead to abnormal congestion and enlargement of the uterus with serious consequences. "Without sufficient data to warrant me in stating positively the fact," he continued, "I would, nevertheless, venture the belief that numberless cases of induration, and finally of organic disease, must be the inevitable consequences."

The Introductory Lecture was published at the request of three of the current medical students, one of whom was Horatio's undergraduate roommate and walking-mate, Gustavus Hay, who had entered the Harvard Medical School in 1854.[12] When the pamphlet appeared a few weeks after the address, the editors of the *Boston Medical and Surgical Journal* wrote an editorial about it which included the following:[13]

Deferring to the judgment of others, whose opinions we all delight to honor, Professor Storer has omitted the very paragraphs, which, in our judgment, should have been allowed to go forth as freely as they were spoken. To whom shall the community look for a verdict upon practices which disgrace our land and prevail to an extent that would hardly be credited, if not to physicians—and, chiefest among them, to medical teachers? For ourselves, we have no fear that *the truth*, as told by the writer of this Address, in reference to the *crime of procuring abortion* and the scarcely less heinous offence of *preventing impregnation*, would do aught but good in this, or in any, city. It would appear that sheer ignorance, in many honest people, is the spring of much of the horrible *intra-uterine murder* which exists among us; why not, then, enlighten this ignorance? It would be far more effectually done by some bold and manly appeal like that to which we allude, than by the private and scattered influence of honorable practitioners alone. In this case we will guarantee that vice would be all the more "hated" the more it was revealed, and would be neither "pitied" nor "embraced."

The editors of the *Boston Medical and Surgical Journal* were Dr. Francis Minot and Dr. William W. Morland. These editors may have been the first to emphasize "ignorance" as a key reason for the rise of the crime, and ignorance about the nature of "foetal" life as culprit in the prevalence of criminal abortion was a theme that Horatio repeated frequently in his articles and books over the next decade. The editors' references to "hated," "pitied," and "embraced," probably were shorthand for the reasons given to suppress the abortion material, whether these reasons were provided second-hand to these editors by David Humphreys Storer or directly by the suppressor (discussed below). These "reasons" may have been that to publicly discuss the "hated" crime would have been to cause the women procuring abortion to be "pitied" and such public discussion would lead to the crime being "embraced" by additional women. After a summary of the suppressed material on the dangers to health from abortion and the possible dangers from contraception, the editors concluded: "We can but express the sincere hope that the omitted portion of this lecture may yet appear in print; it is now a hidden jewel, a sort of lost Pleiad—the constellation is imperfect—let the light shine. From no fitter source, in no better manner, and, we are sure, with no more righteous intention, did ever advice fall from a speaker's lips." [14]

Other reasons for the suppression of the 1855 Introductory Lecture were mentioned in an editorial in the *New-Hampshire Journal of Medicine* of July 1857. Horatio Storer wrote, or strongly influenced, the following paragraph in that editorial: [15]

Fearful however lest its pecuniary interest might suffer, whether at the hands of the public, one of whose prevailing sins had been so boldly and directly assailed, or of the profession, whose lethargy in this matter and subservience to expediency had been rebuked, the college interfered, and at the express desire of its faculty, but, as we now learn, entirely against the author's will, such portions of the address as bore on Criminal Abortion were suppressed in the published copy.

Implicit in "its pecuniary interest might suffer," was the worry that prospective medical students might be prejudiced against Harvard at a time when there was nearly cutthroat competition among medical schools for the fees that students provided directly to the professors.[16]

Years later, when the suppressed portion was finally published, David Humphreys Storer indicated in a brief preface only that the suppressor (singular) thought publication would be "injudicious."[17] However, the most explicit discussion of this suppressor occurred in the May 1872 "Editorial Notes" of Horatio's *Journal of the Gynaecological Society of Boston*. Horatio wrote:[18]

"Injudicious," as it was applied seventeen years ago to an article we published the month before last,* [Footnote: *March, 1872, p. 174] is a word the true meaning of which we all understand. Does not, however, its use in such cases react with terrible force upon those who thus block the wheels of progress?

See what the effects have been in the present instance. A college instructor sums up the result of thirty years' thoughtful observation, and finds that he has discovered the cause, before unknown, of a vast deal of disease and suffering. It is a matter affecting the welfare of the whole community, and clearly within the province of medical men. He is called upon to publicly discourse to a graduating class and to the profession, and, full of enthusiasm, he takes this occasion to announce to the world his inspired conclusions. Then fell the wet blanket—he has told our readers the rest.

The cool assurance of Dr. H. J. Bigelow, or rather his "injudiciousness,"—recollect that it is we ourselves that are now speaking and not the gentleman who has so patiently preserved silence for these long years, lest he might seem by word or deed to injure the school he used so to love,—Dr. B's course was only equalled by that of a prominent officer of the Massachusetts Medical Society towards Dr. Bowditch...

There probably is no major contradiction in Morland and Minot referring to suppressor*s* and this identification of Dr. Henry J. Bigelow, Professor of Surgery, as the single suppressor. As we will see, Bigelow held most of his medical faculty colleagues "under his thumb." Some may have been present and nodding agreement when Bigelow explained the need for suppression to the editors of the *Boston Medical and Surgical Journal*.

Horatio would repeatedly credit this anti-abortion segment of his father's November 1855 "Lecture" and also its strong approval by editors Morland and Minot for starting him on his anti-abortion crusade. For example, in Horatio's *Criminal Abortion: Its Nature, Its, Evidence, and Its Laws*, co-written in 1868 with the Boston lawyer, Franklin Fiske Heard, Horatio wrote: "To ... his father, and to the journalists (Morland and Minot, of Boston), by whom the effort then made was so warmly and eloquently seconded, the writer acknowledged at the time, his indebtedness for the thought of the undertaking, which has culminated, he has reason to believe, in an agitation which is now shaking society, throughout our country, to its very centre."[19] However, Horatio did not begin his anti-abortion crusade immediately after his father's Introductory Lecture. It is possible he thought his "full of enthusiasm" father would continue leadership of the effort. Or Horatio may have been too busy establishing a medical practice, performing his duties at the Boston Lying-in Hospital, and probably assisting his father in some capacity at the Medical School.

With respect to the Lying-in Hospital, Horatio wrote Malcolm in 1901: "Immediately, I insisted upon an uterine ward. After much wrestling with all concerned, save Warren, it was given, and filled at once."[20] When Horatio mentions "all concerned," he at least is talking about the Trustees who included Jonathan Mason Warren and Mr. William H. Foster. He probably also was including the Consulting Physicians. In addition to David Humphreys Storer, these were Drs. Jacob Bigelow, Walter Channing, James Jackson, and Charles G. Putnam.[21] It is thus possible that Horatio may have been opposed by his father in his insistence on a uterine ward.

This gynecological ward was not the only change in the new Boston Lying-in Hospital which took place *after* the opening in June 1855. The *Boston Medical and Surgical Journal* first mentioned the uterine ward in a February 1856 editorial. This indicated the ward "has long been desirable for a large class of females who cannot be properly treated at their own residences."[22] The other change the editors noted was "until now, no *unmarried* females have been admitted as patients." The first reason they mentioned for the hospital trustees' action on this was that almost all married women preferred to have their babies at home. The second reason given for this change was "many *un*married women who seek its shelter are the victims of seduction, rarely of deliberate vice; they are deluded and unfortunate, and by a charitable reception and kind care may be saved from utter ruin." The editors also noted that "this new arrangement may counteract the evils of procuring abortion and of later infanticide so frequent in our midst, and so much to be deprecated; this, at least, would be its tendency." In a brief autobiographical sketch written shortly before his death (presented in Chapter 23), Horatio wrote that it was at *his* insistence that the policy of admitting unmarried mothers was adopted by the Lying-in Hospital. If true, Horatio himself probably argued that this policy would counteract "the evils of procuring abortion and of later infanticide." The editors of the *Boston Medical and Surgical Journal* might even have been quoting Horatio when they gave these reasons for the new policy. This admission of unmarried mothers-to-be to the Lying-in Hospital may have been Horatio's first anti-abortion effort, and it quickly followed, it is even possible that it *preceded*, his father's anti-abortion Introductory Lecture in November 1855.

Horatio resumed regular attendance at meetings of the Boston Society of Natural History upon his return to Boston.[23] In addition, on November 19, 1855 he was proposed by Drs. Samuel Cabot and Calvin Ellis for membership in the Society for Medical Observation.[24] He was elected at the next meeting of that Society.[25] At the following Society meeting, he was present and an active participant in the discussions.[26] Frequent attendance, large participation in discussions, and frequent presentation of papers at both Societies continued for the next two years, until health problems interfered.

An enormous family tragedy was to occur on December 2, 1855. Horatio's daughter Jessie Simpson died of whooping cough.[27] No correspondence or journal from that period has been located that tells of Horatio's and Emily's grief and it is probable that all such reminders of the calamity purposely were destroyed. However, a letter written decades later to Hales Wallace Suter, then Secretary of the Harvard 1850 Class, included: "Thanksgiving Day has for many years been for me one of the saddest in the year because upon it long ago my then only child lay dying."[28]

In later years, Horatio was to advise the beginning physician to write articles for medical journals as a way of establishing a reputation and hence also a medical practice. No doubt, his father and other established physician friends had counseled him similarly and Horatio quickly published a series of "Boston Lying-In Hospital Reports" upon his return to Boston. The first was entitled, "Protracted First Stage of Labor.—Rigidity of Os Uteri."[29] The "os uteri" is the opening into the vagina at the base of the uterus. In this case the amnion or "bag of waters" of the woman had already broken and all of the amniotic fluid discharged. The os was small and slow to dilate with almost no increase in the opening ten hours after the initial examination and more than twelve hours after labor had begun. Horatio noted in his Report that he had read in the most recent *Edinburgh Journal of Medicine* that an antimonial enema had successfully produced dilation in several cases and he administered an enema of one grain of tartarized antimony dissolved in six ounces of tepid water. After fifteen minutes the os was found to be rapidly dilating and was completely dilated thirty minutes after the enema. A normal healthy six-pound girl was delivered ninety minutes later. During the descent and birth of the child, Horatio "freely administered chloroform, during the pains, which were in no way diminished in frequency or force, and with great relief to the patient."[30] He noted that he customarily made such use of chloroform during childbirth.

Horatio's report deserved mention for at least two reasons. One is its demonstration of Horatio's scholarly attention to recent medical literature and the complementary contribution of scientific papers himself. Another is his advocacy of chloroform inhalation to relieve the pains of labor and his claim that this did not reduce the frequency or force of the contractions. The implicit statement was that chloroform was superior to ether which many physicians believed did reduce the force and frequency of contractions. This recommendation of chloroform no doubt raised many medical eyebrows in the city where sulphuric ether was worshipped and every competing anaesthetic was hated, with chloroform, the strongest competitor, the most hated of all. In reporting his views on chloroform, Horatio's showed his courage (or foolhardiness). This is amplified by the fact that only a month earlier the *Boston Medical and Surgical Journal* had published one article describing a death from use of chloroform in Edinburgh[31] and another describing a chloroform anesthesia death in Boston.[32] Morland and Minot were strongly with Horatio on abortion, but were strongly against him on chloroform.

Typically, Horatio presented papers at the Suffolk District Medical Society or the Society for Medical Observation prior to their publication in the *Boston Medical and Surgical Journal* or elsewhere. "Student," the Boston Correspondent of *The Medical and Surgical Reporter*, a New-Jersey-based journal, described these Boston medical societies in a letter published in February 1857:[33]

> The medical societies here are active in their way. There are three of them. First on the list is the Suffolk District Medical Society. I say *first*, because it is the society to which all the regular physicians belong. ... The meetings are usually dull, because there are one or two gentlemen who occupy most of the time in matters peculiarly interesting to themselves. Once or twice within the last year, the hours have been occupied in listening to the complaints of a single member of the profession, who seems to have an idea that he is persecuted, although no one knows why, or how.

"Student" was Dr. Charles E. Buckingham whose friction with both Drs. Storer we already have noted and it is probable that Horatio was the "single member of the profession" singled out in the above. "Student," in the same February Letter, described the other two Boston societies as "very hard to get into." These were the Boston Society for Medical Observation and the Boston Society for Medical Improvement. Buckingham, like Horatio, was a member of the "Observation." David Humphreys Storer was a long-time member of the more prestigious "Improvement," but, Horatio never became a member, nor did Buckingham. Both men had easily acquired the three enemies needed to prevent membership.

A long discussion of vomiting during pregnancy occurred at the Society for Medical Observation early in February.[34] Horatio, who had just advocated anal administration of tartrate of antimony for os dilation, enquired of the physician presenting this serious case whether nutritive enemata had been tried as a means to "keep the stomach at rest." As will be seen, Horatio himself later presented papers on his successful treatments of vomiting during pregnancy. Horatio's primary concern was to prevent abortion which physicians were apt to induce to relieve the extreme distress and even the occasional starvation associated with vomiting during pregnancy.

Another Lying-in Hospital report by Horatio was published in the *Boston Medical and Surgical Journal* on March 13, 1856.[35] It discussed two births where manual removal of the placenta was required. In one there was profuse hemorrhage which Horatio "checked by administration of borax and external applications of ice."[36] Of most biographical significance was the mention that chloroform was administered during both deliveries "with much comfort to the patient and no diminution in the frequency or strength of the uterine contractions." A more timid physician might not have reported any of these cases, or at least not mentioned the somewhat incidental fact that chloroform was administered with good results, given the certain criticism of powerful ether advocates like Dr. Jacob Bigelow and his son. Instead, Horatio appears to have become all the more committed to praising the anaesthetic of choice of his Edinburgh mentor.

On April 3, 1856, a guest editorial signed by "*" appeared in the *Boston Medical and Surgical Journal* entitled "Female Physicians."[37] Twelve years later, Horatio was to include a page-long quote from this editorial in his book *Nurses and Nursing*. Horatio also was to barely paraphrase the following paragraph from this editorial, both in the book on nursing and in his published 1866 letter of resignation from the position of attending surgeon at the New England Hospital for Women.[38]

> The proposition that women, as a sex, cannot practise medicine—that their weak physical organization renders them unfit for such duties and exposures—that their *physiological condition, during a portion of every month*, disqualifies them for such grave responsibilities—is too nearly self evident to require argument. I therefore limit myself to a statement of the facts as regards midwifery alone, for the practice of which it has been especially claimed that they are competent.

This guest editorial was almost certainly written by Horatio, both because of its reappearance in his later writing and because it described the writer's experiences related to female midwives in Paris, Great Britain, and Scotland, all locations where Horatio had recently visited, and doesn't mention the midwives from any country where Horatio was not a visitor. One suspects that Horatio's stern views about women's liabilities for practicing medicine, like many of his other persistent beliefs, originally came from his father. It will be recalled that in medical school Horatio opposed a woman attending classes. Horatio also probably was in contact with many women who were greatly impaired "*during a portion of every month.*" As will be seen, one was his wife, Emily Elvira.

The stated purpose of "Female Physicians" was to counter a pamphlet published in 1848 entitled *Man-Midwifery Exposed* ...[39] which claimed that men should not be involved in the business of delivering babies because the European experience showed that women could do the job and because, as Horatio paraphrased the pamphlet, male "physicians are licentious, and that morality and delicacy require that they should be superseded." Samuel Gregory, the author of the pamphlet, operated a college in Boston for female doctors and was hardly an unbiased pamphleteer. Horatio pointed out that male midwives reduced the mortality during childbirth compared to women and that, in Europe, women midwives were not the preferred alternative, but the inexpensive one or the one resorted to when concealment of birth was the priority. As to the question of the propriety of *male* midwives, Horatio wrote: "But the public have been told, *not by ladies*, but by men whose grossly indelicate works do not go to prove *them* the fittest judges, that the confidence of the sex is abused by physicians, and that to employ them is an offence against the higher sentiments of woman's nature. Every pure-minded lady denies the libel, as regards her trusted medical adviser and the profession at large, as well as herself."[40] As will be seen, much the same words would be required of Horatio fourteen years later to defend the rights of men to practice the young specialty of gynecology and to defend the "pure-mindedness" of their patients.

Although Hermann Jackson Warner's mentions of Horatio in his journal become rarer and rarer, the following did occur on Wednesday, April 2, 1856: "In eve[g] went to Soc[y] of Nat Hist[y]—Storer brought up subject of artificial propagation of fishes—It is very well to turn public attention to it, but it is wholly out of the ordinary & proper course of legislation—It is the theory, no less than the practice of our government to leave such matters to private enterprize—He spoke very fully & very well."[41] Horatio's plan for state support of improved Massachusetts fishing, which Hermann objected to as infringing on the domain of private "enterprize," found its way into the Society *Proceedings*.[42] Among other things, it included the artificial propagation of salmon, trout, shad, and alewives. It will be recalled that in 1852 Horatio had called for elimination of the injurious "race" of bluefish that he believed were decimating the Provincetown mackerel and had discussed local prejudices against "undesirable" fish species that elsewhere were considered delicacies. Expanding the capacity of the sea to produce food and jobs remained one of Horatio's lifelong concerns.

Horatio's initial flurry of "Lying-In Hospital Reports" continued with description of a case of temporary insanity associated with childbirth which he concluded with a note that the "gangrenous state of the cervix uteri is interesting as in accordance with the well-known tendency to such deficiency of vital action in the insane."[43] Whether a valid point or not, the lady's recoveries from madness and painful urination, and the cure of her cervical ulcerations, all occurred together. This may have initiated, but more likely strengthened, Horatio's belief that pelvic disease was a cause of female insanity.

Another "Lying-in Hospital Report" in the *Boston Medical and Surgical Journal* dealt with Horatio's successful surgery for an unpediculated fibrous tumor of the uterus.[44] Two months later, Horatio provided the same journal a review of a new book on obstetric surgery and criticized the author for failing to mention the unpediculated form in his discussion of fibrous tumors. "A successful case of our own, reported in this Journal a few weeks since," Horatio wrote, "well shows how completely and easily many of these hitherto incurable tumors may now be brought within the reach of art."[45] Horatio described the surgery and displayed the tumor at the meeting of the Suffolk District Medical Society on May 31, 1856.[46] There had been considerable hemorrhage associated with Horatio's removal of the tumor, which he controlled by packing the vagina with lint. The Minutes of the Suffolk Medical Society included: "If further trouble should ensue from the hemorrhage, Dr. Storer declared it to be his intention to cauterize the interior of the womb with caustic pot ash." This prompted Secretary Dr. Luther Parks, Jr. to add a footnote to the minutes which read: "The Secretary cannot forebear to express his astonishment at this extraordinary proposition."

There appears to have been bad blood between Horatio and Parks before this footnote. Parks frequently wrote about women's diseases in the *Boston Medical and Surgical Journal* and there may have been some rivalry associated with their common "specialty," although this word was rarely if ever used in that period of general practice. It is likely that Dr. Parks was "the possessor of a most enviable European reputation in one branch of obstetric surgery" singled out by Horatio in October 1855, as one "whose repudiation [of uterine tents] seems to me quite unaccountable."[47] As Secretary of the Suffolk District Medical Society, Parks appears to have taken some advantage of Horatio in the Minutes he prepared of Society proceedings. Horatio was particularly offended by the Secretary's "cannot forebear to express his astonishment" footnote appended to Horatio's potential application of potassa fusa if hemorrhage recurred. At the meeting of the Society on July 26, 1856, Horatio criticized Parks for appending such non-meeting material to his reports and also explained how he was only proposing potassa fusa for the tumor and not the interior of the uterus.[48]

As will be seen, battles between Parks and Horatio would continue for years. Parks was a member of the Boston Society for Medical Improvement and undoubtedly was a factor in Horatio's not being elected, despite being considered highly qualified for membership by some of its members. When Dr. James Clarke White wrote his "Sketch of the Past History of the Boston Society for Medical Improvement," Horatio was probably among the "several of the most able physicians of that day, who would have been an honor and strength to it, [who] were denied admission."[49]

The report of the Lying-in Hospital patient whose fibrous tumor was removed by Horatio included: "May 16.—For the past fortnight, during Dr. Storer's absence, at Detroit, patient attended by Dr. Dupee."[50] Horatio was attending the Ninth Annual Meeting of the American Medical Association. Surprisingly, the outspoken Horatio, although noted as present in the published *Transactions*, was never mentioned as participating in any of the proceedings.[51] By time of this meeting, Horatio probably was aware that Emily Elvira had conceived her second child who would be born early in December. The thought that many women were destroying developing human beings at the stage of development which their own child had reached, may have amplified Horatio's repugnance of the aborting parents and their more-or-less medical accomplices. There was no mention of abortion in the *Transactions* of the Detroit meeting, but the one-man nucleus of a Committee on Criminal Abortion was appointed the next year in Nashville and the full Committee eventually was to include two of the Association Vice-Presidents elected at Detroit (Thomas W. Blatchford of New York and William H. Brisbane of Wisconsin). The Detroit meeting almost certainly provided Horatio the acquaintance of Dr. J. Berrien Lindsley of Tennessee who was key to Horatio being nominated as Chairman of the Committee on Criminal Abortion the next year. It is possible that the initial plans for the future Committee were laid in Detroit in May 1856 with an ebullient father-to-be as architect.

Horatio probably was en route to Detroit when Dr. John Collins Warren died on May 4, 1856. Dr. Warren had been one of the two most important figures in Boston medicine in the early nineteenth century, the other being Dr. James Jackson. To cite just a few of Warren's accomplishments, he held the professorship of anatomy and surgery at the Harvard Medical School from 1815 to 1847. He helped found the Massachusetts General Hospital and on October 16, 1846 performed there the first major operation in the world where the patient was rendered insensible to pain by yet-to-be-named "anaesthesia," the anaesthetic being sulphuric ether.[52] Warren served as President of the Boston Society of Natural History from 1848 until his death and was often visited by Horatio during this period when Horatio made many contributions to that Society.[53] Dr. Warren also was the father of the outstanding surgeon, Jonathan Mason Warren, whom Horatio had defended in print and who had supported Horatio in obtaining his "uterine ward" at the Boston Lying-in Hospital. Hermann Jackson Warner noted in his journal on Wednesday, May 7, 1856: "In eve^g went to meet^g of Bos Soc Nat His—Dr Humphreys Storer read something about Dr Warren ..."[54] The eulogy of Dr. Warren may well have been the reason that David Humphreys Storer did not attend the Detroit meeting, even though he was one of the Vice Presidents of the Association for 1856.

Although it would be a few months before Horatio was to publicly discuss the taboo topic of criminal abortion, his willingness to describe taboo subjects was demonstrated in July 1856 when he read a paper on two cases of nymphomania before the Boston Society for Medical Observation.[55] The first case was a twenty-year-old Irish emigrant who was first examined by Horatio on March 25, 1856. She complained of painful urination and a constant pricking in the region of the bladder. She reported that she had undergone etherization and when Horatio investigated this he learned that Dr. Henry J. Bigelow had removed pins and hairpins from her bladder. Over the next few weeks, Horatio and his colleague, Dr. Dupee, were to remove a series of similar objects from her bladder. Further investigation of her medical history disclosed that corks and silverware had been removed by physicians from the upper part of her vagina.

Given their concern that the patient would "unless restrained, do herself serious injury," she was transferred to the City Lunatic Asylum at South Boston, where after three weeks she was discharged as "not insane," and a day later she was again at Horatio's office complaining of "pricking in the neighborhood of the bladder." Horatio, believing that she had returned to her old habit, refused to treat her, since without restraint this would be useless, and she put herself under the care of another physician. In conclusion for this first case, Horatio wrote: "I am inclined to think that she masturbates, though, as is usual, she denies it. Her manners are those of that habit. Her expression, when unconscious of being observed, is at times decidedly lecherous."

Nymphomania Case 2 was a married women with none of the "genito-urinary proclivities" of the first. The problem was one of inordinate sexual desire apparently associated with an unusually high frequency of intercourse with her husband whom she reported had not missed "having connection with her a single night since marriage, even at times of menstruation. Has frequently come to her three times in a night, and always with a seminal emission."[56] Horatio provided details of the women's "lascivious" dreams, her fantasies while awake, her genital "spasms" and mucous emissions, her generally normal physical presentation, her longing for children, and her belief that this longing had led to her present excess. Horatio continued:[57]

The first interview with the patient was had on May 16th when the following treatment was prescribed, at the same time giving her fully to understand that if she continued her present habits of indulgence, it would probably become necessary to send her to an asylum:—

1. Total abstinence from husband; if not possible otherwise, by temporary entire separation.

2. Meat but once in the day.

3. Brandy and other stimulants not at all.

4. Novel writing to be given up.

5. Hair-pillows and mattress in place of feathers.

6. Cold sponge-bath morning and night.

7. Cold enemata at night.

8. Frequent lotion of anterior vaginal commissure with solution of borax.

9. Two-drachm doses nightly of equal parts of the tinctures of henbane, valerian, and lupulin; ...

10. Iron; gr. iss of the sacch. carb. thrice daily in pill.

11. Exercise, fresh air, and occupation of mind by more and cheerful friends.

The husband left the city, since abstinence from intercourse was not otherwise possible. Horatio reported that after a month of following the difficult prescribed regimen:

> Husband still absent. The lascivious dreams have not occurred for several days, nor the sudden vaginal emissions. The local irritation and heat have also much diminished, and as regards these most troublesome symptoms, she feels greatly relieved. ... I now consider the case much more hopeful as regards the mental symptoms, which, however, will for some time require decided enforcement of very strict laws. Both the wife and the husband must be taught moderation, which done, there seems no very good reason why, after dilation of the os, and perhaps, if it should be needed, application of potassa fusa, the patient should not realize her hopes, and get with child.

His final conclusions with respect to both cases were:

> They both go to prove Duchatelet's opinion, based upon frequent examination of prostitutes, to be correct, that excessive sexual appetite and excessive sexual indulgence are by no means necessarily attended in the female by a clitoris at all enlarged, while Case II is a marked instance of that peculiar and forcible emission, still denied by many, of mucus from the female genital canals during heat, and under mental excitement alone, which, when occurring during intercourse, gave origin to the old and fanciful idea of a true "*semen muliebre.*"

Hermann Jackson Warner's journal entry for Wednesday July 23, 1856 dealt with a Boston Society of Natural History field trip to New Hampshire. It described Hermann's meeting of "the very pleasant" Dr. Calvin Ellis, a key figure in Horatio's life; it also included the following: "I went with Storer & had a good deal of pleasant talk with him—he is under the weather!—not in good spirits—says he has taken $587 in the 8 mos since he has been in practice—Ugh!"[58]   This pinned down the start of Horatio's medical practice as November 1855. Horatio's "$587 in the 8 mos" was a fair salary at the time, and Warner's "Ugh!" probably reflected the sad financial returns from his own law work. Horatio's absence of "good spirits" are hardly consonant with the prospect of a new child in December, but unfortunately, we have no other information about troubles in Horatio's life, unless it be "Student's" description of the "single member of the profession, who seems to have an idea that he is persecuted, although no one knows why, or how."[59]

At the August 30 meeting of the Suffolk District Medical Society,[60] Horatio exhibited a new form of intra-uterine pessary. The intra-uterine pessary was developed by Dr. James Young Simpson. Its purpose was to shift a displaced uterus back to a normal position, and was "worn" more or less permanently within the vagina and uterus. Horatio's version of the pessary allowed precise fitting to the uterine and vaginal cavities and prevented problems associated with pessaries that did not fit. Horatio repeated some of the criticisms he had made in the Preface to Simpson's *Obstetric Memoirs* of Simpson's enemy, Robert Lee. He also discussed problems with a French version of the pessary which was inappropriately altered from Simpson's original design. The "recapitulation" of Horatio's remarks by Secretary Parks also mentioned pessaries' potential for producing abortion:[61]

> 4. He had shown how necessary it was that the instrument should always correspond in size with the uterus and passages to which it was to be applied, and that if this were lost sight of, accidents would undoubtedly be liable to occur. He would also allude to the importance of always thoroughly diagosticating each case, and related an instance of error that had occurred in this city, and had accidentally come to his knowledge. Pregnancy happened to exist, and the instrument, honestly introduced by a most respectable practitioner, had at once induced abortion; the patient, who had really desired this result, then and still supposing it was intentional. On such cases as the one narrated, no fair objection could be based.

Secretary Parks could not resist another long footnote in the Minutes. He downplayed the success that Horatio claimed for the new pessary, praised the "very thorough discussion of it at the French Academy" which Horatio had criticized, and claimed that "all experiments with the intra-uterine pessary should be made only in a cautious and tentative manner." Parks routinely published translations of articles from French journals and was probably trained in France. What looks like Parks versus Storer in these exchanges may also have been Parks' French mentors battling Horatio's Edinburgh mentor.

At the September 1 meeting of the Boston Society for Medical Observation, Horatio was in conflict with Dr. Charles E. Buckingham about Buckingham's unwillingness to make physical examinations of women patients.[62] This problem was related to Dr. Buckingham's case of a uterine polypus successfully terminated without an operation. Horatio criticized Buckingham for not earlier performing a simple operation to clear the surface of the uterus with a spoon, wire or, even better, with a new instrument known as Recamier's Scoop. Buckingham asked for a description of this instrument and indicated his opposition to its employment in any case, since it appeared to him "barbarous—a bad Scrape."

In addition to the implication that Dr. Buckingham's failure to treat the diseased uterus verged on malpractice, both Horatio and Dr. Henry Ingersoll Bowditch took exception at the meeting to Dr. Buckingham's failure to make subsequent examinations of the polypus because of his policy "for reasons of decency" of never making vaginal examinations in his office. Buckingham indicated he would make such examinations in the patient's home, but never alone, or without the consent of her guardians. Horatio was reported to have said he thought Buckingham was wrong on this. "If a woman is of age she can decide for herself," Horatio continued, "and may wish particularly to have it done without the knowledge of her friends." It must have been particularly galling to Horatio that Buckingham, as a long-time member of the faculty of the Boylston Medical School, had probably communicated a similar taboo to the medical examination of women to hundreds of medical students. It perhaps was some comfort that the Boylston Medical School had closed its doors the year before.[63]

In November 1856, Horatio published a review of the *Complete Handbook of Obstetric Surgery* by Charles Clay of Manchester, England.[64] The review could not have been happily received by Dr. Clay. Horatio provided one page of accolades, but he provided five pages of criticism, much of this of serious problems, ranging from Clay's recommendation that the accoucheur tie and divide the umbilical cord under the bedclothing, to Clay's praise of the efforts of Jobert de Lamballe of Paris in treating vesicovaginal fistula, which Horatio had personally observed so consistently to fail. Perhaps the most serious deficiency was Clay's total omission of any reference to the successful techniques developed by Marion Sims for treating vesicovaginal fistulae.

A full page of the review of Clay's book dealt with craniotomy which Horatio indicated was "not a subject on which to select one's words; the deliberately sacrificing an unborn but still living child, in cases where statistics go to prove that the adoption of another mode of delivery, nothing else counter-indicating, would give that child a good chance of successful birth, is nothing short of *wilful murder*, no matter by what schools or by what eminent men it may be sanctioned, and should be branded as such by the profession." Horatio included Clay's table showing the remarkable differences in frequency of this crushing of the child's skull to allow the emptying of the womb in stalled labors. These ranged from one in 128 cases in Ireland and one in 220 in England to one in 1,200 cases in France and one in 1,944 in Germany. Although Clay could not account for these astounding differences, Horatio had no problem in doing so. He claimed that the differences between countries were the differences among their obstetricians in recognition that "the dangers of every labor to both mother and child increase with its length." Horatio continued: "The French and Germans recognise the truth of these propositions, not merely in theory but in practice; whereas the English do not, the Irish do not, and but too frequently, also, the Americans do not. Very many of these maternal and infantile murders may be prevented."

One of the few things in the book which Horatio praised was Clay's preference for chloroform. Horatio added his own view that "ether should always be
preferred for the ordinary operations of surgery; but whenever we use an
anaesthetic in midwifery, and we take so strong grounds in this matter as to
consider such indispensable in almost every case, it is chloroform." Here
Horatio not only was dangerously defending chloroform in Boston, he was
sending a challenge to numerous physicians who opposed use of any anaesthetic
during labor.

Finances at the Boston Lying-in Hospital *apparently* were in desperate
shape and on November 4, 1856 the Trustees voted to close the hospital and the
last patient left two weeks later.[65] "Student," the Boston correspondent of the
New Jersey-based *Medical and Surgical Reporter*, was to cryptically report in
February 1857: "Some say want of funds shut it up, others say that there was
a quarrel between one of its medical staff (for it had three physicians for fifty
patients a year) and the ladies who visited it, which caused the closing up."[66]
Horatio's relations with Consulting Physician, Jacob Bigelow, may have already
deteriorated, and this powerful physician may have recommended against the
contribution of operating funds.

Closing of the Boston Lying-in Hospital was a huge blow to Horatio and
he tried to preserve its operation. One action was to contact the Catholic Bishop
of Boston and determine whether the Church would be interested in taking over
the hospital. The Bishop was willing, and, at first, the Trustees of the Lying-in
Hospital also appeared to support the idea. They backed out later, however.
Boston Diocese records indicated that "although [the Trustees] admitted the plan
to be excellent, [they] had not courage enough to face public opinion and give
the use of the hospital ... to the Catholics. The result did not surprise the
Directors of the Dispensary. They had ever preached it to Dr Storer. But he
would not believe that there was so much opposition."[67]

Frederick C. Irving's history of the Boston Lying-in Hospital (*Safe
Deliverance*) reported what appears to have been an unrelated effort of Horatio
to keep it operating. Irving wrote, "Dr. Horatio Storer thought that he might
lease the property and conduct it as a charitable institution, but after more
mature deliberation he withdrew the offer."[68] The same source indicated that,
"As a last resort they agreed to admit women 'with diseases peculiar to
females'—but even this surrender brought them no greater number of patients."
This, however, is contradicted by Horatio's letter in 1901 where he wrote the
new uterine ward "was filled at once."[69] What is more, the uterine ward was
discussed in February 1856 by the *Boston Medical and Surgical Journal*[70] and
does not seem to have been a "last resort." Unfortunately, the original records
of the Lying-in Hospital have not been located. These might elucidate Horatio's
role in efforts to keep the Hospital open in late 1856 as well as his specific
actions (and their dates) related to creating the uterine ward and admission of

unmarried patients.

Horatio's son, Francis Addison Storer, was born on December 5. Horatio indicated it was at Boston in personal data he provided Harvard University in 1895. However, no record of the birth was found in the Massachusetts State Archives, although the births of Horatio's other two sons are on record. It is possible that Emily Elvira gave birth in another state away from Boston's unpleasant December weather.

The end of the year found Horatio attending meetings of all the Boston societies to which he belonged. At the Society of Natural History he donated "A globular concretion of grass, said to have been formed by the action of waves upon the sea-shore."[71] At the Boston Society for Medical Observation Horatio "mentioned having 2 cases of severe cephalic disease one of which was combined with amenorrhoea, the other with constipation."[72] And at the Suffolk District Medical Society Horatio, among other things, reported the successful use of chloroform to control convulsions of a woman during labor.[73]

Dr. Charles Brown-Séquard, the famous physiologist and endocrinologist, visited Boston again at the end of 1856. He presented a series of five lectures in November, that included the initial results of his pioneering research on the adrenal glands.[74] In his later writings, Horatio referred to a number of inter-actions and consultations with his "friend." Horatio even dedicated an edition of one of his books to Brown-Séquard with the comment, "permitted to couple the present edition with a name far more honored than his own can ever become."[75] It is possible that Brown-Séquard's visit at this time was a stimulus to Horatio to redouble his own efforts to achieve "a far more honored" name. As will be seen, within a few weeks of Brown-Séquard's presentations, Horatio's anti-abortion efforts were in full swing. On the other hand, one can consider that Horatio's public crusade for the unborn had already begun in the Fall of 1856 with his condemnation of the overuse of abortion's cousin, craniot-omy, as "wilful murder."[76]

Another stimulus of Horatio's overt efforts in February against abortion may have been a January 1857 article, "Foeticide," by Dr. Jesse Boring, Professor of Obstetrics at the Atlanta Medical College.[77] Boring's article may have made Horatio aware that another physician might take up the crusade against criminal abortion, and, given Boring's too-strong reliance on the argument that God objected to abortion, he might bungle it.

CHAPTER 6
THE PHYSICIANS' CRUSADE AGAINST ABORTION

The first definite indication that Horatio's anti-abortion crusade was fully underway was a letter from a Boston lawyer written February 17, 1857.[1] John Keith was responding to Horatio's request for information on the laws "respecting procuring abortion, &c." Keith indicated that should the woman die as a consequence, the offence was punishable by not more than twenty years nor less than five years of imprisonment. If she survived, the imprisonment was not more than seven years and not less than one year. Keith also indicated, in response to Horatio's question: "the law makes no distinction between the pregnancy before & after quickening." "These are all the statutes on the subject in this Commonwealth;" Keith continued, "and you can see that causing the premature birth of a child is not under any circumstances murder, though killing the child the *instant* after birth would be."

This information on Massachusetts statutes was part of Horatio's homework for a long presentation he made on the subject of criminal abortion at the February 28 meeting of the Suffolk District Medical Society. Secretary Parks' dubious rendition of Horatio's remarks, omitting even the month of the meeting, follows as published in the *Boston Medical and Surgical Journal*:[2]

> [Storer] desired to bring before the Society a subject which imperatively demanded its early and decisive action. Somewhat over a year ago, the present professor of obstetrics in the University (Dr. Storer, Sen.) had called attention, in a public inaugural address, to the alarming increase of *criminal abortion* in this community, and to the fact that the initiatory steps towards suppressing the crime should come from physicians. When the address alluded to was subsequently published, so much of it as bore upon this question, as also upon a kindred one, the prevention of pregnancy, was suppressed—in deference to the request of other gentlemen of the College Faculty, but entirely against the author's will. That gentleman had since been repeatedly called upon for a reiteration of his views; many months had, however, now elapsed, and as there seemed little or no probability of such being done at present, if at all, his son, after duly ascertaining this fact, had no hesitation in at once bringing the subject before the Society; it being acknowledged by all, in the least degree conversant with this matter, that immediate action was necessary.
>
> Dr. Storer quoted statistics from a recent memoir by Tardieu of

Paris, in the *Annales d'Hygiene Publique et de Med. Legale*, for 1856, showing how common was the crime in this country as compared with others; so common indeed as to have led foreigners to suppose that the procuring [of] criminal abortion was with us an ordinary and well-established branch of industry, not interfered with by the law; as indeed, to intents and purposes, is at present the case.

Dr. S. referred to our statutes on this subject, and to the ignorance prevalent in the community respecting the actual and separate existence of foetal life in the early months of pregnancy. He dwelt on the moral and absolute guilt of the parties offending, and on the necessity of prompt and efficient action by the profession, and called upon the Society, as representing the physicians of Boston, to take such steps as would alike further ensure the innocence in this matter of all its members, and show to the community the sincere abhorrence with which they viewed the crime.

Parks then mentioned that Horatio quoted from the December 1855 editorial of the *Boston Medical and Surgical Journal* that had praised David Humphreys Storer's Introductory Lecture and strongly criticized the suppression of its anti-abortion segment.

David Humphreys was also at the February meeting and, after Horatio's initial speech, was reported to have[3]

expressed his satisfaction that the subject was at last to be brought before the community. He held without abatement the views he had formerly expressed regarding it; the crime, if it existed to the extent all would allow it did exist, should be repressed, and it was the duty of physicians to expose and to denounce it. He disclaimed any collusion with his son in thus bringing up the matter, but was delighted it had been done, and had no doubt of the ultimate result.

One must be cautious in judging whether the phrase, "if it existed to the extent all would allow it did exist," was really David Humphreys Storer's comment or whether it was Secretary Parks' lack of certainty about abortion's high prevalence. There had been no such doubts expressed about the prevalence of the crime in David Humphreys Storer's Introductory Lecture. On the other hand, if David Humphreys Storer really were not as certain about the frequency of abortion as Horatio, it raises the interesting possibility that Horatio had had much influence on the abortion remarks of that Introductory Lecture. Also, if the anti-abortion portion of that Lecture were Horatio's, it could account for the notoriously independent David Humphreys Storer's rare "showing [of] the white feather"[4] in consenting to suppress this portion when it was published. However, Horatio as author of the anti-abortion section of his father's Lecture is *strongly* countered by Horatio's repeated later crediting of his father for starting him on his crusade.

Horatio then proposed a Resolution that a Committee be appointed to determine whether further legislation on the subject of criminal abortion was needed in Massachusetts "and to report to the Society such other means as may seem necessary for the suppression of this abominable, unnatural, and yet common crime."[5] Horatio consented to adding to the Resolution: "And that said report, when accepted by this Society, shall by it be recommended to the Massachusetts Medical Society as a basis for its further action." The amended Resolution passed unanimously, and the Chair appointed Horatio, Dr. Henry Ingersoll Bowditch, and Dr. Calvin Ellis as the Committee with Horatio designated Chairman. Although the amendment to send recommendations of the District Society to the Massachusetts Medical Society for action was probably proposed to increase the effectiveness of the Report of the Committee by giving it a basis beyond Boston, its actual effect was to delay medical recommendations to the Massachusetts Legislature on the issue of criminal abortion.

Parks' Minutes of the Suffolk District Medical Society for the February meeting did not capture the exchange between Horatio and Jacob Bigelow which was to be described at least twice in later years. The following is from an address Horatio gave in 1897 which included a summary of his anti-abortion efforts. Although referring only to "Dr. B.," it actually identified Dr. Bigelow by describing the 1810 beginning of Jacob Bigelow's medical practice:[6]

> ... in 1857, I had brought the question of the prevalence of criminal abortion, as evidenced in gynecological practice, to the attention of the Suffolk District Medical Society, of Boston, ... I was there peremptorily challenged by the older men, who considered the investigation both injudicious and improper. Several of these, ... were determined to prevent the threatened scandal, as they considered it. One of them, a professor at Harvard and the leading physician of Boston, thought to annihilate me by explaining that he had been in practice for nearly fifty years (he began in 1810), and had never known a single instance of criminal abortion, and here was a young man who had been his pupil, soberly relating the histories of scores of such cases. The only answer required was to ask Dr B. if he had ever sought from a patient if her miscarriage had been from an avoidable cause. His reply was, "Never, for it would have been an insult to put to a lady such a question." From that moment the attention and the cordial co-operation of the profession was gained.

Different details of this important meeting, including a specific reference to "Dr. Jacob Bigelow," also were included in Horatio's rendition of the event in his 1901 letter to Malcolm, where he indicated it was at the Suffolk District Medical Society that he "first entered the anti-abortion lists by presenting a year's statistics of such cases, all married ladies in good Society from my practice up at Chester Park. I was at once challenged and given the lie by Dr. Jacob Bigelow, who I have always supposed brought me into the world."[7]

With the blessing of the Suffolk District Society, Horatio then began a huge letter writing campaign to obtain data on the subject of criminal abortion. The following is one of the very few of the many *sent* that still exist:[8]

7 Chester St. Boston
7 March, 1857

Dear Dr.
I am just now working up certain statistics on the subject of *criminal abortion.* If you can put me in the way of ascertaining the proportionate number of still births of later or for a series of years in any of our large American cities, or can furnish me with any other facts bearing on the present frequency or increase of the crime, I shall be greatly obliged.

Yours Sincerely
Horatio R. Storer

Dr Jarvis.

Dr. Edward Jarvis was a physician who was strongly involved in treating insanity, in registration of births and deaths, and in other public health issues. Jarvis apparently forwarded Horatio's request to the Boston City Registrar's Office which provided the data Horatio requested on still-born children both for Boston and for Providence, Rhode Island.[9]

Between March 20, and April 6, 1857, Horatio received letters from physicians in twenty states and territories providing information on their laws related to criminal abortion.[10] Horatio's correspondents for the most part were physicians active in the American Medical Association. One of the responses deserves emphasis.[11] The 1857 Annual Meeting of the American Medical Association was scheduled to be held in Nashville in May. In addition to a request for Tennessee statutes on criminal abortion, Horatio apparently included a request that a Special Committee on Criminal Abortion be created at that convention. Presumably, this was the business that the following letter mentions would "be attended to duly at the meeting."

Nashville March 20

H. Storer
Roxbury
    Dear Dr
Yours to Dr Lindsley is recd. He is absent north—may be in Boston next month early.
Your letter is filed & will be attended to duly at the meeting though we shall expect you at the Association.

There is no statute on the subject of Crim. Ab. in this state, & no decisions in our Courts, as there has never been a case of the crime. Good for Tennessee!
Very truly yours,
James W. Hoyte

The *Medical and Surgical Reporter* for April contained a paragraph about the Suffolk District Medical Society abortion debate.[12] It was written by "Student," who lost his anonymity in September 1857, about half way through his year-and-a-half stint as Boston correspondent for the New-Jersey-based journal, when he (or the *Reporter* editor) started using "C.E.B.," instead of "Student," at the bottom of his "Letter from Boston."[13] In this first "Letter from Boston" with the switched signature, C.E.B. made reference to his previous letter ("Since my last letter..."), and thus there was no switch in correspondent, only in his signature. "Student"/"C.E.B." thus undoubtedly was Dr. Charles Edward Buckingham, who wrote:[14]

At the last meeting of the Suffolk District Medical Society a resolution was passed concerning criminal abortions. It is a great pity that the moral sense of the community cannot be brought to bear upon this subject, but, it is not possible, that the interference of the law should succeed in putting a stop to it. The laws we now have cannot be enforced, and anything more stringent will only feed the operators. I would like to have the profession make a public protest against the practice. Anything beyond this will overshoot the mark. But they owe it to themselves to let the public understand that they in no way countenance it.

As will be seen, Buckingham made similar points in a guest editorial published in May in the *Boston Medical and Surgical Journal* which was signed "B." Buckingham's letters and guest editorial were an ill omen of the problems that the new Committee on Criminal Abortion was to face in its efforts to influence Massachusetts laws on the subject.

Horatio quickly switched from writing letters to writing the Committee Report itself and he had completed a long draft by April 20, 1857 when fellow committee member, Henry Ingersoll Bowditch, wrote:[15]

Boston April 20, 1857

Dear Dr

I have carefully read *twice* your report. It is ably done, but the more I consider the subject the less I see how to meet the object intended, supposing the object to be as you suggest of so grave a nature. From my own *personal* experience, I would not say that the procuring of abortion was *common*. Therefore I could wish in your report that you could have given some proofs of the very great prevalence of the crime. Others may, like myself, have no *personal* proof of the point. To be a Committee man to report more stringent measures when one needs personal acquaintance with a subject to be reported on seems to me absurd.

But let that point pass, I now proceed to lay before you some of the suggestions that have occurred to me during the perusal of the paper. I will refer to pages, at least, at times.

Page 5. It seems to me that the real cause of the inefficiency of the present statutes is more owing 1st to the present *morale* of the community in reference to the subject, & 2d to the great caution observed by all violators of the law & 3d to the fact that the operators & one operated on are both extremely desirous of concealment and therefore the law cannot find witnesses. All the[se] troubles will [be] met by the Prosecuting Attorney in *any* case & under *any* law. Hence I must say I have little hope of any Antiabortion Statute any more than I have confidence in any Maine or Anti-liquor law.

Page 6. Are there not cases where a physician would be justified in suggesting a course such as he would use in Amenorrhoea, even when he might *suspect*, but not be able to *know* of the evidence of pregnancy? Suppose a mother of several children which she has in rapid succession & the physician feels assured that health & possible life will be endangered if another pregnancy occurs, would he be criminal if he were to use common means for amenorrhoea if the menses have been absent six weeks?

Page 7. Are the cases always so plain that a man can decide & may he not balance a choice of evils? This remark is partially answered by the preceding.

Page 8. We are asked to report on Criminal Abortion. Let us keep to that. Prevention of conception may be equally criminal, but we are not called at present to discuss it & we shall have hard work enough, I fear, to persuade the Society, *as a Faculty* to act on the subject of Abortion. Therefore it would be better to avoid all other issues.

Page 15 Let us not go before the Society with any "hastily prepared" draft of a law. But let us wait & only digest the matter. I would lay it before some lawyer & take his advice.

In conclusion, I would remark that I think your plan of making the woman an accomplice is perfectly just.

Yours very sincerely

Henry I. Bowditch

Dr. H R Storer

Bowditch's three causes "of the inefficiency of the present statutes" were added to the Report,[16] and Bowditch's suggestion to omit contraception also was heeded. Despite Bowditch's suggestion, the draft of an abortion statute *was* included. However, Horatio would not have gone against his friend and former teacher lightly and probably did "lay it before some lawyer," and more likely before the "several distinguished lawyers" that Horatio was to mention in later discussions and writing about the Report (discussed below and in Chapter 7). Presumably, these lawyers pronounced the Committee's proposed statute at least an improvement over the current statutes which they indicated could not produce convictions.

Horatio read the Report to the Suffolk District Medical Society on April 25[17] only five days after receiving Bowditch's comments. The Report was printed and distributed to the members of the Society early in May. The Secretary of the Society included a letter dated, May 4, 1857, announcing "a Special Meeting for action on the report" on May 9, 1857.[18] The Report began by describing the high frequency of criminal abortion in Massachusetts and indicated that "it is probably steadily increasing."[19] Horatio also noted that it was "confined to no class of persons" and that "among the married, the crime seems more common than among those who have the excuse of shame." Horatio noted that there were no official statistics to support this claim, but it was recognized by authorities that many reports of still births were really instances of criminal abortion. He also noted "that in no less than *fifteen* instances during the past half-year has the Chairman been called to treat the confessed results, near or remote, of criminal abortion; and, of these patients, all without exception were married and respectable women."[20]

Horatio went on to note that criminal abortion escaped "punishment by law" and had "found public and unblushing defenders, who have so blunted the moral and religious sense of the people, that many respectable women do not hesitate to avow their belief that abortion is no crime." He gave Bowditch's three reasons for the "impunity with which the crime is committed," and added a fourth, "The defective character of the law itself."

Like his father in 1855, he called on physicians to change public opinion about the nature of the fetus and to make the public aware of the crime associated with its destruction. Physicians were "the guardians of the public health" and were the people most apt to learn of the crime. They should "declare its true nature, its prevalence, and its deplorable consequences; to denounce it in unmeasured terms, and, where possible, to point out and to enforce efficient means for its suppression." This the physician could do "In private, among his families; in public from his professor's desk, from the pages of his journal, or from the witness' stand,—the physician is called upon by every dictate of humanity and religion to condemn it."[21]

Horatio devoted the remainder of the Report to how "the profession can control the crime through the laws." He called for laws against abortion that were stringent and "faithfully enforced." They should prevent as well as punish the crime and thus needed to "be simple, easily understood, and not be evaded."

He provided the current Massachusetts statutes which read:

Section I. Laws of 1845. Chap. 27.

"Whoever maliciously, or without lawful justification, with intent
to cause and procure the miscarriage of a woman, then pregnant with
child, shall administer to her, prescribe for her, or advise or direct
her to take or swallow any poison, drug, or medicine, or noxious
thing; or shall cause or procure her, with like intent, to take or
swallow any poison, drug, or medicine or noxious thing;—and
whoever maliciously, and without lawful justification, shall use any
instrument or means whatever with the like intent; and any person,
with the like intent, knowingly aiding and assisting such offender or
offenders,—shall be deemed guilty of felony, if the woman die in
consequence thereof, and shall be imprisoned not more than twenty
years, nor less than five years, in the State Prison. And, if the
woman doth not die in consequence thereof, such offender shall be
guilty of a misdemeanor, and shall be punished by imprisonment not
exceeding seven years, nor less than one year, in the State Prison, or
House of Correction, or Common Jail, and by a fine not exceeding
two thousand dollars."

Section II. Laws of 1847. Chap. 83.

"Every person, who shall knowingly advertise, print, publish,
distribute, or circulate, or knowingly cause to be advertised, printed,
published, distributed, or circulated, any pamphlet, printed paper,
book, newspaper, notice, advertisement, or reference, containing
words or language giving or conveying any notice, hint, or reference,
to any person, or to the name of any person, real or fictitious, from
whom, or to any place, house, shop, or office where any poison,
drug, mixture, preparation, medicine, or noxious thing, or any
instrument or means whatever, or any advice, directions, information,
or knowledge, may be obtained, for the purpose of causing or
procuring the miscarriage of any woman pregnant with child, shall be
punished by imprisonment in the State Prison, House of Correction,
or Common Jail, not more than three years, or by fine not exceeding
one thousand dollars."

Horatio identified why he believed these laws produced few indictments
and even fewer convictions. One reason was the necessity to show that "malice
or want of lawful justification" existed. Another was the need to prove that the
woman was pregnant. Still another was the limitation on aborting agents to a
"poison, drug, or medicine, or noxious thing." He called for a statute which
clearly pointed out that the only excuses for induced abortion were "to save the

life of the mother, or of the foetus within her womb." The law also should specify that this could only be determined "by experienced physicians" and that at least one other physician must agree that abortion was necessary. These changes would place "greater bars" to criminal abortion and increase the chances of punishment when it occurred. The Report continued:

> There could be no injustice to the prisoner, that the burden of proving intent should thus be made to fall upon him. Government, of course, must prove the deed,—in these cases, frequently no easy thing to accomplish; and then should the prisoner be made to show its necessity. If the accused were a medical man, and had held the previous consultation with a brother-practitioner, always proper in cases thus involving life, he would have no difficulty in proving that necessity, if it really had existence.

Horatio noted that pregnancy was almost impossible to determine at the fetal age when most criminal abortions occurred. "Pregnancy should be taken for granted," Horatio wrote, "from the very attempt at abortion." Similarly, the attempt at abortion could involve agents or means other than those specified in the current Massachusetts statute, including many which were not generally considered a "poison, drug, or medicine, or noxious thing."[22]

The Report continued with a discussion of the meager punishment associated with the crime and the major reason for this, which was failure to consider the true victim. He wrote:

> The punishment of criminal abortion, by the present statute, is, in cases where the mother does not happen to lose her life, wholly disproportioned to the enormity of the crime. The law is predicated on an entirely erroneous idea. The real intent is seldom against the life of the mother; in almost every instance, she is herself, not merely an accessory, but one of the principals—in what? Not an attempt at the murder of herself,—for that would be simply absurd,—but the murder of her child.
>
> The law is here fundamentally wrong. It utterly ignores the existence of the living child, though the child is really alive from the very moment of its conception, and from that very moment is and should be considered a distinct being; this the law does not, however, recognize. The foetus is not as has been so often alleged, merely *pars viscerum matris*; though upon such belief our law is evidently based.

Horatio noted the inconsistency of civil law which, unlike "moral" law, recognized the child's existence before birth. He also pointed out that the "perils and dangers" of the uterine existence were no reason for reducing the "criminality" of fetal destruction as some had argued. He noted that perils after birth were as great or greater and these "would hardly be allowed to invalidate a charge of infanticide."

Horatio then argued that the purposeful destruction of a living fetus was "clearly MURDER." However, he recognized that "there are those who will not allow that it should be punished as such." He called for its reclassification from a simple misdemeanor to at least a felony. He also proposed, following an article of the French penal code, that medical persons be punished more for inducing abortion than those not associated with the medical profession. Mothers' punishment also should vary. Horatio noted that the women who obtained abortions were rarely punished under current laws and he called for changes: "Unless proved insane, the wretch who had caused the death of her offspring, perhaps by her own hand, should be made to suffer corresponding exposure and punishment. If married, as is too often the case, her crime should be considered as infinitely increased."

Another controversial plea of Horatio was that anyone who even advocated abortion be charged with a crime. "Much of the public indifference and error on the subject of criminal abortion," he wrote, "is owing to the influence of certain misguided or brutal men, who by their publications or lectures, have given rise to a belief that the induction of abortion is alike the prerogative and duty of the married."[23] Horatio then provided the following paragraph which described physician actions that innocently contributed to the rise of criminal abortion. As will be seen, Dr. Charles Buckingham would request that everything from "the frequent repetition ..." to the end of the paragraph be dropped.

> The resort to craniotomy, where, in some cases at least, the child's life might by other means be saved; the frequent repetition of that operation, or of the premature induction of labor before the seventh month, in the same patient, in accordance with the rule, almost universally acknowledged, but still often WRONG, that the child's life is as nothing in comparison with that of its mother; the neglect of attempts at resuscitating still-born children, especially where, as the phrase goes, "it is a mercy" if the child were born dead; the fear sometimes shown by medical men to denounce the crime in fitting terms to patients who have confided to them their sin; the occasional carelessness in treatment and mistakes in diagnosis, where proper attention and examination would have shown the unmistakable signs of pregnancy; the relying upon a single and unaided opinion, in cases where not one life only, but two, may be involved,—are all instances of apparent disregard of foetal life, that serve with the community as incentives to abortion.

Horatio called for coroners to be selected from physicians and for physicians to become more familiar "with the true principles and with the details of Obstetric Jurisprudence; through ignorance of which, on the part of attorney, medical witness, or judge, not a few perfectly clear cases of criminal abortion have fallen to the ground."[24]   Horatio predicted this would lead to increased certainty of punishment and that this in turn would sharply reduce the incidence of the crime.

Horatio followed with a draft abortion statute which incorporated the changes and additions he had recommended. "But enforce this law," Horatio continued, "and the profession would never allow its then high place in the community to be unworthily degraded; nor, as now, would those be permitted, unchallenged, to remain in fellowship, who were generally believed guilty or suspected of this crime."   The proposed statute read:[25]

Section I.

Whoever, with intent to cause and procure the miscarriage of a woman, shall sell, give, or administer to her, prescribe for her, or advise, or direct, or cause, or procure her to take any medicine, or drug, or substance whatever, or shall use or employ or advise any instrument or other means whatever, with the like intent, unless the same shall have been necessary to preserve the life of such woman or of her unborn child, and shall have been so pronounced by two competent physicians; and any person, with the like intent, knowingly aiding and assisting such offender or offenders,—shall be deemed guilty of felony, whether the woman die or not in consequence thereof, and shall be imprisoned not more than ten, nor less than three years, in the State Prison. And if such offence shall have been committed by a physician or surgeon, or person claiming to be such, midwife, nurse, or druggist, such punishment may be increased at the discretion of the court, to imprisonment not exceeding twenty years in the State Prison.

Section II.

Every woman who shall solicit, purchase, or obtain of any person, or in any other way procure, or receive, any medicine, drug, or substance whatever, and shall take the same, or shall submit to any operation of other means whatever, or shall commit any operation or violence upon herself, with intent thereby to procure a miscarriage, unless the same shall have been by two competent physicians pronounced necessary to preserve her own life or that of her unborn child, shall be deemed guilty of a misdemeanor, and shall be punished by imprisonment in the House of Correction not less than three months nor more than one year, or by a fine not exceeding one thousand dollars, or by both said fine and imprisonment; and, if her child be in consequence born dead, she shall be deemed guilty of felony, and shall be imprisoned not more than ten nor less than three years; and if said offender be a married woman, these punishments may be increased to within twice the limits above-assigned.

Section III.

Whoever shall encourage, by publication, lecture, or otherwise, the procurement of criminal abortion; and whoever shall in any way aid and abet the same, by advertising, selling, or circulating such publication,—shall be deemed guilty of a misdemeanor, and shall be punished by imprisonment in the House of Correction not less than three months, nor more than one year, or by a fine not exceeding one thousand dollars.

The fourth and final section was identical to Section II of the current Massachusetts statute which dealt with advertising abortion services and selling drugs which presumably produced abortion. This draft statute concluded the Report.

At the special Society meeting called to consider the Report on May 9, 1857, Jacob Bigelow indicated his belief that criminal abortion "had been well considered by the legislature when the present laws were passed, and perhaps they could not be improved."[26] He indicated his objections to the Committee's dropping of the Massachusetts requirement for proving pregnancy. "An abortion can not be procured if a woman is not pregnant," he argued, "for there will be nothing to operate upon." He indicated that if this change were made, it "would upset everything in law." He also pointed out that a physician could go to prison for treating amenorrhoea if abortion should follow, even though it was impossible to determine that pregnancy existed. Bigelow also objected to the requirement that two physicians agree as to the necessity of induced abortion. He noted that a "physician in the country might be alone, far distant from any medical brother," and "he could not act on his own judgment without rendering himself liable to punishment." Bigelow's final objection was to the Committee's plan to increase the severity of punishment. This he felt would increase the difficulty of obtaining convictions for the crime, noting that "juries sometimes will not bring in a man guilty of murder because the punishment is so severe." "As to the punishment of the woman," the minutes continued, "Dr Bigelow thought her perhaps the least culpable of all; less so than the physician, for she has frequently the fear of shame and disgrace to urge her on; much less so than her seducer who escapes easily while she suffers severely." Bigelow concluded his speech by arguing that the present abortion statutes were adequate, if they were "well carried out, and if people knew that it was so," and he also indicated that he did not believe the legislature would "act favorably on the report."

Horatio indicated that the Committee "had considered all these objections and differed in opinion." He noted that "several distinguished lawyers" indicated that convictions were not possible with the present law. "As to the punishment of the woman," the minutes continued, "Dr Storer thought that the seducer did not generally share in the crime of procuring abortion." Horatio also pointed out that in the case of the lone physician out in the country, "necessity must be its own law." The minutes also reported that Horatio said:

> As to "proving the existence of pregnancy," a large proportion of these cases occur during the first few months of utero-gestation, when this can not be positively done. The existence of "malice" is also a difficult thing to prove. Dr Storer thought it much easier and much more apt to promote the ends of justice, that the government should be obliged merely to prove the deed, and the prisoner be made to show its necessity.

A Dr. Moore indicated his approval of "the sentiments and opinions contained in the report." He argued that the woman obtaining the abortion should be punished and described a woman who had requested him to perform an abortion. He refused and she "performed the operation on herself by means of a whalebone." Jacob Bigelow then indicated that he "thought the present law sufficiently explicit on" punishment of women. Horatio objected, noting that the current laws "referred only to the person procuring the abortion and not to the child or woman."

It then was Dr. Charles Buckingham's turn. He first emphasized "that regular practitioners do not countenance the production of abortion save in extreme cases, and do not practise it; that the statements to the contrary are made by irregular practitioners to justify themselves." Following this, he indicated his agreement with Dr. Bigelow's objections and cited his additional concern about the greater punishment for married than single women. He acknowledged that married women had more abortions than single women, but noted that once a woman made the decision to abort there was no stopping her, "if she can't get drugs she will operate on herself as in Dr Moore's case, with a piece of whalebone or some other instrument." The minutes then described Buckingham's objections to the Report's paragraph which countered the frequently-accepted belief that "the child's life is as nothing in comparison with that of its mother." Buckingham saw this as "going back too far, to the Roman Catholic laws; making an excuse for the operation of Cesarean Section, a capital and very dangerous operation." Horatio was reported to have indicated

> that the Committee thought it their duty to report the paragraph objected to, and was surprised that Dr. Buckingham should object to it. In cases of deformed pelvis abortion is frequently produced in order to save the life of the mother; it has sometimes been done as often as five times in the same patient. He thought that the lusts of man or woman should not be pandered to in this way. The man should be castrated or the child have a chance. The mother is

responsible if she puts her own life in danger and the crime is against the child. In regard to Dr. Buckingham's statement that if a woman can't get drugs she will operate on herself, Dr. Storer said that was her own risk; the Committee act for the child; the mother is a willing agent and must answer for herself.

The members then decided that still another meeting of the Society was needed to deal with the report. It was moved and carried "that the report be recommitted with instructions to the Committee to make alterations if they thought necessary, and report at the next *regular* meeting" which was scheduled for May 30, 1857.[27]

Although there are several parts of these Minutes that deserve amplification, perhaps the most critical, given recent distortions of the motives of early physician opponents or abortion, is the phrase, "the Committee act for the child; the mother is a willing agent and must answer for herself." It clearly shows that this opposition of physicians to abortion was primarily a concern for the unborn child and *not,* as a 1989 brief submitted to the Supreme Court claimed, primarily a concern for the dangers to the woman of abortion, elimination of irregular practitioners, enforcing gender rules, and/or preventing an increase in the proportion of Catholic immigrants in the population.[28]

The negative criticism Horatio and his report experienced at the May 9 Special Meeting may have been alleviated by two complementary letters which Horatio received from Dr. Stephen Tracy of Andover, Massachusetts[29] and from Dr. Thomas W. Blatchford of Troy, New York.[30] Tracy had read of the February initiation of Horatio's effort in the May 7 *Boston Medical and Surgical Journal* and his letter, *dated May 7*, included, "I feel prompted to express to you the great & sincere pleasure I have this day experienced in reading your remarks ..." Blatchford, Vice President of the American Medical Association in 1856, probably also learned of Horatio's anti-abortion efforts from the May 7 *Boston Medical and Surgical Journal*. Blatchford wrote: "I am glad you have got hold of it. Don't let it go until you have made your exertions tell on [the] community." These encouragements probably were not necessary to make Horatio persist in his efforts, but they surely did not hurt.

Dr. Tracy also provided Horatio with a copy of a book, *The Mother and Her Offspring*, he had written in 1853[31] which included discussion of the fact that abortion was prevalent plus his reasons for believing that abortion was wrong, including: "Its life commenced at the time of the formation of the embryonic cell—at the moment of conception; and no person has any right to destroy it by any means whatever."[32] However, Tracy's lack of success with his book in bringing widespread attention to the problem might have caused Horatio to think hard about his own strategies for effecting change.

Buckingham wrote a guest editorial which appeared in the *Boston Medical and Surgical Journal* on May 28 and which he signed "B."[33] It was highly critical of the Committee Report and we can be sure that it was available for Boston physicians to read two or more days before the May 30 Society meeting was held.[34] It stated in part, that[35]

> The affair was too hastily got up, and ought not to pass in its present form. The writer of it seems to have thrown out of consideration the life of the mother, making that of the unborn child appear of far more consequence, even should the mother have a dozen dependent on her for their daily bread. It cannot be possible that either the profession or the public will be brought to this belief. *Argue as forcibly as they may, to their own satisfaction, the Committee will fail to convince the public that abortion in the early months is a crime, and a large proportion of the medical profession will tacitly support the popular view of the subject.*

Buckingham also reiterated many of the points that Jacob Bigelow and he had made at the Special Meeting on May 9. He indicated that physicians should refrain from attempts to change legislation and concentrate their efforts on changing public attitudes about criminal abortion. However, he believed "this must be approached cautiously: not with denunciation; not refusing aid to her whose defective pelvis, and strong animal instinct, not 'beastly lust' has a second or third time caused her to seek premature delivery at the risk of life; not by a law, which would require a consultation in case of suppressed menses; but by words of warning, and arguments directed in kind language to reasonable women and men." Buckingham claimed that any attempts to change laws would "be absolutely vain." More "rigid" laws would increase concealment of the crime. He then criticized the Committee's proposal to "relieve the government of the necessity of proving malice." "If there is no malicious act proved," he wrote, "there is never any crime proved, as the judge charges the jury upon every murder trial." He then pointed out problems associated with calling abortion "murder."

> But allowing the committing of abortion to be murder, and the writer is not prepared to deny that, although he is less disposed to assert it than he was, before this subject was broached by the Committee, with what consistency can it be proposed to inflict any punishment less than capital for it? Or how can they make it less a murder, if performed upon an unmarried woman, than upon a married one?

"Let the Suffolk District Society utter their protest as strongly as they please," he concluded, "but the making of laws is as much out of their province as the mending of watches."

Horatio and his father were outraged by this guest editorial, not only at

"B.", but at the *Boston Medical and Surgical Journal* editors for publishing something which they *accurately* saw as calculated to prevent acceptance of the Society's Report on Criminal Abortion, and, *inaccurately* saw as libelling physicians (described below). As will be seen, Horatio immediately sought the help of the *New-Hampshire Journal of Medicine* and the *American Medical Gazette*, both of whose editors were in New York, and these editors were more than willing to take on their counterparts at the *Boston Medical and Surgical Journal.*

Although the official minutes of the Suffolk District Medical Society May 30 meeting have been lost, several sources indicate that Buckingham's guest editorial came under intense criticism. The July *New-Hampshire Journal of Medicine* account of that meeting indicated the Report "was warmly contested, but accepted by a close vote."[36] The most comprehensive account of the meeting, was by "Medicus" and published in *The Medical World*,[37] a short-lived journal edited by Dr. Jerome Van Crowningshield Smith, amateur ichthyologist, former editor of the *Boston Medical and Surgical Journal*, and mayor of Boston. The following excerpts provide names of the disputants and other information not elsewhere available:

Suffolk District Medical Society.

The Monthly Meeting of this Society for Medical Improvement was held at their room in Temple Place on Saturday evening, May 30th; and for once, there was a full meeting *without a supper.* ...

After some remarks upon the treatment of *Hemorrhoids* ..., the Herculean labor of the evening was commenced, namely, the consideration of the Report of the Committee upon Criminal Abortions. This Report had been presented at a former meeting, but laid upon the table and printed for the use of the members. It had been noticed in the Boston Medical and Surgical *Journal,* and somewhat severely criticised by a correspondent, signing himself B. Dr. Storer, Jr., the chairman of the Committee, made some remarks, and read those portions of the Report which he wished to be adopted, (leaving out the laws, which the original Report contained,) to be recommended to the Massachusetts Medical Society, and from them to the next Legislature, if they saw fit. Instead of these drafts of Laws, he offered several Resolutions to be presented to the parent Society, ...

This was an improvement upon the former report, inasmuch as it left the law-making business in the hands of those to whom it properly belonged.

But, as this was, in effect, *a new report*, and, as it was difficult to trace the parts which were left out, and those which were retained from the former Report, Dr. Buckingham moved that this new Report, with the Resolutions, be laid upon the table, and printed, to be acted upon at a future meeting.

Dr. Storer, Sen., was very much surprised that any member of the

Society should hesitate for a moment to adopt this Report. He assailed, with considerable severity, the following sentence, in the *Journal* of May 28th, 1857: "Argue as forcibly as they may, to their own satisfaction, the Committee will fail to convince the public that abortion in the early months is a crime, and a large proportion of the medical profession will tacitly support the popular view of the subject." He (Dr. Storer, Sen.,) was surprised that any member of the profession should write thus, and especially, that the man who would make such a statement should not put his whole name to the article, instead of signing it B. He thought he was bound so to do, that the public might know who he was. He had run his eye over the B's in the Society, and could think of no one that would have done it, except a man by the name of Brown, who had been expelled. He was equally surprised that the editors of the *Journal,* whom he held responsible for all that was published in it, should have admitted an article containing such immoral sentiments, &c.

This brought Dr. Morland, the senior editor of the *Journal,* to his feet. He should not be accused of entertaining such sentiments by any man, as had been imputed to him by Dr. Storer, &c.

Dr. Lyman defended the editors of the *Journal,* and thought Dr. Storer in the wrong.

Dr. Buckingham, (with no small share of the dauntless courage of his father, in the days of the "New England *Galaxy,*") arose and said he was the author of the article in the *Journal,* and he did not shrink from assuming the responsibility of all that was there said. He believed it was all true, and was ready to defend it; and that it contained no such sentiments as Dr. S. had tried to make it contain, &c.

Dr. Storer read it again, and renewed his former statements. ...

After an expression of various opinions, (sometimes half a dozen speakers at once,) the report was accepted.

   ...

Medicus.

P. S.—I forgot to name above, that one doctor stated that a female physician had been travelling up and down Cape Cod, teaching the ladies that it was not immoral to produce abortions, and how it could be done! Will not such female doctors also teach the ladies how to escape the laws recommended by male doctors, and made by male legislators?

Invaluable as it was, Medicus' report of the May 30 meeting in the *Medical World* did not identify the specific objections of David Humphreys Storer to Buckingham's published "Argue as forcibly ..." statement. David Humphreys Storer (and no doubt Horatio) had interpreted the statement as claiming that "a large proportion" of physicians shared the public view that abortion was not a crime while it was well-known by physicians that virtually all regular physicians believed abortion was criminal. Hence the "Argue as forcibly ..." statement was claimed by David Humphreys to be "libelling the profession." David Humphreys Storer and Horatio were concerned that this published "deliberate falsehood" about how physicians regarded criminal abortion "would tend to prejudice the profession, wrongfully and dangerously, in public opinion."[38] This we learn from the *New-Hampshire Journal of Medicine* for July which reported the Suffolk District Medical Society abortion doings and strongly criticized the *Boston Medical and Surgical Journal* for publishing "B.s"' piece. The "prejudicial" effect of "B."'s statement on public opinion about physicians, of course, would not matter whether this claim that most physicians did not view abortion as a crime was a deliberate lie; a false belief; actually true; or, as was actually the case, *only an apparent claim resulting from "B."'s bad choice of words*. "B."'s intended meaning of the words "tacitly support the popular view" was given in a June 11 *Boston Medical and Surgical Journal* editorial. The Editors repeated the entire "Argue as forcibly ..." sentence, then wrote:[39]

> We are willing to allow that this is capable of a construction which would imply a "libel" on the profession; but it is also capable of another, and which, to all who know either the writer of the article or the editors of this Journal, will, we believe, be the one most naturally suggested. We should be not a little, and most disagreeably surprised, did we think there was even *one*, in the profession or out of it, who could for a moment imagine we admit that any honorable physician panders, ever so slightly, or even "tacitly," to the procurement of criminal abortion. But that, either from sheer ignorance or a lack of high moral sense, ... the public do not consider "abortion in the early months" a crime, is only too evident—and what we understood by the expression which has excited so much feeling, is that the profession, or a "large proportion" of it, has not hitherto considered, and does not now consider, it worth while to waste time upon people who will not be convinced, and who are nearly always wholly uninformed, upon the *morale* of the act, at least. By admitting the article in question, we in no degree compromised ourselves, or expressed an opinion contrary to the above; neither does the article betray such sentiments on the part of the writer. We presume that even the denunciator of the article will not assert the contrary; indeed, his own complimentary expression in reply to our verbal repudiation of *libellous* intentions and acts, sufficiently prove this. ...

If "B." had said "tacitly *endure* the public view of the subject," or even "tacitly *accept* ...," there would have been no misunderstanding at the time (or now). However, "tacitly *support* the popular view" that early abortion was not a crime, makes it easy, 140 years later when this *is* the belief of many physicians and other people, to believe that "B." was actually saying that most physicians did not believe that early abortion was a crime. "B." made a poor selection of words, as he himself was to indicate in a letter asking his critics to look at his complete article (presented below).

Dr. James C. Mohr was to write in 1978 that "B." "was finally driven to claim that his statements had been misinterpreted ..."[40] "[F]inally driven to claim" suggests, even implies, that "B," was forced to claim something *counter* to his actual belief. However, despite the appearance to the contrary, "B." was *not* claiming in his guest editorial that the medical profession in 1857 supported early abortions or viewed such as not being criminal.

The July *New-Hampshire Journal of Medicine* editorial almost certainly was based on correspondence from Horatio to its New-York-City-based editor, Edward Hazen Parker, including a letter sent *before* the May 30 Society meeting. Horatio may have been trying to counter "B."'s attempt to scuttle the Report as well as entering a protest against what at that time he viewed as the *Boston Medical and Surgical Journal*'s betrayal of their earlier anti-abortion policy. The editorial began:[41]

> Criminal Abortion.—We have watched with much interest the progress of the movement lately commenced by the profession in Boston against Criminal Abortion. This movement has now secured the sanction of the State Medical Society of Massachusetts, and as it will doubtless be participated in by physicians of other States we are inclined to think its history from the outset, obtained from current numbers of the Boston Medical and Surgical Journal, and from the correspondence of a friend may prove not unacceptable to our readers.

Horatio almost certainly was the "friend" providing the "correspondence." The "sanction of the State Medical Society of Massachusetts" was obtained at the June 3 meeting of the Massachusetts Medical Society at New Bedford. On the other hand, it was a weak sanction, if it could be considered such at all. According to the Minutes of the New Bedford meeting, Horatio described the actions of the Suffolk District Medical Society related to the increased frequency of abortion and proposed a Resolution for the Massachusetts Medical Society which would lead to a Committee "to bring before the next Legislature the alarming increase of criminal abortion in this Commonwealth, and to request in the name of this Society a careful revision of the Statutes upon that crime."[42] This single Resolution was a stronger request for legislative change than the two Resolutions that were passed at the Suffolk District Society meeting at the end of May. It was nearly identical to a rejected Resolution. These three Resolutions and the votes for and against them are presented below in "Student's" second letter.

The Minutes of the Massachusetts Medical Society's New Bedford meeting also indicated that there was much discussion where "several of the Fellows advocated the proposition, and others opposed any action which would involve the Society in seeking additional legislation." A Committee consisting of "Drs. Foster Hooper, of Fall River, J. Bigelow, J. Ware, J.C. Dalton, E. Hunt, C. Gordon, and H.R. Storer" was appointed to report at the next Annual Meeting of the Society. As we will see, the Committee made their report prematurely when Horatio was away from Massachusetts for an extended period and this may have been no coincidence, certainly Horatio did not think it was.

The *New-Hampshire Journal of Medicine* version of the New Bedford proceedings predicted that the make-up of the Massachusetts Medical Society Committee was such that they would "not rest till they have secured all they desire. They aim at an open and general condemnation of the crime by the profession, and at thus removing the imputation now so generally considered as resting on its fair name."[43] Given Horatio's strong influence on the *New Hampshire Journal of Medicine* editorial, this shows that Horatio was highly "confident" that the new Massachusetts Medical Society committee would recommend changes in Massachusetts' statutes on abortion, despite the presence on the committee of Dr. Jacob Bigelow who had made efforts to thwart change in the statutes at every 1857 meeting on the issue.

The following final paragraphs of the July *New-Hampshire Journal of Medicine* editorial show that the anti-abortion crusade was viewed as a "war," and show the strong support Horatio's efforts received from many, probably most, physicians. They also indicate why Editor Parker at the outset of the piece, predicted the movement against criminal abortion would be "participated in by physicians of other States."[44]

We feel that we may well be pardoned for first speaking at length as we have, of the connection of our Massachusetts brethren with this subject, as the war seems first to have fairly begun with them; and will only say in addition, that we have personal knowledge that the evil is no less prevalent in our own community. ...

Dr. H. R. Storer has taken a stand in this matter alike creditable to his head and his heart, and we feel that he will receive the hearty thanks of every *true* physician.

That his efforts are appreciated by the profession at large, is evident, from the fact that he was appointed by the American Medical Association at its late meeting at Nashville, as Chairman of a Special Committee "on Criminal Abortion, with a view to its general suppression," to report next year at Washington, and may be regarded as an earnest, that the work now begun, *will be carried forward*.

Buckingham published another criticism of the Suffolk Committee on Criminal Abortion and its Report in the August 1857 *Medical and Surgical Reporter*.[45] The piece, signed "Student," was written on June 4, 1857, one day after the meeting of the Massachusetts Medical Society at New Bedford. "Student" provided additional information about the actual voting on Resolutions, etc., that occurred at the May 30 meeting of the Suffolk District Medical Society which was not available in other accounts. In his "LETTER FROM BOSTON," Buckingham told that:

The subject of criminal abortion is giving great anxiety to some of our Boston brethren, and its discussion has excited so much attention that the number of criminal abortions will probably be increased this year, in consequence. There are those who cannot disconnect any two subjects to which their attention may be called. Physiologists find it necessary to inquire—not what is true—but what agrees with their particular sectarian doctrines. ... In our day it has become necessary to propose the union of morality and medicine, by the aid of the statute law. Some instances of respectability, who claim also to be men of principle, and Christians, doubt the propriety of certain proposed laws, and forthwith they are stigmatized as upholders of crime.

At the meeting of the Suffolk District Medical Society last month, a report, written by Dr. H.R. Storer, of this city, was under discussion. The subject of the report was the prevention of criminal abortions. It contained some of the most uncalled for insinuations, concerning the practice of Boston physicians; a few wild propositions for the protection of morals; and it closed with a law, such as could not be passed, and if it could be passed, would be an abortion of itself. This it was proposed to force down the throats of the Council of the Massachusetts Medical Society, bring before the Massachusetts Legislature, and give to the world as the recommendation of the physicians of Boston. The matter was discussed at two meetings. At the first, interest enough was felt, to bring out less than twenty members of the Society. The second meeting was attended by perhaps twenty-five. Some gentlemen got exceedingly warm, and one indulged himself in the luxury of calling by abusive epithets, a correspondent of the *Boston Medical and Surgical Journal*, whose opinion, concerning the report alluded to, differed from his own, after misrepresenting that opinion.

The profession were not prepared to stand by the report, nor to go for the proposed law. The committee, therefore, very wisely withdrew the latter, and materially changed the former, striking out about all the substance. In place of the law, they offered the following resolutions, of which the second was knocked in the head.

The others would have been, if several of the opponents of the report had not become exhausted, and left in disgust.

"*Resolved,* That the subject of criminal abortion demands the attention of the medical profession of the State. (Adopted—16 to 13.)

"*Resolved,* That in the opinion of the Suffolk District Medical Society, some further legislation seems needed, to prevent the commission of this crime. (Rejected—13 to 17.)

"*Resolved,* That [blank] be a committee to urge upon the Massachusetts Medical Society, to take action in the premises, and if it deem expedient, to present the subject for the consideration of the legislature. (Adopted—14 to 13.)"

...

The end was not yet. The Massachusetts Medical Society were treated to a dose of abortion, yesterday, and one of the committee from Boston informed them, in a very forcible speech, that they *should* take notice of this subject, or he would for them. As they will undoubtedly do nothing, he will have employment enough.

By one of those remarkable coincidences which we sometimes hear of, the American Medical Association appointed a committee upon this same subject, with the same gentleman chairman.

The reader may not need the following explanation, but "Some instances of respectability, who claim also to be men of principle, and Christians, doubt the propriety of certain proposed laws," were those who opposed the Committee's Report and particularly opposed its proposed statute on Criminal Abortion. Foremost among these was "Student," i.e., Buckingham. Those who defended the report strongly, including Horatio and his father, were the ones who "stigmatized" the opponents "as upholders of crime." The "most uncalled for insinuations, concerning the practice of Boston physicians" which "Student" attributed to the Committee Report may have referred to physicians "innocently causing the increase of criminal abortion," but these barely qualify as "most uncalled for insinuations." The Committee Report did not include any claim that Boston physicians were providing abortions, although undoubtedly a few were. Such serious "insinuations, concerning the practice of Boston physicians" may have been made at the May 9 or May 30 meetings of the Society or at the June 3 meeting of the parent society at New Bedford, but were not recorded in the Minutes.

Buckingham may have been led to find these problems with the Report of the Suffolk District Medical Society Committee on Criminal Abortion because of preexisting hostilities with both Drs. Storer. In addition, Buckingham's chairmanship "of the first committee who handled this matter" (described below) may have made him a strong defender of the adequacy of existing laws.

Although Horatio was already aware that he had been selected Chairman of the American Medical Association Special Committee on Criminal Abortion, he received a July 4 letter from J. Berrien Lindsley of Nashville notifying him of this two months after the action was taken. It included:[46]

> The Nominating Committee objected to raising so large a special committee as you wished, but very cordially appointed you Chairman. As such you have the privilege of selecting such Co-adjutors as you may wish. The subject *is* very important as well as interesting, and the Washington meeting will be a good time to bring it up. We all anticipate a very large turn out next year, which will make up for the small attendance at our for the present inaccessible city.

This letter provides considerable information about the "remarkable coincidence" that "Student" mentioned at the end of his letter. Horatio obviously had requested that a large Special Committee on Criminal Abortion be formed in his March letter to Dr. Lindsley of Nashville and no doubt requested that he be a member of it, probably also that he be Chairman. We do not have any indication how large the number was that Horatio proposed for the committee, but the power of nomination of "Co-adjutors" granted by the Nominating Committee was a boon in that it allowed Horatio himself to select those men he believed could best advance the anti-abortion effort.

The furor associated with the Suffolk District Committee Report continued. The *Boston Medical and Surgical Journal* responded on July 23 to the editorial that had appeared in the July *New-Hampshire Journal of Medicine*.[47] They criticized Editor Parker for either discussing something he did not have first-hand knowledge of or of surrendering his editorial function to an actual participant in the Massachusetts Society's criminal abortion discussions. "Certain expressions in the article," the editors wrote, "render the latter supposition not improbable." Obviously, the *Boston Medical and Surgical Journal* editors believed Horatio had made major input to the New Hampshire journal piece. They stuck by their definition of "tacitly support" as "tacitly endure" and rather successfully showed that their editorial positions on the question of criminal abortion had not changed from strong opposition. They also called for physicians to help dispel the ignorance that caused people to "allow, or seek for the perpetration of the crime."

The *New-Hampshire Journal of Medicine* responded in August with an editorial entitled "Criminal Abortion; The Boston Medical and Surgical Journal and its Attempts at Bullying."[48] The editorial pointed out that it had acknowledged the information in their July editorial had come "in part from conversation and correspondence with a personal acquaintance and friend, resident in" Massachusetts. They went on to indicate "we are not conscious of necessarily having displayed either gross ignorance or willful impertinence." The editorial continued: "To the implication that we are not competent or accustomed to write our own editorials, we might if we choose, retort by pointing to a seeming identity in style of the present attack of the Boston Journal upon us, with that objectionable article of its correspondent 'B.'" The editorial also reiterated the claim that "B."'s sentence including "the profession will tacitly support the popular view" would be interpreted by nine out of ten impartial readers as indicating that the profession would agree with the view, not quietly put up with a view they disagreed with. The writer or writers of the editorial added: "Such was our impression before we had written or had heard a word upon the subject, and we are glad that 'B.' has been denounced by one of the New York Journals, as in this matter 'heretical alike to truth and good morals.' Are the Boston editors prepared to quarrel with all who have so thought?" They went on to indicate that now that they knew who "B." was, they too were willing to consider the Boston Journal's interpretation of "tacitly support the popular view." However, they argued that they could not be blamed for assuming a libel on the profession when the author of the sentence was still anonymous. As to the identity of "B.", the editorial indicated this, "was only subsequently and almost compulsorily acknowledged at a Medical Society's meeting, and has never yet been publicly known."

"B.", i.e., Buckingham, was to provide a second letter to the editors of the *Boston Medical and Surgical Journal* which was a rejoinder to all the criticism. It was published in their issue of August 13 and it has highly interesting references to the identity of "the personal acquaintance and friend" of the *New-Hampshire Journal of Medicine* editor. Buckingham wrote:[49]

Messrs. Editors,—"B." is much obliged to you for sending him the copies of the New Hampshire Medical Journal for July and August, in the latter of which the editor pays him his particular respects. "B." is very tenacious of his rights, and does not like to have *his* articles attributed to any one else. He therefore feels compelled to disown the authorship of your article of July 23d, presuming, at the same time, that you write your own editorials.

"B." is very much astonished to learn, that his identity "was almost compulsorily acknowledged at a Medical Society's meeting and has never yet been publicly known." He has good reason to believe that he has been well known as an occasional contributor to your pages, and that he was known to be the author of the article which has created this tempest in the New Hampshire teapot, even by the one who attacked him at the Suffolk District Medical Society.

"B." is forced to the conclusion, that the "personal acquaintance and friend" is one of two individuals, the personal prejudices of one of whom would render him an incompetent witness. The other stands in such a relation to the profession that his evidence would not, by itself, be considered of much worth among the profession in Boston. As "B." was chairman of the first committee who handled this matter, even before Dr. Storer lectured upon the subject, and has

been always active in trying to put an end to the connection of the Society and those who are engaged in irregular practices, his brethren in Boston would probably receive his evidence as quite as valuable as that of the "personal acquaintance and friend." "B." has not heard that he has lost caste with the profession here, nor does he think that the readers of the New Hampshire Journal would look upon him as such a monster of iniquity, if that Journal would re-publish his whole article, in place of the mere sentence which has given so much trouble.

...

As "B." does not take the New York journals, it would gratify him if the New Hampshire Journal would let him know when and in what one he was "denounced." Having written nothing and said nothing which he does not think he can prove, he will pursue the subject further and over his real signature if it is thought proper by the respectable part of the profession, when the New Hampshire Journal will say who their "personal acquaintance and friend" is. Till then, the medical men of Boston will probably deny the competency of that friend's testimony, and how they would receive it afterward remains to be seen.   "B."

Buckingham's claim to having "been always active in trying to put an end to the connection of the Society and those who are engaged in irregular practices" almost certainly was a dig at Horatio whose specialization in the diseases of women had already begun to some extent and which was viewed by many conservative general practitioners as "quackery" or worse.

As mentioned, Horatio almost certainly was the "personal acquaintance and friend" of the editor of the *New-Hampshire Journal of Medicine.* In light of this, and granting the probable accuracy of "B." when he discussed the "two possible individuals" who this could be, "B."'s letter is devastatingly revealing of the way Horatio was viewed by some Boston physicians just two years after Horatio started practice in Boston. "B."'s "possible individual" with "personal prejudices" rendering "him an incompetent witness" probably was David Humphreys Storer who would reasonably be "personally prejudiced" in favor of his son. "B."'s other candidate who "stands in such a relation to the profession that his evidence would not, by itself, be considered of much worth among the profession in Boston" almost certainly was Horatio. Thus we see that advocacy of Boston-tabooed chloroform for midwifery, specialization to some extent in the taboo area of diseases of women, discussion of the taboo topics of criminal abortion and nymphomania, or some combination of these, already had caused Horatio to be blacklisted by some portion of the Boston medical establishment. The "pomposity" that Hermann Jackson Warner had frequently mentioned surely was still extant and no doubt particularly noticeable and offensive to those opposed to Horatio's views and activities.

The following letter was published in the *Boston Medical and Surgical Journal* on August 20, 1857, a week after "B."'s second letter and in response to it:

Messrs. Editors,—Having been an eye- and ear-witness of the proceedings at the Suffolk District Society's meeting holden on the last Saturday of May, I can assert, what doubtless every member of the Society then present will remember, that the gentleman who then denounced the article signed "B." in your issue of May 28th, also distinctly said he was utterly ignorant of the paternity of that article. No one who knows him can for a moment deem him capable of false speaking, or of "mal-reading," which was then charged upon him by "B."

I would ask, then, upon what ground "B." declares, in your issue of August 13th, that he "has good reason to believe that he was known to be the author of the article which has created such a tempest in the New Hampshire teapot, even by the one who attacked him at the Suffolk District Medical Society."

Here we have an impeachment (*direct*, most will say) of Dr. Storer's word, who, we will engage, has always been and continues to be considered "good as gold."

As it is by no means likely that this gentleman will trouble himself to take up this charge, I consider that simple justice demands either a retraction or a verification of the wholesale assertion hazarded by "B." in your issue of the 13th of this month.

Suffolk.

August 15th, 1857.[50]

Even if "Suffolk" is correct that David Humphreys Storer did not know who "B." was when Horatio's father on May 30 began his attack upon the *Boston Medical and Surgical Journal* editors for publishing "B."'s guest editorial, Horatio and his father may have had the incorrect *hunch* that it was the same person, i.e., Henry J. Bigelow, who had influenced the suppression of the abortion section of David Humphreys Storer's November 1855 Introductory Lecture. The signature "B." on the guest editorial probably suggested Bigelow as a possible author. The *Boston Medical and Surgical Journal* editors had strongly criticized that "suppressor" in December 1855, and if they were now presenting a guest editorial by the same person that was timed to produce a "hostile critique" of the Report on Criminal Abortion (discussed below), the contrast between the old editorial "position" of support of Storers and the new editorial position of frustration of Storers would have been all the more salient and vexing. Although all other parties in these disputes have been identified, "Suffolk" remains anonymous. However, this defense of David Humphreys Storer could have come from Horatio's pen. No one would have been more angered by Buckingham's challenge to David Humphreys' veracity than this son with world-class filial piety.

Finally, we get to the New York Journal editorial which "denounced" "B." "as in this matter 'heretical alike to truth and good morals.'" The prefatory paragraph read:

> The following two articles are inserted connectedly, that our readers may see how this important topic is regarded by the medical mind in Boston. The first, being a report of the Committee, is, in our opinion, well considered, and a truthful exposition of a topic which ought to be regarded of the highest interest to the profession and the public. Its ethics are sound and in conformity with the morale of the profession, which has always been on the side of true religion. But the second we regard as heretical alike to truth and good morals, this being a critique on the report of the Committee, and foreshadowing a hostile demonstration to the latter when it shall come before the Society.[51]

This is strong evidence that Horatio believed "B." and the *Boston Medical and Surgical Journal* editors had purposely jeopardized acceptance of the Report on Criminal Abortion. It is also evidence of the swiftness of Horatio's reaction to this threat. The New York journal was the *American Medical Gazette* and it published the editorial in July. The article consisted of the above paragraph, the Suffolk District Committee Report on Criminal Abortion (without the proposed statute), and a total transcript of "B."'s original guest editorial.

Horatio provided at least the Committee Report to D. Meredith Reese, the Editor of the *American Medical Gazette*. Horatio no doubt also described the problem the guest editorial of "B." posed for acceptance by the Society of the Report, namely, "foreshadowing a hostile demonstration to the latter." "Foreshadowing" and the words that followed, "*when*[52] it shall come before the Society," are evidence that Horatio provided material to Reese, and no doubt also to New-York-based Editor Parker of the *New-Hampshire Journal of Medicine, after* "B."'s guest editorial appeared, but *before* the Suffolk District Medical Society meeting only a few days later on May 30, 1857.

Horatio must have realized that the *American Medical Gazette* and the *New-Hampshire Journal of Medicine* could not do anything in time to influence the upcoming May 30 Suffolk District Medical Society vote on the Report on Criminal Abortion. Perhaps he was counting on these journals' help in a later reconsideration of the Report by the Suffolk District Medical Society, if it were rejected on May 30. Or maybe he was just so upset and angry at the *Boston Medical and Surgical Journal* editors for publishing "B."'s guest editorial and what Horatio believed was their change of heart on criminal abortion that he immediately sought solace and retribution from these other medical journal editors.

Other things were happening to Horatio and because of him in 1857. Horatio published a review of a book in the March 1857 issue of a new journal, the *North-American Medico-Chirurgical Review*.[53] The book, *Signs and Symptoms of Pregnancy*, was by W.F. Montgomery, M.D., of Dublin, Ireland, whom Horatio had met, probably on his 1854-1855 trip abroad.[54] Horatio strongly agreed with Montgomery's discussion of the unreliability of many traditional signs of pregnancy, such as breast and vaginal changes and on the high reliability of the fetal heart rate. However, Horatio disagreed with Montgomery on ballottement (feeling the rebound of a fetus after a push on the abdomen) and "active movements of the child, unequivocally felt by another" as being pregnancy signs that were absolutely certain.[55] This discussion of signs of pregnancy allowed Horatio an opportunity to express his views on "quickening." He wrote, "we ignore utterly that cruel and absurd point of law 'quick with child,'"[56] He was referring to what he believed were the "cruel and absurd" differences in legal status of the fetus before and after quickening.

One of Horatio's Boston Lying-in Hospital cases, "Removal of the Cervix Uteri for Non-Malignant Hypertrophy," was published in April 1857 in the *New-Hampshire Journal of Medicine*.[57] The hypertrophied cervix, "almost entirely filling the vagina," was removed by ligation over a period of 27 days using a loop of silver wire that was "tightened almost daily." The patient experienced "marked hysteria" during most of this period and this mental reaction surely strengthened Horatio's beliefs that pelvic abnormalities were the frequent basis for female mental problems.

Horatio's attendance at the Boston Society for Medical Observation continued throughout 1857. "Student," i.e., Buckingham, the Boston correspondent of the *Medical and Surgical Reporter* had also provided in his February 1857 letter the following description of this Boston Society for its readers:[58]

> The other society is the Society for Medical Observation. They say that this society is peculiar in its work. Papers are read by the members in turn, and dissected without much regard to the feelings of writers by the audience. Few men are willing to brave the criticisms to which they are likely to be exposed, and consequently applications are not likely to be numerous for membership.

Horatio's presentations at the "Observation" included discussion of the safety of manual removal of the placenta when it is not immediately thrown off,[59] description of distended abdomens with neither pregnancy nor tumor to blame,[60] cauterization of a birthmark on the face of a young girl, and discussion of individual differences in the dilation of the os by antimonial enemata.[61] However, it was a paper he presented on "cupping" the uterus on October 19 that was the most "dissected without much regards to the feelings" of its author.[62] "Cupping" involved drawing blood from the surface of the uterus with a suction-cup device. The hope was that this "artificial menstruation" would lead to normal menstruation. One of Horatio's patients subject to cupping had been totally amenorrhoeic and the other partially so and both patients had numerous other symptoms judged secondary to their abnormal menses. Although cupping produced an extended flow similar to menstruation, the need for repeat cupping at monthly intervals indicates that it was not all that successful. Dr. Buckingham noted that the patients were anemic and expressed his opinion that amenorrhoea was a normal means for coping with this condition and that "the cases as given were very imperfect." Horatio acknowledged the imperfection of his cases and had presented them "only for what they were worth." However, he claimed the procedure had improved the state of the uterus and cervix of both women and this at least was beneficial.

Horatio published a paper in the October 1857 *American Journal of the Medical Sciences* in which he provided an excellent review of the young history of treatment of vesicovaginal fistula.[63] Vesicovaginal fistulae were openings between the bladder and the vagina typically resulting from abnormally prolonged labor of childbirth. The condition was a curse for its victims because of the odor and other problems associated with uncontrolled flow of urine from the vagina. Horatio's report began with the following history of the adverse medical perceptions and treatment of gynecology and gynecological surgery which he referred to as "Obstetric Surgery," since "Gynaecology" had not come into use:

> None can have failed to notice the remarkable advance made of late by Obstetric Surgery. Within the century this department, aside from midwifery proper, itself then thought almost beneath contempt, was utterly unacknowledged by the profession. Now, on the contrary—although the legitimacy of its every operation, its every means of diagnosis, instrumental or manipulative, and of treatment, ligature, knife, suture, escharotic, compress, injection, are warmly—at times bitterly—contested—it has taken its place as an independent branch, distinct from General Surgery.
>
> In this matter, as in others, general practitioners have been slow to acknowledge the claims of those who, by ill health, abundant worldly means, or ambition, have been enabled or compelled to devote themselves especially to it, although to such subdivision of labour (like that obtaining among lawyers and naturalists), as adopted and practised by physicians of honour, good education, and general experience, all our large communities are fast and willingly and advantageously tending.[64] Impartial conservatism however, nor unfair opposition can longer withhold from obstetric surgery, unconfounded and ununited with midwifery, its honours as both

science and art. Of all the triumphs, early and late, of this department, none excel, as few indeed of general surgery can equal, that which we are now briefly to discuss.

The rational, or at least successful treatment of vesical fistulae in women, dates back hardly ten years—up to which period many, probably most cases were pronounced, even by the best surgeons, incurable; cures where luck gave them, being gotten only by often repeated trial; while now "the surgeon can approach them with a confidence of success before unknown." We need not wonder that with the first approximation to this result was laid at once the foundation of an individual's world-wide fame, and of the Woman's Hospital of New York.[65]

J. Marion Sims was the individual with "world-wide fame" who made the pioneering advance in surgery for vesicovaginal fistula that moved this lesion from virtually incurable to curable with a few exceptions. Horatio presented an extensive discussion of Sims' and others' contributions leading to this success. He noted that the button sutures of Nathan Bozeman virtually eliminated the few failures associated with the clamps that Sims had used to start this surgical revolution and Horatio made reference to his own successful use of button sutures.[66] This was in a case of protrusion of the vagina.[67]

One key prerequisite to Sims' success was his adoption of the knees-and-elbows position of the patient. The following discussion is enlightening in regard to surgery in 1857 which frequently occurred at the patient's own home:[68]

Sims places his patients on an ordinary table, which is not found to answer every indication when an anaesthetic has been administered. Kollock has constructed a special table, with a movable stage—convenient, doubtless, in an operating theatre, but not easily carried from house to house. We have preferred in practice the following plan, suggested in all its details by a colleague, Dr. Nathan Hayward, of Roxbury. Nothing can be simpler, nothing more convenient. A common high-backed chair, or a small old-fashioned wash stand, properly guarded by pillows, is placed on its face upon the bed; over its back the patient is made to bend, her arms extended and secured, her knees at a right angle strapped to the rounds or sides of the frame. She is thus immovably confined in just the posture needed, and the attendance of one or two additional assistants rendered unnecessary. To simplify the matter still more, the anaesthetic may be permanently placed under the patient's face on a cricket, or suspended there from the cross-bars of the frame, or, as in our actual practice, her nightcap may receive the sponge, and then be tied over her face.

Horatio concluded his article by discussing forms of currently unmanageable vaginal fistulae whose "history has yet to be written."[69] Horatio no doubt anticipated contributing to this history.

Horatio's references to "naturalists" in this paper reflected his own continuing strong interest in natural history and his regular attendance at the Boston Society of Natural History. Attendance coincided at least once with that of Hermann Jackson Warner. Hermann noted in his journal for November 18 that Horatio told him he was "going south in a month or two" because his health was poor.[70] Hermann's own medical problem caused another pair of meetings between Hermann and Horatio about six weeks later. Hermann recorded: "Mon 4th January. Went up to Charter Sq after breakfast to see Storer—did not find him in—wanted him to look at my arm—afterwards met him on Washington St, and he came into my office—lanced it—&c—Says he goes to Texas with Nat Hayward in a few days—that his lungs are affected, & he is recommended to try a milder climate."[71] The next day's journal entry of Hermann gives us a rare and far too brief picture of Horatio's domestic situation: "In eve^g went up to see Storer—found him lying in bed—sick—pretty house—money & love together—was ever mortal more blessed?"[72]

The first of a pair of letters to the Smithsonian Institution's Spencer F. Baird[73] announced the trip to Texas and requested "cards of introduction."

> 7 Chester St. Boston
> 15 Dec: 1857
>
> Dear Sir.
> I am just leaving for western Texas on a several months journey—& should be greatly obliged for cards of introduction to any of your correspondents in that region, especially to Heerman.
> Trusting the request will not be allowed to occasion you trouble, I am
> Yours Sincerely
> Horatio R. Storer
>
> Prof. Baird

The second sought means for transporting expected natural history specimens:

> 7 Chester St. Boston
> 5 Jan: 1858
>
> Dear Sir.
> I shall undoubtedly have opportunities of getting hold of various interesting specimens in Texas, but have been at a loss as to *how* to transport them. It has been suggested that you might have collecting

cases on hand, better than anything I could get made here, even if there were time.

I think Samuels spoke of a leather covered valise or pannier.

Should you have one or a pair of such out of use, I shall be glad to use them in the service of the Instit.

I shall leave Boston on the 12th inst.

Yours Sincerely
Horatio R. Storer

Prof. Baird.

"12th inst." means the 12th of the current month. Regrettably, we have no more information about the trip except learning from Hermann that Hayward did *not* go with Horatio and that Horatio was still in Texas on May 30, 1858 when Hermann obtained both pieces of information in a talk with Horatio's mother.[74]

While Horatio was absent, the Committee of the Massachusetts Medical Society chaired by Dr. Hooper met and dealt with "Storer's" Resolution on Criminal Abortion. Referring to the Resolution as "Storer's" instead of the Suffolk District Medical Society's may not just have been an oversight of the Secretary, given the discrepancies between it and those passed on May 30, 1857 by the Suffolk District Medical Society. The Minutes of the Councillors' February meeting indicated:

> The Committee ... reported that they do not recommend any application to the Legislature on the subject, believing that the Laws of the Commonwealth are already sufficiently stringent, provided that they are executed, and offered the following Resolutions, which on motion of Dr. Fiske, of Fiskedale, were taken up separately and unanimously *adopted.*
>
> *Resolved,* That the Fellows of the Massachusetts Medical Society regard with disapprobation and abhorrence all attempts to procure abortion, except in cases where it may be necessary for the preservation of the mother's life.
>
> *Resolved,* That when any Fellow of this Society shall become cognizant of any attempt unlawfully to procure abortion, either by persons in the profession or out of it, it shall be the duty of such Fellow immediately to lodge information with some proper legal officer, to the end that such information may lead to the exposure and conviction of the offender.
>
> *Resolved,* That no person convicted of an attempt to procure criminal abortion can, consistently with its By-Laws, any longer remain a Fellow of this Society.[75]

Although Dr. Hooper was Committee Chairman, Dr. Jacob Bigelow almost certainly drafted the Report,[76] given the similarity of the unusual letter "g" in Bigelow's signature and "g"s in the rest of the document. Also Jacob Bigelow's signature was *not* over a penciled name, unlike the other signatures on the document. As we will see, Horatio strongly disagreed with the Committee's conclusion that existing abortion laws were adequate and would protest their action in his absence and without his knowledge. He also would protest their premature report at the Councillors' meeting in February, instead of at the annual meeting of the Massachusetts Medical Society in June as instructed at New Bedford.

While Horatio was in Texas he was nominated and elected to Boston's prestigious American Academy of Arts and Sciences. The Minutes for May 11, 1858 read: "Dr. Horatio R. Storer in Class II [Natural and Physiological Sciences] Section 4 [Medicine and Surgery] nominated by Professors J. Wyman and Agassiz, Drs. A.A. Gould, J.M. Warren, S. Kneeland Jr. and S.L. Abbott."[77] One suspects that this was no secret to Horatio and that some communications from Horatio directly or indirectly activated these nominators. Perhaps Horatio was providing Wyman and Agassiz the "various interesting specimens" produced by his natural history efforts.

CHAPTER 7

AUTOPSY OF MAGEE, AMA
COMMITTEE ON ABORTION

A third event of much future consequence in Horatio's life which occurred while Horatio was in Texas was the hanging of the convicted murderer, James Magee (also written McGee), commencing at 10:00 in the morning of June 25, 1858. Dr. Calvin Ellis was to perform the autopsy on the criminal. Eight years later, after Ellis picked a quarrel with Horatio related to Horatio's abdominal surgery, Horatio was to accuse Ellis of an "antemortem autopsy" of Magee. A newspaper account of the execution included:[1]

> Execution of McGee.—James McGee who, while a convict in the State Prison, murdered the Deputy Warden, Galen C. Walker, about a year and a half ago, suffered the extreme penalty of the law for the offense, in the rotunda of Cambridge street jail, yesterday morning, at 10 o'clock. ... The noose was adjusted, the black cap drawn over the head, and all being in readiness, the Sheriff put his foot on the fatal spring, and at two minutes past 10 o'clock the trap door fell, and the murderer's spirit passed into eternity. The fall was about 6 feet, and his death was almost instantaneous. There was no movement except a slight contraction of the legs, and the body swung lifeless under the gallows. The body hung 10 minutes, and Drs. Warren, Clark, Storer and Lewis were summoned by the Sheriff to examine it. After a brief examination they pronounced it lifeless, and in half an hour it was taken down, placed on a bier, and covered with a white blanket.

The "Storer" who examined the body of Magee almost certainly was Horatio's father. The "Warren" definitely was Jonathan Mason Warren and his journal for June 25 included the above news article and the following: "*Execution of Mcgee the Murder of the Warden of the State Prison*, Went as witness. Prisoner show no marks of repentance. Died instantly. Examined his heart which beat steadily at 100 the minute for 5 minutes after this gradually diminished & ceased at 11 1/2."[2] Presumably, "11 1/2" means 11:30, but this is open to question, since the autopsy apparently began a little after 11:00. Probably he meant to write "10 1/2." Three days later on Monday June 28, Warren wrote: "Dr. Clark informs me that McGees heart beat up to three o'clock the chest remaining open. No fatal lesion found about the body. No

apoplexy, no lesion of the spine or spinal varices. With artificial respiration &
the use of galvanism he might have probably be recovered."

The report of the autopsy by Dr. Henry G. Clark, Boston City Physician,
was presented at the Society for Medical Improvement and the Society Proceedings, including his report, were published in the *Boston Medical and Surgical
Journal* on July 15.[3] Dr. Calvin Ellis was reported to have proceeded with the
autopsy "a few minutes past 11," which, according to the autopsy report, was
fifty minutes after the last heart sounds had been heard in the patient.
According to the autopsy report this was forty minutes after the body was
lowered, and twenty-five minutes after the rope was removed from the neck.
The report continued:

At 11.30, a slight but regular pulsatory movement was observed in
the right subclavian vein. Upon applying the ear to the chest, this
was ascertained to proceed from the heart itself, which gave a distinct
and regular *single* beat, with a slight impulse, 80 times in a minute.
The chest was then opened, and the heart exposed, without in any
way arresting the pulsatory movements. The right auricle was in full
and regular motion, contracting and dilating with beautiful distinctness
and energy. At 12 o'clock, the spinal cord having been previously
divided, the number of contractions was 40 per minute, having continued with only a short intermission regularly up to this time.

The official autopsy report emphasized that the patient was dead at the time
of the autopsy, with death due to asphyxiation. When the report was presented
at their meeting of June 28, this view that Magee was dead was echoed by other
members of the Society for Medical Improvement, although they were not present at the autopsy. For example, Henry J. Bigelow "considered the motions
of the heart to be solely due to local irritability." The report also mentioned
what Warren had noted in his second journal entry on Magee, but "possibly"
was written rather than "probably." The paragraph included: "Dr. Clark expressed the opinion that, as there was no lesion of any important organ, resuscitation might possibly have been accomplished by artificial respiration, &c., if
efforts to that end had been made immediately upon the lowering of the body
from the scaffold—that is, within half an hour after he fell."

The *Boston Evening Traveller* reported the following on August 2, 1858.
two weeks after the *Boston Medical and Surgical Journal* published the proceedings of the Medical Improvement Society with its report of the autopsy:[4]

The Case of Magee, the Murderer—the Post-Mortem Examination.
    An absurd statement that Magee was alive when dissected, has
been circulated by various newspapers, and as it professed to be
founded on the account of the autopsy as reported in the Medical and
Surgical Journal, it has attracted some attention.

The professional report, however, gives no color for such a statement. On the contrary, it states expressly that when he was cut down all signs of life were absent. The fact that automatic motions of the *right auricle* of the heart, for they were confined to that, continued for some hours afterwards goes for nothing, because it will be observed that they were not interrupted by a division of the spinal marrow itself. ... The supposition that "he might possibly have been resuscitated immediately after he was lowered from the scaffold," was predicated simply upon the fact that there was no apparent injury to the structure of any important organ and that he was in precisely the condition of a drowned or asphyxiated person. ...

If the appearances at the autopsy had offered any encouragement for attempts at resuscitation, we have no doubt that the medical gentlemen present would have felt entirely justified in putting them into operation, leaving the lawyers to settle the question of what should have been done with him in case of recovery.

There are in the medical books several well attested cases of the resuscitation of persons after hanging for the allotted period, but in no case was execution resorted to by the authorities. ...

After indicating that the statement that Magee was alive when the autopsy occurred was "absurd," this mention by the paper of other criminals who survived hanging, must have raised many doubts that such a statement was "absurd."

Two weeks after the *Traveller* report, the editors of the Boston *Medical and Surgical Journal* again discussed the case, since their previous report had given "rise to the erroneous notion that the criminal was still living at the time of the autopsy."[5] Discussion followed of "the inherent irritability of the muscular structure of the heart" and of the muscular contractions frequently following death from cholera. They concluded with the following reference to Dr. Clark's expression of the *possibility* of resuscitation when the patient was lowered from the scaffold:

Nothing was said which would lead one to suppose that Dr. Clark believed such a result to be *probable,* even on the conditions named; but, in fact, the rope was not loosened from the neck until fifteen minutes after the corpse was taken down, nor was the autopsy begun until thirty-five minutes afterward.[6] We believe that under the circumstances it would have been as impossible to resuscitate Magee, after he was removed to the House of Reception, as it would be to restore to life a patient dead of cholera, who exhibited the phenomena of muscular contraction.

As noted, Dr. Warren had recorded that Dr. Clark had said to him "he might have *probably* be recovered." It appears that attempts at resuscitation were more appropriate by Dr. Calvin Ellis than opening Magee's chest.

Horatio was back in New England by July 22. We know this because on that date, Hermann Jackson Warner saw his name and the name of his brother Frank on the Guest Register of a North Conway, New Hampshire resort. However, it is foolish to paraphrase Hermann who wrote: "Saw H R Storer & brother in Register, but no where else."[7] Although Horatio was away for the hanging of Magee, he probably was familiar with the newspaper and *Boston Medical and Surgical Journal* accounts of the controversial autopsy which were published after his return. He also probably discussed the case with his father whom the newspaper said was one of the physicians examining the "corpse" and pronouncing Magee dead. Years later, in the midst of the 1866 quarrel with Ellis, Horatio was to note that he also remembered reading a *London Lancet* editorial that appeared in the New-York-published version of the British Journal in October 1858. It included:

A thief unhung is a sorry sight for honest men; but we know no spectacle more painful than an execution in the house of a medical man. An eager zeal for physiological science has more than once betrayed anatomists into positions of painful dubeity; but we have never seen a more equivocal recital than that which has this week gone the round of the newspapers touching the proceedings of some American surgeons in the examination of a criminal who had been delivered into the hands of the hangman, and upon whom they subsequently performed what would appear to be little less than vivisection. ... The appetite for hoaxes is so strong in America that it might, perhaps, be hoped that some deception was practised in this instance; but the details are given with scientific truthfulness and accuracy.[8]

After repeating many of the details given in the *Boston Medical and Surgical Journal*, the editorial continued:

in the discussion that ensued, Dr. Clark is reported to have expressed the "opinion that, as there was no lesion of any important organ, resuscitation might possibly have been accomplished by artificial respiration, &c., if efforts to that end had been made immediately upon the lowering of the body from the scaffold—that is within half an hour after he fell." That opinion is amply justified by the details given. It amounts, however, to the most serious condemnation of the proceedings adopted. The man was not dead, but in a state of "suspended animation." How then characterize such a vivisection? Every man must shudder at the thought of what is implied, and we do not trust ourselves to speak out the deserved censure.

Dr. Brown-Séquard may have been on the editorial staff of the *Lancet* during this period and there is an indication that he was the author of this editorial.[9] Dr. Charles Buckingham, Boston correspondent to the *Medical & Surgical Reporter*, did not mention the Magee incident in any of his "Letters from Boston." However, Buckingham, out of medical academic work since the Boylston Medical School closed, may have been seeking an appointment at the Harvard Medical School and, like Henry J. Bigelow, could only place an interpretation on the autopsy that would avoid scandal for the school where Calvin Ellis was Assistant in Pathology to Professor J.B.S. Jackson.[10]

On October 25, 1858 Horatio provided an extensive article, "The Use and Abuse of Uterine Tents," to the *American Journal of the Medical Sciences*, where it was published in January 1859.[11] Horatio certainly was the American expert and perhaps the world's expert on uterine tents. The two prime subjects of the article were the continuing medical neglect of tents and their potential for producing abortion if used inappropriately. One paragraph showed that Horatio had already made up his mind to write extensively on criminal abortion.[12]

> It might seem superfluous to add a caution, lest by tents abortion be accidentally and unintentionally induced. Two cases in the practice of friends, however, have satisfied me that the risks are much greater than they might seem. Upon this point I shall speak more fully in another connection,[13] and here merely state, as the safer rule, that ... tents should not be used, or the uterus otherwise disturbed, where the woman is at all liable to pregnancy by marriage or other chance, till the short time sufficient to establish the diagnosis has been allowed to elapse.

Of the 1858 activities of Horatio of which we are aware, the presentation of Horatio's first paper to the prestigious American Academy of Arts and Sciences on December 14, 1858[14] must be considered the highlight. When Horatio provided a history of his anti-abortion efforts in 1897, he described this paper first, apparently considering it more important than the February 1857 Suffolk District Medical Society meetings and Report which actually initiated the campaign.[15] The 1858 paper was entitled the "Decrease of the Rate of Increase of Population" and this reduced rate of increase of the American population was a puzzle in 1858. "I was led to the true answer to the question," he noted in 1897, "not as a medical jurist, philanthropist, or social reformer, but solely as a gynecologist." He noted that he was "struck by the prevalence of certain forms of pelvic disease after abortion, and by the frequency with which patients in easy circumstances acknowledged to me in such cases that there had been an enforced shortening of pregnancy." He asked his colleagues to make similar inquiries of their patients and "soon a body of evidence that justified me in suggesting that criminal abortion, and this alone, afforded the missing link."

Horatio then described the "perfect whirlwind of surprise and indignation in Boston" created by his presentation.

> I was told that to expose them publicly would but increase the evil; was upbraided and condemned for exhibiting, even in the privacy of a scientific society, this blot on the good name of New England, and was begged to postpone publication outside of the medical profession until I had obtained from it a more general corroboration of the position that I had assumed. In deference to the judgment of so many of my seniors and friends, I delayed the publication of the Academy paper, and it did not appear till nearly ten years after, in Silliman's New Haven Journal, *The American Journal of Science and Arts*, for March, 1867.[16]

Horatio provided some additional details on the turmoil his presentation generated in a December 12, 1909 letter to the librarian of the Redwood Library and Athenaeum of Newport, Rhode Island which included: "The Elder Josiah Q[uincy]. (Harv. prex) had me to breakfast at his house in Park St. the next day after my paper at the Academy & with tears in his eyes begged me not to publish. He 'had no doubt as to the facts, but to make them known would ruin N[ew] E[ngland] in the estimation of the world', & it was so with J. Bigelow, Asa Gray, [Joseph] Lovering & the rest almost without exception."[17]

In his Academy of Arts and Sciences paper,[18] Horatio first documented the large drop in births in America from earlier years and also the birth rates in different European countries for the same periods. He noted that the reduction of the increase in the population could not be explained by "certain conjugal habits, ... as unnatural and degrading as they are detrimental to the physical health of both male and female." "We are to consider these pregnancies, not as prevented," he continued, "but as terminated without the birth of a living child." Horatio provided a wide range of statistics supporting his claim that many pregnancies were being ended on purpose. One class showed the sharp rise in still births relative to living births. However, an even more telling statistic, was the large rise in the ratio of premature still births to still births at term. In Massachusetts there were two premature still births per still birth at term for the period 1850-1855. This compared to one premature still birth per five still births at term for 1848-1855 in New York City and this one in five compared to only one in ten in 1838-1847 for the same city. The implication was that the rate of criminal abortion in Massachusetts was much higher than in New York City. Horatio concluded:

> The immense proportion of living births to the pregnancies in the foreign as compared with the native and protestant population of Massachusetts, already referred to, is to be explained by the watchful protection exercised by the Catholic church over foetal life. However

we may regard the dogma on which this rests, the sanctity of infant baptism, there can be no question that it has saved to the world millions of human lives. But of the various corroborative testimony to which I have alluded, and of other matters I shall elsewhere speak.

Were mankind, in following the advice that has been quoted from past and present authorities in political economy, content merely to practice greater abstinence and greater prudence in sexual matters, less blame could justly be laid. But when we find infanticide and criminal abortion thus justified, rendered common and almost legitimated, we may well oppose to the doctrine of these cruel teachers the words of the indeed admirable Percival, "To extinguish the first spark of life is a crime of the same nature, both against our Maker and society, as to destroy an infant, a child, or a man."[19]

Horatio's promise to "elsewhere speak" of "corroborative testimony" and "of other matters" reflected the agreement with Dr. Samuel D. Gross, the editor of the *North-American Medico-Chirurgical Review*, to publish a series of articles on "obstetric jurisprudence." Dr. Gross, the eminent surgeon of his time, provided a preview of Horatio's series in his December number which included:

Commencing with criminal abortion in our January number, Dr. Horatio R. Storer will present our readers with a series of important papers on obstetric jurisprudence, to which no one in this country has paid so much attention as himself, and which in point of fact has never been, as such, touched upon. ... Dr. Storer has taken a very decided and praiseworthy position in the matter, and we hope these papers will serve to awaken the attention of and prepare the minds of the profession for the report on criminal abortion in this country, which Dr. Storer is to make to the American Medical Association.[20]

Horatio identified the different topics of his series of papers in the first article.[21] They would "show the real nature and frequency of the crime: its causes; its victims; its perpetrators and its innocent abettors; its means and its proofs; its excuses, the deficiencies and errors of existing laws, and the various other obstacles to conviction; and, above all, so far as the present series of papers is concerned, the duty of the profession toward its general suppression." For the most part, Horatio's nine articles corresponded to this list of topics. There were small deviations in sequence and this suggests that he was preparing his articles throughout the year and did not have them all ready for publication in January 1859.

The first article was entitled "Contributions to Obstetric Jurisprudence: No. I.—Criminal Abortion." It began:[22]

By the Common Law and by many of our State Codes, foetal life, per se, is almost wholly ignored and its destruction unpunished; abortion in every case being considered an offence mainly against the mother, and as such, unless fatal to her, a mere misdemeanor, or wholly disregarded.

By the Moral Law, THE WILFUL KILLING OF A HUMAN BEING AT ANY STAGE OF ITS EXISTENCE IS MURDER.

He then provided three premises:

First.—That if abortion be ever a crime, it is, of necessity, even in isolated cases, one of no small interest to moralist, jurist, and physician; and that when general and common, this interest is extended to the whole community and fearfully enhanced.

Secondly.—That if the latter assumption be true, both in premise and conclusion, neglected as the crime has been by most ethical writers and political economists, hastily passed over by medical jurists, ... either it cannot in the nature of things be suppressed, as by these facts implied, or its suppression has not been properly attempted. Discarding the former of these alternatives as alike unworthy of belief and proved false by facts hereafter to be shown, it will appear,

Thirdly.—That the discussion now broached is neither supererogatory nor out of place; further, that it is absolutely and necessarily demanded.

A footnote following "jurists" read:

So far as the writer is aware, there exists, in this or any other language, no paper upon the subject at all commensurate with its importance. The chapters devoted to it in medical text-books, though some of them admirable so far as they go, especially that of Beck, are defective and often erroneous; while but little information of any value can be found elsewhere. In the French periodicals have appeared articles on special points hereafter referred to; in Great Britain able arguments regarding the commencement of foetal life have been made by Radford, (1848;) and in this country, with remarks on the frequency of the crime, by Hodge, of Philadelphia, (1839 and 1854,) and by the present Professor of Obstetrics in Harvard University, (1855.) To the latter, his father, and to the journalists (Drs. Morland and Minot, of Boston,) by whom the effort then made was so warmly and eloquently seconded, the writer acknowledges his indebtedness for the thought of the present undertaking.

Horatio then discussed a number of real and apparent objections to discussion of abortion. First was the "natural dislike of any physician to enter upon a subject on some points of which it is probable that a portion of the profession is at variance with him." Horatio may have been thinking that some of those "at variance" could jeopardize his own goals of joining the Harvard Medical School faculty and the Boston Society for Medical Improvement. It should be noted, however, that Horatio did not give as a reason for opinions "at variance with him" *actual support of abortion* by these physicians, only their "disbelief in the alleged increase in abortion" or their preference for "reliance on Providence of itself to abate the evil." Horatio may have known that some "regular" physicians were performing a portion of the numerous abortions that caused Massachusetts' high rate of induced abortion. However, if so, he was unwilling, in 1859, to implicate that guilty fraction.

Other possible objections to discussion of criminal abortion included the physician's "fear" that "by showing the frequency of the crime and its means, he may unhappily cause its still further increase;" his "reluctance" to tell his patients the "most unwelcome truth" about abortion, "thus not merely condemning, but to their own consciences at least, criminating them;" his risk of losing practice because thought more scrupulous than other physicians;[23] his reluctance to come into "contact with the law, even though for ends of justice," and, finally, his "grave doubts lest the statements made, though simple and true, should yet appear so astounding as to shock belief, or so degrading as to tend to lessen all faith in natural affection and general morality."[24]

However, "more than counterbalancing them all" were these arguments *for* speaking out against abortion:

> That medical men are the physical guardians of women and their offspring; from their position and peculiar knowledge necessitated in all obstetric matters to regulate public sentiment and to govern the tribunals of justice. That the discussion by them of this crime may very probably be the means, in great measure, of ultimately restraining or suppressing its perpetration. That such will undoubtedly tend to save much health to the community and many human lives. And, that, were there no other reason, it is clearly a duty.

Horatio went on to show how the Common Law and many American statutes failed to recognize abortion as an offence against the fetus, claiming instead that the person inducing the abortion was committing an offence against the mother. Following this, he pointed out that the very frequency of induced abortion and the high "character and standing" of many of the mothers upon whom abortion was induced were cited as evidence "that the public do not know, or knowing deny, the criminal character of the action performed." Horatio indicated that his patients told him that they thought they were not doing anything wrong in having abortions, believing that the contents of their wombs were "a mere ovarian excretion" that "might be thrown off and expelled from

the system as coolly and as guiltlessly as those from the bladder and rectum."
He continued:[25]

> It having now been shown, directly and by temporary assumption,
> that the law and public sentiment, both by its theory and its practice,
> alike deny to unjustifiable abortion the imputation of crime, it remains
> for us to discuss this question abstractly, and to prove not merely that
> they are wrong, but that the offence is one of the deepest guilt, a
> crime SECOND TO NONE.

Horatio's key to proving "that the offence is one of the deepest guilt," was
to show that the "foetus" was both separate from the mother and alive from
conception. Common sense was the first means used. He wrote, "the mother
and the child within her, in abstract existence, must be entirely identical from
conception to birth, or entirely distinct." Common sense also required that the
"foetus, previous to quickening, as after it, must exist in one of two states,
either death or life." Since the state of death was never followed by a return to
the state of life, "and we can conceive no other state of the foetus save one,
that, namely life, must exist from the beginning."

Although "quickening" presumably was thus demolished as the commencement of human life, it served a key role in many state laws as a marker of when
abortion became a crime, and Horatio singled it out for special discussion.
Quickening was the first sensation of the moving fetus by the mother and
Horatio indicated his belief that quickening mobilized maternal instinct and
"statistics prove that after the perception of these movements criminal abortions
are comparatively rare." He then noted that movement of the fetus occurred
much earlier than when this movement was felt, citing as evidence the sounds
that these movements produced and the visible movements of fetuses born
premature to quickening. "Quickening," Horatio concluded, "is therefore as
unlikely a period for the commencement of foetal life as those others set by
Hippocrates and his successors, varying from the third day after conception, to
that of the Stoics, namely birth, and as false as them all."

The following were the concluding paragraphs of this first of nine
installments. The second paragraph would be used repeatedly in Horatio's
writing over the years.

> If we have proved the existence of foetal life before quickening has
> taken place or can take place, and by all analogy, and a close and
> conclusive process of induction, its commencement at the very
> beginning, at conception itself, we are compelled to believe unjustifi-
> able abortion always a crime.
>
> And now words fail. Of the mother, by consent or by her own
> hand, imbrued with her infant's blood; of the equally guilty father,
> who counsels or allows the crime; of the wretches who by their

wholesale murders far out-Herod Burke and Hare;[26] of the public sentiment which palliates, pardons, and would even praise this so common violation of all law, human and divine, of all instinct, of all reason, all pity, all mercy, all love,—we leave those to speak who can.

We have noted that Horatio was upset that Jacob Bigelow had provided the Report of the Massachusetts Medical Society Committee on Criminal Abortion, of which Horatio was a member, to the Councillors of that Society while Horatio was in Texas, and without Horatio's input or signature. Horatio wrote the following letter in complaint a week before the annual meeting of the Massachusetts Medical Society Councillors:[27]

> Boston
> 27 Jan 1859
>
> To the Councillors of the Mass. Med. Society.
>
> Gentlemen,
>
> The undersigned, ... would hereby enter his respectful protest against the report made by that Committee in Feb. 1858, accepted though it has been by your Board; on the ground that the report was prepared, offered & accepted during his unavoidable absence from this part of the country, & without his knowledge.
>
> And moreover, in as much as it had been voted by the Society that the report should be made to the Councillors "that they may bring the matter before the Society at the next annual meeting,"* [Footnote: *Proceeding of Councillors, 1858. page 77] & as it does not appear from the printed records of that meeting that these instructions were complied with & as the undersigned is prepared with additional reasons & additional proof that the laws of this Commonwealth are not "already sufficiently stringent provided that the are executed" he therefor enters his earnest prayer that the votes by which the report of said Committee, & the resolutions thereto appended were accepted by your honored body, may be reconsidered, & that the whole matter may be either resubmitted to the same Committee, with instructions to again report at an adjourned meeting of your body before the next Annual meeting of the Society, or that the Councillors will themselves hear the remonstrant or permit him to submit a minority report at such adjourned meeting, that the Councillors when bringing the subject before the Society at the Annual Meeting in compliance with their instructions to that effect, may be able to report thereon in accordance with the facts in the case.
>
> All of which is respectfully submitted.
>
> Horatio R. Storer
> Chairman of Committee from the Suff.

> Dist. to the Parent Society, on the sub-
> ject of Criminal Abortion.

The following Councillors' response to Horatio's letter was reported in the Minutes of their February 2, 1859 meeting.[28]

> The Corresponding Secretary read a communication from Dr. H.R. Storer requesting a reconsideration of the vote, by which the Council at the stated meeting in February 1858 accepted the Report of the Committee appointed at the Annual Meeting of the Society in 1857 to consider the Resolution offered by Dr. Storer and the whole subject of the increased frequency of the procuring criminal abortion, and permit him to submit a minority report.
>
> Dr [M.S.] Perry moved that the prayer of the petitioner be granted. Considerable discussion ensued upon the introduction of this motion, when upon motion of Dr. J.C. Dalton of Lowell, the consideration of the subject was indefinitely postponed.

As we will see, Horatio would not let the Councillors forget their indefinite postponement.

Horatio read a paper "Two Cases illustrative of Criminal Abortion" at the Boston Society for Medical Observation on February 7, 1859.[29] The first case was a pregnant woman with "excessive toothache, of nearly two months' standing." All manner of treatments by her former physician failed to relieve the pain, including extraction of her single carious tooth. "After the extraction of the tooth, abortion had threatened," Horatio wrote, "and she now begged that it might be brought on; declaring, if refused, that she would induce it upon herself, rather than endure further pain." Horatio refused her request for abortion. He prescribed pyrethrum and successfully eliminated the pain which he suspected was "entirely neuralgic in its character, reflex, the result of the uterine irritation," and the pregnancy terminated normally. Horatio's major reason for describing the case was to caution physicians to avoid tooth extraction during pregnancy because of the real threat he believed it posed for abortion.

The second case involved a miscarriage which Horatio initially believed was "owing to direct instruments or other violence." His patient denied this, and it was the fact that she was Catholic which "somewhat allayed" his suspicions. Careful reexamination showed that the cervical wounds were from previous labors which had been "exceedingly tedious, and delivery accomplished by instrumental aid." Horatio noted that "in the midst of these physical anomalies, the presentation of an aborting ovum—would raise, I may surely say, in almost every mind the suspicion of foul and criminal interference." If the patient had died, Horatio strongly doubted that the autopsy would have carefully removed the blood clots "obscuring the age of the existing lesions." The point was that a woman and her physician might have been falsely charged with criminal abortion.[30]

The second article of Horatio's series on Criminal Abortion, "Its Frequency, and the Causes Thereof," appeared in March.[31] As Horatio noted, many of his statistics supporting the high frequency of criminal abortion were taken from his December 1858 "decrease of the rate of increase" paper and this was also true for much of the supporting text. The material on "causes thereof," however, was new, as was the discussion of the experience of physicians. He indicated that although requests to regular physicians for abortion were not that frequent, the same was not true for the "quacks," and their willingness to comply led to much work by regular physicians "to treat its acute and immediate effects." Horatio's own experience was confined to the frequent incidence of uterine disease where there was a history of induced abortion. He wrote:[32]

> As a mere matter of individual experience, and from a practice by no means exceptional, the writer some time since reported no less than fifteen such cases as occurring to himself within hardly six months; and of these, all without exception were married and respectable women,* many of them of wealth and high social standing; and subsequently he was able, in consultation, to point out similar cases in the practice of gentlemen who, at that time, had denied the legitimacy of his conclusions. This experience must be a common one, only some lack the courage, as others lack the will, to investigate the matter; should they do so, they can come but to one result.

Maternal deaths "confessedly" from criminal abortion were not infrequent. "It is probable," wrote Horatio, "that in but few of the fatal cases really occurring, is foul play ever thought of."[33] Maternal deaths, of course, occurred in only a fraction of the attempts at abortion, even in 1857, and their not infrequent occurrence also was cited by Horatio as evidence of a very large number of such attempts. Horatio concluded his "frequency" section: "We are compelled, from the preceding considerations, to acknowledge not merely that criminal abortion is of alarming frequency among us, but that its frequency is rapidly increasing; ... Every effort that might possibly check this flood of guilt will, if delayed, have so much the more to accomplish."

The first of the "causes" which Horatio addressed in "Its Frequency, and the Causes Thereof" was the "low *morale* of the community as regards the guilt of the crime." In addition to the primary factor of ignorance about the actual existence of "foetal life" early in pregnancy, Horatio described other erroneous physiological beliefs that contributed. One was the notion that it was detrimental to a woman's health to bear a large number of children and the other was that "the fewer one's children, the more healthy they are likely to be and the more worth to society." Horatio referred to the Spartans who destroyed their weakly children and the many infant victims of the harsh climate and diet of the Scottish Highlanders. Probably believing that his own frailty and long-standing poor health would have made him such a victim if born in Sparta or Scotland, he wrote: "But were this theory true even so far as it goes, the world, our own country, could ill spare its frailer children, who oftenest, perhaps, represent its intellect and its genius."[34]

Horatio then took Thomas Robert Malthus, John Stewart Mill, and other political economists to task for the key role that they inadvertently played in fostering criminal abortion. They were among the strongest proponents of the benefits to the state and the individual of a reduced population and these political economists undoubtedly had been mentioned by his patients when they admitted to a history of induced abortion. "The direct result of remarks like these last," Horatio wrote, "so pointed and plainly to be understood, is seen in the statistics I have so largely given."[35]

Horatio delayed discussion of most of the remaining causes of frequent criminal abortion until later articles in the series. The exception was "fear of child-bed," and this no doubt was discussed early because it captured not only Horatio's commitment against abortion, but his strong commitment to use of anesthetics during labor. "Fear of child-bed, in patients pregnant for the first time, or who had suffered or risked much in previous labors," Horatio wrote, "might formerly have been allowed some weight in excuse, but none at all in these days of anaesthesia."

In the final paragraph of his March installment, Horatio returned to the "cause" of public ignorance of the status and life of the fetus and put on the spot any physician who did not work to remove it. "[Where] ignorance is so evidently and so extensively its foundation," he wrote, "those who, possessing, yet withhold the knowledge which by any chance or in any way would tend to prevent it, themselves become, directly, and in a moral sense, responsibly accountable for the crime."

March 11, 1859 was a big letter writing day for Horatio who was planning to have the Report of the American Medical Association Committee on Criminal Abortion ready for the next Annual Meeting at Louisville. He received several responses to his letters with that date, including the following from a District of Columbia physician who had provided information to Horatio in 1857 and whom Horatio would soon request to become a member of the Committee on Criminal Abortion.[36]

> Washington City
> March 16, 1859
>
> My dear Sir,
> Your letter of the 11th instant has been duly received, and I take my earliest occasion to make reply. I fully agree with you in your

sense of the importance of bringing the subject of Criminal Abortion before the profession, and the proper authorities of society generally, in such imposing form as to lead to such measures as may effectually check the farther growth of so great an evil, and if possible put such an extinguisher upon it as to prevent its becoming a characteristic feature in American "civilization." ... it will afford me great pleasure to do all in my power to assist you in your investigations.

I thank you for calling attention to the papers published on the subject in *N. A. Medico-Chirurgical Review*, and, it will be my purpose, from hereafter to write to you such views as may be called up into my mind on the matter. ...

I will thank you if you indicate more particularly the special inquiries and distinct matters in relation to the subject which you wish to have attended to in furtherance of your report.

In haste...

A. J. Semmes

Dr. Horatio R. Storer
    Boston, Mass.

Another letter from another future Committee member repeats some of the words of Horatio's request:[37]

St. Louis, March 18th '59

Horatio R. Storer, M.D.
    Boston.
        Dear Dr.
        Your kind letter asking me to join in rendering your report on Criminal Abortion to the Am. Med. Association was received on yesterday. I will do so most cheerfully, and hope that your efforts "at the revision and more consistent wording of our laws upon the subject, and to abate the prevailing ignorance of the true character of the crime" may meet with abundant success.

I shall endeavor to meet you if possible in Louisville in May next.

With sincere regards to your Father and Mother and the rest of your family I remain

Yours very truly
Charles A. Pope

A letter agreeing to participate in presentation of the Report also was received from William Henry Brisbane of Wisconsin who became a Committee member.[38] A similar acceptance by Samuel D. Gross[39] was turned down, probably because Gross had recently moved from Kentucky to Philadelphia. Gross included in his letter, "I shall not only have no objection, but feel highly honored to serve with you in presenting your Report on Criminal Abortion to the American Medical Association meeting in May provided you have not already selected some gentlemen from this city or Section of country." Hugh L. Hodge from Philadelphia may have already accepted the Pennsylvania slot. On the other hand, Dr. Edward H. Barton's move from New Orleans, where Horatio wrote, to Columbia, South Carolina, did not jeopardize his place on the Committee.[40]

Only ten days after mailing his first letter indicating his willingness to serve on the Committee, Alexander Semmes mailed the following which shows that Horatio had in the brief interim provided Semmes a draft of the Report on Criminal Abortion:[41]

> Washington
> March 26/59
>
> Dear Doctor:
>
> I have received your letter of the 20th instant, with the enclosed copy of your able Report on Abortion in its criminal aspect, which you propose to make at the ensuing meeting of the Association.
>
> The Report seems to me to say all that is needful for the occasion, while it, at the same time, avoids any degree of that prolixity which might obstruct its favorable consideration.
>
> The Report is clear, pointed and condensed, that nothing from me can improve or amend it.
>
> It will give me the greatest pleasure to sign my name to the Report, which you can do for me. ...
>
> In haste ...
>
> A.J. Semmes

Dr. Hugh L. Hodge's agreement to sign Horatio's Report also suggested a key tactic of the physicians' crusade. His letter included: "I return your Report and shall be gratified to have my name attached to it, trusting that your praiseworthy efforts will meet with their due rewards. Perhaps the probability of success might be increased, if the general association would strongly recommend that each state med. association would press the subject on the legislative bodies of their respective states."[42] Similar letters allowing their signatures to be added to the report were received from Drs. A. Lopez of Mobile,[43] Henry Brisbane of Wisconsin,[44] Thomas Blatchford of New York,[45] and Edward H. Barton of South Carolina.[46] Thus the American Medical Association Committee on Criminal Abortion, first formed at Nashville in May 1857, was rounded out only a little more than a month before its Report on Criminal Abortion was presented at Louisville on May 3, 1859.

Although no draft of the Report on Criminal Abortion has been located, the unanimous approval of Horatio's March effort probably indicates slight changes at most from the final version read at the convention in Louisville and published later that year in the *Transactions of the American Medical Association*. It began: "The heinous guilt of criminal abortion, however viewed by the community, is everywhere acknowledged by medical men.   Its frequency—among all classes of society, rich and poor, single and married—most physicians have been led to suspect; very many, from their own experience of its deplorable results, have known."[47]   Additional evidence of abortion's frequency were "comparisons of the present with our past rates of increase in population, the size of our families, the statistics of our foetal deaths, by themselves considered, and relatively to the births and to the general mortality."

Horatio then moved to the reasons for the large numbers of abortions. First was the "wide-spread popular ignorance of the true character of the crime," because of the "belief, even among mothers themselves, that the foetus is not alive till after the period of quickening." The second reason he cited was innocent abetment of abortion by physicians who "are frequently supposed careless of foetal life." "The third reason for the frightful extent of this crime," the Report continued, "is found in the grave defects of our laws, both common and statute, as regards the independent and actual existence of the child before birth, as a living being." In conjunction with the third, Horatio noted the contrasting legal recognition of the "foetus in utero" for civil purposes. Horatio called attention to his series of articles in the *North-American Medico-Chirurgical Review* as "Abundant proof upon each of these points."

The Report then moved to the duties of physicians toward reduction of criminal abortion. "The case is here of life or death—" he continued, "the life or death of thousands—and it depends, almost wholly, upon ourselves." The recent actions of the Massachusetts Medical Society in his absence probably were on Horatio's mind when he then wrote: "Mere resolutions [condemning the crime] and nothing more, are therefore useless, evasive, cruel." He called on physicians to enlighten the public's ignorance about fetal development, to avoid any appearance of negligence "of the sanctity of foetal life," and to establish an "obstetric code; which, ... would tend to prevent such unnecessary and unjustifiable destruction of human life."

He then turned to the deficient state laws on abortion and called on physicians "as citizens" to improve them. "If the evidence upon this point is especially of a medical character," he continued, "it is our duty to proffer our aid, and in so important a matter to urge it." When the faulty laws reflected "doctrinal errors of the profession in a former age," he called on physicians "by every bond we hold sacred, by our reverence for the fathers in medicine, by our love for our race, and by our responsibility as accountable beings, to see these errors removed and their grievous results abated." The Report concluded:

> In accordance, therefore, with the facts in the case, the Committee would advise that this body, representing, as it does, the physicians of the land, publicly express its abhorrence of the unnatural and now rapidly increasing crime of abortion; that it avow its true nature, as no simple offence against public morality and decency, no mere

misdemeanor, no attempt upon the life of the mother, but the wanton and murderous destruction of her child; and that while it would in no wise transcend its legitimate province or invade the precincts of the law, the Association recommend, by memorial, to the governors and legislatures of the several States, and, as representing the federal district, to the President and Congress, a careful examination and revision of the statutory and of so much of the common law, as relates to this crime. For we hold it to be "a thing deserving all hate and detestation, that a man in his very originall, whiles he is framed, whiles he is enlived, should be put to death under the very hands, and in the shop, of Nature."[48]

The Minutes of the American Medical Association meeting for the first day, May 3, included:[49]

The Committee, appointed in May, 1857, on Criminal Abortion, submitted a report written by Dr. Storer, of Boston, which was read by Dr. Blatchford, of New York, and referred to the Committee on Publication. The following resolutions appended to this report were unanimously adopted:—

"*Resolved*, That while physicians have long been united in condemning the act of producing abortion, at every period of gestation, except as necessary for preserving the life of either mother or child, it has become the duty of this Association, in view of the prevalence and increasing frequency of the crime, publicly to enter an earnest and solemn protest against such unwarrantable destruction of human life.

"*Resolved*, That in pursuance of the grand and noble calling we profess, the saving of human lives, and of the sacred responsibilities thereby devolving upon us, the Association present this subject to the attention of the several legislative assemblies of the Union, with the prayer that the laws by which the crime of procuring abortion is attempted to be controlled may be revised, and that such other action may be taken in the premises as they in their wisdom may deem necessary.

"*Resolved*, That the Association request the zealous co-operation of the various State Medical Societies in pressing this subject upon the legislatures of their respective States, and that the President and Secretaries of the Association are hereby authorized to carry out, by memorial, these resolutions."

Horatio was too ill to travel to Louisville to present his Report and this must have been a huge disappointment to him. We are aware of Horatio's illness because of the following letter from Dr. Blatchford:[50]

Louisville 3 May 59

Dear Dr

I have ordered the paper sent to you daily during our associate existence. You will see that your report was read and the resolutions unanimously adopted. Your report was highly spoken of, not a dissenting voice in any direction. I am sorry my dear Dr to hear from Dr Townsend the cause of your not being with us. I do hope my dear yoke fellow (though I am not the oldest ox) that your illness will be of short duration, and that a little relaxation will restore you to your wanted measure of health and professional ability.

Dr Reese of the N Y Gazette took a deep interest in the subject and so do many others.

Yours truly

Thos W Blatchford

H R Storer M D

The failure to mention the name of the illness that prevented Horatio from attending the meeting, may indicate something not readily discussed. A decade later, Horatio wrote an article on surgical treatment of hemorrhoids and referred to his own frequent bouts with the problem (discussed in Chapter 13). What is more, Blatchford's prescription of "relaxation" is not an unusual one for this condition. It is easy to imagine Horatio was "sitting on pins and needles" in Boston while his Report was being read at Louisville. Another letter from Blatchford two days later included the following: "I cannot tell you the number of Gentlemen who have spoken to me about your Report since I read it nor can I begin to tell you the high encomiums, bestowed upon it without a single drawback. I thought you would like to know it. To know that our labors are appreciated by our brethren when those labors have been bestowed in the cause of humanity is a precious cordial for one's soul in this old and thankless world."[51]

The series of papers in the *North-American Medico-Chirurgical Review* continued with three in the May issue, the first being, "Its Victims."[52] Horatio noted that the ages of aborted fetuses were shown to be concentrated between the third and sixth months, although Horatio indicated these data were largely from the French Morgue and may not have depicted the age of aborted fetuses in America. Horatio also showed that the age of women obtaining abortions covered all child-bearing years and that such women were not primarily unmarried women who were concealing their pregnancies. Similarly, early beliefs that it was largely uneducated and poor women seeking abortions were claimed to be false. He indicated:[53]

But not only must we believe that the crime prevails in our midst to an almost incredible extent among the wealthy and educated and married; we are compelled to admit that Christianity itself, or at least Protestantism, has failed to check the increase of criminal abortion. It is not astonishing to find that the crime was known in ancient times, as shown by evidence previously given, nor that it exists at the present day among savage tribes, excused by ignorance and superstition; but that Christian communities should especially be found to tolerate and to practice it, does almost exceed belief.

Horatio pointed out that Catholics, at least outside of France, rarely sought or obtained abortions. Horatio went on to discuss how Catholic guarding and supervision of foetal life, while reducing abortions, had also led to the death of women during childbirth, when craniotomy was delayed to insure that the foetus was dead. Horatio then showed how to prevent this unnecessary death of the mother through "intra-uterine baptism" which was a part of Catholic doctrine and reduced in the eyes of the Church the tragedy of death of the child. Horatio provided instructions to the physician on how to carry the holy water to the child in the womb by hand, by sponge and staff, or by syringe. He chided physicians who "from fear of ridicule or dislike to sanction what they do not believe in, would shrink from such a duty." "I am not ashamed to acknowledge," he continued, "that for myself, though no Catholic, I have performed this intra-uterine baptism, where delivery without mutilation was impossible ... it was ... simply my duty." The implication for his physician readers was that it was their duty in the same circumstances.

"Its Victims" continued with Horatio noting that many crippled and disfigured children were born because of injuries acquired during attempts at abortion. He also indicated that women who immediately survived attempts at criminal abortion often succumbed within the next week or two from delayed hemorrhage or peritonitis. Horatio then provided a "long and fearful list" of problems, including pelvic cellulitis, various fistulae, adhesions of the os or vagina, inflammatory or malignant diseases of the uterus and ovary, "each, too frequently incurable" which were the direct consequence of "intentional and unjustifiable abortion." The article concluded with the following:[54]

We have seen that in some instances the thought of the crime, coming upon the mind at a time when the physical system is weak and prostrated, is sufficient to occasion death. The same tremendous idea, so laden with the consciousness of guilt against God, humanity, and even mere natural instinct, is undoubtedly able, where not affecting life, to produce insanity. This it may do either by its first and sudden occurrence to the mind; or, subsequently, by those long and unavailing regrets, that remorse, if conscience exist, is sure to bring. Were we wrong in considering death the preferable alternative?

In his fourth article, "Its Proofs,"[55] Horatio first described the difficulties of identifying whether an abortion has taken place and cautioned against jumping to the conclusion that an abortion has occurred. He indicated there had been instances where "women, suffering from retention of menses or from ovarian disease, and suddenly relieved by a critical and spontaneous discharge, have on suspicion of abortion lost character and even their lives." Once it was concluded that there had been an abortion, the problem became one of determining whether the cause was "accidental, natural, or intentional." Horatio noted that proofs of the cause "are both positive and negative; drawn from the history of the case and from personal examination of the patient and the foetus." He pointed out that an absence of local wounds and mutilations in the patient did not preclude an intentional abortion, and, referring to the case reported to the Society for Medical Observation in February, neither did their presence imply that violence had occurred.

Horatio then described the following indicators of probable criminal intent:

If violent purging or vomiting have been resorted to without any apparent reason, or to a greater extent than ordinarily prescribed or required; or if leeches have been applied to the thighs, to the number of an hundred or more, ... there is certainly ground for suspicion.[56]

If the cervix, the portion of the uterus most frequently wounded, is found punctured or lacerated, while the ovum is still retained, there is reason for suspicion; if the membranes are torn and extensively detached, while the cervix is but little dilated, such is increased; and it is made almost a certainty, if with the latter condition, nothing remain of the ovum in the uterine cavity but lacerated fragments. Here the abortion would probably not merely have been intentionally induced, but by the direct introduction and agency of instruments.[57]

On excuses for induced abortion, Horatio claimed:

the plea of Drs. Gordon, Smith, Good, Paris, and Copeland, that as a foetus born before the seventh month has a slender chance of surviving, its murder should be viewed with leniency, [cannot] be allowed. Such arguments, that the perils and dangers to which the foetus is naturally subjected should lessen the criminality of attempts at its destruction, are without foundation, and when advanced by physicians are utterly unworthy the profession.

For all others beside the physician there can be no allowable excuse except, in the mother's case, insanity; which, however common in the true puerperal state, and often no doubt then showing itself by infanticide, has in early pregnancy, and to any extent, still to be observed.

Horatio concluded:[58]

> If the accused be a physician, presumed as he should be, acquainted
> with the great principles of practice, his only plea can be, where the
> means used were unjustifiable and proved such, and where the
> pregnancy was known to others, that he was ignorant of its existence.
> Liable as the profession are at any time to this charge and easy as it
> is in almost every case, especially of instrumental procedure, for us
> to take such preliminary measures as would be likely to settle the
> question of the existence of pregnancy, or to request the presence of
> a witness to our act, it is unjust to ourselves and to each other to omit
> these precautions.

The fifth article in Horatio's series, "Its Perpetrators,"[59] was published
in the same May issue. Horatio noted that in France "where the abortion is not
induced by the mother itself, the offenders are women." "With us," Horatio
indicated, without giving any source, "the same statement is, without doubt,
equally true." As we will see, this was one basis for Horatio's objections to
female physicians. After noting that the mother was out of the reach of most
state laws against abortion, Horatio wrote:

> If the mother does not herself induce the abortion, she seeks it, or
> aids it, or consents to it, and is, therefore, whether ever seeming
> justified or not, fully accountable as a principal. We have already
> seen the position these mothers hold in the community, high as well
> as low, rich as well as poor, intelligent and educated as well as
> ignorant, professedly religious as well as of easy belief, not single
> alone, but married.

Harsh as Horatio was on women seeking abortion, he was harsher on their
accomplices. Among women accomplices he included "friends and acquaintances; nurses; and midwives and female physicians." Among the men, "husbands; quacks and professed abortionists, druggists; and worst of all, though
fortunately extremely rare, physicians of regular standing." Horatio was to take
each "class" in turn starting with the female friends and acquaintances:[60]

> It has been said that misery loves companionship: this is nowhere
> more manifest than in the histories of criminal abortion. In more
> than one instance, from my own experience, has a lady of acknowl-
> edged respectability, who had herself suffered abortion, induced it
> upon several of her friends: thus perhaps endeavoring to persuade an
> uneasy conscience, that, by making an act common, it becomes right.

Such ladies boast to each other of the impunity with which they have aborted, as they do of their expenditures, of their dress, of their success in society. There is a fashion in this, as in all other female customs, good and bad. The wretch whose account with the Almighty is heaviest with guilt, too often becomes a heroine.

Horatio indicated that nurses were apt to be approached by women to perform or assist in an abortion and were "not always found proof against an offered fee." The notorious role of midwives and female physicians in France in both abortion and infanticide was then discussed, including one midwife who had an "account with an undertaker, who was accustomed to smuggle her foetuses into his coffins, by the side of the corpses confided to him for burial." Horatio indicated that midwives and female physicians were even more likely than nurses to be sought out by women seeking abortion and some also would be more than tempted by an offered fee:

By these remarks we would not be supposed endeavoring to excite prejudice against female physicians and midwives, as such, or advocating their suppression. We are now merely considering this crime of abortion, in relation to which they are peculiarly and unfortunately situated. At present everything favors their committing the crime; their relations to women at large, their immunities in practice, the profit of this trade, the difficulty, especially from the fact that they are women, of insuring their conviction. Let better laws be enforced, and let public opinion be enlightened considering the guilt of abortion, and the influence for evil of this class of offenders will in great measure be done away with.

Horatio had less to say about male accomplices. Husbands he saw as aware of their wive's abortion, but rarely performing it and probably rarely compelling it.[61] "Professed abortionists" were men who prepared and distributed drugs, "against the use of which, 'at certain times,' the public are 'earnestly cautioned,'" Druggists were their confessed agents who might not directly recommend the abortifacients, but kept them for sale. Horatio then criticized the newspapers, including religious newspapers, who carried the advertisements for these nostrums and presented the Massachusetts statute prohibiting such advertisements. "The above statute, however, such is the public sentiment on this point," Horatio continued, "is not enforced, or is daily evaded. The press, if it choose, may almost annihilate the crime; it now openly encourages it."[62]

Horatio's final discussion was of regular physicians and abortion:

It has been often alleged, and oftener supposed that *physicians in good standing* not unfrequently, and without lawful justification, induce criminal abortion. This statement, whatever exceptional cases may exist, is wickedly false. The pledge against abortion, to the observance of which Hippocrates compelled his followers by oath, has ever been considered binding, even more strongly of late centuries. The crime is recognized as such in almost every code of medical ethics; its known commission has always been followed by ignominious expulsion from medical fellowships and fraternity. ... The instances, where physicians in good standing are guilty of the crime, are of rare occurrence; the error that has prevailed on this point originating from the self-assumed titles of notorious quacks and knaves. But no condemnation can be too strong for the physician who has thus forgotten his honor; who has used, to destroy life, that sacred knowledge by which he was pledged to preserve it.

William Overend Priestley, Horatio's co-editor of Simpson's *Memoirs*, wrote Horatio in June 1859. Priestley's letter provided some unique information about Horatio's health at that time:[63]

At last a letter from your old Edinburgh friend Priestley who truant and renegade though he be, but right glad to hear from you again and to learn that you were safe and sound in your old city of Boston again. Notwithstanding so long a time has lapsed since I wrote to you. I was at one time most anxious on your account. I was told that you had gone away to some distant and inland part of the country, that you had had some threatening chest symptoms, and that you had some notion of relinquishing medical practice altogether, deeming it prudent rather to relinquish a pursuit which afforded you so much pleasure, than lose your health, which is so important to the interests of your wife and family. Glad I am to hear from Dr. Bowditch that you have come back to work restored again and that all seems well with you.

The letter also mentioned the ill health of their mentor Simpson, and the Edinburgh medical and medical-political ramifications of this. Priestley also brought Horatio up to date on his own professional and family developments. He concluded with: "Is it child or children you have yet?" The answer to Priestley's question in June was "child," but Frank Addison Storer would soon be joined by John Humphreys Storer on September 28.

Horatio's next article in the *North-American Medico-Chirurgical Review* series was "Its Innocent Abettors."[64] It was published in July and represents one of Horatio's most important insights related to the public's ready acceptance of forced abortion. Unlike many of Horatio's pronouncements on the topic, it was not foreshadowed by his father's November 1855 Introductory Lecture. Horatio first discussed how some physicians resorted to premature labor for reasons other than to save the life of the mother or of her child. Craniotomy also was employed far too often, according to Horatio, and he repeated much of the discussion from his review of Clay's *Handbook of Obstetric Surgery*. Horatio then moved to the issue of whether the fetus justified Caesarean section in cases where pelvic irregularities prevented birth of a living child. At that time a Caesarean section was more frequently fatal to the mother than not. Horatio indicated that at least one authority claimed the operation should be forced on the woman who repeatedly became pregnant, even though fully aware of her inability to normally bear a live child. "The question now so plainly put," Horatio wrote, "is one for the profession soberly to discuss and to answer."[65] Horatio also referred to the problem of Catholics who would not allow sacrifice of a living fetus, even to save the mother. However, he sharply criticized those physicians who pretended that the child in such difficult labors was already dead and reminded physicians of their duty to perform intra-uterine baptism.

Referring to Dr. Henry Ingersoll Bowditch only as "one of the most eminent practitioners of the Eastern States," and "my friend," Horatio quoted the paragraph from Bowditch's letter of April 20, 1857 asking whether a physician might not "use common means for amenorrhoea if the menses have been absent six weeks" when a mother's "health, and possibly life," might be endangered by another pregnancy. "Covering, as these questions do, much of the ground already gone over," Horatio began, "we may answer them at once, and decidedly in the negative." "To justify abortion, life must certainly or very probably be endangered, not possibly merely, which is true in every pregnancy, and might be alleged at every trial for the crime."

Other rules for physicians were to immediately perform Caesarean section to extract every foetus old enough to survive in cases of maternal death; to make every effort to prevent threatening miscarriages and to resuscitate still-born children; to avoid "operations of any kind on pregnant women, even tooth-drawing, that might be delayed;" and to avoid "the careless or unnecessary use of ergot" which could produce premature labor. To do otherwise in these situations would not show the highest valuation of the unborn and newly born. People, observing this, might conclude that abortion was no crime.

Horatio's next installment on criminal abortion, entitled "Its Obstacles to Conviction," was published in September.[66] Horatio described how Massachusetts' statutes against abortion were among the most "wisely and completely drawn" as those of any State. However, not one of the thirty-two trials for abortion since they were enacted had led to a conviction. Horatio also mentioned the failure of Jacob Bigelow's Massachusetts Medical Society Committee Report to recommend changes in these laws to the legislature and reiterated his January 1859 "earnest protest against the plainly erroneous opinion avowed in that report." He contradicted their stated belief that the crime could never be controlled by law, claiming that legislation failures were caused by the ignorance of legislators, judges, attorneys, and jurors about the criminality of criminal abortion. What is more, physicians were to blame for this widespread ignorance. The "only source possible for enlightenment" was the medical men from whom they "have hitherto found but few bold and honest statements, and these unindorsed by the mass of the profession."[67] Horatio singled out Drs. Tatum and Joynes of Virginia, and Dr. Brisbane of Wisconsin as among the few physicians who did boldly and honestly speak out on the subject. He praised these physicians for their input to recent changes in their states' abortion laws. However, he noted that "total silence" from the medical profession was far more likely to have been heard by legislators and officers of justice. Horatio optimistically indicated that this "first and great cause," the silence of physicians, "is by no means an essential one."

Horatio turned then to the laws on criminal abortion of the country. He thanked all the physicians who in 1857 had provided information on their state and territory statutes. He also indicated his indebtedness "to my relatives, Woodbury and Bellamy Storer, Esqrs., of Maine and Ohio." These brothers of David Humphreys probably were among the "several distinguished lawyers" who advised Horatio on the draft statute in the original report of the Suffolk District Medical Society Committee on Criminal Abortion.

Horatio discussed the various laws against abortion, presenting the statutes "at length" for the states and territories who had them. He noted the problems with these statutes, starting with "the absurd distinction between the foetus of an early and a later age" that he indicated was the largest of the obstacles to conviction. He also noted that in almost all these statutes "the offence is considered a trifling one, except as affecting the person or life of the mother." Horatio indicated that some statutes encouraged the crime, since a crime existed only if the mother were injured during the attempt. "We have seen," Horatio noted, "that the surest and most efficient means of producing abortion are those where no injury whatever is inflicted upon the mother."[68] Horatio noted that only three states would punish the women, regardless of her involvement in the decision or act. Two states referred to the abortionist as "he," perhaps preventing any prosecution of female abortionists. Horatio then described the common law's schizophrenic treatment of the fetus, noting "that while it recognizes the distinct existence of the foetus for civil purposes, it here considers its being as totally engrossed in that of the mother." "Its Obstacles to Conviction" was quickly acclaimed in the *British Medical Journal*. "Dr. Storer;" the editors wrote, "shows plainly that the legislation in America on the subject of criminal abortion is in a most imperfect state."[69]

Horatio's final two articles on criminal abortion appeared in the November number of the *North-American Medico-Chirurgical Review*. The first, "Can It be at all Controlled by Law?,"[70] began by giving an "unqualified answer in the affirmative." He noted that this was not the case "anywhere," but this was because "laws against abortion do not as yet exist, which are in all respects just, sufficient, and not to be evaded." Horatio then stressed that a law to be just must attempt to prevent a crime as well as to punish it, and this required laws which made detection of abortion likely and punishment of abortion "more certain." Detection would be strongly assisted by improved registration laws that required a physician to certify the cause of death, both in infants and mothers, and by laws against concealment of births and secret burials. Detection of abortion also would be facilitated by requiring that coroners be medical men "skilled in all that pertains to obstetric jurisprudence." This would greatly improve the identification and collection of evidence in cases where criminal abortion may have occurred.

Another means for prevention of the crime recommended by Horatio was the establishment of foundling hospitals by State governments. The expected reduction of criminal abortion would occur in the unmarried who would be less apt to destroy or have destroyed their fetus if there was a place for the child after birth.[71]   Horatio also called for enforcement of statutes preventing the sale of emmenagogues, except by physicians. This would end the notorious newspaper advertisements and other advertisements for these drugs.

Following this discussion of indirect means for controlling abortion, Horatio returned to the need to improve the abortion laws themselves. They should reflect the fact that the criminal intent is against the child. They should only require proof of the attempt at abortion, not its consummation, and this attempt need not involve injury to the mother, or even that she be pregnant. He called for dropping any requirement for determining the age or stage of the fetus. There was no need to prove intent to destroy the child or to consider how the abortion was attempted. There should be no exemption of the mother from penalty, given that she is nearly "always 'an assessory before the fact,' or the principal ..." In addition, he recommended that punishment should be increased, since most was so minimal that it did not deter. "Were the murder of adults to be made answerable by merely a year or two in prison," Horatio wrote, "far more convictions than at present would undoubtedly be secured; but it is certain that the instance of the crime would be fearfully increased." Finally, he argued that standards for when abortion *is* justified should be "fixed by law," and included a draft abortion statute that was nearly identical to that in the May 1857 report to the Suffolk District Medical Society.

Horatio's final installment was "The Duty of the Profession," and Horatio wrote:[72]

We have seen that unjustifiable abortion, alike as concerns the infant and society, is a crime second to none; that it abounds, and is frightfully on the increase; and that on medical grounds alone, mistaken and exploded, a misconception of the time at which man becomes a living being, the law fails to afford to infants and to society that protection which they have an absolute right to receive at its hands, and for the absence of which every individual who has, or can exert, any influence in the matter, is rendered so far responsible.

"Under these circumstances, therefore," Horatio continued, "it becomes the medical profession to look to it, lest the *whole* guilt of this crime rest upon themselves." He was referring to two things. The mistaken notions about "intra-uterine vitality" had come from early medical literature. The second basis for physician guilt was their current "apathy and silence" on the subject, despite the fact that "thousands and hundreds of thousand of lives are thus directly at stake, and are annually sacrificed, ..." The explanations offered for physician "apathy and silence" were "either that we do not yet really believe in the existence of foetal life, though professing to do so, or that we are too timid or slothful to affirm and defend it." It is my aim," he continued, "while setting forth a deliberate and carefully prepared opinion upon this point, to inspire, if possible, in my fellow-practitioners throughout the land, somewhat of the holy enthusiasm sure in a good cause to succeed despite every obstacle, and an earnest, uncompromising hostility to this result of combined error and injustice, the permitted increase of criminal abortion."

Horatio then took on the critics who argued against such speaking out: "But it is asked, is our silence wrong? Is there not danger otherwise of increasing the crime? These are the questions not of wisdom, or prudence, or philanthropy, but of an arrant pusillanimity. Vice and crime, if kept concealed, but grow apace. They should be stripped of such protection, and their apologists, thereby their accomplices, condemned. Answers, however, are ready at hand to the questions proposed." To support this, he provided a dozen quotes from various editorials, articles, and books, which echoed his call for the medical profession "to urge upon individuals the truth regarding this crime, [and] speak out against criminal abortion." However, this was only one obligation he cited for physicians: "it is equally their duty to urge it upon the law, by whose doctrines the people are bound; and upon that people, the community, by whose action the laws are made. And this should be done by us, if we would succeed in suppressing the crime, not by separate action alone, but conjointly, as the profession, grandly representing its highest claim,—the saving of human life."

Horatio also provided a brief history of the American Medical Association Committee on Criminal Abortion, the acceptance of its Report by the Association with "high encomiums" and "without a single drawback," and the Association's unanimous adoption of the resolutions appended to the Report. Horatio gratefully acknowledged this support of the members of the Association in the final paragraph of his nine articles:[73]

In behalf of the committee, of whom he had the honor to be chairman, the writer cannot close this portion of his labors without thanking the physicians of the land, represented as they are by the Association, for their hearty and noble response to the appeal that had been made them. He would express, were it possible, the gratitude not of individuals, but society; for by this act the profession was again true to "its mighty and responsible office of shutting the great gates of human death."

The phrase "close this portion of his labors" implied another "portion" and this was writing the "Memorial" that the American Medical Association sent to the "several legislative assemblies of the Union" and writing the "Address" the Association sent to the "various State medical societies" requesting them to also press their legislatures on this issue.[74]   As will be seen, Dr. Henry Miller, President of the American Medical Association in 1860, later gave sole credit to Horatio for preparing these documents in his Presidential Address.

The Memorial began: *"To the Governor and Legislature of the State of _____ the Memorial of the American Medical Association, an Organization representing the Medical Profession of the United States."* The Memorial then indicated that Criminal Abortion was "the intentional destruction of a child within its parent; and physicians are now agreed, from actual and various proof, that the child is *alive* from the moment of conception." It described the high and increasing rate of criminal abortion which led to the deaths of "hundreds of thousands" and "the serious injury thereby inflicted upon the public morals." In case these were not enough to influence state legislators to take measures to suppress abortion, Horatio described the "decided and detrimental influence ... upon the rate of increase of the nation and upon its material prosperity." "Public sentiment and the natural sense of duty instinctive to parents proving insufficient to check the crime," the Memorial continued, "it would seem that an appeal should be made to the law and to its framers." The various problems with existing statutes were then briefly described, including the inconsistency of the Common Law which "fails to recognize the unborn child as criminally affected, whilst its existence for all civil purposes is nevertheless fully acknowledged." The Memorial then referred to the "duty of the American Medical Association, ... publicly to enter an earnest and solemn protest against such unwarrantable destruction of human life." "The duty would be but half fulfilled," the Memorial continued, "did we not call upon those who alone can check and control the crime, early to give this matter their serious attention." It concluded:

The Association would in no wise transcend its office, but that office is here so plain that it has full confidence in the result. We therefore enter its earnest prayer, that the subject of Criminal Abortion in the state of _____, and the laws in force on the subject in said State may be referred to an appropriate Committee, with directions to report what legislative action may be necessary in the premises.

The Memorial was signed by the Association President Henry Miller and Secretaries S.M. Bemiss and S.G. Hubbard. There was no mention in the one-page document of the Chairman of the Committee on Criminal Abortion who authored it. It included as an enclosure, Horatio's series of articles on Criminal Abortion published in the *North-American Medico-Chirurgical Review*. Horatio himself requested the publisher of the journal to send "extra copies you have printed" to the President of the American Medical Association.[75]

The Address to the State Medical Societies consisted of the three Resolutions on Criminal Abortion adopted by the Association plus the following:

> In pursuance of our instructions, a memorial, of which a copy is herewith enclosed, has been transmitted to the Governor and Legislature of the State of _____, and it now has become our duty earnestly to request of the body you represent, such early and hearty action in furtherance of the memorial of the Association, as may insure its full success against the common, though unnatural crime it aims to check.

It too was signed by Miller, Bemiss, and Hubbard and made no mention of its author. This Address reached the New York State Medical Society sometime before early February 1860 when, at its Annual Meeting, the following Resolutions were provided by the Committee that had previously been appointed to consider the recommendations of the American Medical Association:[76]

> "*Resolved*, That this Society cordially approves of the action of the American Medical Association in its efforts to exhibit the extent of the evils resulting from the procuring of Criminal Abortions, and of the means which are adopted to prevent its commission, and cheerfully comply with the request to a 'zealous co-operation' for furtherance of more stringent legislation in regard to this most destructive and revolting crime, committed almost with impunity, and with appalling frequency.
>
> "*Resolved*, That a committee of three be appointed to present the memorial of the President and Secretaries of the American Medical Association, which has been read, to the Legislature of this State at its present session."

Other state medical societies similarly responded to the Address from the American Medical Association, eventually even the Massachusetts Medical Society.[77]

The nine articles of Horatio in the *North-American Medico-Chirurgical Review* were published in 1860 as a book entitled *On Criminal Abortion in America*.[78] The book's publication was the occasion for the editors of the *Boston Medical and Surgical Journal*, Dr. F.E. Oliver and Dr. Calvin Ellis, to write a strong anti-abortion editorial.[79] They described the new book as coming "from the pen of one of our most painstaking and careful investigators, Dr. H.R. Storer." "This paper contains much interesting information," they continued, "and if it do as much for poor humanity as might be fairly expected, from the ability and good intentions of the author, he will have much reason for pleasant reflection."

Those who may currently believe that physicians at that time opposed abortion only because of concern for the health of the mother, and those who perhaps regard Horatio's many expressions of concern for the "foetus" as an aberration among physicians of the period, should take note of the following final sentence of the Oliver-Ellis editorial:[80]

The physician may do much by warning his patients against the dangers and guilt of this awful crime, and using the "greater vigilance lest he become its innocent and unintentional abettor"; and the moralist may do more by the inculcation of those principles in the young, that shall lead them to regard with abhorrence such a violation of the positive laws of God, involving, as it does, the guilt of murder, and a total indifference to the most sacred privileges with which woman is endowed.

CHAPTER 8

EUTOKIA, PELVIC FACTORS IN FEMALE INSANITY

The American Medical Association held its 1860 Annual Meeting in New Haven, Connecticut during the first week of June and there was a large contingent of physicians from nearby Massachusetts, including David Humphreys Storer. Horatio was not among the delegates, although a Permanent Member and eligible to attend. It is unfortunate that he did not hear the Presidential Address of Henry Miller, much of which was devoted to the work of the Committee on Criminal Abortion and particularly generous in its praise of the Chairman of that Committee. Miller first discussed the American Medical Association Committee and its Report. He described the Resolutions adopted by the Association and the resultant memorials to legislatures and state medical societies. He continued:[1]

> I am happy to acknowledge my obligations to the able Chairman for his valuable assistance, not only in furnishing the documents referred to, but in the preparation of the Memorial as well as of the Address directed to the various State Medical Societies, requesting their co-operation with the Association, in pressing this important subject on the attention of the legislatures of their respective States. The memorial, with the accompanying documents, was transmitted in January last to the President of the United States and the Governor of each of the States and Territories of the Union, the legislatures of several of them being at the time in session. ... the hope may be reasonably indulged that their Excellencies have submitted them to the National, State, and Territorial legislatures, or will embrace the earliest opportunity of doing so.

After a brief aside on the need for better information about the mailing addresses of state medical societies, Miller continued by describing the challenges that remained for physicians and "that obstructions will be thrown in this path of your benevolent operations, which it may require years of ceaseless vigilance and unremitting effort to overcome." He described the major task of enlightening "popular ignorance on this subject" and the need to withstand "the jeers of the flippant, the superficial, and the unthinking in your own ranks." He then gave a primer on fetal development, recognizing that there was still physician ignorance as well as "popular ignorance." Miller then moved to the Association's effort to change state statutes on abortion.[2]

It is difficult for legislation in a free country, where the people are the source of all political power, to rise higher than popular sentiment and intelligence; but is it not the duty of all wise legislators, in questions which can only be elucidated by the science of medical jurisprudence, to endeavor rather to elevate popular sentiment and enlighten popular ignorance than to degrade themselves to their low level? And how can lawmakers better give expression to their estimate of the crime of abortionism than by sedulously providing against its commission? The necessity of more stringent legislation has been clearly pointed out by the Chairman of the Committee, in the papers already referred to, and valuable suggestions, to aid in the enactment of a suitable statute, have been offered by him. May we not hope that our appeal to the different legislative bodies of the Union will not be in vain?

While the American Medical Association was meeting in New Haven, it received a request from the Judiciary Committee of the Connecticut Legislature to "frame a suitable bill to serve as a guide for their action" in compliance with the Association's Memorial. Drs. Hooker and Daggett from Connecticut and Horatio's father were appointed to provide this assistance.[3] Had Horatio been in attendance, this duty probably would have fallen on his shoulders, and one suspects that he assisted his father in preparing the result, which was a unique piece of legislation that combined "into a single forceful act the denial of the quickening doctrine, the notion of women's liability, and anti-advertising principles."[4] It was the forerunner of similar legislation treating the fetus as the victim which would be passed in almost every state in the next few decades.

The Councillors of the Massachusetts Medical Society met on May 30 and took under consideration the Address that Dr. Miller had sent to the Society. The Minutes included:[5]

A communication was read from the Committee of the American Medical Association requesting the aid of the Councillors in furtherance of the Memorial of the Association which has been sent to the Legislature of Massachusetts on the subject of the increased frequency of criminal abortion.

Voted, "To refer the communication to a Special Committee."

The Chair nominated Drs. C.G. Putnam, N.B. Shurtleff and H.R. Storer.

And they were appointed.

This Committee reported back to the Councillors on October 3, recommending that the Society present the American Medical Association Memorial to the Massachusetts Legislature. "The report was adopted," according to the Minutes, "and on motion of Dr. Gordon it was voted that the recommendations be adopted and that the Corresponding Secretary be requested to present them to the Legislature."[6] Horatio must have been somewhat gratified that his efforts had finally enabled him to meet the objective of having physician recommendations for abortion statutes presented to the Massachusetts Legislature. On the other hand, Horatio remained unhappy with the Massachusetts' statutes. Apparently the lawmakers did not heed these recommendations.

Information on Horatio during 1860 is sparse. Dr. J. Mason Warren's journal for Saturday September 22, 1860 included: "Dr Storer called to say that his son intended to set up a Hospital for Women at Blue Hills & to ask that Dr S. & myself would be consulting surgeons to it."[7] Dr. Warren must have quickly agreed and Horatio also must have moved swiftly, given the following announcement a week later:[8]

> Dr. Horatio R. Storer, in pursuance of professional advice, has opened an Establishment for Treatment of The Diseases of Women.
> Drs. J. Mason Warren and Storer, Sen., of Boston, Consulting Surgeons.
> Blue Hills, Milton, near Boston, (Readville Station, Providence Railroad),
> October 1, 1860.

Although 1862 was later described by Horatio as the year when he gave up general practice for specialization in the diseases of women, this announcement suggests he was at least close to this in 1860. As we have earlier noted, specialization itself was frowned upon by many of the physicians of the period, virtually all of whom were general practitioners. Specialization in the diseases of women was particularly despised, with many physicians viewing this as "quackery," or worse, a form of prostitution where the attendant "manipulated" to meet non-medical needs of the "patient."

The years 1861 and 1862 also are almost devoid of information about Horatio. Malcolm's birth in the Spring of 1862 indicates that Horatio was not totally incapacitated during 1861. However, it is curious that the pen that produced hundreds of thousands of published words after his return from abroad apparently produced none from 1860 through 1862.

On January 26, 1862, Hermann Warner provided a brief mention of Horatio in his journal: "Horatio still lives at Milton, rarely coming to town."[9] The Milton address is one probable reason for Horatio's absence from Boston medical science and politics. Another may have been the onset or exacerbation of mental problems in his wife. Horatio would indicate in 1883 that it was the "case" of his wife that led him to turn much of his attention by 1863 to insanity in women. A feature of the "case" was the predictable onset of attacks during menstruation. Horatio had emphasized the problems menstruation posed for women physicians as early as April 1856 and this may mean that early in Horatio's marriage (or earlier), Emily's menstruation-related problems were noted.

A Civil War incident was the basis for correspondence between Horatio and Massachusetts Senator Charles Sumner and between Sumner and President Lincoln. Horatio's initial May 26, 1862 letter included:[10]

> You must pardon my begging your earnest attention to a case of individual distress at a time, of all others, when your energies must all have been severely taxed by public anxieties. ...
>
> The enclosed letters will explain themselves, that dated on the 22d inst. I have this evening received.
>
> The writer John Doyle of the 2d Artillery, now at Fort Delaware has lived with me as farm servant & it was probably in accordance with my advice that he reentered the Army, & risked the fate that he thinks awaits him. I *cannot* however believe that his case can be as he represents it. It must be that his Commanding officer is frightening him as a punishment[,] for what Court martial however severe would visit one who *deserted in peace, & voluntarily re-enlisted during the Country's direst need, with **death**?*
>
> I beg you will at once investigate the case & inform me of it at your earliest moment. Should the boy's fear prove well founded, I am sure that Mr. Lincoln at your intercession would extend the merciful & saving arm. I feel that I can confidently rest upon you in this matter. I would at once go to Washington were it necessary, but the whole thing is better in your hands.

Sumner's letter to President Lincoln follows:[11]

> Senate Chamber
> 28th May '62
>
> Dear Sir,
>
> My attention has been called to the case of John Doyle of the 2nd U.S. Artillery, Fort Delaware, Delaware Bay, who is menaced with the punishment of death for desertion from the army in 1859. It seems to me that this cannot be so. *A desertion in time of peace*, followed by enlistment in time of war, cannot deserve so severe a punishment.
>
> I enclose the letter of the soldier addressed to Dr Storer, a distinguished citizen of Mass who is much interested for the soldier.
>
> Hope that the case will be considered worthy of your clemency.
>
> > Faithfully yours,
> > Charles Sumner
>
> The President

Horatio responded to Sumner on June 1: "You have my sincere thanks."[12] In 1890, Horatio wrote the following paragraph in a letter to Dr. Joseph Toner, a Washington, D.C. physician active in the American Medical Association, which gives only a partial indication of how the Doyle case was resolved:[13]

> When next at the Govt. Insane Asylum, give my regards to the good Dr. in charge & ask him for a memo of the case & result of John Doyle, a soldier who was sent there from Fort Delaware on June 10 (or there abouts), 1862. He had been previously a servant of mine, & in looking over some old letters a day or two ago, was brought to my memory.

Horatio returned to meetings of the American Academy of Arts and Sciences after an absence of three years on May 27, 1862 when he attended the Annual Meeting in company with his brother, Frank, who was a Fellow in the Section on Physics and Chemistry.[14] He was to wait until January 1863 before attending again, but this began a period of regular attendance lasting for several years. It may be no coincidence that Horatio's home address had changed from Blue Hills, Milton, to Hotel Pelham in downtown Boston. The move probably had occurred by December 4, 1862, which marks the date when the following weekly advertisement first appeared on the cover of the *Boston Medical and Surgical Journal*: "DR. H. R. STORER has resumed practice in Boston, attending only to the diseases of women. Office at Hotel Pelham."[15]

Horatio also resumed publication of medical articles with the first dealing with *unintentional* abortion.[16] Horatio initially discussed his earlier articles, their general welcome by the medical community, and "the practical result of the whole matter (which has proved precisely that aimed at in the outset), namely, the awakening of the public mind as to the value of foetal life and the vindication of the character of the profession on this point alike in its own sight, that of the law and of the community, by the unanimous voice of the medical press, are all convincing evidence of the importance and legitimacy of the investigation." Horatio discussed the problems of diagnosis of spontaneous abortions. One was incorrectly diagnosing a spontaneous abortion as a polypus or as menorrhagia. Another was misdiagnosing the spontaneous abortion as intentional with grave ramifications for the character of the women or her attendant.

Horatio indicated the physician's duty when treating spontaneous abortion was, in most cases, to arrest the process. Typically physicians did just the opposite, completing "the abnormal process as soon as possible." He indicated that he often saved the life of the fetus "in cases apparently desperate as far as the foetus is concerned." "Should, however, the expulsion of the ovum be already effected or be beyond prevention," Horatio continued, "it becomes of the utmost importance that the accident should be thoroughly completed."

Horatio noted that spontaneous abortion was much more frequent among women than was generally recognized, with "frequent or constant repetition of the occurrence in the same patient." Horatio followed this with a pitch for "the hands which are more especially called to the treatment of chronic uterine disease" in resolving these questions of the "true frequency of abortion."[17] His "hands" reference may well have magnified the antipathy towards Horatio of the many general practitioners who still opposed specialization in yet-to-be-named "gynaecology." Horatio's son, Malcolm, was to write: "the very name of diseases of women savored strongly of quackery; and it was the honest belief of many a doctor of the old school that the preservation of a man's personal morality was highly dubious if he was constantly engaged in treating the female genitals, while the supposed effect upon the woman can be left to the imagination."[18] As will be seen, Horatio, himself, as editor of the *Journal of the Gynaecological Society of Boston*, was to frequently condemn the activities of "specialists" whose manual treatment of women pandered to the women's sexual appetites.

In 1862, Dr. Marie E. Zakrzewska, a Berlin-born physician, started a hospital for women in Boston on Pleasant Street. She hoped to staff it entirely with women, but was unable to find a competent woman surgeon. Dr. "Z," as she was known, wrote to her future resident physician, Dr. Lucy E. Sewall, on February 20, 1863, that the hospital was going well and that Dr. Storer had called on her the day before and indicated his desire "to extend colleague-ship to me."[19] "Colleague-ship" no doubt was a most rare and welcome offer to Dr. Z., given that most Boston physicians were strongly opposed to women physicians. Dr. Z apparently extended a most tangible colleague-ship offer to Dr. Storer, in turn. Horatio accepted the position of Attending Surgeon on April 3, 1863.[20] He remained in that capacity until he resigned three years later, following imposition of severe restrictions on his surgical prerogatives.

On May 30, 1863, Horatio read a paper, "On Artificial Dilatation of the Os and Cervix Uteri by Fluid Pressure from Above: A Reply to Drs. Keiller, of Edinburgh, and Arnott and Barnes, of London,"[21] at the Suffolk District Medical Society. In May 1859, Horatio had described a water-filled distensible sac for the purpose of such artificial dilation.[22] This 1863 article was basically a review of literature designed to elucidate who first proposed dilation by pressure from above. Horatio granted that Keiller had anticipated himself in applying the technique, although both had published simultaneously on July 1, 1859. He also noted that Murray had beaten them both to publication by more than two months with his description of a technique using an air-filled rubber diaphragm for the purpose.

It is the asides that make this article important for Horatio's biography. "Immediately on entering practice," Horatio wrote, "it became evident to me that the great field for advance in obstetric therapeutics was *the interior* of the uterus,—an opinion that was daily strengthened during the intimate relations to which I was admitted by Prof. Simpson in 1854-55." In addition to this evidence that Horatio practiced medicine *before* leaving for Europe in December

1853, we also note the motivation of Horatio to *advance* medicine and not just to practice it.

Horatio also wrote: "I have not hesitated to impress upon the students at present temporarily in my charge, the extreme caution necessary in manual or operative interference during labor, the impropriety of endeavoring to excite intra-uterine or intra-vaginal respiration, even by the method so ingeniously suggested by Dr. Jacob Bigelow, of this city."[23] The "students at present temporarily in my charge" probably were Harvard Medical School students to whom Horatio was providing clinical instruction at Dr. Zakrzewska's hospital. When Horatio resigned from that hospital in September 1866, he noted in his resignation letter, "I have more than once, previously to the present time, felt that I was occupying a false and undignified position, as when you voted that no male students should be allowed the advantages I have felt it my duty to them to offer." Dr. Henry Orlando Marcy, who obtained his Harvard medical degree in 1864, apparently had Horatio as instructor in some capacity and this would fit with clinical rounds at the Pleasant Street Hospital.

Horatio's reference in the paper to Dr. Jacob Bigelow's method for inserting air into the vagina and uterus, followed by the strong caution that the method could lead to a fatal result, probably was poorly received by Dr. Bigelow, despite Bigelow being praised by Horatio for "ingeniously" suggesting it. If so, this may have compounded Horatio's problems with this powerful physician and with Jacob's son, Henry J. Bigelow, who may have already supplanted Jacob as the major power in Boston medical politics.

On June 17, 1863, Horatio no doubt antagonized the Boston "etherites" more than he ever had previously when he presented the paper, "On the Employment of Anaesthetics in Obstetric Medicine and Surgery," at the Annual Meeting of the Massachusetts Medical Society. Horatio defended anaesthesia in midwifery, advocated the use of chloroform for this purpose, and identified problems if ether were used instead of chloroform.

We have already referred to the strong condemnation by many Boston physicians of any anesthetic other than the anesthetic used in the famous initial Boston demonstrations of anesthesia in 1846. The *Boston Medical and Surgical Journal* editors invariably shared this preference for ether and contempt for other anesthetics (these no doubt were prerequisites for the job). They routinely presented articles or editorials announcing deaths from chloroform anesthesia and showing that deaths when ether was administered were the result of factors other than the anesthetic. Chloroform in midwifery had also been decried on the journal's pages and would be again only seven weeks after Horatio gave his paper praising chloroform for this purpose.

Although Horatio's presentation at the meeting of the Massachusetts Medical Society on anesthetics in obstetrics surely intensified hostility towards him and created it in others, Horatio also had his supporters in Boston and elsewhere. In fact, Horatio gave the following reason for his anesthesia-in-obstetrics presentation: "for the past eight years, and by a large circle of medical friends, I have been importuned to state my convictions regarding it."[24]

Horatio first showed the inappropriateness of objections to anaesthesia in general, including "that anesthetics are hazardous to life," they tend to "develop immoralities, alike in operator and patient," "that it is unnecessary" and contrary to the Bible "to abrogate pain," and that anesthetics produce "ill effects upon the immediate or remote health of the patient." He then listed a number of benefits of anesthesia in gynecology and midwifery, including aiding in diagnoses, relief of pain in disease and labor, shortening labor, prevention of convulsions, and facilitation of instrumental deliveries. Horatio did recommend ether for diagnosis and surgery, "except that immediately pertaining to labor." "Chloroform alone should be used in midwifery," he continued, "to the entire exclusion of ether." The advantages of chloroform over ether for midwifery that Horatio cited were its better smell, less nausea and vomiting after administration, more rapid onset and offset of its effects, less effect on the progress of labor, and its greater efficacy "for restraining or preventing puerperal convulsions and puerperal mania."[25]

Horatio admitted that chloroform had produced deaths, but flatly denied that fatalities had ever resulted in its use in obstetrics. Horatio cited three reasons for chloroform's "immunity in childbed." One was the high level of vitality of the patient during labor which was "the great end for which, sexually and anatomically speaking, woman was formed." Another was the reflex excitation of the nervous system by this uterine event. Finally, there was the assistance to "elimination of carbon from the sanguineous system" of a menstruation-like discharge from the uterus during labor, "normal labor taking place almost precisely at the time of the periodical menstrual molimen." The latter is particularly absurd, and this was not the last time that Horatio would call on this notion of menstruation aiding respiration.[26]

Horatio concluded with guidelines for the effective and safe use of chloroform in midwifery. These included use only of "perfectly pure and reliable" chloroform, delay in its use until the "os uteri has become fairly dilated" unless pain is already great prior to this, administration only during the pains and then only giving a very few breaths of the chloroform, stopping its inhalation prior to complete insensibility, and frequent checks of pulse and respiration rates during administration.

The Massachusetts Medical Society traditionally published the addresses given at its meetings. Several years later, Horatio was to write the following related to the fate of his 1863 address: "It was referred to the Committee upon Publication, Drs. Putnam, Shattuck, and Morland, but containing, as it did, doctrine very unfashionable in Boston, namely, an endorsement of chloroform in midwifery in preference to sulphuric ether, the committee refused to permit it to be printed among the *Medical Communications* of the Society according to the usual custom, and it was subsequently published elsewhere."[27] "Elsewhere" was the *Boston Medical and Surgical Journal*, which published it on October 29, 1863, despite the commitment of the journal and its editors to a strong anti-chloroform view. However, much discussion, writing, and publication about anesthetics in midwifery and about chloroform versus ether for midwifery would occur before this late October publication.

Horatio's June 17 presentation at the Massachusetts Medical Society apparently was effective. In a Prefatory Note to the October publication, Horatio indicated that he removed prejudices against chloroform in Dr. Josiah Bartlett, President of the Massachusetts Medical Society, and Dr. Alden March, President of the American Medical Association.[28] No doubt, many less influential physicians in his large audience were similarly swayed. In fact, it may have been to counter Horatio's effective defense of chloroform in midwifery that the editors of the *Boston Medical and Surgical Journal* published on August 6, 1863 an anti-chloroform paper by Dr. Robert Johns of Dublin, Ireland.[29] The paper, "Practical Observations on the Injurious Effects of Chloroform Inhalation During Labor," appeared originally in the May 1863 issue of the *Dublin Quarterly Journal of Medical Science*. It included numerous quotes from articles, many written in the distant past, all critical of the use of chloroform in obstetrics.

Four days after Johns' paper appeared in the *Boston Medical and Surgical Journal*, Horatio provided editors Samuel L. Abbott and James Clarke White with a long critique of Johns' paper which also took the editors to task for republishing "what after all and though unintentionally on the part of its author, is but an offence against truth, against science and against common sense, which it is the duty of every obstetricist to brand."[30] Despite their own strong anti-chloroform views, they published Horatio's critique on August 20 as their lead article. It was titled, "On Chloroform Inhalation during Labor; With Especial Reference to the Paper by Dr. Johns, of Dublin, Lately Admitted into This Journal."

Horatio began his critique by indicating that much of the impetus for the largely dated anti-chloroform quotations Johns provided were the rivalries between Dublin and Edinburgh and between London and Edinburgh, including that between Robert Lee and James Young Simpson. Horatio, who had twice before taken Lee to task, referred to Lee as "a renegade Scotchman, an unsuccessful candidate for the midwifery chair of Edinburgh, whose spleen thus vented itself, and in many similar ways before and since." Horatio went on to indicate that he had been aware of Johns' publication when he gave his own address in favor of anaesthetics in midwifery in June, but had not referred to it because "Dr. Johns' statements seemed so obviously unfair, so stale and utterly without foundation, as not to merit the slightest acknowledgment among scientific or practical men."[31]

Horatio briefly mentioned the points of his recent Massachusetts Medical Society paper. Induction of anaesthesia during labor was not just a matter of expediency or necessity, "but a sacred duty, which were we women, we should soon recognize." Ether had "overwhelming advantages" for general surgery, but he insisted on chloroform "for the entire and sole control of child-bed." Horatio then declared that Johns was unfit to participate in this, "the most extensive, most interesting and most important medical controversy of the age, whose participants are not to be diverted from their earnest work by grotesque mask of ridicule, or put to flight by bladder-strokes, however loudly sounding or plied with whatever force." Horatio indicated that his strong language was necessary in defense of chloroform because of its important role in increasing the number of live births by shortening labor. He called Johns' paper a "bomb-shell" "charged with gratuitous assumptions, slurs and manifest untruths; [calculated] to light anew our prejudices, wound our personal feelings, and destroy our faith in all that the labor of years has been accomplishing." Horatio's battle imagery continued with the following:

> If, however, this must be; if, as in the case of our Southern rebellion, reform can be had but by contest, the prejudice and apathy of a former age removed but by forcible attrition, and relief to the unnecessary pangs and peril to which ancient superstition has condemned our own flesh and blood, afforded by the power of an enlightened outside public sentiment—let such then be accepted by those who recognize the weight of their mission. To have hastened the coming of its inevitable result will be sufficient reward.

The reference to "enlightened outside public sentiment" suggests that by August 10, when he submitted this critique of Johns' article, Horatio was already considering the publication of his Massachusetts Medical Society paper on anesthetics in midwifery as a pamphlet to be distributed to the general population.

Abbott and White, editors of the *Boston Medical and Surgical Journal*, were to follow Horatio's critique of Johns with an editorial on August 20 defending both Johns and their republication of Johns' article.[32] They took Horatio to task for omitting key phrases when he quoted Johns, noting: "In quoting from another who is the subject of severe criticism, too great accuracy cannot be observed." They also indicated that they did "not consider the question of the propriety of the use of anaesthetics in natural labor as by any means definitely settled." As to the question of chloroform, they wrote that they looked forward to the publication of Horatio's Massachusetts Medical Society presentation "with much interest." It may be that the decision not to publish Horatio's paper in the *Medical Communications* of the Massachusetts Medical Society had not been made or was not known by Abbott and White on August 20 when they indicated their anticipation of the publication of Horatio's paper. Their public expression of "much interest" in its future publication may have been a lever used by Horatio to get them to publish his article, despite the article's sharp conflict with the anti-chloroform views of the editors and of the powerful Harvard Medical School professors who selected and largely controlled these editors.

The October publication of Horatio's paper included the Prefatory Note in which Horatio bragged of his conversion of Dr. Bartlett and Dr. March from their anti-chloroform views. Horatio also referred in this Note to several thousand cases of labor where chloroform had been used successfully in the practices of Dr. Henry Miller, Dr. Theophilus Mack, and a Professor of Obstetrics in Laval University. Horatio indicated he could have presented "a mass of similar testimony," "but my business at this time is not with statistics, which are said, if shrewdly used, to prove almost anything we may desire, but to remove certain prejudices which have hitherto very widely obtained."[33]

Editors Abbott and White followed Horatio's paper a week later with a long anti-chloroform editorial. "Expressing opinions so directly at variance with those which the Editors of this Journal have uniformly held and advocated," they wrote, "our readers will naturally look for some comments from us upon the subject."[34]   They went on to note that there were at least three deaths associated with use of chloroform during childbirth, and that these had been admitted by a London physician *advocating* the use of chloroform. They also contradicted Horatio's claims that chloroform's effects were more transient than ether's.   As to "the correctness of Dr. Storer's theory, that the peculiar condition of the parturient female is in itself a protection against the dangers of chloroform inhalation," they needed to give this "more deliberate consideration" before admitting that this was the case.

Shortly after its publication in the *Boston Medical and Surgical Journal,* Horatio reprinted his Massachusetts Medical Society paper as *Eutokia: A Word to Physicians and to Women upon the Employment of Anaesthetics in Childbirth.*[35] Horatio included a second Prefatory Note, "To the Community." It shows that the topics of women's suffering and criminal abortion were never far from Horatio's thoughts.   The Note, dated November 1863, included:[36]

in placing [these pages] within the reach of those even more interested in their truth than the accoucheur, their own comfort and lives being involved, I am, I conceive, but fulfilling a direct duty, resting myself upon doctrine I have more than once publicly expressed within the past ten years: namely, that while—"but yesterday the man who dared give ether or chloroform in labor was considered as breaking alike the laws of Nature and of God, the time is close at hand when such will be said of all who withhold them, even in natural labor."—(Preface to Simpson's Obstetric Works, 1855, page xvi.)

In so far, moreover, as these words may be of avail in removing ... the now so frequent dread of allowing pregnancy to go on to its fulfillment, ... in so far shall they have done efficient work towards checking and preventing the great social evil of the time, more prevalent even among our rich, our educated and our refined, than among the poor and ignorant, most prevalent among our married! the intentional and criminal induction of abortion and miscarriage.

November 20, 1863 marked the beginning of law school for Horatio. He completed one-and-one-half terms at Harvard, leaving in July 1864. He was eventually to get a law degree, but for some reason this was delayed until 1868.[37] Dr. James Joseph Walsh, a close friend of Horatio in his later years, wrote that Horatio obtained the law training to further his efforts to improve legal treatment of abortion and to improve his standing with the lawyers who prosecuted such cases.[38] Frederick C. Irving, who largely relied on Horatio's descendants for information, claimed it was to prepare himself for teaching medical jurisprudence.[39] On the other hand, criminal abortion was a key topic in medical jurisprudence. Horatio himself was to write the following about his law degree to Malcolm in 1901: "after I had taken LL.B. and the law students were permitted to come in from Cambridge to attend my examinations in medical jurisprudence, I gave instruction to the combined class upon those gynaecological questions equally important for doctors and for lawyers, and not referred to in the textbooks."[40] Horatio was discussing events at the Harvard Medical School during 1865 or 1866 *before* being granted the LL.B. Horatio apparently considered himself to have the LL.B. after his eight months of law schooling. Horatio indicated in the same 1901 letter that at the time he expected an eventual Harvard Medical School professorship. "[A]s I had fitted myself in Edinburgh for special teaching," he wrote, "my father's chair was eventually to be divided, and I was to have gynaecology as a separate and wholly distinct branch." This division envisioned in 1855 for the Chair of Obstetrics and Medical Jurisprudence was apparently into a Chair of Obstetrics and Medical Jurisprudence and another Chair of Diseases of Women. In the 1901 letter, Horatio also discusses a planned subdivision of his father's chair into midwifery, which Horatio's former Lying-in Hospital colleague, William Read, expected to receive, and gynecology and medical jurisprudence, which Horatio expected to receive. Perhaps, in 1863, it was decided by the faculty that the Chair of Diseases of Women was to pick up medical jurisprudence, and Horatio began law school in preparation.[41]

The first known mention of Emily Elvira's mental illness was in the following letter. It was from Horatio to his friend Dr. Edward Jarvis who, after an unsuccessful career as a general practitioner, began a successful private mental institution in Dorchester, Massachusetts.

Hotel Pelham
28 Aug. 1863

My dear Dr.
    I shall be much obliged if you will inform me how many private establishments for the treatment of nervous disease there are in this

State beside your own, & by whom kept. I presume also that you will be able to send me a list of the various public & private institutions, for the same purpose, throughout the Country, outside our own state. Do not trouble yourself however to do so, unless it is perfectly convenient.

Mrs Storer continues in much the same condition as when you saw her, having had three attacks since, one of them on that same evening.

Yours sincerely
Horatio R. Storer

Dr. Jarvis.[42]

Shortly after this letter was written, Horatio became a member of the Massachusetts Commission on Insanity with the Hon. Josiah Quincy, Jr., a former mayor of Boston, and Dr. Alfred Hitchcock, a physician of Fitchburg, Massachusetts who was a member of the Governor's Council. Horatio's query to Dr. Jarvis about "establishments for the treatment of nervous disease" thus may have been related to his wife, to his new Commission duties, or both. The Commission was empowered by Massachusetts to conduct its business "provided, however, that no charge or expense is incurred by the Commonwealth under this resolve."[43] The absence of a budget did not prevent visits "by the Commission or one or more of its members" to each of "the lunatic asylums, public and private, and many of the State and town poor houses in the Commonwealth, as well as the hospitals in Toronto, Quebec, Concord, N.H., Augusta, Me., Kalamazoo, Mich., Indianapolis, Ind., Cincinnati, Ohio, Binghamton and Utica, N.Y., and Providence, R.I." It is not clear whether this remarkable commitment of time and travel at personal expense was shared equally by the three members. It is possible that Horatio joined the Commission, perhaps even somehow concocted the Commission, as a means to increase his general knowledge of insanity and its causes and also to help understand and, hopefully, cure the problems that were commencing or increasing in Emily Elvira.

Early in 1864, Horatio presented a series of five cases "illustrative of obstetric disease" at the Suffolk District Medical Society, and he published a paper on the series several weeks later.[44] These included a uterine abscess, a urethral tumor, and an operation for local enlargement of the vaginal wall. However, these cases were somewhat peripheral to Horatio's major new area of investigation and writing which was insanity in women. In April 1864, Horatio published Case VI which did involve this new interest.[45] Case VI was described to the Suffolk District Medical Society in December 1863 (before Cases I-V) and was also presented to the American Academy of Arts and Sciences in February 1864. Case VI was a woman with a tumor in the right abdomen who committed suicide during her menstrual period. The woman had frankly acknowledged her suicidal desire to Horatio. Rather than place the woman in an asylum, she was provided an attendant who left her by herself only at night and slept just outside her open bedroom door. The lady persuaded this attendant to close the bedroom door one night after she somehow secreted a knife into her bedroom. She slashed first her arm and, when that quit bleeding, repeatedly stabbed her neck until she severed a vein and this led to her death. These efforts apparently were virtually silent, since the attendant did not discover the dead woman until the next morning.

Horatio made special note that "the suicidal impulse reached its maximum and became effective at the catamenial period," and also noted the peculiar tolerance of pain exhibited by this and other insane patients. Horatio then proposed the following "as general laws":

1. In women of insane tendency, accidental or by inheritance, the access of insanity, its increase and its results, are more likely to occur at times of uterine or ovarian excitement, whether periodical and normal, or from disease. Just as we constantly see hysteria more or less marked, at such times, we occasionally find the mental irritation so great as to constitute actual alienation, whether as mania, monomania, melancholia, or the so-called moral insanity.

2. In women, mental derangement, even of extreme character, is very commonly the consequence of uterine or ovarian derangement, however trifling; occurring at puberty, at the grand climacteric, or at any point between them, during virginity, during gestation, during or after labor, or during lactation, from excessive sexual gratification, or excessive sexual abstinence, from self-abuse, from organic or functional local lesion.

3. So large a proportion of the mental derangements of women being sympathetic and reflex, and referable to local derangements, herein differing from what obtains in men, where insanity is more frequently of centric and cerebral origin, there is decided indication for local curative treatment much oftener than it is now resorted to in cases of insane women, either at asylums or in private practice.

"Self-abuse" if you haven't guessed, referred to masturbation, as does "self-pollution." Horatio viewed this as a factor in his Case VI, noting that "upon several occasions after the commencement of the molimen, and just previous to the night of her death, she had practised self-pollution, confessing it soon afterwards with evidence of disgust and regret."

Horatio contrasted his theories of female insanity with those of Dr. Isaac Ray of Providence, Rhode Island. Ray, "while acknowledging the immense frequency of ill health among American women, and its evident connection with insanity, seeks to explain both these results, almost exclusively, by overwork, necessary in the poor, self-imposed in the wealthy—overlooking or ignoring the great causes lying beneath overwork, upon which I would lay such stress."

Horatio's underlying "great causes" were the "uterine or ovarian derangement" factors he had enumerated in his second "law." "Some of these causes I have already called by name," Horatio continued, "but it would be indeed false delicacy and actual cowardice not to hold up as chief among all the predisposing and effective causes of uterine ill health among us here in New England, the so frequent induction of criminal abortion, [and] the so frequent intentional prevention of impregnation, by women, married and unmarried, who have been exposed to its occurrence."

Horatio named the coincidence of menstruation and mental attacks "catamenial mania." "Who is not familiar," he continued, "with the varied phases of despondency, jealousy, erotic desire, the habits of lying, stealing, and other deceit, &c. &c., at these and other times displayed by women who are called and treated as merely nervous, only through mistaken pity or a desire to shield their friends." At least some of these many symptoms no doubt applied to Emily Elvira Storer. Horatio went on to claim that when men exhibited such behaviors they were not shielded and were sent to asylums. The implication was that were it not for "shielding," women would be much more numerous than men in asylums due to the greater complexity of female than male sexual organs and their resultant higher vulnerability to disease. Horatio then quoted an early medical writer, Jean Baptiste van Helmont (1577-1644), who had written *Propter uterum est mulier*, which roughly means "Woman exists for the sake of her womb."[46] "I would not so far commit myself as to accept his statement in all its bearings," Horatio wrote, "but I have no hesitation in averring that in the uterus we shall find the key to many a case of mental malady, ..."[47]

The Massachusetts Commission on Insanity provided its report on February 23, 1864.[48] It called attention to abuses of the insane, particularly at the poorhouses which were charged with keeping "incurables" and which often kept them in cages. The Commissioners claimed that one "incurable" patient they encountered in the Charlestown Almshouse was not insane and should be either restored to liberty or to an asylum. They noted overcrowding at regular asylums and the typical saddling of superintendents with administrative duties while treatment of patients fell on their largely untrained assistants. They called attention to rules that differed for native-born and foreign-born citizens, where the latter were sent to treatment asylums and the former were not, and called for asylum treatment for both classes. They even provided a cost-benefit analysis that showed the economic advantages to the state of the increased cures that would result for native-born insane if they were provided asylum treatment.

One report recommendation was undoubtedly strongly influenced by Horatio, since he was to write frequently about it over the next few years. This was to empower "the trustees of State hospitals to appoint to each a board of consulting physicians." "Especially is this required," the report noted, "for evident reasons, in the case of female patients, as superintendents themselves have stated to the Commission." The report also included a paragraph calling attention to Horatio's recent "Case VI" insanity paper and to his new theory about the causes of female insanity. He indicated these "may prove of interest to scientific men, and of practical benefit to the community."

Horatio had made many earlier references to mental problems associated with abnormal uterine conditions, such as his paper on puerperal mania and the article describing the hysteria associated with ligature of the cervix uteri. What is more, Horatio claimed to have acquired at an early date from his father the belief that sexual factors such as "too timid intercourse"[49] were responsible for abnormal uterine excitation that led directly to nervous conditions. But what a boon it would be for gynecology, Horatio must have thought, if by correcting abnormal uterine conditions one could reduce or eliminate much of the insanity of women! And what an additional indictment of induced abortion if it were a frequent cause of these uterine problems that led to female insanity! Such hypotheses might be difficult to abandon, even if data were encountered that contradicted them. But Horatio claimed that his opportunities as Commissioner on Insanity to study the insane from September 1863 until early 1864 increased his belief in the influence of pelvic factors in female insanity.[50]

This belief that uterine factors were important in female insanity was expressed again by Horatio at the annual meeting of the American Medical Association in New York City early in June. Horatio read a paper before the Section on Practical Medicine and Obstetrics with the long title, "The Relations of Female Patients to Hospitals for the Insane: The Necessity on Their Account of a Board of Consulting Physicians to Every Hospital."[51] In the paper, Horatio cited a case where he had operated on the cervix of a young woman and cured her derangement and her pain. It involved "mechanical dysmenorrhoea" in which the young lady experienced "attacks" of "excessive sexual desire" which were "very clearly coincident with the menstrual period, and so extreme that the patient could with difficulty restrain herself from soliciting the approach of the other sex." In addition, she was unable to "restrain herself from frequent and excessive masturbation." Horatio operated, "freely incising the cervix uteri and dilating its canal." As a result, the woman was freed from "the dysmennor-rhoeal pain," the "morbid desires," and "the disgusting propensity." "They have not since returned," Horatio continued, "save in one single instance, when an acute attack of erotic desire, plainly resulting from indulgence in so-called pepper tea, was at once allayed by the application of potassa fusa to the cervix."

Horatio indicated his belief that symptoms other than excessive erotic desire also were the result of such "sources within the patient herself" which could be relieved by ordinary medical procedures at least while "the mental disturbance retains its original reflex character and has not merged into organic cerebral change." He then made the point that these uterine and ovarian causes of insanity were rarely if ever diagnosed or treated in the patients confined to mental asylums. To change this he called for the appointment "to every asylum in the land a board of consulting physicians, useful in ordinary cases of insanity, but absolutely indispensable in the instance of insane women." He claimed the superintendent of an asylum, or his assistant, could not make pelvic examinations of female patients or effect the necessary treatment of uterine disease because the mentally deranged patient would totally misinterpret such diagnosis and treatment and might describe it, during their stay at the asylum or after their cure, to friends and family as sexual abuse. Presumably, the consulting physician or surgeon might be similarly blamed, but his separate status would reduce or prevent damage to the asylum or its supervisors.

An editorial note at the end of Horatio's published paper indicated that it was "warmly approved by many of" the members of the Section on Obstetrics, which may indicate some "warm" dissent as well. On the other hand, the Resolutions appended to Horatio's report were unanimously endorsed when referred to the Association at large. The first Resolution was to attach "to every public hospital for the insane, one or more consulting physicians, who may be consulted at the discretion of the superintendent; such measure being alike for the interest of the hospital, its medical officers and its patients." The second Resolution was to provide a copy of the first "to the Board of Trustees of each of our public hospitals for the insane; and also to the Secretary of the Association of American Superintendents, with the request that it may be endorsed by that body, and the action proposed be urged upon the respective boards with which its members are officially connected."

On October 1, 1864, Horatio read a related paper, "Advisory Medical Boards Requisite at Asylums," at the Suffolk District Medical Society. The paper was published two weeks later in the *Boston Medical and Surgical Journal.*[52] Horatio first indicated that his experiences since his publication of "Case VI" had strengthened his beliefs about "the causation, nature and more rational treatment of insanity in women," and he described the cordial reception of his views by other medical men. He then restated his belief that much of the insanity of women was "of reflex character and origin," in a majority of these "unattended by organic cerebral change," and thus "it may be prevented, treated, [and] cured by medical and surgical means." He went on to indicate, as he had in his American Medical Association paper, that the patient with a diseased ovary, cervix, or uterus underlying her insanity received neither diagnosis nor treatment at an asylum. Horatio restated the superintendent's difficulty in providing the needed vaginal examinations of their patients, whereas proper diagnosis by the advisory-board physician would help "settle the question of sanity or insanity, of detention or non-detention, of permanent disability or of cure." If the diagnosis prompted a cure, "the delusions involved might have been made to permanently disappear, and an immense amount of scandal and professional disparagement avoided."

Horatio noted an extra advantage to the profession of having advisory boards to asylums. This was the increased pool of physicians qualified for asylum positions such as superintendent. He indicated the current lack of qualified candidates made asylum trustees concerned whenever a vacancy occurred at another asylum because their own superintendent might be lured away.

He indicated that the vacancy at the Northampton Massachusetts Asylum led to a request that he and Dr. Hitchcock of the Commission on Insanity make their names available as candidates. "It is unnecessary to add that in one at least of these instances," Horatio continued, "such position would have been incompatible with other though perhaps not higher aims ..." Finally, Horatio discussed benefits for the community of advisory boards. These were the economic benefits of increased cures, the reduction of frequent trials associated with doubtful cases of insanity in women, and the increased confidence of the public in asylums which would lead to earlier admission of patients, producing even more cures.

As with his crusade against abortion and his crusade for administration of chloroform during childbirth, Horatio soon faced criticism for his views and recommendations on insanity in women. On November 10, a guest editorial signed only "*" appeared in the *Boston Medical and Surgical Journal*.[53] The writer claimed there was no need for such advisory boards, since superintendents already had the power to consult with outside physicians as needed, and that an advisory board would prevent the superintendent from selecting such consultants. The writer claimed that he himself had "acted both as assistant and superintendent in one of the most important of our New England hospitals; ..." As such he had benefitted from consultations, but did "not feel the need of any *permanent* board of advisors, *such as is recommended.*" The anonymous author then raised questions about the Massachusetts Commission on Insanity of which Horatio was a member:

> by what influence was the late board of "Commissioners in Insanity" selected? For what reason were all the well-known "experts," able men and true, omitted from that Board? Without any wish to intimate that said Board was deficient, either in talent, experience or accomplishment for the task required, it is sufficient to say that of the three constituting that Board, two only were physicians, that neither of these was ever heard of as an "expert" in insanity, or as being inside the walls of an insane asylum in any other capacity than as an accidental or curious visitor, before his appointment to examine and report upon the difficult and complicated subject of insanity.

The critic questioned Horatio's claim that he and Dr. Hitchcock were invited to apply for the Northampton vacancy. "If either of the gentlemen *so urged*," he began, "supposed for a moment that by yielding to the advice of his partial but imprudent friends he would have secured the countenance and support of a single member of the intelligent Board who had the power of appointment, he is certainly under a great delusion."

Horatio was most curious about the identity of his new critic. The following is from a letter to Dr. Jarvis written several days *before* Horatio's critic's paper was published.[54]

Your kind note of this morning, with its two alternatives, yet leaves the point I would make untouched. It is not who has been Superintendent without an Assistant, or who has been either Superintendent or assistant, but who has been both Superintendent & assistant, at one time having filled the one office & subsequently the other? So far as I am aware, the gentleman I refer to would seem to be either Dr Prince or Dr Stedman, but I am in doubt.

Horatio was hardly deterred by "Dr. Prince or Dr Stedman." In a paper published in the *Boston Medical and Surgical Journal* two weeks after "*"'s article, Horatio reiterated his positions and took his critic to task for finding fault with the ideas of medical advisory boards for asylums and even more for his indirect attacks on Massachusetts superintendents and for his direct questioning of the makeup of the recent Massachusetts Commission on Insanity. However, Horatio first made far too much sport with his critic's failure to sign his name:[55]

The signature of our friend was that of a star. Of heavenly bodies, the moon is that which has always been supposed the peculiar perquisite of the psychologist, and if any sign manual were intended to be typical of the light to be thrown by such upon the subject under discussion, this would have seemed more to the purpose than that actually employed. ... Representing himself by a lesser luminary than his fellow-workers would have been likely to have done, the critic may have desired modestly to express his own sense of comparative insignificance; or it may be that he had the malign dog-star in mind; or it is possible that in Lucifer, thrust from his high estate, he would typify the fact, with all its probabilities, that he is an ex-superintendent, now no longer in office.

Horatio then noted that his critic had made no criticism of Horatio's claim that female insanity frequently was a reflex of uterine or ovarian problems, and that this was the crux of the need for advisory medical boards which had the expertise and the independence to make these diagnoses and effect necessary treatments. Horatio also tried to show that his critic's arguments against advisory boards were inconsistent and that they appeared to boil down to concern that such boards would infringe or be "a covert attempt at infringement of the superintendent's high prerogatives, of chief steward, chief farmer, chief hostler, chief policeman, chief cook, chief valet de chambre and—physician." Following this, Horatio responded to his critic's questions related to selection of the Board of Commissioners on Insanity:

With regard to the personal attack upon my colleagues, Hon. Josiah Quincy, of Boston, and Dr. Hitchcock, of Fitchburg, it might have been thought that the many public services they have rendered and the position they both hold in private life would have protected them from such ungenerous treatment.

As regards the Commission collectively:—

1. The appointment of the Commission on Insanity was made by the Governor and Council. The charge upon this point has therefore been transferred to these gentlemen, and is an assertion that they were false to their duty and to their oaths.

2. The Commission would hardly have been properly constituted had it been composed merely of superintendents, for with the many questions that came before it in various ways affecting that fraternity, all of which it is to be hoped were fairly and impartially decided, how could they have given a report that would not have been thought biassed?

3. In view of the double character of the questions submitted, it was necessary that the Commission should have been chosen from the two professions it represented. Was it unfair that it should have been constituted by one lawyer to two physicians?"

A fourth item made reference to the Commission's Report and listed the numerous practical results of the Commission which were presented earlier. Horatio mentioned that the Commission's extensive work without compensation and payment of its own travelling expenses "to the extent of several hundred dollars" proved "a novel sort of unfaithfulness to its public duties" and "a novel sort of incompetence to accomplish its work."

Horatio also indicated he had sent letters to the superintendents with whom the Commission had dealt to see if they shared his critic's views. He provided the response of Dr. Bemis, the Superintendent of the State Asylum at Worcester, Massachusetts. Bemis indicated the Commission faithfully and impartially performed its duties; that it should *not* have been made up of superintendents and should have included a lawyer; that it was more sympathetic to his problems that he expected; and that he wished the Commission had visited more frequently, stayed longer, and would be made permanent. As to the critic's claim that no member of the Northampton board would have considered Commission members for the superintendency, Horatio wrote: "one of these gentlemen, whose name had been submitted to that Board without his knowledge, did receive by a Committee from a majority of the Board an informal tender of the superintendency; which invitation was declined." Horatio invited "*" to visit him and examine the evidence for this; thus one can surely conclude that Horatio was that Commissioner.

Horatio angrily concluded with the following which included his first published use of the term *gynaecologist*:[56]

it will have been made evident, from his own admissions, that he could hardly have been fitted for the moral treatment, as he was certainly unfitted for the physical treatment of insane women. The very inaccuracies of thought and of expression and of statement which he has evinced, the reckless way in which by his allusions to the opinions and conduct of his brother-superintendents he has scattered firebrands within his own household, are in themselves sufficient answer to the intolerant and intolerable attempt to withhold from all save the little circle of hospital experts the privilege of knowing or of stating anything concerning insanity. The time has passed for such an assumption as this; it would probably not be made by another physician in the country; and there is good reason for believing that the new door now opened by gynaecologists for reaching, analogically and from their other diseases, insanity in women, none will more gladly acknowledge and more faithfully employ than superintendents themselves.

The critic responded to Horatio in a paper published on January 5, 1865.[57] "It may not be thought a recent discovery that physical disease often exists with and aggravates mental alienation, and health returning, the mind improves;" he wrote, "but that any amount of physical suffering is sufficient, without predisposition, to *produce* insanity, has never been demonstrated." He restated his objections to advisory medical boards: their uselessness, given that consultations are already possible, and the nuisance and evil such a board with powers and privileges would become to the competent superintendent. He then provided a new objection, "more serious than any before urged." Female patients learning that such special advisors were available would exaggerate every sensation associated with their sex "and there would be no peace for the patients until the *knight of the speculum* had been summoned, a search for the imaginary demon instituted, and an attempt made to drag him from his hidden retreat."[58] "*" then denied that any superintendents he knew approved of "such a board of advisors as recommended." He indicated the complete concurrence with his own views of a "well-known" writer on insanity and mentioned another whom he quoted: "'There is just as much occasion to have an oculist, an aurist, a chiropodist, to the end of the chapter on specialties, attached to our institutions for the insane, as one for that under consideration.'" He also quoted "a physician sound in judgment and of acute observation" (it may well have been Jacob or Henry J. Bigelow):

"The general practitioner has often to witness and lament the deleterious influence of some specialist in the department named. The minds of a few women in a neighborhood become disturbed with the idea that something is *wrong* about the *womb*. The disease (imaginary) becomes contagious; the delusion extends, and the panic becomes general, till most of the women in the community are made anxious and miserable."

Finally, "*" challenged Horatio's claim that little was being attempted or achieved in public hospitals for the cure of insane women. "Does he mean to say," he continued, "that superintendents have not discharged, *as cured*, as many women as men?" Such claims without statistics to back them "are neither creditable to the author nor complimentary to living superintendents, and are a stigma upon the hard-earned fame and revered memory of the honored dead."

Horatio's only immediate response was the following footnote to a paper dealing with other diseases published a week later in the *Boston Medical and Surgical Journal*:[59]

> In view of the fact, tolerably well known by physicians in this vicinity, that I have uniformly protested against the unnecessarily frequent use of the speculum and nitrate of silver, so generally considered indispensable by those professing an acquaintance with uterine disease, one may well be amused at the especially ill-fitting epithet applied to me in the last week's Journal by the gentleman who has undertaken to criticize my proposal of Advisory Medical Boards at Insane Hospitals, for the cases of female patients. The term "knight of the speculum" seems hardly applicable in this instance, except on the principle of *lucus a non lucendo*, very much as seems to have been the case with the part taken by my doughty opponent, whose zeal in this controversy and the arguments that he has advanced alike seem based upon an utter want of knowledge as to the real principles which should govern the treatment of insane women.

Horatio presented a longer response to "*" at the Suffolk District Medical Society on January 28, 1865. It was submitted to the *Boston Medical and Surgical Journal* for publication. However, the following letter to Horatio from one of the editors, indicated that "*" would get the last word:[60]

Office of B. M. & S. Journal
Feb. 15th 1865.

Dear Dr.

The Editors of the Journal came to the conclusion after the publication of the last article relating to this discussion, that enough space had already been given to it, and that they would decline any further communications on the subject.

Very truly yours
James C. White.

CHAPTER 9

THE AMA MEETS IN BOSTON, PRIZE ESSAY, HYSTERECTOMY

Horatio was on the Nominating Committee at the 1864 Annual Meeting of the American Medical Association in New York. One of the Committee's first tasks was to nominate the founder of the American Medical Association, Dr. Nathan S. Davis, as President and this was accepted by the Association. Another approved recommendation of the Committee was to hold the 1865 meeting at Boston and this no doubt was a factor in the designation of Horatio as Assistant Secretary of the Association. Horatio also was designated to be Chairman of the Committee on Insanity, even though the former Chairman continued in that status.[1] The Committee on Prize Essays was traditionally made up of physicians from the host city and the Nominating Committee selected Horatio's friends, Drs. Jonathan Mason Warren, Henry Ingersoll Bowditch, and John H. Dix, with David Humphreys Storer nominated to be Chairman. These nominations too were approved by the Association.

Two pieces of business on the last day of the 1864 New York Association meeting would directly affect Horatio at the 1865 Boston meeting. One was a proposed resolution by Michigan delegates that the Association "offer a premium for the best *short and comprehensive tract* calculated for circulation among females, and designed to enlighten them upon the criminality and physical evils of forced abortion."[2] This had been agreed on by members of the Northeastern District Medical Association of Michigan at their annual meeting three weeks earlier. This resolution was approved by the American Medical Association and referred to the new Committee on Prize Essays. The other piece of business involving Horatio dealt with the new phenomenon of medical specialization. Horatio and four other physicians were appointed to a Committee "to define the position of specialists, and the duties of the profession towards specialists, as well as the duties of the specialists towards the profession."[3] Horatio's appointment no doubt was because his own step into specialism had attracted national attention.

Horatio must have been even busier than usual in the weeks before the June 1865 American Medical Association meeting in Boston. As Chairman of the Committee on Insanity he prepared a report that was to take up 136 pages of the *Transactions*.[4] His winning essay, "The Criminality and Physical Evils of Forced Abortions," would occupy nearly forty pages.[5] He also prepared a minority report for the Committee on Medical Specialism. As Assistant Secretary to a distant Permanent Secretary, he was also busy with preparations for the meeting, not the least of which was *making sure the meeting actually occurred*. Horatio in later years was to make reference to a conspiracy among four Boston physicians to prevent the meeting from taking place with this being viewed as a way to destroy the American Medical Association itself, given that in 1865 the Association was facing "the most precarious period of its history."[6] The precariousness was related to the several years' hiatus of truly national meetings due to the Civil War.   Two conspirators mentioned by name by Horatio several years later were Dr. Henry J. Bigelow[7] and Dr. Henry W. Williams.[8]   Bigelow was Chairman and Williams a member of the Committee of Arrangements for the Boston meeting and they were in a fine position to prevent the necessary arrangements. Bigelow and his followers probably already could be classed as Horatio's opponents or even enemies, and Horatio's key role in bringing the meeting to Boston, may have made the meeting all the more undesirable to them. The thought may have been that since Boston was the "Hub of the Solar System," what need was there for a superfluous American Medical Association, the dissolution of which would also be most displeasing to the upstart Horatio Storer?

An editorial in the *Boston Medical and Surgical Journal* for May 11 announced the upcoming meeting of the Association on June 6, but also included: "The doubts which partly occupied the minds of some of us, as to the practicability of holding the meeting this year, while the storm of war still hung over the country, are dissipated in this new sunshine of peace."[9]   Jonathan Mason Warren provided another Storer-independent indication of jeopardy for the Boston meeting in his journal for February 1, 1865: "Meeting of the Councillors of Mass Med Soc. ... Dr H. J. Bigelow brought up the question of having the Am. Med. Assc. meet here next June, & asked the opinion of the Councillors on it. Dr Bowditch introduced a substitution for Dr B's question—Dr Shattuck [introduced] an amendment against having them[.] carried with but ten nays."[10]   Assuming that Warren's handwriting is deciphered correctly, all but ten of the forty-eight Massachusetts Medical Society Councillors present were obstacles, and it is not clear how this powerful group was thwarted in their attempts to prevent the meeting.   Given Dr. George C. Shattuck's "amendment against," he, like Bigelow and Williams, appears to have been active in the opposition. However, the meeting in Boston occurred as scheduled and Horatio's important role in preserving it was mentioned, without specifics, a few years later by the "Salutatory by the Publisher" in the first issue of the *Journal of the Gynaecological Society of Boston.*[11]   Horatio himself mentioned his Association-saving effort in a later letter,[12] also, unfortunately, without any details.

On the first day of the Boston meeting, Horatio read his Committee on Insanity Report.[13]   There had been a Committee on Insanity for many years, but this was the first time that Committee had produced a Report. Horatio's report was long, but the length was not to make up for the previous delinquent Insanity Committees, only to buttress Horatio's case that much female insanity was caused by factors ovarian, uterine, or otherwise sex-related. Horatio's approach was to avoid the data of "gynaecologists" and present material by "psychologists," as the asylum superintendents were then called. Horatio felt this necessary to adequately persuade his fellow members of the Committee and others in his audience who *were* "psychologists" that they needed to be more concerned about "reflex" insanity produced by pelvic factors. Horatio justified his "insanity in women" theme for the Committee Report with the following:

> As it is, having been chosen by the Association to this work in consequence, as I suppose, of having long been delving in the special field of hysteria, and the reflex nervous and neuralgic demonstrations of invalid women, I take it for granted that what is expected at my hands is, to a certain extent, of a special character, although of necessity, as all specialism rests upon general principles, I shall endeavor not to lose sight of the general basis upon which it lies.

It will be recalled that Horatio was a member of the Nominating Committee at New York that determined the members and Chairman of the Committee on Insanity. According to a footnote of Horatio, this Committee was formed *despite the fact that the previous Chairman had requested and been granted an extension of time to provide his report.* This earlier Chairman was told that the "organic law of the Association" required a new committee.[14] It seems that, in 1864, Horatio would let nothing preclude this Chairmanship he desired!

Horatio began his report by claiming that one did not have to be a superintendent or ex-superintendent of an asylum to "know much about insanity;" that his non-asylum position would prevent bias; and that his success in treating insanity in his civil practice made his conclusions "apt to carry with them conviction." Horatio indicated that the other members of his Committee were willing to grant that his position had validity, but at least one worried that allowing Horatio's important idea of pelvic causation of much insanity "to absorb the whole report would but partially and imperfectly discuss the great points of interest pertaining to insanity in this country." However, Horatio was not deterred or sidetracked and began by listing what he was *not* claiming about female insanity, but which he had been earlier misunderstood as claiming. These included "universality of causation or of treatment;" that psychologists were not already aware of the key role of women's sex; that there were no other "predisposing, exciting, or continuing causes at work;" and that its treatment "should always and only be local." He followed with his proposal for advisory boards at asylums, with reassurances for "psychologists" in his audience "that such aid was only to be made use of at the discretion of the superintendent." Horatio then claimed that the brain, typically the subject of autopsies at asylums, was rarely the cause of insanity, although it was certainly the "seat" of it. He then gave numerous instances where "psychologists" and other insanity writers had also theorized about or described abnormal processes in distant organs which caused insanity and provided evidence that in women pelvic organs frequently were the culprits. The following were his comments about why the sexual system of women was more apt to produce insanity than the "merely subsidiary" genital apparatus of men:

> Not only is she subject to a host of diseases peculiar to her sex, to which we find neither homologue nor analogue in man, but they are capable of so modifying herself as entirely to change her natural disposition and character. In health, we find her still obedient to a special law. The subject here also, we might even say the victim, of periodicity, her life is one perpetual change, and these changes even are still subdivided.

Horatio again made reference to van Helmont, but this time did not quote him in Latin, providing instead: "Van Helmont was not far wrong when he contended that woman was what she is, in health, in character, in her charms alike of body, mind, and soul, because of her womb alone." Horatio also credited the womb as the source of a major part of her characteristics in disease and, as a result, "in longer refusing for the female insane that study, special examination and treatment, without which, in all other forms of disease, women cannot be properly cared for, any person laying claim to the honorable office of physician must be deemed guilty of gross neglect, blindness from too great conservatism, or inhumanity." Horatio admitted this was strong language, but denied that it was "intended as personal." "I am but working for a general principle in one of the many fields of its application," he continued, "and in behalf of the sex, to the alleviation of whose sufferings some of us are devoting our lives."

Horatio then presented a long passage from a paper, "Considerations on the Reciprocal Influence of the Physical Organization and Mental Manifestations," which a Dr. Kellogg of the Utica Asylum had published in the April-1856 *American Journal of Insanity*. It indicated that one fourth of the insanity in both sexes was related to disturbances of the reproductive organs, but that the effect was larger in the female because of the greater intricacy of female organs and the greater role they played. Kellogg's paper sounded very much like Horatio's articles in 1864 in the *Boston Medical and Surgical Journal*. Horatio criticized the asylum superintendents who had not properly responded to Kellogg's decade-earlier ideas. He then described an absurd claim of another article in the same insanity journal where Kellogg's paper had been published. It was that "parasitic animals of various kinds" infest women's frontal sinuses. This absurdity had gone unchallenged by "psychologists" in that or in subsequent issues of the journal and Horatio concluded that Kellogg's cogent message had also been ignored by them.

In arguing for connections between pelvic organs and mental functions, Horatio also cited mental events as causes of amenorrhea, menorrhagia, and increased pain in dysmenorrhea. He also cited numerous cases reported by asylum superintendents showing insanity resulting from physical causes, and particularly from pelvic causes. As additional evidence of uterine factors in insanity, Horatio presented examples of serious mental problems associated with pregnancy and with other normal uterine events such as puberty.

Horatio discussed one ramification of his strong belief in the influence of pelvic factors on mental states. This was that treatment of pregnant women who committed capital crimes was wrong. "I believe not only that the execution of pregnant women should be stayed for the sake of the life of the child," he wrote, "but that no pregnant or parturient woman, for a crime committed during her gestation, or shortly after her confinement, should ever be executed at all."

Horatio argued that the only evidence against his position that pelvic factors were important in insanity was negative and failed to counter the positive evidence he had compiled. He mentioned that his critics had argued that menstruation often remained normal during the onset, course, and cure of insanity; that insane women frequently do not complain of pelvic pain; and that many women with *bona fide* uterine disease remained sane. "As well might be asserted," Horatio commented on the last, "that because some persons with musket wounds have recovered, therefore a bullet never kills."

Horatio described how his Insanity Commission had encountered terrible conditions in some of the poor houses where the insane people judged incurable by asylums were maintained. He pointed out that while the asylums themselves were no longer guilty of such abuses, their failure to adopt "any means or measure that may tend to the cure of a patient, or a class of patients, is in reality almost as grievous a wrong as a harm intentionally inflicted." Horatio also described the general absence of any special treatment of insane women among current practices of asylums. He mentioned his *Boston Medical and Surgical Journal* critic's question, "Where are the statistics [showing a failure to cure women]?" which had followed Horatio's claim of such a failure. After describing the *Boston Medical and Surgical Journal's* refusal to publish his statistics, he provided the statistics he claimed showed that asylum cures of women were "not in reality cases of cure," since it was common for these patients to return to asylums. In addition, Horatio claimed that males' greater susceptibility to fatal forms of insanity, and the generally higher death rates of men in institutions required the excess of female cures over males to be much larger than it was, if treatment of both were equivalent. Horatio's conclusion was "that all justifiable resources of medical treatment can scarcely have been put in requisition at asylums." However, this presentation could hardly have convinced "*", given the reliance of Horatio's argument on a too-small excess of female cures over male cures.

The second day of the American Medical Association meeting in Boston, Wednesday, June 7, 1865, was another big day for Horatio. The Minutes included:[15]

The Committee on Prize Essays, Dr. D. Humphreys Storer, of Massachusetts, Chairman, reported as follows:—

"The Committee on Prize Essays beg leave to report that they have received a dissertation 'On the Surgical Treatment of Morbid Growths within the Larynx,' bearing the motto '*Quod vidi, scripsi*,' which they would unanimously recommend as worthy the usual prize of the Association.

"They would also award the premium offered at the last annual meeting of the Association for 'the best short and comprehensive tract calculated for circulation among females, and designed to enlighten them upon the criminality and physical evils of abortion' to an essay with the motto '*Casta placent superis, castâ cum mente venito, et manibus puris sumito fontis aquam*.'

"In the preface to which the writer very modestly remarks: 'If it be considered by the Committee worthy its end, they will please adjudge it no fee, nor measure it by any pecuniary recompense. Were the finances of the Association such as to warrant it in more than the most absolutely necessary expenditures, yet would the approbation of the Committee and of the profession at large be more grateful to the writer than any tangible, and therefore, trivial reward.'

> D. Humphreys Storer,
> J. Mason Warren,
> H. I. Bowditch,
> John H. Dix."

The seals were then broken, and Dr. Louis Elsberg, of New York, proved to be the successful competitor for the first of the prizes mentioned, and Dr. Horatio R. Storer, of Massachusetts, the author of the Essay on Criminal Abortion.

On motion, the report was accepted and the essays referred to the Committee of Publication.

No mention is made in the Minutes of the number of entries submitted for the regular or for the special prize. A May 10 entry in J. Mason Warren's journal had included, "Returned Dissertation on *Abortion* to Dr Storer." This would have been to the Chairman of their Prize Committee. Warren's handwriting is poor, but it is almost certainly "dissertation" and not "dissertation*s*," and this could mean that Horatio was the sole entrant. However, if there had been other entries, Horatio's intensive research on abortion gave him a unique perspective on the subject that made his essay highly likely to capture the prize.

Horatio attempted to hide his identity to the Prize Committee by referring in his essay to the author of his own published papers on criminal abortion in the third person. For example:[16]

I am constrained to acknowledge my indebtedness to the various publications of the writer from whom I have quoted, for much of the evidence I shall now present upon the subject of forced abortions. I trust that thus offered it may lose none of its freshness, point, and force. My frequent extracts from one who has given more thought to the subject than probably any other person in the country, will I am sure need no excuse.

Horatio no doubt believed that anyone else making reference to his publications would have used such favorable terms to describe them and the efforts that produced them.

"The writer," Horatio began Prefatory Remarks to his essay, "who knew nothing of the project to elicit a direct and effective appeal to women upon the subject of criminal abortion, until after it had been decided at the New York meeting, has long been a member of the Association." One might suspect that Horatio had planted the idea for such a Horatio-serving essay contest in the Michigan physicians who brought the resolution before the American Medical Association the year before. What is more, Horatio had been visiting asylums in Michigan in late 1863 or early 1864. However, if Horatio's statement that he "knew nothing of the project ..." were false, this would exceed any misrepresentation of the facts by Horatio Storer this author has encountered.

Horatio declared that he had opportunity to note the high frequency of criminal abortion, its disastrous effects on the country, and the increase in physicians' desire to "arrest" abortion since the 1859 American Medical Association Report of the Committee on Criminal Abortion. He went on to discuss the coincidence that Boston was the original source of the Association's first action "in 1857" against criminal abortion and now the site for its appeal to the community to abstain from the practice. This coincidence no doubt was news to members of the Prize Committee (with the possible exception of his father) who would have been unaware that it was a Boston-originating letter to the Nominating Committee at Nashville in 1857 that led to formation of the American Medical Association's Special Committee on Criminal Abortion. A second-mentioned coincidence was that the Chairman of the Prize Committee, David Humphreys Storer, was the man "who, in New England, first appreciated the frequency of criminal abortions, pointed out their true character, and denounced them."[17] Anyone who had done their homework by reading Horatio's 1859 articles would indeed have been aware of this second "coincidence."

"If the essay prove successful," Horatio ended his Prefatory Remarks, "its author only asks that the seal which covers his identity may not be broken until the announcement is made upon the platform of the convention, pledging himself that this is but a whim of his own, and that he is well, and he trusts favorably, known by many of the best men of the Association throughout the Union." An associated footnote in the *published* paper read: "Now that the decision of the Prize Committee has been made, the purpose of the above stipulation becomes evident. The committee consisted of Drs. D. Humphreys Storer, Henry I.

Bowditch, J. Mason Warren, and John H. Dix, of Boston; the chairman of the committee being the writer's father." The breaking of the seal on the platform, at least partially removed the onus of favoritism in awarding the prize to Horatio, since it could be argued that no one knew the author of the essay until the seal was broken. However, one can hardly imagine that any member of the committee, and particularly its chairman, was totally surprised to see Horatio's name under the seal. Yet that is exactly what one physician was to note in a letter written to Horatio a few months after the event. "Nothing pleased me so much as the gratification so pleasantly expressed by your good father," wrote his Philadelphia friend, "as he so unexpectedly found his son to be the essayist. For that reason, I am much pleased that you requested, 'for a whim,' to have the seals broken upon the platform."[18]

Some uncertainty *may* have existed in the minds of Prize Committee members, even that of David Humphreys, as to the author of the Prize Essay. Horatio demonstrated his capability of concealing authorship in a later prize competition when he had his entry mailed from Pittsburgh, to reduce the likelihood that the Boston judges would identify its source. Horatio may have had this 1865 essay sent from some other city and he probably took the lesser step of having the essay copied by another person to eliminate the cue of his distinctive handwriting. What is more, other submitted essays also would have made extensive reference to Horatio's *North-American Medico-Chirurgical Review* papers, since these papers represented the only scholarly American investigations of criminal abortion. Nor would these competitors hesitate to heap praise on the son of the Chairman of the Prize Committee, as Horatio did in his essay, particularly since Horatio's work was indeed praiseworthy. The "gratification so pleasantly expressed" by David Humphreys "as he so unexpectedly found his son to be the essayist" *may* have been an expression of surprise, but more likely was one appropriate for confirmation of an expectation. On the other hand, David Humphreys Storer may have been a good actor.

Horatio began the actual essay by testifying to its importance. He noted that this may have been the first occasion when the profession had chosen to "directly address itself to the judgment and to the hearts of women upon a question vital to themselves and to the nation, ..." "To women, on the other hand," Horatio continued, "how interesting the topic!" He enumerated the various bearings of the essay on women's discretion, conscience, moral character, peace of mind, sanity, domestic happiness, and self-respect. He described "the frightful extent of the evil that exists in our homes," noted that both the community and medical profession bore responsibility for this, and presented his plan for showing in the essay that induced abortions were "a crime against life, the child being always alive," as well as crimes against the mother, nature, public interest, and morality. Horatio then noted that even if one disregarded the ethical aspects of induced abortions, "they are so dangerous to the woman's health, her own physical and domestic best interests, that their induction, permittal, or solicitation by one cognizant of their true character, should almost be looked upon as proof of actual insanity."[19]

Horatio then provided a historical account of the medical profession's long silence on abortion; the efforts of Hodge and two Storers to break that silence; the American Medical Association's outstanding performance after being enlisted in the campaign; and the fine support to the campaign provided by medical journalists and medical text book writers. He decried the incorrect popular belief that reputable physicians ever performed abortions for reasons other than to save the mother, but did admit that physicians had sometimes appeared to devalue human life when the child at birth was destroyed for the sake of saving the mother, and in cases where abortions were inappropriately performed by physicians to remedy otherwise treatable conditions such as excessive vomiting. He indicated that no abortion should ever be performed by a physician without concurrence of a second physician. He then showed the need for laws making this a requirement:

> How much more requisite is it that in the question we are now considering, to one mode of deciding which the physician may be prompted by pity, by personal sympathy, the entreaties of a favorite patient, and not seldom by the direct offer of comparatively enormous pecuniary compensation, the law should offer him its protecting shield, saving him even from himself, and helping him to see that the fee for an unnecessarily induced or allowed abortion is in reality the price of blood.

The next section of the Prize Essay discussed inappropriate intentional abortions. "Physicians have now arrived at the unanimous opinion," he wrote, "that the foetus in utero is *alive* from the very moment of conception." This was followed by the quotes from Percival and *Man Transformed* which he had incorporated in his earlier articles and reports. "The law, whose judgments are arrived at so deliberately, and usually so safely, has come to the same conclusion," he continued, "and though in some of its decisions it has lost sight of this fundamental truth, it has averred, in most pithy and empathic language, that 'quick with child, is having conceived.'" "By that higher than human law, which, though scoffed at by many a tongue, is yet acknowledged by every conscience," Horatio continued, then quoted himself, "'the wilful killing of a human being, at any stage of its existence, is murder.'"

Horatio then became a biology teacher, noting that before the egg leaves the ovary and is impregnated "it may perhaps be considered as a part and parcel of herself, but not afterwards." He compared the temporary attachment of the fertilized egg to the womb to the attachment of the born child to the breast, throwing in the interesting and somewhat intermediate case of the tiny kangaroo fetus "born into the world at an extremely early stage of development" and placed by its mother in the external pouch to spend weeks attached to a teat therein before "in reality to be born." He continued: "Many women suppose that the child is not alive till quickening has occurred, others that it is practically dead till it has breathed. As well one of these suppositions as the other; they are both of them erroneous."

Quickening was discussed with the major point that it is but a sensation of the mother and that movement of the fetus occurs much earlier. "These motions must be allowed to prove life," Horatio continued, "and independent life." He then asked: "In what does this life really differ from that of the child five minutes in the world?" Horatio's own answer is implicit in the following:

> In the majority of instances of forced abortion, the act is committed prior to the usual period of quickening. There are other women, who have confessed to me that they have destroyed their children long after they have felt them leap within their womb. There are others still, whom I have known to wilfully suffocate them during birth, or to prevent the air from reaching them under the bedclothes; and there are others, who have wilfully killed their wholly separated and breathing offspring, by strangling them or drowning them, or throwing them into a noisome vault. Wherein among all these criminals does there in reality exist any difference in guilt?

Although much of this essay was taken verbatim from Horatio's earlier articles written for physicians, the following new paragraph was written for his female audience *and* for physicians:

> I would gladly arrive at, and avow any other conviction than that I have now presented, were it possible in the light of fact and of science, for I know it must carry grief and remorse to many an otherwise innocent bosom. The truth is, that our silence has rendered all of us accessory to the crime, and now that the time has come to strip down the veil, and apply the searching caustic or knife to this foul sore in the body politic, the physician needs courage as well as his patient, and may well overflow with regretful sympathy.

Horatio next discussed "The Inherent Dangers of Abortion to a Woman's Health and to her Life." Much of the material was taken from the article, "Its Victims," of the *North-American Medico-Chirurgical Review* series, including a direct quote several pages in length. Horatio described the short-term, medium-term, and long-term consequences of induced abortion to women's health, including the very real possibility of death which he claimed was much more frequent than believed, due to misdiagnosis and to concealment of the source of death of many women who died following induced abortions. The non-fatal problems were judged due to premature interruption of the numerous preparations of the woman's body for birth and nursing, to incomplete abortion, and to damage of tissues during invasion of the womb. Horatio then noted that should the woman avoid physical impairment, there still was the potential mental problem:[20]

> Add to this that even though the occurrence of any such feeling may be denied, there is probably always a certain measure of compunction for the deed in the woman's heart—a touch of pity for the little being about to be sacrificed—a trace of regret for the child that, if born, would have proved so dear—a trace of shame at casting from her the pledge of a husband's or lover's affection—a trace of remorse for what she knows to be a wrong, no matter to what small extent, or how justifiable it may seem to herself, and we have an explanation of the additional element in these intentional abortions, which increases the evil effect upon the mother, not as regards her bodily health alone, but in some sad cases to the extent even of utterly overthrowing her reason.

As in the 1859 article, Horatio strongly emphasized the long-term physical health problems caused by the abortion even when it was followed by no immediate consequences. Uterine displacements, he indicated, were particularly likely following abortion and he cited a host of symptoms which could occur as a result. He concluded the section by pointing out the increased vulnerability of the woman undergoing a forced abortion to health problems at menopause.

Horatio's next section was "The Frequency of Forced Abortions, even among the Married." Horatio summarized the statistics that comprised much of his earliest writing on abortion. He noted the sharp differences in abortion rates between Protestant and Catholic women, probably hoping to utilize the anti-Catholic sentiment of his primarily Protestant women readers and induce them thereby to bear their children to prevent the population from becoming increasingly Catholic. He discussed his belief that abortion was more frequent among the married, and indicated that one reason was that the married woman was more apt to recognize a pregnancy at the early stage when most abortions took place. Horatio also wrote that he believed the frequency of abortion was still increasing, which seems somewhat contradictory to his earlier claim that the medical profession was taking strong steps to arrest it. It may have been just an excuse to provide the following strict admonition taken largely from his earlier writing for a physician audience:

> But not only is abortion of excessively frequent occurrence; the nefarious practice is yearly extending, as does every vice that custom and habit have rendered familiar. It is foolish to trust that a change for the better may be spontaneously effected. "Longer silence and waiting by the profession would be criminal. If these wretched women, these married, lawful mothers, ay, and these Christian husbands, are thus murdering their children by thousands, through

ignorance, they must be taught the truth; but if, as there is reason to believe is too often the case, they have been influenced to do so by fashion, extravagance of living, or lust, no language of condemnation can be too strong."

Next was "The Excuses and Pretexts that are given for the Act." This dealt with matters of ignorance, ill health, fear of childbed, and effects on living children, using many of the same paragraphs of Horatio's earlier article, "Its Frequency, and the Causes Thereof." The final section was "Alternatives, Public and Private, and Measures of Relief." The initial paragraph dealt with women's "most valid excuse for the crime." This was the effect of the state of gestation on the woman's mind, and Horatio put in a plug for "the authority I have so freely drawn from," who, he claimed, also had provided the most thorough investigation of such gestation-mind effects. This factor made the woman "liable to thoughts, convictions even, that at other times she would turn from in disgust or dismay ..." It will be recalled that Horatio had earlier cited this as the reason that women committing murder during pregnancy or shortly thereafter should not be executed. Its inclusion in the Prize Essay perhaps reflected Horatio's hope that by telling women that such thoughts and convictions during pregnancy were crazy, the pregnant woman would somehow not continue to hold them or at least would not act on them. On the other hand, he may have realized the futility of this and was talking to relatives or friends who might dissuade or otherwise prevent the more-or-less temporarily insane woman from exercising her conviction to abort.

Horatio asked, "Is there no alternative but for women, when married and prone to conception to occasionally bear children?" His answer was that this was certainly in their best interests "for length of days and immunity from disease." He indicated that both prevention of pregnancy by artificial means and termination of pregnancy were "disastrous to a woman's mental, moral, and physical well-being."

Horatio again indicated the need for foundling hospitals, as he had done in November 1859. Not only would this prevent infanticide and abortion by the unwed mother, "they would save her from one element of the self-condemnation and hatred which so often hurries the victim of seduction downward to the life of the brothel." Horatio continued:

But for the married, who have not this strong stimulus of necessity, and the excuse of having been led astray or deceived, there need be no public channel provided, through which to purchase safety for their children. Is it not, indeed, inconceivable that the very women who, when their darlings of a month old or a year are snatched from them by disease, find the parting attended with so acute a pang, can so deliberately provide for and congratulate themselves, and each other, upon a willful abortion? Here words fail us.

This was the cue for Horatio to quote his "Of the mother, ... we leave those to speak who can" statement, which had ended the first article of his 1859 series on criminal abortion. Instead of stopping with this powerful ending, Horatio continued with a final section where he included a series of quotes from his earlier work and elsewhere which, to some extent, recapitulated what had been presented in the essay. He also mentioned his strong interest in "the great territories of the far West," and asked "shall it be filled by our own children or by those of aliens?" "Aliens" were the recent immigrants who were not restricting their families by contraception or abortion. "This is a question that our own women must answer," Horatio continued; "upon their loins depends the future destiny of the nation."

In conclusion, Horatio wrote:

> In the hope that the present appeal may do somewhat to stem the tide of fashion and depraved public opinion; that it may tend to persuade our women that forced abortions are alike unchristian, immoral, and physically detrimental; that it may dissipate the ignorance concerning the existence of foetal life that so extensively prevails, and be the means of promoting the ratio of increase of our national population, so unnaturally kept down, the National Medical Association addresses itself to all American mothers; for thus, in the closing words of the essay from which I have so frequently and so freely drawn, would "the profession again be true to its mighty and responsible office of shutting the great gates of human death."

One of the last pieces of business of the Boston meeting of the American Medical Association was a request for the Committee on Publication, of which Horatio was a member, "to adopt such appropriate measures as will insure a speedy and general circulation of the Prize Essay on Abortion, provided this can be done without expense to the Association."[21] This seemingly contradictory request to do something in a hurry without spending any money was the authorization of Horatio to publish the Prize Essay himself. The controversial title Horatio selected for this publication was *Why Not? A Book for Every Woman*. The title gave no indication of the topic of the book, and a reader who did learn from some source that the topic was induced abortion, might expect from the question, "Why Not?", a justification rather than a proscription of induced abortion. Perhaps Horatio was hoping to attract as readers women seeking justification to end an unwanted pregnancy, expecting that his book would convince them to have the child instead.

If the long paper on female insanity and the popular essay on criminal abortion were not enough, Horatio also presented a minority report at the Boston meeting as a member of the Committee on Medical Specialism. Committee Chairman Dr. Julius Homberger, of New York, presented a Committee report "signed only by himself." Horatio afterwards read his minority report. The minutes indicate both reports were "laid on the table."[22] The minutes continued: "Drs. W. Hooker, of Connecticut, and T. C. Brinsmade of New York, of the same Committee, reported that the Committee had never been called together, and that they had not seen either report, until at so recent a date as to allow no time for consideration." The fact that Horatio, unlike his fellow committee members, had time not only for "consideration" of Dr. Homberger's report, but time to prepare a substantial minority report in response to it, certainly shows the remarkable industry of Horatio and may not reflect at all on Drs. Hooker and Brinsmade.

The *Boston Medical and Surgical Journal* made reference to the "conceited and arrogant assumptions" in these 1865 reports a year later, when discussing the 1866 reports by Homberger and Bowditch of the Committee on Medical Ethics to which the subject had been referred.[23] What were the "conceited and arrogant assumptions" presented by Horatio in Boston? His paper was entitled "Specialism and Especialism; Their Respective Relations to the Profession," and was published five years later in the *Journal of the Gynaecological Society of Boston*.[24] Horatio began:

> The undersigned, a member of the Committee upon Specialists, and their relations to the medical Profession, has found himself unable to sign the report presented by its chairman. From the position, however, that he himself occupies, not merely as a specialist, but as one of the only two practitioners[25] in this country, so far as he is aware, in regular standing in the profession, who are as yet wholly devoted to the treatment of the diseases of women,—a specialist claiming for a branch hitherto supposed the peculiar province of charlatans, its practical recognition as a legitimate field of labor,—he cannot consistently by silence allow it to be inferred either that he endorses entirely the report referred to, or that he will acknowledge his own course, in assuming the position of a specialist in the profession, to have been unwise or improper.

In other words, by not signing Homberger's Report and by not providing a minority report, there was the danger that it would be assumed that he was opposed to specialism itself, instead of opposed to the claim by Homberger that specialists were better off *without* a thorough knowledge of general practice and somewhat opposed to another Homberger claim that the specialist had the right to advertise their practice in non-medical journals.

The first thing that Horatio did in his minority report was to refer to the propositions of Dr. Homberger, to which "assent must be freely rendered by every philosophical or impartial mind." These were that a specialist is more likely to successfully treat his class of diseases and to make medical advances for these diseases than the general practitioner; that the competent specialist is a benefit to the community and profession and thus deserves respect; and that great success requires that the specialist practice in a large city that serves "extensive tracts of country." Great success also required that he be widely known, and Horatio would grant any means to the specialist, whose prime motive was financial, to "present himself in a business way to the community, if he can bring his mind solely to view his labors as a matter of mere barter and sale ..."

Horatio provided the following reflection about motivation of the specialist, which recalls the words from *Henry V* which Horatio had declaimed in 1848:

> But there is a higher gain than that of lucre, and one of the labor for which no honorable man need be ashamed. To attain fame and earthly honor is no mean ambition; to strive worthily to fill the highest niche, faithfully to work the largest field, first or most safely to carry, by some new suggestion or some method of practice developed to its fullest extent, the boon of life to the largest number, or to generations yet unborn, is a higher aspiration still, beyond which man can hardly soar. Can the profession, if this be in reality the end for which means otherwise in questionable taste are employed, consistently strive to prevent it?[26]

If this did not smack of "conceited and arrogant assumptions" to the conservative general practitioners of Boston and the editors of the *Boston Medical and Surgical Journal*, his following comment surely did:

> The question of the influence of specialists upon the profession is also one that irrevocable time has taken from our hands. Many of the most active medical scientists of the present day, of the most authoritative teachers, whether as lecturers or writers, are from the class that would formerly have been stigmatized as men of one idea, who, catching a glimpse of new truth in its mazy labyrinth, have patiently pursued it to its ultimate retreat, and there overtaken have compelled it to an unconditional surrender, alike to the honor of the individual and of the profession at large. Is it asking too much to claim for such men that they are in reality the leaders of the profession, and that the mass of general practitioners, however excellently they may have assimilated to themselves the results of all past research, are but in reality the rank and file?

Horatio not only downplayed the importance for medical advancement of the general practitioner, he claimed that the specialist with a "thorough knowledge of general principles, gained by participation, for a longer or shorter period, in the manifold cares, duties, and labors of general medical and surgical practice" was "in fact the best general practitioner." In a later paper, Horatio was to note that this "assertion was derided by some and considered presumptuous by others," but that the famous physiologist, Brown-Séquard, made this same point at the next year's meeting of the American Medical Association in Baltimore "in almost the same identical language," and this "was applauded to the echo." In a comment which sounded much like his college friend, Hermann Jackson Warner, Horatio added, "Thus the world moves."[27]

"The belief that a thorough knowledge of general practice is unnecessary for a skilled specialist we consider an erroneous one," Horatio continued in his Minority Report, "and that this is in reality the weak point of our colleague's report." Horatio discussed his own years of general-practice "probation" and indicated that it was the "imperative necessity of relinquishing all night work" which caused him to give up general practice. On the other hand, Horatio acknowledged that in some specialties many "step at once from the schools into full and successful practice, [and] we must yet confess that it is possible ..." Ophthalmology was singled out as producing "instances in this city, as doubtless in many others, to which we may all refer with pride." One suspects that his "chum," Gus Hay, now ophthalmologist, Dr. Gustavus Hay, was on Horatio's mind as this was written.

Horatio pointed out the difference between specialists and those for whom he coined the term "especialists." He reserved specialist for one like himself solely devoted to his specialty. The especialist was the general practitioner who maintained his general practice while also devoting time to a specialty. He pointed out that the general practitioner had much more to fear from the especialist who might appropriate the general practitioner's patients as well as providing special treatment to them. As he would note in future discussions, the general practitioner who sent a woman to an "especialist" in obstetrics for delivery of her baby might find the woman later chose that same physician to provide the new child a smallpox vaccination. In effect, the general practitioner might never see his patient again.

Horatio discussed the increasing numbers of specialists and their "right to legitimate recognition." He also provided advice to physicians considering specialization and noted special problems faced by the specialist in gynecology:[28]

> Here, as elsewhere, success is not for the faint of heart. Whatever a man is minded to do, if to this he devotes his life, with sincerity, persistency, and true moral courage, he is sure, with whatever measure of external success, at least one priceless treasure,—the approval of his own conscience.
>
> He is sure, besides, of the support of the profession. These are personal matters, affecting every one of us in smaller or greater degree; and in the discussion of a question so important, personal testimony is neither irrelevant, conceited, or invidious. For one, I can only say that the bulk of my own practice comes to me directly

from medical men; it has always been so, and with each year I have the greater reason to be thankful that in this respect I had not misunderstood the signs of the times, and this in a department which even yet the profession are perhaps least inclined of all to acknowledge as legitimate. It is with private practices as with special hospitals,—if well conducted they will be recognized and supported by the profession at large.

Finally, Horatio made a plea to permanently table the issue. "Thus quietly and practically would be conceded," he concluded, "what every specialist will otherwise be sure to claim as his right, that each is free to exercise that taste in pursuing his own professional course which will mark him as being, or not, devoted to his noble work through higher than personal motives, a man of honor and a gentleman."

Horatio must have been disappointed that his Minority Report was not published in the *Transactions* of the Association. Such disappointment was justified. It was cogent in its arguments for proper recognition of the specialist, tempered in its criticism of the Chairman's desire for open advertising by physicians, and wise in its recommendations to the association for permanently tabling the matter. It certainly was the best of the three papers Horatio presented at the Boston meeting. Only massive prejudice among Boston general practitioners against specialists and gynecology, and personally against Horatio,[29] plus, of course, a reluctance to be relegated to the "rank and file," could have colored their judgments that it displayed "conceited and arrogant assumptions."

Years later, in 1883, the Medical Superintendents of American Institutions for the Insane met in Newport where Horatio lived. Horatio helped host their meeting and attended their sessions. He spoke of his 1865 paper and described the distinction he had made between the specialist and the especialist. He noted that his father was present at the 1865 session and indicated the following incident had occurred:[30]

> In submitting this view of the subject at the general session of the National Association, I came, unexpectedly, though pleasantly, in contact with my own father, who was present at the meeting. He quickly rose and said, "I do not wish the gentleman to use any such terms, at least as applied to myself; if he does, I declare that I am a general practitioner, and will never become a specialist; I will go against the whole system and will remain only a general practitioner."
> It gave rise to some laughter. This was many years ago.

David Humphreys Storer probably was indicating that he would "never become an *especialist*" who would steal the patients of general practitioners.

Still another piece of American Medical Association business at the Boston meeting directly affected Horatio. He was appointed delegate to attend the upcoming meeting of the Association of Medical Superintendents of Insane Asylums. One of his duties was "to urge upon that Association the advantage, for all purposes of science, of a more intimate union with this Association."

Following this memorable Boston American Medical Association meeting, Horatio apparently took at least a partial vacation. He wrote Dr. Zakrzewska, head of the Women's Hospital: "During July and August, I shall be able to visit the Hospital only on Saturdays. During my absence, I wish Dr. Tyng, in accordance with her duties as assistant surgeon, to take my place as concerns both the Dispensary and the Surgical Wards. Of course operations of any magnitude will be reserved until the days of my attendance."[31] Dr. Anita E. Tyng (ca.1840-1913) was a graduate of the Women's Medical College of Pennsylvania and in 1864 or 1865 became Storer's assistant in his private practice and also at the New England Hospital for Women. She was to remain a lifelong friend of Dr. Storer, and was described by Horatio as an exception when he publicly criticized women physicians in his 1866 letter of resignation from the Hospital for Women. Dr. Tyng was "obliged to resign her position" at the hospital a few years after Horatio left. As we will see, the reason may have been because she continued to associate in some capacity with Horatio.

On September 23, 1865, Horatio successfully performed an operation for the removal of a uterus and ovaries. His case was only the sixth successful hysterectomy out of a world-wide total of twenty-four such operations. The unmarried forty-seven-year-old patient, a Miss Colcord, was sent to him by Dr. John L. Sullivan, of Malden, Massachusetts.[32] The report of the hysterectomy was published in the *American Journal of the Medical Sciences* in January 1866.[33]

"Miss C. is now larger than a woman at the full term with twins," Horatio noted at the time of her first examination, "walks with difficulty, cannot lie down without dyspnoea, is emaciated, very anxious about herself, and desires relief." Although not certain as to the exact nature of the unusual tumor, Horatio admitted her to his "private hospital in Boylston Place." A consultation with his father led to the decision to keep her under observation and prepare her for possible surgery. "After mature reflection," Horatio continued, "I decided to operate, being persuaded that the tumour, whatever its nature, would, unremoved, eventually destroy the patient." Horatio continued, "I can only say that I expected to find, as I did find, my case very unlike any that I had ever seen before, and that I never for a moment entertained the thought of not completing the operation after the first incision had been made."

The patient was to change her mind about surgery. Horatio wrote:

as the day of trial approached, her courage entirely failed, and I was compelled, as I consider it is often our duty in desperate cases to do, to take the sole responsibility of advising the operation and carrying it into effect; herein differing from many of the profession, who make their only standard of necessity the request or the supplications of the patient. ... In my patient's unbounded gratitude, now that she has been saved from the fate that had been impending, I find my sufficient excuse and my reward.

Horatio started the incision from just below the umbilicus and continued downward for five inches. The exposed tumor was found to almost completely fill the abdomen and after severing adhesions and making wire ligations of large vessels which fed the tumor, he determined that the abdominal mass was "continuous with another also of large size, and of very irregular outline, completely filling the cavity of the pelvis." The great weight of the mass, later determined to be thirty-seven pounds and more than twice as heavy as any previously removed, prevented severing of the pelvic portion from the vaginal septum. For this reason the abdominal mass first was separated from the pelvic portion using the ecraseur, a loop of wire (or chain) that was tightened around the tissues or organ and cut through them. The incision was then increased slightly to allow removal of the severed abdominal portion. The pelvic mass then "was lifted up with great difficulty sufficiently to allow a clamp to be passed beneath it; this protected the vaginal septum from being opened, the broadened cervix was after much taxis got wholly within its grasp, and the instrument fastened tightly." The pelvic mass then was severed with the ecraseur and also removed. "Oozing from the extensive surface of the adhesions" repeatedly filled the cavity with blood. This was corrected by exposure of the cavity to the air for an extended period before closing the incision. "Theoretically, this course should have killed the patient," Horatio wrote; "practically she had never a bad symptom."

The healing and recovery of Miss Colcord proceeded rapidly. "Upon the third day," Horatio continued, "it was evident that adhesion of the lips of the abdominal wound had completely taken place; there had never been any gaping of it from the very beginning; on the tenth day the wires were untwisted, and on the thirteenth and fourteenth they were removed." The patient begged to sit up on the fifth day after surgery, was finally allowed to do so on the twenty-first, was out of bed on the twenty-eighth, and went home on the thirty-seventh. Ten days later, Horatio visited her "and found her perfectly well."

Horatio reported that, although for eighteen days after the operation "there was no discharge whatever from the vagina," at the normal time for the patient's period there occurred "a sanguinous effusion, attended by feelings of lassitude, backache, etc., lasting thirty hours, and being an evident attempt at the re-establishment of menstruation; a very curious circumstance, and of great physiological interest, when it is recollected that the uterus and both ovaries had been removed." This was not repeated, however, at the time for her next period.[34]

Horatio's pathologist friend, Calvin Ellis, examined the tumor and provided a description which Horatio included in the article. In brief, the removed mass consisted of some forty tumors of various sizes congregated closely with a large part of the uterus, the ovaries, Fallopian tubes, etc., and so deforming the uterus "as to render it unrecognizable except by its appendages." Horatio donated the specimen to the Harvard Medical College's anatomical museum. Professor J.B.S. Jackson, Curator of the museum, exhibited it at the Suffolk District Medical Society a week after the operation and demonstrated "its character and relations." Horatio himself described the details of his operation at the same meeting.

Horatio pointed out that although there had been only six successful cases, these were from the more recent operations and he criticized the recommendations of many surgeons that this operation was too dangerous to be performed. Horatio also provided advice on preventing the three conditions most likely to produce a fatal result, namely shock, hemorrhage, and inflammation. "In conclusion," wrote Horatio, "I shall best serve my friends in this department of practice if I now express my creed, as to abdominal sections, in a few succinct general formulae." These were:

1. Almost all ovarian tumours, a far greater majority than has been generally supposed, may be safely removed by abdominal section.

2. A certain proportion, as yet not ascertained, of uterine tumors, fibroid or fibro-cystic, may be safely removed in a similar manner.

3. A large proportion of the fatal instances of either operation referred to, may be traced to neglect of simple precautions, prophylactic, immediate or subsequent.

4. Others still, to the fact that the patient was allowed to linger without assistance, till she was already practically moribund, before the commencement of the operation; and

5. Still others, that the surgeon's heart failed him after the abdomen had been opened, and the operation was not completed.

In *bona fide* conclusion, Horatio provided the following quote from West's *Diseases of Women*:

"Your duty and mine," says West, "is not to sit down in apathetic indifference, doing nothing, trying nothing, for a patient's cure, because her disease is one which hitherto has proved almost invariably mortal; but rather, patiently, carefully, with much mistrust of our own powers, much watchful scrutiny of our own motives, to apply ourselves to the trial of every means by which suffering may be mitigated or life prolonged. To this our common humanity prompts, our obligations as medical men compel us. It is to misinterpret both very grievously, if we not merely content ourselves with doing nothing, but take shelter under noisy censure of the conduct and uncharitable construction of the motives of those who read their duty differently."

Regrettably for Horatio's professional dreams, some of the most powerful "do-nothing"-"try-nothing" physicians and surgeons of Boston were to take the latter "uncharitable construction of the motives" course with respect to Horatio's pioneering surgery. Horatio was even to report that shortly after his successful hysterectomy "a prominent hospital surgeon had expressed his regret that this patient had recovered."[35] Dr. Henry J. Bigelow is the likely candidate. On the other hand, Horatio's hysterectomy report was quickly read by Dr. William Mayo of Rochester, Minnesota who wrote Horatio for advice related to a patient of his own with an abdominal mass.[36] (Dr. Mayo's physician sons started the Mayo Clinic.)

Much credit for the survival of Miss Colcord after hysterectomy belonged to Horatio's assistant, Dr. Anita Tyng. Dr. Tyng was a friend of the prominent Caroline Dall of Boston and, some years after the hysterectomy, Mrs. Dall recorded in her diary the following about the Tyng-Storer-Colcord relationship:[37]

> Dr. Storer's objection to *monthly period.* She [Dr. Tyng] asked him if she could perform operations in ovariotomy. He said yes, but he would advise her not to do it at her *monthly period.* Now in Miss Colcord's case, Anita took charge next to himself, watched, supplied the instruments, etc., took the first watch of fifteen hours, administering ice and drugs every five minutes, wrote the notes, and afterwards wrote out the whole report of the case, in the very climax of the menstrual period, and yet he told her that he owed his success in that case to her care. He left her in charge for three weeks half of every night and half of every day, Miss Chafee a nurse of her own training, taking the alternate periods. Dr. Storer then went to Berkshire and left her with the whole care of the case. During this period Miss Colcord had the menstrual discharge of which so much has been said. Anita took all the observations, made the microscopic examinations, wrote all the notes of the case and copied out the Reports as published. Dr. Storer never saw the discharge, and owes all he knows of it to her report. During this time also she was the Resident Physician of his special Hospital.

These Dall references to Anita Tyng in her diary between May 16 and June 14, 1870 while visiting Rhode Island included another passage which supports Horatio's claims to the high frequency of abortion and probably also his belief that female physicians were frequently involved in producing them. Dall wrote: "[Dr. Tyng] Had to stave off applications for abortions, many in Boston from the middle class." There apparently was an expectation in expectant mothers that a female physician would perform abortions and hence Dr. Tyng's need "to stave off" such requests. Her refusals suggest that Anita Tyng was as opposed to abortion as were many regular male physicians, perhaps as opposed as Horatio.

Dall's "Dr. Storer then went to Berkshire" reflects the fact that Horatio accepted the appointment of Professor of Obstetrics and the Diseases of Women at the Berkshire Medical College. Horatio listed his various affiliations in a paper published in the Fall of 1865 and included both: "Assistant in Obstetrics and Medical Jurisprudence in Harvard University and Professor of Obstetrics and the Diseases of Women in Berkshire Medical College."[38] There was little overlap between the Berkshire and Harvard terms and thus there was no "temporal" conflict in holding both positions.

The Berkshire Medical College was located in Pittsfield in the western part of Massachusetts. It had been producing medical school graduates for more than forty years, but because railroads had made attendance less difficult at medical schools in large cities with much greater opportunities for clinical instruction, its numbers of students had declined sharply by 1865. The school was to close its doors before the end of the decade.[39] Horatio described his Berkshire post in his 1901 letter to Malcolm:[40]

> When called to Pittsfield, I was asked by Dr. Holmes,[41] acting as he said for the Faculty, not to go, as it would jeopardize my chance of the Harvard professorship, and yet he, I believe, had lectured there or at Dartmouth. At Pittsfield, I gave courses of sixty lectures on gynaecology, which, so far as I know, had never been attempted at all here before, with shorter courses on Midwifery and Med Jurisprudence as there were good textbooks for these.

The 1901 letter also discussed Horatio's post-graduate teaching of gynecology to physicians and this included: "I had previously had vaginal and rectal expositions at my Pittsfield lectures, and this also seems not to have been attempted before,—Prof. James P. White of Buffalo having merely shown cases of labor in his lecture room, and been incontinently condemned therefor." One can imagine there also was considerable controversy when Horatio brought "vaginal and rectal expositions" into the classroom.

Horatio provided his most complete account of his Berkshire experience, including the school's relationships to the nearby Albany Medical College and the distant Harvard Medical School, in a later discussion of the Albany physician, Alden March:[42]

> Eventually, upon my accepting a chair at the then Berkshire Medical College at Pittsfield, the acquaintance [with Dr. Alden March of Albany] became more intimate. In those days there was some professional jealousy between Western and Eastern Massachusetts, or,

rather, between Albany and Boston. The Harvard School and the Massachusetts General Hospital, to a great degree identical, very naturally sought to dominate New England, as has now occurred. Western Massachusetts as naturally resented this, and was long able to postpone its realization through the very influential and extremely militant president of the Pittsfield School, the late Dr. H. H. Childs. Far from jealousy of this college, that at Albany was its champion. They were allies, through self-interest, against Boston. As a subordinate teacher in the Harvard School, I was greatly blamed for joining my then minor influence with that of its adversary. The Pittsfield students were, however, of admirable material, mostly farmers' sons with their living to earn, not a dude among them.

Horatio published a paper, "A Medico-legal Study of Rape," in the *New York Medical Journal* for November 1865. He began by noting that rape was a subject upon which "much conflict of opinion has arisen, both upon abstract points and the circumstances of individual cases; it is also one of those happily rare questions where the sympathies of a jury are apt to be found instinctively tending against the prisoner." He indicated that large changes in thinking and the law on rape had occurred over the years. As a result, "the literature and the law of rape have alike become effete and need careful revision." Despite this general need, Horatio's particular stimulus for the paper was a case "where four young men have been sentenced *to the State-prison for life* for compelling intercourse from a notorious strumpet, and their so severe punishment, apparently indorsed by the entire community, warrants my examining into details that, though repulsive in themselves, are of value as establishing upon a firmer basis the rights of a woman to her chastity, however infinitesimally small this may be."[43] Horatio noted that cases of rape were on the increase and attributed this to the return of former Civil War soldiers "whose blood has been heated by a Southern sun and by long privations." One reason Horatio gave for examining the subject was so the accused rapist "may not come to harm greater than he in reality deserves." Another was that "those exerting themselves in the interests of justice may wield a sharper sword."

After reviewing various legal definitions of rape, most requiring violence or artifice and destruction of the woman's "chastity," Horatio provided the simpler definition: "Carnal knowledge *without* or *against* consent." Horatio then discussed legal interpretations of carnal knowledge and dismissed former requirements for semen in the vagina, evidence of penetration sufficient to rupture the hymen, etc., and then recommended relaxation of this to partial penetration or even just "reciprocal contact of the generative organs of the two parties."

The term "*without* consent" applied to "children of tender age, insane persons, and idiots." It also applied to those in natural or drug-induced "deep sleep" or those who had fainted prior to the intercourse. *Against* consent required examination of each individual case's circumstances. "The chance of wrongful allegation," Horatio continued, "is so great that these circumstances can not be too closely scrutinized, by the parties on both sides having the case in charge." Horatio reminded lawyers and medical experts that presumption of innocence required the presumption "that rape was not committed, and that if intercourse were effected, it was with the full consent of the female."

Horatio discussed various proofs that reciprocal genital contact had occurred and the problems associated with the reliability of each. Semen, blood stains, and marks of violence could come from non-rape sources. The hymen sometimes did not exist in women or had been ruptured by earlier non-rape activities. Impregnation was irrelevant as a defense, although once considered evidence that the woman had cooperated in the intercourse, since it was believed that "fright, disgust and aversion" would prevent conception. Matching venereal disease in accused and victim was strong evidence, but venereal lesions on the genitals, even of children, could come from non-rape sources. On the other hand, absence of transmission of a rapist's venereal disease to the victim was not a defense.

"Carnal knowledge having been effected," Horatio concluded, "was it without or against the consent of the woman?" He promised evidence for and against this second criterion for rape in a forthcoming article. However, "forthcoming" would be more than two years afterwards when he published a paper, "The Law of Rape."[44] He returned to the subject which "more pressing duties" had delayed, after a physician who impregnated a woman patient was freed on appeal by the Supreme Court of New York of an earlier charge of rape. Horatio argued convincingly that the woman, despite observing what she was reluctantly allowing to take place, was not consenting to sexual intercourse, since she had been convinced that she was being treated for a disease of her womb. In fact, it was only the resultant pregnancy that led her to recognize that something was involved other than therapy and that something criminal was involved.

The major thrust of the new paper was that consent obtained by fraud was not consent. He again discussed the impossibility of consent of the insane and idiot and of the person under anesthesia, narcotics, or deep sleep. As to the physician who impregnated his patient, Horatio noted that some in the medical profession might welcome his successful appeal of the charge of rape. Horatio, on the other hand, claimed "it becomes our duty, through the channels of the medical press, and of the National Association, to protest against the decision of the Supreme Court of New York, and to call upon the profession to repudiate it."[45]

CHAPTER 10

QUARREL WITH ELLIS, WOMEN'S HOSPITAL RESIGNATION, *A BOOK FOR EVERY WOMAN*

Horatio performed major surgery on a woman with an umbilical hernia on February 4, 1866 and described the operation at the Suffolk District Medical Society later that month. The report of the case, "A New Operation for Umbilical Hernia," was published in the *New York Medical Record* on April 9, 1866.[1] "The method pursued in the case," Horatio wrote, "is so far as I am aware, a novel one." Horatio's willingness to attempt a new surgical procedure no doubt reflected the fact that he was brimming with confidence in his surgical skills, given that he had just a few months "since" removed the largest tumor in history via an abdominal incision and given that the patient herself was brimming with health.

Horatio's new patient, a forty-one-year-old woman with long-standing liver disease, had developed ascites, i.e, an accumulation of fluid in her abdomen, and had been under Horatio's care since June 1865. "I admitted her to the Woman's Hospital, contrary to my usual custom in other than purely pelvic disease," Horatio wrote, "because there had been some slight menstrual derangement, and I thought that to this, as indicating the approach of the climacteric, might be referred the change, ascitic effusion, that had occurred in the progress of her case." Horatio continued:[2]

> From this time forward the ascitic symptoms became more and more marked. The woman's condition at admission was feeble, so that I did not anticipate she could be kept living more than a few weeks; no less than nine months, however, elapsed before her death. Towards the close of this period, the effusion of fluid was so rapid that it became necessary to tap her twice a week; the amount removed varying from two to three gallons, according as she was able to bear more or less upward pressure upon the diaphragm, and the dyspnoea that it produced.

The patient persuaded Horatio to make an exploratory incision which she hoped would disclose that the "disease was dependent upon some outgrowth capable of removal." Horatio "long demurred," but on November 21 made an incision "downwards, from just below the umbilicus, and of a length freely to admit the index and middle fingers." The abdominal cavity was found "free from outgrowth of any kind," the ovaries normal, the uterus slightly enlarged, the liver atrophied, "and the gall-bladder distended and tense." The wound healed quickly and the patient seemed improved, but there was no change in the ascites. Early in 1866, Horatio noted that the umbilicus "had been gradually becoming more and more patulous until it was, when distended, but little more than a thin membrane, partially, however, regaining its contractility whenever, by tapping, the pressure from within was withdrawn." To prevent rupture, Horatio increased the frequency of tapping. The distended umbilicus also became "very painful to the patient."

The following extensive report of the surgery and demise of the patient is provided, since this operation was criticized by Horatio's "friends," and the controversial exchange of criticism became a key factor in Horatio's leaving his position of "Assistant in Obstetrics and Medical Jurisprudence" at Harvard. Horatio decided to operate because he felt that rupture of the umbilicus was imminent with extensive laceration leading to "profound discharge" and probable death "by shock," particularly if rupture occurred at night. Horatio described the surgery as follows:[3]

Upon the 4th of February, the patient having been tapped for the forty-fifth time, she was again etherized, and at 9 a.m. the operation commenced. I had determined to resort to a double incision, of so great a length that, upon bringing the edges of the wound together, there would be no gathering, puckering or wrinkling, as must else have inevitably obtained. I therefore commenced my incisions at a point some three inches below the lower level of the umbilicus, and terminated them at a corresponding point some two and a half inches above the upper edge, their whole length being about seven and a half inches. They were therefore divergent for the first of the spaces named, nearly parallel for two inches, and again convergent till they met.

I worked from below upwards, for convenience sake, since I had determined to prevent, if possible, any the slightest protrusion of intestine; and in this, by the simple expedient of inserting the sutures as fast as the incisions were made, I succeeded perfectly. These sutures were metallic, and twenty-one in number. From the moment they were twisted, not a drop of serum escaped through the wound;
...

The patient rallied perfectly after the operation, requiring but little in the way of direct stimulant, and, as in her former section, she was very shortly put upon small but frequently repeated doses of beef tea and boiled milk and flour. She did as well as could have been desired for twenty-four hours; at the end of this period she received a sudden fright, whose effects were immediately perceptible upon her. She rapidly sank and died at midnight of the 5th, of secondary shock, thirty-eight hours after the operation.

At the autopsy, on the following day, upon removal of the sutures, the wound was found completely united; throughout the greater part of its thickness for its whole extent, considerable traction upon the integument upon each side being unable to open the wound, and at no point of its surface could the smallest probe be passed.

The operation therefore, as an operation, was a success.

Horatio then discussed the criticism he received when he reported the case at the Suffolk District Medical Society on February 24. "Some of my friends then present were, however, of so different an opinion," he wrote, "that I have thought the question of sufficient importance in its scientific aspects, and as establishing a precedent for the future treatment of similar cases, to submit it for decision to the profession at large." He recorded their "strictures" and allowed Ellis, Hodges and Minot to review and revise them before submitting them for publication. These "edited" strictures were:

"Prof. Calvin Ellis thought the operation liable to criticism. It had not been claimed that its performance was undertaken with the hope of curing the patient, nor that, with the single exception of guarding against rupture of the umbilicus, it could have materially prolonged her days, or have done away with the necessity of frequent tapping. Abdominal section was too grave an operation, was attended with too severe immediate risks, to be resorted to for the prevention of a possible accident, the removal of a danger that merely threatened. According to the reporter's own showing, there was reason to believe that there existed no abdominal or pelvic tumor capable of removal, and therefore the first [exploratory] section could hardly have been required.

"Prof. Richard M. Hodges could not see why removal of the umbilicus without opening the peritoneum would not have been an equally efficient operation, and far preferable because less dangerous. It was well known that such a method had been frequently employed in diseases of the umbilicus. As regards the question of securing immediate union of the abdominal wounds, in cases where there had been previous distension, he thought if the patient lived long enough there could be seldom any difficulty in effecting it. This was particularly the case in sections for the removal of ovarian tumors, in which the subsequent laxity of the integuments, the edges of the wound were brought into very close apposition. He had frequently seen immediate union under such circumstances.

"In answer to the inquiry whether such union had been throughout the whole length of the wound, Dr. H. excepted, of course, the points where a pedicle or ligature had been brought through.

"In conversation after the meeting, Dr. Minot, who had presided, expressed the opinion that rather than perform the operation, the umbilicus should have been allowed to rupture; that there would have been very little risk to the patient from this, even had it occurred at night. He would have punctured the distended umbilicus in preference to tapping elsewhere, and allowed the canula to remain in permanently. He did not consider that anything could justify the operation of excision of the umbilicus in such a case."

Horatio discussed each of these criticisms in his paper, handling some better than others. First he pointed out that it would not have been possible to leave the peritoneum intact in this case as Hodges had recommended, because it was so distended that it would under the pressure of the ascitic effusion have expanded and forced open the more superficial wound produced by the lesser procedure. Tapping of the umbilicus would have not worked because the holes produced would not have healed in the "thin and membranous" integument. Attempts to leave the drainage tube had been tried, but had produced so much pain that they had to be withdrawn. As to Minot's recommendation to let rupture of the umbilicus happen, Horatio claimed that all previous medical opinion made this of far too serious consequence to risk.

Ellis' criticism—that there was too little benefit to be gained from the earlier exploratory surgery, since there was little expectation of finding anything requiring removal, and from removal of the umbilicus itself, since it would not prevent the requirement for tapping and since it could only prevent a possible accident—was dealt with in two ways. First Horatio claimed that much careful consideration of gains and losses occurred prior to surgery and that full knowledge of the situation required it. "We must take our patients, ... as we find them," Horatio argued; "we are not to quietly fold our hands and do nothing, merely because their condition is not wholly satisfactorily to us."

Horatio's second way of dealing with Ellis' criticism was related to his own belief that it represented "the imputation" that Horatio and his associates had "been hasty or injudicious" in carrying out the surgery. Horatio thus responded by showing that Ellis' criticism was being cast from a crystalline edifice. "On the 25th of June, 1858," he began, "an examination, to which the term vivisection was at the time applied, was made of a man in the Dead House attached to the Jail in Boston." Horatio then repeated from the report of the Magee autopsy the discussion of the heartbeat that preceded opening of the hanged convict's chest, and the continuing "full and regular motion" of the right auricle after the heart was exposed. Horatio continued:

It is not my intention to refer to any of the medico-legal aspects of this case, though in view of the laws defining criminal responsibility, it will hardly establish a precedent that can safely be followed—nor will I dwell upon the fact that the man thus incised, and incised to death, for exploratory purposes, was a criminal whose end the judicial officers, who alone are justified in committing homicide for legal ends, had failed to accomplish. I need merely say that this *antemortem autopsy* showed most conclusively that all the vital organs of the body had escaped serious injury during the fall from the scaffold, "a small space under the left ear having escaped active compression, so that some circulation might have continued through the carotid and jugular of that side," and that, as was acknowledged by the reporter of the examination, "resuscitation might possibly have been accomplished within half an hour after he fell;" and if at that time, probably also an hour later, at the time of the section. I allude to this case with hesitation, for it reopens a most delicate though important question in medical jurisprudence, that might else remain at rest; but in relieving ourselves from the imputation of having been hasty or injudicious in our conduct, we cannot but recognise the pertinency of collateral illustration.[4]

Although censure of Ellis for performing an autopsy on Magee instead of an attempt at Magee's resuscitation would have been appropriate in 1858, Horatio must have been extremely wounded by Calvin Ellis' criticism of what Horatio viewed as an advance of general surgery to proffer this "low blow" eight years after Ellis' probable mistake. Horatio saw his "excision of the umbilicus by deep incisions" as an important new means for "satisfactorily treating abdominal hernia," and here was Ellis telling him that he should not have done it at all!

Horatio justified his publishing the report of the umbilicus removal in *The Medical Record* instead of a "local journal," on the one hand, because it was a public question requiring a journal with "more than local circulation" and on the other because the *Boston Medical and Surgical Journal* had turned down his response to "*" more than a year earlier and he expected that his new article would be refused as well. Three weeks later, on April 26, 1866, the *Boston Medical and Surgical Journal* indicated that Horatio's expectation of their refusal to publish his paper was well founded. Their editorial included:[5]

The Boston Medical and Surgical Journal has reached its 74th volume; it is one of a very few which survived the war, and was the only weekly in the country which appeared uninterruptedly during that period. It had more than a local circulation then, it has a larger circulation now. We lost no subscribers by closing our pages to a controversy of an unpleasantly personal character, and we certainly should have refused an article in such very bad taste, to use the mildest expression we can think of, and betraying such entire ignorance of the laws of physiology as that published in the *Medical Record*. We would recommend to that journal, which has attained its 4th number, the observance of a similar precaution, if it desires an equally successful existence.

J. Mason Warren's entry in his journal for Saturday, April 28, 1866, included: "Suff dis med soc. Dr. H.R. Storer's attack on Dr. Ellis was referred to a committee. ... "[6] Horatio was absent and would claim at the Society's next meeting that this action in his absence was inappropriate. Horatio's views on the controversy associated with his umbilical hernia operation and his raising of the Magee incident eight years after its occurrence were reported in a June 8 letter to *The Medical Record*. The following excerpt describes the reaction from Boston physicians:[7]

> Immediately upon the appearance of the paper, I became aware that I had touched a loud and long resounding string. Believing that the case in its scientific aspects was a very important one, I was not surprised at the interest immediately evinced in it by those who had never heard of, or had forgotten it. I was astonished, however, in view of my published disclaimer of any personal feeling, that my remarks upon the case should have been considered by any one as a personal attack upon Dr. Ellis, for whom, both as a physician and a gentleman, I have ever had the most profound respect, and whose friendship I have always valued. Finding that my motives were misunderstood by some, or perversely misstated, I endeavored, as soon as might be, to correct the matter, and in case I had really committed an error, to make, as I am always ready to do under such circumstances, the *amende honorable*. It was asserted, both privately and publicly, that I had violated all rules of medical criticism, had misrepresented the facts in the case, and had evinced gross ignorance of the simplest physiological principles. I hardly saw matters in this light, but nevertheless set myself earnestly and soberly to repair any wrong that I might have committed.

The following described Horatio's efforts to "repair any wrong":

> I now offered to state in your pages that there existed doubts in some minds as to the relevance of my citation, the propriety of my exhuming a fact, even though very important in its scientific aspects and legal relations, that on some accounts had better have remained buried in the past, and even the correctness of my physiology, and I offered, moreover, to refer this latter point to the decision of any competent and impartial authority, say to Dr. Brown-Séquard. These offers, however, were declined, and I was told that nothing could suffice save the recantation of my abstract scientific opinion, which of course, being unconvinced of error, I could not give.

"These offers" may have been to Ellis, Hodges, and Minot. As we will see, Horatio was to later describe Hodges and Minot as unwillingly forced into the quarrel, presumably by Ellis. However, it is more likely that Horatio's "offers" were to the superiors of these three at the Harvard Medical School who were in position to determine Horatio's career as a Harvard Medical Professor. By June 8, the controversy involved the senior Harvard medical faculty, including at least "Holmes and Bigelow and Jackson," whom Horatio would mention in the same sentence with Ellis, Hodges, and Minot four years later in an editorial that discussed Horatio's 1866 break with the Harvard Medical School and this quarrel that precipitated it.[8] "Holmes," of course, was Oliver Wendell. "Bigelow" was Henry J., the famous surgeon. "Jackson" was J.B.S., whom Horatio had always gotten along well with. "White" also was mentioned in Horatio's editorial, and this was James Clarke White, lecturer at the Harvard Medical School and one of the two editors of the *Boston Medical and Surgical Journal* in June 1866.

Horatio then described in his published letter the Suffolk District Medical Society meeting of April 27, where, in his absence, his "attack on Dr. Ellis" was discussed and sent to committee:[9]

> Meanwhile, and during my absence at Baltimore as delegate to the American Medical Association, the affair was brought before one of our medical societies, the Suffolk district, isolated extracts were read from my paper in the Record, and a committee appointed to investigate them. At the first meeting of the Society after my return, I stigmatized this unusual procedure as, under the circumstances, alike uncourteous and improper, for it had received charges, by implication, if not direct, against a member, and had undertaken to pass upon them during his absence; the matter in question, my paper in the Record, being one with which, as a society, it had no concern. I therefore simply denied its authority, ignored its committee, refused, as circumstances then were, to give any explanation whatever, and demanded that such action should be taken as justice to myself required. A special meeting of the society was accordingly held, at which the committee appointed for investigation reported that no charges had been made, and that they should render no report. The attempt at pressure thus being withdrawn, I read the entire paper from the Record, and volunteered the explanation that I could not have been forced into making; asserting however, that my opinion of the vivisection was still unchanged.

The "explanation" Horatio "volunteered" probably was the following which he provided two paragraphs later:

> I considered my allusion [to the Magee autopsy] a proper one; for the

official papers that I cited were published, and are therefore the property of the profession, alike for reference and for criticism. I considered it a relevant one, for the gentleman had stated that he considered exploratory sections unwarrantable; he had ventured to sit in judgement upon my own, and it seemed fair to test his decision by his own previous practice. I thought, moreover, that my language, though strong, was yet not inappropriate. I had been told that my operation was unjustifiable. Successful though it had been as an operation, the woman had died; if it were unjustifiable, I had therefore "incised my patient to death."

The minutes of this May 31 Special Meeting of the Suffolk District Medical Society give many fewer details than Horatio's rendition, but they do indicate a large turnout, perhaps four or five times that at meetings prior to and following that on May 31, 1866. The minutes also identify "Drs D.H. Storer, H.R. Storer, Ordway, Johnson, Bowditch, Dix, J.L. Moore, H.G. Clark, Upham, H.J. Bigelow & White" as participants in the "animated discussion." "On motion of Dr. Ordway," continued the Minutes, "the whole matter was indefinitely postponed by a vote of 39 to 30."[10]   The next paragraph of Horatio's published letter read:[11]

Inasmuch as, during the discussion that ensued, the charge of ignorance of physiology in reference to this special topic was distinctly and deliberately repeated by the gentlemen who had previously preferred it against me, the editors of the *Boston Medical and Surgical Journal*, I am compelled to prolong this controversy. For myself, I can only say that I am forced into it against my will, having no leisure just now for such matters, and being anxious to do what I can to restore and to preserve professional harmony. I shall beg you to assist me in keeping the discussion, based as it clearly is, so far as I am concerned, upon difference of opinion as to a scientific point, free from all personalities whatever.

Horatio unwisely continued:

Viewing the matter, however, in the light that some have done, I see that the cases, though analogous, were yet not identical; Dr. Ellis having undoubtedly supposed his subject dead, while I knew that mine was alive, and meant to keep her so if I could, performing the section at her own request. I therefore regret sincerely that I applied the remarks that I did to Dr. Ellis.

Horatio ended his letter with the following comment which must have been perceived as a threat, although "another communication" never appeared:[12]

In another communication, and as a contribution to medical jurisprudence, I may take occasion to discuss the questions: 1st, as to whether it is proper, advisable, or necessary, to ascertain whether criminals are alive or not at the time of their dissection; 2d, as to what constitutes in such cases probable, and what decisive, evidence of the persistence of human life; and 3d, as to whether medical men, if careless or ignorant of physiology, may become *criminally* responsible to the laws of the land. The profession shall then decide as to which of the parties in this controversy—for it will be found to include more than originally entered it—are sound in their physiology, and which have contributed to, or desired to interfere with, the advancement of their science.

It is appropriate to shed as much additional light as possible on this controversy which led to Horatio's resignation or firing from the Harvard Medical School. In Horatio's 1901 letter to Malcolm, he indicated that the squabble with Ellis, Hodges, and Minot was related to Horatio's preceding autonomous behavior as Assistant in Obstetrics and Medical Jurisprudence. He wrote:[13]

my father's chair was eventually to be divided, and I was to have gynaecology as a separate and wholly distinct branch. Meanwhile I was made his assistant, just as Hodges was with H.J. Bigelow, Ellis with J.B.S. Jackson, and Minot with J. Bigelow or John Ware. ... After a while the other assistants began to complain to the Faculty that they heard from the students I was exceeding my powers, and was discoursing upon subjects not contained in the textbooks or in my father's lectures. This was true. I was called upon by the Dean, then Dr. Shattuck, to explain, and I merely stated that as the matters referred to were fully as essential as those that were given, I must be allowed to continue, or else resign. In the same way, after I had taken LL.B. and the law students were permitted to come in from Cambridge to attend my examinations in medical jurisprudence, I gave instruction to the combined class upon those gynaecological questions equally important for doctors and for lawyers, and not referred to in the textbooks. For this I was again reprimanded,—as also for holding the examinations in my father's classroom instead of in the library, which proved too small when the law students came in that the overflow clung to the stairs to H.J. Bigelow's quarters. In both instances I was told that I was acting entirely beyond my duties as assistant. None of the other assistants had such necessities, and they could not endure them in me. As Bowditch said, if I had but waited till both my feet were more firmly in the stirrups, I should not have been thrown,—but I was acting in good faith, and foolishly thought that others were also.

Horatio's self-written sketch of himself for the Carney Hospital Album included:

> An assistant instructor in the Harvard Medical School, he was dropped from his place in 1866, "in order to do penance," the faculty espousing a private quarrel into which he had been forced by three of his fellow-subordinates. This apparent disgrace he accounts the great good fortune of his life, for it couched his blindness as an alumnus of Harvard, to the arrogance, nepotism, and injustice of those claiming to control the profession in eastern New England.[14]

As Editor of the *Journal of the Gynaecological Society of Boston* from 1869 to 1872, Horatio was provided with a forum for further discussion of the subject of his conflict with Ellis and others at the Harvard Medical School. The following from the August 1870 "Editorial Notes" referred first to "discoverer" Ellis, to "antagonist" Horatio, and then to "Rip Van Winkle" Holmes.[15]

> ... where the discoverer of the "oscillatory wave of the subclavian vein," according to Tardieu, the "most curious" suggestion of all medico-legal science,—dictates the expulsion of an antagonist first attacked by himself whose attempt at obtaining a fair hearing he pronounces "a sudden fit of mental aberration;" and whence his own Rip Van Winkle of physiological lore periodically emerges, ... the least egotistic of men, and therefore applying the term with the best of grace to others,—a propounder of "penance" and a doer thereof, ..."

Oliver Wendell Holmes obviously shared Hermann Jackson Warner's view of Horatio as "egotistic."

Unfortunately, attempts to locate perspectives on this controversy from Ellis' and Ellis' defenders' perspective have not been successful. In fairness to the memory of Dr. Calvin Ellis, no physician other than Horatio may have so criticized this outstanding physician, pathologist, and medical educator, except perhaps for a few distant physicians shortly after the Magee autopsy. Ellis' classmate at Harvard, long-serving U.S. Senator George Frisbie Hoar, in Hoar's autobiography,[16] was to rate Ellis as one of the two most distinguished members of their Harvard class, "entitled to hold a greater place than any others in the memory of future generations ..."

Horatio's father presided at the annual meeting of the American Medical Association in Baltimore in May 1866. His Presidential Address was on the subject of specialties, and in many respects it mimicked Horatio's own minority report of the year before. It was a resounding claim for the legitimacy of the specialist and of the key role the specialist played in advancing medical science.[17]

Horatio presented two papers at this meeting. The first was on the clamp shield which he had developed when the need for a stronger clamp was shown during the removal of Miss Colcord's uterus.[18] Horatio first indicated that if it had been available, his new clamp also would have been useful in his second hysterectomy which he performed on March 11, 1866. The "strongest ovarian clamp" had not prevented the ecraseur from pulling and severing tissue from the clamped area. As a result, "both the internal iliac artery and vein of the right side were opened, and very profuse hemorrhage occasioned in consequence." However, this hemorrhage was controlled and the ovarian clamp had prevented what would otherwise have been uncontrollable hemorrhage from the extensive pelvic adhesions of the tumor. "As it was," Horatio continued, "my patient rallied completely from the shock of the operation, and succumbed only to an increase of the previously existing peritonitis, on the third day."[19]

Horatio then went on to describe his new clamp shield, which provided a much stronger clamp on the uterine pedicle and which shielded "tissues beneath and around it from being lacerated." It also served to lift "the uterus, so as to bring as much as possible of the cervix within its grasp," and "lessens the number of ligatures necessary to be subsequently applied." Numerous reports of Horatio's surgery in the future would credit this clamp shield for successful outcomes. However, two months afterward, on July 25, 1866, Horatio reported at the Berkshire District Medical Society, that its first use in extirpation of uterus and ovaries was another instance of a successful operation where the patient died. "The tumor was very vascular," Horatio reported, "and without the clamp shield, so large and so numerous were the vessels it was necessary to divide, I should undoubtedly have lost my patient from primary shock." The patient rallied, "and would probably have recovered had she had a more reliable and competent nurse." Horatio published his Berkshire District Medical Society presentation in the *Medical Record*, and added the following footnote:[20]

> I have also tested the instrument, since the above paper was read, in four cases of ovariotomy, three of them in my own practice, and the other performed by my colleague, Prof. Greene, of Pittsfield, which he will doubtless report in this Journal. In each of these cases the clamp shield was found to be just what was required; in two of them, indeed, the operation could hardly have been completed without it, on account of the shortness of the pedicle and the risk of extensive haemorrhage.

Horatio's second presentation at the Baltimore meeting was his Report as Delegate to the Association of Medical Superintendents of Insane Asylums.[21] Horatio had attended the meeting of the superintendents in Pittsburgh four days after the AMA meeting in Boston in 1865. Horatio reported that he was treated courteously, but the Superintendents rejected the proposal of the American

Medical Association that they meet at the same time and place as the American Medical Association and form "a more intimate union" with the national association "alike for the purposes of science and effectual practice." Horatio decried their unwillingness to conduct their business as part of the national association:

> In all specialties—and the care of the insane is but such—the practitioner has little reason to separate himself from his fellows. He is incompetent for his work unless he has himself been tried in the furnace of general practice; he is unfit for it if he is unwilling to freely communicate with the mass of his profession. Researches merely for the benefit of a limited circle, publications merely for a few selected readers, alike fail of the two great ends that alone should be sought by the true physician—the general edification of his professional brethren, and the general relief of those sick persons whom he professes to wish to cure.

Horatio then described the benefits of such a closer union for the American Medical Association, the profession at large, the insane, the community, and the superintendents. Surprisingly, Horatio said nothing for once about pelvic factors in female insanity. However, Horatio did make a strong case for increased emphasis on medical jurisprudence in medical schools, noting that "of all the cases interesting to medical jurists that enter our civil and criminal courts, those of insanity are the most perplexing." He noted that if medical jurisprudence was not completely ignored in the curriculum of medical schools, it was often appended to some other branch of medicine considered more important. He called attention to Dr. John Odronaux, of New York, who was one of the few "masters alike of medicine and of the law," and whose lectures at two law schools and three medical schools were "almost the only instances in which this science is as yet at all properly taught in the country." "Almost" allowed the other exceptions of his own medical jurisprudence program at Pittsfield and his father's at the Harvard Medical School. Horatio again showed great restraint and did not remind his readers that he also had both law and medical training.

Horatio concluded his report by offering two resolutions which were unanimously adopted by the Association. One was that "the Association recommend to the several medical and law schools of the country the establishment of an independent chair of medical jurisprudence, to be filled, if possible, by teachers who have studied both law and medicine; attendance upon one full course of lectures from whom shall be deemed necessary before the medical degree is conferred." The other was that the Association "still is of opinion that such union [Superintendents of American Asylums for the Insane with the American Medical Association] is for their mutual and reciprocal advantage, and that it ought to be effected without further delay."

Horatio himself was the subject of one 1866 Resolution of the American

Medical Association which read:[22]

> *Whereas*, Dr. H. R. Storer, the author of the essay to which the
> prize of $100 from this Association was awarded in 1865, declined
> to receive the amount thus awarded, consequently increasing the
> resources of this Association to that amount; therefore,
>   *Resolved*, That the thanks of this Association are hereby tendered
> to Dr. H. R. Storer for this display of liberality.

Severe problems for Horatio at the New England Hospital for Women
where he was Attending Surgeon probably date from a June 2, 1866 letter of
resignation of Dr. Samuel Cabot, one of its Consulting Surgeons. Cabot's letter
included:[23]

> Feeling as I do the very warmest interest in the cause of female
> education and advancement, and believing as I do that the path of
> medicine and surgery, as well as every other path to honor and profit,
> should be open to women as well as to men—still, I feel constrained
> to send you my resignation of the office of Consulting Surgeon ...
> and to request you at your earliest convenience to accept it and to
> appoint my successor.
>   I cannot enter into any explanation of my reasons for this step,
> and can only ask you to believe that it is from no loss of interest in
> the cause you represent nor from any dissatisfaction with the ladies
> connected with the Hospital.

Dr. Samuel Cabot was not only a highly respected surgeon, his strong interest
in birds had made him a particular favorite of Horatio during his college days
when Horatio frequently visited the physician and natural scientist. Dr. Cabot
and Dr. Calvin Ellis had nominated Horatio to membership in the Society for
Medical Observation in 1855. Dr. Cabot would be one of the physicians
treating Horatio in his near-fatal bout with blood-poisoning in 1872. However,
despite the strong friendships before and after 1866, Dr. Agnes Vietor, a
biographer of Dr Zakrzewska, mentioned Cabot's resignation letter as "the first
outward manifestation" of the storm associated with Horatio's resignation a few
months later. Vietor indicated that Horatio's problem may have been "a
technical disagreement as to the limits of the respective domains of attending and
consulting staffs—always a subject filled with delicate possibilities."[24]
    Vietor also quoted Dr. Mary Putnam-Jacobi as saying "it was because the
successful outcome of Dr. Storer's operations fell too often below the boldness
of his conceptions of them." She also noted that the records of the Hospital for
1866 indicated "'Only three deaths have occurred among our patients, and all
these took place in the surgical wards after hazardous operations.'" One of

these was the February umbilical hernia operation that sparked the controversy with Ellis and eventually with the senior Harvard medical faculty. Horatio's fatal March hysterectomy probably also occurred at this Hospital. One suspects that Consulting Surgeon Cabot was embarrassed by Horatio's bold surgical efforts which were leading to the deaths of patients. The ongoing controversy related to Horatio's umbilical hernia surgery and the local vilification of Horatio for his *Medical Record* attack on Ellis, were undoubtedly also factors in Dr. Cabot's displeasure and one suspects that his resignation was to remove himself from the criticism of Horatio which no doubt now was great enough to include the New England Hospital for Women, its consulting staff, and its Directors. The following resolution was passed by the Directors and sent to Horatio on August 13, 1866: "That in all unusual or difficult cases in medicine or where a capital surgical operation is proposed, the attending and resident physicians and surgeons shall hold mutual consultation and if any one of these shall doubt as to the propriety of the proposed treatment or operation, one or more of the consulting physicians or surgeons shall be invited to examine and decide upon the case."[25]

Horatio responded on August 30 with his letter of resignation which he also sent to the *Boston Medical and Surgical Journal*[26] and the *New York Medical Journal*.[27] It was mailed from Pittsfield, where Horatio was in the midst of the Berkshire Medical College term. He indicated that the delay in his response reflected the importance of the matter and its requirement for mature reflection "that I might act, whatever my decision, only deliberately and upon conviction." Horatio first dealt with the new requirement to submit his "cases of difficulty or danger" for review by "attending and resident physicians" and by "one or more of the consulting physicians or surgeons, whose decision shall in such event be final." He pointed out that decisions about surgery should not be shifted to the non-surgical staff, "even in case it were proposed to do so by the surgeon himself." "Consultations among medical men are not matters of compulsion," he continued, "they are made upon the request of the patient or at the desire of the attendant." He indicated that the new policy would deny hospital admittance to severe cases and he was "compelled to resign" from the hospital since the policy was "incompatible with my own self respect, my duty to my patients, and the best interests of the hospital." He then noted that this was not his first problem with the hospital:[28]

> I have more than once, previously to the present time, felt that I was occupying a false and undignified position, as when you voted that no male students should be allowed the advantages I have felt it my duty to them to offer, and the duty of the hospital, as a charity, to extend to the profession at large, and when you ordered that in future no patients shall be admitted to the hospital save those paying their full expenses. By such restrictions the hospital has in reality lost its essential and only claim upon the sympathies of the community, and

has been degraded below the level of an ordinary boarding house, where patients can at least obtain such attendance as they themselves may elect.

Horatio went on to discuss how he accepted the position in the first place because of the large need for a public hospital for invalid women and had done this contrary to the advice of "Drs. James Jackson, Jacob Bigelow, J. Mason Warren, and others of similar standing." He indicated he had been willing "incidentally, and only incidentally" to participate in "the experiment of testing the ability of women to become fitted to practise as general physicians." He indicated that his position on this experiment had "been one of perfectly good faith" and he had worked to the end of fitting "better educated" women to be competent physicians in the hope that the medical profession "might be purged ... of many claimants utterly unfitted for its membership." He continued:

> Since receiving your communication, I have been better able than before to dispassionately consider and weigh the whole matter. ... It is sufficient for me to say, that despite certain exceptional cases upon which so much stress has been laid, exceptions in every sense of the word, I think that the experiment has been a failure; and that were there no other reason than for a physiological one, perfectly patent, though its importance has been so much lost sight of, women can never, as a class, become so competent, safe and reliable medical practitioners as men, no matter what their zeal or opportunities for pupilage.

The "exceptional cases" included Dr. Zakrzewska, who "may well challenge comparison in practice with a certain percentage of my own sex," and Anita Tyng, who "has such natural tastes and inclinations as fit her, more than I should have supposed any woman could have become fitted, for the anxieties, the nervous strain and shocks of the practice of surgery." The letter concluded:

> You yourselves have placed me where I could view the matter in a truer light than might otherwise have been possible. Many things have hitherto conspired to warp my judgment; the opposition and violent denunciations of former associates, the knowledge that to my own personal exertions has been owing much of your pecuniary success, and to my own professional reputation, whatever this may be, very many of the applicants for medical and surgical aid, and above all, my habit of never abandoning an experiment until it has been tried to my full satisfaction. The attainment of that point you have now assisted me in recognizing; and in yielding to the irresistible logic of facts, I thank you all for the many marks of confidence I have up to this moment received at your hands, and trust that you

may find for my post a successor with as much sincere desire to render good service to his profession and to the suffering poor, as I think I may claim to have brought to it.

Yours very respectfully,

Horatio Robinson Storer.

Horatio had little choice but to resign, given the stringent restrictions on his prerogatives as Attending Surgeon. No doubt, the lady hospital directors expected their resolution to produce Horatio's resignation and Horatio viewed it as such a request. Spite thus might have been the basis for Horatio's attack on the directors, describing their institution as "below the level of a boarding house."[29] However, spite probably was not the main reason for Horatio's criticism of women physicians. He had made the argument that menstruation periodically made a woman an unreliable physician or surgeon ten years earlier in his *Boston Medical and Surgical Journal* guest editorial and in future years he would again repeat this view.

Correspondence, between Dr. Tyng and Dr. Storer[30] later in their lives indicates that their friendship survived, despite Horatio's resignation attack on the women's hospital and on female physicians. Their continuing friendship may have been one reason, perhaps *the* reason, that Dr. Tyng was forced to resign from the hospital a few years later. As will be seen, Mrs. Dall blamed Anita Tyng's friendship with Horatio for the fact that Dr. Tyng had been "shabbily treated" by the medical profession in Boston.

Finally, one notes in Horatio's resignation letter the reference to "the opposition and violent denunciations of former associates." The Ellis challenge, or Ellis-Hodges-Minot challenge, was a dominating factor in Horatio's thoughts. This challenge and Horatio's counter challenge of 1858 misconduct by Ellis no doubt were having the ramification of removing Horatio from Harvard at the very time he was resigning from the New England Hospital for Women. This must have been a very low point emotionally for Horatio, and, ironically, it was occurring at the peak of his medical and surgical career.

Horatio was not to be long without a woman's hospital. Horatio was listed as "Surgeon to the Franciscan Hospital for Women" in the 2nd Edition of *Why Not? A Book for Every Woman*, which was published in March 1867. The Franciscan Hospital was started by Sister Superior Frances Sophia MacKenzie, probably in close partnership with Horatio. It was certainly open to women who could not pay "their full expenses." Although Roman Catholic and called "Sister," Frances Sophia MacKenzie and the women associated with her at the Franciscan hospital were not traditional nuns, but members of a "lay" order. They were free to marry and Frances Sophia MacKenzie would become Horatio's third wife in 1876.

A pair of Horatio's achievements in 1866 dealt with criminal abortion. His Prize Essay was published as *Why Not? A Book for Every Woman* with no changes other than a few unplanned omissions of quotation marks and foot-notes.[31] Horatio did add to the "Prefatory Remarks" and added an "Appendix" where he discussed his views on anesthetics during labor.[32] He indicated that these views, unlike his views on criminal abortion, were not universally held by physicians of the American Medical Association. This disclaimer was prompted by a letter from a Philadelphia friend who requested that Horatio drop the recommendations in the essay for "use of anaesthesia in all cases of labor."

Why Not? was reviewed by the *Medical and Surgical Reporter* in their issue of May 26, 1866.[33] This review was generally favorable and included the recommendation: "we wish and hope for it an extended circulation and many readers." However, they indicated their "regret that in a few instances the earnestness of the author leads him to speak in a tone almost of exaggeration, which in this, as in *every* case, must so far weaken the cause upheld." One instance was Horatio's claim that some means for preventing pregnancy led to the "'evils and dangers, mental and physical, of self-abuse.'"

The *Boston Medical and Surgical Journal* did not get around to their mention and brief review of *Why Not?* until the end of August.[34] This three-month delay may have been related to some lingering animosity of the editors who had condemned Horatio in late April for his *Medical Record* article accusing Ellis of "vivisection." Their review was generally positive, although the editors did question whether criminal abortion "be so general as some, whose special practice is the most likely to bring them into cognizance of it, are led to believe." They also indicated that they feared that many women would not listen to or heed its advice, "preferring to be guided by the assurance of impunity from those by whose advice they are tempted to its commission." They indicated that the title would better have made some actual reference to the subject of the book. "It will be likely to excite curiosity," they concluded, "among those who are too young to need to have the subject presented to their minds; and who, in our estimation, had better not know anything of such things until maturity of years or the marriage relation has drawn aside the veil with which we should prefer to keep them enshrouded."

The *New Orleans Medical and Surgical Journal* did not let the publication of *Why Not?* go by without taking another swipe at Horatio, although they waited a year after the book's first publication, presenting their highly critical review in July 1867. It is possible that Bennett Dowler, who had castigated Horatio for his Preface to Simpson's *Obstetric Memoirs*, was its author, given the strong similarities of both attacks. One illustrative paragraph read:[35]

> While we admit the general incumbency upon writers for a medical journal to avoid all disparaging personal allusions to authors whose works are being reviewed, our sense of duty leads us, in this instance, to a different course. We honestly believe that, if we can, by truthful statements or well-sustained suspicions disparaging to this book or its author, counteract its general circulation, we shall thereby

subserve the cause of virtue and morality.

The following indicates some of their objections:

> The title of the book is, in itself, such an offence against public
> decorum and good manners, that it justifies a relentless crusade for
> its expulsion from general marts of literature. It presents obtrusive
> and immodest claims for general notice; it is not a book for some
> women, for certain women, for those women whom it may concern,
> but it is "a book for *every* woman" (so-called). No lady can enter a
> book store which tolerates such literature upon its shelves, without
> danger of being victimized by the Yankee ingenuity of the title, so
> prettily printed in gilt letters upon the cover.

Horatio quickly became aware of this diatribe against him and his book, and
even against New England and the North. Horatio recommended it "to all
lovers of truly scientific criticism" in an article on masturbation in women
published a month after the scathing review appeared.[36]

On June 5, 1866, Mrs. Caroline Dall, of Boston, "a lady of great intellectual and moral worth, well known indeed throughout the country" (as Horatio
described her in his next book), wrote a long and highly complementary letter
to Horatio related to *Why Not?* which she had just "laid down." Her letter may
have had much to do with Horatio's authorship of a second book, *Is It I? A
Book for Every Man*, and Horatio was to copy much of Mrs. Dall's letter in *Is
It I?*. One paragraph of her letter included: "But the book needs a counterpart
addressed to *men*. Till *they* are willing to spend as freely for wife and children
as for the mistress, hidden but a few doors off, women will hardly be free
agents in this matter. No woman dreads her travail, as she dreads the loss of
what she calls, in her unhappy ignorance and blindness, her husband's love."[37]
Horatio responded to Mrs. Dall with the following:[38]

Hotel Pelham
18 June 1866

My dear Madam,
    Want of a moment's leisure has prevented me from acknowledging
your kind note till now. Your comments are very just, & I may take
occasion to print them, in part or in whole, in case my publishers
think best to issue another edition of "Why Not?" & you do not
object. Were you to send a terse & Dallian notice of the book to one
of our Journals, say to the Atlantic, I doubt not it would aid greatly
in its circulation.
    As for myself, my time is now so wholly engrossed that I am
unable to look after the welfare of any such fledgling once launched

from the nest.

Yrs sincerely
Horatio R. Storer

Mrs. Dall

One could argue that the above request for a "terse & Dallian notice of the book to one of our journals," represented very much a "look after the welfare" of his "fledgling" *Why Not?*.

    The *Boston Medical and Surgical Journal* was to make two more references to *Why Not?* in their seventy-fifth volume. One was a long letter published November 1, 1866 entitled, "'Why Not? A Book for Every Woman.' A Woman's View."[39] The associated footnote of the journal editors indicated that the author was "the wife of a Christian physician," from "one of our most distant New England towns" and not from Massachusetts. The editors hoped her delicate and truthful expression of "the universal feeling of her sex" on the subject "might find its way, in some more popular form than our pages afford, to the eyes of every husband in the land." The thrust of the lady's letter was that many women were victims of husbands who forced sex on them indiscriminately, preventing the timing of intercourse that could prevent unwanted pregnancy. These husbands' lack of consideration continued after pregnancy, sometimes even taking the form of blame of the woman for her condition. Under such circumstances, it was understandable that some women, so denied control of conception, would opt for measures to prevent birth, particularly if they believed that they were not taking a life when the abortion was induced early in pregnancy. She claimed that abortion was not a consideration of women with sympathetic husbands. For the "worthy husband," "careful for her comfort and her preferences," "be she ever so slight and fragile, ever so much adverse to motherhood," "she will bear it all, even to the end, cheerfully." Her last paragraph included what may be the first *public* mention of a book for men: "If Dr. Storer will perform as noble service for our brothers and husbands, as for ourselves, and send the two books out hand in hand, they will bring him back a rich harvest of gratitude, and amendment in morals."

    The woman's letter so closely mimicked Horatio's views on use of chloroform during childbirth; the high and increasing frequency of criminal abortion; the agony of childbirth, "akin to nothing else on earth;" and the unspeakable vice of holding fashion as god that it could have been written by Horatio himself. However, Horatio would later expressly deny any knowledge of who wrote it when he called attention to it in *Is It I?*.

    A few weeks later, the *Boston Medical and Surgical Journal* published a letter from someone signed "A Fighter for the Right against Wrong" praising the letter providing "A Woman's View." It too is a little incredible, but Horatio later also indicated no knowledge of the author of the following:[40]

Messrs. Editors,—I cannot refrain from expressing my feelings of thankfulness at your publication of "A Woman's View," in a late number of your Journal, relative to abortion. Dr. Storer's work had already been brought to my attention with—as must be the result to every right-minded man—approval; but the addenda, or rather complement, of his valuable little book, lies in that "nutshell of pertinence," the article referred to. I lit upon your Journal by the merest chance. I am on the eve of marriage myself, and though not a whit more sensual than most men, cannot be too grateful for having thus forcibly brought to my mind a view which I for one had doubtless scarce otherwise considered. I would to God that it might meet and claim the serious consideration of every man born of woman's agony. Yours very truly,

A Fighter for the Right Against Wrong.

Many coincidences were required to produce this letter. The author, though male, had read and approved *Why Not? A Book for Every Woman*; though apparently not involved in medicine, he had read the issue of the *Boston Medical and Surgical Journal* with the lady's "view;" and though single, he was unusually aware of woman's agony during childbirth. Not the least coincidence was the remarkable pertinence of "A Fighter's" letter for another book which would communicate "to every man" "A Woman's View." Still, there is another plausible explanation for the letter from "A Fighter" and for "A Woman's View" other than Horatio lying about not being the writer. Despite his problems with the medical powers of Boston and Harvard, we know that Henry Orlando Marcy and other students at the Harvard Medical School strongly supported Horatio in his battles with the establishment. Marcy in 1910 referred to his own "ardent" early defence of Horatio in the following:

There is no doubt that Dr. Storer was the "best-hated" member of the profession in Massachusetts. A long and dangerous illness removed him from the active arena and years were spent in Europe in quest of health, unfortunately never fully restored. He gave brilliant promise of being the leader of gynecology in America, notwithstanding the vituperative abuse unsparingly showered on him by men who should have known better. A generous share of this attention was bestowed on me as his ardent defender. I have somewhere a letter of his, written at the time, containing a touching appeal to forget him and his service to suffering humanity lest it work my ruin. He is a man of strong magnetic power, quick of thought and action, fluent of speech, equally ready to attack his enemies and to defend himself; and there are yet many who hold his service in grateful remembrance.[41]

It may have been a pair of these strong supporters, perhaps including Marcy himself, plus one of their spouses, who provided to the *Boston Medical and Surgical Journal* this pair of letters which were so very favorable to Horatio, to some of his most controversial ideas, and to his new supplemental career as an author of popular books on criminal abortion.

The other important abortion-related event in 1866 was Horatio's presentation of the paper, "The Abetment of Criminal Abortion by Medical Men," at the May 30 annual meeting of the Massachusetts Medical Society.[42]   In many respects the paper was a history of the physicians' crusade against abortion, which was largely the history of Horatio's own efforts. Again he gave credit to his father for first bringing up the frequency of New England abortions and the health problems they produced, and he discussed the suppression of the abortion portion of David Humphreys' 1855 address when it was printed. Horatio expressed his concern that his beloved Harvard had been party to this suppression of the truth. "If our alma mater, in any of her provinces, ever fears to allow the truth to be spoken," Horatio said, "she is recreant both *Christo et Ecclesioe* [sic] and to all her old traditions, and one at least of her sons will not hesitate to upbraid her for violating the ethics she herself has taught him." Horatio criticized critics who argued that public discussion of criminal abortion was inappropriate. "To cure a fetid and burrowing sore," he wrote, "it must be freely laid open and exposed."[43]

Horatio then referred to his 1859 *North-American Medico-Chirurgical Review* "abetment" article and its theme that "by any apparent disregard of the existence or sanctity of foetal life, however evinced, we in reality increased its disregard by the community." He provided a new example of physician abetment of criminal abortion that involved the Councillors of the group he was addressing and this probably was the prime reason for his presentation. He called attention to the 1858 actions of the Massachusetts Medical Society while he was in Texas, when the Committee of which he was a member, "decided that 'the laws of the commonwealth are already sufficiently stringent, provided they are executed'." Horatio also pointed out that his "earnest protest" against the Committee's action in his absence "seems never to have been acted upon." Horatio noted that when the claim that existing abortion statutes were sufficiently stringent if executed had been made, Massachusetts had had thirty-two trials for abortion in the previous eight years, but not a single conviction. He also pointed out that it was not severity of punishment, but the law's inappropriate definition of the crime which was the problem. He noted that as these laws were written, if the mother survived, "the crime practically goes unpunished." He then described the strong action of the New York State Medical Society in appealing to their legislature for improved abortion legislation and contrasted this with the failure of the Massachusetts Society.

Undoubtedly, some of the members of the audience who had been on the Committee Horatio was accusing of abetment must have bristled at this charge. Most angered no doubt was Jacob Bigelow who had opposed new abortion legislation from Horatio's first proposal for changes early in 1857 and who drafted and prematurely submitted the Report to the Councillors of the Massachusetts Medical Society without contacting Horatio and without his signature. If these "guilty" parties in his audience were concerned that their anger or other emotions might make them conspicuous, Horatio gave them no choice, since he proceeded to name each of the six other members of the 1857-1858 Committee. Horatio then spread the blame to the rest of the Councillors who had approved the 1858 Resolutions that omitted the recommendation to address the legislature. Horatio cited this as another instance "where the profession become directly accountable for the increased frequency of the crime."

Horatio went on to discuss other physician actions that abetted abortion, including the frequent resort to unnecessary craniotomy when "turning," long forceps, or prematurely induced labor would allow the survival of the child; failure to use anesthetics in child-bed, despite its improvement of the chance of survival of child and mother; use of ergot to speed labor unnecessarily, thereby jeopardizing the fetus; and accepting the mother's refusal to nurse, "although the breast of its own parent when in health is undoubtedly the best one on all accounts for her child, and far safer for its life than any artificial feeding." Most serious, however, in his list of physician "abetments" was the induction of abortion for medical reasons, other than for saving the life of child or mother.

Horatio quoted his long paragraph from the "Its Perpetrators" article of his original abortion series, claiming that abortion was almost never performed by regular physicians and providing reasons that this popular but false belief existed. He then waffled on this point considerably in the following paragraph near the end of his address:[44]

> On the other hand, it is no uncommon thing for women of good position to assert to me that abortion has been induced for them by gentlemen of excellent standing in the profession, especially among the older men, and I am constantly conferred with by other physicians to whom similar charges have been made. Allowing, as I cheerfully do, that many, perhaps the majority, of such allegations must be false, still there is in a certain number of cases a foundation in truth.

No doubt some of the women willing to tell Horatio about their induced abortions would have also identified the abortionist without any prompting on his part. When Horatio strongly suggested that some of "the older men" may have been abortionists it is possible that he was aiming a barb at specific members of his Massachusetts Medical Society audience who had been so identified by these women, particularly if any were among the Councillors of the Society who had generated a Committee Report without his signature, accepted the deficient document, or refused to act on his January 1859 protest of these actions.

References to Horatio's paper in the minutes of that Massachusetts Medical Society meeting indicated:[45]

> Dr H. R. Storer read a paper on "The Abetment of Criminal Abortion by Medical Men."
> Dr Hartwell (of Southboro') moved a vote of thanks, & also that Dr Storer's Essay be published by the Society. An Amendment was offered that it be submitted to the Committee on Publications. Dr Ordway spoke against the Amendment. The Amendment was carried; and the original motion withdrawn.

Horatio apparently did not even receive the "vote of thanks" portion of Dr. Hartwell's motion. The Committee on Publications turned the paper down, even as that Committee had similarly refused to publish Horatio's 1863 paper on chloroform anesthesia in obstetrics. Horatio published it in the September 1866 issue of the *New York Medical Journal*.

At the end of 1866, the *Boston Medical and Surgical Journal*, published the following apology from Horatio to Calvin Ellis:[46]

> Boston, Christmas Eve, 1866
> Messrs. Editors,—Will you afford me a brief space in your Journal that I may express my regret at having published in the New York *Medical Record* anything which my friends tell me was calculated to injure Dr. Calvin Ellis, one whom I regarded as a neighbor and a friend, and whom I would not have injured or insulted intentionally. I wish to make all amends in my power, and to persevere in efforts to do so. Without referring to scientific opinions and convictions, I would thus publicly say that I regret having so expressed myself as to injure or cause pain or annoyance to one towards whom I should be sorry to entertain any other feelings than those of kindliness and respect.
> Horatio R. Storer

"We comply with the request made by the writer of this letter," the editors added, "and are glad to learn that the reiterated disclaimer by Dr. Storer of any intention to annoy or injure has been accepted by Dr. Ellis." There is a hitch in the above apology which is, "Without referring to scientific opinions and convictions, ..." As we will see, Horatio still was not admitting that he was ignorant of physiology or that Magee was sufficiently dead to be autopsied.

It will be recalled that Horatio had called for the establishment of foundling hospitals in November 1859 and again in his *Why Not? A Book for Every Woman* as one means to reduce abortion and infanticide. Horatio was one of the principal organizers of such an institution in Boston. At a meeting held on January 11, 1867 "to consider the subject of Deserted and Destitute Infants, and what further provisions should be made for them," Horatio was reported to have "stated his convictions of the great need existing of an asylum for infants, and that the establishment of such a home would tend to check the crime of infanticide." He was also reported to have spoken "in answer to several of the questions, especially in regard to the importance of breast milk for raising children, and of the value of the Sisters of Charity as nurses."[47]

The "questions" were a long list related to the need for and possible effectiveness of a home for destitute and deserted infants. Question 27, for example, read, "Would it tend to diminish infanticide and criminal abortion?" The questions were distributed and mailed to people with experience that might allow insights into the benefits and problems of a foundling hospitals. One such expert was a Mrs. Stewart, who was involved in efforts for foundlings in Detroit. She was described by Dr. Pilcher of the University of Michigan as "the daughter of an eminent clergyman and the wife of one of our most respectable physicians." Her answer to Question 27 was "Infanticide certainly to a measure—criminal abortion will be practiced just as far as women have the pecuniary means and physical courage and pride to accomplish it." This apparently shows that there was some resistance to the physicians' crusade from an unexpected source. However, one wonders whether Mrs. Stewart, and the "most respectable" Dr. Stewart of Michigan agreed on the issue of criminal abortion. A Dr. Morse Stewart presented a paper before the Wayne County (Michigan) Medical Society in December 1866 which frequently quoted Horatio's anti-abortion views and indicated total agreement with Horatio on the issue.[48] Assuming that Mrs. Stewart from Detroit was the wife of Dr. Morse Stewart from Detroit, this discrepancy in views is so astounding, that one suspects that Mrs. Stewart's answer to Question 27 was distorted in the above report by a Boston recorder who believed that abortion was the province of courageous and proud women.

It was mentioned that Horatio's relations with some, perhaps many of the students he came in contact with while Assistant in Obstetrics and Medical Jurisprudence at Harvard, were excellent. One was Albert Day who obtained his Harvard M.D. in 1866 and was Superintendent and Physician of the Washingtonian Home of Boston, an asylum for inebriates. Day wrote a small book on alcohol-related insanity, entitled *Methomania*, and requested Horatio to contribute his views on the subject. Horatio agreed and his words were included as an Appendix.[49] He praised Day's book; discussed the subject of institutionalization of people with alcohol problems, particularly women; mentioned reflex action, as the basis of insanity and the failure of asylums to adequately diagnose and treat this; and discussed the physical and mental problems of children whose parents were addicted to alcohol, foreshadowing "fetal alcohol syndrome." However, Horatio's major thrust was pointing out the problems that physicians caused by prescribing alcoholic spirits and medicines containing alcohol. He referred to a case early in his own practice where his prescription caused his patient to return to problem drinking. He described the worse situation where physicians actually caused the problem by their medications.

Horatio noted that women were much more victimized than men by addiction to alcohol. "We look to see them a little nearer to the angels than ourselves," he wrote, "and so their fall seems greater." He noted that in his thirteen years of practice he had encountered "many sad instances of habitual drunkenness" among his women patients and that a large proportion of them had first had liquor prescribed by a physician, nurse, or relative to relieve the "infinitely oftener causes for suffering" that women had compared to men. Other prescriptions of spirits were frequently made to counter "the lassitude of lactation and of early pregnancy, the faintings of hysteria, and the fatigues following marriage." He observed that[50]

> Such is still done by some obstinate or over-conservative men, to the ruin of their victims, to their own eternal disgrace, and, may we hope, to their eventual remorse. Cases of the kind referred have been frequently sent to me for treatment, or I have been called in consultation to them. Here the exciting cause of their sad condition was an attempt to relieve weakness or to still pain. But pain and weakness are not in themselves generally the disease itself: they are but its symptoms; and to prescribe for them alone, as is still too frequently done in the case of sick women, without ascertaining in what the actual disease which excites them consists, is alike unscientific, empirical, and inexcusable. To this fact I have more than once called the attention of the profession: in exciting to it the anxiety of women themselves, and of their protectors by blood or by bond, I am but fulfilling the physician's highest duty.

In late February 1867, Horatio was a guest of the New York State Medical Society and presented a paper on "The So-called Chronic Metritis, and its Rational Treatment" which was published in their *Transactions* for that year.[51] It is perhaps less important for its questionable recommendations of use of a new tool for scarification of the mucous membrane lining the uterus and producing a "therapeutic" discharge of blood than for its vilification of various other bad treatments that had been used over the years for the ill-defined disease. These ranged from leeches applied to the cervix, with their occasional scary escapes into the uterus, to "daily or frequent use of the uterine sound, or worse still, the finger of the operator, as the only means employed to elevate the uterus or to produce a cure ..." Horatio described the latter as "often but the grossest abuse of a license granted only to supposed scientific acquirements, and to a decent and honest man." "These so-called manipulators or movement workers," he continued, "of whom I have now known very many instances, are exposed to the chance they too often find a certainty, of awakening in their patient a slumbering passion, or but pandering to the vilest of lusts."

There were some physicians who denied that there was such a disease as chronic metritis. Horatio dealt with them in the following paragraph which also shows Horatio's preoccupation with cycles of medical science and medical scientists when he himself was only thirty-seven.

> The frequency of the disease, or class of diseases we are considering, to which the specific or generic and frequently inappropriate name of chronic metritis has been applied, is now admitted by all who know anything soever of uterine pathology. I am aware indeed that there are many unduly influenced by that spirit of conservatism which is in other respects the salvation of the profession, who deny its frequency and even its very existence, as is sometimes done of every other form of uterine disease. The time, however, of these gentlemen has passed. Skepticism in this direction has culminated, and those under its sway are beginning to be viewed with mingled feelings of wonder and pity, tempered perhaps with pride at the earlier achievements of these very persons, and with regret that the evil days of being left behind in the march are so rapidly drawing near for ourselves.

Horatio concluded by noting that the prognosis for some patients with chronic metritis was bad.

> If the woman is left to the unbridled caresses of even a considerate husband, or is allowed to indulge in any of the conjugal indecencies of the present day, preventing impregnation by the use of a sponge, or by cold injections, or by the employment of condoms or the so-called womb guard, or that worst measure of all, incomplete intercourse, the practitioner's hands are tied. He cannot expect to effect a cure.

CHAPTER 11
IS IT I?, SELF-ABUSE IN WOMEN, *NURSING*, EVERSION OF THE RECTUM

Horatio's next major effort was his treatise on criminal abortion written primarily for husbands.[1] We have already described possible etiologies of this companion book, including letters from Mrs. Caroline Dall, the Christian physician's wife, and "A Fighter for the Right Against Wrong." Still another was described in a letter from Horatio to Thomas Addis Emmet,[2] to whom he dedicated the book. Horatio told Emmet that the publisher wanted a second book, given the high sales of the first, as did "many physicians and many lady patients."

The book's Prefatory Remarks indicate that Horatio's strategy was similar to that of the earlier book, i.e., to submit it to the American Medical Association as an offering for its annual prize. However, unlike in 1864-1865, there was no special category related to a popular book on the subject, and Horatio placed it in competition with more medically oriented essays. Horatio noted that "it was distanced by the essays of Drs. Black ... and Pallen ..., treating as these did of subjects of more direct and especial interest to the medical profession." The Chairman of the Prize Committee provided a letter which Horatio published in the book and claimed (with little basis) gained his object of an American Medical Association sanction. It included: "I have read your essay with very great interest, and hope that you will publish it. It certainly will do good. The subject, although one of great delicacy, is handled with marked ability. The whole profession ought to feel grateful for your efforts to check the fearful amount of crime in relation to abortions. Your essay will, I have no doubt, meet with the general approval of the Association."[3]

Is It I? A Book for Every Man went to press shortly after August 1, 1867, the date at the end of the "Publishers' Note" that preceded the text. This "Publishers' Note" is a unique personal account of Horatio during this most tempestuous and productive period of his life. The author was at least a close friend and intimately aware of recent events and people affecting Horatio. It is possible that it was written by Horatio himself. It told that[4]

Professor Storer's writings are no inapt index to his own character. He is thoroughly alive to his duties; sagacious to discern the truth, fearless in asserting it. Progressive, without being too radical, he is still sufficiently conservative to respect the opinions of others, even though at variance with his own. Perhaps no American physician of his own age, holds at the present time a more prominent position in his profession. He has already been quoted as authority by European writers; and in this country he seems everywhere to have received the most flattering acknowledgment of his scientific labors, save here in his own city, where for many years he has met with uninterrupted opposition, and even personal abuse, from a professional clique the result, doubtless of jealousy on their part, envy, and that spirit of antagonism which has long rendered the disagreements of physicians a by-word.

If Horatio did not actually dictate or write this description of an opposing and abusing "clique of local physicians," he let it stand, and it appeared again in the second edition of *Is It I?*. Henry J. Bigelow, the powerful Boston surgeon and Harvard Professor of Surgery, surely viewed Horatio as foe by 1867, and Bigelow's followers, whom the members of the future Gynaecological Society of Boston would describe as sycophants, no doubt were in agreement.

The Note revealed a key reason why Horatio was not "appreciated by those in his own immediate vicinity," namely his zealous support of "the celebrated Sir James Y. Simpson, the discoverer of chloroform as an anaesthetic." This matter had placed Horatio "in opposition to the many disciples of the French and Viennese schools among his contemporaries." Henry J. Bigelow, perhaps the strongest opponent of Simpson and chloroform, studied in Paris, and Calvin Ellis and Richard Manning Hodges studied in Vienna. We thus have clues about some who comprised the "clique." The Note continued:

It has been asserted of Dr. Storer that, when engaged in professional controversy, he is pitiless and unsparing. These statements seem traceable to opponents who have been worsted, and speak from bitter experience. There may, however, be some reason to believe, that, like his teacher, Dr. Simpson, he has profited by the advice of Polonius:—

"Beware
"Of entrance to a quarrel; but being in,
"Bear it that the opposer may beware of thee."

Here we are given some insight into Horatio's dredging up the 1858 Magee case in his quarrel with Ellis. With both his beloved Simpson and his beloved Shakespeare recommending that one should bear a quarrel in a way that made the opposer "beware of thee," Horatio may have seen himself as simply following mentors' orders in accusing Calvin Ellis of an "antemortem autopsy" of Magee. The Note also told that[5]

The character of the weapons that have been used against our author may be judged by an extract from a personal attack contained—without a word of palliation or excuse from the editors—in one of the latest numbers of the Boston Medical and Surgical Journal.

In attempting to save a poor invalid—sure otherwise soon to perish—Dr. Storer had performed one of the most tedious and difficult operations in surgery, hitherto successful in a most notable instance at his hands, namely, the removal of the womb by incision through the abdomen: an operation with which his name will be forever identified. In commenting upon it, the would-be critic used the following language:

The Publishers' Note then included *only* the final sentence from the following letter:[6]

Messrs. Editors,—I have learned this afternoon of the death of a very estimable lady in Cambridgeport, thirty-six hours after the removal of a large fibrous tumor and with it nearly the entire uterus. This is the second lady formerly a patient of mine who has lost her life by like reckless and injudicious treatment. Please allow me publicly to protest most solemnly against such practice, and earnestly to beg of my professional brethren everywhere to use their utmost influence to prevent their patients and friends from employing or consulting such practitioners.

Yours respectfully,
Asa Millet, M.D.

Bridgewater, June 8, 1867.

Dr. Millet may have had reason to complain, although it is not certain that Horatio was the operator in the first of the two deaths. On the other hand, Horatio no doubt believed that the patient or patients would have soon died without the surgery and that the chance of a restoration of health, *a la* Miss Colcord, justified the effort.

The Note continued: "Abuse like this is sure, of course, to react upon those who employ it, and to gain for its object the sympathy and active interest of all lovers of fair play and justice. By a happy coincidence, the article referred to chanced to be followed, on the same page, by another which we also quote:—"[7] The Note then provided the following resolutions of Horatio's first class of graduate physicians:

"*Whereas*, We, the attendants upon Prof. H.R. Storer's first private course of lectures on the Surgical Diseases of Women, being regular practising physicians and surgeons, have long experienced the disadvantages arising from the very imperfect manner in which these subjects have been treated in our various text-books, and by the professors in our colleges; many of the most important diseases and operations being entirely ignored, by men who think deeply and reason candidly in all other matters pertaining to medicine and surgery; and whereas, we cannot but feel that this class of diseases is the most important, believing it to be the cause of more suffering than any other, therefore,

"*Resolved*. That we tender to Dr. Storer our sincere Gratitude for taking the advanced step which he has, thereby giving us, as we hope he will hereafter give others, the opportunity of hearing these subjects discussed thoroughly and impartially.

"*Resolved*. That a copy of these resolutions be presented to Prof. Storer, and sent to the Boston Medical and Surgical Journal and the New York Medical Record for publication."

"These resolutions derive their significance," the Note continued, "from the fact that the signers are neither students nor recent graduates, but practitioners, chiefly of many years standing, who have become alive to the importance of the special diseases of women." Horatio's classes for physicians would continue twice a year for several years and constituted the first post-graduate medical education in the country, perhaps the first American post-graduate education in any field.

The Note claimed that, despite his young age, Horatio had "already attained the highest medical honor, save one, that can be conferred in this country." The reference was to his recent selection as Vice President of the American Medical Association at its annual meeting in Cincinnati. "The success ... will not be wondered at," the Note pointed out, "when the extent and variety of the contributions that he has made to medical science are taken into consideration." This was followed by a list of forty-three publications of Horatio. However, "forty-three" understated the number of his publications, since the list included as number "III" a half dozen of Horatio's Boston Lying-In Hospital Reports which as readily could have been numbers "III" through "VIII." Similar combinations of articles under a single Roman numeral occurred in other instances making the total number of papers at least fifty-six. Probably no physician or medical scientist in the country produced more medical papers from 1855 to 1867.

Horatio began the "Prefatory Remarks" for *Is It I?* by describing the history of the earlier *Why Not?*. The "propriety" of the American Medical Association's resolution to distribute the Prize Essay is claimed to be shown on the one hand by the huge demand for the essay and the fact that every medical journal in the country had given the book "kindly notice."[8] Newspapers and some of the religious papers also had "praised the profession for its united effort thus to enlighten the so general ignorance upon a professional topic." Horatio next briefly summarized *Why Not?*, discussing the criminality of induced abortion and also its effects on the woman's health, her family, and society. "The nail upon which society is to hang its faith has been driven;" Horatio continued, referring to *Why Not?*, "to clinch it, and so to render its hold secure, another blow is needed. The necessity I proceed to show, and the stroke to give, only regretting that my feeble arm is not that of some one of the Association's stronger men, and my pen tipped with the flame which should cause these words to burn their way to the very hearts of those to whom they are addressed."

Horatio mentioned the letters of the "wife of a Christian physician" and "A Fighter for the Right Against Wrong," which discussed the need for widespread education of men on the subject of criminal abortion and men's large contribution to the problem. He noted that both letters were "apparently made in the most perfectly good faith," and that he knew nothing of the "personal identity of their authors." Horatio indicated that the arguments of the former "are so weighty, and they are so well put, that I copy the letter entire in an Appendix to this essay." Horatio must have thought no less of the letter from "A Fighter for the Right Against Wrong," since he copied much of it immediately in the Prefatory Remarks.

The first chapter of *Is It I?* was called "It is not Good to be Alone." The major subjects were the dangers for a youth associated with the premature excitation of his sexuality, the near impossibility of avoiding mistakes along these lines, and the admission of the near necessity of experiencing the consequences of such mistakes in order to learn the self-control needed for their future avoidance. The period between puberty and marriage was shown to be difficult for the parents of the youth and particularly difficult and perilous for the youth himself. Sexuality while "alone," i.e., masturbation, was mentioned, but the primary subject of "It is not Good to be Alone" was man's instinctual need for a mate.

"Marriage as a Sanitary Measure" was the second chapter and marriage, prostitution, the keeping of a mistress or mistresses, and masturbation were the major topics. Marriage was cited as the preferable means of satisfying the instinctive sexual urge. The dangers of prostitution were described, including that of venereal disease, and the man with a mistress was deluding himself if he thought he was safe from such infection. Horatio described the not infrequent tragic event where a married man contracted the disease from a prostitute or mistress, did not manifest the symptoms, transmitted it to his wife and then believed infidelity on her part was the source of the disease in the family. Next came the dangers of masturbation. "It is customary," Horatio continued, "but still a grave error, to preserve silence upon this subject," "physiologically a worse crime against nature" than resorting to prostitution. The dangers were such that Horatio appeared to pledge to undertake a physicians' campaign against masturbation when he wrote: "If the subject is decided, as I believe will be the case, to be of the importance that is claimed by every philosophical physician who has looked into the matter, a voice will go out into every corner of the land, caught up and re-echoed by all the medical men thereof, that will cause those who care either for their souls or their bodies, to pause and tremble."[9]

Horatio used an extensive quote of nearly eight pages from an 1850 treatise of his former Medical School Professor, Dr. John Ware, for the background on how masturbation is acquired, its direct connection to future licentiousness, and all of its other bad effects. According to Ware: "The deleterious, the sometimes appalling consequences of this vice upon the health, the constitution, the mind itself, are some of the common matters of medical observation." Specifically, these included:[10]

"an impaired nutrition of the body; a diminution of the rotundity which belongs to childhood and youth; a general lassitude and languour, with weakness of the limbs and back; indisposition and incapacity for study or labor; dullness of apprehension; a deficient power of attention; dizziness; headaches; pains in the sides, back, and limbs; affections of the eyes. In cases of extreme indulgence, these symptoms become more strongly marked, and are followed by others. The emaciation becomes excessive; the bodily powers become more completely prostrated; the memory and the whole mind partake in the ruin; and idiocy or insanity, in their most intractable forms, close the train of evils. It not unfrequently happens that, from the consequences of this vice, when carried to an extreme, not even repentance and reformation liberate the unhappy victim."

If Ware were correct about only half of these problems, there surely was need for a national campaign to reduce masturbation. Whether in anticipation of heading such a campaign or not, Horatio was to publish a paper on the occurrence of "self-abuse" in women in August 1867.

After reiterating the various "sanitary" benefits of marriage, Horatio moved to "How Early in Life is Marriage to be Advised?" Recommendations of others that men wait until they were twenty-five were cited, but Horatio (who married at twenty-three) did not see this as important in an expanding country, where there was need for the increased children one would predict with earlier marriage. In line with this, he pronounced long engagements to be decidedly bad.

Horatio's fourth chapter finally impinged on the original reasons given for writing the book. It was called "The Rights of the Husband." Horatio noted that these rights "are usually considered total and indisputable. Till now they have seldom been challenged; certainly seldom of men by men." In the following, Horatio not only explained his atypical male defense of women's rights, he referred to his experience as father of a daughter, which must have been painful, given the brevity of that father-daughter relationship.

What, then, do we [men] usually claim? All that the law, and still more tyrannical custom, grants to us, in our wives; all that they have, and all that they are, in person and in very life. And here let me say, that I intend no ultra ground; that I am neither a fanatic or professed philanthrope; and that in loosing, as I hope to do, some of woman's present chains, it is solely for professional purposes, to increase her health, prolong her life, extend the benefits she confers upon society—in a word, selfishly to enhance her value to ourselves; and yet there is somewhat in this effort, as I believe there is also in the hearts of all those who will peruse it, of gratitude to her for the love with which she has solaced us, as mother, and sister, and wife, and daughter,—all of which I have myself possessed; unhappy he who has not.[11]

After discussing women's slave status in primitive times, the frequent killing of wives for disobedience or infidelity in "former days," and the possession of multiple wives "in by-gone times, and among heathen, as at present in a remote valley of our own great land," Horatio finally got around to the subject of abortion. He asked whether the slaughter of new-borns by the Spartans was less wicked than

the pre-natal murders of the present day, daily in occurrence, fashionable even, and be-praised by professing Christians, repeated over and over again by the same married woman and mother? You will exclaim with horror that it is not! And yet, in a very large proportion of instances, this shocking and atrocious act is advised and abetted, if not compelled by the husband—by us men. Who enjoys asking now, "Is it I?"[12]

Horatio indicated that the woman had a "certain measure of excuse," but "For her husband none." He continued:

This is a matter concerning which the public mind is now undergoing a radical change. Slow to set in motion, but every day gaining more rapidly in force, the world's revival proceeds. In "Why Not?" or "Why should women not commit this crime?" I have sounded almost a trump to wake the dead. Would, indeed, that it might arouse a better life in every man who reads these words: ...

Then followed the "Of the mother, ... we leave those to speak who can" passage from his first *North-American Medico-Chirurgical Review* article.

Next, Horatio gave the following progress report on women's rights and tied this to the need to prohibit wife rape and abortion:[13]

Formerly men had control, exclusive and entire, of any possession their wives might bring them. Now, and with us at least, the law has very materially curtailed the husband's power in this respect, save it be granted him by the wife's consent. Will the time come, think ye, when husbands can no longer, as they now frequently do, commit the crime of rape upon their unwilling wives, and persuade them or compel them to allow a still more dreadful violence to be wreaked upon the children nestling within them—children fully alive from the very moment of conception, that have already been fully detached from all organic connection with their parent, and only re-attached to her for the purposes of nutriment and growth, and to destroy whom "is a crime of the same nature, both against our Maker and society, as to destroy an infant, a child, or a man"?*

After further discussion of abortion as a moral problem, he mentioned the problems of increased "ill health of women" and "the gradual dying out of our native population." He also indicated that insanity was sometimes caused by abortion, several cases observed by himself, and his claim had also been recently backed by Dr. John Gray, the Utica, New York Asylum Superintendent in his asylum's annual report. Thus, as in *Why Not?*, Horatio recognized that moral persuasion would not work with at least some of his audience, and he appealed to self-interest as well.

Horatio's next chapter was "Are these Rights Absolute, or Reciprocal, with Duties?" The following final paragraph gives the answer and the gist of the chapter:[14]

> For these [conjugal] rights, of which I have been speaking, are, in reality, not absolute, but reciprocal with duties. How can we ourselves expect enjoyment, if perchance we are inflicting terrible suffering? How can we look for constant and untiring affection, if inconsiderate or brutal, we compel what would be withheld perhaps, however reluctantly, by ill health? Is it thus we would cherish? As we sow, even so must we reap. No true conjugal enjoyment can exist, unless it is mutual. We cannot be loved, unless we are respected. We cannot be respected, even by our wives, unless we respect them. The true rule should be to take only what is freely given; were this the case, far more freely would gifts be offered.

The next chapter was "Should mere Instinct, or Reason, be the Rule?" Horatio claimed that excessive sexuality was harmful to the health of the woman. Bearing of children was essential, but not too frequently. The recommended interval between births was two-and-a-half or three years. Breast feeding was important for avoiding uterine disease. Pleasure was an appropriate reason for sex, but the wife must not be compelled to do anything "she herself does not freely assent to." As had been argued by the "wife of a Christian physician," forcing women to engage in sex was a major reason for women averting "impending maternity."

Horatio's next chapter on divorce called for less of it and certainly no change of statutes that would make divorce easier. Forgiveness of human errors was cited as the key to avoiding divorce. One notable passage was:[15]

> Were divorces more common, or more readily obtained, the very foundation of all society and civil government would be uprooted. The stability of the state rests upon that of the element of which it is composed. When these return to chaos, or dissolve themselves into the thinnest air, the commonwealth itself must prove a bubble, collapsing as soon as pricked by circumstance.

Horatio's final chapter, "A Plea for Woman," was basically a recapitulation of the book. However, it also brought in more of Dr. Ware's recommendations for preventing sexual indulgence in youth and other suggestions to youth and men for controlling themselves. It also included the letter from Mrs. Dall praising *Why Not?*, which suggested that a book for men also be written, and which reinforced Horatio's claims about the frequency of abortion in general and its high frequency among the married. Horatio again stressed the frequent lack of consideration husbands showed for the complaints of their wives. Although "there almost always exists a physical cause for all the many peculiar woes that women suffer," Horatio claimed that many husbands, and even some physicians, passed these off as "vain imaginings of a distempered mind, or the restless chafing of a soured and impatient disposition," which it was best not to encourage. "Courteous to strangers," he added, "we should be still more so to our own, and so be most truly brave in fighting down and conquering ourselves." "Let each of my readers," he concluded, "before closing this book, again ask himself, 'Is It I?'"[16]

We have mentioned Horatio's letter to Dr. Thomas Addis Emmet requesting permission to dedicate the book to him. The actual dedication may be unique in including a footnote. The dedication and footnote read:[17]

> To Dr. Thomas Addis Emmet, of New York, Surgeon to the State Woman's Hospital; One of the only two purely uterine specialists as yet practising in America;* The pupil and successor of Marion Sims, and himself as an operator, his great master's more than equal.
>
> *As contradistinguished from especialists, of whom there are many.

When Emmet finally saw this dedication he provided the following thank-you note. It indicates that Horatio had achieved considerable fame for his successful extirpation of a uterus.[18]

73 Madison Av: NY
June 5th 1867

My dear Doctor
With our friend Dr Brown-Séquard,[19]
I also deem it something more than a compliment in dedicating your book to me. I feel highly flattered at the compliment & your appreciation of the little I have yet accomplished, (for I have not yet taken the Uterus out) but between ourselves I can not help stating that I really think you have laid it on pretty thick in your dedication. With every wish for the accomplishment of all that you would ask from the book

I am yours sincerely
T.A. Emmet

In February 1868, the following book review of *Is It I?* by a guest editor appeared in the *Boston Medical and Surgical Journal*.[20] It was signed "P.," almost certainly Horatio's old enemy, Dr. Luther Parks, Jr. Parks had just relinquished co-editorship of this journal two issues earlier and "P." included a phrase with "*we*" which suggests it was actually written earlier while Parks was a co-editor. It constituted a scathing attack on Horatio:

According to the standard which makes a pamphlet on the use of tents for the dilation of the os uteri suitable for distribution in social circles,[21] this work might be deemed "a book for every man." For ourselves, we find nothing in it likely to produce any great impression on any married man or woman; but much calculated to do mischief to the young unmarried persons of both sexes, who constitute the majority of readers of works of this class. Notwithstanding the opinions of some eminent men, we do not believe in the advantage of solemnly calling the attention of very young people to the sexual function with the purpose of warning them against certain dangers. … we believe that the feelings thus excited are not again repressed by any such words of warning, be they ever so judiciously put. What can be said, then, of a book like that we are now called upon to notice, where the sensational elements so largely prevails in title and contents—particularly when we see it conspicuously placed on the counter of a bookstore much frequented by school-girls, and other persons of various ages and classes?

The review stated that the Publishers' Note "enrolls the author among the noble army of martyrs," and this was followed by quotation of those portions of the Note postulating a clique of Boston physicians who harassed Horatio and which contrasted this to the widespread "acknowledgment of his scientific labors" by physicians elsewhere. "P." then noted: "The 'publishers' note' thus seems to proclaim that Dr. H.R. Storer is in advance of his time; and that he is not honored by all 'in his own city.'" The review continued with the "character of the weapons that have been used against our author" sentence from the Note that was reproduced earlier and this was followed by the full text of Dr. Asa Millet's letter, presumably showing why no "word of palliation or excuse from the editors" was required. Following some comments about Horatio's first graduate course for physicians and a questioning of Horatio's refusal to give a certificate to one "unworthy aspirant" in Horatio's recently-completed second course, "P." repeated the Publishers' Note's preamble to the list of Horatio's publications, then concluded:[22]

> The publication of this list—including reference to articles on "cases of Nymphomania"; on the "uterine dilator; a a [sic] new method of reaching the uterine cavity, and of inducing premature labor"; and on a "medico-legal study of rape," &c.,—is charmingly appropriate in a book designed for general circulation. Fortunately for the public, the papers themselves have not been added. P.

Given the tenor of this review, one suspects that if "P." first learned of the clique that was out to get Horatio from the "Publishers' Note," he quickly applied for membership.

The 1867 Annual Meeting of the American Medical Association was held in Cincinnati from May 7 to May 10. Horatio and his father attended and probably stayed at the home of his father's brother, Bellamy, who already had achieved fame as lawyer, judge, and politician. Certainly the most significant thing occurring for the Storers at the meeting was Horatio's election as one of the Association's Vice Presidents. Some Boston physicians, contemptuous as they were of the national association, would have scoffed at this being "The highest medical honor, save one, that can be conferred in this country," but Horatio and his father no doubt believed it, along with most other members of the American Medical Association.

The Cincinnati meeting led directly to Horatio's next published paper, "Self Abuse in Women: Its Causation and Rational Treatment."[23] Horatio saw the need for this article since "the subject is very generally misinterpreted, is as frequently treated upon erroneous principles of practice, and is too often entirely overlooked." He claimed that the source of his information was "not of thought alone, but of many hundreds of confessions, and many years observation of sick women." He began with the following general discussion:

> Now I venture to say at the outset, that self abuse in women is not of rare occurrence; that it prevails alike in those who are married and who are unmarried; in the young, and in the old; that it is not necessarily a vice, nor primary, but that it may be the result of physical causes, and therefore less amenable to moral than to physical

treatment; that it is not always a sign of partial insanity, its effect or its cause; that while far less frequently than in the male, productive of extreme nervous exhaustion, it is even more frequently than in him productive of partial or extreme nervous irritation, explaining many of the cases of so-called hysteria; and that in many instances the habit initiates from no normal or abnormal longing of the woman's own heart, from no direct or indirect physical sensation upon her part, from no endeavor to simulate previous sexual intercourse had with husband or lover, but from manual caresses conferred by some half-timid man, or from the measures injudiciously or too frequently employed, however honestly, by a medical attendant, or from certain legitimate and very common employments of life, such, for instance as the use of the sewing machine. I have space but for a few words as to the causation of self abuse in women. The greater portion of my remarks I shall endeavor to devote to its rational treatment.

Horatio discussed criminal abortion because it and self-abuse both were "matters of very delicate character; concerning both of them, physician and patient would gladly preserve silence, were it not that by this means the evils referred to with all their train of deplorable results, would be sure to proceed unchecked." Horatio noted that he had been recently criticized by the *New Orleans Medical and Surgical Journal* of "indelicacy" in discussing subjects such as abortion. "Indelicacy in the physician," Horatio said, "lies rather in ignoring these pains and aches, and sufferings, these problems, that lie beneath all social life and all domestic happiness, than in sensibly studying their phenomena, and throwing upon them the light of science."

Horatio described many examples of self-abuse that were prompted by irritation from pinworms, body lice, hemorrhoids, constipation, etc. "If this be the case," Horatio wrote, "the patient is a fitter subject by far for medical treatment than for the madhouse or nunnery, and yet I have known both of these latter methods resorted to instead of the first." These innocent beginnings, however, could be problematic. "The procedure, commenced as it were in self-defense," he continued, "may easily merge into voluptuous self-abandonment." Horatio described the case of a woman for whom the "pruritus assumed such intensity that it was thought necessary to remove her to an insane asylum" where, despite a strait jacket, she "would yet rub herself upon her heel, and this openly and before the medical attendants." In this particular case, the itching was a symptom of uterine disease which Horatio "long since removed by appropriate treatment, ..." Horatio did not describe the disease or the treatment, but earlier discussions of the irritating effects of uterine discharges suggest something of this nature.

The bad consequences of self-abuse presumably were understood by the medical audience for whom Horatio was writing, and he briefly noted: "its effects, just as its frequency, have been much underrated. It accompanies, both as a symptom and as a cause, many of the apparently inexplicable and intractable cases of long confinement to the couch; it explains many a fitful temper, many a restless disposition, many a suicide."[24]

Horatio indicated that an Illinois clergyman had written him, praising his "plain, manly statements concerning abortion" and asked him for information about self-abuse in the youth of both sexes, but particularly women. The minister described in his parish "'no less than *four* young women whose physical and mental vigor are entirely wasted, and who, if they do not die from its effects, must lead miserable lives, a burden to themselves and to every one else.'" The clergyman continued: "You have taken a noble stand regarding 'fashionable murder.' If you have any such attack on physical, mental and moral suicide, I wish to obtain it. ... If there is no such book, would it not be doing a good work, blessing humanity and serving God, to take steps for its preparation." Such published requests in medical journals for popular books had typically been followed by the requested book, but Horatio apparently did not take up this suggestion.

Horatio devoted a page of his article to treatment. Lice or pinworms should be removed, hemorrhoids excised, and anal fissures treated by rupturing the anal sphincter. Uterine, ovarian, or other disease producing the irritation should be treated. Excision of hypertrophied nymphae had been successful for Horatio, but he had never had success with clitoridectomy and he condemned Baker-Brown's overuse of the procedure. Drinking large doses of the bromide of potassium had been "quite often" successful. "In some instances, no doubt, marriage is indicated;" he continued, "in others, where conjugal intercourse is already excessive, lessening its amount occasions relief." Horatio criticized institutionalization for cure of self-abuse:[25]

> To place a woman addicted to self abuse, at an asylum, where everything that can take her mind off her physical condition is sedulously interdicted; where moral restraint, so-called, is chiefly relied upon, with or without the straight jacket or camisole, which, while it may confine her hands, does not confine those of her imagination, and where, as yet, many superintendents ridicule the idea of the local or pelvic causation of a local or vulval sensation, is, to say the least, a very solemn farce.

Finally, Horatio reiterated his claim that physicians must discuss such subjects and again took the critical New Orleans editor to task for saying otherwise. "The day of such prudery has passed," he concluded, "and he best serves his profession and the cause of humanity for which we are all laboring, who detects the existence, the cause and the course of any obscure disease, and points out its proper treatment. Especially is this true of the too much neglected diseases of women."

Early in the article on self-abuse, Horatio questioned a reference to him by the editor of the *Western Journal of Medicine* in the June issue of the journal which was then called the *Cincinnati Journal of Medicine*. It dealt with the recent meeting of the American Medical Association and Horatio transcribed: "'We had the pleasure of conducting one of the Superintendents of Insane Asylums to the room devoted to Psychology. But he found himself alone in his glory—not one single alienist to meet him; not even Dr. Storer came to teach, or be taught, whereat our wonder was doubtless greater than our friend's disappointment.'"[26] In the August issue of the journal, the editor, Dr. Theophilus Parvin, included an explanatory note—the meeting of the Section on Psychology had adjourned without day—and an apology of sorts. The latter read:[27]

> we would unhesitatingly express our sincere regrets that such reference was made, had it not contributed, in part at least to secure so excellent an article as that which he has furnished for the present number of the Western Journal. Certainly we shall never again for a moment suspect that one who has made such important efforts for the salvation of the offspring of others, should fail in the least iota in his duties to that "Section" which, though not his by original paternity, at least is his by fostering care, and by the most important contribution to its character.

This is an example of how well Horatio and his efforts were regarded by many, probably most, members of the medical profession who were involved in advancing medical science. One might forget this when reading about his treatment by Dr. Parks, Dr. Henry J. Bigelow, Dr. Charles Buckingham, and some of the other members of the profession in his home city.

Much to Horatio's dismay, there were only a few members of the clergy who echoed the physicians' outcry against criminal abortion. One prominent exception was the Reverend John Todd of Pittsfield, Massachusetts. He wrote an anti-abortion article for a religious publication which was republished as a pamphlet entitled *Serpents in the Dove's Nest*. It noted, in part, that[28]

> As a class, the medical profession have taken a noble stand. The desolations have become so fearful, that, as the guardians of human life, they were compelled to do so; and society owes a debt of gratitude to Dr. H. R. Storer, of Boston, especially, for his powerful arguments, lucid arrangement of facts, patient investigations, and earnest and eloquent remonstrances. Among his writings on this subject, the little work entitled "Why Not?" is a "book for every woman." and I wish every woman might carefully read it.

In a fascinating biography of his father, Todd's son wrote that *Serpents in the Dove's Nest* "secured for him the hearty sympathy and thanks of the medical profession. One of the most eminent in it wrote: 'This noble step of yours will carry joy and courage to thousands of hearts in the medical profession; and in their name, and in the name of science and humanity, allow me most sincerely to thank you. The influence of this little work will be incalculable.'"[29] A few years later, Horatio referred to "our old friend, the Rev. Dr. John Todd, of Pittsfield,"[30] and Horatio may have been this "most eminent" physician. Todd's son also wrote that his father received much mail "filled with invective and insult," because of his anti-abortion pamphlet. This suggests that Horatio may have received similar responses to *Why Not?* and *Is It I?*. If so, these were not preserved or mentioned in his writing.

The famous London ovariotomist, Mr. T. Spencer Wells, and Dr. Randolph Edmund Peaslee, of New York, who also had successfully performed the surgery, were guests of the Boston Society for Medical Improvement on September 23, 1867. Horatio's father had invited them to "give the society the results of their experience and their opinion as to the propriety of the operation." Mr. Wells discussed his impressive overall record of 162 recoveries and sixty-six deaths with only four deaths in his most recent twenty-eight cases. The Minutes of the meeting included the following comments from Horatio's nemesis:[31]

> Dr. H. J. Bigelow said he had listened with interest to these remarks; he had often quoted the case in which this washing out was first done by Dr Peaslee and thought the proceeding admirable. He himself had done the operation twice unsuccessfully in 1849-50 and had had numerous applications to do it again, but never had, preferring, as a matter of taste, not to do the operation. Statistics as to this operation are imperfect; many fatal cases here are never reported and probably elsewhere the same concealment is made.

Horatio later was to indicate that as a result of Bigelow's comments, "Mr. Spencer Wells received what he considered the grossest insult of his life."[32]

The Minutes also told that "Dr Jackson said no Boston surgeon had had a successful case save Dr Clark, and death took place in that case from cancer of the ovary. (He afterwards begged pardon for forgetfulness & said that Dr H. R. Storer had had 2 or 3 successful results.)"[33] It is possible that Mr. Wells, himself, corrected Dr. J.B.S. Jackson's "forgetfulness." Only that morning, Wells had been present at, and participated in, an ovariotomy of Horatio's. An ovarian tumor of "some two years' standing" and weighing forty-three pounds was removed from a forty-one-year-old woman from Tennessee.[34] The clamp shield was applied to the pedicle and the ovary and its tumor separated from the pedicle with scissors. Hemorrhage did not occur until the clamp was relaxed and then from only one artery which was secured with an iron wire ligature. Horatio performed the surgery and for the first time "pocketed the pedicle."

The patient recovered quickly and was discharged by her attending physician, Dr. Wheeler of Chelsea, a month later and just before Mr. Wells sailed back to England.

The closing of the incision and the "pocketing" were described as follows:

> Mr. Wells having passed his hand into the abdominal cavity and found the right ovary in a healthy condition, the walls of the primary incision were united by twenty sutures of iron wire; *the extremity of the pedicle being brought between the inner lips of the wound, at its lower angle, and there 'pocketed;'* this being effected by passing three of the stitches through itself and both inner edges of the abdominal wound, and then bringing the external edges closely together; the raw surface of the pedicle being in apposition to the raw surfaces of the wound, and yet covered over fairly and completely by the line of superficial union.

Horatio reasoned that the novel procedure of "pocketing the pedicle," would avoid a number of problems that had beset ovariotomy, including primary and secondary hemorrhage, fetid discharge from the stump, and suppuration in adjacent tissues. Years later, Dr. Henry Orlando Marcy was to write Horatio about the "discovery" of the procedure at Johns Hopkins in 1891.[35] Marcy would also describe pocketing the pedicle as one of the most significant advances in his 1910 article on the history of abdominal surgery.[36]

It will be recalled, that the "Publishers' Note" for *Is It I?* discussed Horatio's June lecture to physicians and included their resolutions thanking Horatio for "taking the advanced step" that gave them "the opportunity of hearing these subjects discussed thoroughly and impartially." The second class of physicians met in December 1867 and they provided similar resolutions which were published in the *Boston Medical and Surgical Journal* in December 1867.[37] The *Whereases* are of interest:

> *Whereas,* an unjust prejudice, founded, partly on ignorance and professional jealousy, and partly on a false conservatism, exists in the minds of many or our profession, against those who give special attention to the diseases of women; and, *whereas,* many of these diseases are either altogether ignored, or imperfectly treated of, in our text-books, and by the teachers of medical science in our schools; and *whereas,* Prof. H. R. Storer, in instituting and carrying out, as he has done, a plan for the more thorough instruction of physicians on these important subjects, and in taking a bold stand as a Uterine Specialist, has incurred a certain degree of misrepresentation and abuse; therefore
> *Resolved, ...*

The eleven physicians signing the Resolutions thanking Horatio for his course and requesting publication of the Resolutions included Alexander J. Stone, who already was Horatio's assistant. Stone had been a Harvard medical student in 1865-1866, but moved to the Berkshire Medical School where he obtained his degree in 1867.[38] Horatio was already at Pittsfield and no doubt Stone had been a prize pupil whom Horatio invited to help with his Boston practice.[39] Stone was to become a key figure in medical education and medical journalism in Minnesota.

Horatio included the following discussion of his lectures to physicians in his 1901 letter to Malcolm.[40]

After the trouble with Hodges, Minot, and Ellis, and my being dropped from Harvard rather than apologize for what was no concern of its Faculty, I began my lectures to physicians, two courses yearly. They came from far and near. The lectures were advertised in the medical journals, and were given in my large offices at Hotel Pelham, with diagrams, demonstrations upon patients during each lecture, and operations at St. Elizabeth's.

Horatio also noted in this letter that his lectures "are supposed by many to have been the first anticipation of the post-graduate schools." Horatio's 1901 letter also made reference to a much more ambitious post-graduate-education effort. It was to be "a combination of lectures upon the remaining specialties by a dozen others who had all promised to cooperate with me, the prospectus having been printed and circulated." The prospectus reads:[41]

SPECIAL INSTRUCTION
IN
MEDICAL SCIENCE.

In compliance with the desire of the profession, as indicated by the resolutions of the Convention of Teachers at Cincinnati in May last, unanimously endorsed by the American Medical Association at its subsequent meeting, that the Standard of Medical Education in this country should be raised and its limits extended, the undersigned have associated themselves together for the purpose of giving instruction in their respective departments to advanced students and to physicians who may be desirous of fitting themselves for special practice.

It is thought that this action will be appreciated by those intending to visit Europe, who can do so to better advantage after mastering the details of a special department, as well as by those who are unable to go abroad and are yet anxious to avail themselves of every opportunity of reaching the same plane with their more fortunate neighbors. There seems little reason why much the same instruction cannot be afforded at home that is now sought in Europe, and sought to so little purpose by those unacquainted with foreign languages.

It is thought, also, that there are many general practitioners who will be glad to refresh their memories after years of engrossing labor.

The courses will be delivered during the winter term of the Medical College, at such hours as will not interfere with the collegiate curriculum.

At the summer session it is intended, with the assistance of additional instructors, to cover the whole range of legitimate specialties.

Fee for each course, $25. The classes will be limited, and certificates of attendance will be issued at the close of the term.

Applications for tickets to be made to Dr. H. R. Storer, Hotel Pelham.

Boston, 1 Nov. 1867.

This was followed by the names of the dozen lecturers, their lecture topics, and their impressive affiliations and educations. Gustavus Hay was among these and his specialty was ophthalmology. It is gratifying to see that Horatio's friendship with Gus Hay continued beyond their undergraduate years and also to see the large body of other eminent Boston physicians who were willing to cooperate with Horatio, given his bad treatment by the Boston "clique."

Horatio also described in his 1901 letter how this attempt "was frustrated by the treachery of Dr Buckingham, who, although my father's open enemy, received his professorship as reward ..." Unfortunately, little has turned up to elucidate "the treachery" of Charles Buckingham that prevented the courses of the above prospectus. A best guess is that he was contacted as a possible obstetrics lecturer and not only declined, but blew the whistle on the effort to someone who could pressure the other cooperating physicians to change their minds. David Humphreys Storer was to resign his Professorship of Obstetrics and Medical Jurisprudence the next summer and was replaced by Buckingham. If Buckingham obtained the post as a "reward" for frustrating this post-graduate medical instruction, some powerful physician or physicians at the Medical School wanted the effort frustrated. Henry J. Bigelow is one that comes to mind.

A double ovariotomy was performed by Horatio late in November on a forty-three-year-old Canadian woman and the report was published in the *Canada Medical Journal*.[42] Following removal of the first large ovarian tumor, the patient's pulse disappeared and the rate of respiration dropped. Attempts to revive her continued for seventy minutes, finally with success. Since the clamp shield which had remained in place was preventing hemorrhage, the exhausted resuscitators took the opportunity "to enjoy a hearty dinner." The operation resumed with the pedicle "sutured rather than ligatured." Examination of the other ovary showed it also was diseased. With much difficulty the tumor, the size of a child's head, was dislodged from its wedged position in the pelvis, the clamp shield applied, and "division effected as before" with a scissors. The smaller tumor weighed two-and-one-half pounds and the larger more than thirty-three pounds. Thanks to the fine post-operative care of Dr. Wheeler of Chelsea, the lady survived and travelled back to St. Johns, New Brunswick five weeks and three days after the surgery.

The double ovariotomy report included a progress report on "removal of the uterus from above." Horatio's great record of one survivor out of one operation had by then declined to one survivor out of five. Horatio noted, "all of the cases having been of dire necessity, and the worst of them having recovered; while in the unsuccessfully [sic] four, primary haemorrhage, the more usual cause of death, was easily and entirely prevented by my clamp shield." Horatio also mentioned his umbilical hernia operation, noting that "death was from extraneous causes." Horatio obviously viewed all six of these abdominal surgeries as successes since he made reference to them "only as bearing upon the general question of abdominal section, and as tending to strengthen the hands and cheer the hearts of that great army of the brethren, who, slow to take the responsibility in a doubtful case, are quick and ready to follow a successful precedent."[43]

It will be recalled that Horatio on Christmas Eve of 1866 provided an apology to Calvin Ellis which was published in the *Boston Medical and Surgical Journal*. The following letter to Oliver Wendell Holmes indicates he was again thinking of Ellis' autopsy at Christmas time:[44]

> Hotel Pelham
> 28 Dec. 1867
>
> My dear Dr.
>
> I have become satisfied that I was wrong in the opinion I have till now entertained, that the convict Magee was alive at the time of his examination. It is therefore clearly my duty to make all possible amends to Dr Ellis for the injury I may have occasioned him, & necessary that the revocation of my views should be as complete & public as was their avowal.
>
> To this end I am now preparing for immediate publication in the New York Medical Record, the journal in which my obnoxious article appeared, a paper that I hope will put this unfortunate subject finally at rest.
>
> To do this will however involve a careful resumé of all the features of the Magee case, & as there were certain points observed, such as, the contraction of the ventricles, the regular beat of 80 to the minute, prior to opening the thorax, &c &c, which under the circumstances must subvert the hitherto received doctrines of physiologists. I shall esteem it a great favor if you will furnish me at your very first leisure with such arguments as will serve to destroy forever the position I have hitherto taken in the premises—and end I am now as anxious as yourself to accomplish.

yrs sincerely
Horatio R. Storer

Prof. Holmes—

Dr. Holmes responded quickly with the following from which is omitted two-and-one-half handwritten pages of references on this subject:[45]

164 Charles St
Dec 30th 1867

Dear Dr Storer,
    The treatises on Physiology, many of which I have examined, are very barren of information on the point to which you refer. I can, however, give you a few references which may prove of service.
        Heart beating after death.
"First to live and last to die." Galen, as given in the "Index Brassacoli"

    ...

    I give you these references to the books on my own shelves. The journals will present plenty more, no doubt, but some of these may be useful. I think from these alone it would appear that an accusation could not be supported on the grounds alleged, so far as I understand them. I am therefore very glad that you wish to review your position, and I shall be happy to hand you any further aid if I can do so, especially by referring you to the pages I have cited from works at hand.

Yours very truly
O.W. Holmes

No apology of Horatio to Ellis published in the New York journal has been located. What is more, Horatio was to discuss the Magee case again four years later, claiming that Magee could and should have been resuscitated after being lowered from the gallows. Horatio's failure to carry out his promise to Holmes to publicly proclaim that he was wrong is puzzling to say the least. The less unflattering explanation is that he changed his mind *again* after reviewing the additional information that Holmes provided, deciding that it did not "subvert the hitherto received doctrines of physiologists," i.e., show that Magee was dead when autopsied.

    Much of Horatio's time in the early months of 1868 must have been occupied writing the book *Nurses and Nursing*.[46] Unlike two of Horatio's later books which were largely the republication of earlier articles, reports, or books, *Nurses and Nursing* was written from scratch. The book may be considered a labor of love for at least two reasons. It was concerned primarily with nursing of the women patients to whom Horatio had devoted his practice and his life.

In addition, it was dedicated to Sister Superior Frances Sophia MacKenzie, a woman whom Horatio would marry two-and-one-half years after the death of his second wife, but a woman whom he no doubt loved much earlier. The book has the following dedication:

TO
FRANCES S. MACKENZIE,
SISTER-SUPERIOR OF THE FRANCISCAN HOSPITAL,
HERSELF A REALIZATION OF THE PICTURE
DRAWN OF THE GOOD NURSE BY
ST. VINCENT DE PAUL.[47]

A great-grandson of Horatio has Frances' hardbound copy of the book which includes in Horatio's hand:

"Sister Frances"
With Sincere Regard
19 June 1868

The cover page also includes "*Published for the Benefit of the Franciscan Hospital for Women.*" The book was used as a training manual for nurses by the hospital and it may be that proceeds from its sale went to the Hospital which Frances founded.

Training of nurses had barely begun anywhere when the book was written and the efforts of the "irresponsible" and "incompetent" personnel at the notorious Boston Female Medical School of Samuel Gregory in this direction were most deficient. Horatio's first paragraph reads:[48]

The need of a more thorough preparation for their duties by those intrusted with the care of the sick,—more especially where these invalids are women,—seems already to have been felt. Attempts have been made to supply this want, but usually by parties irresponsible or incompetent, who have, therefore, not secured general confidence, and have failed. Under these circumstances, I might well shirk from undertaking any portion of a task of such importance, and to which there has been attached so disagreeable a prejudice, did I not rely upon my readers' forbearance and cordial cooperation.

Horatio further criticized "irresponsible or incompetent" men like Gregory who had called for female attendants for midwifery and treatment of women's diseases because employment of men "is an offence against the higher sentiments of woman's nature." Horatio quoted a long paragraph from his anonymous editorial, "Female Physicians," in the April 1856 *Boston Medical and Surgical Journal* which challenged the view that physicians behaved inappropriately with their women patients. He noted that such inappropriate criticisms of male physicians probably had deterred physicians from providing the instruction and assistance to women that otherwise would have already generated a competent force of nurses. Horatio also provided definitions of "nurse":[49]

> A nurse, say Worcester, Webster, and other lexicographers, is one who is in charge of a sick person. For my own nurses, however, I enlarge upon this definition, and expect a light and delicate hand, a noiseless step, gentle voice, and quick eye; neatness and a sense of order, perfect obedience, presence of mind, cheerfulness, sobriety, patience, forbearance, judgment, and kindness of heart. They must be intelligent and discreet, and must be actuated by high religious feelings and principles of duty.

Sister Superior MacKenzie may have been the model for such a high standard.

Horatio made highly specific recommendations on a range of subjects including nurse-patient relations, nurse-family relations, nurse-servant relations, the sick room, the patient's bed, etc. Requirements for the sick room included a proper temperature range during day and night, the need for adequate ventilation, the need for humidifiers, and the proper fuel for heating (never anthracite coal). Horatio's prescription for the condition of sick room air showed Horatio's early knowledge and application of Lister's principles of antisepsis. The paragraph included:[50]

> An excellent disinfectant, but one as yet but lately known, is the ordinary coal-tar of the gasworks. Mixed intimately with fine coal ashes, or any similar absorbent, it may be used like powdered charcoal; or its essential element, carbolic acid, whose effect in preventing the growth of the microscopic and disease-causing sporules crowding the atmosphere, is very marked, may be used in solution, and diffused through the air by the atomizer.

Horatio indicated that a candidate required many months of instruction in these "principles of nursing," and this could only properly take place in "a sick chamber or the wards of a hospital." He called for "scholarships" at hospitals which would allow women to acquire nursing skills. These would prompt many capable women "to gladly offer their services gratuitously in return for such privileges, and the honorable certificate a faithful performance of duty might justly receive." "Instruction might thus be afforded to nurses," Horatio continued, "not merely at general, but at special hospitals, the advantages of which are becoming recognized in every large city, and to aid in the establishment of one of which this book has been written." Horatio then described the Franciscan Hospital, its original connection with St. Joseph's Home for unemployed domestics and its later transfer to its current limited 30-bed facility.

He indicated the need for expansion to a new "edifice without vain show, or unnecessary architectural finish, but of size sufficient for from fifty to one hundred beds; a building capable of sheltering whatever poor women, requiring its aid, may knock at its doors;—a blessing to the community, and an honor to the city."

The key contribution of nursing to the "excellence" of the Franciscan Hospital was described in the concluding passage of *Nurses and Nursing*:[51]

> In ordinary hospitals, the nurse is merely a hired subordinate, with no other aim than the acquisition of her scanty pittance. Here, on the contrary, she enters already tried, having been selected from many applicants for her apparent fitness for the work, and under the immediate supervision of one who has herself been trained by a previous hospital service. She takes a deep and special interest in every patient; she sees in each an intimation and precedent of those to come under her care in the future, and she feels that, upon her success and faithfulness, her own reward, not on earth, but in heaven, is to depend; while, to the invalids under her charge there comes a sense of the devotion with which they are attended,—in itself no slight guarantee at once of security and of recovery, and going far to secure the latter end.

This paragraph includes a hint about Frances Sophia MacKenzie's largely unknown past, as one "who has herself been trained by a previous hospital service." But we don't know where or when.

In 1868, Horatio also commenced a series of papers on "The Rectum in its Relations to Uterine Disease," the first of which appeared in May 1868 in the new *American Journal of Obstetrics*.[52] Horatio began the first installment by denouncing the near-total lack of rectal examinations by physicians and noted as well that vaginal examinations still were not performed as frequently as they should be when diagnosing and treating uterine disease. What is more, he "knew men of great reputation as gynecological experts, ... who do not, in their ordinary examinations, practically recognize the existence of the rectum, at least so far as its exploration is concerned." He also noted that some gynecologists, including one of the most eminent, felt that the "treatment of rectal disease in women as in men should rest only with the general surgeon." Horatio argued that the intimate interrelationships between rectal and uterine disease vitiated these views.

Although not given as the *reason* that gynecologists should treat rectal disease in women, Horatio had a unique awareness that female anatomy made diagnosis and treatment of the rectum in women quite a different thing than it was for men. At some point in training or practice, Horatio developed the technique of *vaginal eversion of the rectum* and his first published description of it was in this article in the May issue of the *American Journal of Obstetrics*. The technique involved insertion of the finger into the vagina, then the rectum is "everted through its sphincter like the finger of a glove." Horatio indicated that he had practiced this for "many years" and shown it to a great many physicians present at his operations and examinations. None had ever reported seeing or hearing of it before, but Horatio suspected that although original with himself, it may have been "but the rediscovery of something already well known."[53]

Vaginal eversion of the rectum allowed diagnosis and treatment of many conditions such as hemorrhoids much more rapidly and simply than would otherwise be possible. Sometimes it was necessary to rupture the anal sphincter to achieve satisfactory eversion. This was not considered by Horatio to produce any long-term problems, although he frequently administered ether prior to doing it. Horatio concluded his initial article by describing a case that highlighted his major points. Vaginal eversion of the rectum disclosed primary intestinal disease which was found to be the underlying cause of the patient's "uterine and other pelvic disturbances."[54]

Early in May, Horatio faced "the most difficult [case] that had ever presented itself to me in practice."[55] So he described it during the initial stage of the operation to his associates who were assisting him. The case was a young woman whose physician had accidentally inserted a hard rubber "horseshoe pessary" eight-and-one-half inches in outside length into the bladder instead of the uterus. The lady was in a great deal of pain and requested removal of the instrument which had been inserted five days earlier. After his original vaginal examination, Horatio told the woman she must have been mistaken in her belief that her physician had inserted the device. A subsequent rectal examination also was negative. Only the lady's persistent claims that she had a pessary finally led Horatio to the two-handed examination of the bladder that suggested presence of the two blunt points of the instrument. The uterine sound was inserted through the urethra and confirmed the existence of the pessary. "The pessary was completely within the cavity of the bladder," he wrote, "which it had distended to the utmost, and was lying with the centre of its closed portion directly opposite the outlet, but with its convexity, instead of its concavity, forwards."

Horatio admitted the woman to the hospital, and the next afternoon "proceeded to operate" with the assistance of several physicians. All potential incisions such as those for removing bladder stones were considered and judged "unavailing, or very dangerous." The only course that appeared at all promising was removal of the instrument via the route it had entered. Horatio tells the rest too well to paraphrase:[56]

> I now, by graduated uterine bougies, dilated the canal sufficiently to receive the tip of the little finger of my right hand, the patient being upon her left side. By steady, continuous pressure, or rather coaxing, I succeeded in inserting this finger entirely, and could then

only touch the centre of the pessary at the posterior portion of the bladder; the points, even when extreme pressure was made above the pubes, could not be brought within reach. Efforts were made to rotate the pessary by the aid of the forefinger of the left hand within the vagina, but without avail; and very shortly I was compelled to desist on the account of the severe pain I was suffering myself, the position of the centre of the pessary being such that I could only reach it with my right little finger by stretching this away from those adjoining it, the hand being supine, while upon turning it with the palm downwards, the remaining fingers of the hand, by closing the vulval outlet, effectually prevented any assistance by introducing the forefinger of the other hand.

I now tried the little finger of the left hand with no better result, although I am ambidexter [sic]. So far I had accomplished nothing. Forceps was introduced, and the insurmountable character of the obstacles already indicated was practically shown, while haemorrhage, which now began to show itself despite all the care that had been taken, warned me against further essaying what was, at least by this means, an impossibility. Determined, however, to succeed if success was possible, I now rapidly and forcibly passed my right forefinger, and, to my great delight, found that I could grasp the bar with the pulp of the first phalanx, much as an elephant seizes an object with the tip of his proboscis, and I now felt that the case was practically my own. For some twenty minutes, or half an hour, with the active assistance of my friends, who controlled, as they best could, the points of the instrument through the thick abdominal wall, I essayed the required evolution—one forefinger being in the bladder, the other in the vagina. It was necessary that the position of the pessary should be completely reversed and that the right bar of the instrument—this looking forward, the concavity being upward, and the patient still lying upon her left side—should enter the outlet. Otherwise, of course, extraction would be impossible, as every one familiar with the vaginal use of the horse-shoe will at once perceive. So that I not only had with the tip of my forefinger, which was aching badly from the compression to which it was subjected, to bring one of the distant extremities of the pessary to, and into, the opening which my finger already occupied, but it was necessary also to make a selection between them, and not merely this but to see to it that the pessary was right side up, its concavity looking forward else my efforts must be in vain. I have often thought, when turning the foetus in utero, how completely the mind and the touch must coincide in order to effect success, and have been even more impressed with this when essaying version where the membranes have remained unbroken; but how simple and easy were these procedures in comparison with the present!

Several times I all but succeeded, and each time the upper limb, in its rotation, impinged upon the arch of the pubes or one of the rami, and the instrument slipped back in an instant; but, at last, by a fortunate coincidence of position, continued manipulation and forcible pressure, a point of the instrument was engaged in the urethral aperture, was protruded by pressure behind from within the vagina, was seized, the three-quarters rotation was effected and, to the joy of us all there came the safe deliverance.

The patient quickly recovered, including "at once" regaining control of the vesical sphincter. Rather than criticize the doctor who put the pessary in the wrong place, Horatio wrote:

Fortunate for him that the case fell into friendly hands. There are those who might have called this accident an unpardonable error, instead of seeing in it only an instance to warn themselves of the possibility of its occurrence. Those only who have never, in passing the female catheter, found its point sliding down into the vaginal rather that into the urethral orifice, can have the right to miscall the gentleman's misfortune. None such, however, exist.

In the Summer of 1868, David Humphreys Storer sent a letter to his long-time friend and colleague, Dr. Oliver Wendell Holmes, announcing his resignation from the Harvard Medical School and giving his reasons for doing so:[57]

I have forwarded to the Corporation of Harvard University my resignation as a Professor in the Medical School. You, I feel have a right to know the reasons which have influenced me in taking this step. In 1855, you did me the honor to propose me as a suitable person to fill this Chair of Obstetrics. I accepted this trust and from that hour, until the present, I have endeavored untiringly, faithfully, to discharge the duties devolving upon me. I have felt a pleasure and a pride in this position, and have striven to sustain its aspirations.

For years, it was always grateful to meet my colleagues—freely, unreservedly to express my sentiments—knowing that if I differed from them, they would never doubt the purity of my motives—and that sometimes my suggestions might even be thought worthy of consideration never having any object in view save the good of our Institution, I felt that my presence at our meetings was not unacceptable.

During the past two years, a revolution has taken place—a new policy has been inaugurated. Several of the elements which have been added to our numbers since the dissolution of the Tremont St School have destroyed almost entirely our former unity. ...

A course has been pursued of late which I most sincerely, most honestly believe must be injurious to the welfare of the School. I have endeavored faithfully to avert it. I have at all times freely and fearlessly expressed my views—long after it was evident that to express them was to call forth an almost unanimous approbation. A sense of duty has compelled me to relinquish my post—a duty to you as well as to myself.

This sad letter does not specify who and what were the problems that prematurely ended the sixty-four-year-old professor's career, although it may be no coincidence that among the "Several of the elements which have been added to our numbers" was Charles Edward Buckingham.

David Humphreys' Harvard Medical School colleagues, J.B.S. Jackson, Oliver Wendell Holmes, Henry J. Bigelow, George C. Shattuck, Edward H. Clarke, John Bacon, Richard M. Hodges, and James C. White, expressed their sorrow at his departure in single letter dated July 8, 1868.[58] Dr. Buckingham provided the following separate but accompanying letter:[59]

Boston, July 8, 1868

D. Humphreys Storer, M.D.
My Dear Sir.

You will not deem it strange that my name is not appended to the accompanying letter. Indeed your feelings of regard for our colleagues would be diminished, were it to appear with theirs. You will, however, allow me to express my respect for the position you have taken in the school, and for the untimely faithfulness with which your work has been performed.

The differences between us have been of many years standing, and had their origin, undoubtedly, aside from professional matters.

Allow me to ask that all past disagreement be forgotten, and that when we meet, it may be without the coolness of the past. As the younger man, I propose this, and am

Very respectfully yours,
Chas. E. Buckingham

Despite this attempt at resolving past problems, we will learn that Buckingham was to denigrate David Humphreys from his new pulpit.

J.B.S. Jackson, also sent a separate letter of regret[60] which included a second source for regret. He wrote: "how much disappointed I was that you were not chosen President of the Mass. Medical Society." Jackson noted that Dr. Charles Putnam, the actual recipient, "has not the first requisite for a presiding officer, nor has he ever done anything for the Society to entitle him to the honor conferred upon him, nor do I believe that he cares a straw for it. He ought to have declined at once." It is likely that David Humphreys Storer was greatly disappointed not to have received this highest honor in Massachusetts medicine. He probably would occasionally attribute it to the fact that his son was held in such low estimation by a few powerful Boston physicians who dispensed such honors.

The summer of 1868 marked a "new" book written by Horatio in conjunction with a Boston lawyer, Franklin Fiske Heard. The book was entitled *Criminal Abortion: Its Nature, Its Evidence, and Its Law.*[61] Its preface indicated that "Book I" was "rewritten from" the 1859 *North-American Medico-Chirurgical Review* articles. This "rewrite" involved relatively minor changes and only a small amount of new material. "Book II" aimed at exhausting the subject of the Criminal Law as it pertained to abortion. "The cases have been stated so fully," the authors noted in the Preface, "as to preclude the necessity of examining the volumes of Reports from which they are taken."

In 1859, Horatio had written in his first chapter: "To ... his father, and to the journalists ... by whom the effort then made was so warmly and eloquently seconded, the writer acknowledges his indebtedness for the thought of the present undertaking." In the new book, "thought of the *present* undertaking," became, "thought of the undertaking, *which has culminated, he has reason to believe, in an agitation which is now shaking society, throughout our country, in its very centre.*"[62] Horatio also added a long paragraph which further described the large progress of the crusade by physicians since its inception a decade earlier. It summarized the efforts of himself, the American Medical Association, Rev. John Todd, and others, and also noted that: "The importance of the subject is rapidly becoming recognized by the legal as well as by the medical profession; and extracts from the author's writings upon the subject, presented through the pages of Elwell's treatise on Malpractice and Medical Evidence, and the later American edition of Taylor's Medical Jurisprudence, have already affected the ruling of courts."[63]

In Horatio's second chapter, "Its Frequency, and the Causes Thereof," Horatio repeated the data originally presented in 1859 along with a few additional recent supporting statistics. He added a key footnote following the 1859 paragraph claiming that abortion's "frequency is rapidly increasing." It read: "Thus we wrote in 1859. Since then, though so great a flood of light has been poured upon the subject, the times seem little changed. Let us hope, however, that the apparent fact may be owing to the unveiling of what was formerly more frequently practised, but kept concealed."[64]

An addition to a footnote in a succeeding chapter, "Its Victims," expanded on the differences between Catholics and Protestants in the frequency of criminal abortion noting that "several hundred" of Protestant women had obtained abortions compared to seven Catholic women. What is more, Horatio had learned "upon further inquiry, that all but two [Catholics] were only nominally so, not going to the confession."[65]

Horatio had claimed in 1859 that insanity could result from abortion via "consciousness of guilt against God, humanity, and even mere natural instinct ..." In 1868 he added: "The mental aberration may also be produced, and undoubtedly frequently is, by the reflex cerebral irritation induced by either of the pelvic lesions, that we have instanced as directly resulting from abortion." Thus we see that Horatio's ideas about reflex insanity from pelvic sources had matured, or at least changed, considerably in nine years. Horatio's undiminished belief that abortion was a factor in female insanity and that asylums could improve their treatment of their female patients is shown by this footnote that immediately followed the above quoted sentence:[66]

> To the decided effect, akin to neuralgia, very frequently produced upon the mental system by uterine and ovarian disease, we have had occasion to direct the attention of the medical profession. ... Inasmuch as several of the gentlemen charged with the supervision of our lunatic hospitals have been slow to apply towards the cure of their patients the practical suggestions that we have made, the evidence lately afforded by one of their own number upon the causation of insanity by abortion will read with interest. "I have for many years," says Dr. Gray, of the New York State Asylum at Utica, "received and treated patients whose insanity was directly traceable to this crime through its moral and physical effects."

Horatio in 1859 had claimed that insanity was "still to be observed" in early pregnancy. A new footnote included:[67]

> We must frankly avow, however, our belief that, during the whole period of pregnancy, women are not quite as accountable morally, however they may be legally, as when not in this condition; just as in the non-puerperal state, their minds are ordinarily somewhat differently affected at the menstrual periods than during the interval; a fact acknowledged by every woman who honestly confesses to her own sensations, and noticed by every observant medical practitioner, indeed by most married men.

As Horatio himself confirmed in his speech to Asylum Superintendents in 1883, Emily Elvira's mental state was strongly altered during her menstrual period.[68] Given her eventual move to a mental asylum or residential facility of some sort, she undoubtedly had days during each menstrual cycle prior to that move when she appeared somewhat "insane." Horatio's possible generalization from this unfortunate experience with his wife to other women is shown by a new long footnote a few pages later reiterating his claim of the large liability of menstruation for female physicians.[69]

Horatio in his 1859 "Its Innocent Abettors" chapter had taken the controversial position that a woman with a deformed pelvis which had repeatedly led to the death of her child during birth should after some number of infant deaths be required to have a Caesarean section in the event of another pregnancy. Horatio added the following paragraph in 1868, indicating that his mentor Simpson totally agreed:

> Said Professor Simpson to the British Medical Association, in August 1867, at Dublin, which has always been the headquarters of craniotomy, "If a woman with a deformed pelvis would go on putting herself in the way of becoming pregnant, she ought to be made to take the risks of the Caesarean operation, rather than be encouraged in her course by sacrificing the life of her child." [70]

Simpson may have expressed this to Horatio in 1854 or 1855, and it might have been a factor in Horatio's strong concern for fetal life, but no published words of Simpson to this effect have been located. It is possible that Simpson had read, accepted, and was repeating Horatio's view on the matter.

The following admission of his own accidental productions of abortion was added to Horatio's discussion of abortion being induced by medical procedures when the attendant had no expectation the woman was pregnant:

> He has himself, in two cases reported by him to the Suffolk District Medical Society, in a somewhat similar manner, unintentionally induced miscarriage. In one of these cases, the woman had aborted but a short time before. To abate its apparent effects, a strong caustic was applied within the uterine cavity, the patient declaring that no intercourse had occurred since her previous mishap. The result was as already indicated. In the other instance, a lady supposed to be passing the grand climacteric, and who had not had children for many years, was operated upon for artificial perineum; she also, as well as her husband, alleged that coitus had not been indulged in for several months. Some ten days or a fortnight after the operation, she miscarried. [71]

Suffolk District Medical Society proceedings frequently went unreported in the *Boston Medical and Surgical Journal* or elsewhere and this appears to have been the case when Horatio reported these two unintentional abortions which he himself had caused. On the other hand, the Society Secretary may have purposely omitted reference to these particular reports.

Considerable reshuffling of 1859 material occurred in the final chapters of the 1868 book, but almost all of it is there. The notable exceptions were the various state statutes on criminal abortion (or lack of same) and the analyses of these that Horatio had provided in the "Its Obstacles to Conviction," article.

These might have been expected to be covered in Book 2, "From the Standpoint of Law," which as Horatio indicated in the Preface was produced by the lawyer, Franklin Fiske Heard. However, they were not, and Book 2 seems a rather weak effort that Horatio may have been dissociating himself from when he wrote "the latter half is wholly due to his accomplished colleague, Mr. Heard," in the initial footnote of the book.

Horatio closed his portion of *Criminal Abortion: Its Nature, Its Evidence, and Its Law* with a new footnote including an optimistic view about the American Medical Association's Memorial which had been provided to governors and legislatures of the states and territories some nine years earlier. "There is good reason to believe," he concluded, "directly and indirectly, it was productive of a great deal of good."[72]

On September 9, 1868, Mrs. Caroline Dall sent a letter to Horatio in which she said[73]

> I have a great desire that Dr. Tyng should retain her office in Boston, and be here at least two days in the week as she was last winter. She hesitates about it, and I think a word from you might decide her. I have two reasons for wishing it, one at least ought also to be a reason with you. In the first place I think Dr. Tyng has been very shabbily treated here by those who ought to have shown themselves her friends, chiefly on account of her being a favorite of your own. I want her to succeed in spite of the efforts to prevent it.

Thus we learn that Anita Tyng was a "favorite" of Horatio's and she suffered shabby treatment from Boston physicians because of this. This supports the *Is It I?* "Publishers' Note" and other reports of Horatio's own shabby treatment by some Boston physicians. Despite this rude treatment of Horatio and Horatio's friend by Boston, the city was favored in Horatio's next published paper entitled, "A Modification of Cusco's Speculum, by which it Becomes also a Retractor."[74] Horatio viewed his new speculum as such a valuable advance that he published this description, despite the fact that "it has been asserted that every accoucheur feels it incumbent upon him to invent a new midwifery forceps and every gynaecologist a speculum." The key feature was that the "duckbill" blades of Horatio's new speculum could be reversed "by a slight touch of the finger" and the instrument then became a retractor. "If it is as appropriate for an inventor as for a naturalist to attach to a novelty its specific name," Horatio concluded his note, "I would request that my instrument should be known as the Boston speculum, as I am anxious to do what little I can for the credit of my native city."

CHAPTER 12
THE GYNAECOLOGICAL SOCIETY AND ITS *JOURNAL*, SIMPSON'S "FREEDOM"

Horatio was appointed Consulting Surgeon to the Catholic-run Carney Hospital in south Boston when a new wing was opened in July 1868.[1] In early 1868, the Hospital started an Album which contained pictures and self-written descriptions of its associated physicians. Horatio apparently wrote his sketch shortly after the formation of the Gynaecological Society of Boston in early 1869, since his sketch ended with: "A founder & first Secretary of the Gynae-cological Society of Boston." The handwritten sketch is revealing of his achievements as he himself viewed them and also of his perception of the conflict that led to his leaving the Harvard Medical School.[2]

Horatio Robinson Storer—born in Boston, 27 Feb 1830—Public Latin School 1840-46, (H.U.) A.B. 1850; A.M. & M.D. 1853; LL.B. 1868. Private pupil of Agassiz, and Brown-Séquard, and for a year, after studying on the Continent, of Sir James Simpson, of Edinburgh. Fellow of the American Academy of Arts & Sciences, Member of the Obstetrical Society of Edinburgh, the Medico-Chirurgical Society &c. Member of the State Commission on Lunacy in 1863. One of the incorporators of the Mass. Infant Asylum. Physician to the Boston Lying-in Hospital, St. Joseph's (Catholic) Home, & St. Elizabeth's Hospital for Women. Professor of Obstetrics & Med. Jurisprudence in the Berkshire Medical College. Probably the first physician in America to give a complete collegiate course (60 lectures) upon the Diseases of Women as distinct from Midwifery, & the first to give private courses upon the subject to physicians. Prize Essayist & Secretary Am. Med. Association 1865, & Vice-President 1868.

An Assistant Instructor in the Harvard Medical School, he was dishonorably dropped from his place in 1866, "in order to do penance", the Faculty espousing a private quarrel into which he had been forced by three of his fellow subordinates. This apparent disgrace he accounts the great good fortune of his life, for it couched his blindness as an alumnus of Harvard, to the arrogance, nepotism & injustice of those claiming to control the profession in eastern New England.

Horatio had only one page in the Album for his sketch, and the full paragraph related to loss of his Assistant Instructor position shows the dominance of this event in his life and thoughts two-and-a-half years later. "Prize Essayist" is the only reference to the anti-abortion work that he would later describe as the most important of his life.

"In 1868, I think it was," Horatio wrote Malcolm in 1901, "it occurred to me that through a purely gynaecological society, the teaching in this department could be greatly extended and hastened."[3] The meeting that actually established the Gynaecological Society of Boston was held January 22, 1869. The seven original physician members and their offices in the new Society were Winslow Lewis (President), Horatio R. Storer (Secretary), George H. Bixby (Treasurer), Samuel L. Dutton, Levi Farr Warner, William G. Wheeler (the three-man Membership Committee), Henry M. Field, and John C. Sharp (both on the Committee on Foreign Literature).[4] All except Dr. Wheeler had positions at the St. Elizabeth's Hospital on November 1, 1869 when an advertisement for the Hospital was printed.[5] Dr. Warner was Attending Physician, Horatio was Attending Surgeon; Dr. Sharp was Assistant Physician, Dr. Bixby was Assistant Surgeon, and Dr. Winslow Lewis was Consulting Surgeon. Horatio's father was Consulting Physician to St. Elizabeth's but was *not* one of the founders of the Society. Horatio in his 1901 letter to Malcolm mentioned that "None of the prominent men in Boston" were willing to aid him. David Humphreys Storer's unwillingness must have been a great disappointment to Horatio. His father was to occasionally attend Society meetings, however, and became one of the Society's first Honorary Members.

A number of arguments were stated for founding the Society at the First Regular Meeting. These included "to stimulate its members and the profession generally to a deeper sense of the importance of the diseases peculiar to women," since the diseases of women were "but partially understood or entirely unknown;" that these diseases are extremely important "not merely to the individual sufferer, but with reference to her relations to her family and to society;" "That their importance, their variety, and their frequency are but partially appreciated by the profession, and still less by the community;" that the science of gynecology was undergoing large advances, with promise of "still more rapid progress in time to come;" and that it is not a disgrace, but an honor for physicians to be interested in uterine disease. The last of these reasons for forming the Society read:

> And, were there no other reason, the fact that every man owes to woman for her love in his infancy, in his childhood, and in his manhood, a debt that no devotion can ever repay;—and when as physicians we reflect that her special diseases are manifold more in number, worse in severity, and more dangerous to physical and mental integrity, than any affliction we ourselves are called to suffer, we should offer no less a sacrifice to the other sex than a life's work.[6]

After favorable discussion of the above reasons for a new Society, the Society formally resolved "in every honorable way to exert an educative and persuasive influence upon the profession at large." A specific objective was to change the disgraceful practice of some physicians who still prescribed "at random for married women complaining of pelvic symptoms." The members also made it explicit that "all impurity of thought, and even the mental appreciation of a difference in sex, are lost by the physician, and an imputation of them would be resented as an insult by the profession."

The group then adopted a Constitution which limited membership to graduate physicians "in good professional standing" and willing to uphold the objectives of advancing the science and art of gynecology and advancing its recognition "both in Boston and throughout the country." The Constitution also adopted the Code of Ethics of the American Medical Association. By-Laws were adopted which defined Active members, Honorary Members, and Corresponding Members. The number of Active members was limited to twelve for the first six months and twenty-four thereafter. The By-Laws specified meetings every two weeks and an annual meeting the first Tuesday of January.

The Proceedings of the first meeting then concluded on a somewhat racy note, at least from the standpoint of those of us with some difficulty shedding "the mental appreciation of a difference in sex." Horatio presented a fifty-year-old unmarried patient. She was "masked," and this probably was her only garment. She was described as having "an inordinate longing for the opposite sex, and frequent indulgence in masturbation." She had delusions that every Irish person she met was aware of her sexual intercourse twenty-five years earlier with a mill overseer. Contact with the Irish "starts, through her morbid self-consciousness and remorse, the old disordered train of ideas, and these, reflexly and always, kindle the vulval congestion, which almost invariably culminates in orgasm." An associated physical symptom was "a troublesome pruritus and a constant twitching of the clitoridal region," similar to a twitching of the eye. The use of "clitoridal region" reflected the fact that before the patient had come to Horatio her clitoris had been excised, "no benefit being obtained." Horatio's attempts to allay the physical and mental symptoms had been only partially successful, and he "therefore appealed to the Society for aid" in hope that they might suggest some remaining "reasonable ground of treatment."

Drs. Warner, Bixby, and Dutton had already studied the case prior to the meeting. "Dr. Wheeler, after carefully examining the case, remarked that it was certainly a very unusual and interesting one" justifying local treatment, but he did not suggest any additional measure. Dr. Field regretted that physicians could not recommend "a fortnight of sexual hard labor" at a brothel, since this "might prove her salvation." He saw masturbation in this instance providing important "temporary relief" of a symptom "whose influence upon the mind, if not thus relieved, might prove more disastrous." Dr. Sharp suggested galvanism and "an appeal in succession to the various regions of the spinal cord." Following that, the first meeting of the Society, and perhaps the most unusual meeting in the history of any medical society, adjourned.

The second Society meeting two weeks later included the Society's first guests: "Drs. J. G. Pinkham, of Lynn, and E. A. Perkins, of Boston."[7] Horatio presented a paper "Two New Methods of Exploring and Operating upon Lesions of the Female Rectum." Horatio also exhibited another masked patient. The case involved "hemorrhoids, external and internal, and a polypoid outgrowth above the unnaturally contractile sphincter ani, by which it was prevented from revealing itself to any of the usual methods of diagnosis." Horatio then demonstrated "how instantaneously, painlessly, and perfectly the diagnosis became possible by eversion of the rectum by pressure from within the vagina."

The meetings of the Society continued every other Tuesday. On February 2, a letter was read from the Secretary of the American Medical Association who wished the Society success, indicated its uniqueness in the United States, and invited a representative at the next annual meeting of the American Medical Association.[8] The Editor of the *American Journal of Obstetrics* indicated by letter his willingness to publish the Transactions of the Society, as did the Editor of the *American Journal of the Medical Sciences.* Horatio made arrangements for this with the former and communicated to the latter the Society's intention to allow them to publish some of the papers presented at the Society.[9]

At the fourth meeting on February 16, 1869, Horatio read the paper "Upon Pocketing the Pedicle in Ovariotomy: A Reply to Certain Strictures by Dr. Kimball, of Lowell."[10] Dr. Gilman Kimball had published a paper "Ovariotomy" in the *Boston Medical and Surgical Journal* of September 17, 1868.[11] Kimball discussed different methods of treating the ovarian pedicle. Kimball indicated in a footnote his surprise that Horatio claimed that pocketing the pedicle was a new method and "an important improvement upon the ordinary mode of operating." He indicated that he himself had done the same thing several times when the pedicle was unusually short. "By ovariotomists generally," Kimball's footnote concluded, "the '*pocketing*' practice of Dr. Storer will probably never be considered as furnishing anything new or essentially important in practice; much less will it be likely to supersede or materially modify the practice so long and so successfully pursued by Spencer Wells and other European ovariotomists."

"In the present communication," Horatio began, "I do not intend to discuss the merits or demerits of my method of treating the ovarian pedicle, known as 'pocketing,' but simply to correct a misrepresentation. My answer to Dr. Kimball would long ago have appeared in the Journal where his insult was given, had I not been refused the opportunity by its gentlemanly editor, Dr. Luther Parks." After repeating Kimball's "insulting" footnote, he wrote,[12]

Putting aside for another occasion the statement that my proposal contains nothing "essentially important in practice," I would call attention to the fact that three distinct charges are made against me by Dr. Kimball in the above paragraphs; for his reiterated expression of surprise means nothing less than that I set forth as new an old method; that I had intentionally done this; and that I had taken my idea from him. The last two charges I declare to be false. The first of the three I believe to be false also.

Horatio described the operation on the Tennessee woman he had performed with Wells and provided the reason Kimball was "a bystander" to the surgery: "I called, in consequence of an appointment we had together, for Mr. Spencer Wells, at the Revere House. There I found Dr. Kimball, vainly importuning Mr. Wells to visit the factories at Lowell. Disliking to seem uncivil to Dr. Kimball, I invited him to join us."

Horatio indicated that when he pocketed the pedicle, "Mr. Wells expressed his surprise, asking me where I got the idea, and remarking that it would have occurred to no one save a Yankee; Dr. Kimball meanwhile saying never a word." Horatio then described the ride home and this gives some unique insights about an "excitable" Horatio:[13]

But to return to the ride from Chelsea. Mr. Wells had much to say, all of it very kindly, concerning the merits of my method, and that generally employed by himself, which, as is well known, consists of fastening the pedicle outside the wound by a clamp. As every earnest operator would have done, he warmly defended his method. Dr. Kimball said very little, save in echo of Mr. Wells. I do not think he uttered one word in disparagement of the novelty of pocketing the pedicle. I am quite sure of this, for being a little excited at having ventured to perform an important operation in the presence of the greatest living authority upon the subject, by a method which that gentleman had evidently never heard of, I took occasion to note down our conversation before going to my bed that night.

Horatio wrote Wells to see if he remembered whether Dr. Kimball had mentioned having performed Horatio's procedure. He indicated that Wells responded: "I have also a sort of indistinct idea that Dr. K. said he had once tried a plan somewhat similar, but did not like it. Of this, however, I am very far from certain." Horatio indicated that Wells also told Horatio in his letter that both he and Kimball after the operation had told Horatio that he would have better used the clamp than pocketing the pedicle. Horatio continued:[14]

Now, if Dr. Kimball had really performed my operation, it is not at all likely, ... that he would have refrained, out of regard to my feelings, from expressing himself in such a way as would be remembered both by Mr. Wells, even at this distance of time, and by myself for half-a-dozen hours after the event occurred; and it is also not at all likely, had he done so, that I should have deliberately set myself down, as I did that very night, to prepare for publication the description of a method, as an original one, upon which I was not only to stake my reputation as a scientific, but as a truthful man.

Horatio then described the judgment of various New York physicians, including one "better posted in the history of all procedures in gynaecological surgery than any other man in America," as to the originality of Horatio's procedure. These were made at a "meeting of the N.Y. Academy of Medicine, held specially for the discussion of my method, on 19th December, 1867." Horatio took leave of Dr. Kimball "without" mentioning "the details of a case where I performed his vaunted operation of everting the lips of the abdominal wound by quilled sutures, and satisfied myself of its inutility [sic], before any publication by himself upon the subject was made; nor will I avail myself of evidence in my possession, tending to show his unfitness to sit in judgment upon other men's practice."

Horatio's response to Kimball was published in August 1869, six months after he read the paper. In July 1869, Dr. J. Ford Prioleau of South Carolina provided a favorable discussion of "pocketing the pedicle" in the *American Journal of the Medical Sciences*. Horatio mentioned Prioleau's praise and indicated it "is sufficient balm for" the "wound" of a Louisville medical journal editor who had read Kendall's footnote and written: "'Storer's operation, for pocketing the pedicle, proves to be an old one, though there is no reason to believe that the fact was known to the doctor.'" Among the nice things that Dr. Prioleau said was: "In those instances in which the pedicle is of sufficient length to accommodate itself to any condition of the abdomen, this mode of treatment I regard as eminently superior to any heretofore suggested, and I think that Prof. Storer has indeed by it '*won an additional laurel to American surgery.*'"[15]

In less than a month from its organization, the Gynaecological Society of Boston showed that it believed its obligations extended well beyond Boston. The members resolved that each of the medical colleges in the country be requested "in the name of the Society" to establish "a separate chair or lectureship of Gynaecology, as distinguished from Obstetrics or Midwifery." They also resolved that "a memorial be transmitted to the American Medical Association ... praying that the circular sent to the colleges by the Society may receive the formal approval of the Association, and be indorsed to that effect by its president and permanent secretary."[16]

At the meeting of the Society on March 2, Horatio read a paper entitled "Golden Rules for the Treatment of Ovarian Diseases."[17] These included "never tap;" "if exploratory section reveals a cystic ovary, remove it at once;" "disregard abdominal adhesions, even if firm;" and "the surgeon should not refuse to operate even in an apparently unfavorable case." In discussion of this last, Horatio wrote:

> To decline operating lest one should thereby injure his reputation is not only very selfish, but very unwise. The worst cases often do the best. Says Mr. Spencer Wells: "I have operated lately, and shall soon be driven to again, in very unfavorable cases,—cases almost hopeless,—by a feeling that it is impossible to resist the prayer of a dying woman to try and save her life;" and the experience of this surgeon during the past year has been five lives saved out of every six cases undertaken. Without ovariotomy every one of these women would have died; and yet some physicians still *dare* to persuade their patients that the operation is more dangerous than its non-performance.

"Upon motion of Dr. Warner, seconded by Dr. Dutton," according to the Proceedings, "Dr. Storer's 'Golden Rules' were declared formally endorsed by the Society."[18]

Horatio afterwards offered designs for a Society Seal and the members voted to adopt a seal with the legend "Propter uterum est mulier, 1869," encircling the initials "G. S. of B." It will be recalled that Van Helmont was the author of "Propter uterum est mulier," one translation of which was: "Woman exists for the sake of her womb." A year-and-a-half later at another meeting of the Society, Horatio was to note that this motto "was not to be pushed to a degree unauthorized by the facts in the case."[19] This suggests that there may have been early criticism of this near equation of woman to her womb.

At the next meeting of the Society, letters were read from "D. Humphreys Storer and J.B.S. Jackson, of Boston," acknowledging their election as Honorary Members of the Society.[20] The meeting included a presentation by Horatio, entitled "Physicians in their Relations to Invalid Women,"[21] which was a response to a letter in the *New England Medical Gazette*, a Homeopathic journal.[22] The letter was by the same Caroline Dall who had praised *Why Not?* and also written in regard to Dr. Tyng. Mrs. Dall claimed that men had no proper place in the treatment of women's diseases and this was one reason more women physicians needed to be trained. Horatio reproduced a portion of her letter then summarized her charges as follows:[23]

> 1. That a physician's presence in the sick-chamber is impossible without creating a morbid activity of the sexual sense, that is to say, an unchaste thought, if not an unchaste longing, even in the purest women.
>
> 2. That a vast amount of female disease is merely simulated.
>
> 3. That physicians, themselves a disturbing influence, do not recognize this fact, are unable to detect malingering where it really

exists, and are so incompetent to practise.

4. As they are, also, for the reason that "it is impossible for any man to penetrate the mysteries of an organism that he does not share."

Mrs. Dall's letter must have produced *deja vu* in Horatio who in 1856 had countered similar claims related to the inappropriateness of male physicians delivering babies.[24]   He indicated that had Mrs. Dall just leveled charges against physicians he would have remained silent, "but an imputation upon the character of their patients has been made, which, unless changed, would tend to prevent the disclosure of much real suffering, and the bestowal of much real aid, and besides to lower the moral standard of professional and social intercourse with women." "It would be wicked to believe that she spoke from any personal experience;" Horatio wrote, "but there can be no doubt that she has totally misrepresented the general experience of her sex." He continued:

If Mrs. Dall has not committed a fearful error of judgment, not only are physicians universally a curse to the community, but the daily meeting of clergyman with parishioner, of teacher with scholar, of friend with friend, unattended as these are by the disgust which is so constantly present in the case of the medical attendant, are productive of so direct and intense a degree of sexual excitement, "even in the purest women," that the very name of continence is a delusion, and of chastity a lie.[25]

Drs. Bixby and Field were appointed "to consider whether some further action ought not to be taken by the Society relative to counteracting the mischievous influence of Mrs. Dall's late article."[26] At the next meeting, they recommended and it was approved that Horatio's response "should be offered for immediate publication to the Boston Medical and Surgical Journal."[27] When the Proceedings were published several months later in the *Journal of the Gynaecological Society of Boston*, a footnote followed which read: "In consequence of certain offensive conduct of the editor of the journal referred to, it was thought best to reserve Dr. Storer's paper for publication elsewhere." The Editor of the *Boston Medical and Surgical Journal* in April 1869 was again Dr. Luther Parks, Jr.

The April 6 meeting also included exhibition by Horatio of the "pelvic viscera from a patient dead of criminal abortion, the case being one then in court." The abortion was induced by a midwife in a woman five-months pregnant. She died several weeks later and the autopsy showed extensive pelvic cellulitis and "complete disorganization of the left ovary." This led to a discussion of medical testimony in criminal abortion trials. Horatio noted that "medical experts must be very careful, when put upon the stand, lest by turning counsel they let their zeal destroy the value of their testimony."[28]   He then described "the reluctance of physicians to assist in bringing to justice these gross offenders who strike at man's life in the very citadel of its commencement." He also indicated that a physician in a nearby county was performing abortions, but was "still accredited as a member of the Massachusetts Medical Society, whose disgrace it was that it had not yet moved in the affair." Another significant event of the April 6 meeting was that "the officers of the Society were authorized, ex officio, to enter upon the publication of a new medical journal, to be entitled 'The Journal of the Gynaecological Society of Boston.'"

Three days later, the First *Special* Meeting of the Society was held in the "capacious and elegant apartments" of Horatio's friend and Hotel-Pelham neighbor, Dr. Dix. At the meeting, Dr. F.G. Lemercier of Paris gave a presentation on the Physiology of Reproduction. In addition to seven Active and Corresponding Members of the Society, there were "some two hundred medical gentlemen of Boston and the immediate vicinity."[29] It is comforting to know that such a large number of Boston-area physicians were willing to attend a meeting of Horatio's Gynaecological Society of Boston. The opposing and abusing clique referred to in the "Publishers' Note" in *Is It I?* obviously was just a small portion of the Boston medical community.

At the regular meeting of April 20, Horatio described the draft legislation related to criminal abortion which the New York State Medical Society had prepared and recently sent to the State Legislature. Horatio discussed the etiology of this draft statute, beginning with the Suffolk District Medical Society and American Medical Association Committees on Criminal Abortion, the latter's Memorial to the State Medical Societies, the resolution of a Troy, New York physician urging compliance with the Memorial, unavoidable delays "inseparable from the successful progress of any great reform," and a series of resolutions submitted a year earlier by the New York State Medical Society to the State Assembly prior to their draft bill. After noting that he had had the honor of being consulted during the drafting of these resolutions,[30] Horatio said: "How different from what has obtained in our own State! It was here that the advance was initiated, which has received the benediction of the whole country. Having given the key-note to other States, the courage of our brethren failed them,—Boston, which claims to control the opinions and actions of the rest of the State, first showing the white feather."[31] Following this, the Gynaecological Society of Boston Committee on Criminal Abortion was formed "to report at a future meeting such action as may seem advisable to assist in preventing the crime of abortion." Its members were Horatio, Dr. Dutton, and Dr. Sullivan. The final business reported was "that negotiations were in progress with a responsible publisher, for the establishment of the new journal authorized by the Society."

At the meeting of May 4, 1869, a letter was read from J. Marion Sims acknowledging his Honorary Membership in the Society.[32] Horatio then presented a paper, "The Frequency and Causation of Uterine Disease in America."[33] One key point was that uterine disease was frequent with two of three women in New England probably requiring occasional treatment. A related point was that this was largely unappreciated by medical men. Some who failed to recognize the frequency of uterine disease had "defective training or erroneous methods of observation."

> There are others, equally honest in their purpose, who are deterred from making the necessary investigation, from a twofold timidity: fear of the ridicule of their fellows, and of being misunderstood by their patients. There are others still, who, from jealousy, natural incompetency, the love of mischief, or ingrained malice, would keep from the laborer his most satisfying recompense, by stigmatizing the records of his cases as false or overdrawn, and as imaginary the diseases that they represent.

"During the sixteen years since we graduated in medicine," Horatio continued,[34]

> we have never once prescribed for a married woman with any, the slightest, pelvic symptoms,—and this is what perhaps no other living man can say,—without a careful digital examination; and while in a small proportion of cases we have found so healthful a local condition that we were able to dismiss the pelvic region from all participation in treatment, in scores upon scores of other cases, where not the slightest suspicion had existed on the part of the patient that there was here any cause for anxiety, we have detected the grave, effective, and real exciting cause of the distant or apparently constitutional disorder previously recognized.

Horatio noted that digital examination for the *unmarried* was "reserved for cases whose pelvic character is evident, or where ordinary treatment has failed."

Horatio also described the great need for more gynecologists: "It is strange that young men complain that our profession is more than full, when there is everywhere, in city and country alike, a wealth of legitimate and lucrative employment as yet almost unopened, awaiting the zeal of the special worker, and the surest key, for him who desires to use it, to the best general family practice."

Horatio then discussed the manifold causes of uterine disease. Singled out for special attention were criminal abortion, prevention of pregnancy, self-abuse, and the sewing machine. Honorable mentions were given to high-heeled shoes, faulty leverage in dress, inheritance, long betrothals, and avoidance of breast-feeding. Although granting that many causes of uterine disease were new or increasing, Horatio concluded, "there were in the old times behind us, that we are wrongly taught were golden, deaths without number from pelvic causes unsuspected, ovarian dropsies supposed ascitic, uterine hypertrophies, outgrowths and degenerations misnamed affections of the liver, and all sorts of disease from oversight and neglect by the physician, special in their causation, and wrongly designated as by the providence of God."

Although "The Frequency and Causation of Uterine Disease in America," was not the first paper that Horatio presented at the new Society, he chose it before earlier papers for publication in the first number of the *Journal of the Gynaecological Society of Boston* when the journal made its debut in July 1869. As will be seen, Horatio later quoted extensively from "The Frequency and Causation ..." in the paper, "Female Hygiene," which he presented in California in 1871.

The June 1 meeting of the Society included, "by invitation" ten physicians from around the country who were the students in Horatio's Lectures upon the Surgical Diseases of Women.[35] Dr. Storer exhibited a portable gas furnace for heating cauterizing irons. The paragraph describing this adds to our knowledge of Horatio's past. He indicated that while in Paris, Jobert de Lamballe had shown him the huge benefits of this "actual cautery" "in softening down indurations, and lessening hypertrophies, as well as for checking hemorrhage." Horatio also indicated that he had used the portable furnace for "some three years" and had it constructed for the Franciscan Hospital. If it were exactly three years, this would mean that Horatio was surgeon to the Franciscan Hospital in May 1866, some four months *prior* to severing his connection with the New England Hospital for Women. However, "some three years" is not specific enough to let us assume that the Franciscan Hospital was Horatio's "golden parachute" when he sent his September 1866 letter of resignation to the Board of Directors of the New England Hospital for Women.

In what probably was simply an extension of the Eleventh Regular Meeting on June 1, the Second Special Meeting was devoted to Horatio's first lecture of his series to the physicians attending his semiannual course. Horatio provided an overview of his twelve two-hour lectures and then concentrated on "certain matters fundamental to a correct appreciation of pelvic surgery." His following discussion of pelvic surgery pointed out a surgeon-blindness parallel to the physician-blindness to uterine disease that Horatio had discussed some weeks before in "The Frequency and Causation ..."[36]

> Pelvic surgery had suffered great neglect at the hands of professed surgeons. Often, indeed, it had received their open contempt. The great advances in gynaecology had, however, not been made by them. The dilation of the cervical canal by tents, and its incision when necessary, the removal of ovarian cysts, the closure of vesico-vaginal fistulae,—these were triumphs achieved by the special worker, and this was true, moreover, of the introduction into practice of metallic sutures, and of acupressure, and of the great advances made in our knowledge of the causation, true character, and proper treatment of

surgical fever.

The Third Special Meeting of the Society, occurred the next day and was the second lecture of Horatio's course to physicians.[37] Preparation of the patient for surgery was discussed as was anesthesia. Here we see a shift in views by Horatio who had always recommended ether for surgery other than obstetric surgery. "In Boston and its neighborhood there existed a prejudice in favor of ether, very natural under all the circumstances;" Horatio wrote, "and yet there was reason to believe that chloroform, with all the risks, great or small, that have been attributed to it, was in reality safer than ether, in consequence of its less likelihood to cause nausea and retching, which were so fatal as causing secondary hemorrhage and as keeping up or increasing general exhaustion."

Horatio went on to discuss the "gauntlet to be run" after every severe pelvic operation. The points of this gauntlet were "shock, primary and secondary hemorrhage, exhaustion or secondary collapse, peritonitis, septicaemia,—these were each to be anticipated and guarded against." Each was discussed in turn with special attention given to avoidance of primary hemorrhage through use of his clamp shield and avoidance of secondary hemorrhage by using metallic instead of organic sutures. Horatio's presentation on prevention of peritonitis gave the clearest exposition that Horatio was aware of the need for antiseptic surgery, and even for aseptic surgery. Horatio also called for "vicarious transfusion of blood to avert death from hemorrhage or toxaemia." The blood in this case was the patient's own, collected from the site of hemorrhage. The following concluding paragraph of the Proceedings of the Third Special Meeting reiterated the need for cleanliness and provided other points of interest, including the risk to the surgeon of septicemia, and this would also prove prophetic:[38]

> There were many points concerning the details of diagnosis, of great interest and practical importance, to which there was only time for the most passing allusion; such were the necessity of ambidexterity upon the part of the surgeon, alike in examination and in operating; the risks to which he was exposed, of digital syphilitic and septicaemic infection, and of damage from other sources, to his good name; the danger, unless his hands and instruments were kept scrupulously clean, of inoculating the patient with specific or other virus; the advantage of always preceding the examination with the speculum by careful palpation, both by the vagina and abdomen, and these combined; the benefit, in the case of nervous patients and abdominal enlargements, of employing an anaesthetic; the need of care with reference to the presence of pregnancy, and to the patient's moral welfare; the proper methods of making instrumental examination, the errors of observation liable to be made, and the physical injuries to

be avoided.

At the Thirteenth Regular Meeting on July 6, William Overend Priestley acknowledged by letter his Corresponding Membership by letter, as did Alexander J. Stone, now in Stillwater, Minnesota.[39] The tone of the meeting must have been unusually negative. There was discussion of two failures of members to diagnose pregnancy which had led to "treatments" producing abortion. Dr. Wheeler presented an ovariotomy case, in which he was assisted by Storer, Bixby, and Bean, which led to death from shock a few hours after the surgery. At the next meeting two weeks later, the operations described were successful. A letter requesting suggestions for treating nymphomania was read. However, of most significance, "Dr. Storer laid upon the President's desk a copy of the first number of the Society's Journal, for July, 1869."[40]

The first entry in this first number of the *Journal* was a "Salutatory by the Editors," which began:[41]

Till within a very short time the workers in Uterine Medicine and Surgery have been few and far between in New England, scarce a practitioner having dared to claim for these branches more than an ordinary interest. Now, there is no department of professional science, not even that of ophthalmology, which has so many devotees, general practitioners though most of them necessarily continue; and while to other sections of the country there must be yielded a great predominance so far as individual reputations are concerned, it has remained to New England to establish the first active association of gynaecologists in existence.

This was followed by a statement of the reasons for forming the Gynaecological Society of Boston, the recognition that the Proceedings of its meetings could benefit other physicians, and the problems the Society had experienced by having these Proceedings published in existing journals.

Under these circumstances, it has been decided by the Society to itself undertake the publication of its transactions, and at the same time to take advantage of the opportunity thus afforded to call the attention of the profession to *matters of collateral interest.*

The importance of the diseases of women is as yet hardly recognized at our medical colleges; at our hospitals they are but seldom treated, and are not always diagnosticated. *There still exists in New England, as in many places elsewhere, that measure of despotism, miscalled conservative, whereby the many are overridden by the semblance of a transmitted authority. To the progress of gynaecology, as of other branches of medical science, this has proved a hindrance. It will be one of the duties of the editors to assist in breaking it down. With cliques or "rings" they will have nothing to do.* The pages of the Journal will be open for the freest [sic] discussion, provided only that it is conducted in a courteous and scientific spirit.

When a second school, more alive to the wants of the age,—a Woman's Hospital, in the fullest sense a charity,—a free profession, in which the degree of every first-class medical college is recognized to be as respectable as that of any other,—and a due appreciation of the diseases of women,—exist in the city which ought long ago to have been the centre of American Medicine, then perhaps will their pens grow weary and their labors end.

W.L.
H.R.S.
G.H.B.

The italics above were not in the original. These italicized passages show that publishing the Society's Proceedings was not the only goal, perhaps not even the prime goal of the Editors, or, more correctly, of the Editor.

The "Salutatory by the Editors" was followed by a "Salutatory by the Publisher."[42] It described the three Editors, and much of what publisher James Campbell wrote could only have come from extensive conversations with the three men and primarily with Horatio. For example, it is hard to believe that Dr. Winslow Lewis said this about himself:

Dr. Lewis has always disbelieved in the too great centralization of power, applying the same rule to the medical profession that governs, in this country, the rest of the community. It is not impossible that certain articles of his creed may at times manifest themselves in the pages of this Journal,—opposing, as he ever has done, the subordination of the mass of the profession to a few self-appointed rulers, the transmission of authority by these to their parasites, and the assumption of superiority by the metropolis in the distribution of State medical offices. He is no coward himself, and he cannot brook an unmanly fear in others.

By contrast, it is hard to believe that anyone *other* than Horatio wrote, or at least said, the following about Horatio:

The second of the editors, Dr. Storer, is to many a riddle, and is accordingly variously judged by them, as scientific and expert, an enthusiast, an empiric, egotist, fool. Resembling Dr. Lewis in his vivacity, ardor, and general professional attainments, he has differed from him, in that from the moment of his graduation he has steadily kept a single object in view, namely, the building up in New England of a belief in and respect for the diseases of women.

This self-consecration was at first misunderstood. His early professional career was considered aggressive, and attempts were long made by those most interested in retaining mastery of the field, to eliminate from it the obnoxious competitor; the attacks made upon Dr. S. having at times been of the most unwarrantable and disgraceful character. They but served, however, to strengthen his purpose, and, as our business gives us excellent opportunities for knowing, the tide of professional sentiment long ago turned, and is now setting very strongly in his favor.

Compelled eight years since, by ill health, to exchange the general practice, in which he had been laboring an equal period, for the comparative leisure and comfort of a specialty, he was *dared* to do this, and was assured that the profession in New England would never tolerate in its ranks an avowed gynaecologist. The insult referred to accomplished what no money could have done,—it kept him at home. Accepting the challenge so defiantly made, refusing a kindly and attractive invitation to remove to New York,—the city of all others in this country that he thinks worth living and working in, and of all others the most to be proud of its medical men,—he has remained, engaged in what from that moment had been to him a missionary work. Unmindful of personal advancement, careless of the abuse that has so unsparingly been heaped upon him, accepting seeming injury as ultimate gain, he has kept ever before him the development of what were to him great and living truths.

Still in the prime of life, Dr. S. is an indefatigable worker; and though he has always had a large and lucrative practice, he has yet found time to contribute much to the literature of the profession. A catalogue of a portion only of his publications, that was compiled by Messrs. Lee & Shepard, comprises the titles of over forty articles. From the remarkable opportunities of observation enjoyed by Dr. S., even while a very young man, and from the reputation he has already achieved,—for outside of a circle ten miles distant from Boston he has a host of professional friends,—we anticipate much advantage to the Journal from his connection with it.

The Publisher quoted from the Carney Album sketch of Horatio, including the "in order to do penance" paragraph which described Horatio's forced separation from the Harvard Medical School. He then provided more discussion of Horatio's past: "It is not generally known that to Dr. Storer's decision and inflexibility of purpose the American Medical Association owes its escape, in 1865, from what would probably have proved its death-blow, a deep-laid and powerful conspiracy having been formed in Boston to prevent the meeting of the Association, at probably the most precarious period of its history."

The third editor, George Bixby, was also described, including his extensive European training in gynecology, his service during the Civil War, his practice in St. Louis, his additional year of European study, and his recent decision to practice in Boston. The Publisher's Salutatory concluded:[43]

> Thus officered, the Journal of the Gynaecological Society cannot fail of success. Not being obstetrical, it will leave that department, Midwifery, as well as the Diseases of Children, to the excellent New York quarterly, which so well illustrates those branches of medicine, and being to a great extent official in its character, it will endeavor in no way to run counter to, or injure, the venerable weekly which has for so many years, from its very solitude, enjoyed the privilege of irresponsibility.
>
> It will be to our own aim to present to the profession a magazine that will yield the palm to none in the country for general typographical excellence.
>
> J. C.

It will be noted that it only took to the end of a sentence before the *Journal of the Gynaecological Society of Boston* failed in its "endeavor" not to injure the "irresponsible" *Boston Medical and Surgical Journal.*

We have already quoted extensively from the July issue of the journal which covered the first two meetings of the Society and included Horatio's "The Frequency and Causation of Uterine Disease in America." At the end of the issue appeared a section entitled "Editorial Notes," which would be a regular feature of each monthly number. This was the future site of the promised battles for improved medical education, for a Woman's Hospital, against the forces opposed to gynaecology, and against the preferential treatment of Harvard Medical School graduates when applying for entry into the Massachusetts Medical Society.

In Horatio's first "Editorial Notes" he discussed the large ignorance of most obstetricians of gynecology and the huge deficiencies in the medical schools of the country in providing training and clinical experience on the subject.[44] He described the problems associated with this new medical specialty where "undue stress may be laid upon trivial affections, hazardous operations be unnecessarily performed, and incompetent practitioners consider themselves, and lead others to think them, masters of the art." In support of these a long paragraph of Matthews Duncan of Edinburgh was reproduced which closed with the claim that "great progress is certainly being made" in gyne-cology, "but 'blinding dust' is the chief result of the labor of many of its most notorious if not famous promoters." As we will see, the famed abolitionist, William Lloyd Garrison, was to extract passages from the Duncan quote and use these as ammunition against Horatio and the Gynaecological Society of Boston when Garrison came to the defense of Mrs. Dall in her call for women to replace men as gynecologists.

Horatio devoted five pages of small print to reproduction of a portion of the Annual Report of the Board of State Charities of Massachusetts which was written by Dr. Samuel Gridley Howe, "one of the most practical philosophers, most thoughtful workers, and most reasonable philanthropists of the age." Howe's passage emphasized the family, "the most important of all social institutions," since it alone developed the critical restraining powers of reason which prevented each and everyone from perpetrating crimes and engaging in social vices. Howe recommended that the State foster and strengthen the family and, wherever possible, use it as a means to nurture the reason and self-restraint of wards of the state who now were typically institutionalized in huge barracks. Where actual families could not be used, as for dangerous lunatics or criminals, state establishments should be modeled "as nearly upon the family system as could be."

The next item in this initial "Editorial Notes" section praised the formation of the American Association of Medical Editors at the recent annual meeting of the American Medical Association and praised its President, Dr. Nathan Davis. "Here in the East," Horatio wrote, "where three years ago he so ably brought order from chaos, and attuned conflicting elements to the most perfect harmony, making of the meeting that fair-weather prophets had doomed to an ignominious failure, the most perfect success, there has since but one adjective been applied to Dr. Davis, as to his then administration, and that, the word magnificent."

"The discussion of local questions, conducted with reference to their general bearing," Horatio continued, "becomes of interest to far-distant readers. We shall therefore offer no apology, when commenting, as we often may, upon public needs, mistakes, or abuses, especially if of gynaecological character." Horatio then objected to "local" plans to change the site of the proposed Boston lunatic asylum from a Winthrop farm that provided view and sound of the sea and access to it for walks, yachting excursions, etc., all judged highly therapeutic for the patients, to another location favored by powerful speculators. He called on the physician mayor, Dr. Nathaniel Shurtleff, and the city physician, Dr. William Read, to protest the action to change the site of the asylum.

Given that there presumably were three editors of the *Journal of the Gynaecological Society of Boston*, we would not refer to the Editorial Notes as Horatio's writing were it not for Horatio's own admissions of this, such as the following discussion of the Gynaecological Society of Boston and its journal in his 1901 letter to Malcolm:[45]

The Gynaecological Society of Boston was the first of its kind in existence, and by associating many distinguished practitioners with it as Hon. and Corr. members, at home and abroad, it acquired a reputation that has not even yet ceased. ... The fighting character of its Journal, though I disliked very much to employ such measures, was highly approved by many, even in Boston, who did not dare themselves to speak. I had given open notice that having been prevented from working within its walls for the progress of the Medical School, I would do so outside them,—and you will find in the Journal, *all of whose editorials until I broke down, and the presidential annual addresses of Dr. Winslow Lewis as well, were written by me,*[46] appeals for and foreshadowing of most of the great changes that have been made of late years in the general plan and details of the School. I have had more than one letter, then and since, from Pres. Eliot, thanking me for suggestions, and in later days congratulating me on seeing carried into effect what he was good enough to speak of as my methods and ideas. The Journal of the Gyn. Society had a very large subscription list. Many who disagreed with me took it, merely because they believed in a fair field and no favor. My being chosen president of the Association of American Medical Journals in 1871, just before I broke down, brought the Journal into even greater prominence. The fact that my Boston opponents, like Croker here in N. Y. till yesterday,[47] took refuge in the policy of silence, told strongly in my favor. How they felt, however, is shown by this. The Journal was stereotyped, and when I returned in 1877, there were many requests for its renewal, and for back copies. *None, however, were to be had, and it was explained that Henry Bigelow had bought up the plates and had them destroyed.*[48]

Among the many things which kept Horatio busy in the Summer of 1869 was the Caesarean section he performed on July 21, 1869 which was immediately followed by extirpation of the patient's uterus. Horatio's unsuccessful surgery occurred nearly six years before Edoardo Porro of Pavia, Italy performed this operation on May 21, 1875. Porro's patient survived and the operation today is known as Porro's.

The report of Horatio's surgery was prepared by Dr. George H. Bixby, presumably because the patient was his.[49] "Mrs. H., aged thirty-seven, native of Pennsylvania, residing at 52 Spring Street," Bixby began, "consulted Dr. H. R. Storer, on July 16th, 1869, for pregnancy complicated by a large obscure abdominal tumor." Other physicians had previously diagnosed an ovarian tumor and one a fibrous tumor of the uterus. Several had "told her it was impossible for her to live through her confinement." She was already more than nine-months pregnant and fully aware of her "desperate condition" when she consulted Horatio.

The irregular tumor was judged to obstruct normal delivery of the fetus, even if the skull were crushed. A few days later, when labor may have begun, Dr. Bixby found the cervix dilated enough to get his finger into the uterus and past the obstructing tumor to the head of the fetus. Labor did not proceed because of the tumor and Horatio decided that an abdominal section was the only chance for saving the woman's life. Exploratory surgery "established the existence of a fibro-cystic tumor of the left and lower anterior wall of the uterus, with an outgrowth nearly the size of the foetal head, originally pediculated, but now firmly adherent low down to the walls of the pelvis." Another exploratory incision into the tumor led to a substance-filled cavity produced apparently by "degeneration of the fibroid." Bixby continued:

> The hemorrhage being already very profuse, and the danger from shock and exhaustion imminent, with a few rapid strokes of the knife, Dr. Storer extended his incision into the cavity of the uterus, and with all expedition removed a male child, weighing eight pounds; it being, as well as the placenta, in an advanced state of decomposition. This accomplished, the next question to be decided was, what should be done with the mass left behind, including uterus and tumor. ... It was apparent that the tumor in the uterine wall would necessarily prevent a perfect contraction of the organ, and thus render suppression of the hemorrhage impossible, contrary to what obtains in ordinary uncomplicated cases of Caesarean section.
>
> With his usual self-possession, Dr. Storer decided to remove the whole mass as far as possible, which would include the uterus, as well as the fibro-cystic tumor of the left wall, necessarily leaving behind the outgrowth posteriorly, the firm adhesions of which to the pelvis it was found impossible to dissect away or break down.

Removal of the uterus was accomplished with the ecraseur. The stump was seared by the hot iron, and in addition Horatio applied the clamp shield. Hemorrhage was eliminated, "the abdomen carefully cleansed of all coagula, and the wound brought together by ten deep silver sutures, which involved the peritoneum." The operation lasted three hours. Chloroform anesthesia continued at a lower rate for another hour "to ensure rest." The patient returned to consciousness "in the happiest way, without complaining of the least pain or discomfort." However, a day-and-a-half later she showed the first negative sign, "face flushed; foetid discharge from wound." The pulse slowly rose, then became rapid and she died three days after the operation was completed. Bixby concluded:

> The case now reported is probably the first one in which the removal of the puerperal uterus has ever been performed; and it is undoubtedly the most heroic of the bold procedures as yet resorted to by Dr. Storer in extreme gynaecological emergencies. Nothing else could have been done; the patient begged for the chance of life, however small, and it was a matter of surprise to all concerned, in view of the

terrific character of the operation, that she should have survived it at all, and still more so for so long a time.

Ironically, when this surgical achievement of Horatio was discussed at the Society on August 10, 1869, Horatio was absent for the first time.[50] Following Bixby's description of Horatio's extirpation of the pregnant uterus, there was discussion of the problems associated with ether anesthesia (this may have been Horatio's first Boston use of chloroform for major surgery). President Winslow Lewis "reminded the gentlemen that they were venturing on dangerous ground, to speak thus freely of the comparative disadvantages of employing sulphuric ether, here in Boston."

The August "Editorial Notes" included discussion of the history of Boston medical politics. Starting with the beneficial alliance between Drs. James Jackson and John C. Warren that gave rise to the Massachusetts General Hospital, it went on to sharply criticize the Harvard Medical School and the Massachusetts Medical Society.[51]

> With the wheat sown by Jackson and Warren, there were also planted tares, and, as often happens, the bad stock has grown apace. Monopolies were established that, in their infancy, were for the general good; and for this reason, and their very infancy's sake, were protected by artificial shelter. The monopolies referred to, thus fostered, soon attained a controlling power. The Medical School succeeded in destroying that attempted to be established by Brown University, prevented that essayed by Dr. Huntington and his associates at Lowell, persistently endeavored to strangle the Berkshire Medical Institution at its birth and after; a process it has since tried to accomplish in the late legislative conflicts concerning the giving the right to Tufts College to confer medical degrees, and the establishment of the Boston Dental College.
>
> The Massachusetts Medical Society came soon to be managed, as indeed it had always been in great measure, by Boston graduates, and in the interests of the school there was established that discriminating tariff upon the alumni of other medical colleges desiring to practise in this Commonwealth, which is still in full practical force,—a disgrace to us all.

The "discriminating tariff" on other medical school graduates was that they, unlike graduates from Harvard, were faced with an examination prior to admission to the Massachusetts Medical Society. Elimination of this "tariff" became one of Horatio's major crusades and his recruitment of the American Medical Association in support would cause bad feeling between Boston medical men and that Association for decades.

Horatio began the next month's Editorial Notes" by praising the State Legislature for establishing a State Board of Health and the choice of Dr. Henry Ingersoll Bowditch and Dr. George Derby as two of its three physician members. Horatio identified some health problems for the new Board to deal with.[52]

> Lime is still burned from putrefying shells at South Boston, ... and there are still, without doubt, city fathers who think the horrible stench an excellent antiseptic. Still do the ore-heaps at Point Shirley, ... belch forth their poisonous fumes. ... Had the will existed to accomplish what the public health has long demanded, power would have been found by the city, or obtained, if not already possessed, to abate this excessive nuisance of the Revere Copper Company. And so with the slaughter-houses at Brighton. Let an alarm of cholera be given, and, under its stimulus, talk will be had of their suppression or improvement; but soon the power of invested capital resumes its sway, and sanitary claims are again disregarded. ...
>
> In making these remarks we may perhaps wound the sensibilities of some; we are pretty sure to receive the condemnation of others. Better to do this, however, than by our silence become accessory to the continuance of public evils whose influence in causing disease and death is more than commensurate, oftentimes, with their age or apparent importance. Every life lost is not an isolated one; *every life saved is, as a general rule, the precursor of others that else would not have been called into existence.*

The phrase in italics no doubt indicated Horatio's awareness of the ramifications of a successful campaign against criminal abortion as well as a successful campaign against disease-causing pollution. A demonstration of Horatio's continuing fierce antipathy to criminal abortion quickly followed in these September "Notes."

> We desire to call its [State Board of Health's] attention, and that of our professional brethren, to the fact, that in a neighboring city, not more than ten miles distant from Boston, a member of the Massachusetts Medical Society, in regular standing, who bears the reputation, well earned, no doubt, of being an unblushing abortionist, resides, and practices his nefarious art without let or hindrance.
>
> More than once has the law striven to vindicate its violated authority and failed of its object, being struck spellbound by the all-potent charms of Mammon. More than once have dying lips borne testimony to the blood-guiltiness of this monster in human form. ...
>
> The wretched mothers who lose their lives in this mad attempt to set at defiance the laws of God and man, may be virtually suicides,

but their educated accomplice is, in a far truer sense, a murderer.

There cannot be the slightest doubt in regard to the truth of the statements which we have made, and yet the members of the District Medical Society, and of the Medical Association in his own city, allow this man to go in his course, without a single vigorous effort to arrest the diabolical work which is demoralizing the community, and tarnishing their own good name. Shame on the profession which makes such high pretension, and tolerates such baseness! Shame on the manhood of those who retain in their fellowship, and admit, ay, to their very homes, and to a leading place in their councils, this professional Herod, whose garments are indelibly crimsoned with the blood of unborn innocence!! Dare any man who has virtually taken the solemn oath of Hippocrates, who has sworn to regulate his conduct by the noblest maxims of justice, purity, and benevolence, give countenance to the most cowardly of assassins, and even clasp his bloody fingers as those of a friend? If so, then farewell honor! farewell integrity! farewell all that is lofty and worthy of regard in human character!

Finally in the September "Editorial Notes," Horatio contrasted Boston's medical climate, rife with petty jealousies, with New York where "to acknowledge another's merit is for the common good." No doubt much to the dismay of the Harvard Medical School faculty, Horatio concluded: "we advise, with even greater emphasis, that they improve every opportunity, whether they be physician or student, to seek New York for their gynaecological studies."

October's "Editorial Notes" were almost exclusively devoted to criticism of the Massachusetts Medical Society's by-law that automatically admitted Harvard M.D.s, but required an examination prior to membership of anyone with a non-Harvard degree.[53] Horatio indicated why the examination of non-Harvard graduates was such a serious matter. Massachusetts physicians typically refused to consult with any physician who was not a member of the Massachusetts Medical Society and this made it imperative that a physician in Massachusetts join the Society. Horatio pointed out that such differential treatment of Harvard and non-Harvard graduates was contrary to the Code of Ethics of the American Medical Association, which the Massachusetts Medical Society had committed itself to uphold by sending delegates to the national association.

Horatio's concern was more than a general one. The new Massachusetts arrivals, Dr. George Bixby and Dr. Levi Farr Warner, both had out-of-state M.D.s and both were tested by the "censors" of the Massachusetts Medical Society in June. Warner passed, but Bixby, "in his excitement, became confused, as any other person might have done, and did himself apparent discredit."[54] Although two of the four censors passed Bixby, he was judged to have failed the examination. Horatio mentioned in the "Editorial Notes" that the failure may have been related to the fact that the Prospectus for the *Journal of the Gynaecological Society of Boston* had previously been circulated with Bixby listed as one of the future editors. One of the censors had indicated his concern that their failure of Bixby might be "interpreted as persecution," given Bixby's connection to the new journal. Obviously, the prospect of a "new and more independent journal" was not a welcome one in some Boston medical circles.

After describing Bixby's distinguished professional credentials and career, including "honorable work" with the Navy during the whole Civil War, which Horatio claimed more than qualified Bixby for Massachusetts Medical Society membership, and after making reference to the insult that Bixby's "ostracism" was to the Dartmouth Medical School and to Bixby's distinguished preceptor, Dr. Randolph Edmund Peaslee, of New York, Horatio wrote: "This is no fulsome overstatement of facts; they will probably all be made patent enough at the next annual meeting of the [Massachusetts Medical] Society, and at that of the American Medical Association,—a body which, if it cannot redress a wrong, can at least rebuke one, and hold its agents up to general execration."

This was actually the second warning that Horatio made to the Fellows and Councillors of the Massachusetts Medical Society that they would face problems at the next annual meeting of the American Medical Association unless their "discriminative tariff" against non-Harvard M.D.s and their other Code of Ethics violations were not remedied. Horatio first gave this warning verbally to the Massachusetts Medical Society at their June annual meeting a day or two before Bixby's unsuccessful trial. In an attempt to insure that all of the Fellows of the Massachusetts Medical Society were aware of this challenge and the warning of problems awaiting at the next annual meeting of the American Medical Association if change were not effected, the related "Editorial Notes" for October were reprinted in pamphlet form and sent to each Fellow of the Society with a cover letter dated October 1, 1869.[55]

The meeting of the Gynaecological Society of Boston on October 5, 1869 included description of Horatio's fourth double ovariotomy where "The ovaries and their contents, some twenty-seven quarts of a greenish treacly fluid, weighed in the neighborhood of sixty pounds."[56] Perhaps most significant, however, was that Horatio used chloroform instead of ether for anesthesia of the patient. Asked his current opinion of chloroform versus ether, Horatio reiterated his preference of chloroform for obstetrics, then claimed that he might "entirely discard the use of ether, as has been done in almost every place in the world save Boston." He indicated the initial slightly higher risk of death from chloroform was more than balanced by ether's increase of retching and other post-surgery risks. "There could be no doubt," he added, "that should a patient be lost here from chloroform, there would occur a temporary uproar; but he was not accustomed to allow the outcries of partisans to disturb his equanimity."

The ether discussion was capped by a tribute to Dr. Henry J. Bigelow, who was certainly no friend of its maker. Horatio either had just written or was about to write the following similar tribute to Dr. Bigelow for the "Editorial Notes" of the November issue of the *Journal of the Gynaecological Society of Boston*. The paragraph reads:[57]

> Jackson's four years' silence would have remained a life-long one; Morton's enthusiasm, hampered by the very natural conservatism of the medical profession, had succeeded in procuring the application of anaesthesia to a few cases of minor surgery. Now came the crucial experiment, the amputation of a thigh at the Massachusetts General Hospital,—their first capital operation in which ether was ever employed. The elder Warren had given but a half-willing, passive consent; his son had withheld a positive expression of opinion; while Hayward, by decidedly objecting to the experiment, had thrown his great influence adversely into the scale. Everything depended upon the verdict of this surgical staff; had it been unfavorable, there is probably not an operator, in public or private practice, who would have ventured thereafter to have given ether in a serious case. But the man for the emergency was not wanting. By his courage and decision he brought it to pass that the ether was administered to Alice Mohan, and under its influence her limb removed, and from this moment it was that anaesthesia passed into general use. It is not to the host of surgeons that have since then employed ether that the credit of its introduction is due, for each of these contributed but an infinitesimal fraction towards the end attained. The third man in the discovery, equal in his part to Jackson and Morton, was Dr. Henry J. Bigelow, who was so appropriately selected to transfer to the city authorities the beautiful monument upon the Public Garden.

At the Society's meeting on November 2, 1869, Horatio exhibited a modification of his "Boston Speculum" which the instrument maker had both improved (sturdier) and worsened (too-large a gape at the vaginal extremity). He noted that "the demand for the speculum was now so great that the Messrs. C[odman] and S[hurtleff] had to devote the whole time of one of their workmen to its manufacture."[58] Horatio's father was at this meeting and commented upon a paper on "The Reflex Sympathetic Affections Produced by Uterine Disease," noting that it did not sufficiently stress "the peculiar pain or pressure at the top of the head, complained of by many patients, and which he was almost inclined to consider pathognomonic of uterine disease, and more especially of displacements" of the uterus. One wonders whether David Humphreys influenced Horatio, or *vice versa*, in their strong belief in reflex effects of the abnormal uterus.

The "Reflex Sympathetic Affections" paper also stimulated discussion of reflex insanity. Horatio is recorded to have indicated that "proper local treatment" had produced marked improvement in several of his current cases.

He discussed his efforts to convince asylum superintendents to more carefully investigate such causes of mental disturbance in their female patients and "was glad to state that there was at last commencing a change from the general apathy upon this subject."

As if enough of Horatio's pet theories had not been raised at the meeting, someone made allusion to "the fitness of women to practice medicine." Horatio indicated that many of the objections to women physicians were untenable, since some of the women wishing to practice medicine had the needed education and motivation, "and were as unflinching in the presence of suffering or at the sight of blood, as were many male practitioners." However,

> like the rest of their sex, lady doctors, until they are practically old women, regularly have their courses, and are therefore subject to those alternations of mental condition, observable in every woman under these circumstances, which so universally affect temporarily their faculties of reasoning and judgment. That these faculties are thus affected at the times referred to is universally acknowledged. That the fact obtains to an injurious degree in the persons of many lady doctors, and to a greater or less degree in them all, had been acknowledged to Dr. Storer by more than one representative woman of the would-be medical type.

November's "Editorial Notes" mentioned Henry J. Bigelow's contribution to Boston's discovery of anaesthesia, as has already been cited. They also continued the theme that New York was a much better place for a medical student to train to be a gynecologist than Boston. There was no Chair of Gynecology at the Harvard Medical School and "the Obstetrical Chair has remained, as it has always been, the exponent merely of midwifery as an art ..." Horatio expressed his belief that Obstetrics now was not handled as ably as it had been by Walter Channing and, particularly as it had been handled "by Channing's successor."[59] Channing's successor, of course, was David Humphreys Storer, and the current holder of the Chair was Dr. Charles Buckingham who must have read this particular sentence with even more displeasure than that typically reserved for Horatio's "Editorial Notes." Buckingham would have liked even less Horatio's subsequent statement that Dr. Alexander D. Sinclair, rather than Buckingham, should have obtained the Chair of Obstetrics.

Horatio described the enormous numbers of women treated at the various charitable hospitals and other institutions in Boston and the opportunities these cases would provide for clinical instruction in the diseases of women. "Of the whole mass of disease thus indicated," he asked, "how large a proportion of it was properly diagnosticated, and how much properly treated?" And he answered: "The scoffs that are here so current concerning gynaecology and [concerning] those most interested in its scientific development, are a sufficient answer to these questions." Horatio continued, probably hinting at a new medical school:

> When asked by physicians or students, as we are so constantly, by
> letter or otherwise, whether Boston affords anything like the
> instruction in this department, that it so blatantly proclaims has been
> provided for every other special study, we are compelled to answer
> in the negative. We believe, however, that the influence of the
> Gynaecological Society, already making itself felt in more than one
> responsible quarter, will soon be sufficient to effect the required
> change.

Horatio then took up the cause of Navy physicians who were not given
opportunities for advancement commensurate with other Navy officers. He also
provided a progress report on "The points at issue between the American Medical Profession, and the State Society of Massachusetts, to which we called
attention last month, ..." These had been referred by the Councillors of the
Society to a committee chaired by Dr. Calvin Ellis, now Dean of the Medical
School, and Drs. Wellington and Hunt. Horatio called again for dropping the
automatic admission of Harvard M.D.s to the Massachusetts Medical Society
and also for "an apology from those who officially exceeded their duty" in
rejecting Fellowship for Dr. Bixby. The November 1869 "Editorial Notes"
concluded with the following tongue-in-cheek announcement:

> pleasure will be felt by our friends, particular here at home, to learn
> that the Journal of the Society is proving pecuniarily a success. The
> first few months of the existence of a periodical, like that of a child,
> are usually its most precarious ones, that is, supposing it to be
> endowed with an ordinary degree of vitality. There are those here
> who have been volunteering the opinion, indeed sedulously circulating
> it, that our publisher would prove a few thousands out of pocket,
> even at the outset of the undertaking. These gentlemen will, of
> course, rejoice with us that the end of the first quarter shows a
> balance in favor of the Journal, and this although neither any
> extended advertising nor canvassing have as yet been resorted to.

The December "Editorial Notes" consisted primarily of a transcript of the
ceremonies in Edinburgh, Scotland, in late October where Sir James Young
Simpson received the "freedom of the city of Edinburgh."[60] In the following
discussion of this tribute to Simpson, Horatio almost appears to be describing
his own struggles and perhaps his hope that someday his city might similarly
honor him:

> In the fact that our master has lived to obtain this spontaneous
> recognition *at home* of his great services to humanity, we heartily

rejoice, for it is the most valuable of all the triumphs that he has achieved, and is the legitimate result of a life of faithful endeavor. To some of the details of Prof. Simpson's earlier history, his struggles, long but successful, against adverse circumstances, false friends, and bitter professional enemies, the worst of whom were his own townsmen, we ourselves were permitted, many years since, to call the attention of the medical world.

Of the many achievements of Simpson that Edinburgh's Lord Provost honored in his speech, Simpson's discovery of chloroform was most heralded. The following comments of the Lord Provost did not sit well in Boston, since they appeared to indicate Simpson had discovered anesthesia itself:

"I will not dwell on what you have accomplished in medical science. I will only allude to your discovery—the greatest of all discoveries in modern times—of the application of chloroform in the assuagement of human suffering. (Loud applause.) That was a great gift to mankind at large, and it well befits us, the Corporation of Edinburgh, to mark our sense of the great act of beneficence on your part by this small compliment."

Horatio also quoted the following portion of an editorial from the *Edinburgh Daily Review* which Horatio saw as "probably the great secret of Simpson's so successful life:—"

"In short, Sir James Simpson is known to the lovers of progress, and to the lovers of humanity, as nearly, if not quite, the foremost man among them; a man of the highest scientific reputation, who carefully and boldly utilizes science for the diminution of human suffering,—using science in its highest possible manner. Some scientific men dislike Christianity. Some Christians, foolish people, we think, dread the light of science. Sir James Simpson, as a scientific man and a Christian, does neither. Deeply loving Christianity, he never fears, for one instant, that true science will lead anywhere but to the truth, and that the truth is Christianity."

Horatio followed these tributes to Simpson with the information that Dr. Jacob Bigelow had denied "the justice of the honors rendered to the discoverer of the anaesthetic properties of chloroform." Bigelow had written a guest editorial for the November 25, 1869 issue of the *Boston Medical and Surgical Journal*. Bigelow blamed Simpson, in his acceptance of the "freedom of the city of Edinburgh" speech, for not clarifying the fact that ether was the agent involved in the discovery of anaesthesia and that the discovery had occurred in Boston. Horatio referred readers to the transcript of the Edinburgh presentation, noting "it was not so much the general discovery that was under discussion as the man of the day, and the agent that, at the peril of his life, and after repeated experiments upon himself with deadly and unknown drugs, he had deliberately secured for mankind." And he added:

> Were Boston physicians, and in particular the past and present attendants at the Massachusetts Hospital, a little more chary in asserting their own claims, and a little more magnanimous towards those of others, there would be far less jealous apprehension among us of unintended slights.
>
> When chloroform shall have superseded ether in this city, as it eventually and assuredly will, then will Boston and Edinburgh stand side by side in the world's gratitude; the punctilious "hub" being content with having performed its customary duty, of sending out an idea for the rest of the universe to develop, and, if it can, improve.

Horatio thus had made a complete turnabout on the relative merits of ether and chloroform for surgery. His "When chloroform shall have superseded ether in this city," sentence must have caused a new level of antipathy among his opponents, particularly Jacob Bigelow, who was not just defending Boston's discovery of anesthesia, but ether.

A rare personal letter of Horatio's from this time period was found among family papers. It was dated December 27 and was to a "Dear Miss Minnie," probably the daughter of Horatio's Uncle Robert Boyd Storer and sister of William Brandt Storer, who had served in the Civil War and rose to the rank of Colonel. Minnie had been a member of a large party sharing the previous Summer's vacation, probably at Mt. Desert on the Maine coast. The letter strongly suggests that Horatio's wife, Emily Elvira, was still at home and functioning as lady of the house. The following key paragraph ending the letter gives indications of the stresses and strains that had been wearing heavily on Horatio in the Summer of 1869. It also indicates a new religious awakening, almost certainly his conversion from Unitarianism to belief in the Trinity via Reverend Phillips Brooks.[61]

> I often laugh to myself when I think of last Summers varied experiences with the tangled skeins of so many lives knotting themselves together to make the confusion a little the worse confounded. I fear I was very moody & self-absorbed, very tired in mind I know, & I don't think I ever felt so much like drifting like a log on the waves of each day. I've been ashamed of it a great many times since, for it was certainly very, very uncivil, but I was carrying heavy business cares at the time, aside from my profession, & was in the midst of a conflict with uncertainties, doubts & downright disbelief of which

young ladies, the angels may conceive, but not themselves know. There was but one issue to such a strife. Compelled humbly to surrender to the Master my life had denied, I find a peace of which before I had had no conception, & then strangely enough, the harbor of refuge for which my ships at sea had been so long & so ineffectually struggling was reached at last on Christmas Eve. Your father will be glad to know that Col Storer has completed good negotiating here at home for his iron working & goes in a few days to Troy, in pursuance of an arrangement within Mr Griswold's firm.

With a happy year, if wishes can bring it

HRS

CHAPTER 13

ANNUAL ADDRESS, GARRISON FIGHT, 1870 AMA MEETING, SIMPSON'S DEATH

Horatio's January 1870 "Editorial Notes" discussed a formal resolution relative to the controversial location of the new City Lunatic Hospital which the Gynaecological Society passed a month earlier and sent to the Mayor, Aldermen, and Common Council. Among the "Whereases" to the resolution were the strong gynaecological role in the cure of female insanity and the wise judgments of insanity experts that the new facility should be located at the city-owned "Winthrop Farm." The resolution protested "the crude, hasty, and trivial opinions expressed by Drs. Putnam, Buckingham, and others, being allowed by the city government to affect its action, as against the matured and judicious advice of asylum superintendents, who have examined the several sites suggested, and of the Board of Directors of Public Institutions, who have so long given the subject thoughtful attention."[1] Horatio followed this with two more pages of "Editorial Notes" reiterating the Society's position and further criticizing the President of the Massachusetts Medical Society (Putnam) and his followers, who had publicly opposed the Winthrop Farm site advocated by experts on insanity and who had derided these experts in the process. He felt that

> there can be nothing more contemptible, or more damaging to the real welfare of the profession, than for medical men to allow themselves to become cat's-paws for those who shrewdly love a civic kernel. There can be nothing more cowardly than an attempt, whether open or underhanded, by general practitioners to bring discredit by ridicule upon so respectable a body of special workers as are the medical superintendents of insane asylums in this country. ... Commenting upon it as we have done, the editors of the Journal are but breaking another link in the chain which has so long bound, it was once thought hopelessly, professional freedom in Eastern New England.

The increased stridency of Horatio's attacks in the "Editorial Notes" was not lost on the subject of criminal abortion. He noted that the abortionist described in September had recently been "charged with causing the death of a young woman from a distant town," but had never appeared for trial. "Report has it," Horatio wrote, "that three thousand dollars in greenbacks answered as a sufficient hypnotic for the conscience of the prosecuting attorney as well as anodyne for the agonized feeling of the fond parents." He continued:

It is clearly the duty of the County Medical Society to disown

Dr._____, if guilty, and to make an emphatic public protest against his acts, whether it attempt to procure his conviction and punishment, or not. It should do this for its own sake, and that of the community. Right here, in professedly Christian Massachusetts, where the crime of induced abortion is perhaps more frequent than anywhere else in the world, and where public opinion, stringent on so many points of morality, is unaccountably lax on this, should the brave Christian work begin of stemming the torrent of evil, that it may not gain such strength and volume as to overflow and devastate the world. Why are philanthropists and good men so timid? Do they love their own ease and pecuniary interests more than they do the cause of virtue and righteousness in the earth? Do they forget that the career of the professed follower of Christ is to be one of continual warfare, and that he is not to regard even life itself in the service of his Master? Significant indeed is that passage in the Apocalypse which speaks of the "fearful," in company with the "unbelieving," and with "liars" and "murderers," as receiving the final punishment described under the dreadful image of a lake burning with fire and brimstone.

In conclusion, we earnestly request our brethren to whose jurisdiction the case under consideration belongs, to shake off their apathy, and set an example worthy of being imitated by every medical society in the country.

The ends of the year and the first volume of the Society's *Journal* provided Horatio with an occasion for the following philosophical thoughts, stock-taking, plus a warning or two:

Christmas and New Year's are occasions for editorial as for other friendly salutations. Every advent of advanced thought and work has in itself the element of a higher progress still; every change from an effete December, even of professional attainment, to a renewal of vigor, gives earnest of grander future, to help towards which is the duty of all, though its full completion none living may see.

This Journal rounds the new corner in time, to find before it, we trust, even a wider field of usefulness. It has already lived down ridicule; it has assailed even to their fall more than one wrong and abuse; and it has combined a very powerful opposition to the over-conservatism of disbelievers in medical improvement. Its work, however, has but just begun. There are a score or more of professional deformities here at home, and elsewhere many others, already ticketed for admission to treatment; and, if ordinary pressure does not suffice for their cure, the knife will be resorted to with unfaltering hand. The personality of those coming to grief will be wholly lost sight of; to us they are merely unfortunate patients requiring the probe, or still more unfortunate delinquents demanding discipline.

To our friends we send a kindly greeting; we shall have, willingly, no enemies. In the name of the Society we extend to all fellow-workers an invitation to join with it in contributing to the common harvest.

The first *Annual* Meeting of the Gynaecological Society of Boston was held at 4 P.M. on January 4, 1870 at St. Francis' Hospital in Somerville, by invitation of Sister Superior Frances Sophia MacKenzie. In addition to nine of the Active Members, there were "by invitation, quite a number of medical gentlemen of Boston and vicinity."[2] The Hospital meeting site allowed not only discussion of a successful recent ovariotomy of Horatio's and exhibition of the ovarian tumor, weighing with its contents twenty-four pounds, but the recovering patient herself was viewed by many attendees. The major event of the evening, however, was delivery of the Presidential Address. Given its important theme and message and given that Horatio was the actual author of these Presidential Addresses, much of it is quoted below. The title was "The Demands upon Every Thoughtful Physician to Give Closer and More Intelligent Heed to the Diseases Peculiar to Women."[3] Before actually addressing this subject, Winslow Lewis recounted some of the founding principles and some of the accomplishments of the Society over its first year. He noted that "nearly every distinguished writer or practitioner" of gynecology had been selected as Honorary or Corresponding Members "and their acceptance has been conveyed in terms highly flattering to the Society." The *Journal* of the Society was discussed and ten of its most important articles identified. The Society's extensive library of books and journals and its important collections of "diagrams elucidating the phenomena of uterine disease" and surgical instruments were mentioned. He also mentioned "the opportunities which are now afforded, in a measure through the leading spirits of the Society, of studying uterine disease upon a scale never before possible in New England" at "the hospitals established by the good Franciscan Sisters."

The following main portion of the address, provides much of importance related to the struggles of the specialty of gynecology, the Society, and the Society's Secretary, Horatio Storer:

I myself, as is very generally known, am an old man; in the medical and surgical harness before many gentlemen now in active practice were born. I have passed through all the several stages of professional opinion in my estimate of the claims, the value, the respectability even of gynaecology. When I commenced life, no such thing as special diseases, as such, peculiar to the female, and unshared by the other sex, was dreamed off [sic]. It was known that women had tumors, it was true, and that they were sometimes uterine, and sometimes ovarian, but no one had yet claimed that they could be differentially diagnosticated from diseases of the spleen, liver, or kidney, and, still less, from each other. The true character of the menstrual function, and its wonderful influence upon the whole general economy of women, had been surmised, no doubt; but so far as a scientific demonstration was concerned they were all unknown. The speculum had not yet been resuscitated from the ashes of Pompeii, and the uterine sound, that attenuated prolongation of the human finger, though known to the ancients, had been for ages forgotten. The uterine cavity was a crypt whose entrance was sealed, and so, for all scientific exploration, was the vagina also. Just as indeed has always been, for all practical purposes, the rectum, so important in the relation its diseases hold to those of the other pelvic viscera, *until the late discovery, by the Secretary of this Society, of that simple method of exploration and treatment, in the female, so easy, so interesting, and so perfectly efficient, with which his name will pass down in honorable association to the physicians and surgeons of all future time.*[4]

In my youth, large numbers of women, old and young, were hopelessly bedridden, and hundreds of others, known to be invalid, were permitted to die of diseases now known to be easily, and indeed certainly, curable, without an effort being made to save them, simply because physicians did not know how to examine them, did not dare to attempt it, would not have understood the nature of the disease had they found it, nor have known how to treat it, had they ascertained its character.

Since then, everything has changed, and how greatly! The fear of proposing an examination has given way to the more rational ways of thinking of a more enlightened, and, let us hope, a more moral age. The fact is beginning to become acknowledged, and to be appreciated, that the diseases of all special regions of the body, whether organic or functional, are governed by the same general principles, and that there is no more real mystery about the cradle of mankind, than about the brain, the heart, the lungs, the teeth, the skin; and, strangest of all, that there exists a latent, but still very appreciable, sympathy between all the other organs of the body, in the female, and those of the pelvis, by which a thousand distant lesions, at first sight perfectly idiopathic, are found to be wholly secondary; neuralgias or neuropathies, stubbornly resistant to direct treatment, but under appropriate measures yielding like wax to a flame.

These are general statements, to the truth of which, assent must be given by all at all cognizant with the subject. And yet in practice, how continually do we still see them denied or forgotten! One would think that the appreciation felt by every physician of the female members of his own family, so dear to him, would lead to a general application among patients of those measures which experience has now proved of such inestimable value. Alas for poor human nature! and alas, too, that the petty motives which sway toward the bad, as well as toward the good, all mankind, should be found to prevail even among medical men! An ultra-conservatism, with its bad logic, and its worse selfishness; a dislike to acknowledge that the golden age is before, rather than behind, us; a disinclination to accept from mere boys, as we older men are but too apt to consider them, the priceless treasures that they offer us from the mines of their hard-acquired knowledge; the fear of ridicule by our fellows; and, still worse, the determination not to confess that we have been all along in the wrong,—these are the grounds upon which so many of us still allow our most interesting patients to linger in hopeless and most poignant suffering, however patiently, or to perish from causes, not to detect and remove which it is simply cruel, abominable, infamous.

I know, that for speaking so strongly as I have done, I may be censured by many of my older friends, and perhaps by some of my younger brethren also. If so, I can only say, that I am sorry for them. I am, however, and I do not hesitate to confess it, a convert to the new doctrines, and I state only that which I have seen. If any endeavor to find in this but evidence of second childishness, or dotage, I can only pity their stubbornness and hardness of heart. Having eyes, they see not; having ears, they do not hear, neither do they understand.

To bring the remarks thus far made, to a practical working, every-day lesson; who is there in practice however skilled, who does not every little while have a female patient about whose case he feels some doubt? He hesitates about proposing a consultation, for fear he should alarm his patient, confess his ignorance, or lose the case. He continues to trust to nature for a cure, knowing in his heart, however, all the time, that the more chronic the disease becomes, the less likely will recovery be to take place. He hopes against hope, that the accession of the grand climacteric, which is perhaps a dozen years away, may bring improvement, although he knows perfectly well that it is a critical period, fraught with an increase of danger. He herein performs a mean, pitiful act, which he would scout in any other man, and, did he not steel his conscience to it by frequent repetition, which he would condemn even in himself.

Why, then, do men continue in such evil doing? There seems no answer to this, that can be given, unless to say, that it is the fashion,—an evil custom far "more honored in the breach than in the observance." If the Gynaecological Society should effect nothing more than to bring the profession to a true sense of this but too

prevalent enormity, it will have accomplished a most excellent work.
...

There is one piece of advice I would give to those who, slow to be convinced that they have been wrong, or are still so, may yet desire to act in this matter as befits the honorable profession to which they belong; and that is, to look at the *general* aspect of questions with which they are not too familiar, instead of at their minute and often perplexing *details*. There are gentlemen, for instance, who spend much time and many words in the endless discussion regarding the respective merits of ether and chloroform, who yet, in practice, neglect to employ anaesthesia, by any agent, for the relief of the pangs of parturition, the spasmodic strictures of whatever mucous canal, to relax the tonicity of a doubtful abdomen, or to prevent, to a delicate moral sense, the shock of a necessary personal examination. There are others who will quarrel about the value of the several methods of reducing chronic uterine inversion, and yet allow a patient to sink to her grave from exhaustion, for want of any attempt to reduce this lesion. And there are still a great many who discuss the claims of the more prominent champions of ovariotomy, permitting, nevertheless, all of their own patients, who are afflicted with cystic disease, to go the way so many have untimely trod, because they have not the courage to operate themselves, or the manliness to advise that it should be done by others.

And, worse than all this, there are but too many, who, by their carelessness, their silence, or their cowardice, directly or indirectly encourage that scourge and hellish offence of the land, the induction of criminal abortion. Woe to him, who, by word or deed, in commission or omission of either, lends himself to this work accursed of the Lord!

But I have said enough, I think, to vindicate the work of this Society, and to prove my hearty desire to co-operate therein. I only trust that my words may sink deep into the hearts of all to whom they may come. We may meet with rebuffs, and we must expect them, but "Truth is mighty, and will prevail."

The Proceedings noted that the Presidential Address "elicited many expressions of applause from those present."[5]

Two weeks later, the Society met at its usual location in Horatio's offices at the Hotel Pelham. The Secretary made reference to ovariotomies reported in several medical journals which had successfully pocketed the pedicle. An unsolicited letter from a Boston physician was read and it indicated that the physician had weighed the evidence relative to "pocketing." "That you operated, demonstrated, and fixed professional opinion," he wrote, "while Dr.

Kimball was 'fondly dreaming' of some such result, is conclusively true."[6] Dr. Levi Farr Warner exhibited a patient whose cancerous breast was removed by Dr. Storer's operation of "lacing," and pointed out that no other method could have attained such a small scar. A new member of the Society, John G. Blake, was most impressed with the result and requested details on the operation since he had not yet been elected an Active Member when Horatio had presented a paper on the technique,[7] and Horatio obliged. Following presentation and discussion of several other cases, the Proceedings concluded with the following notice: "The Secretary presented a copy of the New York 'Independent,' of Dec. 23d, 1869, containing an attack by Mr. Wm. Lloyd Garrison upon the Society and its action with regard to an absurd argument adduced by Mrs. Dall in behalf of some physicians, and an answer that he had prepared to be forwarded to the editor of the paper referred to."[8] Garrison's article was entitled "Fair Play for Woman in the Medical Profession."[9] Garrison was responding to Horatio's letter to Mrs. Dall which had appeared in the Society's *Journal* in September. Although Horatio overlooked it and claimed otherwise, Garrison also made reference to Horatio's "Physicians in their Relations to Invalid Women," which was published in the November 1869 issue of the *Journal*.

Before discussing the Garrison article, the following letter from the editor of the *New England Medical Gazette* to Mrs. Dall is relevant. It indicates that Mrs. Dall was invited to provide "sharp surgical treatment" of the *Journal of the Gynaecological Society of Boston*.[10]

> *New England Medical Gazette.*
> No. 31 Mt. Vernon Street,
> Boston, Oct 25th 1869.
>
> Dear Mrs. Dall;
> I have not sent you the journal with the "unpronounceable name," because you looked so poorly that I did not think it right even to add a little burden to your cares and thoughts. If you are really feeling better this morning I will send for your perusal a bundle neither interesting nor agreeable, but which I think deserves sharp surgical treatment.
> If it should suit you to do so, I should be happy to give place to a communication from you on the subject, in the November number of the Gazette.
> I will try and see you in a day or two, and remain,
> Very sincerely;
> I. T. Talbot

Thus we see it is not only Horatio who made requests to Mrs. Dall for "Dallian notices." No published Dall paper on the "journal with the 'unpronounceable name'" appeared in the November *Gazette* or elsewhere. One suspects that

Editor Talbot found Mrs. Dall unwilling and turned instead to William Lloyd Garrison, enclosing in his letter the "bundle ... which I think deserves sharp surgical treatment."

Garrison provided a spirited defense of Mrs. Dall's call for the training of women physicians. He emphasized her main reason for this, namely that women and not men should be treating women's diseases. Garrison found passages in the early issues of the *Journal of the Gynaecological Society of Boston* which he claimed strongly supported Dall's notions that it was improper for "impure" women in all cases and pure women under the abnormal mental conditions of pelvic disease to be attended by a male, because this would excite in such women sexual feelings that would interfere with treatment. These passages included Horatio's attacks on "manipulators," some of whom "pandered to the vilest of lusts." They also included Horatio's quotes of Matthews Duncan, who had complained of many "foolish and unscrupulous" men working in the area of women's diseases. Garrison noted that even if these "unscrupulous" men were a small minority, having women attendants instead would prevent such abuse.

Garrison then quoted and belittled passages from Horatio's "The Relations of Physicians to Invalid Women: "Yet with vast assurance, Dr. Storer declares: 'We can only believe that their authoress was unaware what she penned'! or, 'if she has not committed a fearful error of judgment, then are physicians universally a curse to the community'! Was ever a more lame and impotent conclusion than this?"[11] Garrison also cleverly played on Horatio's advice to young physicians to specialize in the uncrowded area of women's diseases:

> Suppose some half a dozen female physicians in Boston had formed an association exclusively to themselves, for the avowed purpose of attending to *the peculiar diseases of men*, and had established a journal wherein coarsely to recount their "explorations" and modes of treatment; and suppose they had enticingly summoned young women in quest of employment to make these diseases their special study, as furnishing a lucrative field to cultivate—in what estimation would they be held, and how would they be described by the members of the Gynaecological Society? Would they give the consolatory assurances that "all impurity of thought, and even the mental appreciation of a difference in sex, are lost by the physician"? Certainly, they would do no such thing. Yet the rights of the sex are equal in this matter.

Garrison concluded by discussing bad attitudes of male students and faculty related to training of women physicians in Philadelphia and good ones in New York and Chicago. Despite his review of several articles from the *Journal of the Gynaecological Society of Boston*, he did not pick up on, or at least did not address, Horatio's main reason for opposing women physicians, namely the

mental and physical debilities associated with menstruation that Horatio believed
made women unreliable practitioners.

Horatio's "answer" was sent to the *Independent* who turned it down, and
it was published in the Society's journal.[12] It strongly reemphasized Horatio's
concerns about the inability of women physicians to perform during a portion
of their menstrual cycle. He denied that it was for selfish reasons that most
male physicians opposed women physicians. As for those male physicians who
supported women in the profession, he wrote:

> there is hardly a physician of any note in this country who favors the
> movement: Atlee [Washington L.], of Philadelphia, Bowditch, of
> Boston, and perhaps half-a-dozen others, are all, and these, more-
> over, are gentlemen extremely impulsive, however high-minded and
> honorable. The remaining few who are held up to us as representa-
> tive men are mostly those who, for other reasons, are considered as
> technically irregular, or who seek the petty profit that may directly
> accrue from consulting with women, or who are paid indirectly by the
> surgical practice they receive from their fair associates, or who, like
> certain hospital attendants and college lecturers in New York and this
> city, yield temporarily, unwillingly, and but partially, to the outside
> pressure, hoping that by so doing they may be able covertly to check
> the frenzy of the bacchantes of the present day.

Horatio then described his "experiment" at the New England Hospital for
Women which convinced him that women should not be physicians. He also
mentioned his belief "that there is an especial liability of women physicians
becoming principals in" criminal abortion. Horatio then returned to Mrs. Dall's
"repulsive argument" that the presence of a male attendant "must necessarily
induce ... thoughts and longings of an improper character."

> So far as concerns Mrs. Dall's new and repulsive argument, which
> is the only point they undertook to discuss, the members of the
> Gynaecological Society were united in condemning it, and there is
> probably not a reader of the "Independent," should he or she take the
> trouble to look it up, who will not do the same. The venerable
> President of the Society, and our associate in the editorial conduct of
> its Journal, Dr. Winslow Lewis, well known for his previous
> courtesies to lady physicians, took no pains to conceal his disgust.
> And Dr. Bowditch, to whom we have referred as for the present still
> giving nominal recognition to female practitioners, exclaimed, upon
> being shown the lady's denunciation of the purity of her own sex, that
> it was "perfectly outrageous for such a thought to have entered her
> mind," and that, "after it had done so, it should not have been loosed
> therefrom upon the community." To-day he states to us that he as

carefully reperused her article, and that he attaches to it the same stigma.

Finally, Horatio recommended that Garrison read his "The Relations of Physicians to Invalid Women," since he erroneously believed that Garrison had not seen it, although as we noted above, Garrison had actually provided quotes from it. "When he shall have read it," Horatio concluded, "and appreciates to what scandalous doctrine he now seems to lend defence, he will probably recall the very pertinent old saying, that it is sometimes better to let sleeping dogs lie."

As mentioned, the *Independent* refused to publish Horatio's "answer." "If Mr. Garrison has unwittingly misrepresented you," its Editor wrote, "we will allow you to say wherein in the briefest terms; but we cannot allow you to reply to his arguments." He claimed it was against their rules to "allow space for one writer to reply to another." Horatio included the Editor's letter in the February 1870 "Editorial Notes" and also noted there that this was hardly appropriate treatment of the Gynaecological Society of Boston since the *Independent* "had at least lent the opportunity to unjustly malign it." Horatio took advantage of the meager offer by the editor of the *Independent* and his new "answer" was published in their issue of January 13, 1870. Horatio indicated that Garrison had not done his homework, since he had not read Dall's article or Horatio's original criticism of it.[13]

> Had Mr. Garrison read this last, he could not have committed the error into which he has fallen. When he shall have received the copy ..., he will perceive that the statement of Mrs. Dall, in support of which he occupied so many columns of your issue for 23d December, was no less than this: "that the entrance of her medical attendant into the chamber of 'even the purest woman' necessarily excites in that woman's mind the most improper thoughts and longings." It was this statement which was stigmatized by us as unkind and untrue, and detrimental to the community. It alone was discussed by the Society; and Mr. Garrison has done injustice by ignoring this fact, and raising an entirely extraneous issue.

Israel T. Talbot, editor of the homeopathic *New England Medical Gazette*, who almost certainly incited Garrison to take on the *Journal of the Gynaecological Society of Boston*, provided the following comment on Garrison's article and on the *Journal* in his February 1870 number:[14]

> **The Gynaecologists Again.**—Since our last issue we have received a copy of the *New York Independent* containing a very severe but just criticism on some of the published transactions of the newly-formed Gynaecological Society of Boston. For unblushing indecency, some of the articles published by that society are unparalleled in medical

literature. Take, for instance, the reported cases of erotomania or nymphomania, and the comments made upon them; they are as disgusting as the treatment is unscientific. To think of removing the distressing malady by the vile means proposed would be like subduing the drunkard's appetite by administering alcohol, or curing a case of kleptomania by permitting the person to steal.

This publication has been six months before the world, and if it continues in the same course, it might very properly change its name to "Journal of the Gynaecological Society of Boston, devoted to the advancement of immorality, indecency, and kindred sciences!"

When discussing a case of erotomania before the Gynaecological Society of Boston, Dr. John L. Sullivan had argued "that the most successful treatment in many instances was to allow excessive intercourse."[15] The Proceedings of that July 20, 1869 meeting were published in January 1870 and it no doubt was this Sullivan comment that Talbot referred to in his February 1870 editorial. Horatio was associated with Sullivan as a partner in practice for about a year, and they also were partners in challenging the credentials of Massachusetts Medical Society delegates at the American Medical Association convention in Washington in May 1870. However, as will be seen, Horatio terminated this professional partnership after Sullivan pretended to be the absent Horatio to gain a patient seeking Horatio's services. We will also learn that Sullivan would be part of an 1878 conspiracy to obtain the extensive library of the Gynaecological Society.

In contrast to Talbot's panning of the *Journal of the Gynaecological Society of Boston*, the editor of the Minnesota-based *Northwestern Medical & Surgical Journal* wrote in its first number: "The Gynaecological Journal is supplying a need long felt in the country, and meets with a welcome at every physician's table. We predict that, ere ten years elapse, it will have the largest circulation of any medical periodical in the world."[16] The editor of the new journal was Dr. Alexander J. Stone, Horatio's former student and former assistant. Horatio no doubt was as pleased that his friend and associate also was now editor of a medical journal as he was for Stone's biased prediction for the *Journal of the Gynaecological Society of Boston*.

The first entries in the February 1870 "Editorial Notes" surely cemented Horatio's bad relationship with Jacob Bigelow, Jacob's son, and with *Boston Medical and Surgical Journal* Editor, Dr. Luther Parks. Horatio resumed his December criticism of Bigelow's criticism of Sir James Young Simpson with the following:[17]

The communication from Prof. Simpson, of Edinburgh, which we to-day publish, in answer to the uncalled for, ungenerous, and unjust attack by Prof. Jacob Bigelow, of this city, will be read with interest by all, whether within or without the profession, who delight to see false currency nailed to the counter. Our townsman seems to have stated what he must have known, or at least, ought to have known, was unfounded.

Possibly, it is true, as we intimated in our December number, the course of Dr. Bigelow may be attributed to the forgetfulness of age. This excuse, however, cannot be urged for the editor of the journal who welcomed the tirade to his columns, with a preface of fulsome laudation ... Nor can it avail those suborned claqueurs, so ready always for their prompter's nod, who so assiduously ladled that week's milk and water into the runnels of the secular press.[18]

As Dr. Parks, known by us all for his largeness of soul, and love of fair play, will of course hasten to copy Prof. Simpson's reply to Dr. Bigelow, into the journal of which he is the responsible editor, we would not be behind in courtesy. We therefore present below, the criticism of Dr. Bigelow as adorned by Dr. Parks, asking pardon from the former gentleman if we allow his postilion to precede him.

The Parks' "preface of fulsome laudation" included:[19]

when the now venerable author of the famous essays on Nature in Disease comes forth, as in the following communication, from his retirement of literary leisure,—a repose well earned by a life of activity as full of honors as of years,—to vindicate the claims of the land which gave to the world one of the greatest medical discoveries ever vouchsafed to mankind, it becomes us to vacate the chief place in this Journal, and leave it to be graced for the time by his distinguished occupancy.

Jacob Bigelow's November criticism, which Horatio reprinted,[20] began by noting the award to Simpson of the Freedom of the City and quoting Lord Provost Chambers: "I will only allude to your discovery,—the greatest of all discoveries in modern times,—the application of chloroform to the assuagement of human suffering." Bigelow next complained that when Simpson replied to the Lord Provost, "he complacently accepts the crown of borrowed plumes thus tendered to him, [but] makes not the slightest allusion to the country from which they were plucked, in which country anaesthetic inhalation, with more agents than one, was established, vindicated, and successfully practised long before it was heard of in Edinburgh or any part of Europe." Bigelow then gave a brief history of anaesthesia, "first used in the extraction of teeth, and afterwards in capital operations in the Mass. Gen. Hospital, and in obstetrical practice." He concluded by discussing ether and chloroform as the two major anesthetics and claimed that ether was far safer.

Simpson's "Answer to Jacob Bigelow" occupied six pages of the *Journal of the Gynaecological Society of Boston.*[21]   Simpson noted that he could not have been expected to give the full history of anesthetic agents in his off-the-cuff response to the Lord Provost's speech, the history of which "has always taken me a full hour in my University Lectures." Simpson then gave a fairly extensive history of such agents, and although he gave much credit to Boston's Dr. Morton, he also discussed Sir Humphrey Davy's proposal to use nitrous oxide during surgery "some seventy years ago." He even inquired whether Bigelow would have had him mention "other soporific vapors and measures employed by different olden surgeons, in Greek, Roman, and Mediaeval times, with the view of rendering their operations painless to the Patient?" Simpson also indicated that anesthesia in obstetrics was first used in Edinburgh and not in Boston as was suggested by Bigelow.

Horatio concluded this February presentation and discussion of the Bigelow-Simpson exchange with the following quote from a letter Simpson wrote to Horatio:[22]

> "Of the very misdemeanor with which he [Bigelow] charges me, he is guilty, while I am innocent. Certainly the Provost, Mr. William Chambers, the publisher, made no allusion whatever to the history of anaesthesia, upon which I could have hung any remark upon Morton, or Davy, or any one else. I don't know if his observations are correctly reported, as we had no written address; but even as given by the reporter, his one or two sentences on anaesthesia refer to chloroform only.
>
> "I think that, in common courtesy, Dr. Bigelow should have sent me some copy or another of his attack. In this and other respects, it has the character of what in England is called a 'foul' blow."

February's "Editorial Notes" also continued The Gynaecological Society's war on the Massachusetts Medical Society and the Harvard Medical School for the policy that gave automatic Society fellowship to Harvard Medical School graduates while stigmatizing graduates of all other schools. Horatio reported a rumor that the Society would evade the charges Horatio had made at the Annual Meeting or stifle their discussion. Horatio gave another warning that these violations of the "Code of Ethics of the American Medical Association" could lead the Association to refuse the right of representation of members of the Massachusetts Medical Society and Harvard College. Horatio reproduced a portion of an editorial from the *Cincinnati Medical Repertory* written in support of Horatio's October 1869 editorial criticism of the Massachusetts Medical Society's unfair connection with the Harvard Medical School. The editors found it "truly astonishing" that the Massachusetts Medical Society "could be induced to make such a discrimination—subjecting some to examination before admitting them as members of their Society, *because they did not graduate at particular schools*, and omitting it with others *because they did—..."* The italics were the editor's who also had the following advice for the Harvard Medical School: "Colleges which make use of such means to compel patronage should be classed among the irregular schools, and their courses of lectures not recognized by other institutions. It is dirty work, gentlemen, and the sooner you discard it the better."

Also among February's "Editorial Notes" were deflections of a pair of challenges about who was "first." The Louisville Obstetrical Society claimed it was the first society "to give especial attention to the new science of the medical and surgical diseases of women, as well as to midwifery." This one was easily handled when Horatio indicated that the Gynaecological Society of Boston was "not partially, nor chiefly, but wholly devoted to the diseases of women." The other challenge was from a Dr. Newman of Louisville who claimed he was the first to lecture on the surgical diseases of women in the Fall of 1865, more than six months before Horatio did. Newman apparently believed Horatio's initial post-graduate course constituted his first lectures on the topic. Horatio indicated that Newman was wrong and that Horatio had begun his series of lectures to students at the Berkshire Medical College in October 1865, "that is to say, at the same time with Dr. Newman if not before him."

The "Editorial Notes" for March 1870, began:[23]

We are glad that the "Boston Medical and Surgical Journal" has followed our suggestion with regard to the propriety of inserting in its columns Sir James Simpson's reply to Dr. Jacob Bigelow, published by us last month, and we do not share in the general laughter that our contemporary should have preferred to wait a fortnight for the London simultaneous issue[24] rather than copy from us. Under all the circumstances, Dr. Parks' course was a very natural one, and therefore should not be ridiculed.

We are also glad that our successive numbers have thus far received, without a single exception, the cordial endorsement of our brother,—to our every assertion and comment there seems to have been his sincere amen. All over the world, silence is acknowledged to mean consent, and it is, of course, a great satisfaction to us to know that the respect we entertain for our neighbor is so fully reciprocated. Long may he preserve this present friendly discretion, which is always the better part of valor.

The latter paragraph reflected the fact that the *Boston Medical and Surgical Journal* had not made any mention whatever of the existence of the *Journal of the Gynaecological Society of Boston*.

The March "Editorial Notes" went into some discussion of the controversy about whether W.T.G. Morton or Dr. Charles T. Jackson discovered ether anesthesia and stated the Society's conclusion, following its investigation of the facts, that the discoverer was Jackson. In a related vein, Horatio took Boston to task for arguing that it was the site of first use of ether in midwifery. However, Horatio expressed even more concern that Boston probably had less use of anesthesia to allay the "Agony" of parturition than any other large city in the world. He cited a pair of reasons for this, namely, Boston accoucheurs' "ungrounded dread of chloroform" and their "personal disgust at ether."

The March "Editorial Notes" also contained the latest on the Massachusetts Medical Society and its way of dealing with Horatio's proposal to eliminate the unethical favoritism the Society granted to Harvard Medical School graduates. Horatio indicated that the Committee appointed by the Councillors of the Massachusetts Medical Society to consider the issue "rendered the anticipated report, recommending that no change be made." Horatio noted that the favoritism problem continued, then raised the issue of another Code of Ethics violation by the Massachusetts Medical Society. This was the inclusion of irregular practitioners among its members. These typically were Harvard M.D.s who had opted to become Homeopaths. Horatio, in the following, made all the more explicit his threat that Massachusetts Medical Society and Harvard Medical School delegates to the American Medical Association meeting would be denied access:

> "What!" we were soberly asked, but a month or two ago, by a very influential physician, "do you really suppose that we Boston men care a pin for the authority of the American Association? We can attend to our own affairs, and as for coercion,—bah!" We replied then, as now, that events will prove. If we do not wholly misjudge the American profession, its National Association is alike a refuge for the oppressed and a judge for the guilty, and with power, too, fully sufficient to enforce its decrees. To it we confidently appeal.

Dr. Henry W. Williams, one of the physicians who tried to scuttle the American Medical Association in 1865, was twice criticized in the March "Editorial Notes," first for his defense of the status quo on Harvard graduate favoritism at a meeting of the Massachusetts Medical Society Councillors and second for opposing both a grant to the City Lunatic Hospital and the hospital's relocation. Williams was the current President of the American Ophthalmological Society, and Horatio pointed out his vulnerability as "a specialist, and therefore liable to be viewed by very many of the profession as a superfluous ornament." Horatio concluded: "It is no mark of wisdom for the eye to say to the brain, 'What have I to do with thee, or what need have I of thee?' They are too near neighbors for that."

Horatio also discussed the reprimand by the Harvard Medical School of Dr. David W. Cheever. Cheever received censure "for giving formal instruction in surgical anatomy to the students dissecting under his eye, an alleged usurpation of the province of the Professor of Surgery, [and] resigned his position as Demonstrator at the College." The Professor of Surgery, of course, was Henry J. Bigelow. Horatio indicated in the following that Cheever had more than *survived* this reprimand:

> That he accepted the promotion then immediately offered him, and went back as an Adjunct Professor, was no eating of dirt,—it was a victory. The Faculty could not afford to lose so valuable a servant, and therefore they paid his price. Had they hesitated it would have cost them far more.
>
> To teach this lesson, even though it required him to postpone for a while the leading surgeonship of New England, and to defer for a little making the City Hospital what it will yet become, a second Bellevue, was at the time the duty of the gentleman to whom we have referred. It may prove to have been, after all, but reserving the seed for a soil that should be ploughed a trifle deeper by retributive justice, and enriched by the falling to dust of fossils thus upheaved.

It will be recalled that a second Medical School in Boston was one major initial goal of Horatio and of the Gynaecological Society of Boston. The above no doubt reflected Horatio's expectation that the City Hospital would provide the clinical instruction for such a new school, that Dr. Cheever would be the Professor of Surgery, and in Cheever's hands this would become "the leading surgeonship in New England." It was probably to avoid the start of such a new medical school that Harvard quickly promoted Cheever, after his reprimand for offending Henry J. Bigelow.

The March "Editorial Notes" also included Horatio's first reference to the death of Mrs. Darwin Barnard following childbirth on September 5, 1869. Dr. Charles E. Buckingham had been the attending obstetrician and was assisted by a Dr. Swan. Horatio provided a pair of rules from a recent edition of *Swayne's Obstetric Aphorisms*, which dealt with what Horatio undoubtedly believed were the situations leading to the woman's death. Horatio wrote:[25]

> These aphorisms of Swayne are many of them good; one of them in particular we would commend, just at the present moment, to the attention of the President of the Obstetrical Society of this city [Buckingham], as we understand that he is collecting authorities on the subject. It is upon post-partum hemorrhage, and reads as follows: "In all cases where there is any reason to apprehend hemorrhage, the pulse should be frequently felt, and the uterus examined. The patient should be asked whether she feels any discharge running from her; and the napkin should be frequently removed and inspected." An extract from Gooch is also given, which is particularly pertinent in the present connection: "The life of the patient depends on the man who is on the spot; he must stand to his gun. A practitioner who is

not fully competent to undertake these cases of hemorrhage can never conscientiously cross the threshold of a lying-in chamber."

At about this time, Buckingham published a pamphlet with the correspondence related to the tragic death.[26] This was primarily letters between himself and Mr. Barnard, but also included letters Buckingham exchanged with Horatio's father. Buckingham described the death as "a fatal case of placenta proevia," but it appears to have been a more typical case of hemorrhage following the normal live birth of the child. A republication by Mr. Barnard of the correspondence added sworn affidavits by persons present that his wife had been left unattended for a substantial period following the birth and even for several minutes after the woman herself had called out that she was bleeding.[27] The twice-published correspondence indicated that Barnard initially had accepted the Buckingham verdict that nothing could have been done to save his wife. However, routine questions from family and friends had caused him to doubt this. Barnard contacted Buckingham several weeks after the death of his wife and child (who lived only a few days) to obtain reassurance that his wife's death was not due to neglect or malpractice. Buckingham, however, became defensive and refused to answer Barnard's questions and requested that these questions be put in writing and that the answers to them would then be made in the presence of physicians selected by himself and Barnard. Buckingham also suggested that Barnard was put up to his "charges" by some enemy of Buckingham.

Barnard's heartrending letter in response described the grief of himself and his wife's family at the death of mother and child and the concerns that family and friends had raised related to measures *not* taken, such as failure to use ice, although much ice was available in the household. It also indicated that Barnard had contacted David Humphreys Storer and other physicians about these raised concerns, only because Dr. Buckingham was away. Barnard indicated that at least some of these physicians had expressed their surprise that more was not done by Buckingham to stem the hemorrhage. As originally published by Buckingham, this correspondence appears to provide damning evidence of Buckingham's neglect and malpractice. This was strongly reinforced by the subsequent publication by Barnard of the same material plus Barnard's views on what had taken place and sworn affidavits by three women present at Mrs. Barnard's death that Dr. Buckingham and his assistant Dr. Swan were not, as the two claimed, always with the patient. These women also denied seeing the doctors compress the uterus as was claimed by Dr. Buckingham. These pamphlets would receive intense discussion in subsequent "Editorial Notes."

Horatio devoted the last portion of the March "Editorial Notes" to discussion of various periodicals, both medical and non-medical. He singled out a San Francisco magazine, "Overland Monthly," and a book, "Sunset Land," by "our old friend, the Rev. Dr. John Todd, of Pittsfield," citing both for their "fascinating occidental charm—for the West outvies the East in interest to us Americans." It certainly did for Horatio, given his award-winning "Mississippi" thesis, his six-month trip to the West in 1858, and a major interest in the expeditions in that area. In a year, he himself would travel to Utah and California when the American Medical Association met in San Francisco. Horatio also noted the criticism the Reverend Todd received for his anti-abortion tract, *Serpents in the Dove's Nest*, which had praised Horatio.

There was also the following paragraph which praised a magazine of the famous brother of Horatio's college friend, Charles Hale. It also indicates some of the groundwork that was unconsciously being laid for Horatio's trip to southern Europe, when he himself sought a cure in 1872.[28]

> "Old and New," edited by Edward Everett Hale, and published by H. O. Houghton & Co., of Boston, brings to us each month a wealth of material for restful thought. Doctors and doctors' families are but men and women after all, and to them, as to all the rest of the working world, mental as well as physical relaxation is a necessary change. In the March number is an article, entitled "In Search of a Climate," of peculiar interest to gynaecologists and the patients whom they may send to Europe, inasmuch as it describes with minute detail Mentone, the favorite wintering-place, in Southern France, of Dr. Henry Bennet, of London.

Horatio concluded the March "Editorial Notes" with the following lofty statement of the mission of the Gynaecological Society of Boston and its Journal:

> The establishment of the Gynaecological Society was, in truth, but a birth of which the time had long been pregnant; its Journal, the pioneer from the old and obscure ways of the past to a new and fresh and more perfect understanding of questions in our art, very vital in themselves, and in their application touching, most emphatically, social science, State medicine, and the public happiness.
>
> In Schiller's "Columbus," Mr. Hale's Prologue for February, we find no inapt conclusion to what we have just now said of the Society and its work:—

> "On, brave sailor! though the men of worldly wisdom mock thee!
> Though the helmsman in his place let fall his lazy hand!
> Westward! westward ever! Yonder must be the shore,
> Which mirrored in thy mind so clear and shining lies!
> Trust God's guiding angel—trust the silent sea.
> Were the land not there, still from the flood 'twould rise.
> Nature is linked with Genius in eternal bonds—
> That which the one foretells, the other must fulfil!"

The March 1 meeting of the Society included a reading by Dr. Bixby of the initial portion of a monograph on "Insanity Occasioned by Disease of the Pelvic Organs" by Professor Louis Mayer of Berlin. Bixby was translating Mayer's paper from the German "at Dr. Storer's suggestion,"[29] and Bixby's translation would be published serially in the *Journal of the Gynaecological Society of Boston*. Horatio indicated his satisfaction that his own ideas of 1864 about pelvic causation of insanity in women were being "fully corroborated by Prof. Mayer, who has established, by gynaecological evidence, every point that had previously been made ..."

Of particular interest at the March 1 meeting was Horatio's reading of his memoir on the surgical treatment of hemorrhoids and fistulo in ano which was published the next month in the Society's journal.[30] It will be recalled that Horatio won the Boylston Medical Prize in 1851 for his paper, "The Pelvis." One of the subjects for prizes in 1869 was "the surgical treatment of hemorrhoids, and the surgical treatment of fistulo in ano with the result." Horatio had frequently dealt with both rectal conditions in his practice and had developed surgical procedures for both which were distinctly at variance with the use of ligatures, the practice that prevailed at the Massachusetts General Hospital. No doubt, Horatio thought himself the world's foremost expert on the subject of hemorrhoids, and perhaps he actually was.

Why would Horatio deign to submit what he must have believed to be the state-of-the-art essay on this topic to judges with questionable competence and almost certainly with biases against its strong recommendation for surgical treatment and its condemnation of ligatures? And why did Horatio take deliberate pains to conceal his authorship? Horatio himself indicated his four reasons in the following "subjoined letter of reclamation" sent to Henry J. Bigelow, Secretary of the Boylston Prize Committee:[31]

Hotel Pelham, Boston, 19th Nov., 1869.

Dear Sir:— I sent to Dr. John Jeffries the other day to reclaim a dissertation upon hemorrhoids forwarded last spring from Pittsburg [sic], Pa., to the Committee of which you are Secretary, and enclosed the express receipt therefor. As Dr. J. states that the MS. referred to is in your hands, you will please deliver it to Dr. Warner, who will give you this. You may very likely have already appreciated that the dissertation was written not so much for the sum offered by the committee as to ascertain, what is much more valuable,

1. Whether hospital surgeons in Boston have a better knowledge of the diseases in question than their practice indicates.

2. Whether, as unprejudiced members of a prize committee, they prefer mere compilations to original researches.

3. Whether advances initiated in a certain quarter would be recognized as such in this city; and

4. Whether the work of strangers, or what purports to be such, gets impartial judgment in Boston.

These points have plainly enough been settled by the action of the committee. In anticipation of their decision, a signature was appended indicative of the position assumed by its members.

> "O God! Horatio, what a wounded name,
> "Things standing thus unknown, shall live behind me!
> "Hamlet, Act V. Scene II."

The dissertation will now be published, with the statement of the facts in the case, in the Journal of the Gynaecological Society of Boston.

Yours sincerely,

H.R.S.

To Dr. H.J. Bigelow, *Secretary, etc.*

This letter was included in a footnote to the published essay. Not the least significant thing about the letter is that it indicates an unwillingness to personally visit Henry J. Bigelow. Obviously, the rift between the two men was very large. The following preceded the letter:

> The above paper is a "Rejected Address." It has been condemned by Drs. Jeffries, Sen., Reynolds, Sen., Townsend, J.B.S. Jackson, Putnam, M. Wyman, Bigelow, Jr., Hodges, and one other,[32] ... "none of the dissertations presented being considered worthy of a prize." To this adjudgment, "unanimous save a single dissenting voice," as stated by Dr. Jeffries, the writer makes no objection, the paper having accomplished the ends for which it was written, as will appear hereafter. ... It will be seen that the writer speaks of himself in the third person, and in no very complimentary terms, for reasons that will be apparent enough, in the light of the subjoined letter of reclamation, sent to the Secretary of the Boylston Committee.

Horatio began the paper:

> If it was more particularly intended by those having the matter in charge to elicit lengthy disquisitions from young gentlemen just entering practice and with leisure to translate from foreign languages, or to dress over from their own, what has been hitherto written upon the subject selected, the committee need not trouble themselves to read farther the present communication, for it will not suit them. It merely narrates, with great brevity, the personal experience of a very practical man, who, for the nearly twenty years since he entered the profession, has had, in his hospital wards and in private practice, good opportunities for knowing whereof he speaks.

Horatio fairly quickly referred to vaginal eversion of the rectum and this produced the following illustration of third-person treatment of Dr. H.R. Storer "in no very complimentary terms":[33]

> How to make such diagnosis [distinguishing "outgrowths or hypertrophies from simple prolapsus"] as to avoid the chance of this [cutting into Douglas' fossa], is a question apparently never yet asked or answered. It is simply, however, to pass a sound and elevate the uterus posteriorly by throwing it forward, and then to evert the anus and lower rectum by digital pressure from within the vagina. (The second part of this procedure, beautiful in its simplicity and as effective in all the diagnostics of the rectum, has been claimed as original by Dr. H. R. Storer, of your city. Putting aside the improbabilities of anything so important having been overlooked by the thousands of surgeons who have worked at the rectum, and the scores who have written upon it, I can only say that I have myself for several years employed the method referred to, and have demonstrated it both publicly and privately to numbers of medical men. The gentleman's course in claiming it as his own seems paralleled by that he pursued regarding what he calls "pocketing the ovarian pedicle," which Dr. Kimball, of Lowell, calls an old method, a useless method, and one he himself had previously tried and cast aside. I hope the committee will pardon what is not intended as a personality, but only an honest outburst of indignation, under the circumstances allowable.)

The general thrust of Horatio's paper was that the knife, scissors, and ecraseur were much more satisfactory than ligatures in dealing with these rectal problems. Rupture of the sphincter ani often was recommended for diagnosing and treating both hemorrhoids and fistula. With respect to sphincter rupture, Horatio warned: "If the forefingers are relied upon, as more easily introduced [than the thumbs], one must be careful for personal comfort in what direction the pressure is made. I thus once induced a partial lateral dislocation of my own finger, the use of which I did not fully recover for many months." We also learn that Horatio himself was a hemorrhoid sufferer. "Personal experience as a sufferer has, moreover, given me the right to ignore medical treatment," he wrote, "from which I got only brief reprieves, and to value the knife, from which came the years of subsequent comfort."

Sometimes Horatio seemed seriously to be seeking the Boylston Prize. On the other hand, the following comment may have been intended as a direct insult of Henry J. Bigelow, Secretary of the Prize Committee, even if he were only generally implicated:

> Much has been written upon the method of using the knife in fistula. A single word will suffice. Instead of three assistants, "one for

flexing the upper thigh and supporting the buttock, a second for straightening the lower thigh, and the third for depressing the lower buttock and holding one of the instruments," none is in reality required, if an anaesthetic be given, unless they are smuggled in under the pretence of necessity, but in reality to behold the operation; though I would by no means imply that surgeons are always happier in proportion as they are surrounded by admiring disciples.

The prize topic was "the surgical treatment of hemorrhoids, and the surgical treatment of fistulo in ano with the result," and Horatio included the following few sentences related to "the result." The passage concluded with his apology for not including any surgical cases, fashioned, no doubt, to infuriate:[34]

> As to the result of the methods of treating hemorrhoids and fistula that have now been described. That of the old way of operating is familiar, experimentally, to every member of the committee. That of the new methods, based, as they may be allowed to be, upon general surgical principles, has been to the writer far more satisfactory that what had been his earlier experience. Success is now his rule; failure, even to a partial extent, the very rare exception, and this has been the verdict, in their own practice, of many of his friends and pupils who have followed his teaching. Had he the time to do more than present this outline of his views, which he trusts has not proved wholly uninteresting to the committee, he would have presented a long series of illustrative cases, well aware that such often win the applause of the profession, however barren or erroneous the principles that they embody. He is not unwilling, however, to avoid the appearance of what is so often but an *ad captandum* argument, and will leave it to other competitors to present selections from perhaps more slender stores, merely adding that if any member of the committee ever finds himself in his section of the country, it will give him great pleasure to perform before him each or any of the methods now described, and to verify every word that has been said in their favor.

Horatio gave statistics in the next month's (May) "Editorial Notes" of the Society's *Journal* which were obtained from the Resident Medical Superintendent of the Massachusetts General Hospital and which indicated that all of the hemorrhoid cases in 1868-1869 had been treated "by ligature,—a practice as tedious and barbarous as it is dangerous, comparatively liable as it is to produce septicaemia." He then contrasted their cases with those of Dr. Cheever at the City Hospital, "all by excision, in accordance with a cardinal principal of modern surgery."[35] Horatio then characterized those surgeons, such as Dr. Henry J. Bigelow, who were on the staff of the Massachusetts General Hospital and who taught at the Harvard Medical College as: "Men who sneer at the importance of rectal disease, who are blind to its comparative severity and disturbing influence in women, and who, if operating at all, rather than step from a time-honored routine, would subject a patient to dangers realized in a most notable instance here in Boston but a few months ago, are so far unfit for college teachers or hospital attendants." Horatio added the following additional reference to the Boylston Prize Committee:

> With regard to the action of the Boylston Committee, to which we referred last month. There are those, at a distance, who may consider that it was owing to an instinctive desire upon the part of the Committee to shield a townsman from what appeared an unjust attack from Pittsburg; for the publication of which, were the memoir accepted, the members might have seemed to themselves responsible. So charming an instance, however, of professional *espirit de corps* as this may be common enough at the West or South; we have no doubt that it is. It has not occurred in Boston.

The Gynaecological Society's *Journal's* April 1870 "Editorial Notes" began with criticism of both Drs. Bigelow. Horatio referred to two *Boston Medical and Surgical Journal* articles, the first of February 24, 1870, in which the younger Bigelow claimed that he and not Dr. Gunn was the first to propose an easy method for overcoming dislocation of the hip;[36] and the second of March 10, 1870, where Jacob replied to Simpson's response.[37] Both Bigelows had indicated they had given their final answer, and Horatio wrote: "An ultimatum is hardly possible in controversies so serious as are these. Self-asserting medical autocrats are well enough for spokesmen or butt of a breakfast-table, but the great republic of the profession does not tolerate them."[38] "Breakfast-table" "spokesmen or butt" were the province of Dr. Oliver Wendell Holmes, whose humorous pieces appeared in the *Atlantic Monthly* and were published as books such as *The Autocrat at the Breakfast Table*.

Horatio then censured the close link between the *Boston Medical and Surgical Journal* and the Boston newspapers. The newspapers were apt to publish summaries of the medical journal articles even before the medical journal itself had been published. A most troubling one for Horatio was an abstract of Bigelow's March 10 letter which was "very laudatory of course of Dr. Bigelow, and very unkind and ungenerous to Prof. Simpson." Horatio next compared the current effort of Luther Parks, Jr., Editor of the *Boston Medical and Surgical Journal*, to compile all the evidence of chloroform's deadly effects to the similar effort of Dr. Johns which Horatio had criticized in 1863. Horatio provided two pages of quotes from his 1863 paper which he believed applied as well to Parks' more recent compilation, which was referred to by these critics of chloroform as a "martyrology." Horatio observed that ether also had its fatal victims, had more severe effects on subsequent health than chloroform, and "is in reality more deadly and unsafe." As to proposals by the "Etherites" to legally ban the use of chloroform and to erect a monument to the martyrs of chloroform, he wrote, "we simply hold them up to be laughed at by the world."

The meeting of the Society on April 19, 1870 was the last prior to the American Medical Association meeting in Washington.[39] Horatio listed three initiatives and interests of the Gynaecological Society of Boston. One was a reconsideration of "the Memorial of the Society in behalf of a proper system of instruction in gynaecology at American Medical Colleges." Since no Society member had been at the previous annual meeting, discussion had been postponed. The second was "the action of the Society condemnatory of the resolution passed by the Association last year relative to the insertion of their cards in medical journals by special practitioners." Third was "the discriminative and prohibitory tariff laid upon the graduates of other medical colleges, save Harvard, in the matter of admission to the Massachusetts Medical Society." "Upon motion," the Proceedings continued, "the Secretary was directed to bring these several matters, in behalf of the Society, to the attention of the Association, presenting the latter of them by a formal memorial, to be signed by himself and the President."

Before Horatio went off to Washington to the annual meeting of the American Medical Association, he prepared the "Editorial Notes" for the May 1870 *Journal*. Horatio virtually accused Buckingham of the malpractice in the death of Mrs. Darwin Barnard, which Horatio had only hinted at in March. The "Notes" began:[40]

> In accordance with its author's evident desire, we call attention to the extraordinary pamphlet prepared by Dr. Charles Edward Buckingham, ... Though a little affair of only twenty-nine pages, every copy has a duplicate title-leaf, reiterating the fact that the author is the Professor of Midwifery and Medical Jurisprudence in Harvard College; the verbiage being ... one of a series of shallow artifices towards accomplishing a certain end. We are told upon three consecutive pages, that "for the benefit of the medical profession," rather than as an impotent attempt to warp public opinion, in anticipation of an expected and degrading exposure, this cruel outrage upon the grief of heart-broken mourners has been committed. What else, however, could have been expected from one who could say to a dying mother, that the child which she had feared all through her pregnancy might prove deformed, was, though perfect, a frightful thing, "half horse, half alligator!" to use his own elegant bar-room language?

As mentioned earlier, Buckingham's pamphlet contained letters from the widower of the victim charging Buckingham with malpractice and also letters from David Humphreys Storer. The latter were solicited "under the impression that they were to be considered as private," but published anyway. One letter, the last from David Humphreys to Buckingham, included: "I am not a little surprised that you should say 'you had given me no account of the treatment!' If you had not done so, how could I say 'I thought you had discharged your duty'?"[41] As to Buckingham's "half horse, half alligator!" comment, Horatio gave no explanation in the May 1870 "Editorial Notes." However, it was described in Barnard's republication of Buckingham's pamphlet. The comment was made to Mrs. Barnard shortly after the birth of her child, and was a pun on her question about the sound of her child's voice. Mr. Barnard wrote:[42]

> A few minutes before her death, Mrs. Barnard, in a faint tone, remarked that the voice of the child, who was crying at the time, sounded hoarse. Dr. Buckingham, after asking her what she had said—causing her to repeat the remark, answered, *"It is half horse and half alligator."* The young mother who had borne an anxiety common to all in her situation, lest her offspring might not be perfect, died without seeing her child, and nearly the last words which came to her ear, fell from the lips of the physician who was attending her, your child is half horse and half alligator.

Buckingham's pun on *hoarse* no doubt indicates that Buckingham still thought his dying patient was fine and that a joke was not inappropriate.

Horatio concluded discussion of this Buckingham episode by calling for "an immediate and thorough investigation of the whole matter by the Faculty of the Medical College." "With the Webster case not yet forgotten,"[43] Horatio continued, "and with their part in the Ellis controversy that a single word may open again with all its terrible questions, as yet unatoned for, they will hardly dare to avoid the present issue."[44] This shows that Horatio had not concluded that Calvin Ellis had done the correct thing in his autopsy of Magee, despite Horatio's letter to Professor Oliver Wendell Holmes claiming this in December 1867. What is more, Horatio believed that the "Faculty of the Medical College" had participated in an inappropriate way in the Ellis controversy that was "as yet unatoned." Presumably, he was referring to their denials of wrongdoing on Ellis' part. The juxtaposition of the Ellis and Buckingham events (and even the Parkman murder) suggests that in Horatio's mind they were similar grave errors deserving major censure, no doubt including removal of at least Ellis and Buckingham from the Harvard Medical School faculty.

Horatio next indicated that Buckingham obtained his earlier Adjunct Professorship in the Department of Theory and Practice at the Harvard Medical School, "by the merest accident, having been taken as bait to hold the hospital with which he happened to be connected ..." "The hospital" was the City Hospital and there is a parallel here with the Harvard appointment of Dr. Cheever. Apparently in both cases a real threat existed of formation of a competing medical school which would use the City Hospital as its clinical resource. Horatio also indicated in these "Notes" that Buckingham quickly bit the hand that fed him when he took over David Humphreys Storer's Professorship. Horatio wrote that Buckingham "spoke to his class of their previous beloved preceptor, as 'good enough' for the place he had voluntarily vacated after so many years of faithful labor, 'but behind the age,' even while accepting that predecessor's free gift of all the rich appliances of the chair." Horatio then made the following prediction: "The miserable man, upon whose case we comment, seems of his own accord to have placed himself, bound and helpless, within the guillotine of professional opinion. It is with sincere pity that we see him lie shivering beneath the now, we fear, inevitable axe." Nevertheless, Buckingham survived in his Professorship until his death at age fifty-five in 1877.

Horatio next made a self-serving reference in the May "Editorial Notes" to the publication of Professor Louis Mayer of Berlin which Bixby was translating and which was being published in installments in the Society's *Journal*. He referred to the numerous scoffers at his theories that pelvic disease was a frequent cause of insanity in women and indicated that Mayer's doctrines provided "a metal that will turn the edge of their hardest weapon." Horatio then justified, or perhaps, rationalized, his trait of being "too self-assertive." He discussed how this "vindication and triumph" of his female insanity theories by Mayer might "smack of the grossest egotism" to those personally unfamiliar "with the toil and struggle of ideas that to their possessors are as clear and precious as crystal," for

> others in the profession, perhaps more competent judges, who believe that without correctness or intentness of vision no point in advance of the general practice can be discerned; that without enthusiasm, no pioneer, however brave, can reach that goal; and without a blending of self, motive, and work together, even to that extent that the first may at times seem to outcrop, however unintentionally, just as it does in every real missionary labor,—a general adoption of special views can never be, as it were, enforced. Philanthropy, education, and all other agencies for good, move still by force, after all.[45]

Horatio's attacks on various Boston medical men such as Buckingham and the Bigelows may have appeared one-sided. However, his enemies were not without their own devices. Horatio described one tactic used by some of his enemies in the following excerpt from the May "Editorial Notes":

> We have now to expose a more cowardly procedure than that [the leak to the newspapers of Bigelow's journal letter against Simpson],—and though it is one the full malice of which has been dealt upon ourselves, during several years and without comment or complaint from us till now, we feel that it has become high time to

end it, in view of the conclusive proofs that have come into our possession.

One of the editors of this Journal has a namesake in this city, whose initials (H. B. S.) are very nearly the same as his own. This gentleman, whom we happen never even to have seen, is undoubtedly a very worthy man, and entitled to respect. He is, however, by profession a lecturer upon Spiritualism, and a peripatetic at that, travelling up and down over the face of the country. Neither of ourselves have any, even the slightest, sympathy whatever with the peculiar views referred to. We therefore submit that it is a dastardly act for Boston physicians of high standing, who are well aware of the distinctness from each other of the two individuals in question, to report to their patients and to physicians far and wide, as they have done, that it is the Spiritualist who is the Secretary of the Gynaecological Society and one of the editors of this Journal.

The same unbrotherly conduct has been resorted to by medical men pretending to our face to be friends, who have been written to from a distance concerning our standing, both as has regarded proposed consultations and attendance upon our lectures to physicians. Such acts always recoil upon their perpetrators. We claim to be no better, wiser, or more skilful than our neighbors; but we are not a Spiritualist, and we tolerate neither in ourselves nor in others anything at variance with the code of Ethics of the American Medical Association.

Dr. H.*B*. Storer's practice is illustrated by a letter from him to Clara Barton. It requested a lock of her hair and statement of her age.[46] A week later she received the results of the "Clairvoyant Examination of Miss C. Barton."[47] The cost was two dollars. One would think that nurse Clara Barton would have known better than to participate in such quackery.

Dr. Bixby served as Secretary at the May 3, 1870 meeting of the Society where a pair of letters from Sir James Young Simpson were read.[48] One, dictated from what Simpson anticipated was his death bed, was a reply to Jacob Bigelow's second letter criticizing Simpson and it credited Horace Wells with the discovery of anaesthesia. According to the Proceedings, it "was written especially for the Society, and, as Dr. Simpson himself states in his letter, it would be his last offering to it and to Science." The letter was immediately published in a special Supplement of the *Journal of the Gynaecological Society of Boston*, since the May issue already had gone to press. Also at this meeting the following Resolution from the Society's Committee that had investigated anesthesia and its origins was read and unanimously adopted: "*Resolved*, That, after careful investigation of all the evidence presented, the honor of the solution of the problem of practical anaesthesia, as distinguished from the suggestion of any special agent, belongs without the shadow of a doubt to the late Dr. Horace Wells, of Hartford, Ct." This was telegraphed to the delegates at the American Medical Association meeting in Washington "in furtherance of any attempt that might be made to render a tardy justice to the memory of the late Dr. Horace Wells."

The American Medical Association meeting in Washington began with the challenge to the delegates from the Massachusetts Medical Society that Horatio had repeatedly warned about. The younger Dr. John Collins Warren, the son of Jonathan Mason Warren, was a delegate to the meeting from the Suffolk District Medical Society. The manuscript papers of John Collins Warren include his notes or someone else's notes for a formal letter of protest.[49] These convey some of the shock that must have been experienced by the Massachusetts delegates who were not aware of Horatio's repeated threat, or, if aware, had not taken it seriously. Warren's notes read:

[In pencil at top] This coolness between the M.M.S & the A.M.A. lasted until the meeting in 190?[50] when the new Harvard Medical School was incorporated.

1870 c May

To the Councillors of the Mass Med. Society:

The undersigned a majority of the delegates fr. the Mass Med. Soc. to the last meeting of the Amer. Med. Asso. held in Washington on May 3rd respectfully submit the following report—

that when certain of the delegates presented their credentials before the organization of the Association they were informed that delegates fr. the Mass. Med Soc. were not received as a protest had been entered by certain parties against their admission. They were referred to the permanent sec. of the association for future information & he informed them that "tremendous charges" had been made against the Soc. by Drs Storer & Sullivan of Boston & that the Committee on Credentials had refused to receive any delegates of said Soc. after the protest had been entered.

Soon after the organization of the Association[,] on motion of Dr. [Oramel] Martin of Worcester[,] the subject was referred to the Committee on Ethics, consisting of Drs. Stillé of Phila., Davis of Chicago, Woodward of Washington,

This Committee in private session immediately took up the subject: Drs. Storer & Sullivan were called in succession before the Committee & their testimony taken at great length. Drs. Savory, Allen, Martin were afterwards called in & gave testimony. The precise nature of the charges against the Mass. Med. Soc. we are ignorant of & can only judge of their general tenor fr. hearsay & fr. the report of the Committee wh. after a protracted session of fr. 3-4 hours adjourned. The following morning the Committee on Ethics

submitted the following report wh. was accepted by the Association-
Report.[51]
We would respectfully state that as the protest was wholly unexpected
no one was prepared to meet the deliberate & premeditated attack of
the parties supporting the accusation who came to Washington with
the apparent intention of bringing your Society into disrepute.
Boston May 1870.

The "Report" condemned the presence of "irregulars" in the Massachusetts
Medical Society and unless they were removed, future representation of Massachusetts Medical Society delegates at the American Medical Association would
be denied. However, it noted that Horatio and Dr. Sullivan had not properly
protested the "irregulars" to the Massachusetts Medical Society before bringing
the matter to the American Medical Association, and thus the Massachusetts
Medical Society delegation was granted admission to the meeting.

Other activities involving Horatio or the Gynaecological Society of Boston
included the motion to rescind the ban on cards by specialists which was "laid
on the table,"[52] and Horatio's appointment as delegate to attend the Canadian
Medical Association meeting. The Association also resolved that it "views with
approval the suggestions made by the Gynaecological Society of Boston, with
reference to collegiate instruction upon the diseases of women, and recommends
to the schools their more general adoption." The Association also adopted the
resolution offered by Horatio, "That the honor of the discovery of practical
anaesthesia is due to the late Dr. Horace Wells, of Connecticut."[53] However,
this was somewhat more controversial than indicated in the brief notes indicating
adoption of the resolution in the "Minutes" of the *Transactions* and in the
"Report of the Section on the Practice of Medicine and Obstetrics of the
same.[54] A letter published in the *Boston Medical and Surgical Journal* on June
30, 1870 echoed the journal's earlier stated concern about a "snap" judgment
in the matter.[55] The writer of the letter described the rudeness of a member
who, when the Section on the Practice of Medicine and Obstetrics proposed to
return the resolution without discussion, walked out of the meeting "calling upon
his auxiliaries to go out with him, which they did." The writer indicated that
the next day a "packed body" of the Section passed the resolution unanimously
with "a great part of those voting knowing little of its merits and caring less,
and influenced mainly by a good-natured desire to gratify the gentleman who
had pushed the matter with so much zeal." No name was mentioned, but the
zealous advocate of Wells almost certainly must have been the man who brought
the resolution before the full Association the next day, i.e., Horatio Robinson
Storer. Given that the critic was at all accurate in his discussion of events, this
certainly shows Horatio's ability to make friends, influence people, and make
enemies.

At the meeting, Horatio also defused a tense racial situation related to
exclusion of Howard University Medical Department delegates who would have

been the first blacks admitted to the American Medical Association. There were charges that these delegates were members of another organization (the National Medical Association) which included "as members medical men who were not licensed to practice." However, there were many who were opposing the delegation from Howard for their race alone, and Horatio did not please some extremists on both sides by proposing the following resolution which was adopted by a vote of 112 to thirty-four:[56]

> *Resolved*, That inasmuch as it has been distinctly stated and proved that the consideration of race and color has had nothing whatsoever to do with the decision of the question of the reception of the Washington delegates, and inasmuch as charges have been distinctly made in open session to-day attaching the stigma of dishonor to parties implicated, which charges have not been denied by them, though present, therefore
>
> The report of the majority of the Committee on Ethics [denying representation to members of the National Medical Association] be declared, as to all intents and purposes, unanimously adopted by the Association.

Shortly after the American Medical Association adjourned its annual meeting on Friday, May 6, 1870, Horatio received a telegram from Sir James Young Simpson's son indicating that Simpson had just died.[57] Many of the other delegates also were still in Washington and were reconvened for a memorial session held in the Army Medical Museum at noon on the following Monday. Horatio was a key speaker, although his remarks were relatively brief, perhaps because of his own great grief. He noted Simpson's very recent contribution to the American Medical Association's late resolution on Dr. Horace Wells and noted that Simpson's name was "never to be forgotten, so long as the primal curse, from which, through God's great grace, he took the sting, shall lie upon suffering woman." Among the numerous tributes, the Army surgeon, Dr. George A. Otis, described chloroform's use on the battlefield. His following statement illustrates the great medical value of Simpson's discovery:[58]

> But whether more dangerous or not, ether is not suited for use on the battle-field, because it is impossible for the attendants to carry an adequate quantity of ether upon the actual field, whereas the surgeon may take on his person, in a flask, a sufficient quantity of chloroform to produce anaesthesia in all the cases he is likely to be called upon to attend. You well know the history of the use of chloroform in the Crimean and Italian campaigns, where it was employed without a single disaster; and I am informed by Langenbeck and Stromeyer that a similar result attended the seven weeks' Austro-Prussian war. In

our own unhappy struggle chloroform was administered in more than one hundred and twenty thousand cases, and I am unable to learn of more than eight cases in which a fatal result can be fairly traceable to its use.

Following Horatio's return to Boston, the May 17 meeting of the Gynaecological Society was another memorial to Sir James Young Simpson.[59] Dr. John L. Sullivan began the tributes and included high praise of Simpson's discovery of the anesthetic properties of chloroform, particularly noting the pain and anguish prevented or relieved on the world's battlefields. Horatio followed Sullivan. He first described the memorial for Simpson that followed the American Medical Association meeting and then enlarged his tribute with the following:[60]

"Philanthropy, education, and all other agencies for good move still by force, after all." When you and I, Mr. President, penned these words but a short month since, in the Society's Journal, we little imagined that we should so soon be gauging with them the completed character of this loved friend. It was just, however, the personal force of Simpson which rounded and made effective the learning, so thorough and complete; the persuasive and convincing philosophy which so perfectly carried to the minds of others those great ideas which have revolutionized, not merely gynaecology, but general medicine and surgery; and the prophetic and patient perseverance through which those ideas were enabled to develop themselves into practical, acknowledged perfection. Manly in his presence, he was such in his standard of thought and in his every action. Seldom stirred to anger, and never unless with cause, he detested all meanness, hypocrisy, and time-serving. Gentle in heart as a woman, no lion surpassed him in courage when occasion, of whatever nature, needed his defence or support.

There are those, faint hearts, or self-convicted of wrong, who, pointing to his conflicts with Robert Lee, of London, Collins, of Dublin, Meigs, of Philadelphia, and of late with Jacob Bigelow, have called Dr. Simpson a seeker of controversy. Skilled, however, though he was in its every weapon, nothing was more distasteful to him. Long years ago, he subjected the self-sufficiency that is natural to every young worker for the truth and the right, to that dependence upon a Higher Power which can alone give sufficiency unto death,—a sufficiency which, with every trial that it was given him to bear, repeated and heavy as they were, was but increased. Thus armed with the sword of the Lord, he always left the field as its victor. He was a man longing for peace, and yet pre-eminently a fighting man. We hold with Mr. Hughes [author of] *Tom Brown's School Days* that the world would be far happier were there more such. "After all, what would life be without fighting, I should like to know. From the cradle to the grave, fighting, rightly understood, is the business, the real, highest, honestest business of every son of man. Every man who is worth his salt has his enemies who must be beaten, be they evil thoughts and habits in himself, or spiritual wickedness in high places, or Russians, or border-ruffians, or Bill, Tom, or Harry, who will not let him live his life in quiet till he has thrashed them."*[61] Having fought the good fight, he now has found the peace that passeth understanding.

Society President Winslow Lewis afterwards praised Simpson and offered Resolutions about the "irreparable loss" of the Gynaecological Society of Boston and "scientific bodies throughout the world" due to Simpson's death and offering sympathy to Simpson's family. Horatio's father "most cordially, most heartily" seconded the resolutions, praising Simpson as a peerless advancer of medical science in the process. The resolutions were adopted and Rev. Dr. James B. Dunn of Boston was invited "to deliver a public eulogy in honor of the deceased." Rev. Dr. Dunn accepted the invitation and delivered his eulogy on June 19, 1870 at the Beach Street Presbyterian Church of Boston. As we will learn, Dr. Alexander D. Sinclair, a Scotchman like Dr. Dunn, and a former assistant to Dr. Simpson like Horatio, tried to dissuade Dr. Dunn from delivering this eulogy. Horatio was to learn of Sinclair's unsuccessful attempt and it led to a rift between the two physicians who had once been friends.

The "Editorial Notes" for June 1870 were the source for much of the information about the Washington and Hotel Pelham memorials to Simpson described above. Horatio's began these "Notes" with the following:[62]

From his death-bed over the seas, there came to us last month, just in season to bind with this Journal as it went from the press, the Reply of Sir James Y. Simpson to the Second Letter of Dr. Jacob Bigelow, concerning the history of Practical Anaesthesia; his "last offering to the Gynaecological Society of Boston, to use as they may see fit." Looking into the grave that was open at his feet, for he felt that his sickness was to be mortal, he wrote to us these solemn words: "There never was a more unjust or unjustifiable attack than Dr. Bigelow's. I know from the inmost depths of my own conscience that I never said or wrote a single word to detract from the mightiness of the discovery of anaesthesia by sulphuric ether at Boston in 1846. But surely the discovery of another anaesthetic by me, a year afterwards, more powerful, practical, and useful than sulphuric ether, was in itself a fact of no small moment." The closing sentence of that magnificent plea for justice, completed with the closing life, in which he vindicated the pre-eminent claim of Dr. Horace Wells, will not soon be forgotten. He was speaking of his many friends in this country, "whose friendship I regard so very highly that I shall not regret this attempt—my last perhaps—at professional writing as altogether useless on my part, if it tend to fix my name and memory duly in their love and esteem." To the private note to ourselves he added: "My assistant, Dr. Coghill, has just told me that a patient of mine, who has been here from America for some months, has received a copy of Dr. Bigelow's letter from America by the last post. I suppose that shows how active some Bostonian physicians are against me in this matter. Surely in common courtesy Dr. Bigelow ought to have sent me a proper and authenticated copy. Probably the strife has been fanned—it is suggested to me—by one or two medical men in this city, for there are one or two in our city who have quarrelled bitterly with me, though I have never quarrelled with them. They are old pupils, who ought to have felt deep gratitude for what I had done for them; but I have found, what many others have found, that what ought to be deep gratitude, sometimes, and without any apparent cause whatever, becomes deep malignity. I forgive them most willingly all they have done. God has made my life sufficiently successful, to a degree beyond my deserts, and I have ever been happy in doing the work with he has allotted to me. May He ever prosper you in your work, and hold you under the guidance of His eye."

Horatio thus made public the last "private note" of his mentor which blessed Boston's "most-hated" physician and castigated Boston's most-"venerable" physician. No doubt the Bigelows began making plans to purchase and destroy the plates of the *Journal of the Gynaecological Society of Boston*, should they ever be for sale.

LEFT: Horatio's father's friend, John James Audubon, whose 1833 voyage to Labrador was mimicked by Horatio in 1849. *Photo courtesy of the National Portrait Gallery, Smithsonian Institution.* RIGHT: Captain Nathaniel Atwood who hosted Horatio, his brother Frank, and Dr. Jeffries Wyman on Atwood's sloop, *J. Sawyer,* for the Labrador trip. *Original photo with Storer Family Papers.*

Figure from Horatio's report on the fishes of Labrador. The lower fish was a new species which Horatio dedicated to his father. *Journal of the Boston Society of Natural History,* 6 (October 1850): 247–270.

The Natural History Society Rooms at Harvard. *Photo courtesy of the Harvard University Archives.* Horatio was a member of the Society for three years and served as the Society's President when he was a senior. He may have been the model for the cartoon by his classmate and later medical associate, Nathan Hayward. *Figure courtesy of the Massachusetts Historical Society, H.J. Warner Collection.*

Sparrow Stalking by a member of that sporting fraternity The Natural History Society.

29

FROM LEFT-TO-RIGHT AND TOP-TO-BOTTOM: David Humphreys Storer. *Photo from Storer Family Papers*. Jeffries Wyman, Louis Rodolphe Agassiz, and Asa Gray. These natural scientists were key to the scientific development of the young Horatio Storer. *The source of the Wyman and Agassiz photos is the History of Medicine Division of the National Library of Medicine. Gray photo courtesy of the Harvard University Archives.*

Horatio's first wife, Emily Elvira Gilmore Storer, and his second, her sister, Augusta Caroline Gilmore Storer. BOTTOM: Emily Elvira with Jessie Simpson Storer. *Photos among Storer Family Papers.*

Strong supporters of Horatio. TOP-LEFT: his Edinburgh mentor, Sir James Young Simpson. TOP-RIGHT: Henry Orlando Marcy. BOTTOM-LEFT: Jonathan Mason Warren. BOTTOM-RIGHT: Henry Ingersoll Bowditch. *Source: History of Medicine Division of the National Library of Medicine.*

FROM LEFT-TO-RIGHT AND TOP-TO-BOTTOM: Charles Edward Buckingham, Calvin Ellis, Jacob Bigelow, and Henry J. Bigelow. All were thorns in Horatio's side, Buckingham earliest and the Bigelows deepest. *Source: History of Medicine Division of the National Library of Medicine.*

The early American gynecologists. FROM LEFT-TO-RIGHT AND TOP-TO-BOTTOM: Marion Sims, Horatio Robinson Storer, T. Gaillard Thomas, and Thomas Addis Emmet. *Storer photo in Storer Family Papers. Source of the others is the History of Medicine Division of the National Library of Medicine.*

TOP LEFT: Harvard President, Charles W. Eliot, who made "grave" changes in the Harvard Medical School, perhaps at Horatio's direction. TOP RIGHT: Horatio's brother and Eliot's brother-in-law, Francis Humphreys Storer, Professor of Agricultural Chemistry at the Harvard Bussey Institute. *Both photos courtesy of the Harvard University Archives.* BOTTOM LEFT: Dr. Anita Tyng who was Horatio's assistant for several years. *Photo in Storer Family Papers.* BOTTOM RIGHT: Dr. Marie Elizabeth Zakrzeswka, who hired Horatio as Surgeon at her New England Hospital for Women. *Photo courtesy of the Sophia Smith Collection, Smith College.*

Hermann Jackson Warner at the Latin School, as a young Boston lawyer, and in later years in Europe. Mrs. Caroline Dall, prominent Bostonian who supported Horatio on abortion, but claimed gynecologists should be women. *Photos courtesy of the Massachusetts Historical Society.*

IS IT I?

A BOOK FOR EVERY MAN.

A COMPANION TO

WHY NOT?

A BOOK FOR EVERY WOMAN.

BY

PROF. HORATIO ROBINSON STORER, M.D.,

OF BOSTON,

Vice-President of the American Medical Association.

Homo sum, humani nihil a me alienum puto. TERENCE.

BOSTON:

LEE AND SHEPARD.

1868.

WHY NOT?

A BOOK FOR EVERY WOMAN.

THE PRIZE ESSAY

TO WHICH THE AMERICAN MEDICAL ASSOCIATION
AWARDED THE GOLD MEDAL
FOR MDCCCLXV.

BY

HORATIO ROBINSON STORER, M.D.,

OF BOSTON,

Surgeon to the Providence Hospital for Women; Professor of Obstetrics and the Diseases of Women
in Berkshire Medical College; Fellow of the American Academy
of Arts and Sciences, etc.

ISSUED FOR GENERAL CIRCULATION,

BY ORDER OF THE AMERICAN MEDICAL ASSOCIATION.

*Casta placent superis. Casta cum mente venito,
Et manibus puris fontis adito aquam.*

BOSTON:

LEE AND SHEPARD.

1868.

Horatio's books on abortion written for popular audiences.

Vol. 5.   OCTOBER, 1871.   No. 4.

THE

JOURNAL

OF THE

Gynæcological Society

OF

BOSTON.

DEVOTED TO THE ADVANCEMENT OF THE KNOWLEDGE
OF THE DISEASES OF WOMEN.

EDITED BY

WINSLOW LEWIS, M. D.   HORATIO R. STORER, M. D.
GEORGE H. BIXBY, M. D.

PRINCIPAL AGENTS.

New York—AMERICAN NEWS COMPANY, NEW YORK NEWS COMPANY, WILLIAM
WOOD & CO., *Philadelphia*—J. B. LIPPINCOTT & CO., LINDSAY & BLAKISTON.
Boston—A. WILLIAMS & CO., NEW ENGLAND NEWS CO. *Cincinnati*—R.
CLARK & CO., R. W. CARROL & CO. *Chicago*—WESTERN NEWS CO., S.
C. GRIGGS & CO., W. B. KEENE & CO. *St. Louis*—ST. LOUIS BOOK
AND NEWS CO. *Baltimore*—H. TAYLOR & CO., KELLY, PIET & CO.
Louisville—CRUMP & MILLER. *Detroit*—W. E. TUNIS. *San
Francisco*—A. ROMAN & CO., H. H. BANCROFT & CO.
Toronto, Canada—W. C. CHEWITT & CO. *Montreal,
Canada*—DAWSON BROTHERS.

BOSTON:

JAMES CAMPBELL, 18 TREMONT STREET,
L. W. SCHMIDT, NEW YORK; AND LEIPZIG, GERMANY.

Rockwell & Churchill, Printers, Boston.

Cover of Horatio's *Journal of the Gynaecological Society of Boston*. It includes the
Society's seal with its Van Helmont quote.

Horatio and his four surviving children. FROM LEFT-TO-RIGHT: Malcolm, Horatio, John Humphreys, Agnes, and Francis Addison.

Malcolm, Horatio (with stiff left leg), John Humphreys, Jr., and great-granddaughter, Ethel. *Both photos among Storer Family Papers.*

CHAPTER 14

THE LYNN ABORTIONIST, MASSACHUSETTS MEDICAL SOCIETY BATTLES

The June 7, 1870 meeting of the Gynaecological Society of Boston included four visitors from out-of-state who no doubt were Horatio's physician students.[1] If they were the complete class, it was the smallest class of graduate physicians he had taught. Following discussion of several gynecological topics, Horatio reported the results of the Society's efforts at the recent American Medical Association meeting. We have already referred to these, except for his report of the results of the Society's memorial against the Massachusetts Medical Society's improper cabal with Harvard College and its harboring of "notorious and acknowledged charlatans." "Upon the filing of this complaint," Horatio wrote, "and in accordance with the custom of the Association, the credentials of delegates from the Massachusetts Medical Society ... were not received until the case had been adjudged." The "adjudgment" given the next morning consisted of the Committee on Ethics threatening a future bar to representation if the irregular practitioners in the Massachusetts Medical Society were not removed. As to the improper Society-Harvard connection, Horatio reported the Committee on Ethics indicated "the exposure that had been made ought to be sufficient to check the abuse."[2]

The Massachusetts Medical Society had held its annual meeting a few days earlier and Horatio also reported that, thanks to the actions of the Gynaecological Society, all irregular practitioners were expelled and the Councillors had been instructed "by an unmistakable vote, to cancel the iniquitous arrangements in favor of Harvard College." However, Horatio also indicated that he feared the Councillors would somehow try to evade change of these "iniquitous arrangements." Also at this Gynaecological Society of Boston meeting, a petition by Dr. J.B.S. Jackson to sever his Honorary Membership was read. Jackson undoubtedly was receiving heat from his Harvard Medical School colleagues, such as Henry J. Bigelow and Buckingham, for being associated with the Society of their enemy. Horatio was "directed to obtain from Dr. Jackson the reasons for his extraordinary request." The Proceedings of the meeting two weeks later on June 21, 1870 indicate that Horatio tried: "The Secretary read a letter from Dr. J.B.S. Jackson, declining to give reasons for wishing to resign his honorable connection with the Society. Upon motion, it was therefore decided that Dr. Jackson's resignation should not be accepted."[3]

Horatio invited two physicians with recent experience in criminal abortion prosecutions to the meeting on June 7, 1870, and an unusual and frank discussion of the role of regular physicians in providing criminal abortions resulted. Horatio had denied any such role in his 1859 articles, though strongly criticizing physicians for their apparent and their occasional real disregard for the life of the unborn. Discussion of the topic began with a letter from a Lynn physician, who wrote:[4]

> "I hope the Gynaecological Society will not fail to take immediate and decided action in regard to the 'Lynn Abortionist.' The prosecuting officers of the Commonwealth complain that public sentiment is against them in their efforts to procure the conviction of this class of criminals, and in a measure they are right, although their own timidity makes the matter seem worse than it is. The Society has it in its power to create, or control, public sentiment by bold action in a case like this. If it leads the van bravely in the good fight, scores will join its ranks who now stand aloof from sheer cowardice,—men whose consciences have long tormented them for their culpable inaction. Come out in the way that may seem best to you, but *come out by all means, and that at once.*"

Horatio then "reminded" members that "many years ago" he had called on the Massachusetts Medical Society "to cease its notorious harborage of habitual abortionists" and had been frustrated "by the allegation that to do so would be but to 'stir a dunghill'." "In consequence partly of this professional and most criminal apathy," he continued, "the public sentiment had become more and more blunted, until it was given as a reason by the public prosecuting officers that a jury could not be found in Boston to convict of this crime, even in the most flagrant and indisputable cases of maternal death." He then introduced the visiting Drs. Whittier and Weston. The former "had zealously labored during the past year to bring some of these professional as well as unlicensed wretches to their deserts." Dr. Weston was coroner in a nearby county and "had lately placed evidence of the strongest character in the hands of the State constabulary, but without avail." A long discussion followed of the public's acceptance of abortion, the unwillingness of district attorneys to prosecute abortionists, the apathy of some physicians about the problem, and the actual conduct of abortions by some regular physicians. The visiting Dr. Whittier saw district attorneys' unwillingness to prosecute because the law "was too stringent, abortion being made a State-prison offence for a term of years." This provoked a sharp response from both Dr. Henry A. Martin and Dr. John G. Blake who "considered this punishment none too severe, the crime being second to none."

Several instances of regular physicians who performed abortions were cited by various members. One who was arrested had the case dropped when he told prosecutors "that he had several years ago attended the woman for syphilis, and that therefore he did not do wrong in destroying her offspring." Dr. Martin, "as evidence of the appalling state of public opinion and the recklessness with which this crime is committed," described the small fee (five dollars) charged by the Lynn abortionist and "the peculiar nonchalance with which women apply for the procurement of abortion." Discussion followed of the need to purge the Massachusetts Medical Society of its abortionists. Dr. Martin expressed the opinion that the Councillors of that Society "would fail to give that endorsement which might be needed to render the action effective." Horatio disagreed: "To rid the Society of its pests did not require the alteration of any by-law, and the Councillors, therefore, in their corporate capacity had nothing to do with it." The discussion concluded with the adoption of the following Resolutions:[5]

> I. That the Gynaecological Society is ready to receive such evidence as may be sufficient to convict a Fellow of the Massachusetts Medical Society of criminal abortion, and to present the case and prosecute the same before the officers of that Society, with a view to his expulsion.
>
> II. That the Society address the Governor of the State, by memorial, setting forth the failure of his prosecuting officers to take cognizance of this crime, and requesting that he direct them to perform the duties of their office, or supply their place, if he can legally do so, by more competent men.

This discussion belies Horatio's repeated insistence in his earlier writing that regular physicians were almost never performing criminal abortions. One wonders whether Horatio in 1859 was naive; whether he had just been defending the name of the graduates of legitimate medical schools, despite the guilt of some; or whether regular physicians had commenced the practice since 1859. His statement "that many years ago he had urged upon the Massachusetts Medical Society to cease its notorious harborage of habitual abortionists," is his first published mention of this. He may have spoken this during his 1866 presentation on "physician abetment" before that group, but did not include it in his published report.

One implication of this effort of the Gynaecological Society of Boston to get rid of the regular physicians who performed criminal abortions, is that their crusade was not aimed primarily at the irregulars performing abortions, but at the practice itself. Another implication is that more than a decade of strong opposition from Horatio and the American Medical Association had not stifled criminal abortion in Massachusetts. It is possible that some influential Boston physicians were so opposed to Horatio for one or more reasons, that this led them to thwart his anti-abortion efforts by not working to eliminate the problem and even by being a direct part of it. It will be recalled that Buckingham, as "B.," wrote: "But allowing the committing of abortion to be murder, and the writer is not prepared to deny that, although he is less disposed to assert it than he was, before this subject was broached by the Committee."[6] We also will learn from a Gynaecological Society of Boston presentation in 1886 that abortion "is advocated by gentlemen of great professional influence in this city."

In the July "Editorial Notes," after still another tribute to Simpson, Horatio described the high honor he received while at Washington of being elected President of the Association of the Editors of the American Medical Journals, and he tied it to the success of the Gynaecological Society of Boston and its *Journal*:[7]

> We have reason indeed to be thankful; and yet in all our success we see only an appreciation of the Society and of its devoted missionary work. When the Association of the Editors of the American Medical Journals, in session at Washington on the evening of May 2d, appointed Dr. H. R. Storer, of Boston, as its President for the ensuing year, ... it was only a mark of respect from the brethren for the department of science to which he is devoted, for the dear old city he would so gladly see again assuming its place in the medical advance guard, and for the patience and perseverance that at the end of seventeen years of labor are but fresher than ever.

The apparent purchase and destruction by Henry J. Bigelow of the plates of the *Journal of the Gynaecological Society of Boston* sometime after it ended publication in 1872, adds credence to Horatio's next claim.[8]

> That journalists, professional as well as secular, mould the thoughts of their readers, is as true as that they reflect them. What indeed, can compare with the influence of the press? Before its batteries those who oppose the world's progress go down as so many broken reeds. Whether it be a single man or an organization of men,—a medical college, for instance, that has dared an act of wrong,—let but a certain little black cross be made in sober earnest against the name, and that individual or circle of individuals, makes amends or it is doomed. Their exposure reaches to thousands of miles away, and as blow follows blow, each harder and harder, friend after friend falls away from the evil-doers, the fountains of their support are dried, and if, as we have instanced, it is an illy cemented medical school, containing within itself the elements of its own ruin,—dry rot and burrowing vermin,—it totters to its fall.

Horatio then discussed the huge responsibility associated with this journalistic power to "make a man, or lower him." Hopefully, he was still contemplating this when he referred to "certain parties here in Boston" as:

> Traducers, slanderers,—we do not like to add, wilful falsifiers of history,—it remains to be seen whether they are also, in the face of

the threefold decision that has now been rendered in favor of Dr. Horace Wells as the discoverer of practical anaesthesia, to remain apologists for the unblushing, deliberate, and wicked theft committed when what belongs to Hartford, Ct., is claimed for the Massachusetts General Hospital and for the city of Boston.

After presenting a letter of Simpson's received after his death which bolstered the claim of Wells and called attention to the "strange and narrow-minded policy of the profession" of Boston that would cabal his student Dr. Sinclair were he to use chloroform, Horatio added more to the Simpson discussion:[9]

> There are those in this city who are now, their false glories stripped from them by that dead hand, going about our streets with poltroon courage and with flippant tongue, defaming Dr. Simpson's truthfulness, honesty of purpose, and mental equipoise. There has indeed been lying done, but not by him. He was the very soul of honor. There have indeed strange instances of forgetfulness gone upon the record, and of lack besides of self-control. Did these, however, occur in Edinburgh? Is it possible that the great Boston authorities, to whom we have bowed so servilely all these years, are but poor, weak mortals like the rest of us, after all?

It is somewhat ironic that Luther Parks was the editor of the *Boston Medical and Surgical Journal* when Simpson made his deathbed request that Horatio ask that *Journal's* editor to publish his "Reply to Dr. Bigelow's Second Letter." "At the request of Dr. Simpson, contained in one of those letters from his dying chamber," Horatio wrote, "we compelled ourselves, very reluctantly, to temporarily reopen communication with a person for whom, for some fifteen years, we have entertained only the most supreme indifference." Horatio then described Parks' initial refusal to publish Simpson's "Reply" ("It occupies about twenty pages, but contains little that is new; and nothing, as it seems to me, that invalidates the positions taken by Dr. Bigelow."), then his agreement to publish it. While criticizing Parks, Horatio added the following which was primarily aimed at Dr. Calvin Ellis:[10]

> It is an odd coincidence to have a *Luther* behaving in this way, and at the same time to have come into possession of proof, from more than one gentleman with whom he has spoken, that a certain *Calvin*, once in controversy with us, by forcing his unwilling colleagues into the quarrel, and by explaining his non-denial of our charge by the most craven of excuses, was guilty of the meanest of cowardly acts, the attempting to destroy an antagonist by secret blows. Meant to be mortal, they have but awakened us to a quicker life. We pardoned

the first offence, but for these there can be forgiveness only after
acknowledged repentance.

What were these recent offenses by Ellis involving secret "cowardly acts" aimed
"to destroy" Horatio? The "first-offence" referred to was the 1866 quarrel that
officially started when Ellis criticized Horatio's exploratory surgery, abdominal
sections, and his operation to correct the umbilical hernia. These recent Ellis
offenses sound more serious than claiming Horatio was the Spiritualist Storer or
denigrating Horatio when queried by physicians interested in his course or in
consultations with Horatio, but these appear the most likely candidates. Ellis
now was Dean of the Harvard Medical School and would no doubt be considered an authoritative source on Horatio's professional and teaching qualifications. Horatio's surprisingly small physician class may have indicated the
effectiveness of such an anti-Horatio campaign.

Horatio also discussed the Gynaecological Society's success in changing the
improper practices of the Massachusetts Medical Society. Horatio indicated
that, at its May Annual Meeting, the Massachusetts Medical Society had re-
pealed the section of the By-Laws which gave the unfair advantage to Harvard
graduates. It also "expelled from its fellowship 'all those who publicly profess
to practise in accordance with any exclusive dogma, whether calling themselves
homeopaths, hydropaths, eclectics, or what not, in violation of the Code of
Ethics of the American Medical Association.'"[11] These actions were by the
full membership of the Massachusetts Medical Society and Horatio indicated the
by-law change related to Harvard still required endorsement of the Councillors
at their next meeting in October. He indicated that the expulsion of irregular
physicians "does not require the concurrence of the Councillors, no alteration
of any by-law being involved." "The Society understands that, in correcting the
two abuses above indicated," continued Horatio, "it has but commenced the
work of reform." As we will see, Horatio was a bit premature in believing that
both abuses had been corrected.

The July 5, 1870 meeting of the Society included the next installment in
J.B.S. Jackson's efforts to end his Honorary Membership. Jackson indicated his
reasons "were purely of a personal character, and directed against the Secretary." Horatio moved that Jackson be allowed to retire. This was turned down
"and a Committee, consisting of Drs. Martin, Lewis, and Weston, was appointed with instructions to convey to Dr. Jackson such rebuke as the reflections
upon the Society contained in his communication might appear to deserve."[12]

The August "Editorial Notes" began with "an obituary notice of a living
man."[13] Horatio's enemy of a decade and a half, Dr. Luther J. Parks, Jr., resigned from the editorship of the *Boston Medical and Surgical Journal* at the end
of June. Horatio first warned that one might expect sarcasm when the attitude
of the "deceased" toward the obituary writer is negative, and the following
shows it—in spades:

He has vanished. The pages of his past, sparkling, as the profession had a right to expect that they should, with the coruscations characteristic of an elegant leisure; using wealth, education, inherent intellectual brightness, and a manly, generous disposition, only for the benefit of others, and never for narrow, sinister, or selfish ends,—will ever remind us of the dear departed. They present, what the many readers of "Alice's Adventures in Wonderland"*[14] will remember as the most tantalizing of conceivable deprivations, the feline "grin without the cat."

To us, the loss is an inconsolable one. We had hoped, for years yet, of the reasonable and true enjoyment that the contemplation of him, his intellectual feats, and his generous acts, has hitherto afforded us. But it seems that this was not to be. Like a brave general upon the battle-field, at the time of the most imminent peril he has crept to the rear, and there, without confession of wound, he has given up the editorial ghost.

Luther Parks was to spend the last years of his life in Europe. Perhaps we know one reason why. Horatio afterwards discussed Park's replacement, Dr. Francis H. Brown, noting that "our friend shows a heroism worthy a better cause, when he becomes the calker of a sinking ship." Horatio praised Brown's initial editorials "acknowledging the power that specialism in medicine has now acquired," stating his vow of "independence of the clique and school," and disclaiming "all intention of acknowledging personal issues." Horatio indicated that the journal and its editor also had an obligation to admit to and atone for its past mistakes such as "the late attempt at whitewashing Prof. B[uckingham]. of Harvard College."[15] This referred to a *Journal* editorial of April 21, 1870 which, among other things, said: "we feel perfectly assured that no feasible measure for [Mrs. Barnard's] safety and comfort was omitted or for an instant remitted."[16] Horatio then discussed the letter from Dr. J.B.S. Jackson:[17]

We have been a good deal amused by a letter formally sent to the Gynaecological Society by one of the oldest professors in the Medical School of this city; upon the reflections against the Society, ... Whether or not the seemingly official document was intended to express the feelings of the whole Faculty, we do not know, and it don't [sic] much matter. However this may be, the letter distinctly states that it was inspired by what occurred at the annual meeting of the Massachusetts Medical Society, when, as will be well recollected, that Society, partly at the instigation of the Gynaecological, took from the diploma of the Harvard School its undue advantage over those of every other college in this country, and expelled the horde of its graduates, who, under cover of that hitherto omnipotent document, "had chosen to walk in the paths of pseudo-science."

Having started on the Harvard Medical School, Horatio went all out describing various internal squabbles such as the Bigelow-Cheever dispute, and others involving Drs. Jackson, Oliver, Jeffries, Williams, Ellis, and Holmes. Particularly relevant to Horatio was the following:

> From that shining galaxy it was that a late Professor of Obstetrics and Medical Jurisprudence, indignant at the injustice done to his son for simply speaking the truth, would four years ago have severed himself. Persuaded against his wish to remain, lest his resignation, so it was pleaded, might injure the University, and blinded by evil wiles to the fact that his silence and his tarry were interpreted, as it was intended that they should be, in condemnation of that son's course, he for the time tied the hands that were lifted in self-defence; for a blow then struck would have seemed parricidal. Thence at last, but none too late, the father has emerged, and the son's hands, none the weaker for their enforced delay, are again free.

Charles Buckingham need not have felt neglected, since Horatio then devoted a page of the "Editorial Notes" to him and to Harvard's "delay" in dealing with the Barnard case. The following paragraph shows that Horatio had no doubt that malpractice existed:[18]

> If the school can afford this delay, so can the profession at large. The community, it is true, have already become disastrously influenced as against their medical advisers; for if this, it is generally very plausibly argued, were the representative obstetrician, what in the name of humanity must be the ordinary average of practitioners? And there is growing a very visible tendency to trust parturition to the unwatched powers of nature, rather than employ attendants who are charged in effect with meddlesome midwifery, covering unpardonably uncombated bleeding to death by the technical term of "shock," and calling post-partum hemorrhage, ordinary "placenta proevia."

Horatio then called on the new editor of the *Boston Medical and Surgical Journal* to publish "the explanation [of the Barnard case] that it has been understood has been read before the Boston Obstetrical Society." If he refused, Horatio offered the Society's journal for this purpose.

Horatio next took Dr. Alexander D. Sinclair to task for Sinclair's attempt to convince the Rev. James B. Dunn, another Scotchman, not to provide the "Eulogy upon Sir James Simpson" that the Gynaecological Society of Boston requested. Sinclair was reported to have indicated to the minister that to do so would disgrace himself, presumably because of the strong feeling against Simpson that had been generated in Boston by some of the popular press who had echoed Jacob Bigelow's views in the *Boston Medical and Surgical Journal*. Sinclair and Horatio had been allies in "the fray of 1867," "when certain gay deceivers here when down before the American Medical Association."[19] Horatio had frequently praised Sinclair and recommended him as the proper candidate for David Humphreys Storer's chair which went to Buckingham and had more recently recommended replacement of the "injured" Buckingham with Sinclair. Horatio must have been deeply hurt by what he saw as Sinclair's betrayal of Simpson.

In his writing of later years, Horatio was to claim much influence in producing the major reforms of the deficient Harvard Medical School that started in 1870. The August 1870 "Editorial Notes" mentioned "the case of Dr. Hawes, of the Dental School, who, treated with indignity, for no reason that we can conjecture, except his having read a paper before the Gynaecological Society, sends in his resignation as a subordinate, and is immediately promoted to the position of assistant professor, ..." It is probable that this good outcome of a bad situation for Dr. Hawes was influenced by Horatio, given the following:[20]

> While the matter was still in abeyance, we suggested to President Eliot, exercising the right of every alumnus, that it was his duty to put a stop to these disgraceful attempts at injustice, which of late years have brought such deserved discredit upon the school. It is possible that their free ventilation may accomplish the reform which the late Dr. W. J. Walker had so much at heart, and which, delayed, at last more surely comes.

In "exercising the right of every alumnus" Horatio was also exercising the access afforded by the fact that Eliot's sister was soon to marry Horatio's brother and also the access afforded by common summer vacations of Eliots and Storers at Mt. Desert in Maine.

Horatio had earned the epithet "arch-disturber of the public peace." However, the following "Editorial Notes" discussion of events at the May annual meeting of the Massachusetts Medical Society indicate that he was not alone in disturbing "the public peace":[21]

> "Whenever the polarities meet," says Emerson, "whenever the fresh moral sentiment, the instinct of freedom and duty, come in direct opposition to fossil conservatism, the spark will pass."
> It was thus the great May victory, to be but the precursor of others yet to come, was gained by the Massachusetts Medical Society over the parasites who have so long been living upon its life. Potent though unexpected aid was there from abroad, an earnest of the

support furnished by the American Medical Association to those who acknowledge and uphold its authority. The Society met, it was generally said beforehand, to give the "arch-disturber of the public peace" his "final" quietus. Let those who were not present imagine the confusion of those who, expecting to be executioners, were compelled to listen to such unaccustomed truths as the following. We quote from the remarks of Dr. Henry Darwin Didama, of Syracuse, delegate from the New York State Medical Society. These pithy, electric sentences were like the match to gunpowder. The rock was quickly riven.

"I should esteem it a high honor," thus [began] Dr. Diderman, as the "Boston Medical and Surgical Journal" vengefully spelled his name,* "to represent the New York State Medical Society anywhere; but to be a delegate to the Massachusetts Medical Society, sitting in Boston, is a rare felicity.

"For Boston is not only the hub, from which all good things radiate to us poor fellows in the distance, but it is the social and intellectual Mecca to which we must all make our pilgrimage, if we would live in style, and die in peace.

"So entirely does Boston occupy our thoughts and affections, in the rural districts, that when our mothers are in a certain delicate but coveted condition, they delight to speak of themselves as 'on the road to Boston.' And after we are fairly born, we are 'trot-trotted to Boston to buy a loaf of bread,' as a panacea for all our infantile pains and griefs.

"The Massachusetts Medical Society occupies a high position in the medical world. Your opinions influence, if they do not control, us.

"When you refuse to admit to your favored circle the graduates of foreign schools, unless they shall first pass an examination before your Board of Censors, we meekly accept the conditions, and lament that we are but ignorant outside barbarians.

"The dictum, attributed to one of your early and most distinguished physicians, that 'the best treatment for inflammatory rheumatism is six weeks,' has undoubtedly condemned many a poor wretch to a month of needless suffering.

"Your Society, it is well known, tabooed chloroform. Now, such is our confidence in your decisions, that although we, in the western wilds, venture to use chloroform occasionally, we always do so with great fear and trembling. I know that my friend S____ has a charitable word for the European anaesthetic; but then you are all aware that S____ is regarded here in Boston as little better than a heathen man and a publican.*[22]

"You have a wise and witty poet-physiologist belonging to your

Society [Holmes]. Some time ago he declared that medicines do as much harm as good. Our respect for his judgment and experience was such that we were restrained from casting the contents of all our drug shops into the sea, only by our sharing with him a tender regard for the welfare of the fishes.

"You may well be proud of your Society; for although we foreigners do sometimes complain of your exclusiveness and your rigid adherence to Boston notions, we are happy to admit that you preserve the medical faith in its purity; that you stand fast by the Code of Ethics; that you preserve your garments unspotted from contact with irregular practitioners; and that you labor, wisely and well, to elevate the standard of medical education."

It is somewhat remarkable that Dr. Didama was allowed to speak such pro-Storer, anti-ether, anti-Harvard, and anti-Massachusetts-Medical-Society remarks at the Massachusetts Medical Society. Horatio probably was both involved in Didama's nomination by his own New York State Medical Society (or invitation by the Massachusetts Medical Society) and for much of the content of Didama's speech. Horatio followed Didama's speech with: "We regret that such a volley of sarcasm as this had come to be required. It served, however, to show our mutual admirationists the contempt with which they are viewed by the leaders of opinion elsewhere." It also surely aided Horatio in obtaining the expulsion of the homeopaths and the initiation of the changes leading to removal of Harvard medical graduates' "free pass" into the Massachusetts Medical Society. The outrage of that Society's Councillors against Horatio, exemplified by J.B.S. Jackson's resignation letter and Ellis' wish that Storer "was hung" (described in the previous endnote), suggests that Horatio's presentations at that Massachusetts Medical Society meeting, like Dr. Didama's, were marvelous.

The August "Editorial Notes" concluded with discussion of the Gynaecological Society of Boston's recent vote to expel the abortionists from the Massachusetts Medical Society and invited "evidence of such a character as shall ensure conviction, with reference to any case that may have occurred within the limits of Massachusetts." Also the physicians in the neighborhood of the Lynn abortionist were congratulated for taking steps "to vindicate, so far as they are concerned, the good name of the profession." At the August 2, 1870 meeting of the Society, Horatio reported the result of the Society's memorial to the Massachusetts Governor complaining of the laxity of "Executive and Prosecuting officers with regard to the crime." Governor Claflin promised cooperation in preventing abortionists from going free.[23]

Horatio was absent two weeks later at the Fortieth Regular Meeting of the Society. Dr. J.B.S. Jackson's reply was read and it indicated the "highest respect for the members of the Society collectively, and acknowledging that his action had been wholly based upon personal feelings towards the Secretary." The Society voted to stand by its original decision to refuse his resignation of

Honorary Membership. To do otherwise would "tend to bring discredit upon the Society," and "would tend, moreover, to bring disgrace upon Prof. Jackson himself, and this the Society, in view of their mutual relations to each other, could not force itself to permit."[24]

In early September 1870, Horatio served as the American Medical Association's delegate to the Canadian Medical Association in Ottawa, and, at the September 20 meeting of the Gynaecological Society of Boston, Dr. W. Bayard of St. John, New Brunswick was an invited guest. The Canadian commented on the quality of M.D.s graduating from Harvard, noting that "as one of the Examiners for Registration in New Brunswick, [he] had been compelled to reject graduates of that school because of the grossest incompetency."[25]

In October, Dr. Didama was again featured in the "Editorial Notes."[26] Horatio provided excerpts from Didama's Presidential Address to the Medical Association of Central New York which was printed in the *Rochester Daily Democrat*, for June 22, 1870. Dr. Didama addressed "the necessity of specialties and the reluctance of the profession to tolerate them." He used as his vehicle "the history of gynaecology." He first described how Dr. James Henry Bennet, of London, had published a book on uterine disease in the mid 1840s and for it "was assailed, by his brothers in the profession, with abuse and misrepresentation, so unmeasured in violence and so malignant in spirit, that his success would have been assured, had he been an apostle of error instead of the messenger of truth." In time, the "prejudice and ignorance were vanquished; and all the intelligent scoffers became, by easy gradation, sullen listeners, penitent learners, and zealous converts." Didama mentioned how Sims, Emmet, and other New York gynecologists had "'pursued their beneficent calling without molestation.'" However,

"In Boston, when —————, who had been the student and companion of the eminent Sir James Y. Simpson, proposed to devote himself to the treatment of woman's diseases, he was gravely and significantly warned by the oracles of the Hub that the respectability of the Hub would never tolerate any such specialty. The young surgeon, happening to possess manliness as well as genius, audaciously determined to follow his own convictions of duty, and, if necessary, to fight, single-handed, the entire force of respectable conservatism.

"The war was opened with vigor, and prosecuted with unrelenting bitterness. The old London arguments were re-hashed, and spiced with much original gall.

"They began with the complacent assurance that Boston ladies would never, no, never, admit that they were subject to diseases incident elsewhere to the sex, and tapered down to the fearful whine and sneer that Boston ladies were no better than they should be, after all.

"The profession in the rural districts rallied to the support of their persecuted brother,—whose business increased to magnificent proportions,—while the conservatives only caught a Tartar convert, in the person of a Mrs. Dall, who overdid the business, and brought ridicule and confusion upon her friends, by declaring that the presence of a male physician, in the sick chamber of a lady patient, always excites her sexual propensities.

"'Hoist by their own petard,' the conservatives at once dropped the delicacy and morality dodge, and watched with more or less satisfaction, the growth of the Boston Gynaecological Society, which already numbers amongst its members many of the best surgeons in this country and Europe."

Didama's essay was followed by a long statement of editorial mission and editorial progress of the *Journal of the Gynaecological Society of Boston* which Horatio wrote while vacationing in what is now Acadia National Park on the Maine coast.[27]

Writing at Mount Desert that delightful bridal-place of mountain and sea, where every breath is a ten-fold renewal of life and a few days' vacation restores a vigor almost forgotten, we yield ourselves, not unwillingly, to its softening influences. Meeting here but kindly faces, how can one preserve even in his thoughts the semblance of any antagonism, or feel other than a brother's interest in all that pertains to the welfare of those distant medical circles at home? We take the opportunity for peaceful reflection upon issues no more personal than public, that have from time to time been forced upon us, and it is true that we have not hesitated to accept.

At heart originally very conservative, so far as concerns holding to the old landmarks, we have become, almost in spite of ourselves, one of the leaders in what is acknowledged to be already a very powerful Opposition; and we have it in our power, we find, to widen or close rifts in the profession which are rapidly ceasing to be local in their character. Old friends, new friends, have counselled us. We have listened to them or not, as occasion seemed to require. And now, as we rest from the turmoil of the moment in this sweet quiet, there come back to us varied words of admonition, encouragement, denunciation, written and spoken, by living and dead. To all of them we give patient heed.

Musing as we are doing in print, it is with no intention of putting ourselves upon any defence. There are those, however, who have desired, and they have the right, to know why, as editors of a journal which has secured an unexpected degree of success, we have assumed what has been termed, and approved as, a distinctive policy.*[28]

1. We have gently touched, first upon this side and then upon that, as with a shepherd's crook,—which directs, imperceptibly it may be, but usually surely enough, towards any desired end, provided that this be well defined, duly determined upon, in itself proper, and followed with persistence,—certain public institutions, well known to the profession throughout the country, and supposed by the inhabitants of this city to be models of their kind.

2. We have referred, disrespectfully some say, to individuals, towards several of whom, apart from their connection with the institutions referred to, we still entertain a personal regard.

3. We have initiated, or assisted in, the correction of abuses, in opinion and in practice, to which these institutions have been committed, or towards confirming others in which their influence, both public and private, has been uniformly exerted.

4. We have alluded, in sufficiently distinct terms, to the fact that our native city, charming place of residence though it be, etc., etc., does not constitute, as seems to have been supposed by some of its residents, the whole universe, hub, spokes, rim, and tire. And it is said, that,

5. While aiming at breaking the power of a certain little local "ring" of professional politicians, we have assisted in establishing a clique whose prospective influence, just as its aim and resources, is, in comparison with the power it is supplanting, simply boundless.

And what interest, it has been asked by those who have opposed us, can this Boston ferment, general though it has become, possibly have for the distant subscribers to the Society's Journal?

A single word will answer this question. Every point in "medical politics," as we have termed it, that interests one physician, interests all. Whether in Calcutta or in Edinburgh, Denver or East Eden, a right or a wrong lies at the foundation of every local question that can be agitated, and there exists beneath and beyond this, moreover, an identity in the questions themselves which renders every petty and every major solution of absorbing interest to the intelligent reader. Whether it be Evans of Paris and Marion Sims at blows about the conducting of ambulances, or Sayre of New York coming unscathed from the courts, or Hibberd of Indiana and Martin of Boston Highlands insisting upon the necessity of general, compulsory vaccination, there is but one fundamental inquiry, Wherein lies the right? To find this out, concerns all men. It concerns all, likewise, that the right shall finally prevail.

But why, we are asked, do you place yourselves, or, as we prefer to word it, permit yourselves to be placed, eternally in antagonism? "To what?" we merely reply. We are not in antagonism to real professional advance, of whatever sort or of whatever character. We believe that we shall be found working side by side with all good and true men, as regards the improvement of medical education, the weeding of ignorance, deceit, and crime from the professional field, the solution of vexed questions in theory and practice, and the recognition of individual merit. Is it in antagonism to the opponents of such progress that we are charged with being? If so, we frankly acknowledge the truth of the allegation; and may our hand forget its cunning ere we cease from the strife.

With reference to certain specific statements to which we have alluded, it is perfectly understood in Boston, and the fact is well enough appreciated by the host of physicians elsewhere who have had residence here of longer than a week's duration, that the whole affair, dating from its true outset, lies in a nutshell: a determination upon the part of a few—and at first they were indeed a very few—that gynecology should be acknowledged and treated with becoming respect, and upon the part of the many that it should not be. Every personal misunderstanding in which as editors, and we might also say as individuals, has had herein its point of departure.

"Is this possible?" we are asked. "Is it really true of the position, every day growing more and more serious, that you have assumed with regard to the Medical School of Harvard University?" We soberly ask ourselves the same question, down here in the wilds of Mt. Desert, and we reply, in all sincerity, that therein the whole trouble began. Ellis and Hodges and Minot, Holmes and Bigelow and Jackson and White (Buckingham we count out as having practically placed himself beyond the circle referred to),—all those, in a word, of the group who may have found themselves under the editorial ban, with trouble for themselves in the past or future, owe it to one or another of their own number, and not, we can truly say, to ourselves. They may affect not to remember, it might be inconvenient for them to do so, the real beginning of the breach.

"Just as though it were his mother," President Eliot once wrote to us, "when a man strikes his Alma Mater, the presumption is against him." To that extent, and only in default of valid reason to the contrary, we acknowledge that the presumption does lie. But there's a limit to parental discipline, and when a child, or an alumnus, is disciplined without due cause, the parent sometimes comes, with justice, to a greater grief.

"How could he deliberately forfeit," was asked of a friend the other day, by one of the teachers in The School, "his certainty of a professorship in Harvard University?" "Why," it was replied, "is it possible that you think that he has no higher ambition than a chair in a second-rate medical college?"

No man has reason to have, or has, a higher respect for the University than ourselves. No man has a more sincere belief in what the Medical School, in other hands than the present, may yet become. For our own part, having long since relinquished the dream of our younger life, when denied the privilege of teaching youthful students, we turned to the higher task of removing the rust from full-grown men. We have personally nothing to gain and nothing to lose by our course towards the college. Maturer judgment has taught us that, rather than work for the establishment of a second school, which a couple of years back would have been opened had it not been for the treachery of one in whom we had confided against our better reason,[29] it were better to examine into the foundations of the old concern. If our gentle taps reveal now and then a flaw or a bit of decay, so much the better in the end for the college and the true interests of the profession.

There's a power at last at work as certain and as resistless as death. Strange changes have occurred at Cambridge within a twelvemonth. Stranger than these are yet to come. We have repeatedly scourged in this Journal the Boston tendency to deprecate the great medical centre of this country, New York. In our May number we referred to the Faculty of the Long Island School, with the wish that certain of them were only here to do much needed missionary work. In our August number we alluded to the unfitness for his post, of the then incumbent of the Physiological chair at the Harvard School. Is it a mere coincidence that within a month from that time, at a special meeting of the Board of Overseers of the University, there was appointed to lecture in the department of Physiology, Dr. Lusk,—a gentleman competent, there is every reason to believe, to redeem it from the disrepute into which of late years it had justly fallen,—who is at once a resident of New York city and a professor in the Brooklyn School?

One more strip from the old rag known as the Boston Policy torn off and gone to the winds! Another soon.

And so, listening to the rote of the sea and drinking in these refreshing draughts from a purer atmosphere, we have answered our own and our friends' questionings, and we patiently bide our time.

Horatio next discussed Canadian medical policies and education. He indicated with "much pleasure" that the Canadian Association had included two six-month courses of study on the diseases of women, independent from obstetrics, as the minimum requirement for the M.D. However, Horatio indicated his displeasure with the fact that the Medical Council of Ontario was recognizing Homeopaths and Eclectics, and even including them on their Examining and Licensing Board. That Board had encountered Harvard Medical graduates and

Horatio described the result as follows:[30]

> It was a painful shock to us, as Harvard men, to hear it stated in open session that in Ontario the Cambridge degree had been pointedly refused recognition by the Examining Board, because of the gross incompetence of persons who had presented themselves fresh from graduation at that school. Well known as it is that scores of provincial students for many years have flocked to Boston to get their diplomas more easily than at home, and that the college by the means familiar to canvassers has particularly bid for this class of students, the fact we refer to becomes the more distasteful.

This Ontario Board action against Harvard M.D.s and the similar action of the New Brunswick Examiners for Registration, indicate that Horatio's frequent complaints in the "Editorial Notes" about the performances of Harvard's Medical Faculty were not just "personalities."

Horatio next referred to "a Star-chamber Committee" which was to report to the Councillors at their October meeting on "what shall be done with certain physicians of this city and State, who were instrumental in procuring the action by the American Medical Association, in May last, with reference to the Society mentioned, irregular practitioners, and the Medical College." Horatio then defended his and Sullivan's actions at the American Medical Association meeting with the following:[31]

> Inasmuch as the action in question was wholly based upon a formal memorial from the Gynaecological Society to the Association, duly presented and considered by that body, and was not obtained by any individual or individuals as such, we look with curiosity for the report of the committee. It is intimated that an attempt will be made to evade the question by laying the matter upon the table, or affecting to consider the Massachusetts Medical Society as the victim of a stupendous joke. This, however, we do not intend to permit. We demand that the report be made. When this has been done, it will be time for us to consider who are the parties to be pilloried.

Afterwards, Horatio discussed the expulsion of the Lynn abortionist from the Massachusetts Medical Society, and congratulated the Lynn physicians who "have done their duty tardily but well." The following portion of this discussion shows Horatio's belief that criminal abortion continued at a high rate, but also in the possibility of its reduction, if physicians did their duty:[32]

> His expulsion has purged our ranks of one dishonorable name. Are there any others? Let us look well to it! A ball has been set in motion which should not cease rolling; a movement has been

inaugurated which should not be arrested until it has overthrown the grim Moloch to whom our children are being yearly sacrificed in numbers that would seem incredible to one not familiar with the statistics of the abominable rite. Earnest, persistent labor is required, both inside and outside of the profession. In our keeping, fellow-physicians, lies the great issue. We can, in time, create a healthy public sentiment where it does not now exist. We can speak out boldly and let people know what we, who have had the best opportunities for investigating the subject, think of criminal abortion, both in its medical and legal aspects. In this way we can at least drive the harpy from the abodes of the virtuous and good, where it too often makes its foul nest, and banish it to regions inhabited by persons of no doubtful character.

At the October 4 meeting of the Society, Horatio exhibited a large vaginal polypus which he had removed since the last meeting from a patient who "had been bleeding for several years, was very much reduced, and had been told by her previous attendants that she could not possibly survive an operation." "One of these gentlemen," the Proceedings continued, "had indeed gone so far as to call upon her after it was decided that she should pass into Dr. Storer's hands, for the purpose of dissuading her from being 'led like a lamb to the slaughter.'" Horatio indicated that the patient had already returned to her home, perfectly well.[33] Horatio also showed malignant mammary tumors he had removed a few days earlier. "In both cases," the Proceedings continued, "the operation was by 'enucleation,' as is now done, when possible, by several leading operators in London, in preference to removing the whole breast ..." A discussion of "induction of menstruation" followed, and Drs. Lewis, Wheeler, and Warner all agreed that it was common for physicians to give abortifacients in the early months of pregnancy. Warner, in fact, indicated a majority did it, "shielding themselves under the *possibility* that impregnation might not have occurred." An octogenarian invitee, Dr. McNab, of Woodsville, New Hampshire, indicated that "there was more of this wickedness pursued in the country districts than they had any idea of, many women inducing the miscarriage themselves." Horatio indicated that he was glad that the Society members were concerned about criminal abortion, but that until more physicians shared this concern there could be no expectation "to awake the public conscience." "There were sins of omission," he continued, referring to silence of many physicians on the issue, "that were as reprehensible as the direct commission of crime."[34]

Four days later, a Special Meeting of the Society was called where Horatio made the members aware of the "censure" of Storer and Sullivan by the Councillors of the Massachusetts Medical Society because of the charges they had brought against the Massachusetts Medical Society at the meeting of the American Medical Association.[35] As reported in the *Boston Medical and Surgical Journal* of October 27, the Councillors voted unanimously that Horatio and Sullivan had not given proper notice to the Massachusetts Medical Society of their intentions to present their objections to the American Medical Association and that the apparently premeditated failure "to give such notice was to say the least, an act of discourtesy which deserves censure."[36] However, the *Boston Medical and Surgical Journal* report omitted the following sentence of the Massachusetts Medical Society Committee Report that followed *censure*: "And your Committee are of opinion that the circumstance that Drs. Storer and Sullivan, in interposing the objections aforesaid professed to act, or acted, as representatives of a society called the Boston Gynaecological Society, constitutes no justification of the course pursued by them."[37] The Proceedings indicate that Drs. Warner and Martin were unwilling "to stand quietly by and see such iniquitous proceedings as those of the Councillors tamely submitted to." Dr. Martin offered a set of resolutions, seconded by Warner, and passed unanimously, indicating that the Storer-Sullivan censure by the Massachusetts Medical Society was a gross violation of that Society's by-laws, and, since illegal, null and void. They also indicated that any "credit or demerit of the results thereof belongs to the Gynaecological Society," which "does hereby demand for itself a trial* being alone responsible for the Memorial presented to the American Medical Association."[38] The footnote following "trial" read: "Incidentally to the main question, and as bearing upon that of animus, all the facts in both the Ellis and the Buckingham cases will now have to be brought to light. In regard to the former of these gentlemen, it will be borne in mind that his friends have forced the issue upon us. Our pity might else have spared him."

At the October 18 meeting of the Society, Horatio exhibited two ovarian tumors he had recently removed. One weighed 108.5 pounds and had "extensive and very firm adhesions, not merely to the omentum and peritoneum, but to the liver, and these could only be separated by force." Despite excessive hemorrhage, the patient survived for two days before succumbing from exhaustion association with excessive vomiting. The growth of this huge tumor was blamed on her attending homeopath who had promised a "spontaneous cure." The other ovariotomy patient "recovered without any drawback" despite an appearance "anything but favorable." In this second case, Horatio for the first time purposely left a portion of the wound open to the atmosphere with good results.[39] These operations led to a discussion on ovariotomy and Horatio condemned as malpractice the fact that many physicians still insisted that the operation should never be performed. He himself had cured many such patients who had been condemned to death by such attendants ignorant of or blind to the high success rate in ovariotomy. "Gentlemen would remember that it was in this city that Mr. Spencer Wells received what he considered the grossest insult of his life," Horatio continued, "being told ... that to perform ovariotomy or not was a mere matter of taste; and this in the face of many repeated series of eight cases out of ten, saved by the operation, when, otherwise, all would have died."

In response, Dr. Martin indicated "that none but the veriest sycophants" would have "permitted so grave an affront to their distinguished guest."

The November "Editorial Notes" described the next triumph of the Gynaecological Society.[40] This was the Councillors' revocation of the By-Law giving Harvard Medical School graduates automatic fellowship in the Massachusetts Medical Society by simply presenting their diploma. The "Notes" summarized Horatio's initial attempt to make this change in May 1869, the decision of the Councillors that Fall that change was unnecessary, Horatio's repeated warnings that the issue would be brought before the American Medical Association, the "gentle reprimand" of the Massachusetts Medical Society by the American Medical Association Committee on Ethics, the 180-degree turn by Calvin Ellis shortly afterwards, and Henry J. Bigelow's motion to revoke the By-Law in October. Bigelow was reported to have said that the privilege given to Harvard was illegal, was "never used," and that three-fourths of the Faculty were ignorant of it or had forgotten it. Such forgetfulness was then described in the "Editorial Notes" to be highly prevalent in Boston and Harvard medical circles:[41]

> It was "forgetfulness" rather than malice that dealt the "foul blow" at Sir James Simpson from the hand of an ex-professor in The School. It was "forgetfulness" rather than ignorance that disgraced the physicians of New England in the matter of the little pamphlet that was issued from its Obstetric Chair "for the benefit of the medical profession."
>
> And, to ourselves personally the most amusing instance of all, it was "forgetfulness" of a certain insult once attempted to be given by the College Faculty to H. R. Storer,—the atonement for which the Fates are now so steadily bringing,—that wrote us so lately as July 13, 1870, the following note. It is from one of the most prominent professors now in The School: "I had entirely forgotten the action of the Medical Faculty in regard to yourself; of course I have no recollection of any part that I took in it."
>
> After such an exhibition as this, who can feel for poor Rip Van Winkle [Holmes]—whether asleep or awake again, and whatever the chair that he nominally fills—other than a sense of pitying sympathy, or do else than try to forget likewise, however hard it may be to forgive?

"Forgetfulness" continued in Horatio's discussion of the various inappropriate actions of the Harvard Medical School over the years. He indicated forgetfulness provided the "excuse" for false information in the school catalog, for delay of building the City Hospital until it was controlled by the Medical School, for the attempt to prevent Tufts College granting the M.D., for incorrect reports of high numbers of students enrolled at the Harvard Medical School, and certainly of most importance from the Gynaecological Society's standpoint: "It is 'forget-fulness' of the importance, nay, of the very existence, of gynaecology, and of the exhortation of the American Medical Association that a chair should be established for its instruction at every medical college, and of the fact that most of the other schools have already done so, that still prevents their good example from being followed in Boston."

Horatio then called for "the beneficent and efficient besom [broom]," i.e., the new Harvard President, Charles Eliot, to find his way to the "dust" and "spiders" of the Medical School:[42]

> These have been instances of petty trickery unworthy the name and the fame of a great University, as every one of its sons must truthfully claim old Harvard to be. Such, we shame to confess it, such has been the history of the Medical School. It is time that the beneficent and efficient besom that is so rapidly sweeping professorial spiders from their lurking-places, and whisking from ancient stones and mummies the dust that for years has been settling upon them, should find its way to the corner where so much work awaits it. We trust, sincerely, that the class about matriculating will prove the largest that has ever entered itself, and in this respect resemble that of the undergraduates at Cambridge the present year. We trust, besides, for the coming of the day when The School shall be made worthy of its high calling and its admirable opportunities, with the best men that can be found in the country to occupy its every chair, and with new lectureships added, if necessary, so as to cover every recognized department of medicine.
>
> It is surely an editor's duty to help, so far as he may be able, the speedy coming of that time.

Horatio described the beneficial changes that had taken place at the Harvard Medical School and recommended still others, even providing names of physicians who should be added in the various departments. Horatio's willingness to mention these men by name reflected a change in Boston physicians perceptions of the Gynaecological Society of Boston and its *Journal*. He wrote:[43]

> The Society, however, and its Journal, are beginning to be better understood by the profession. They have neither of them favors to ask; but they grant them, sometimes, and when they do so it is in sincerity and good faith. The younger men are commencing to perceive that pioneers, of muscle and good heart, are no disadvantage in clearing a path for those who would fain run but else must walk; and the older ones, upon their side, are learning that a dead or misshapen growth but invites the axe. There's a better time coming,

and as fast as certain nobodies are slipped from their places by the constant, unremitting, and merciless pressure, these younger men now clustering about them like bees upon a comb, will enter in and take possession.

Horatio concluded discussion of the Harvard Medical School by noting that the superb combination of Dr. James P. White and Dr. Fordyce Barker at the Bellevue Hospital Medical College in New York provided a superiority of "instruction in the diseases of women, over that of this city, where there is none, [that] is simply infinite, and students do well who act accordingly." However, this probably was calculated to inspire and hasten improvements in instruction in gynecology at the Harvard Medical School more than to penalize it by sending good students to New York.

Horatio also discussed the unanimous acceptance by the Councillors of the Massachusetts Medical Society of their Committee's Report that Storer and Sullivan "deserved censure" for their actions at the May American Medical Association meeting. He then listed in a footnote the names of the fifty-one Councillors present at the October 5, 1870 meeting, including David Humphreys Storer, but noted that his father was not present when the vote was taken. Horatio indicated that if David Humphreys had voted that Horatio and Sullivan "deserved censure" "we should indeed have felt annoyance." The footnote with the fifty-one names included the comment, "We need not repeat what we said last month as to who would prove 'to be pilloried.'"

The Massachusetts Medical Society Councillors also had unanimously approved a recommendation that "no Delegates from the Society be sent to the next Annual Meeting of the American Medical Association." Most also voted that "a committee be appointed to make a formal representation to the American Medical Association at its next Annual Meeting, with a view of procuring a reconsideration of its action in the premises." Those who voted against formation of this committee wanted "no notice be taken of the Association, except by omitting to send delegates in the future." Horatio scoffed at these actions of the Councillors:[44]

What do the distant members of the American Medical Association say to the above proposition? A party under sentence of non-representation till certain duties, distinctly stated, shall have been performed, coolly proclaims that it shall appoint no delegates till the Central and Controlling power makes an apology for its own self-assertion. We can predict the verdict at San Francisco. Massachusetts has tolerated no secession from the Union of States. By its own doctrine it is now to be judged.

In a final segment of the November "Editorial Notes," Horatio described another achievement of the Gynaecological Society. The "First Annual Report of the State Board of Health, of Massachusetts" addressed the problem of un-regulated slaughter-houses around Boston that Horatio had called attention to in September 1869. The Board of Health Report also made reference to irresponsible sale of poisons and Horatio made two recommendations on this issue. One was to add the full address of the seller on the label of dangerous drugs. The other was to use women in the compounding and dispensing of drugs. He reiterated in general terms that women were unfit for certain "duties," but saw their superiority over men for "the niceties of chemical manipulation," given "their care in matters of petty detail, and their greater sense of responsibility."

CHAPTER **15**

EMILY'S ILLNESS, MEDICAL SCHOOL CHANGES, A WYMAN VILLAIN

We know little about Horatio's family life, but given his wife's mental problems, it was certainly not routine. Years later, in 1883, Horatio described a case of mental illness exacerbated during menstruation. This case almost certainly was Emily Elvira. She was not identified directly, but Horatio's discussion of Charles Brown-Séquard, Henry Ingersoll Bowditch, and David Humphreys Storer as personal friends of the "patient," of her unsuccessful institutionalization, and of her early death without relief of her condition, all point to her.[1] A number of letters to Horatio's second son, John, were preserved and those dating to 1870 were almost all written by "Aunt Carrie," the sister of Horatio's wife. This was Augusta Caroline Gilmore who was a few years younger than Emily Elvira and apparently functioned much as the children's mother, both before and after Emily Elvira was institutionalized in late summer or early fall of 1870. Aunt Carrie's letters provide the only discussion of the departure of Emily Elvira from her family to Worcester, either to the state asylum or to some nearby residential facility.[2]

Horatio sent his long 1865 American Medical Association Report, "The Causation, Course, and Treatment of Reflex Insanity in Women," to the publishers on November 1, 1870.[3] Horatio indicated he was led to publish the paper, with "no material changes in it whatsoever," because of the recent publication of Professor Louis Mayer of Berlin on the relation of female sexual organs to mental disease, and the ongoing serial publication of Dr. Bixby's English translation of this work in the Society's *Journal*. He indicated in the Preface that he had hoped to "prepare a work upon this interesting subject of reflex insanity more worthy its intrinsic and practical importance," but had not found time for this. He dedicated the book "To the Members of the Gynaecological Society of Boston, thoughtful, working, fearless gentlemen, already a power in the land."

The Forty-fifth Regular Meeting of the Society occurred on November 1, 1870.[4] One of the invited guests was Dr. Henry Orlando Marcy of Cambridgeport whose defenses of Horatio had already gotten him into trouble with the Boston medical establishment. Marcy had recently returned from Europe where, by Horatio's arrangement, he had planned to work with Simpson.[5] Simpson's death led Marcy to work instead with Dr. Joseph Lister. Marcy was to become one of the foremost surgeons in America and President of the American Medical Association in 1891. He wrote articles on the history of medicine which praised both Horatio and Horatio's father.[6] Fortunately, Horatio would still be alive to read them. Much of the meeting was occupied with discussions of enlarged spleens and malaria with Dr. Marcy noting the high frequency of the enlarged spleen in the South among Civil War soldiers under his care. There also was discussion of "conjugal fraud," i.e., intercourse where ejaculation was delayed or suppressed. Dr. Martin reported that an Oneida Community physician indicated no ill effects had been noted over many years of this common practice. Horatio saw no validity in this and indicated a "mass of positive evidence which outweighed all such negations." "Every practical gynaecologist must have recognized the evil effects so constantly produced upon women," he continued, "by attempts to evade or improve upon the ways of the Creator during the generative act."[7]

Horatio announced at this meeting that the editor of the *Boston Medical and Surgical Journal*, Dr. Francis H. Brown, had refused to publish the Resolutions of the Gynaecological Society of Boston protesting the Councillors' "censure" of Horatio and Sullivan for their actions in behalf of the Gynaecological Society. Dr. Martin was appointed by President Lewis to be a committee of one "To take charge of all matters growing out of the mission of Drs. Storer and Sullivan in Washington on behalf of the Society."[8] The censure of Horatio and Dr. Sullivan also was discussed at the next Society meeting. The Councillors apparently were regretting their decision and claiming that their statement: "to give such notice was to say the least, an act of discourtesy which deserves censure," did not mean that they had actually inflicted censure. Dr. Martin disagreed and indicated he would continue in his efforts to expose their improper actions.[9]

The December "Editorial Notes" began with the following references to President Ulysses S. Grant's Proclamation for a Day of Public Thanksgiving and Praise and to its implications for the medical profession:[10]

> The duty of Public Thanksgiving to Almighty God, at the season set apart by government for such glad service, bears with the same force upon individual men and classes of them as upon a people collectively. It is not merely for "general prosperity, abundant harvests, exemption from pestilence, foreign war, and civil strife," that we of the medical profession should thank Him, but for all the glimpses that we are permitted of that beneficent Providence that rules alike the seasons, the tides, and the beating of our hearts, and with Whom life is but death, and death the renewal of a better life.

Horatio indicated a special reason for gynecologists to be thankful. This was the increased acceptance of "this hitherto most underrated and most abused of the departments of medical science." "There has been, there still is, resistance to the work;" he continued, "but for the harrow of opposition there should also be thanksgiving, for it but hastens the coming of the harvest." Horatio then described the Boston "harrow."

> The Journal has been laughed at here in Boston, and in every way derided; copies of it with sentences underlined are at this very

moment being passed from hand to hand among its professional enemies, and shown by them to their patients. Its policy has been
misstated and intentionally perverted from the reality. Ourselves have
been threatened so often with personal violence, that we have learned
to look for every new message of the kind with the same expectancy
as does the gunner, who tells by the faint crash from the distant wall
whether his shot is doing or not its work. As for the realization of
such baby-threats, men know that to lay a finger upon the hand that
wields this pen, would be to invite a lash of scorpions, whose every
sting would be worse than that of death. We have never written
anything really *bitter*, as yet, but we might, should occasion require.

Horatio then addressed the Massachusetts Medical Society Councillors'
decision not to send delegates to the next annual meeting of the American
Medical Association. He pointed out that both demands of the American Medical Association had been met and called on the District Societies in the state to
ignore the Councillors and appoint delegates. "To vote, as they did at their
meeting of October 5th," Horatio wrote, "that no delegates should be sent from
the State Society of Massachusetts to California next spring, was a fresh
usurpation of powers that belong, gentlemen of the Society at large, to yourselves." Horatio next attacked the *Boston Medical and Surgical Journal* and its
subservience "to the will of Napoleon the Little," undoubtedly "to the will of"
Dr. Henry J. Bigelow:[11]

It will be recalled that we have once or twice referred to the course
that used to characterize what was then the only medical journal in
New England. Under the management of a large proportion of its
frequently changing editors, it was nominally in the interest of the
profession, actually in that of a selfish little clique; it was nominally
fair, honest, and fearless; actually unjust, tricky, and subservient to
the will of Napoleon the Little, who aped the magnificent autocracy
of a surgeon now in his grave [John Collins Warren]; nominally an
arena of the largest freedom, but, in fact, a pile of lumber, behind
which cut-throats might skulk. We spoke frankly, for we had had
personal experience of all these facts, and it was with no other malice
than actuates a man, who, in part for the sake of his neighbors, cap-
tures and hands over to punishment a public enemy. We but referred
to what by common consent must be acknowledged to have existed.

Horatio returned to the failure of the *Boston Medical and Surgical Journal*
to include the phrase that indicated Storer and Sullivan were working "as representatives of the Boston Gynaecological Society" in its report of the Councillors' meeting. The *Journal* editor, Dr. Brown, indicated to Dr. Martin that he
had published "brief notes that had been furnished him by some nameless person

who had been present at that meeting." "We do not say that Dr. Brown himself was aware of all these facts," continued Horatio; "his letter indeed, to Dr. Martin conveys the impression of an outside hand,—but we do say, and deliberately, that the person who 'inspired' what he published is a coward; and the Journal, as of old, is again affording harborage to a 'cut-throat,' whoever he may be, or however high his professional standing." Horatio continued:[12]

> Not satisfied with what they had done, the parties in whose sly hands Dr. Brown was, we think, but the cat's-paw, determined to increase, if possible, the damage they had attempted to inflict upon the representatives of the Gynaecological Society at Washington. A reprint of the bogus report of the Councillors' Meeting was therefor struck off from the Journal types, upon a separate sheet, and, as though it were an official publication of the State Society, it has been sent by mail to its Fellows, and, for aught we know, scattered throughout the country. Every copy of this document was intended to be, and is, an additional stab at those it was sought to injure. Now, by whom was this done? It involved, of course, considerable expense for printing and postage, and it has been done anonymously,—that device of the lowest poltroon.

Horatio speculated about this culprit, but reported no conclusion, noting that the Committee of the Gynaecological Society of Boston would follow up the matter "as long as may be necessary." Horatio apologized for being "compelled to confront the profession, month after month, with these unpleasant, these disgusting disclosures." And he repeated his earlier view "that a science, in this instance Gynaecology, like a man, reaches success only by persistent struggle, and if there be intentional opposition, by beating it down."

Horatio then reported the latest on the refusal of the *Boston Medical and Surgical Journal* to publish the Resolutions of the Gynaecological Society of Boston related to the illegal "censure." The Editor's plea was that the Massachusetts Medical Society had taken final action on the matter and that the communication of the Gynaecological Society of Boston "To the Fellows of the Massachusetts Medical Society" was not directed to the proper route for an appeal which must be made to the Councillors. "The Councillors, it will have been perceived," Horatio wrote, "have claimed that so far from being but the representatives of the State Society, they are the Society itself; and their tool [Editor Brown], dazed by their very impudence, dares to endorse their pretence. Let them reap a common infamy."

Horatio also discussed "deserve censure" and the devious motives of the fifty Councillors who selected these words:[13]

> The Councillors are endeavoring, as every one expected they would, to avail themselves of what we last month stigmatized as "a cowardly

quibble with the word 'deserve'" "To say men 'deserve censure' is
no more formally censuring them," they assert far and wide, "than
to say that a person deserves to be hung is an execution." Common
usage, however, has decided that the expressions are not parallel.
We are informed that the trick, so far as the Councillors are
concerned, is a stale one, and that in years past discipline has more
than once been attempted to be inflicted by them in this cowardly
manner; the expression being intended to convey, conveying, and
being understood to convey, all that it implied. The only difference
is that till now no one has dared to face these wolves and drive them
back howling,—more than one of them stretched at his feet, life-
less,—like so many curs.

Horatio ended December's "Editorial Notes" by calling attention to the
following announcement printed in the *Boston Medical and Surgical Journal* in
late November: "in answer to numerous inquiries, we are requested to state that,
at present, no one can enter the Massachusetts Medical Society without
examination."[14] Horatio was puzzled by the "at present" and wondered whether
there might not be an effort to lobby the Massachusetts Legislature "to annul the
Act of 1859" which required that "no person shall hereafter become a member
of the Massachusetts Medical Society, except upon examination by the Censors
of said Society." "The fact that there is a Massachusetts Medical Society, at
large, may be forgotten," concluded Horatio; "but it will not be safe to forget
that there is an American Medical Association."
    The December 6, 1870 meeting of the Gynaecological Society included
description of a patient who had experienced serious hemorrhage for years and
was "very anaemic."[15] She had been treated by a number of different physicians, "not one of whom had suggested the propriety of an examination." An
examination finally occurred disclosing a uterine polypus the size of a cranberry.
This was removed by Horatio and the hemorrhage ended. This illustrated the
sorry state of "diagnostication" and treatment of women's diseases that still
existed in some Massachusetts quarters. Such frequent failures to provide
proper medical treatment to women make Horatio's monthly lashings of his and
gynecology's enemies appear much the philanthropic attempts to advance gynecology that Horatio no doubt viewed them.
    The final meeting of the year on December 20 was highlighted by a dis-
cussion of ether and chloroform anesthesia.[16] Deaths during ether anesthesia
in Boston were described and it was noted that one had even been reported in
the *Boston Medical and Surgical Journal*. However, the editor was criticized
by members of the Society for describing it as an "overdose," when in reality
it was a small dose, and for "putting it down in the table of contents as an
'Alleged death from the effects of sulphuric ether.'"[17] Dr. John G. Blake, an
Active Member with atypical connections to the Massachusetts General and City
Hospitals, stoutly defended ether and criticized chloroform. He indicated he

"had administered ether in some six or seven thousand cases during the last ten or twelve years without seeing any untoward effects." Dr. Martin could not resist mentioning that he doubted that anesthesia had been administered that often in Boston since its discovery.

Given Horatio's frequent references to God from the days of his youth, and given his frequent praise of the devout Christianity of his mentor Simpson, one would have hardly considered him "A free-thinking, restless, unbelieving man" at any time of his life. However, the following paragraph from an essay in the January 1871 "Editorial Notes" almost certainly is self-descriptive:[18]

There are few physicians who do not accept what is known as natural religion. It is the truths of Revelation upon which so many stumble and fall,—to their own constant, even though silent, regret. We speak of these things plainly,—foolishly so, it may be deemed by some. We, however, think otherwise. If at this sacred Christmas time we can, by any feeble word of ours, cause the Christ to be born in the heart of any weary or sorrowing professional brother,—if but to a single soul it is granted us to bring the glad tidings of great joy, then we shall indeed be repaid for any misinterpretation. To have said the word in season, how good is it! A free-thinking, restless, unbelieving man, his professional first plans thwarted, the best hopes of his life one after another disappointed, his every year a continual and fruitless battle with himself, the world, the flesh, and the devil,—there came to him in his mature manhood that great conviction which alone can give one rest or peace. Many long months since then have gone by. Long, do we say? They would have seemed long in that unquiet past. There are readers of ours who know, through experience, the rest and peace of which we have spoken. There are others to whom we pray that they [this?] may come.

But we shall at once be asked, here in Boston, have you yourselves forgiven those who have so despitefully used you? Would you yourselves wreak vengeance? We reply, that for forgiveness there must be repentance. We cherish no malice, excepting no man. It is abuses that we correct, not individuals. We have our work to do, not for ourselves nor the Society merely, but for Gynaecology. There are those now aiding us who were once our ill-wishers; without act of our own, save to forgive when they came penitent, they now strengthen our hands. We would that it were so with others. They would be cheerfully welcomed.

And so, to all, we wish A MERRY CHRISTMAS AND A HAPPY NEW YEAR! H.R.S.

The initials were unusual. Perhaps Horatio thought he might embarrass Lewis and Bixby with this sermon.

In the same "Editorial Notes," Horatio emphasized that the Active Members of the Gynaecological Society of Boston were not to be blamed for the "Editorial Notes" of the Society's Journal. The members apparently had been receiving heat from the Notes' victims. Horatio added the following note which, like his 1901 letter, designated him as the author of the editorials:[19]

> One, Two, Three,—the editors. But just as these do not shelter themselves behind their fellow-members,... so in the same manner does Number Two desire that for whatever unpleasant word may occasionally have to appear in these Notes, when the mirror is being held to Nature, neither Number One, an older man than himself,—nor Number Three, a younger,—shall be spoken of with unkind epithet. So far, on the other hand, as concerns the agreeable and acceptable things that may be written, ... let full credit be given to his colleagues, for they are gentle-men. Conjoined, we shall endeavor to make the Journal, as a scientific exposition of the specialty, a necessity to every practitioner. Into it we have aimed to infuse a little of that missionary spirit, the old martyr-leaven, men may call it, which kindles wherever it goes, in Florida or on the upper Saskatchewan, a responsive flame of interest in, and of work for, the advance of Gynaecology.

The sad state of medical education in the United States in this period has already been noted. The physician wishing to maximize his skill and knowledge was obligated to study abroad as Horatio and many of the other American-educated M.D.s did. The American Medical Association had been trying to improve the medical schools in America since its inception in 1846. They had recommended lengthening the term of study and called for increased demonstration of competence of graduates, additional scientific and laboratory training, and a university education prior to matriculation. However, competition between the numerous medical schools for student fees paid directly to the medical professors was a major obstacle to such reforms. The way to attract students was to make it easier and quicker to become an M.D. The Harvard Medical School made a major shift towards reform of its education just prior to the November 1870 start of classes. At about the same time, the large apartment house where Horatio lived was one of the first large buildings to be actually moved from one location to another. The following paragraphs compare these two events and give the Gynaecological Society of Boston and its *Journal* more than a little credit for the shift at Harvard:[20]

> In April, 1870, at the time of the Convention of Medical Teachers at Washington, Harvard College still held to its determination, put upon record in 1867, not to lend its influence towards elevating the

standard of medical education. ... In November, 1870, six months afterwards, the Harvard Medical School attempts to lead the van of the most ultra reformers! This complete somersault might seem very remarkable to those not conversant with the daily progress of events here in Boston. It has been not more so, however, than the removal from one place to another of certain heavy buildings would have appeared to the summer's absentees, who upon their return to the city have found the undertaking ... completed. In both instances there has been "constant unremitting pressure"* from without, no initiatory movement at all from within. In both, the jack-screws have seemed insignificant and wholly unfitted for such ponderous work; in both, the laborers too few for the apparently hopeless task. An occasional lifting of one's hand, however,—no haste or impatience, but simply faith in the laws that govern both stones and men,—and the work, in both instances, has been accomplished. It is just eighteen months today since, the trenches dug and the screws all in place, we threw off our jackets and took the levers in hand.[21] Already we sit at our ease and enjoy the surprise of passers-by at the result that they had considered impossible.

The forthcoming changes at the Harvard Medical School were announced in the Introductory Lecture delivered, as always, at the beginning of the term in early November. It was given by Dr. James Clarke White, who was Adjunct Professor of Chemistry, but whose major interest was dermatology. The following from White's Lecture, which Horatio reproduced in his Society's *Journal*, makes well the point that American medical schools were inadequate:[22]

"To those who may say that I am taking an unpatriotic view of the matter, that my estimate of medical education and our profession in America is too low, and unfounded in fact, I will only reply: When I find the young men of Europe flocking to our shores and crowding our native students from their seats and from the bedside; when the fees of our best lecturers are mostly paid in foreign coin, and when thousands of wealthy invalids from across the sea fill the waiting rooms of our physicians, then I will confess that I am wrong, and that of the two systems of education ours is the best. Until then I shall seek in the spirit and working of their schools the secret of their success, the cause of our failings."

White's Lecture angered Henry J. Bigelow and certainly separates James Clarke White from the Bigelow sycophants. In White's *Sketches from My Life* he wrote that his Introductory Lecture "aroused a violent and active hostility on the part of some members of the medical faculty and hospital staff." Prior to his Introductory Lecture, White had, "after long-continued agitation," started a skin-disease ward at the Massachusetts General Hospital. After the Lecture, Henry J. Bigelow and his supporters apparently declared war on this ward and it was closed "before it had time to grow."[23] It is easy in writing about Horatio Robinson Storer to view Dr. Henry J. Bigelow as something of a villain. It is even easier to do so when one finds that others who were committed to reforms that conflicted with Bigelow's goals were similarly flayed by Boston's most powerful surgeon and medical professor.

The first Society meeting of the new year took place on January 3, 1871.[24] Horatio was home ill and Dr. Bixby served as Secretary pro tem. After the annual election in which all officers were reelected, Dr. Lewis read the Annual Address for 1871 which was entitled, "The Gynaecological Society, and its Work During 1870," Lewis' Annual Addresses, it will be recalled, were composed by Horatio. Lewis (Storer) began by discussing changes in the Society since the first Annual Address: "Then the Society was an infant,—lusty, it is true,and full of promise, but still in its swaddling-clothes,and with prophecies upon it of death during the first dentition. To-day, it is a full-grown man, the peer of any in the land, proud in its strength, looked up to by the oppressed, aiding zealously in all good work, and feared and hated by evildoers."[25] The Address described the various topics discussed at meetings and the topics of papers published in the journal. It also described political actions such as the expression of "its abhorrence of that scourge of modern civilization, the induction of criminal abortion," its advising "systematic instruction in gynaecology at the medical colleges," and its defense of Sir James Young Simpson from the "unjustifiable attack" of Dr. Jacob Bigelow. Much praise was given the Gynaecological Society of Boston for its success in changing the Massachusetts Medical Society. "Lewis" also mentioned that the Gynaecological Society of Boston's support of the American Medical Association in these various Society efforts had been returned in the Association's appointment of two members as representatives to the Canadian Medical Association meeting and the bestowal on "your Secretary" of "the crowning honor of medicine in this country, the Presidency of the Association of American Medical Editors."[26]

"Lewis" then touched on the journal's editorials and his words give additional assurance that there were three editors in name only. "Our readers can judge," he spoke, "as to our associate's logic, his power of language, his masterly skill." A concluding paragraph refuted the claim that much of the editorial labor was "for the fostering of personal quarrels, and thus for the division of the profession into private partisans."[27]

> I need not say that I believe this charge to be as unjust as it is unkind. That one of your staff, "Number Two," as he terms himself, was forced into battle is true; but it was because of his zeal as a gynaecologist. He was expelled from the position that he held as teacher at the Medical School of this city,—a subordinate post, to be sure, but at the time the chief delight and honor of his life; but it was

simply because he had turned upon his assailants, fellow-instructors of his at that school, their own weapons. He was accused of gross physiological ignorance, because he asserted, as Brown-Séquard had already done, that a certain criminal, who had been cut down from the scaffold as dead, by the officers of the law, was not at the time of his dissection "as yet a cadaver," ... and he has been called a monomaniac upon the subject by those involved in this charge. I happen, however, to have seen an affidavit, gentlemen of the Society, not as yet published, though it yet may be, *written by an eye-witness of the so-called execution*, sworn to before the Secretary of the Board of Overseers of Harvard College, and under the city seal. It bears strongly on this very important topic, and it tends to exonerate our Secretary from the aspersion that he was actuated by any but a perfectly justifiable motive in his comments upon that proceeding.

Horatio's reiteration, via Lewis, of the Ellis-Magee episode, prompts even those of us generations later to view Horatio, along with Ellis, Hodges, Minot, and their senior Faculty supporters in the 1866 quarrel, as "a monomaniac" on that quarrel that Ellis started, but which Horatio refused to let be finished, and which included a "foul blow" which "zeal as a gynaecologist" hardly justified. Brown-Séquard almost certainly was *not* in the United States when Magee was executed. The reference to him may mean that Brown-Séquard wrote the October 1858 *Lancet* editorial that was critical of the autopsy of the body with a beating heart, since Brown-Séquard may have been associated at the time with that journal. The affidavit, "sworn to before the Secretary of the Board of Overseers of Harvard College, and under the city seal," has not been located.

Horatio was back for the Fiftieth Regular Meeting of the Society on January 17.[28] A California suit for malpractice against a California physician was discussed and, given information provided by disinterested parties knowledgeable of the case, it appeared almost certainly to have been trumped up by a professional enemy. The Society voted to send official approval of the medical treatment that was challenged as malpractice and approved a general policy for the Society of supporting "any competent gynaecologist who was unjustly accused of malpractice."[29]

The February 1871 "Editorial Notes" continued the discussion of the changes at Harvard announced in Dr. White's Introductory Address and gave more praise to White.[30] As evidence that change was in fact a reality, the previously unheard of appointments of non-Boston physicians to the Medical School and to the Massachusetts General Hospital were mentioned. However, it was also noted that there was "a most grievous division in their councils after all," not all of the Faculty of the Harvard Medical School backed White's proposals for change. As we will see, Dr. Henry J. Bigelow was the key dissenter.[31]

Horatio claimed in his later writing that the President of Harvard, Dr.

Charles Eliot, acknowledged Horatio's contributions to the changes of the Harvard Medical School.[32] Eliot's sister and Horatio's brother Frank became engaged in February 1871. Frank at the time was Professor of Agricultural Chemistry at the Bussey Institute of Harvard and he and Charles Eliot had collaborated earlier on important chemistry textbooks. The marriage of Catherine Atkins Eliot and Francis Humphreys Storer would occur in June 1871. No doubt numerous family gatherings related to Frank's engagement and wedding provided opportunities for Charles Eliot and Horatio to interact, as did their sharing of Mt. Desert as a vacation place. It is doubtful that either could resist talking about a favorite subject, Harvard University.

The source of information on the engagement was a letter written by Horatio to his son John Humphreys at boarding school.[33] The letter also related that "Dr. Sullivan is no longer my partner, so that Dr Warner & myself are again over-engrossed with work." Dr. Sullivan's departure from partnership with Horatio was not voluntary. Despite being in the thick of the Code of Ethics controversy between the American Medical Association and the Massachusetts Medical Society, Sullivan apparently was to behave most unethically in his own medical practice. Horatio wrote in 1901 to Malcolm that, unlike Marion Sims, he had avoided problems with his associates "except in the case of my assistant Dr. J.L. Sullivan, of Malden, whom I had to discharge for personating me and offering to do a laparotomy as H.R.S."[34] Sullivan disappeared from the meetings of the Gynaecological Society of Boston after December 20, 1870. No doubt Sullivan's "personation" was shortly after that, probably around January 3, 1871, when Horatio was too ill to attend the meeting of the Society and no doubt also absent from the office.

The February 7, 1871 Society meeting included reading of letters from two Boston physicians and one Somerville physician requesting Active Membership.[35] This supports the Annual-Address claim that the Society and Dr. Storer were well regarded locally. Numerous uterine problems and their treatment were discussed at the meeting and Dr. Warner made note that many of his patients "after menstruation speak as though they were recovering from a severe fit of sickness or a surgical operation." He also noted that his remarks applied to "apparently healthy women" as well. "In this light," Warner continued, "the physiological objection to women physicians, that had been so clearly stated to the Society at a previous meeting, by Dr. Storer, was a most valid one, and that it would be eventually and universally accepted by the community."[36] (One suspects that not only Henry J. Bigelow had sycophants!)

A number of letters from editors of medical journals to Horatio early in February indicate that he was actively in the process of adding such editors to the American Association of Medical Editors.[37] As we will see, Horatio was tremendously successful in expanding the organization, even into Canada!

At the next meeting of the Gynaecological Society of Boston on February 21, 1871, the diseased uterus of a woman who had had four intentional abortions was described along with the somewhat successful treatment of her case.[38]

Horatio then described another abortion case, "occurring in good society," where a wife was forced to have the abortion, being physically tied by him to her bed while it was performed by a Fellow of the Massachusetts Medical Society. Dr. Martin bravely indicated his disbelief. Horatio defended himself and Dr. Warner also came to Horatio's defense, noting "that the incidental way in which the fact had been mentioned to Dr. Storer was, to his mind, strong proof of its reality."[39]

Horatio began the March 1871 "Editorial Notes" with discussion of an ambitious Memorial to James Young Simpson. Priestley had requested Horatio's involvement in the erection of a memorial which would include a monument and statue in Edinburgh, a bust in Westminster Abbey, and a Hospital for Women in Edinburgh, with similar hospitals in London and Dublin, if funds permitted. Horatio made an impassioned plea for contributions from America and called on the gynecologists across the country to act as centers for collection. For those reluctant to contribute to a foreign project, he wrote:[40]

> And let none say that they cannot give to a memorial that is to be founded in a foreign land. As Jerusalem to the Christian,—we speak it with reverence,—so will Edinburgh be, for all time, to every gynaecologist, and to every general practitioner, whose wife or daughter or mother, perhaps, has, by her sufferings, brought nearer home to him the diseases of those whom he daily treats,—the Holy City,—and the offering now to be made, a willing tribute, not to Simpson's genius alone, but to the Mercy by which it was inspired;—a gift offered not to him, but to the One with whom he is now at rest.

Horatio also noted that Brown-Séquard was back "just in time to prevent the chair of Physiology from descending again to its former deadliest of levels." Horatio would later praise Oliver Wendell Holmes as almost unrivaled as a teacher of anatomy. This rough treatment in 1871 was related to Holmes' teaching of *physiology* and no doubt was tied to Holmes' claim that Magee was unquestionably dead when autopsied by Ellis, despite the regular heartbeat.[41]

Charles Buckingham, Professor of Obstetrics and Medical Jurisprudence, although not mentioned by name, was the subject of the following news:[42]

> It is rumored, of late pretty audibly, that a change is near at hand in another Chair. When students understand the state of things so well that a respectable handful cannot be got to attend the lectures of any given professor, especially if his be a course which was formerly the one that perhaps was most thronged of all, seasonable resignation sometimes prevents a more disagreeable necessity. It would of course be followed by the customary vote of thanks; heartfelt enough, for the relief, they would be in the present instance.

To recall the senior Storer, who did so much for the success of the School, and who possesses we trust strength for many years' lecturing yet, would, under all the circumstances that attended his resignation, be the most proper thing. ... Should it be found impossible to retrace the lost ground, by obtaining Dr. Storer, there is no physician here so well fitted as Dr. [John P.] Reynolds for the teaching both of Obstetrical Theory and Practice, ... By and by there will be constituted a Chair for the Diseases of Women. There are at last many gentlemen in Boston, who would be available candidates.

This time Dr. Alexander D. Sinclair was not mentioned as one of the "available candidates." In fact, Horatio criticized Sinclair for a paper on "peri-uterine inflammation" in the "Report of the Boston City Hospital." Horatio wrote that Sinclair appeared to advocate letting "patients linger along or die, rather than resort to surgical interference." In contrast, Horatio strongly praised John G. Blake who advocated aggressive measures to eliminate pus from "abscesses about the peritoneal organs." Sir James Y. Simpson was mentioned once by name and once by mane in the following concluding paragraph:[43]

Simpson used to hold, as Bowditch, that opening an abscess was preferable to permitting death or lingering disease. Dr. Blake, of the City Hospital, whose article upon Rheumatism is one of the best contained in the "Report," showed far better knowledge of the most approved modern practice, in his paper upon Pelvic Abscess, read to the Gynaecological Society a year since, than the gentleman who is said by his friends to have kicked a dead lion. We will not, however, credit, even from them, so unkind an assertion.

At the March 7, 1871 meeting of the Society, Horatio exhibited a multi-locular cyst he had removed three days earlier. There had been numerous attachments of the cyst which when broken produced profuse hemorrhage, but the operation was successful and the patient was doing well. This was another instance where the patient's physician had tried to talk her out of the surgery since "it would inevitably prove fatal." As in a previous successful operation, the upper portion of the incision was allowed to remain open.[44] Dr. Theophilus Mack of Ontario was an invited guest at this meeting. After describing a successful operation of his own and the importance of publishing the results of unsuccessful ones, he expressed the following view about allowing wounds to remain open:[45]

Dr. Mack considered that the absence of dread regarding extended exposure of the peritoneum to the external atmosphere, took from the operation one of its greatest anxieties. He considered that more credit was due to Dr. H. R. Storer, for the improved practice in this respect, than to all other authorities combined; many writers of the present day, as Byford, Thomas, and others, still teaching that the peritoneal cavity should be closed as quickly as possible. It was often of the greatest importance to keep it open, even for several hours, until hemorrhage from ruptured adhesions, etc., had entirely ceased.

Perhaps the most interesting event of the meeting was Dr. Levi Farr Warner's discussion of an incident that he considered a "gross violation of the Code of Ethics of the American Medical Association." The violator was Dr. Morrill Wyman, the older brother of Horatio's companion on the trip to Labrador. Dr. Warner in consultation with Horatio and Dr. Bowditch had recommended an operation for a perinephritic abscess. Friends of the patient's family requested that Dr. Wyman see the patient with Dr. Warner. Dr. Warner set up a time for this joint meeting, but Wyman "not only refused to 'consult with any physician who practised that specialty,'... but offered to see the patient alone, by himself, before the hour appointed by Dr. Warner; although distinctly told by the husband that that gentleman was to continue in charge of the case." After seeing the patient, Wyman advised against an operation, although Warner noted "she was rapidly sinking, having already passed into the condition of septicaemia." Dr. Warner called in a Dr. Hooker who agreed that surgery was needed and two weeks after the initially planned date for the operation, it was performed by Horatio. Although the surgery was nearly too late, the patient, "though very feeble, was now doing well."[46]

> Dr. Warner reported the case as one in which nearly all the chances of a patient's life had been sacrificed to a jealous professional selfishness, and as an instance of gross violation of the code of ethics of the American Medical Association. He would say, moreover, that Dr. Bowditch, upon writing to Dr. Wyman for an explanation of this strange conduct, had been told in reply, that Dr. W. did not wish to give Dr. Bowditch any unnecessary pain, but that Dr. Warner "had been or was associated in practice with Dr. H. R. Storer."

Dr. Warner then criticized Dr. Wyman, slightly for refusing to consult with him, and sharply for visiting the patient in the absence of her regular physician. "It was not to his credit, besides," the Proceedings continued, "when he spoke in so contemptuous a manner of gentlemen, who, like the members of this Society, acknowledge and endeavor to relieve the diseases of women." Other members expressed their shock and surprise at Wyman's behavior. Dr. Martin suggested a Massachusetts Medical Society Board of Trial, but there is no evidence that Wyman faced any Board of Trial, other than this one-sided one in Horatio's widely-read journal. Thirteen years later, Dr. Morrill Wyman wrote a letter to Francis Humphreys Storer[47] which indicates he was Francis' wife's attending physician and which asked Francis to give his best wishes to David

Humphreys Storer for the latter's return to health. For Horatio's brother to have Morrill as friend and physician, one suspects that either Morrill and Horatio made up sometime after 1871, or that Horatio and his brother Francis had a rift. As will be seen, there are indications that it may have been the latter.

A March 28, 1871 letter from Horatio to John Humphreys at boarding school included mention of the illness of Horatio's wife: "Mamma has had a very tedious time of it too. She is easier to day but she has suffered severely from the painful measures thought advisable for her by Dr Brown-Séquard. I only hope that she may receive permanent benefit, though this is far from certain."[48] One hopes that Emily Elvira was not faced with the incredibly painful "moxa" treatment that Brown-Séquard prescribed for Senator Sumner in which "the naked skin was burned with inflamed agaric ... or some other very combustible substance."[49]

The "Editorial Notes" for April 1871 dealt largely with the Massachusetts Medical Society Councillors whom Horatio charged with illegally countering the full Society's vote to expel irregulars, including printing a new official register "containing all the obnoxious names."[50] The Councillors also persisted in their order that no delegates attend the Annual Meeting and in their protest against the Association's actions at Washington in 1870 as "ill-considered and unwarranted." Horatio wondered how the protest would be delivered, given that no delegates were to attend, and offered to carry it for them if the Councillors employed "sufficient pomp and ceremony" in requesting this errand from the Gynaecological Society. Professor Oliver Wendell Holmes received more flack in these April "Editorial Notes" for spending time writing poetry instead of concentrating on medical research and teaching, but though reproduced by Horatio, Holmes' flack was self-inflicted. Holmes had just given the Commencement Address at the Bellevue Hospital Medical College in New York where he warned the students against "ambitious aspirations" outside of medicine and indicated they should not be found "in the spasm of an ode," but instead found providing medical aid to the suffering. "Had we first used them of their author," Horatio wrote of Holmes' words, "how unkind it would have seemed of us!"[51]

The April 4 meeting of the Gynaecological Society of Boston was the last attended by Horatio before his trip to California. A letter was read from Dr. John Scott of California, who had treated "'three cases of bad puerperal mania, all of whom had been in asylums, and had come out worse than ever.'" None had previously been examined for uterine disease which was found "well-marked" in all. Local treatment quickly cured one, greatly improved another, and allowed removal of a long-term strait jacket in the third whom he thought was "likely to get well." This information was provided in conjunction with Scott's praise and endorsement of Horatio's "new" book on insanity in women.[52]

The May 1871 "Editorial Notes" probably were written by Horatio before departing for California and dealt almost exclusively with the Massachusetts Medical Society's inappropriate restriction of its members from attending the San Francisco meeting of the American Medical Association.[53] Dr. Henry W. Williams came in for some vicious swipes for saying: "'Massachusetts should no more allow herself to be governed by the American Medical Association than by the Medical Society of the pettiest State, Rhode Island for instance.'" And also for saying: "'If she chooses to violate the Code of Ethics, and to tolerate irregular practitioners as Fellows of the State Medical Society, she will not allow herself to be disciplined therefor.'"

June's "Editorial Notes," like May's, were written before Horatio went West.[54] The theme was the resuscitation of criminals who had been judged "hanged till dead." Horatio had requested and obtained from a Missouri physician information pertaining to the hanging of a Missouri criminal named Skaggs, whom the physician, Dr. Jackson, had brought back to life, despite objections of the sheriff and the populace, some 2,500 of whom had witnessed the execution. The hanging had occurred at 1:00 P.M. and the prisoner died at 4:00 A.M. the next morning, and would have survived much longer except that Jackson and his colleague were forced by the public to end their efforts at resuscitation. Horatio's reasons for presenting the case were to illustrate "the length of time during which aid may reasonably be possible after apparent death from hemorrhage, ether, anaesthesia, and the like,—and its bearing on a certain now world-known medico-legal case that once occurred here in Boston." Horatio's primary reason no doubt was presented second. Horatio concluded:[55]

> In Skaggs' case, the sheriff failed to observe this formality [release of control after medical judgement of death], and retained his hold upon the prisoner. In that of Magee, upon the contrary, a living man was formally pronounced dead by a jury of physicians selected by the sheriff to decide this point, and, as a dead man, he was given up for an autopsy. The requirements of the law had all been complied with, and it legally released its hold upon the prisoner. Had McGee been resuscitated, as there is evidence that he might have been, he would have been, in law, whether as a man newly born or not, entitled to his life, and free to repent perhaps of his sins, and become a sober member of society.
>
> In law, whoso takes a life, unofficially, is responsible therefor. It is a physician's first and only duty, whether it be a still-born foetus, a submerged person, or one otherwise asphyxiated, that is under his hands, to save and not to destroy.

Horatio once accused Calvin Ellis of "attempting to destroy an antagonist by secret blows." The repeated "blows" of Horatio against Ellis, were hardly "secret," but one suspects that even Horatio regretted them in later years.

CHAPTER 16

CALIFORNIA, THIRD ANNUAL ADDRESS, EMILY'S DEATH

Horatio's California trip was made with at least his two oldest sons, Frank Addison and John Humphreys. Emily Elvira apparently did not accompany them, but Augusta Caroline was along.[1] Horatio's itinerary was a busy one, with the major event being his Presidential Address to the American Association of Medical Editors on the evening of May 1, 1871, the day before the American Medical Association meeting.[2] Prior to this, however, he gave an invited address, "Female Hygiene," to the California State Board of Health at Sacramento on April 28,[3] and he would give the same address to the physicians of San Francisco on May 25. He also would present a paper "The Propriety of Operating for Malignant Ovarian Disease" to the San Francisco Medical Society on July 25.[4]

The Sacramento/San Francisco "Female Hygiene" address began:[5]

> To a tired man, just preparing for a month's respite from constant and harassing care, by crowding that month's work in advance into the busy weeks preceding it, there came most unexpectedly Dr. Logan's kind request to add an Alp to the already too heavy burden. The very idea of preparing for delivery, under the auspices of the California State Board of Health, a lecture upon Female Hygiene in any way worthy the intrinsic importance of the subject, seemed like raising for the traveller a far more impassable barrier betwixt Boston and Sacramento than would once have been the dizzy heights, the floods, the wilderness, that intervene.

Horatio accepted the challenge, however, and, in his address, he first discounted the claims of some physicians that California women were more subject to pelvic disease, although he did note that California appeared to be as much plagued by criminal abortion as other sections of the country. Horatio then discussed various bases for women's medical problems, quoting several pages from his, "The Frequency and Causation of Uterine Disease in America," mentioning, among other things, abortion, contraception, and the sewing machine.

Horatio then called attention to the vast amount of female hygiene that remained unknown, particularly that related to sexuality. He "did not" discuss, but certainly raised questions related to the proper sites for education of girls and the related problem when girls left "the mother's watchful protection," for "the mill, the shop, or the service of strangers." He warned of "The terrible instincts that a chance word or look may awake into activity, never again to be put at rest,—which, for the world's good, cause yet its greatest dangers,—are there always and everywhere. Happy she who, till the day of her change of name, never becomes conscious of their existence." He then referred to the many problems that that marriage state could present:[6]

> From the dawning of that day, however,—nay, from the time it is first looked forward to,—a host of hygienic questions troop upon the stage. The amount and the character of intimacy that is advisable, or even safe, so far as health is concerned, between young people who are affianced; whether marriages, in a sanitary light, are best made early or later in life; the advantage of pregnancy within the first year or two of wedlock; the care that should be taken of the woman during gestation, parturition and the puerperal state; the fearful risks of miscarriage, to life and to subsequent health, even where complete recovery seems for the time to have taken place; the so-called social evil [induced abortion], and the specious arguments by which the devil would tempt his victims to make its toleration seem a positive safeguard to the virtuous portion of the community,—these are all matters of which you have clearly to do, but to which I shall only refer.

Horatio compared polygamy, which he had just studied in Utah on his trip West, with the common keeping of mistresses elsewhere and related them to female hygiene. "Each state has, in its way, its mental frets, its physical ills," he continued; "each in its way furnishes material for the profoundest study to the medical scientist." Horatio then cited a number of activities that were judged beneficial to women by some experts and disastrous by others. These included gymnastics, horseback riding, and sea-bathing. On the other hand, women's dress and their long continued enforced positions at the piano, business desk, and counter were judged most often bad. Horatio was particularly concerned about certain *non*-sea-bathing and certain drugs: "The voluptuous warm bath may cause, indulged too frequently or incautiously, as perfect ruin to the health as slavery to opium or alcohol; and these, first taken for the relief of pain, and perhaps by the advice of a physician, may prove—they often do—a flight of steps descending to an early grave, or, far worse, to a prolonged death in life."

Horatio expressed his belief that to properly value Female Hygiene "men must first value, better than ever yet has been done, woman herself." He then indicated the why and how of this, sounding many of the same notes he had in his *Is It I?*:

> The state and its every citizen must value her as one entitled to the

tenderest care and sympathy, without whom the world would be a wretched place, but who bears its heaviest burdens; whose hours of pain are tenfold—nay, a thousandfold—those of man; and this, not to mention the agony of childbirth, of whose exquisite poignancy he knows absolutely nothing, and which, were it not wrong to do so, might justly be said to approach more closely than can any other experience of mortals, the physical portion of the Passion upon the Cross. Does she seek sympathy, it is her due; or confess to suffering, she is to be believed; or exhibit nervous disturbance, it is far more difficult to bear than mere pain would be; or at times seem capricious, unreasonable, or a severe and cruel despot? A fortunate woman she is, if her temper has never been tried, if her powers of mental endurance have never been overtaxed, if the angel within her has never been slighted or openly denied. What seems vice in woman, man alone is often to blame for. Where this is not the case, as often it is but disease.

He concluded:[7]

As I said to you at the outset, it's the most delicate things that are the most precious. The very evil chances that so preponderate in the case of the health of the gentler sex should caution you to guard its members from every harm, with a more anxious care, a closer watchfulness,—appreciating the fact that every wise or kind act that men can do for the safety of the health of women is done in reality, and in the sense of simplest self-interest, well understood, for themselves.

Three days later in San Francisco, Horatio delivered his Presidential Address, "The Mutual Relations of the Medical Profession, Its Press, and the Community," to the American Association of Medical Editors. Horatio first described the medical profession of the country and offered little to be pleased about. "Were every physician what he should be," he spoke, "a thoroughly honest, straightforward man, anxious only for his patients' welfare, laboring for the development of his science, and not alone for gain, liberalized by education, humanized in the highest sense by a constant entering into the sufferings he is compelled to meet, and, above and beyond all else, spiritualized by the recognition that his every success is but a vouchsafement of God's great mercy, and he but its humble instrument,—what a different art were medicine, what a different place the world!"[8] "That the ideal I have presented to you is constantly fallen far short of," he continued,[9]

is no argument against its appropriateness or its possibility. Allowances are to be made for the infirmities of man's nature. Even after there has occurred that newness of heart, so essential to truly holy living, through which a man turns from the world's allurements to a nobler walk and conversation, he will sometimes cast a lingering look behind, such is instinct and the power of former habits of life.

It must not be forgotten, however, that there is nearly as much danger of underrating actual goodness and purity, as of extolling imperfection. Eyes as of a microscope are upon us all, ever quick to detect the slightest flaw. Malfeasance in morality is an easier charge to make against a physician than malpractice in art. For every uttered breath of scandal, ten thousand suspicions exist unspoken,—for mortals are prone to judge each other from what they themselves might do in similar opportunity, and they catch exultingly the faintest whispers of the wind. What gynaecologist is there, for instance, who does not daily pass between walls of fire, liable as he constantly is to be misunderstood, misrepresented, by the distempered imaginations his sad duty it is to seek to heal?

The sad state of medical education in the country was cited as a major factor in physicians being so far from the ideal. "If the medical colleges are content to underbid each other, and year after year to pursue the suicidal warfare," Horatio spoke, "they should not grieve that their students, [once] become practitioners, so often are starvelings and so frequently do them discredit." He called on his fellow editors "to convince students, and the public which is to employ them, that the best education is none too good for those who are ever to stand betwixt life and death."

Horatio then brought up "the press," and described the high duties of his audience "as purveyors to the profession of the best fruits of the medical mind; the preservers from oblivion of its choicest discoveries; the directors, and the creators, in all essential matters, of public opinion; the tribunal, indeed, before which professional reputations are made or fall." He decried the low rate of journal use by the profession, noting that only a "small number subscribe for more than a single journal, and that a very, very great many take none at all." These negligent physicians were failing to take advantage of the "ever-swelling tide of discovery and improvement in practice" provided by medical journals. Cost was believed by Horatio to be a key factor in some of these physicians' failure to keep up with medical literature. He indicated that the physician who subscribed to and read journals "obtained his money back again, at compound interest."[10]

Turning to "the community," Horatio hoped that the editors could restore lost prestige to the physician whom many people view "as simply their servant, to be paid his wages, and not always when due; at their beck by day and by night; and to be discharged when the whim takes them, as summarily as their horses' groom." Horatio saw physicians themselves as much of the problem: "The moment a medical man descends to underbidding or decrying his neighbor, that moment he becomes, to the commonest intelligence, a mere market man, to be haggled with, browbeaten, or taken advantage of himself." Horatio described the criticality of union of the members of their Association for effective action and defense against enemies, and the role in this of charismatic leaders. One suspects he had himself in mind when he said:[11]

> In our union, as in all others, there lies the chief secret of strength. There may be instances, within our circle, of men of pre-eminent energy, and of such magnetic force or power or persuasion, that every frost of indifference and brazen wall of opposition melts down before them. Such, however, are few. Accept them if you choose, and they are otherwise worthy the trust, as leaders; but still do not neglect that closing in of the ranks, and that hand-touch together, without which you become an easy prey to every foe, and can never reach to any really great accomplishment for the general good.

Horatio then discussed the relationship of medical journal editors to the American Medical Association itself:

> Far more than the college professors, ... *we* constitute the power behind the throne, and the measures which we initiate will give its toe and pith to the action of the National Association, upon any topic to which we may earnestly devote ourselves. Let a measure be proposed by a member for personal or improper ends, and how quickly he is scathed through our pages. Let even so august a person as its presiding officer undertake to force upon the profession any Utopian views of his own, whether they regard the acknowledgment of female physicians, for instance, or any other pet heresy, and it were better he had never accepted the chair, whose attainment constitutes the most laudable ambition of every physician in the country. It requires a steady hand, a calm pulse, and a cool brain, so to fulfil the duties of the presidency of the American Medical Association as to give satisfaction to, and receive efficient support from, the little group of ability-gaugers, who comprise this Editorial Association.

Horatio identified a number of issues requiring editorial elaboration and scrutiny by his audience. Almost every editor had written him "that the standard of medical education in this country *must be raised*." He referred to the changes that President Charles Eliot was making which made "Massachusetts, long so laggard," now, "foremost in this matter." Other worthy topics for editorials were a National Medical School, a National Medical Journal, a National System of Quarantine, a Board of General Scrutineers to examine the credentials of Association delegates, and "founding of a National Board of Censors, with branches in every state, whose examination should stamp, as worthy or not, the

standing of every physician already holding a college diploma."
Horatio then outlined another editorial requirement:

> I have exhorted you to be kindly affectioned one to another, and
> towards all mankind. But at the same time I warn you, would you
> preserve your influence, that of this Association, and your own self-
> respect, never to palliate wrong, never to afford shelter to the evil-
> doer. To do so seems often the easiest course,—it indeed may be for
> the time,—while to act uprightly may involve temporary misconcep-
> tion, remonstrance, or blame.

Horatio then recited details of the Massachusetts Medical Society controversies
that were then providing so much "misconception, remonstrance," *and* "blame"
on his own editorial shoulders. Horatio indicated that the *Journal of the
Gynaecological Society of Boston's* editorial opposition to the Councillors of the
Massachusetts Medical Society had produced "an ocean of communications, in
commendation, of inquiry, and in fierce denunciation, from physicians in every
part of the country." "It has also been the means," he spoke, "I doubt not,
through your kind favor, of placing one of those editors, at the present moment,
in this honorable chair."[12]

Horatio then asked for editorial support of the Memorial to Sir James
Young Simpson; praised Dr. Joseph Toner's compilation of the names of the
50,000 physicians practicing in the country; and described a system for
exchanging their journals with the journals of other countries that he had set up
via the Smithsonian Institution. He concluded his address by describing how he
had brought twenty-six more medical journals and their editors into the fold of
their Association, including two from Canada, "making a total of thirty-eight"
"out of the forty-one that are so-called regular, at present existing in the
country." He said that one of the three absent did not join because the editor
could not attend meetings, another had not responded and was probably absent
or ill, and, as to the third:[13]

> But a single journal in the whole country—I say it with pride—has
> flatly refused to associate itself with its contemporaries; and this, as
> a Boston man I say it with shame, the "Medical and Surgical Journal"
> of my own city, the plea of its editor, Dr. Francis H. Brown, being
> that "he does not think it advisable, at present, at least, to bind
> himself by the rules which such an organization might see fit to
> impose upon him"!

Boston's failure again to support Horatio, this time its major medical journal,
probably because of implicit or explicit pressure from the opposing "clique,"
raises the interesting question of what Horatio might have accomplished had
Boston seen fit to support him, or, had he not become ill and been forced to

leave the arena, whether or *not* Boston had seen fit to support him.

The Annual Meeting of the American Medical Association began the following day. Horatio again made his pitch for the Simpson Memorial at the San Francisco meeting. As a result, the Association adopted a Resolution which "recommended to the members to take this opportunity, so far as they may be able, of discharging somewhat of this nation's obligation."[14] However, the most interesting thing from Horatio's standpoint was the following putdown of the Massachusetts Medical Society Councillors in the Report of the Committee on Ethics:[15]

> Concerning the protest of the Massachusetts Medical Society, the Committee offer the report here attached:—
> Among the papers referred to your Committee is one purporting to be a protest of the "Councillors of the Massachusetts Medical Society" against the action of this Association at its last annual session. Inasmuch as there is nothing in the paper, or accompanying it, showing that it had either been submitted to, or approved by, the Massachusetts Medical Society; and inasmuch as this Association has no knowledge of any organization called the "Councillors" of that Society, your Committee do not deem it necessary to recommend any action concerning such protest. We learn, from the records of the last annual meeting of the Massachusetts Medical Society, that the following resolution was adopted by that body:—
> "*Resolved*, That the Massachusetts Medical Society hereby expels from fellowship all those who publicly profess to practice in accordance with any exclusive dogma, whether calling themselves homeopaths, hydropaths, eclectics, or what not, in violation of the Code of Ethics of the American Medical Association."
> Which action we regard as sufficient evidence that said society is disposed to comply with the Code of Ethics, and is therefore fully entitled to representation in this Association.

Horatio was not a member of the Committee on Ethics, but as one of only four Massachusetts physicians attending the California meeting, one suspects that if Horatio did not actually write the above, he made much input to it.

Horatio's major involvement in the annual meeting was in opposition to an amendment to the Constitution that would have allowed women physicians to become members of the American Medical Association and to a related resolution that would have allowed consultation with "the graduates and teachers of Women's Medical Colleges." The *Boston Medical and Surgical Journal* on May 25 and June 2 printed portions of the debate on the women physician resolutions which they copied from San Francisco newspapers. The following excerpts from Horatio's long speech may not be totally accurate, given stenographer error, but they provide the best clues about Horatio's behavior in public meetings when defending a strongly held view.[16]

... But, Mr. President, there is another point underlying all this. We will grant that some exceptional women are as interested in our science as ourselves. That some of them have those peculiar qualities, that especial temperament, that gives them not merely a taste for anatomy and surgery, but courage to face the greatest dangers and anxiety in surgery; that there are some women who are able to go out in inclement weather and brave the storm; we may grant that women, some of them, may have had peculiar means, or favorable opportunities which allow them to get this same education that men have; we may grant that, and grant it freely that in some matters, intellectually, women are as completely mistresses of their subject as we are masters of ours; but beyond this there is a point that is fundamental to the whole matter, and out of very many physicians that have discussed the matter with me—I may say out of many of my patients who have discussed the matter—I have to see the first one that does not agree with me in it; and that is this inherent quality in their sex, that uncertain equilibrium, that varying from month to month, according to the time of the month, in each woman, that unfits her from taking these responsibilities of judgment which, as I said this morning, are to control the question often of life and death. Women may be and are undoubtedly the best nurses—they may carry out to the letter the direction of the physician; but every physician who is familiar with women, and every woman, almost without exception, who expresses an honest opinion in this matter, will say that women from month to month and week to week vary—up and down; that they are not the same one time that they are another; that their diagnosis varies, and comparing the average of women with the average of men to-day, they are inferior in the matter of judgment.

Now, I know there are many sides to a question. Dr. Thomas read to you a list of leading men in the profession who allow their names to be used as consulting physicians, or directors, or trustees of various educational establishments, and it is claimed that use of their names is a guaranty that the system is endorsed. We all of us know that very many men are compelled to allow their names to be used, in the same way that they endorse Seltzer water and surgical instruments; and I have no doubt, from the statement made upon both sides of the question by one prominent gentleman in this assembly, that it is possible that his heart may direct him one way and his judgment another. I said this morning that I would not imply that any man of standing in the profession would be governed in his profession by pecuniary considerations, but it is evident that gentlemen who are practising in a certain department, providing their organizations allow them to endorse female physicians, are thereby sure of an increase in their consultation fees.

Horatio's expressed views prompted a sharp reaction from Dr. Washington Atlee, of Pennsylvania, who had made the resolution that members be allowed to consult with women physicians. He denied that pecuniary considerations motivated his resolution and demanded an apology from Storer before the Association for the insinuation that they did. A gap in the stenographer's report is indicated following Atlee's speech, and it is not known how or even whether Horatio responded.

At this same 1871 meeting, Washington Atlee and D.A. O'Donnell provided a long Report on Criminal Abortion.[17] Like the 1859 report written by Horatio, it strongly opposed the practice. Their report quoted Dr. Allen of Massachusetts, who had frequently referred to Horatio's research. However, the Atlee-O'Donnell report avoided any mention of Horatio, of the preceding 1859 Association Report on Criminal Abortion, of its supporting literature published in the *North-American Medico-Chirurgical Review*, or of the Association's memorials to state legislatures and state medical societies that had caused and were causing major revisions in the abortion laws of many states. The antipathy of Atlee toward Horatio that had been demonstrated in their debate on women physicians, no doubt preceded the 1871 San Francisco meeting, probably survived it, and almost certainly explains the failure of Atlee to mention Horatio in the 1871 Report on Criminal Abortion which would be tantamount to failing to mention Einstein in a treatise on the Theory of Relativity.

Horatio wrote July's "Editorial Notes" in California after the meeting of the American Medical Association. They included the long Protest of the Councillors of the Massachusetts Medical Society and the brief brush-off by the Committee on Ethics which was provided above. Horatio commented: "The Sierra Nevada fairly groaned as it was being delivered of that Protest of the Councillors of the Massachusetts Medical Society against last year's action of the American Medical Association. See what a ridiculous little mouse it proved to be when finally laid upon the table at San Francisco."[18]

The August "Editorial Notes" were written "still from the shore of the Pacific," and written shortly after Horatio learned of the speech by Harvard President Eliot to the Massachusetts Medical Society announcing "the grave change which has taken place in the Medical School of the University" as Eliot himself referred to it.[19] The reforms included extension of the school year; study of anatomy, physiology, and chemistry prior to the more advanced medical subjects; increased laboratory work; and the requirement that the student now would have to "pass a satisfactory examination in every one of the main subjects of medical instruction." Horatio reproduced Eliot's speech in his

"Editorial Notes." Horatio also formally renounced the former editorial opposition of the Society's *Journal* to the College. "The ends for which we have striven, with such earnestness and persistency, have all been accomplished;" he wrote, "and it is with pleasure that we now cast down the sword." He then reiterated: "The changes that this Journal has so often suggested, have been accepted, President Eliot has stated 'by the unanimous consent of the College Faculty.' This being the case, we bury the past, and shall endeavor, as best we may, to strengthen the hands of those who, willingly or unwillingly, have at last taken a stand worthy of the name they bear."

Contrary to Eliot's avowal that the changes had been effected "by the unanimous consent," they had met with extreme resistance from Dr. Henry J. Bigelow, and Bigelow controlled many of his faculty colleagues who echoed his opposition to reform. Dr. Oliver Wendell Holmes was one of those who was influenced by Dr. Bigelow, but Holmes was to eventually vote against him. Following the faculty meeting where Holmes finally defected from Bigelow, President Eliot indicated that Holmes: "came up to me and said, 'Mr. President, you have undoubtedly seen what is the matter with me.' I could not say that I had. Screwing the ball of his thumb round on the top of the table, Dr. Holmes went on: 'I have been under Dr. Bigelow's thumb so long, that I have not been able to get out from under'."[20]

Horatio's paper, "The Propriety of Operating for Malignant Ovarian Disease," presented before the San Francisco Medical Society on July 25, 1871, was an objection to a paper on this same topic by Professor T. Gaillard Thomas published in the May 1871 *American Journal of Obstetrics*.[21] Thomas did not operate in the several cases he discussed in his paper because his diagnosis indicated that the ovarian tumors were malignant. Horatio challenged the accuracy of Thomas' cancer diagnoses and criticized Thomas' failures to operate on the women. On the one hand, Horatio indicated the relative rarity of ovarian cancer, on the other, was Thomas' failure to conduct exploratory surgery in one diagnosis. Horatio also noted that even if cancer were found, there was a real possibility for successful cure by surgery if the neighboring tissues were not affected.[22] The following excerpt from Horatio's paper was aimed at the critics of "reckless" surgical operations:[23]

I have said enough, I think, to call the attention of operators, and the profession generally, to the true point upon which the decision of this question of operating in malignant, and a fortiori in doubtful, cases of ovarian disease must turn. As elsewhere, the patient should have the benefit of the doubt. With the operation, she has a fair chance of recovery; without it, she has none. ... To avoid the risk of an unsuccessful operation, it is very easy to decline receiving a doubtful case, but it is far more creditable to save a life that would otherwise have been lost, by simply pursuing the same course that would be taken in every other problem of surgery, and that is, where a disease is evidently killing the patient, is practically isolable, and can be removed with less risk that to leave it alone, then to remove it.

Horatio persisted in California, "chained" there, as he noted in the September "Editorial Notes."[24] Horatio discussed the failure of the California delegates to unite which would have led to one of their state being elected President of the American Medical Association. Dr. David W. Yandell of Kentucky was finally selected. Yandell had been a Vice-President in 1868 when Horatio also had that honor and it is possible that Horatio might also have been in the running for the office. His discussion of the requirement for a "steady hand, a calm pulse, and a cool brain, so to fulfil the duties of the presidency of the American Medical Association as to give satisfaction to, and receive efficient support from, the little group of ability-gaugers, who comprise this Editorial Association," may have been a pitch to the medical editors for their support of Horatio's hand, pulse, and brain. However, no information that Horatio was or was not in the running has been located.

Horatio contributed to the October 1871 "Editorial Notes," while still in San Francisco.[25] He discussed the prevalence of malaria in the West and its contribution to uterine disease. He also discussed the climate and the proposals for sanitation in San Francisco that would make the city "the healthiest city of its size upon the continent." Dr. Bixby concluded the October "Notes" with a discussion of a recent Boston newspaper editorial on criminal abortion. "We heartily commend it," he wrote, "for its truthfulness, boldness, and for the clear and comprehensive manner in which the editor has treated the subject." Bixby noted that the newspaper editor had claimed "'much can be done by the Press.'" Bixby agreed, and continued in an Horatio-like vein:[26]

A free discussion of this subject by every respectable journal in the land, would, we believe, carry conviction into many, many hearts, and save to the world innumerable precious lives, and untold moral and physical pangs. But what would be the use of free discussion, and such united action as that suggested in the noble sentiment of the editorial in question, when over against it in the same issue, or perhaps in a more conspicuous column, there appear the flaming announcements of notorious quacks and abortionists, or long lists of lauded nostrums, with their insidious cautions to women, in italics, against "their use by ladies in an interesting condition"?

Is the press intended for the public weal or public woe? According to our observation in nine-tenths of the cases of criminal abortion, so often resulting in the death of both mother and child, the poor victim has found her information in the columns of some respectable newspaper.

When we consider the extent of this crying evil, the very thought is appalling. We cannot serve God and mammon. We doubt the efficacy of the prayer of "Good God and Good Devil." No, gentlemen of the press, either lend us your powerful influence, undivided and unalloyed, in this humane, ennobling, Christianizing work,—an object worthy of the highest aspiration of the human soul,—or forever hold your peace.—G. H. B.

As will be seen, Bixby's loyalty to Horatio would wane after Horatio's coming illness and departure from Boston. One result would be Horatio's exclusion from the American Gynaecological Society which Bixby was a principal in founding in 1876 while Horatio was convalescing abroad.

There was a recess in meetings of the Gynaecological Society of Boston from June 6, 1871 to August 8, 1871, and another from that date to September 26, 1871 when only four members were present. Obviously, Society meetings were not as satisfying to the members with Horatio absent. At the September 26 meeting, Dr. Bixby proposed a resolution thanking a New York City judge for his strident attack against abortionists and this was unanimously adopted.[27] There was also a description of a new gynecological instrument invented by Dr. Field which he called the shielded applicator, which allowed treatment of the womb without use of the speculum. The woodcut figure of this instrument was cut out of its page of the journal at the Emory University Medical Library.[28] Some Southern subscriber probably gave this picture to his local maker of medical instruments so that he could have his own "shielded applicator." This hole in the journal page is strong testimony of the relevance of the *Journal of the Gynaecological Society of Boston* to its subscribers.

The October 3, 1871 meeting was much better attended. Horatio was back and "the heartiest welcome was given him by the President and members."[29] Among other discussions, Horatio noted that insane asylums in California were extremely crowded and that if it were not for the healthy climate, there would undoubtedly be epidemics of disease as a result. He also noted that the Superintendent of at least one of them was much more open than eastern superintendents to reflex causation of insanity in women. At the next Society meeting on October 17, the Society offered its support to Honorary and Corresponding Members of the Society who had suffered losses in the recent great fire in Chicago.[30] It also voted formal thanks to President Eliot and the Corporation of Harvard University "for the wise and persistent energy with which they have of late examined into, remodelled, and infused with new life the Medical School under their charge." The members also indicated their hope "that such further changes may from time to time be made, as may be necessary to bring the school up to the standard recommended for several years past by the American Medical Association."[31]

The "Editorial Notes" for November began:[32]

At home once more, after an absence of half a year, we have occupied ourselves, with equal interest and pleasure, in resurveying the old, familiar ground; making ourselves again—we say it in no offensive sense—"master of the situation." Let us see whether we have not succeeded.

Last April, tired and weary, both in body and mind, and, withal, blood-poisoned from a dissection wound, we sought, in change of scene and climate, the recreation these so often afford. At that time, certain forces had been set at work here in Boston, chiefly through the instrumentality of the Gynaecological Society, whose results we both foresaw and foretold. ...

We left our friends confident in the continuous success ... of the party of the Future as against that of the Past. Let us see how nearly we were right in our opinion.

Horatio then documented the successes of "the party of the Future." First was the "overwhelming rebuke of the Councillors of the Massachusetts Medical Society by the American Medical Association." Second was the announced "grave change" at the Harvard Medical School which "had adopted the advice so often urged upon it by this Journal, and which, it had been openly alleged, should, for that very reason, never be accepted." In the following, Horatio "refused" any claim for the Harvard Medical School changes.[33]

The influence of the Gynaecological Society, it may be said, had nothing whatsoever to do with this change. It was purely the spontaneous act, we may be told, of a progressive and lively Faculty, who had always striven to keep in advance of all the requirements of the medical age.* We cheerfully grant all this, for we have promised henceforth to do what we can to strengthen the now cheerful zeal of these gentlemen; and we have reason to believe that there are influences actively at work in their midst which they dare not ignore, and cannot resist. Should, however, there be any of our readers who think that they recollect any articles to have appeared in this Journal which might possibly have had to do with the result that has been obtained, we are sufficiently magnanimous to agree with the Faculty that it could not have been the case. There are those, however, who affirm that, in the College change of base, the Society, and the Future that it so feebly represents, had won again.

The third success of the party of the Future was the triumph of specialties in the new Harvard Faculty, with Professors added in Ophthalmology, Dermatology, and Mental Disease; two instructors added in Otology "(for each ear, perhaps)"; and Syphilis made a separate branch of instruction "as though it were the prince of all diseases." The fourth success was location of the City Lunatic Hospital at the Winthrop site, which the asylum experts and the Gynaecological Society of Boston had recommended rather than in the site which speculators had apparently desired and which had been backed by "certain of our most prominent medical men." Horatio concluded the segment on the successes of the "party of the Future" by saying: "And so we might go on. We do not care, however, to weary our readers. What we have said may serve to show those who feared, how groundless was their alarm, and those who boasted, that their pride has been only equalled by their fall. As for ourselves, we resume the editorial chair with renewed health, patience, and courage."

Horatio then turned his attention to the local climate for gynecology.[34]

We may be asked, however, if the gynaecological climate, so to speak, of Boston, is already an unexceptionable [sic] one. As yet, of course, it is not; but the change for the better has been very rapid and satisfactory. Is the Society, for instance, yet recognized by those whom this Journal has been sending down into history, like pretty insects preserved upon pins? It would have been folly to have expected so much the present year.

Then he discussed the October 5, 1871 *Boston Medical and Surgical Journal*, which the editors referred to as the "Student's Number," but which he indicated was better described as the Harvard Medical School's number. Horatio pointed out that the issue failed to include the Gynaecological Society of Boston in its list of "Medical Societies in Boston" and failed to mention the City Lunatic Hospital, the Carney Hospital, and St. Elizabeth's Hospital in its list of "Hospitals in Boston." These were seen as a continuing Faculty animosity to gynecology, but in reality "trifles, little sparks from the cooling ashes, we hope, of a fire that ought, in view of the changed relations of the College Faculty to the outside profession, to be allowed to die out." He continued:

we have promised our aid to the University in its every effort to advance and improve its system of medical instruction, and no petty exhibition of their former temper, upon the part of individuals, can make us forget that, as members of the Press, and therefore, so far as our influence extends, controllers of public opinion, we occupy a higher level than themselves. The success of the School, in its new role, depends in great measure upon agencies that, however it may affect to do so, it cannot afford to despise. No amount of self-conceit, or of mutual admiration, upon the part of its instructors, can take the place of outside approbation and aid.

Horatio indicated that there would be future needs for change at the Medical School and "we shall continue from time to time, and as circumstances may seem to require, to offer them such suggestions as may be needed, confi-

dent, as we are, that our tender of advice will be sure of immediate acceptance."
He then immediately offered "such suggestions," noting that the improved curriculum, with it expansion to specialties, still did not cover "the whole range of
the special branches of practice, that are now recognized *by the profession* as
legitimate." Horatio singled out the diseases of infants and children as one not
covered, and he proposed a full professorship be immediately instituted and
named three qualified persons who could fill it. These magnanimously included
Francis Minot, who had been part of the Ellis, Hodges, Minot quarrel of 1866,
and Francis Brown, the current editor of the *Boston Medical and Surgical
Journal* who, among other slights of Horatio and the Gynaecological Society of
Boston, had allowed the omission of the Gynaecological Society of Boston from
his journal's list of Boston Medical Societies.

Horatio then dwelled on Medical Jurisprudence, which in theory was covered, but which had always been a stepchild taught either by a medical man with
no extensive knowledge of law or by a lawyer ignorant of medicine. He suggested the names of four physicians with law degrees who would do justice to
the College. Although Horatio did not name himself, there is much informative
self-reference in his related discussion:[35]

> There is another light in which this subject of Medical Jurisprudence
> must be viewed by the Overseers of the College, that has not been
> appreciated as yet, it would seem, by the Faculty. We refer to the
> fact that the science of which we are speaking is as important in its
> theory and its practice to the members of the bar as to medical men.
> So truly is this the fact, that were public lectures, say under the
> auspices of the Lowell Institute, to be given in this city by some first-
> class man, fitted for his work in the way of which we have spoken,
> they would be largely attended by legal practitioners. This being the
> case, it would be a simple measure of worldly wisdom to open the
> college course, which properly initiated at the Medical School, also
> to the members of the Law Class at Cambridge. Should it be thought
> that such action would be futile or but an experiment, we answer that
> one of the past Deans of the Medical School, Dr. Shattuck, will
> testify that there was a time, some years ago, when at the suggestion
> of the young enthusiast who then occupied the place of "assistant"
> during the summer session, the Faculty invited the students of the
> Law School to attend his "recitations" upon Medical Jurisprudence.
> It was found, so great was the throng that attended, that the Library,
> which had heretofore sufficed for the summer instruction, and was
> then fully large enough for the classes of the other teachers, was
> altogether too small to hold the conjoined students. The janitor,
> perplexed, threw open one of the "lecture-rooms," and it was used
> for the purpose. The Dean may have forgotten the reprimand which
> he sent to the "assistant," in the name of the Faculty, for violating a

sacred custom by teaching the class in a room that was to be used only by a full Professor,—as also the second rebuke that so soon followed because it was dared to fill to the class "by lecture" certain gaps concerning points in medical jurisprudence that were untouched by Casper, or Taylor, or Wharton & Stillé. We too would like to forget those old times of red tape, official jealousy, and suppression of young and earnest men by those who have culminated; but the two little notes, in the Dean's handwriting, are just at this moment upon our table. The dead, indeed, sometimes come back to do good service.

Was Horatio offering his services to the school as the Medical Jurisprudence Professor and to the Lowell Lecture platform? This is the probable meaning for the "dead" returning to "do good service." Horatio, at forty-one in 1871, no doubt would have packed them in as well as he did at thirty-six in 1866.

"Many who have regretted or condemned our course," Horatio editorialized in December, "now tender us their congratulations and their apologies."[36] He was referring to the Society's and its *Journal*'s earlier attacks on the Harvard Medical School and the recent "complete reconstruction of the school" which proved their legitimacy. Horatio referred to the recent appointment of Dr. Francis Minot to a clinical professorship of diseases of infants and children "*and those of women also!*" However, whether he had already been selected at that time, whether the *Journal* editorial had influenced Minot's selection, or whether he was selected despite the *Journal*'s endorsement, is not known.

Horatio next reported that the conservative Medical Faculty had succeeded in preventing the Board of Overseers of the University from establishing a Full Professorship of the Diseases of Women, despite a recommendation to do so from President Eliot and the Corporation. The Faculty's strongest argument apparently "was that as yet no action in this direction had been taken by the other schools." Horatio then listed the six medical colleges in the United States with full professorships of gynecology, eight others with professorships of gynecology and diseases of children, and another with a clinical lectureship in gynecology. Horatio also noted that not only had the Faculty indicated that other schools did not have such a Professorship, there had been a threat of resignation by those professors providing "unexampled" opposition to a Professorship of Gynecology. This led Horatio to conclude:[37]

But, it has been asserted by those who think they know, should the Overseers become convinced of the wisdom of the recommendation made by the higher board, proceed to found the professorship, and elect a man of world-wide reputation,—like Fordyce Barker, or Peaslee, of New York, for instance,—whose very name would bring a crowd of students, and perhaps even of practitioners, to the school for special instruction, it is possible that some one or more of these protesting professors might resign, in their great indignation. Supposing, however, so deplorable a circumstance to happen, it is also possible that the University and the outside world might stand the shock.

But who dreams of the possibility of such a fiasco, even in such an event? Resignations have been threatened before for similar cause, but they never take place; for such vacancies could be too easily filled. It was said, not so very long ago, that if Mr. Charles Eliot dared even to suggest any change in the school, however trivial, the whole Faculty as a unit would vacate their places. They have now been turned topsy-turvy, over and over again, and every man of them, as if for dear life, clings to his chair.

Horatio's references to a "man of world-wide reputation" would apply to himself and he had long demonstrated the ability to bring in practitioners "for special instruction." It seems probable that Horatio was thinking that he himself might be the candidate if such a full professorship of gynecology were made at Harvard. It is possible that when the Chair of Diseases of Women was proposed, Horatio had been proposed to fill it. This could have accounted for the "unexampled" opposition to the proposal.

Horatio closed the December "Notes" with a plea for Christmas gifts to the Women's Hospital of Chicago whose resources had been depleted and whose patient load had been increased by the recent great fire. He also included the following conciliatory paragraph which was somewhat prophetic, given his own near demise a few months later:[38]

To the physician, Christmas should come with a peculiarly softening and persuasive power, for it is he, of all persons, who is brought the nearest to God's deep mysteries, and he, of all, who should recognize most fully the love that underlies the universe, and how near to death is the quickest life. Before another recurrence of this time, one's self, or those with whom he has differed, may be taken away, and the opportunity for reconciliation have passed. To forgive, then, our enemies, persecutors, and slanderers, as we hope ourselves at last to be forgiven, and to pray Him to turn their hearts,—such, at this season, of all others, is surely no unworthy thing for us each to do.

At the Sixty-fifth Regular Meeting of the Society on December 5, 1871, Dr. Martin indicated that surgeons were taking too long to complete surgery. Horatio expressed his own preference for taking a good bit of time and reminded the group of the successful double ovariotomy that was interrupted by a half hour in restoring the respiration and circulation of the patient following her collapse, and another half hour when the surgeon and assistants "enjoyed a hearty dinner."[39] Next was discussion of a case involving "differential diagnosis of uterine fibro-cysts." Perhaps because Horatio's track record on uterus extirpation had become so bad, he closed the incision when exploratory surgery confirmed "an immense interstitial fibroid, occupying the whole anterior wall of the uterus," instead of cystic disease of both ovaries.[40]

At the next meeting of the Society on December 19, 1871, Horatio read a long account by Dr. Logan, Secretary of the California State Board of Health, of a midnight visit Horatio, Dr. Logan, and a guide "had made to the worst portions of the Chinese quarter."[41] This described remarkable overcrowding, unsanitary conditions, and depravity that included prostitution, opium smoking, gambling, and "habitually committed" "crimes that cannot be named." Given Horatio's lack of reluctance to name unnameable things such as abortion, nymphomania, and female masturbation, one is hard-pressed to identify "crimes that cannot be named." A strong possibility is homosexual behavior which was not specifically named in any of Horatio's articles or books. In the "Editorial Notes" for January 1872, Horatio again made reference to the midnight trip to the Chinese Quarter which he described as "not unlike the most horrible conceptions of Dante, and we can hardly look back upon it, even now, after the lapse of many months, without a shudder."[42] Horatio also quoted in these "Notes" his Chinese-Quarter-visit companion, Dr. Logan, who wrote about female hygiene in the General Report of his California State Board of Health in November. Horatio reproduced Logan's discussion of the particular vulnerability of women to impaired health, which concluded:[43]

> "We believe, also, that there is a great amount of communicable information [about female hygiene] withheld by the medical profession, which it is their duty to spread abroad and make common for the public good. Actuated by such considerations we extended an invitation to a physician of Boston, who has made the diseases of women a special study, to deliver a public lecture on 'Female Hygiene,' that would meet all the issues at question. Many physicians appear to entertain the idea that their knowledge cannot be imparted to the people without infringing upon their obligations to their profession, and that it is better, in fact, that the world should not be possessed of such recondite information as theirs. We are happy to be able to state that Dr. Storer was influenced by no such obsolete and non-progressive ideas, but cheerfully acceded to our wishes. His lecture, which is now published in the Appendix of this Report, for more general diffusion, was delivered in May last, both in San Francisco and Sacramento, before appreciative audiences of ladies and gentlemen, and we are gratified to be able to add that it was well received, and is calculated, in our opinion, to redound to the good of the State."

The Third Annual Meeting of the Gynaecological Society of Boston was held January 2, 1872. The Presidential Address written by Horatio for Dr. Lewis was entitled, "The History and Progress of Gynaecology in New England." "Lewis" began:[44]

> The position as your President, while it has been very grateful to me, from your kindness, has had its inconveniences and troubles. It has brought me into a quasi collision with many; and, in one instance, into a rebuke of words, so very acrimonious, that it would not have been tolerated, but from the well-known fact that the attack was made by one of a family belonging to the "genus irritable." Living continually "in hot water" does not agree with my constitution; I prefer the more pleasant temperature which soothes and represses the exacerbations of morbid humors and violent eruptions.

A good guess on the family member from the "genus irritable" was Jacob Bigelow or his son, Henry J. Bigelow. "Lewis" then summarized much of what Horatio had earlier written in a paper, "Outline History of American Gynaecology,"[45] giving authors and titles of early papers on women's diseases. This was followed by a discussion of teaching of women's diseases and obstetrics at the different New England medical schools. The Address became much more interesting when Lewis moved on to the individual practitioners who had worked to legitimize gynecology in New England. He began with Dr. Channing, who had been the second physician to be selected by the Society for Honorary Membership. (Simpson was first.) Horatio wrote and Lewis spoke:[46]

> To Dr. Walter Channing, the first Professor of Obstetrics in Harvard University, there is due great praise for having for a long series of years given especial attention to the diagnosis and treatment of uterine disease. He was, indeed, in many respects, wholly in advance of his time. While still a very young man, he was called to the Obstetrical Chair, which was made for him virtually by Dr. Jacob Bigelow, to offset the arrangement, for offence and defence, then existing between Drs. James Jackson and John C. Warren. There then ensued a double alliance. It was early found, by these four gentlemen, that to combine their forces at any sacrifice, even of personal inclination, was far wiser than to waste their strength in mutual rivalry or conflict. As a consequence, the balance of power was secured, and for nearly fifty years the quartette governed the medical profession of Massachusetts, as with a rod of iron; and even at the present day, with two of them deceased, and the other two fast nearing the inevitable hour, these powers of the past still exercise a baneful influence, in repressing that spirit of independence and self-assertion which should be possessed, in a measure, by every member of a

liberal profession, and without which he is no freeman, but the veriest sycophant and slave.

Horatio's father was next to be cited:[47]

> Dr. D. Humphreys Storer, also one of our Honorary Members,— would that he could have seen it his duty, by a closer affiliation with us by attendance upon our meetings, to have given us, of his large experience, that aid and countenance that every gynaecologist has a right to expect of his elder brethren!—the elder Storer succeeded to Dr. Channing in the Obstetrical Chair of the University. For many years previously, namely from 1838 to 1854 he had taught, as I have said, in the Tremont Street Medical School; to which, private though it was at first, belongs the proud honor of having initiated that better and more thorough system of medical instruction, which slowly, and aided by much pressure from without, has at last culminated in the late new birth of the Harvard Medical College. Dr. Storer, though not a writer, has been always known as a genial, whole-souled man, devoted to his profession, and beloved by his students, and to his influence, more than to that of any other man, has been due the prosperity that the college has of late years enjoyed. Had it not been for the dastardly treatment to which his son, at the time his class-assistant, was subjected by his associates in the conduct of the school, and which eventuated also in his own withdrawal, Dr. Storer would undoubtedly at the present moment be occupying the chair that he so long honored, and the fulfillment of whose duties he so much enjoyed.

After briefer discussions of two other gynecological pioneers, Dr. Gilman Kimball of Lowell and Dr. E.D. Miller of Dorchester, "Lewis" referred to the younger gynecologists in the area, noting that "it would hardly be right for me to speak by name" of these "who are doing so much among us to establish for gynaecology its rightful place among the departments of medicine." He noted that without exception, they were members of the Gynaecological Society of Boston, either accepting invitations to attend meetings or applying on their own to join. "Can I, however," he continued, "fail to speak of our 'ruling spirit,' as he has truthfully been called by those who have opposed this organization, acknowledging, as they have done, by their very fear of him, his power." "Lewis" continued his praise of Horatio:[48]

> He was practically the first in this country to recognize gynaecology in all its length and breadth, as a distinct department of medicine, I should almost say indeed a distinct science; and while I appreciate all that Sims and a host of others have done to perfect special operations,

and to advance our knowledge of certain isolated diseases, I believe that to him, above them all, is owing the present enthusiastic recognition of the diseases of women by the great mass of the American profession. By his influence at home, and in the National Association, and by those ringing editorials it has always been my delight to endorse,—so long and so convincingly pointing out the necessity of the reform,—it is to him more than to any other man, beside the President of Harvard University, that those masterly changes have been made which have regenerated the Medical School of this city, and have placed it again in advance of all others in America.

Sooner or later,—patient as ever, he is biding that time,—it will be found that, in the great professional chess-match of our time, it is he that has won. To me, who have studied that game from its very commencement, it has seemed that this must be impossible, so great were the efforts made to break him down and drive him from the city. Seeming losses, however, immense though at the time they may appear to be, are sometimes, in the end, but greater gain.

True, or nearly true, as much of this appears, it is too bad that we must attribute the words to Horatio, and not to Dr. Winslow Lewis. However, there is no evidence that Lewis, seventy years of age in 1871, was incapacitated. He would not have read this tribute to Horatio had he not believed it.

Two weeks later, at the next meeting of the Gynaecological Society, there was discussion about medicating and feeding patients via rectal suppositories and enemata. Horatio indicated that this had been claimed to be impossible at a recent meeting of the Suffolk District Medical Society "and that a quotation had been read from Trousseau to the effect that said T. utterly disbelieved in rectal absorption." The Proceedings continued:[49]

Such being the case, it had truly been said, "so much the worse for Trousseau." For his own part, he had so often kept patients along by nutrient enemata and in tolerably good condition, who were suffering from malignant and other disabling gastric diseases, who would have starved if left to the usual method of receiving their food, that he must still recommend to those who differed from him than sooner than let their patients die from inanition they had better be on the safe side and fall back upon the rectum, even though they suppose it to possess no absorbent.

The February "Editorial Notes" contained a long reprint of an English article indicating the dangers of addicting patients to alcohol when it is administered as a drug. It was noted that it could be "read with profit by certain prominent physicians of this city" who had testified under oath to the State

Legislature "that no harm had ever been occasioned, at the hands of the medical profession, by the careless or indiscriminate prescription of alcoholic cordials and stomachics, placeboes, or anodynes."[50] Horatio's strong concern for this issue, and the fact that in 1863 he had almost started an institution for well-to-do women alcoholics,[51] suggests that alcohol may have contributed to Emily Elvira's problems.

Another essay reprinted in the "Editorial Notes" was related to hereditary factors in disease. Horatio introduced it by mentioning Darwin's "theory of progressive development" and clearly showed his own belief in the theory of evolution.[52] However, Horatio also noted "that to suppose a gradual evolution of life from a lower to a higher plane is none the less to accept an intelligent and ever-presiding power, than to hold to the successive introduction upon the earth of animal types, each different from their predecessors and perfect in themselves from their beginning." Here Horatio was echoing Asa Gray's position on God and evolution and it is unfortunate that we have not located any correspondence showing how Horatio came, perhaps agonizingly, to his anti-Agassiz, pro-Darwin position.

Horatio was depending to an unprecedented extent on the writing of others for the "Editorial Notes" of 1872. One suspects that Emily Elvira was very ill, and that this was the reason. However, Horatio ended the February "Notes" with a fairly lengthy self-composed piece, on the one hand, congratulating the Harvard Medical school for appointing his friend, Dr. John P. Reynolds, as Instructor in Obstetrics, and, on the other hand, chastising them for failing to provide clinical instruction in the subject. He called on the Medical School to quickly make arrangements with the Carney Hospital to remedy this deficit.

The meeting of the Society on February 6 included discussion of the imprisonment of a notorious abortionist in the Nebraska Territory, which was elaborated on in the Proceedings by the following note: "Dr. Storer commented upon the growing sentiment of the community that this crime must be suppressed. It was evident that efforts that a few earnest men had made in the face of doubt and ridicule were now producing their perfect work throughout the country."[53] The second meeting of the Gynaecological Society in February indicated that Horatio was still operating, perhaps fully healthy, having just prior to the meeting removed a chestnut-sized cervical polypus which was exhibited by Dr. Warner.[54] Horatio read the suppressed portion of his father's Introductory Lecture of November 1855 which dealt with the country's new source of uterine disease, criminal abortion. Horatio also discussed the reasons for the suppression of this section of his father's Introductory Lecture and the failure of some recent authorities to give his father proper credit for bringing the moral and medical problem to the attention of the profession. The Proceedings told that:[55]

> Dr. H. R. Storer stated the circumstances under which his father's paper had been written (in 1855,) and those under which its publica-

tion had been suppressed. He himself had always regretted that the "injudicious" counsel had been followed. So far from the publication having been likely to have injured the interest of the Harvard Medical School, it was well known that the school had been very nearly ruined by just such a timid, vacillating no-policy, of whose fear of taking a manly stand, even upon purely scientific matters, the present was one among many proofs. He regretted the long suppression of the paper all the more, in that the suggestions made therein by his father, though read only at the college commencement, had been seized upon with avidity by members of the profession, to whom much unwarranted credit had been given. In his own publication upon the detrimental physical effects of abortion and incomplete intercourse, he had repeatedly made mention of this fact.[56]

A visitor at the meeting, Dr. Rooney, who had been "in practice for many years," indicated that he "he had seen and known of more criminal abortions and attempts at criminal abortion since he removed to Boston a year since, than in all his life before." Horatio then discussed the history of local efforts to improve the laws against abortion and proposed the Society take further action on this. The Proceedings indicate that Horatio reminded the members of the failure of the Massachusetts Medical Society to recommend to the legislature changes of its abortion laws and of his protest of Bigelow's action in his 1858 absence. They also recorded that:

The Gynaecological Society had since that time memorialized the Executive of the State with reference to the reluctance of its prosecuting officers to attempt trials for the crime, and the Governor had pointed to their valid excuse [defective laws]. Dr. Storer thought that the time had at last come, so great a revolution was occurring in public sentiment, when steps for a betterment of the statutes might be taken with success. The New York Medico-Legal Society for instance, had lately been acting with vigor and success. He would therefore move the appointment of a committee to consider the propriety of a memorial from the Society to the Legislature. He himself should decline serving upon it, as he feared he was considered by his friends a fanatic upon this subject, but he would aid the committee by every means in his power.

The motion was seconded by Dr. Hazelton, and Drs. Greeley, Hazelton and Bixby were appointed.

Horatio's March "Editorial Notes" expressed his concerns about some of the Massachusetts Medical Society's Councillors' attempts to reassert their power, and he condemned Henry J. Bigelow's characterization of the American Medical Association as "volunteer delegates, having primarily in view the agreeable and commendable object of a journey to break the monotony of medical practice, and give them an apology for leaving their homes and their patients at a pleasant season of the year."[57] The March "Editorial Notes" no doubt were submitted to the publisher just a few days before the death of Emily Elvira. She died on February 27, 1872, at Worcester, possibly at the State Asylum, with the "Immediate Cause of Death" noted on the death record as "Pneumonia." Adding to this tragedy, was the fact that she died on Horatio's forty-second birthday. She was buried two days later in Forest Hills Cemetery in Jamaica Plain. Horatio would join her fifty years and seven months later.

Nonetheless, Horatio was present for the March 5, 1872 meeting of the Gynaecological Society of Boston. As Secretary, he must have suppressed the sympathies undoubtedly expressed to him by those in attendance, since the Proceedings give no indication of Emily's death. A key feature of the meeting was Horatio's list of gynecological instruments. A Tennessee practitioner had requested the "necessary appliances" for making "somewhat a specialty of Diseases of Women," and Horatio named the following:[58]

DR STORER's LIST OF "ESSENTIAL INSTRUMENTS."

5 specula.
   3 sizes bivalve and retractor.
   1 size quadrivalve.
   1 of wood or horn for actual cautery.
1 cauterizing iron.
2 vaginal forceps.
   1 slender dressing.
   1 with ratchet and as curette.
2 sponge holders, plain.
3 caustic holders, different sizes. (Byford's.)
1 sound, Simpson's, plain.
1 scarifier and punctuator. (Scott's.)
1 applicator. (Warner's.)
12 dilators, graduated—German silver—with handle in common.
2 canulated, needles—folding.
2 ecraseurs.
   1 large with long curved chain
   1 smaller for stout wire.
2 clamps for ovariotomy.
1 clamp-shield. (Storer's.)
1 trocar, medium size, but long.
1 pneumatic aspirator.
1 wire twister.
1 hollow sound.
1 circular scissors, (Emmet's.)

2 catheters.
  1 silver.
  1 gum elastic.
12 tents,—carbolized, sponge and sea-tangle, assorted sizes.
1 case for liquids and powders.
  with six cut glass bottles.
  wire-annealed iron, silver plated.
  acupresure and other needles.
1 colpeurynter for flooding, etc. (Braun's.)

No mention is made of pessaries because, when needed at all, they can be selected, like medicinal agents, according to the requirement of the individual case.

Horatio also was present for the March 19, 1872 meeting of the Society and described recent surgery including his removal earlier that day of a large blood clot from a painful anal thrombus.[59] No mention was made of the surgical or dissection wound that soon was to lay him low.

The "Editorial Notes" for April 1872 included praise for the Society's Dr. Martin for his efforts in providing a safe small-pox vaccine to curb the new epidemic of that disease and described the members' defense of Martin's publication of an article in support of this vaccination effort in an irregular homeopathic journal.[60] Horatio also took the railroads to task for not providing discounts to physicians traveling to the upcoming annual meeting of the American Medical Association in Philadelphia.

Horatio's last attendance at a meeting of the Gynaecological Society of Boston prior to his illness was on April 2, 1872. He discussed two operations since the last meeting both of which involved "free incisions for the discharge of pus" one for an abscess between the uterus and bladder and another from the breast.[61] Again there was no mention of any surgical accident to Horatio or of any illness. There also was no attenuation of the Proceedings which might have been expected had Horatio been incapacitated. Horatio and Dr. Bixby were even appointed delegates from the Gynaecological Society of Boston to the upcoming May meeting of the American Medical Association in Philadelphia.

Two weeks later, when the Society met at Hotel Pelham which was both Horatio's home and office, Horatio was absent and so was Dr. Bixby. The Proceedings made no mention of any illness of Horatio.[62] At the next meeting on May 7, "Dr. Bixby said that he had been delegated by Dr. H. R. Storer to state that owing to a painful illness, which has already confined him to his bed for more than four weeks, and bids fair to do so much longer, he is compelled to tender his resignation as Secretary."[63] Since Horatio was confined to his bed from early in April, the May 1872 "Editorial Notes" probably were written about the time the suppressed portion of his father's Introductory Lecture of 1855 was published in the March 1872 Journal.[64] For the most part, they were a restatement of the circumstances surrounding suppression of that portion of the Introductory Lecture. Novel, however, in this rendition was attribution of the opposition in 1855 that caused the portion on criminal abortion and contraception to be suppressed, *to Dr. Henry J. Bigelow and apparently to him alone.* Horatio also made reference to a physician's paper and quoted extensively from a Catholic theologian, both of which sources described the huge increase in techniques for "securing the pleasures of matrimony without its burdens." Horatio implied that the suppression in 1855 of the "leaven" of his father's Lecture was not incidental to this sharp increase in the practice of contraception. The following was Horatio's concluding paragraph of his final "Editorial Notes":[65]

We have reproduced the above in no unfriendly spirit towards theologians, but that the medical profession may judge to what a frightful extent the great cause [producer] of uterine disease that Dr. Storer, senior, first pointed out as such, is now playing its part in the disorganization, physical as well as spiritual, of the world.

CHAPTER 17
KNEE SURGERY, EUROPE, A NEW WIFE, DAUGHTER AGNES, STEP-MOTHER FRANCES

The interval from the May 7 meeting, at which Horatio's resignation as Secretary was announced to the next meeting was four weeks instead of the usual two. The next meeting after the June meeting was on *October 8, 1872.* The appropriateness of calling Horatio the "ruling spirit" of the Society, is no better demonstrated than by this languishing of the Society in his absence.

A letter from Dr. Alexander Stone of Minnesota to Dr. Joseph Toner told that he had visited Horatio on May 13, after the AMA Convention. It included: "I left Phila. for N.Y. & Boston on the 5 oclk P. M. train Saturday reaching Boston Monday morning to find poor Storer on what I greatly fear was his death bed. There chances seemed entirely against him and little short of a miracle can restore him."[1] Stone's "death bed" phrase suggests that he fully expected that Horatio was dead when he was writing to Toner.

"Aunty Carrie," Horatio's sister-in-law, had been taking care of the household even before the death of Emily Elvira. She did not date the following letters to John Humphreys Storer telling him and us about Horatio's illness, but they presumably were written in late Spring and early Summer:[2]

My dear John,
    Dear Papa is no better today, He suffers very much, & it is so harsh that we can do so little to relieve him.
    You shall hear from us every day Dear, if it is only a few words. This afternoon Dr. Cheever is to having another surgeon in consultation & they will decide what more it is best to do. I will finish my note after they have been.
    evening
    The Doctors have decided that their must be an operation upon the *bone* tomorrow afternoon.
    You shall hear again Saturday.
                    Good night
                    Aunty. Thursday evening

Dear John,
    We have received your letters. Dear Papa was operated upon again day before yesterday, He is *very* sick darling John, but we

think he is going to get well. We cannot *know*, but Dr. Cheever &
Dr. Cabot think he will get well, but it will be a long long time
before that happy time comes. I have written to Dr. Lowell by
today's mail & perhaps he will allow you to come down to see us
before long.

Good bye now

Aunty

Horatio's illness was named septicemia by some and pyemia by others.
Dr. Bixby provided the following "Editorial Note" in the July 1872 issue of the
Society's Journal describing Horatio's condition:[3]

It affords us great pleasure to announce the progressing convalescence
of our colleague, Dr. H. R. Storer, after four months of severe
illness. His disease, which seems to have been the culmination of
many successive poisonings from operating and dissecting wounds,
has been inflammation of the head of the left tibia, resulting in deep
suppuration. Trephining was resorted to; but the pus not being
reached, subsequently borrowed through into the knee joint, and
finally from thence into the soft parts of the femur, where it formed
large sinuses. He has had to submit to three distinct operations
requiring anaesthesia, besides numerous minor ones, not to mention
the pain attending the daily dressing, the discomfort arising from this
summer's unusually severe heat, the weight of his professional duties
continually forcing themselves upon his mind, and the prolonged
confinement so tedious and irksome to one of such active habits. It
was our privilege to contribute somewhat to his comfort, and our
sorrowful duty to witness much of his agonizing suffering. We are
able to attest to his patient submission and fortitude under those
severe trials. Dr. Storer is still confined to bed, and it will yet be
many months before he will eventually have recovered the use of his
limb. Meanwhile he has the sympathy and best wishes of his numerous friends. G.H.B.

The following letter from Aunt Carrie to John appears to have followed the
various surgeries, since Dr. Cheever probably was the surgeon. It indicated that
Dr. Anita Tyng still maintained friendship. "Mr. Brooks" no doubt was Reverend Phillips Brooks:[4]

Monday

Dear John,

We have just received yr. Sunday's letter and have been quite
amused by yr. joking! I shall read it to Papa by & by when he is
stronger. Miss Tyng has been here this morning. Also Mr. Brooks

& Aunt Margaret & Mrs March. Grandma has gone out to dine with Aunt Augusta this morning. You knew Aunt A. sails for Europe tomorrow. Dr. Cheever goes out in the same steamer with her, and Dr. Cabot is going to take care of Papa. Dear Papa is very sick yet, but we think he is a little bit better than he was two days ago. I will write you in a day or two whether Frank will go up to spend this next Sunday with you. I think he will. Have you told Dr. Lowell of Papa's illness?

Good bye, lovingly, Aunty

Horatio's successful convalescence is shown by the following passage from a July 15, 1872 letter to Horatio's sons, John and Frank, from, "Aunt Abby," Horatio's sister, which read: "I have seen your Father several times, and I certainly think if his appetite continues, that we shall have him a fat man yet."[5] About the same date, Aunt Carrie sent a letter to John telling of another milestone in Horatio's recovery: "When [the tea table] was all ready we opened the folding doors & moved it up to his bed & he took tea with us. Sister F. on one side & I on the other. The next night Dr. Bixby at a fourth seat. Now every evening Papa expects us regularly to tea with him & he enjoys it greatly."[6] "Sister F." undoubtedly was Sister Superior Frances Sophia MacKenzie. It appears that she had moved into Horatio's Hotel Pelham apartment to provide him with the personal care that had inspired Horatio to dedicate *Nurses and Nursing* to her. Carrie's letter concluded: "Dr. Cabot says this morning that Papa is doing so well that in a week or two he is going to have him sit up & by the 1st of August he hopes to send him out of town somewhere! I think that will hardly be, but we shall see."

Cabot's prediction must have been fairly good. In the following Editorial Note for October 1872, Dr. Bixby informed the journal's readers of Horatio's trip to Europe in search of a cure.[7]

Our friend and colleague, Dr. H. R. Storer, sailed with his family for Europe on the 5th inst. We are glad to announce their safe arrival out, after a short passage. Recent letters report his having borne the fatigues of the voyage tolerably well, and as being as well as could be expected under the circumstances. Dr. Storer will spend the autumn in Germany, and the winter in Italy. We hope the genial climate of the Mediterranean coast will do much toward restoring his health. G.H.B.

With the exceptions of Bixby's pair of brief notes reproduced above, the "Editorial Notes" of the *Journal of the Gynaecological Society of Boston* came to an end with Horatio's May entry. The *Journal* itself continued with a final volume for July through December 1872, but it was largely made up of Proceedings of meetings from December 1871 through April 1872 when Horatio was still attending, and, as Secretary, writing these Proceedings. The final issue was for both November and December, this being the only time that a separate monthly number was not published.

The party for the trip abroad was a large one. The list of cabin passengers of the Steamship *Main,* which sailed on Saturday, October 5, 1872 for Bremen via Southampton, included Horatio, his three sons, Mrs. Addison Gilmore, Augusta Caroline Gilmore, and Frances Sophia MacKenzie.[8] Frances obviously had given up her position at St. Elizabeth's Hospital to nurse Horatio.

Presumably, Bixby's "autumn in Germany, and the winter in Italy" was somewhat accurate, although no additional information about Horatio's location for the rest of 1872 has been located. A saved January 4, 1873 rent receipt for a villa in Mentone, France may mark his move to that city.[9] Horatio had referred to Dr. Henry Bennet and that physician's favorite wintering-place of Mentone, France in the March 1870 "Editorial Notes" of the Society's *Journal* and it surely is no coincidence that Horatio became Dr. Bennet's patient at Mentone. Horatio described this in the following paragraph of a paper on his technique of digitally everting the rectum via the vagina, published in the May 31, 1873 *Lancet* of London:[10]

> In the Lancet for 18th January, 1873, Mr. Christopher Heath devotes a considerable portion of a first lecture upon the diseases of the rectum to a description of the various methods of examination of that canal. It is not unreasonable to presume that a surgeon of this gentleman's reputation should have stated in the above paper all the methods with which he was personally familiar or that are ordinarily employed in Great Britain. Such being the case, the mention of what will be found to constitute a very decided practical advance in rectal diagnosis and the possibility of exact localised treatment may prove interesting to English medical men. The present communication is written, it should be stated, at the instance of Dr. Henry Bennet, under whose care the writer has been passing the winter at Mentone, and by whom, despite his experience in pelvic examination and familiarity with what has been published upon the subject, the procedures referred to had been hitherto unknown.

Somewhat later in Mentone, Horatio wrote to the American Medical Association "asking that he might be appointed on a committee to inquire into and make a report on the relative advantages of American and foreign winter cures," and he was "appointed chairman of a committee"[11] to do just that, indicating that Horatio may have been planning on at least one more winter in Europe.

On July 31, 1873, Horatio was miles inland from the Mediterranean in Frankfort-on-the-Main, Germany. There, and on that date, he married "Aunt Carrie," i.e., his sister-in-law, Augusta Caroline Gilmore.[12] A sketch of Horatio's son, John Humphreys Storer, indicates he went to school for one year at Frankfort-on-the-Main and three years in Italy.[13]   Horatio's stays in Germany and Italy probably correspond to this. Horatio was to describe the summer which included Frankfort-on-the-Main as spent "throughout Central Europe,"[14] and his 1901 letter to Malcolm indicated he first saw Vienna in 1873. By April 22, 1874, Horatio was in Sorrento, Italy, where Augusta Caroline gave birth to a daughter. Harriet Beecher Stowe had written *Agnes of Sorrento* in 1862 and Horatio was to mention Stowe's book in his *Southern Italy as a Health Station for Invalids*. Stowe's glowing account of Sorrento may have influenced Horatio and his family to travel there. Horatio in later years referred to his daughter as Agnes of Sorrento, and it is possible that Augusta Caroline and Horatio chose the name "Agnes" because of Stowe's novel.

Tragically, Augusta Caroline was to die four days after Agnes' birth of something referred to as "Roman fever." Phillips Brooks, pastor of Boston's Trinity Church, wrote the following letter of sympathy, which provides us with almost all that we know of Augusta Caroline:[15]

Boston
May 16, 1874

My dear Doctor,

I cannot help thinking how long it will be before you get this note & wishing with all my heart this morning that I could talk to you directly & tell you how sorry I am for you in your great sorrow of which I have just heard. I have thought of you so often I silently wished your happiness in the new home which your wife had made for you & I have thought of her so often with her quiet earnestness & patient self-sacrifice. And now it is almost impossible to realize that it is over for this world. I think that even you can hardly realize it & it is more difficult still for us who are so far away & have not seen her for so long.

I remember your wife from the first day I saw her. I felt as if I knew her much better than probably it seemed to her, but the simplicity & freshness & kindliness of her nature did not allow her to remain a stranger. And I have known nobody to whom the best hopes & finest inspirations of religion seemed to come so simply & easily. The pure love for the Savior was very real to her & very beautiful to see in her. She was one of the people who are so simply & genuinely good that they do not make other people say or even notice how good they are.

In the midst of all your sorrow, I am very thankful for you, my dear friend. I am thankful for the happy days which God has given you with her whom He as taken, and I am thankful that you have felt the assurance of her love, the happy knowledge that the change which has come to her has not broken the affection between you. May God give you this knowledge more & more. He is putting your faith to its severest test. May He make it strong under the trial & all the stronger for the trial.

When shall we see you at home? Perhaps I may see you in Europe first, for I am going for a few weeks this Summer. My kind love to Mrs Gilmore & your boys. May God bless & keep you always

Your friend

Phillips Brooks

The following excerpt of a letter from Horatio's aunt, Margaret Susannah Storer, written about the same time to her friend, Mrs. Hobart Williams, gives us additional information about the family tragedy:[16]

And I have not told you of the sadness, the grief, which came to us, in the affliction of my dear nephew (Dr Storer) who has been abroad with his family the past two years. He went for his health (now a confirmed cripple on crutches), passing through agonies of suffering enduring all with saint-like sweet patience and submission.

He has just lost his precious wife, of Roman fever, she left a little daughter two or three days old! He is *almost* crushed by the blow. She was indeed a ministering angel to him and the dear children.

She was very dear to me. There was deep and *true* sympathy between us. The *disparity of years* was no barrier to the most perfect confidence and love. They were both confirmed three years ago, at Trinity, and were most earnest and growing Christians. I felt that I must tell you this as I cannot see you now face to face. ...

The 1875 meeting of the American Medical Association the first week of May in Louisville included the appointment of Horatio as a delegate to the Italian Medical Association."[17] One wonders if Horatio talked to Dr. Edoardo Porro of Pavia, Italy about removing a pregnant uterus at that meeting. As was noted earlier, Porro first performed the surgery that bears his name on May 21, 1875.[18] Horatio's earlier charge by the American Medical Association to prepare a paper on European winter-cure locations, was completed and the paper forwarded to the Association. Dr. Davis' review of it in the 1875 *Transactions* indicated that although "well written," it would be better placed in "one of the more widely circulated professional or even literary magazines."[19] Horatio included portions of the report in a book entitled, *Southern Italy as a Health Station for Invalids*. This is a beautiful seventy-page book which includes photos of the various resorts and cities described. The following dedication confirms the "blow" associated with the Sorrento death of Augusta Caroline and also Horatio's respect for the late President of the Gynaecological Society of Boston who died on August 3, 1875:[20]

TO
THE LATE **WINSLOW LEWIS** OF BOSTON,
THE FIRST SURGEON TO EMPLOY ANAESTHESIA IN ITALY,
AND TO ANOTHER,
WHOSE DUST, LYING IN ITALY,
HAS MADE IT THE AUTHOR'S HOME,
IN LOVING MEMORY.

The Preface to *Southern Italy as a Health Station for Invalids* reads:

This pamphlet is in great measure reprinted from a series of letters, during 1874, to the "American Register" of Paris. They were written in part to show that Italy may be visited with advantage by invalids, provided only reasonably cautious as to exposure and overfatigue, and in part to warn against the real dangers of the country, which belong not so much to its climate as to causes easily preventible, and which even so slight a contribution as this towards the spread of sanitary knowledge may do somewhat to remove.

Horatio began the book with a chapter on "General Considerations regarding European Health Resorts." The following excerpt no doubt describes the huge benefit Horatio derived from leaving his Boston battlefield and his belief that no American health resort could have provided it to the same degree:[21]

For the American invalid coming to Europe there exists a very great benefit ... It is that here, as never at home, one can change the current of the thoughts, can shake off the cares of business, and the little frets of every day life, and thus ensure a mental and consequent bodily freshness and elasticity otherwise well nigh impossible. The value of this towards regaining regularity of sleep and of digestion, and towards hastening convalescence from any chronic malady, whatever its character, cannot be over-estimated.

In defending Southern Italy as a health resort, Horatio's book countered statements by Dr. Bennet of Mentone that invalids should avoid Southern Italy. Horatio noted the sanitary problems, particularly in Naples, but argued convincingly that cities near Naples and the islands of Ischia and Capri had unique advantages, some for year-round convalescence and enjoyment. One sanitation problem Horatio admitted existed was public urination, and Horatio must have blushed a little when he echoed Jacob Bigelow in the following defense of existing statutes: "As to the disregard of public decency, involving also a danger to the public health, which is everywhere observable in Italy, sufficiently stringent laws already exist for its suppression, the only trouble being that they are not enforced."[22]

Sorrento, where Augusta Caroline died of fever, got a surprisingly positive recommendation. The weather was favorable, particularly in the summer. Walking and riding in the mountains "opens out an endless succession of as enchanting views of land and sea as can well be found in the world." For the boater, grottos and cliff views provided "a pleasurable excitement to those capable of such enjoyments, that can never satiate or fatigue." Horatio compared fevers in America and Italy in the following passage: "The variously styled slow fevers of our South and the typhoid of the North, seem just as prevalent, and treated with the utmost discretion they often prove as fatal. Besides, there can be no question that Rome and Florence, and even Naples, are each credited with many more cases of fever every year than really belong to them." This was followed by the following footnote discussing the fever that struck Caroline:

> The ink was scarcely dry with which the above words were written, when death overshadowed the writer's own household. By strange coincidence, it was fever—sudden, intense, and wholly resistless, despite the efforts of skilful professional friends—Sorrentine, English, and Neapolitan—who gave their aid. The dearest of all, at whose suggestion it was that these letters were commenced, was taken.
>
> Several months afterwards, and this time, indeed, as a labor of love, the notes were once more gathered in hand, for careful revision, and with the determination to change or even erase every statement already made that could not bear the added light of such bitter experience.
>
> The first impulse under such circumstances would be, hastily to pack one's trunks and flee, lest there might occur a repetition of the calamity. It seemed, however, the better course to remain, and to subject the climate to a still more searching study. Another year has now passed, and of one thing the writer remains quite certain, that there are localities in Southern Italy where, with proper precautions, the risks of self-originating fever are not so great as has been generally supposed to obtain throughout the country.

Horatio's own activities during his stay in the Naples area no doubt were similar to the numerous ones he recommended. He first described the tourist activities of the typical "flying" Neapolitan visit: the Museum, Palace, Convent of San Martino, Capodimonte, Vesuvius, Pompeii, Capri's grottos, and Sorrento or Ischia. He also described a host of other things to do:[23]

> The student of languages will find much to interest him in its dialect, so many of whose words are of direct Greek origin, and differ from those used in Central, and still more in Northern Italy. For the lover of art, the Pompeian Schools have more than a momentary attraction.

The antiquarian can nowhere find a richer field. There are most interesting discoveries awaiting the historian who cares to sift the vast public and private libraries and collections of manuscript. There are unrivalled subjects for the painter of land or sea. For the student of natural history, there is the finest aquarium in existence, with most admirable laboratories attached for private research; while every step that the geologist, mineralogist or botanist may take upon this enchanted ground will be found to afford the most satisfactory results.

In addition to the above activities, or at least, some of the above, Horatio became a member of the Medical Society of Sorrento. He and his sons also collected real and confederate Roman coins and became at least somewhat expert at separating the groups.

Horatio concluded the book on Southern Italy with excerpts from his American Medical Association Report which dealt largely with the relative rarity of deaths of Americans in Naples, despite the hundreds of such visitors to the city, many who were chronically ill. He also indicated the large advantages of Naples and its surrounding cities for the invalid from America who was seeking a year-round residence, since Horatio judged Mentone and other Riviera sites to be suitable only in the winter.[24] At the end of the book were a dozen pages of advertisements from hotels and shops in Naples and the surrounding area. Horatio was still in Southern Italy on January 17, 1876 when he added and dated a note to this section recommending the Villa Ropolo.

Horatio and family apparently left Italy in July 1876. A letter to Horatio from J.A. Menzies, a sometimes resident of Edinburgh, but writing from Naples, mentioned Horatio's expected arrival in Liverpool by the first or second of August and encouraged him to travel immediately to Edinburgh, before the faculty at the University all dispersed after the August 2 graduation.[25] Menzies' letter indicates that Horatio's party included "Miss McK.," John, Malcolm, and Agnes. Menzies' letter indicated that Agnes was subject to seizures, but sufficiently minor that by the time they got chloroform ready to treat them they were over. Possible Edinburgh schools for the boys also were discussed and much of the letter indicated the problems Horatio would have as an Episcopalian in Presbyterian Scotland. Other than that, Menzies did not indicate what Horatio's plans were, and, as we will see, Horatio himself was quite uncertain about his future.

Horatio attended the "session of the British Medical Association" at Sheffield, England which took place from August 1 to August 4, 1876. Horatio is reported in the meeting "Proceedings" to have responded to a toast to "The Foreign Guests" with "a graceful tribute to England, as the centre to which American physicians turned for their best medical literature. [*Cheers.*]"[26] Horatio met J. Marion Sims at the Sheffield meeting and learned of the formation of the American Gynaecological Society.[27] This Society was perhaps unsurpassed among all societies in its snobbish exclusion of Horatio. At the time, Horatio probably did not recognize that this was to be the case, or at least hoped that it was not, since he prepared a paper for the new Society. Before discussing Horatio's paper, we provide his remarks on the formation of the American Gynaecological Society which he provided Malcolm in 1901:[28]

> After 1872, Chadwick and John Homans, who till then had not appeared, could but succeed. I had left the field, and the tide had turned. Till I fell ill, Chadwick was unknown, while Cushing and Baker were later creations.
>
> It had been determined by the Gynaecological Society, prior to my illness, to form a national society as well as the local one, since almost every man in the United States who was beginning to give attention to gynaecology was upon our membership list, and we were receiving enthusiastic letters from them, almost without exception. Before leaving for Europe with the rest of you, I placed my private papers, as well as every thing connected with the Society, in Dr. Bixby's hands,—for he had been my trusted assistant, and besides owed me gratitude for forcing him into the Mass. Med. Society after he had been plucked upon examination as a graduate from Dartmouth. Before we returned, Dr. Lyman got hold of him, they subsequently married sisters, and Chadwick joined the conspiracy, although he may possibly not have understood all the circumstances. Lyman had written an essay upon ovarian disease, but had never operated, and had been wholly unknown otherwise as a gynaecologist. The American Gyn. Society was formed by them upon our exact plan and data, and I was excluded. Bixby afterwards attempted to explain that as I had become a confirmed invalid he supposed that I wouldn't care and that the others told him it would be all right,—though Dr. Warner did not hesitate at the time to tell him that he was an ingrate and traitor.

David Humphreys Storer *was* one of the more than three dozen "Founders" of the American Gynaecological Society.[29] This may have been an insult added to the injury of Horatio's exclusion, possibly even an inter-family insult. It will be recalled that David Humphreys was not willing to be among the founders of Horatio's Gynaecological Society of Boston.[30] However, Horatio does not mention his father's connection to the American Gynaecological Society in the 1901 letter to Malcolm and it may be that the seventy-two-year-old David Humphreys Storer had no inkling that Horatio was excluded when he accepted the "honor" of being a founder from the *bona fide* founders of the new Society. What is more, David Humphreys Storer was not at the inauguration of the American Gynaecological Society in New York called by Chadwick, and he also was not present at the Annual Meeting of the American Gynecological Society, September 13-15, 1876, at the Academy of Medicine in New York.[31]

Horatio's paper for the new Society was entitled "The Importance of the

Uterine Ebb as a Factor in Pelvic Surgery." Although Horatio was not present, the paper was presented at the Annual Meeting. Horatio began:[32]

> Upon returning to England from a four years' absence upon the Continent, I was informed by Dr. Marion Sims at Sheffield, during the session of the British Medical Association, that a project often discussed during 1870-1871 between myself and my then associates, Drs. Warner and Bixby of Boston, had at last been carried out, in the establishment of the American Gynaecological Society. At Professor Alexander Simpson's in Edinburgh, I have since been shown the prospectus of the Society, and perceiving that papers are solicited for the first annual meeting, it gives me pleasure to add my mite towards elucidating one of the important problems for whose settlement the Society has been formed.

Horatio's paper claimed that there were an ebb and peak in each menstrual cycle and the ebb reached its nadir a week following cessation of menstruation itself. The data backing this were more than a little weak, calling for example on birth normally occurring at the "tenth" menstrual period, and that the dual shocks of birth and lactation could not be handled by a woman were it not thus occurring at the uterine "ebb." A related practical consequence was that the shock of pelvic operations could be handled better and were much safer during the uterine ebb than at other times. Horatio repeated some of his earlier claims about the mental changes produced by menstruation and these too were cited as evidence of an ebb and peak of uterine function. One sentence almost surely described his experiences with the late Emily Elvira whose mental problems finally required her to leave home. "Scarcely a healthy woman," Horatio wrote, "in whom the observer cannot after a while detect traces of this phenomenon; while in the insane, in whom the tendency may be uncontrollable, either by the will or by the checks of ordinary domestic and social life, the mental disease often plainly evidences, by its exacerbations and other changes, the time, almost the very day indeed, of the personal month."

"By the kindness of the Society," Horatio wrote in a footnote, "the writer has been permitted to decide where the paper shall be published." Given that Horatio was not invited to be a member of the American Gynecological Society, this might be interpreted in a less favorable light than appears. It is possible that the paper was not accepted for full publication in the *Transactions of the American Gynaecological Society*, where it was very briefly summarized on page 22 of Volume I. Horatio appears to have had no problem publishing it in the *Edinburgh Medical Journal*, however.

An invitation to dinner from J. Matthews Duncan on August 14[33] indicates that Horatio travelled to Edinburgh fairly soon after arriving in England. A letter from J. Marion Sims in Paris to Horatio (who was probably in Edinburgh), dated August 30,[34] indicates that Horatio was planning to visit Sims in Paris, but this trip may have been canceled, since Dr. Sims indicated he was returning to the United States and would not be available. Sims might have been expected to be at the First Annual Meeting of the American Gynaecological Society, but, like David Humphreys Storer, he was not among the twenty-eight reporting Fellows.

Charles Brown-Séquard wrote a letter to Horatio from Brighton on September 13, 1876 which is the best evidence of the friendship with Brown-Séquard of which Horatio was so proud. It also indicated that Horatio entertained thoughts of practicing medicine in Great Britain:[35]

> I hope you have found friends in Edinburgh. It is, as I told you, a question whether you would or not, succeed in getting a large practice in this country. But if it became well known that you have occupied, and deservedly so, the highest rank in your special line of practice, in the United States, and that your success in ovariotomy & the treatment of uterine & other affections of women has been considerable, I would be sure of your obtaining here, (I mean in Great Britain) and before very long, a preeminent position.

Even before leaving Italy, Horatio had written J. Marion Sims asking for a recommendation letter related to practice in Great Britain. Sims' response from Paris included:[36]

> Of course my dear Doctor I will with the greatest pleasure write you such a letter as you want. But rest assured you are underrating your position in the profession, and the claims that you have upon its proper recognition by this. You have made for yourself a reputation that no endorsement from any man can augment and no detraction by any can diminish. It is based upon work that cannot be undone by anyone.

On September 20, 1876, Horatio married Frances Sophia MacKenzie in Edinburgh. The marriage was in St. Mary's Church "After Banns according to the Forms of the Roman Catholic Church." The Marriage Register indicates Frances' age as forty-three and her parents are listed as "Peter McKenzie [sic], Wholesale Biscuit Manufacturer, Deceased; and Catherine McKenzie [sic], Ms. Fraser, Deceased." Malcolm Storer, now fourteen years old, signed the Register as a witness.[37] That Horatio at least considered making his residence in Great Britain, is proved by his application for a license to practice there in late September or early October. On December 7, 1876 he received notification that the Branch Medical Committee for England had "Resolved—That the name of Horatio Robinson Storer be placed upon the Register as "Doctor of Medicine (1853) of Harvard University, Boston."[38] As will be seen, Horatio would indicate that this was the first time a Harvard M.D., perhaps any American physician, had ever been so honored.

A letter inviting Horatio to attend a private case of T. Spencer Wells[39] indicates that Horatio was in London in October. Another letter dated November 10 also mentions Horatio's London location.[40] This was from the minister who baptized Agnes in Sorrento, Dr. Niam E. Emmet, but who was at the time in "Bukhamster," apparently south of London. He made mention of the fact that he was "so sorry that Mrs Storer is not strong." Frances' and Horatio's health problems probably were the main reason for their leaving England in less than a year. A letter from a Dr. Mann of San Francisco dated November 20, 1876 indicates that Horatio was contemplating a move to California.[41] Dr. Mann encouraged him to do so and suggested that he restart the *Journal of the Gynaecological Society of Boston* and publish it there.

Aunt Margaret Susannah Storer comes again as a source of much information about Horatio and his family in the following letter addressed to 29 South St. Park Lane W., London, England:[42]

Cambridge Dec. 8th, 1876

Dear Frances,

You doubtless think I have been a long while waiting to thank you for your affectionate and trusting letter. I will assure you that I fully appreciated all your anxieties and sincerely sympathize with you in your increased responsibilities, and sacred duties of your new relation towards one ever so dear to me, and to the precious little motherless Agnes, thus committed to your care as a sacred trust. ...

I am very sorry to hear that your own health and dear Horatio's are unfavorably affected by the climate of Eng. But I sincerely hope you will not be induced to go again to the south of Europe, where there has already been so much suffering to remember. Do not go any *further away*. It seems to me that the bright day *will* dawn ere long. I cannot tell how glad we all were to see Mrs. Gilmore and the dear boys again. John is constantly at school, and very much interested in his studies. Frank, dear boy, looks to me quite feeble, though they all say he is much better that he was before he left Italy. He walks out[43] often and seems cheerful and bright. ... tell me *always* of dear Horatio's health, and the dear little Agnes. I was so glad and *grateful* that she has been taught to say "Aunt Margaret." Would that I could here it from her own lips. May it not be some time, that I shall? With my ever dear love to Horatio. I shall write to him in a few days. Mrs. Storer and the daughters desire their kind regards, & hope sometime to know you personally. Affectionately yrs.

Aunt Margaret.

I hope you receive the Churchman regularly.

A typographical error and an unintentional negative reference to Simpson in the "Uterine Ebb" paper led to another paper a month later in the same *Edinburgh Medical Journal*.[44] Its cumbersome title read: "As to the Practically Absolute Safety of Profoundly Induced Anaesthesia in Childbirth, as Compared with its Employment in General Surgery." Horatio had meant to say in the earlier paper, "Even if profound, anaesthesia may be borne during childbirth without danger." What was incorrectly published was "Anaesthesia, even if performed without danger, may be borne during childbirth." In the "Ebb" paper Horatio had written that Simpson had never described women's near immunity to death from anesthesia during childbirth or at least "had not arrived at its full explanation." Horatio was concerned that some might think that he was denigrating Sir James in saying this, and he concluded:[45]

To the profession in general in America, and to many physicians and surgeons in Great Britain whose personal acquaintance the writer enjoys, the explanation now given would have seemed superfluous. There may be those, however, who have wondered at his language as it appeared in the January number of this Journal. The writer has often been laughed at at home for his egotism, arrogance, pluck, or simplicity, as his various critics have phrased it, in confessing that whatever he may have hoped to become in the profession would have been owing to Edinburgh, and especially to Simpson, who first truly taught him what to observe, how to observe, and what to do with the observations made. It would have been a sorry thing, after Boston's attempt to steal his laurels from Simpson's dying brow, for the Bostonian who had so persistently endeavored through all these twenty-two years to secure him simple justice, to have seemed, and on Scotch ground too, to detract a hair's weight from his work and his memory.

John Codman Ropes was a noted Boston lawyer, law journal editor, and military historian. He was a very close friend of Horatio's, and should his personal correspondence ever be located, it probably would include many letters from Horatio which would shed additional light on Horatio's life. Horatio apparently had written Ropes from London in mid-January about where Horatio should practice medicine. Ropes responded:[46]

> 40 State Street:
> 21 February—1877.

My dear Doctor:
    I sit down at length, after a delay which I trust your goodness will pardon, to reply to your letter of the 14/16 ultm. I should say that

there were two things mainly to be considered in making up you mind where to practice medicine; first, health, of yourself & wife, second, prospects, professional friends, &c. ...

My own idea for you, and I think I mentioned it to you on the beautiful Porch of our house at Ischia, is to go to San Francisco, living there in the winter, with a country house at Santa Barbara or San Diego or even San Jose. You would, I think, enjoy California. The climate is invigorating, but not irritating to the lungs. The society is Cosmopolitan, not at all like anything our side of the Alleghanies. You would have things to a great extent your own way there, you won't be *the* great authority, you could, if you found surgery too exhausting, pay special attention to pulmonary complaints, and find lots of patients who are sent out there from New England every year. Then you are within a weeks' ride of your parents & sisters & brothers & sons. I feel pretty sure you & Mrs. Storer would both like California.

We had a magnificent consecration of our new Trinity Church on the 9th. It is really a noble edifice & in its *interior* is by far the most ornate church in the U.S.

I see your boys occasionally. Frank seems to me quite well & strong, for him. John is now hard at work, studying some? of an evening & I have only seen him at intervals. He is doing first rate. Mrs Gilmore seems very well.

Give my kind regards to Mrs Storer & my love to Malcolm & the baby.
Ever sincerely yours
John C. Ropes　　　　

Dr. Horatio R. Storer

The letter mentions at least two bases for the friendship between Horatio and John Codman Ropes. One was Trinity Church whose doctrine had proved such a boon to Horatio's equanimity. The other was Ischia, the island a few miles from Naples, which obviously was a favorite of both men.

During the visit to Great Britain, Horatio spent time on the Isle of Wight at the very southern tip of the country. Like the Riviera and Southern Italy, it was a popular residence for invalids. Horatio was to write later that Thomas Wentworth Higginson wrote him at Ventnor in 1877, indicating that several Newport families were familiar with the Isle of Wight and described Newport as "a sunny Isle of Wight."[47] This correspondence from an old comrade from the Boston Society of Natural History and an uncle of Anita Tyng could well have inspired or cemented Horatio's plan to settle in Newport after returning to the United States.

CHAPTER 18

ROCKY MOUNTAIN SKETCH, NEWPORT SANITATION, A TB DEBATE

Horatio was back in Boston sometime in late August. The first evidence of this is the following letter:[1]

49 Washington St.
Newport, R.I.
1 Sept. 1877

My dear Dr Toner,

On returning to Boston a few days ago after five years absence in Europe, I found a very kind letter from Dr John Morris of Baltimore, informing me of the approaching publication of your History of the Rocky Mountain Medical Association. It has given me great pleasure to subscribe for a copy, & I shall value it all the more highly because the work of a most esteemed friend.

That I did not answer the one or two letters of inquiry you sent me regarding my own professional life, you must pardon. I was sick in body & weary in mind, & was keenly alive to the fact that I have accomplished but very little that is worth remembering.

Though permanently crippled in limb, I have however been making through all these years a tolerably fair convalescence, & may yet hope to do some worthy labor. It is a joy to return again to the old field, & I gladly look forward to meeting again my brethren of the American and Rocky Mountain Medical Associations. Pardon me that I have placed the National body first. I used to be bitterly condemned for asserting its authority as above that of the members of my native state. The lapse of time, & that sober meditation that illness & exile naturally induce, have but strengthened me in my allegiance to that organization that represents our whole country.

I hope you are in all respects as you yourself would desire; like good wine, but improving with the years.

Remember me to each of my old Washington & Georgetown friends as you may chance to meet, & believe me

ever sincerely yours
Horatio R. Storer

Dr. J.M. Toner.

The Rocky Mountain Medical Association was the group of physicians who had

crossed those mountains to attend the American Medical Association meeting in
1871. A version of the sketch of Horatio for Toner's "History of the Rocky
Mountain Medical Association," apparently accompanied the following:[2]

Newport, R.I.
2 Oct. 1877

My dear Dr Toner,

Pardon my delay in acknowledging your very kind letter of the
4th ult. It has been owing to my strong disinclination for anything
like notoriety, & were it not that it would be alike unkind & wrong
to neglect assisting towards the completeness of your book, I should
probably withhold the brief outline that I now enclose. So far from
occupying the same honored position as our friends Drs Atlee &
Davis, yourself, & a few others of the elder brethren, I feel like
Keats, as I have already intimated to you, that my name "has been
writ in water." Not that I would in any way have changed my record
save to add to it, & to intensify & deepen some of its lines. Life or
rather one's active health, is but short, & our Art is very long.
There remains much that I wished to do, & that I might indeed have
accomplished had I but recognized my time. Instead of giving me
"eight pages" like the first leaders to whom you have referred, let a
dozen lines suffice.

The great satisfaction that I take in my medical history is from
having been able to help, under much condemnation, in removing
some of the obstacles toward the honorable recognition by the general
profession of the department to which I had devoted myself, & in
believing that I was instrumental, both at Washington & at Boston,
in preserving under still greater obloquy the very existence of the
American Medical Association during the most troublous times of its
history, at the close of the Civil War.

...

ever yrs sincerely
Horatio R. Storer

Dr. Toner.

Horatio mentioned his key role in preserving the American Medical Association
at its "close of the Civil War" crisis at Boston. It is regrettable that his specific
actions were never discussed in his later writing or that letters or other
documents recording these actions have not been found. Hopefully, someone
may still find a letter to a friend or some other discussion which indicates how
Horatio, perhaps with the assistance of Dr. Sinclair, frustrated the wishes of Dr.
Henry J. Bigelow, Dr. Henry W. Williams, and others to prevent the 1865
American Medical Association meeting and thereby deal a blow to the
Association from which the Boston "clique" hoped it would not recover.

Horatio's sketch occupied seven pages in the Memorial Volume by Toner, plus another seven-page listing of his publications. The sketch included: "He has now returned to this country, and for the present has established himself, because of the comparatively mild climate, and to escape the engrossing work that would have been inevitable for him at Boston, at Newport, R. I."[3] Some hint of what the engrossing Boston work would have been exists in the following from Horatio's 1901 letter to Malcolm:[4]

That [the 1870 post-AMA-meeting tribute to Simpson] was derided in Boston was of a piece with the fact that when we came back in 1877 and the Sisters at the Carney insisted that, though so disabled, I not merely resume the position I had so long held as Consulting Surgeon, but should accept even a much closer connection and make the hospital as available for gynaecological practice, public and private, and teaching, as St. Elizabeth's, plans for this being repeatedly discussed and virtually arranged—Dr. Elliott and the Shattucks protested and made so much trouble, threatening that the attending staff would one and all resign, that I threw it all up in disgust. Fortunately, for I had not really the physical strength to resist them.

Dr. James Read Chadwick it will be recalled was one of the founders of the American Gynaecological Society that excluded Horatio. Chadwick was also the key figure in formation and management of the Boston Medical Library which opened in October 1875. He apparently used John Codman Ropes to request the large number of books and journals belonging to the Gynaecological Society of Boston for his new Library. Ropes wrote Chadwick on September 3, 1877 and included a transcription of this letter that Horatio had sent to Ropes from Newport:[5]

While in Boston, I was mindful of what you wrote me concerning Dr. Chadwick's wish that the books collected by the Gynaecological Society, should be added to his General Medical Library. I believe that I wrote you from London, that as at present arranged, when the books pass from my custody, they will have to go to the Boston Public Library. I think however that my old associates have still the power to determine this point, and I judge from some little conversation that I had with one or two of them, that they might be willing to make the change indicated. Should Dr. Chadwick still desire it, he would therefore do well to send an explicit request to that effect, either addressed to me officially as Secretary of the Society, or not, as he may prefer. I would then see that it was acted upon at the earliest moment. His application would be the more likely to be successful, should he incidentally allude to the fact that the Gynaecological Society of Boston as an organization for this special work dissociated from the kindred department of Obstetrics, (Midwifery) dated prior to all others that have ever been established.

I cannot act in the matter on my own responsibility, and could more easily effect in the way indicated what Dr. Chadwick desires than otherwise.

Signed

Horatio R. Storer.

A day or two after telling Ropes that he was willing to be contacted by Chadwick, Horatio provided the following to Chadwick. His purpose may have been to give him his address and indicate his openness to contact more than to provide belated thanks:[6]

> 49 Washington St.
> Newport, R. I.
> 4 Sept. 1877

Dear Sir,

I fear that I may have neglected to acknowledge the volume & one pamphlet that you were kind enough to send me in London. Accept my thanks for these.

> Yours sincerely
> Horatio R. Storer

Dr Chadwick.

It could be that Chadwick waited until October 8, 1877 to contact Horatio, given the reference to "8th ult." in the following letter. Horatio himself waited nearly a month to provide this response to Chadwick.[7]

> Newport, R. I.
> 2 Nov. 1877

Dear Sir,

Yours of the 8th ult., & a letter from Dr. Wadsworth as Clerk of the B M S J, have both been received. As soon as I can find time to do so, probably during the present month, I shall take pleasure in communicating them both to the members of the Gyn. Soc.

Remember me kindly to Dr Lyman, & believe me

> yrs sincerely
> Horatio R. Storer

Dr Chadwick.

Horatio seems most gracious in his willingness to have the Society donate its library to Chadwick's, since Chadwick's American Gynaecological Society had excluded Horatio, who had probably done more for American gynecology than any other man. One can hardly fault Horatio for wanting to see some recognition of the Gynaecological Society of Boston, and at least implicitly, himself as its founder, since his Boston Society provided the model, and perhaps the actual plan, for the national organization.

Horatio's friend and former partner, Dr. Levi Farr Warner, provided Horatio a list of the members of the Gynaecological Society of Boston and their addresses on December 13, 1877, presumably for Horatio to set up a meeting of the Society. He added the following: "I do not find the paper on Arsenical Atmosphere in the London Lancet. I have looked them over quite carefully. We are all well, &c. The blackboard and easel are in the storeroom in b[al]lr[oo]m of Hotel Pelham."[8]

The revived Gynaecological Society of Boston met on January 1, 1878. Horatio wrote John Codman Ropes shortly thereafter and described the meeting where he presented the formal request for the Society's library from the Executive Committee of Chadwick's Boston Medical Library Association. The letter included:[9]

By its Constitution, should our own Society ever be absolutely dissolved, its library must go to the Public Library of Boston. There seemed no alternative therefore, in order to meet Dr Chadwick's wishes, but to revive the Society ...

The extent of what I anticipated was that yearly or possibly quarterly meetings might be held, merely to keep up the organization of the Society, for I had been given to understand that with my illness, & the coincident cessation of the Society's meetings & discontinuance of its Journal, almost every particle of life in it had been quenched.

To my exceeding surprise, the meeting yesterday was attended by a large proportion of the immediate members ... They proved as one man enthusiastic in their greeting, & most kind in their expression as to the future, & while cordially assenting to Dr Chadwick's desire, they utterly objected to & overthrew all my plans for a quiescent state, voting to immediately recommence, & continue as formerly, frequent & hardworking meetings, & capped the climax (shall I say of their absurdity?), by electing me to the Presidential Chair, that had been vacated during my absence by Dr Winslow Lewis' death.

Horatio also indicated to Ropes: "since Dr Chadwick & his friends have taken the initiative by their courteous and very fairly worded communications, ... there must be nothing from this moment to disturb the present general tranquillity." The letter concluded:

The Society's Journal, of which from the outset I was the responsible editor, was conducted at the joint risk and expense of myself & Mr

James Campbell of Fremont St, the only medical bookseller & publisher in town. ... The copyright stood in my own name, & the Journal had always been stereotyped. Now I was told yesterday, to my great surprise, by Dr Chadwick, librarian, & Dr Hingham, who was one of my old pupils at the Harvard School before the Faculty turned me out of the humble position that was then my comfort & pride, that the file of our Journal is very frequently consulted by Boston physicians, & that it is entirely out of print. I should like to know, in this connection, what has become of the stereotype plates, if they are still in existence. Perhaps Mr Dexter, if you will kindly ask him, may recollect what arrangement was made concerning them when he obtained my release from Mr Campbell's claims, & whether I still retain the copyright. ﹀

If still available, the plates might be made of use to the Society in effecting the increase of the library strength as systems of exchange.

It may have been "Mr. Dexter" who, as a result of this request, learned that Henry J. Bigelow purchased the plates and destroyed them as Horatio reported happened in his 1901 letter to Malcolm. If true, as is likely, there may be no higher tribute to the effectiveness of Horatio's "Editorial Notes" in countering the corrupt Boston medical establishment.

A description of the January 1878 meeting of the Gynaecological Society and of a few earlier meetings when Horatio was in Europe occurred a year later when the *American Journal of Obstetrics* began printing the Transactions of the rejuvenated Society:[10]

The Gynecological [sic] Society of Boston held its regular meetings, after the suspension of publication of its journal, throughout a portion of the year 1873. Thereafter, the death of its President, Dr. Winslow Lewis, and the continued illness and residence abroad of its Secretary, Dr. Horatio R. Storer, led to a discontinuance of its sessions and work. Upon a call issued, however, for the 1st Jan., 1878, many of its members met at the house of Dr. Bixby in Boston, on the occasion of the tenth annual, and eighty-sixth[11] regular, session. The meeting was organized with the election of H. R. Storer, M.D., to the chair, and of G. H. Bixby, M.D., as Secretary. At a subsequent meeting, Dr. Bixby resigned both his active membership and his office, and Dr. H. M. Field was elected Secretary. Since, 1878, the Society has held its regular monthly meetings, with the same general organization as was then declared.

Among the 21 Society members present was Dr. John L. Sullivan. It will be recalled that Sullivan quit attending Society meetings late in 1870 or early 1871 immediately after Horatio ended their partnership because Sullivan pretended he was Dr. Storer to a patient seeking Horatio's services. Dr. Chadwick apparently prevailed on Sullivan to attend meetings of the rejuvenated Gynaecological Society of Boston long enough to vote the transfer of its valuable library. Sullivan included the following in a January 14, 1878 letter to Chadwick:[12]

> The second meeting of the resuscitated Gyn. Soc. will be holden on the first Tuesday of next month. I intended for wording my resignation today, but am willing to postpone doing so until after the coming reunion, in order to aid in making the change in the constitution we spoke of last evn'g. Meanwhile, will you have time to interest J.G. Blake or Martin or Bixby in favor of the change, so that it may be proposed at the Feb'y meeting and if possible acted upon immediately I don't want to prolong my quasi connection with the illustrious pair (H.R.S. L.F.W.)[13] a moment longer than I can be of service to the Library Association.
>
> I dare not initiate any change in the Constitution, as, coming from me, it would meet with opposition which it would not otherwise encounter. Anything *Blake* proposes will be done, I am confident.

George Bixby's brief cooperation with the rejuvenation of the Gynaecological Society of Boston in 1878, including housing the January 1 meeting and accepting the Secretaryship, and his quick resignation are probably of the same nefarious kind as the "quasi connection" Sullivan mentions in his letter to Chadwick. Sullivan and Chadwick probably anticipated opposition to the library transfer, which Horatio's letter to Ropes indicates did not actually exist. Levi Farr Warner apparently told Bixby "he was an ingrate and traitor" for excluding Horatio from the American Gynaecological Society.[14] He may have had a few more choice words for Bixby following this betrayal of the Gynaecological Society of Boston.

Having committed the Society's library, Horatio went to surprisingly great lengths to add to it and one can only conclude that he was still devoted to Boston and wanted to serve it through its new Medical Library. Letters from Brown-Séquard[15] and Fordyce Barker[16] to Horatio indicate that Horatio had requested both men to provide material. A letter to Dr. Toner of Washington also included requests for the Boston library, but its most interesting content was the request for 1,000 reprints of the Rocky Mountain Medical Society volume sketch of Horatio.[17] Horatio obviously liked it!

In his December letter, Levi Farr Warner had asked Horatio about the paper that Horatio published in the September 29, 1877 *London Lancet*.[18] In the paper, Horatio described the beneficial arsenical vapors and waters from the Solfatara, which was the spring at a "semi-extinct" volcanic crater at Pozzuoli near Naples. Much of the paper dealt with his very ill oldest son, Frank Addison, who was initially carried to the spring and almost immediately improved as a result of breathing the vapors, drinking the water, and other measures, unrelated to the Solfatara, taken for his health. Frank Addison was described as "extremely tall for his age, feeble and ill-nourished." Horatio's "much-improved" son then spent the winter of 1875-1876 in Naples, after which he returned to America.

For some unknown reason, Horatio's father changed his will of 1870 in December 1877 in a way unfavorable to Horatio. The fifth of the estate which was to go to Horatio at David Humphreys' death now was to be placed with his brother Francis in trust for distribution to Horatio's children when they reached twenty-one years of age. Horatio was to get $1,000. It is probably no coincidence that this change occurred only three months after Horatio's return to America. A later codicil (1883) was less unfavorable to Horatio. This left the fifth in trust to an individual outside the family, but gave the income to Horatio and, at Horatio's death, the fifth was to be divided among Horatio's children.[19] As will be seen, Horatio first learned of his differential treatment from David Humphreys' other children when his father's will was read, and he was highly disappointed.

That Horatio's course for physicians prior to his "breakdown" was valued is shown by a letter[20] he received in May from a graduate requesting a duplicate of the certificate of attendance, since his original had been lost in a fire. In addition, at least two inquiries occurred after Horatio's return related to whether he would conduct additional classes.[21] There is no evidence that he did, however.

Horatio attended the American Medical Association meeting at Buffalo in 1878 and presented a paper about "inherited" syphilis and its relationships to tuberculosis.[22] Its discussions were much further from reality than those in many of his earlier papers. The problem may have been his new dependence on other people's data. There were some unique data presented in the paper, however, which showed that the death rate from tuberculosis was substantially higher in Massachusetts than in Rhode Island. As will be seen, Horatio later presented a paper that attempted to account for this fact. An interesting admission occurred at the Buffalo meeting. It will be recalled that Horatio's initial extirpation of a uterus and its tumor had been wonderfully successful. However, the *Transactions* for 1878, reported that "Dr. H. R. Storer said that he had removed seven uteri as a *dernier resort*, with one recovery. He would deprecate a too frequent resort to the operation."[23]

Horatio wrote Dr. Toner shortly after the Association meeting in Buffalo.[24] The letter indicated Horatio had returned to the task of returning the power that had been usurped by the Massachusetts Medical Society Councillors to the Society's members. This initial effort, however, was frustrated and it appears that Horatio did not persevere in this attempt to reform the Massachusetts Society from his new Rhode Island home. This letter to Toner revealed that Dr. Henry Ingersoll Bowditch had also recently criticized the Councillors of the Massachusetts Medical Society. On the other hand, Bowditch's

"LETTER FROM BUFFALO" described the 1870 challenge of Massachusetts Medical Society delegates' credentials as a "gross insult":[25]

> Mr. Editor.—I know of nothing which seems to me more unwise than the feeling on the part of many of the junior members of the Massachusetts Medical Society, that because a gross insult was offered to the Massachusetts delegation some eight or ten years since, therefore they and all gentlemen from Massachusetts should hereafter keep aloof from every meeting of the American Association. I know very well that this feeling is still encouraged by some few influential older leaders of the profession, but I am thankful to see that their influence is waning in this matter. ...
>
> It was intimated recently at a meeting of the councilors of the Massachusetts Medical Society that it was hardly fit to amend our by-laws so as to make it incumbent on the various committees for nominations of officers to select annually delegates to the American Medical Association, because, as the opponent said, "one can't tell how long that body will continue in existence!". This recent meeting presents two cogent arguments against that absurd statement: ...

"Gross insult" is hardly a favorable representation by Bowditch of Horatio's and the Gynaecological Society of Boston's action at the 1870 meeting of the Association in Washington. On the other hand, Dr. Bowditch sounds like Horatio himself in condemning those older Massachusetts Medical Society Councillors who severely deprecated the American Medical Association. The following letter from Bowditch to Horatio a few weeks later was a response to a "note" from Horatio which probably was a protest of Bowditch's reference to Horatio's 1870 challenge of delegates' credentials as a "gross insult." Bowditch dealt with the long-term Horatio, however, and showed that Horatio's willingness to upset establishments over the years was viewed by one of Boston's most noteworthy physicians as, on balance, positive, if not, highly positive.[26]

July 17 1878

My dear Dr.

I always had a feeling of affectionate respect for you, and often argued with them who considered you *rather inclined to decisive measures*. "Wait a little. He is earnest now, perhaps, too much &c. but he sees sharply, & sometimes imperfectly, but he has a solid basis of honesty. Wait a little, treat him kindly, not roughly, and out of *that Storer blood* will come a noble man." That is what I have said even when I "felt mad" at your outbursts. I have said so behind your back & after your last note I feel I must say it to you openly.

My dear Dr I thank God in thinking of you, that it has been my good fortune to meet one or two men, later your self, who were not afraid to say "your souls are your own," and that "by the Eternal" their souls should not be hindered from bold expression of those souls' cherished opinions. The majority (Oh! what a vast majority) of men are essentially *sneaks*, *afraid to* be *improvident*, even in a noble cause. Therefore I honor those who "cry aloud & spare not" when they think they are right, and the cause of *others* is risked by their silence. But I honor also the sweet spirit shown in your last. My dear Dr., I will not say that you could not appeal in a suitable manner to the M M S members to change their position, But I will affirm that I believe 99 in 100 would still hold to the opinion that the treatment of our delegates by the A M A at Washington, as inaugurated by yourself and Sullivan, was highly indecorous, not to say insulting. ...

Well dear Dr. I finish as I began. Keep me always as one, who loves and respects you & whether you agree with me or not, I do not care a farthing. In fact I think the world would be a *humdrum place if all thought alike*.

Sincerely yours
Henry I Bowditch

PS This is my wedding day, 40! years ago! Phoebus what an old fellow I feel I am rapidly becoming.

The revived Gynaecological Society of Boston met monthly during 1878, and Horatio presented a paper, "New or Unappreciated Aids in the Treatment of Strumous Disease,"[27] at the meeting on November 7. The first "treatment aid" Horatio discussed was "residence." Horatio again presented data showing a higher rate of death from tuberculosis for those residing in Massachusetts than those residing in neighboring Rhode Island. He also identified a higher rate of tuberculosis death in Providence, Rhode Island than in nearby Newport. He cited the increased salinity of the Newport atmosphere as producing the difference and argued that it was the closeness to the sea of the Riviera and of the towns on the Isle of Wight that produced "much of the benefit of these famed local climates." He recommended the atomization of sea water in the rooms of consumptives to provide these benefits in areas away from the ocean.

Horatio then turned to "diet" and "medicine" as treatment aids. Sea food was recommended, particularly the oily fishes such as shad, alewife, and menhaden. Cod-liver oil was taken for granted as beneficial for treating tuberculosis, but Horatio recommended the liver oil of skates and sharks as equally good. He also recommended consumption of the actual livers, "cooked in a variety of ways," as a more pleasant way to take the oil. "External applications" came next. Fish oil was seen as a possibility and it smelled "no worse than many remedial agents that are constantly prescribed." Sea water, however, received the largest attention. He wrote: "Sea water is so easily procured, so close at hand to many of our profession, that we are apt to forget that it is, in reality, a 'mineral water' of exceeding value. Let the same, or very nearly the same formula be discovered in any spring existing inland, as is the case with some of the most famous health resorts in this country and Europe, and language in praise of it is exhausted by medical men."

Horatio then described the benefits of various sea plants such as kelp and rock-weed for "assisting in the treatment of strumous disease." He suggested in the following that both these sea weed preparations and cod liver oil be prepared at home: "Indeed, just as cod liver oil, of more worth than much of that in the market, may be extracted from the fresh livers by any housewife over her kitchen fire, it is probable that efficient infusions, etc., of algae, of greater value than the much vaunted 'sea-weed tonics' of empiricism, may be prepared in the same homely way." Horatio concluded with an echo of the concerns for helping people to make their living from the sea that he had voiced thirty years earlier at the Boston Society of Natural History.[28]

> In the presence of consumption and equally fatal forms of strumous disease, and indeed in many other constitutional conditions familiar to the gynaecologist and general practitioner, we cannot wonder that simples like these are so often employed by the friends of the patient, to the neglect of our own more costly prescriptions, and we do well if we ourselves try to utilize and direct them. In this belief, I have suggested to one of the Newport fishermen, Mr. James O. Swan, that he make the experiment of supplying to the profession these various sea products, in fresh and reliable condition, and at prices that will merely remunerate him for his time and labor. To do this, it is my impression, has never, as yet, been systematically attempted by any one in this country.

Sea-products also were the reason for a pair of queries to Spencer F. Baird, U.S. Commissioner of Fish and Fisheries and also Secretary of the Smithsonian Institution. Horatio first asked about methods for capturing lobsters (Baird offered only the name of a Boston expert.[29]) and later about equipment for dredging the ocean bottom, presumably for marine specimens. "A mawl with an 8 ft. beam," Baird wrote, "could easily be worked from a yacht of 10 or 15 tons."[30] One suspects Horatio already had such a yacht, and we know that he and his sons later dredged for specimens and also became somewhat of a threat to the swordfish and other sport fish in the waters around Newport.

On November 13, 1878, Horatio answered a survey by the Overseers of Harvard University and it apparently indicated a complete change of heart related to education of female physicians at Harvard and, presumably, in general. A copy with Horatio's responses reads:[31]

The Joint Committee appointed by the Corporation and Overseers of Harvard College to examine and report on the question of admitting women to the Medical School respectfully ask your opinion on the following points:-

1. Are you in favor of admitting women to the Medical School? **yes**

2. Are you in favor of admitting women on equal terms with men? **yes**

3. Are you in favor of a separate school for women? **no**

4. If in favor of medical co-education, specify the subjects which, in your opinion, can be taught in common, and those in which men and women should receive separate instruction. **All common**

Will you have the kindness to write "Yes" or "No" against 1, 2, 3, and "Common" or "Separate" against the subjects of 4, on the back of the enclosed postal card, and mail at your earliest convenience?

ALEXANDER AGASSIZ,
Chairman

Horatio presented the Annual Presidential Address of the Gynaecological Society of Boston at the meeting of January 2, 1879. It was a summary of achievements of the Society in its first decade. The published Transactions included the following summary:[32]

He reminded the Society that it had completed the first decade of its existence and recalled the unpopularity of its work and purposes at the time of its origin. He congratulated the members upon the success which had attended their efforts, and with which they had carried out the grand object of the Society's organization, viz., the recognition of gynecology as an art and science separate from obstetrics, and as a worthy, and at times essential, department of the service of the general practitioner. He recalled, in terms at once eloquent and filial, the memory and the worth of the first President, Dr. Winslow Lewis. He then proceeded to illustrate in various ways the work the Society had accomplished during the first ten years of its existence. "Ten years ago, the New England practitioners, who avowed themselves interested in the diseases of women, might almost be counted on the hand." At that time, ovariotomy was, as it were, under the ban of the profession. In Boston, in 1869, gynecology was repudiated in name and in practice by the profession, with but few exceptions; while of the small number who had the candor to admit the honesty of such as were devoted to this department of practice, but very few had the moral courage to treat their own pelvic cases. The great change which has come over the community and the profession, in sentiments held on these subjects, was then portrayed, and the direct influence of the Society traced in these important transformations.

Horatio also was reported to have discussed the history of the Society's library, "the first success[ful] effort of the kind in this country," and to have thanked the many corresponding and honorary Society members for their "valuable and prominent service in the cultivation of gynecic science and art." The summary of the address concluded: "The President closed in language calculated to remind the Society of its duties and privileges, and exhorting it to leave behind those asperities which are inseparably associated with the inception of a new and grand undertaking, urged that its members should enter with courage and confidence upon the more prosperous work of the assured present and future."

At the next meeting of the Gynaecological Society, Horatio read the paper "The New 'Protective' Principle in Public Sanitation."[33] He described the Newport Sanitary Protection Association which he had started and which had been formally established on November 11, 1878. He indicated that Newport's serious sanitary problems had led to its creation and noted such organizations "may aid in the prevention, always so much better than relief, of a great amount of uterine disease." The following paragraph from his paper gives a history of Horatio's efforts to correct Newport sanitation problems:[34]

Upon removing to Newport for residence some eighteen months ago, ... I soon became aware of sanitary defects in the city, both public and private, which seemed the more regrettable because so many of its people are delicate strangers, there temporarily, boarding or in hired houses, and in consequence wholly incapable of righting matters themselves. There was no local board of health ... A memorial to the city government was immediately prepared, asking for the appointment of a local board of health, and it was signed by every regular physician in Newport. No attention was given to it by the city council. ... There at first sight seemed no alternative save submission to such misrule. I then recalled having noticed in a foreign journal* that Fleming Jenkin, Professor of Engineering in the University of Edinburgh, had conceived the idea of a system of mutual sanitary protection, through private combination, and wholly independent of civic control. ... I soon obtained the working details, through the kindness of Prof. Grainger Stewart, and they were found to be simple and practical. Briefly they are as follows:

"1. To provide the members, at moderate cost, with such advice and supervision as shall insure the proper sanitary condition of their own dwellings.

"2. To enable members to procure practical advice, on moderate terms, as to the best means of remedying defects in houses of the poorer class in which they may be interested.

"3. To aid in improving the sanitary condition of the city."

One key feature in the above was that *every* physician in Newport was willing to cooperate with Horatio in signing the memorial to the city government. One can appreciate why Horatio did not move from Newport.

Horatio then described how his research had disclosed that death rates in Newport were generally low except for deaths from "diseases originating in filth," such as typhoid fever, which were higher in Newport than in Providence. These data were presented to Newport residents and convinced enough to join the Sanitary Protection Association to make the enterprise work. For a small membership fee, the Association provided each member with an inspection of their home and a test of their water. The Association also made inspections and reports of Newport public buildings such as schools and churches without charge. Horatio concluded his paper with a discussion of the gynecological problems associated with women's reluctance to use outhouses. This included the following quote of the Consulting Engineer of the Newport Sanitary Protection Association:[35]

> "In view of the foregoing facts I make no apology for calling attention to this important matter, believing that all will concede that, however much of elegance and comfort may surround them in the appointments of their homes, the mode of life of women is neither decent, civilized, nor safe, unless they are provided with the conveniences that the water-closet and the earth-closet alone make possible."

Any Newport house being inspected by Engineer George E. Waring, Jr., surely got demerits for an outside toilet!

The March 6, 1879 meeting of the Gynaecological Society of Boston was its 100th Regular Meeting and Horatio used the occasion to cite the names of the one Active Member, twenty-one Honorary Members, and twenty-six Corresponding Members who had died since the Society began.[36] Horatio was absent for the next two meetings, but was back for the June 5 meeting and indicated his regrets that he had not been present on May 1, 1879 when Dr. Field had discussed a pair of incidents where Field had inadvertently induced abortions by probing the uteri of women who had inflammation of the cervix.[37] Both women were convinced that they were not pregnant before the aborting incident and the condition itself was presumed to preclude impregnation. Dr. Field had asked the members their beliefs about liability in these instances for malpractice, but the published Transactions indicate only a single comment in direct answer. Horatio returned to this subject on June 5, 1879 and indicated the dangers to the physician when their justifiable acts produce abortion or even when abortion occurs for other reasons, but the abortion is blamed on the attending physician by the patient or her family. He moved that the Society form a committee "to prepare and present to the Society a report upon 'accidentally produced abortion in its medico-legal relations.'" This motion was carried, and Horatio appointed Drs. Field and Pinkham to undertake the task.[38]

Horatio submitted a paper on his Newport Sanitary Protection Association at the American Medical Association Annual Meeting in Atlanta in May 1879, although he himself did not attend.[39] The paper repeated what he had presented to the Gynaecological Society of Boston with additional quotes from the Edinburgh originator of the idea and a copy of the form used to conduct the house inspection. At the same American Medical Association meeting, Dr. E.S. Lewis of Louisiana presented an obstetric review to the Section on Obstetrics and Diseases of Women and Children. It made reference to the "operation of Porro, of Pavia, or rather that of Dr. Storer, as he was the first to perform it (in 1869), consisting in the removal of the uterus and ovaries after the Caesarean section."[40] Over the years, others would note Horatio's precedence, but Porro remained the name associated with extirpation of the pregnant uterus.

The *Providence Daily Journal* provided the following note on June 10, 1878:[41]

A CONVERT TO ROME.—There was a distinguished conversion to the Catholic Church last Sunday. Dr. Horatio R. Storer of Newport, formerly of Boston, and once Vice President of the Massachusetts Medical Society, being baptized by Rev. Thomas Clinton, C.C. Dr. Storer is well known in New York.

This incorrectly named Horatio as Vice President of the Massachusetts Medical Society instead of the American Medical Association. Hopefully, it is otherwise correct. Marriage to Frances Sophia MacKenzie undoubtedly contributed to Horatio's Catholic conversion. Previous essential ground work for this was Horatio's shift from Unitarianism to Phillips Brooks' church in the early 1870s.

The July 1879 meeting of the Gynaecological Society of Boston was presided over by Horatio and it included description by Dr. Martin of a case of a woman with "atresia ani."[42] Martin reported that she "had not had a really natural movement from her bowels for two years." He mentioned that not one of her many attending physicians had ever examined her, although the woman's condition drove her "to lay aside her usual modesty" and beg for a local examination. Following his examination and appropriate local treatment, Martin was able to cure her in two weeks.[43] Thus we see that, even in 1879, many general practitioners were failing to examine their female patients. The next (August) meeting of the Society included the report of the Committee on "accidentally produced abortion."[44] Dr. Field's portion discussed the extreme difficulty of detecting pregnancy in its early stages. Dr. Pinkham's indicated that it was unlikely that any accidentally produced abortion would be prosecuted, since there would be no intent to commit a crime. Dr. Martin, sounding like the Horatio of the earlier Society, indicated that the uterine sound should never be used if there were even a remote chance of pregnancy.

The few letters and other records for 1880 indicate Horatio was as much concerned about marine science as medical science. Spencer F. Baird, U. S. Commissioner of Fish and Fisheries, spent the summer and early fall in the Newport area and wrote Horatio to apologize for not meeting with him.[45]

> I have called twice at your house and was so unfortunate as not to find you at home. I have been so driven by the work connected with my three departments—the Smithsonian, National Nurseries and Fish Commission, that I have had very little time for visiting. I have been but four times on our steamer when she was away from the dock, and did not accompany her on a single business trip outside of Newport harbor.
> We have made many interesting discoveries especially on the border of the Gulf Stream, having discovered fifteen fishes new to science with (at present) innumerable species of invertebrates.

Despite this apology from Baird, Horatio indicated his great disappointment that his concerted attempts to contact and assist Baird during the summer had all been frustrated and that invalids "cannot always help being sensitive." He wrote Baird:[46]

> To me this was a source of extreme regret. I had looked forward to the coming of the Commission with great anticipation, & had promised myself a daily visit to its laboratory, & should gladly have put the whole time of myself, my three grown sons (who were then at home with us), & my boatman at your service as collectors, for with much of the bottom for ten miles in every direction we are now tolerably familiar.
> I called some four times at Mrs. Ive's, leaving my card each time, & twice I endeavored to see Mrs Baird as well as yourself. Three times I went to the Lead Works, the first time finding no one, the second time only a student, & the last time Messrs Vermill & Smith, who were certainly extremely cordial. ... I had then, for perhaps two minutes, my only glimpse of you for the whole summer, & as I received no invitation ... to go to the place again, I of course made no attempt to do so. You will perhaps say that this was too hasty action upon my part, hurried by many duties of many kinds as I know you to have been. Invalids, however cannot always help being sensitive, & find it difficult at times to appreciate that they have ceased to be of use. It was, as I have said, a great & permanent disappointment

to have seen nothing of the practical working of the Commission.

Horatio's obvious hurt produced a rapid apology from Baird, since only nine days after Horatio's "regret" letter Horatio sent a letter replying to Baird which included:[47]

> I had hoped that in the cause, Newport vs. Woods Holl, the fact that a station here would be visited by such a host of influential people, aside from members of Congress & foreigners, might have some weight. ... To have a permanent station here need in no way interfere with your annual flying visits to other portions of the Coast. It would however give us the pleasure of seeing yourself occasionally, & it would add very greatly to the present attractions of Newport.

However, Horatio did not succeed in his efforts to secure a Fish and Fisheries Commission facility that would help his adopted Newport and reward his own interests in marine science.

The Newport Sanitary Protection Association had twenty-six members in July 1880, a year and a half after it was formally organized. By December 1, the number had increased to forty-one, "each of them representing a dwelling-house that it is supposed is now in the best possible condition obtainable by skilled experts, ..." This information was reported in a paper written by Horatio for the New Orleans meeting of the American Public Health Association in December. It described the early progress of the Newport Sanitary Protection Association, including mention of its initial reception with "disfavor" by the people of Newport. It also included the following discussion of Newport's remaining sanitation needs:[48]

> The natural conditions of the place are favorable for health and longevity. A good many of the past generation, ... have attained here a green old age; but within a very few years Newport has doubled its population, and consequently its sources of filth. So that until there exists a proper system of sewerage (as yet there is none at all); until the soil-water is reduced at least to its natural level (as yet no provision has been made for the escape, other than through the soil, of an abundant aqueduct supply that is now in domestic use in all portions of the city); until the city has consented to have hydrants for fire and general sanitary purposes (as yet it refuses, though the aqueduct water is running under every street); until many of the old cesspools that now contaminate the wells are filled up or removed; until the real-estate agents are directed by city ordinance to furnish evidence, certified to by a competent inspector, that the houses they offer to strangers are safe to live in, and not mere death-traps like

several already examined by the inspecting engineer of the Sanitary Association; and until, over and above all, there is here a permanent board of health officials, who will care for these and other sanitary matters systematically, and not as now at haphazard,—it will be just as well for intending residents to wait a little longer, perhaps a year or two even, before purchasing an estate. The time will eventually arrive when people can, in reality, safely come here to live. To speed that time is at present one of the great objects of the Sanitary Protection Association.

In 1881, Horatio bought the historic house next door to his residence,[49] apparently with the plan to eventually make it a private gynecological hospital. Horatio had in mind a staff of himself and Malcolm. Malcolm was to study medicine and to also specialize in gynecology. However, despite numerous entreaties by Horatio and Agnes, Malcolm chose to live and practice in Boston.

One communication from Italy during 1881 indicated the plight of a former servant following a tremendous earthquake and Horatio made a substantial contribution on her behalf.[50] Another 1881 letter from Italy was a response to Horatio's query. It indicated that the grave of Augusta Caroline was in good shape, "The Tablet clean & practically surrounded by ivy & the grave covered with the periwinkle plant."[51]

Horatio's December 1880 paper to the American Public Health Association was republished in May 1881 in *The Sanitarian*. In the list of remaining Newport sanitary problems, there was now included a footnote indicating that one goal of the Association of providing fire hydrants "had been carried the affirmative, after a very bitter and protracted contest."[52] Obviously, Horatio's combative skills were not totally losing their edge by being removed from Boston. There still was no Board of Health, however, and this issue too was apparently hard fought. After it was won in 1886, Horatio wrote: "It is not five years, since two of those most active in securing the health board that is now doing so much for Newport, were deliberately and in earnest threatened by the 'Newport Mercury' with suspension from a street lamp-post; and now, another instance of the repetition of itself by history, that very journal is praising what a more enlightened public sentiment has come to perceive is for its highest good."[53] There is little doubt that Horatio, as founder of the Association, was included among the "two of those" proposed for lamp-post suspension. The other probably was George E. Waring, Jr., its Consulting Engineer.

Dr. Levi Farr Warner, Horatio's associate in practice prior to his illness, succeeded in convincing Horatio to rejoin him in practice "on Thursdays, from 12 to 4 o'clock, at their old place of business, Hotel Pelham, corner of Boylston and Tremont Streets."[54] This apparently was on a very limited basis and probably of short duration. If Horatio had returned to active practice, especially to surgery, there probably would have been publications in this period related to it, and none has been located. However, Horatio's wish to be considered one of the surgeons of America is shown by the following letter to the "king of surgeons," Dr. Samuel D. Gross.[55]

> Newport, R. I.
> 20 Sept. 1882

My dear Sir,

The card, void of all save your name, has assured me of your safe return to Phil[a], & has reminded me of what was said of the Surgical Association. I do not know your rules, or the necessary qualifications of members, & can therefore only say that when a vacancy occurs in your number, I should esteem it an honor to be considered a candidate for a place among the elect of American Surgeons, & to be permitted thus to become one of your own professional children.

The enclosed outline of much attempted & but little done, ought perhaps not to have been granted to the solicitation of our good friend Dr. Toner. ... The removal of the distended sac in umbilical hernia, to prolong a constantly threatened life, may have possibly served to establish a precedent in similar exceptional cases. Unjustifiable interference with gestation has become recognized as a potent factor in the rendering permanent certain conditions of pregnancy, & in otherwise inducing pelvic disease. Eversion of the rectum for diagnosis & treatment, by digital pressure from within the vagina, is practised now by every surgeon, & reflex, curable, insanity in women is at last acknowledged as one of the inherent "rights" of their sex.

But these are all trifles to our rex chirurgorum.

> ever sincerely yours
> Horatio R. Storer

Prof Gross.

Horatio's "outline of much attempted & but little done" was the Toner sketch with its seven pages of bibliography.[56] Despite this plea of Horatio and a promise from Gross in a letter to Horatio written four days later "to spare no pains to secure your election as a Fellow of the American Surgical Association at the meeting at Cincinnati next spring,"[57] Horatio was not among the five surgeons admitted to the Association in 1883,[58] and it is doubtful that he ever was granted membership, since he never mentioned it as being among his memberships in later years. This failure to be elected to this prestigious group may have resulted because Horatio was no longer actively engaged in surgery. However, there were members of that Association, such as Dr. Richard Manning Hodges of Boston, who might not have forgotten previous conflicts with Horatio and who prevented his election, despite Gross' support.

Most of Gross' letter referred to Horatio's "outline of much attempted &

but little done." The letter began:

> I thank you for your kind letter & the copy of Dr. Toner's sketch,
> which has interested me very much. I am amazed at the extent of the
> catalogue of your literary productions. It is far greater than I could
> possibly have supposed; it displays great mental activity, & a desire
> to be useful. I believe you are a just man, just to every body, except
> to yourself. I make this remark in order to declare to you my
> conviction that you owe it to yourself & to the profession to publish
> your papers in a collected form. Scattered as they now are they are
> of no use or value to any one. There are enough gynecologists alone
> in the country to absorb a reasonable edition, & there are many other
> members of the profession who would hasten to secure the work. I
> pray you to give this matter your serious consideration.

Unfortunately, Horatio never acted on Gross' suggestion.

Horatio would certainly have been described as a "workaholic" had that
term existed during his lifetime. The following delightful effort of Horatio to
communicate a strong work ethic to his daughter occurred when Agnes was
eight:[59]

Christmas Eve—

1882

My dear daughter,
> There is an old saying that
> "All work and no play,
> > "would make John a dull boy,
> > > "and
> "All play and no work
> > "would make John a mere toy".

Now what is true of John, or Jack, as they called him, is just as
true of his Sister Agnes. The best way for all is to work part of the
time, and then to play for a while, or rest, which is play for old
people like your papa and mama—and then, after resting or playing
for a while, to work again. Knowing this, I hope you will have a
great many happy hours while *playing* upon your piano, and then for
that change that I have said was necessary for us all, I hope you will
have a great many more and just as happy hours with the *work*
basket. I shall now be able to take you all my buttons, & my
stockings, so that dear mama may find a little play, in rest—
> > With love
> > > your father.

On November 14, 1882 Horatio presented the paper "Newport, R.I., as a Winter Resort for Consumptives"[60] before the Newport Sanitary Protection Association. It began with a large number of statistics showing the remarkably low rate of tuberculosis in Newport compared to the rest of the country, including other parts of Rhode Island. Horatio again cited the salinity of the air as one reason. He also mentioned the small changes in temperature from season to season as another. With improved drainage to eliminate the damp soil (the expert, Henry Ingersoll Bowditch, viewed this as a major cause of tuberculosis) the city of Newport would "eventually" become an even better place for avoiding tuberculosis and for treating consumptive patients.

Dr. J. Hilgard Tyndale of New York took issue with Horatio's claims in a letter to the *Boston Medical and Surgical Journal*.[61] Tyndale's point was: "The concurrence of excessive moisture, sudden fluctuations of the thermometer, and high winds favor the development of" "acute inflammations of the lungs." Thus, despite the data of Horatio showing Newport's low rate of death from tuberculosis, Tyndale argued that Newport was *not* a good "winter resort for consumptives." In support of his claim, Tyndale cited high rates of death "from pneumonia and congestion of lungs" for Newport. Tyndale also voiced his suspicions that it was the high economic status of Newport residents that contributed to the low tuberculosis rate.

Horatio may have been delighted to have a new adversary. He quickly fashioned a reply and sent it to the *Boston Medical and Surgical Journal*.[62] Although Horatio had not discussed pneumonia in his original paper, he provided more precise statistics than Tyndale did, showing that when considered relative to population, pneumonia fatalities in Newport were unusually *low*. As to Tyndale's suggestion that the low death rate was related to the well-heeled residents of Newport, Horatio noted that half of Newport's population were European immigrants, primarily laborers, and of the "Americans," "a great many were very poor,—sailors, fishermen, and the like." Horatio also took the opportunity to provide statistics showing that Newport tuberculosis deaths were substantially lower than in the rest of Rhode Island and that Rhode Island deaths from the disease were only three-fourths those of Massachusetts.

Tyndale returned for another round, claiming "that the ideal climate for vulnerable individuals, of whom consumptive candidates form a large contingent, is to be found where these three elements of elevation, dryness, and equability are combined as is the case in some parts of the Andes, in South America."[63] He claimed Newport was not a suitable place for consumptives because it "has no equability of temperature, no elevation, no dryness." Tyndale concluded by presenting statistics showing Rhode Island having no lower rate of death from consumption than New York or Connecticut. Horatio responded with a letter published on April 26.[64] Horatio pointed out, as he had originally, that for Tyndale, Newport's climate "was not suitable for the special end that he had in view, namely, the making the facts which exist conform to his theory." Horatio also identified errors in Tyndale's quotes of Henry

Ingersoll Bowditch, and provided statistics showing that Newport had a substantially lower rate of death from tuberculosis than Rhode Island, New York, or Connecticut. Horatio also noted that Newport might not be the ideal place for consumptives, but it was much more assessable for people of moderate means than the Andes.

We have already mentioned that Horatio was involved with arrangements for a Newport meeting of the Insane Asylum Superintendents in 1883. This was the 37th Annual Session of the Association of Medical Superintendents of American Institutions for the Insane (now the American Psychiatric Association) and it was held from June 26 to June 29.[65] When the meeting commenced, the members invited Horatio and others, including "the Medical Press now at Newport," "to take seats with the Association." At the meeting, Horatio spoke extensively in response to a report by Dr. W.B. Goldsmith of "A Case of Moral Insanity,"[66] Goldsmith's patient's problems were temper tantrums often associated with menstruation and they reminded Horatio of a "case" of his own which undoubtedly was Emily Elvira. Horatio's comments are a unique discussion of his first wife and of several other features of the most personally troubled period of his life. With a few exceptions, Horatio's comments are provided as they were recorded in the Proceedings of the Association.[67]

> I would say that I was intensely interested in the case referred to by Dr. Goldsmith; and I would further say that some of the gentlemen may remember a certain case that, years ago, I had some experience with, since they were consulted by me concerning it. In regard to the treatment of this great class of cases, (of which the one in question was a somewhat unusual representative,) there is often difficulty. I know that in the case I was then attending, I became even more interested at the time than before in the possible causation of the mental diseases of sick women. Very many cases, more or less similar in character, in my professional career, have come into my hands. ... I soon came to take the ground that while the brain certainly was the seat of the derangement in insane women, it was not always the seat of the cause.
>
> But to return: Professor Mayer, of Berlin, came to recognize the interdependence of pelvic irritation and cerebral symptoms in women, and as soon as his views were published in this country, my own ceased to be thought irrational or extravagant. Thus was the way paved for some of the successes of the present day. For example, there was the case to which I have referred, for which I failed to afford any relief and I could obtain none from others. The question came up, whether the removing of the ovaries was justifiable, for the purpose of anticipating the climacteric. I argued that if there were peripheral and pelvic irritation, though apparently of only a functional

character, its removal might possibly allay cerebral and central derangement. The question was submitted to a jury of our wisest men in Boston, who in their several departments stood pre-eminent—Professors Brown-Sequard [sic] and Bowditch, Dr. John E. Tyler and my own father. They were each personal friends of the patient as well as deeply interested in her case. My father said, "Has this operation ever been performed for this special indication?" "Well," I replied, "there are apparently as yet no cases on record where it has been performed for this purpose." Brown-Sequard declared that "all experiments were justified to restore reason, just as to save life, in default of more accredited procedure." Dr. Bowditch sympathized with this view. Dr. Tyler said no man could wish a cure more than he did, but the patient had not as yet been in an asylum, and the operation should not be attempted until this treatment had been tried. The result was that the operation was not performed, and the patient subsequently died, her malady unrelieved. Two or three years later, a letter came to me from Dr. Battey, of Georgia. He was just going to operate for the first time, and he kindly wrote me, consulting me considering the general question, which was entirely his own, as my case had not been published. That letter did not reach me until many months afterwards; I was seriously ill at the time, my life despaired of, with septicaemia. I did not see it until, like Minerva from the brain of Jove, his operation had startled the world, and he had acquired the reputation which was justly his due. ... The removal of the ovaries to quiet a mental affection is always an experiment, just as the occurrence of the climacteric is so far but an experiment, though a physiological one. ... No surgeon would be very apt to advise a medical superintendent of an asylum to incur such a responsibility without careful consideration. On another hand, if the result were to prove absolutely negative as regards the mental symptoms, such a result would be no more than often occurs from other methods of treatment; and finally, if death ensued, the poor patient would be removed from further suffering, especially that most terrible of all mental experiences, that of knowing during her lucid intervals, if such occurred, that her case was undoubtedly hopeless, and that it was to life-long insanity that she was doomed.

Emily Elvira no doubt had experienced the above "most terrible of all mental experiences" and Horatio also must have been devastated during *both* her "lucid intervals" and her non-lucid ones.

Dr. Robert Battey first performed his operation to remove normal ovaries on August 27, 1872, "curing" a 30-year-old invalid. Battey reported to his biographer, that "a band of men, among them prominent physicians of his vicinity, awaited the results of this first case, intending in case of the patient's death, to have him arrested and prosecuted for murder."[68] "Battey's Operation," as it came to be known, was performed by Battey over 300 times, but is now viewed as both unnecessary and inappropriate. Given Horatio's view on the suitability of the operation in 1883, he probably would have performed "Battey's Operation" had he not become an invalid and withdrawn from surgery.

At the end of their meeting, the Superintendents adopted the following Resolution, among others:[69]

> *Resolved*, That the Association particularly esteems the cordial and appreciative manner in which our distinguished professional brother, Dr. Horatio R. Storer, President of the Newport Medical Society, greeted its members at the opening session of this meeting, and assisted by Drs. S. W. Francis, W. L. Wheeler, L. H. Rankin, W. C. Rives and C. L. Fisher of the same society, continued to lay and carry into effect plans to take them to see the beautiful harbor and its military defences, the most interesting public institutions and some of the princely private residences of the town.

Five years later when the American Medical Association was considering holding its annual meeting at Newport, Horatio wrote to his friend Dr. Toner: "two or three years ago I made great efforts toward proper entertainment of the Assoc[n] of Superintendents of Am. Insane Asylums when holding their annual session here, & though feebly seconded & the alienists expressing themselves as grateful, it was altogether too much of an undertaking for a partial invalid to attempt again."[70]

We learn that Horatio was proposing a new Catholic parish for Newport from a letter from Monsignor Cleary of Providence in July, 1883.[71] Cleary indicated that no priest was available for such a parish. Horatio would eventually succeed in the formation of Newport's St. Joseph's, but continuing efforts to get Spencer Baird to bring a Fish and Fisheries Commission facility to Newport were not successful.

Horatio read a paper, "The Mild Winter Climate of Newport, R.I., As the Effect of the Gulf Stream," before the Newport Medical Society on November 6, 1883.[72] and it was published in *The Medical Record*. Horatio claimed that Newport marked a boundary, north of which was cold water with arctic flora and fauna, and south of which was the Gulf Stream with southern sea plants and fish. This Gulf Stream produced a mild climate in winter that made Newport attractive to those invalids not wishing to travel a long distance from their New England homes. The following paragraph describes Horatio's initial choice of Newport as a residence and his "retirement":

> That the writer sought Newport as an invalid six years ago, and solely for its winter climate; that he has remained there, partially convalescent, but in far better health than theoretically he could ever

have hoped to regain, and that he is no longer in active practice, may possibly render his opinion, as to the advantages of the place as a winter health resort, of the more weight with the profession.

The lower western shore of the city of Newport was and is known as the "Point," and this was the location of Horatio's "Moss Bank Cottage." In his article, Horatio recommended the "Point" as the quarter of the city that was best suited for a winter residence. Horatio's own survival to the oldest living Harvard graduate was to add an additional datum in support of this recommendation made nearly 40 years prior to his death. Horatio also reported progress in Newport sanitation in this paper. A sewer system would soon be completed and there now was "conformity by hotels, boarding-houses, and dwellings for lease, to the requirements of modern hygiene."

A letter written in 1884 by Richard Manning Hodges to Horatio's father indicates that David Humphreys Storer was working hard to get Dr. Henry J. Bigelow elected President of the Massachusetts Medical Society.[73] It thus would seem that there was a basic difference between Horatio and his father in their attitudes toward Henry J. Bigelow. On the other hand, there is reason to believe that Horatio's attitude may have changed since the days of the *Journal of the Gynaecological Society of Boston*. Henry J. Bigelow had recently operated successfully on David Humphreys Storer for vesical calculus.[74] Prior to the surgery, David Humphreys had been confined to his home for "nearly nine months" and had suffered greatly with his condition considered critical. The relief provided by Bigelow, perhaps even the saving of David Humphreys Storer's life, no doubt was a great reducer of anger and producer of gratitude in both Storer senior and junior. Hodge's letter included:[75]

> From all I can learn I think there is little doubt but that Dr. Bigelow will be nominated for the next presidency of the Mass. Med. Soc. ... I hope nothing will be said to him about his election, lest he might take some measure to prevent it. I have never alluded to the subject in any conversation with Dr. Bigelow, and have no knowledge what his feelings would be in case he were nominated; but as you have expressed so much interest in the subject I write this note to let you know I have not been unmindful of your request that I should move in the matter.

Dr. Charles D. Homans succeeded Dr. Alfred Hosmer as President of the Massachusetts Medical Society in 1884 and remained in that position until 1886, so these efforts of Hodges and David Humphreys Storer on behalf of Henry J. Bigelow, like Horatio's to get a Fish and Fisheries Commission station for Newport, came to naught.

CHAPTER 19

HISTORIAN, MEDICAL MEDALS, THE NEWPORT AMA MEETING

Horatio had published papers on the history of gynecology in the *Journal of the Gynaecological Society of Boston* and the last decades of Horatio's life would be largely devoted to medical history as it was illustrated by medals struck to commemorate medical pioneers and medical events. Given this interest, it is not surprising that Horatio became a member and officer of the Newport Historical Society. In November 1884, he made a speech before this Society at the opening of its new quarters in a renovated old Seventh Day Baptist Society Church.[1] His first theme was the important, but generally unappreciated role of the historian, and this included some unique observations on the varying perspectives on history and historians of youth, middle age, and old age. He began by noting how the young and most "grown people also" could not understand the efforts of the historian.[2]

Such are the mass of mankind. The very exceptions, you who are present at this moment, but prove the rule. For every single student of the past there are a thousand persons who are careless of history and its most useful lessons, who throw down an old book or print or manuscript or medal after a moment's glance, as the average man and woman turn with disdain from the sands of the seashore, the grasses of the field, the snowflake, the bee improving its hour, in all of which there are to those whose eyes have been opened so that they can really see what is ever before them, not merely constant material for ever increasing admiration and wonder, but the everywhere present evidence of the power and wisdom and beneficence of Almighty God.

The very fact therefore of a person's interest in the history of the past proves that his tastes are exceptional, and upon a higher than the general plane. ... Doubtless he may be thought peculiar, possibly a trifle weak in intellect, and he may receive politely concealed commiseration should he touch upon any topic connected with his studies, among his friends. And yet he is all the time conferring upon them most gentle and precious service. ... He bestows upon their prosaic selves and environments, a somewhat that does not of right belong to them,—a fragrance as of spice and perfume that has been laid away with the past, the echo of AEolian or distant music, a sense of lofty achievements and endeavor, still possible in the present because accomplished in the past, and not by fabulous heroes or demigods, but by men like themselves. If such is the effect that a single historical student can produce, upon individuals and upon communities, that of a society like our own is infinitely greater. Not only are doubtful questions in history thus and here elucidated, with greater certainty and ease, by the application to them of diverse minds in concert, ... but the very town where such an institution exists receives thereby a higher reputation among scholars and thoughtful people, an estimate which wealth, powerful as it is, can never purchase.

Another theme of Horatio's speech was the sordid history of Newport which included the nation's first slave markets; the importation of sugar cane juice and its conversion to rum by twenty distilleries; and, worst of all, pirates controlled by prosperous Newport ship owners, who preyed on both friend and foe on the high seas. However, these sins of the past had been ameliorated somewhat by later events. Horatio wrote:[3]

Responsible as was Newport for the introduction into America of negro servitude, with all its disastrous influences and results, ... it was here and at a time when it required the highest moral courage, that the first warning voice, by the Rev. Dr. Samuel Hopkins, was raised against it. Identified as was Newport with the first distillation of ardent spirits in America, that one of our home industries subsequently and still most sedulously protected by Congress, destructive though it be of every other occupation, whether of farmer, mariner, professional man, educator or artizan, it is but right and proper that in Newport, of all places in the country, a determined and general stand should at last be made, as now seems probable in the very near future, against this giant evil of our time.*

Horatio offered the hope that historians using data on the past sins of the city might help current Newport residents improve their behavior and help our children to avoid "the retribution that will [otherwise] surely be visited upon them for our own sins." He then listed "our own sins":

For the African slavery of early Newport, we now have servitude to one or the other of two parties, and to the traffic [alcoholic beverages] which is acknowledged to control them both. For piracy upon the high seas, we now have defalcations and perversion of public trust throughout the national domain. For the expulsion of the loyalists, we now have the abstinence of our best citizens, to a marked degree, from active participation in public affairs, save, and then half bewildered, at the quadrennial spasm of the Presidential election,—and their almost universal refusal to accept, or become candidate for, any office within the gift of the people. An aristocracy, it is said, means from its derivation a government by the best. God help us all, if much longer we are to be ruled in our ideal democracy by those who in the light of their own and all past history, so often prove, when great moral issues are at stake, the very worst.

Horatio's involvement in the history of Newport is also shown by a long paper he wrote on Dr. John Clarke, a key early settler who, like Horatio, was a physician from Boston and persecuted in that city before becoming a valued Newport resident. The paper, "The Life of Dr John Clarke, Founder of Newport & of the Civil Polity of Rhode Island," was apparently presented to the Newport Medical Society and a later longer version was presented to the Newport Historical Society. The major thrusts were the large sacrifices that Clarke made for the sake of Newport and Rhode Island and that Clarke, not Roger Williams, was responsible for the unique clause included in the 1663 Charter of Rhode Island which guaranteed religious freedom to the citizens. No published version of Horatio's Clarke history has been located.[4] Horatio no doubt planned to publish the paper since it is extensively footnoted and Horatio described it as the most complete history of Clarke that had ever been written. However, Horatio's message that Clarke's achievements overshadowed Williams' may not have been well received by the many prominent Rhode Island citizens who were descendants of Roger Williams. Clarke's only daughter died at 11 and Clarke had no descendant allies to counter them. It may be that Horatio's Clarke history was not welcome in the Newport Historical Society *Proceedings* where it logically should have appeared. Horatio and the Newport *Medical* Society were responsible for a two-foot by four-foot marble plaque in tribute to Dr. Clarke at the Newport Historical Society. It is still on the wall of the old converted church, and reads:

TO
JOHN CLARKE, PHYSICIAN
1609.—1676.
FOUNDER OF NEWPORT,
AND OF THE CIVIL POLITY OF RHODE ISLAND
ERECTED BY THE NEWPORT MEDICAL SOCIETY.
DEC. 1885.

Horatio's long-time friend, Dr. John P. Reynolds, provided the following confirmation of Bowditch's 1878 point that Horatio's earlier Boston behavior was highly regarded by some Boston physicians. Reynolds may have been the first to speculate about what Horatio might have achieved in Boston.[5]

Nahant, Mass:
12th September, 1885.

Dear doctor Horatio,

I was very glad to get your friendly note. We cherish in Boston the memory of your earlier, and your later, achievements. I often think how different an obstetrical life Boston might have had, if we could have kept here your hardihood, energy and courage. I am delighted that any words of mine have attracted your notice, and have given me the pleasure of a letter from you. ...

With sincere regard
John P. Reynolds

In December 1880, Horatio had withheld a full-blown advocacy of Newport as a health resort until certain sanitation problems were corrected. In the Fall of 1885 he decided it was time to make this leap and did so in the article, "A Sea Change." Horatio first made reference to his 1880 concerns and then gave this progress report:[6]

Newport has now an efficient Board of Health, three members of which are physicians. It has adopted a general plan of sewerage, the main features of which are being rapidly carried out. In proportion as this is done, the level of the ground-water is being lowered and damp cellars made dry. Public hydrants are everywhere. The cesspools and privy-vaults are disappearing. One of the leading real estate firms refuses to lease houses of the better class unless possessing the certificate of the Sanitary Protection Association; and most recent of all, a mayor and city government have just been elected who are in sympathy with the advances insisted upon by the Association named and by the Newport Medical Society.

Horatio's concluding paragraphs stated the benefits of Newport for "medical and surgical, even 'hopeless' cases" and also indicate a new partner in medical practice and, like John L. Sullivan fifteen years earlier, one whom he was soon to regret:

The conditions at Newport may be thus briefly stated. Its climate is distinctly insular, to a great extent oceanic, being materially affected by the Gulf Stream, and milder than that of the coast-line, even where this is but a very few miles distant. The seasons are markedly prolonged into each other. The atmosphere, though moist, is distinctly saline. Rheumatism and the various nervous hyperasthenias are rare as originating, and when brought are almost always relieved. Pneumonia, and even phthisis, save as here for treatment, are exceptional. The winters are comparatively mild, and though snow and ice are of course present for portions of each winter, it is to a much less extent and for a shorter period than upon the mainland. There are many patients who could be made comfortable here during winter who are now carried South, to their own inconvenience and that of their friends, or remain at home in much less favorable local climates.

I can only add that, should chronic cases of any kind, or convalescents, be confided to my charge, I will endeavor to carry out the wishes of the medical men to whom I may owe them. To accomplish this the more satisfactorily, I have associated with myself in practice Dr. W. Thornton Parker (Munich), late Acting Assistant-Surgeon, U.S.A[rmy]., and together we shall do what we can to make Newport generally recognized, aside from all its social attractions, as a valuable therapeutic aid to the American medical profession.

The following letter was sent by Horatio to Robert Treat Paine, the future father-in-law of John Humphreys Storer. John was now twenty-six years old and engaged to Edith Paine, whom he would marry on November 18, 1885. Paine was a great-grandson of the Declaration of Independence signer of the same name. He was already famous for his philanthropic efforts in Boston and also for the contributions which made the new Trinity Church "not a little thing in a side street which one must hunt to find," as Paine's Latin School and Harvard classmate, Rev. Phillips Brooks, was to later note.[7]

> Newport, R. I.
> 9 Nov. 1885

My dear Sir,

The receipt of the formal invitation today reminds me that ever since our young people found in each other their ideals, I have been wishing to make your personal acquaintance. That I have not more actively attempted it has resulted in part from persistence of semi-invalidism, & of late from resumption of the active practice of my profession, extremely fatiguing to one who had been a long time at rest, & who is possibly several years your senior. I shall hope that the interest, & now the affection, that we each have felt for a child of the other, may hereafter ripen into mutual respect & esteem.

With kindest remembrance to Mrs. Paine.

> Sincerely yours
> Horatio R. Storer

Mr. Robt. Treat Paine.

The following letter to Dr. Toner is typical of almost all of the correspondence to and from Horatio for 1886, in centering on Horatio's collection of medals and coins which were related to medicine. Horatio's interest in coins came from David Humphreys Storer, and the letter shows that Horatio, in turn, communicated this interest in numismatics to both John Humphreys and Malcolm.[8]

Newport, R.I.
5 April, 1886

Dear Dr Toner,

I enclose further slips relating to Dr. Francis; the longer one by his brother, Val. Mott F.

You may also be interested in the progress of Church matters here. Our new parish is only a year old, but already firmly founded.
...

If I can ask you to take so much trouble, I wish you would have copied for me, of course at my expense, the cards of Dr Lee's catalogue & of any other medical medals of the Surg. Gen. Cabinet. ... I believe fully in centralization, as regards making Government collections, of whatever kind the best in the country, & I only wish that this principle could be practically applied to the coin cabinet at the U.S. Mint, which does not possess a single copy of a very great many of even its own issues. There is nothing I would like better, were it possible, than that my son, a young lawyer in Boston, who is Curator of the Coins & Medals of Harvard University, or I myself who hold the same office for the Newport Historical Society, might obtain some non-salaried connection with the Mint Cabinet. ... I have another son, a student at present in the Harvard Medical School, who is also an expert numismatist, & whom I think you will some day know as as staunch in his loyalty to the Am. Med. Association as his father & grandfather before him.

Sincerely yours
Horatio R. Storer

Collecting medical medals no doubt was particularly appealing to Horatio because it combined his long-time interests in numismatics and medical history. Although in 1886 Horatio had been collecting medical medals "for several years," completing this collection appears to have become one of his major goals, given that several letters related to medical medals have been preserved for the year 1886, scores thereafter, but none related to the topic have been located for earlier periods. The first paper that Horatio published in this area of medical medals was titled "The Medals, Jetons and Tokens Illustrative of Midwifery and the Diseases of Women." It appeared in two installments in the *New England Medical Monthly* for November and December 1886.[9] Although the list and descriptions of these medals, jetons, and tokens is of small interest

to anyone outside the numismatic ranks, the following initial paragraphs are
instructive as to Horatio's goals and efforts in medical numismatics:

> It is my wish to direct the attention of practitioners, ... to a fas-
> cinating study, as yet very unusual in this country, that of the history
> of medicine as illustrated by numismatics. For several years it has
> served to occupy my own spare time. ... Nothing, to my knowledge,
> as yet exists, however brief, upon modern medical numismatics in the
> English language. From whatever direction approached, the subject
> will be found full of interest. In the present communication I shall
> describe only the medals and tokens relative to obstetrics and gynae-
> cology, so far as I have been able to discover them.

Horatio also maintained his interest in natural history. He was the prime
mover of the Newport Natural History Society, was Corresponding Secretary of
the group in the 1880s and President in the 1890s.[10] Certainly a sad event for
Horatio in 1886 was the death of his Boston Society of Natural History colleague and Labrador companion, Captain Nathaniel E. Atwood, which occurred
in Provincetown on November 7. This self-educated fisherman, delivered a
series of the prestigious Lowell lectures on the topic "food fishes."[11] The
remarkable Atwood also served in the Massachusetts senate, where he was
Chairman of the Committee on Fishes.[12]

Horatio's disappointment in being excluded in 1876 from the American
Gynecological Society and in 1882 from the American Surgical Association may
have been partially ameliorated by his 1886 appointment as one of the Vice
Presidents of the Gynecology Section of the 9th International Medical Congress.
The Congress would meet in September 1887 in Washington, D.C.[13] The
President of the Section on Gynecology was Horatio's long-time advocate, Dr.
Henry Orlando Marcy. Other U.S. Vice Presidents of the Section were Nathan
Bozeman, of New York City, Gilman Kimball of Lowell, Massachusetts, and
T. Gaillard Thomas of New York City.[14]

Another feather in Horatio's cap was being chosen President of the Rocky
Mountain Medical Association. In one of his rare appearances outside Rhode
Island, Horatio delivered his Presidential Address before the Society in Chicago
on June 5, 1887. It was titled "The Importance and Eradication of Syphilis."[15]
Despite the title, the paper was largely a history of the 1871 California experience and statement of the regrettable fact that the survivors who made the
trip over the Rocky Mountains were so quickly diminishing. The small medical
portion of the paper was largely a repetition of his 1878 paper on strumous
disease and syphilis. Horatio urged strong measures to eradicate syphilis. He
argued that a key benefit of this would be to reduce the incidence of the major
killer, tuberculosis.

In his Presidential Address, Horatio also mentioned his goal of preparing
a comprehensive treatise on the "Medallic History of Medicine." However, the

first series of papers which he published were on medals associated with the tangential area of sanitation with the first installment appearing in 1887 in the *Sanitarian*.[16] This was followed by another twenty-eight installments in the same journal over the next seven years. Horatio began publication of his main series, "The Medals, Jetons, and Tokens Illustrative of the Science of Medicine," early in 1889 in the *American Journal of Numismatics*.[17] Installments were to continue in that journal regularly until January 1913!

The brief period of *active* medical practice in 1885 and 1886, apparently Horatio's only active practice after his 1872 illness, is documented by a paper "presented" by Horatio's new partner to the Gynaecological Society of Boston on November 9, 1886. The Proceedings recorded that[18]

> In the absence of Dr. Thornton Parker, his paper, entitled THE REMOVAL OF A LARGE VAGINAL TUMOR, was read by the Secretary.
>
> This case occurred in the practice of Dr. H. R. Storer, of Newport, R. I. Patient 35 years old; twice married, and has had one child at a normal labor. Health good until four years ago, when she became seriously menorrhagic. When medical aid was sought it was found that the vagina was entirely filled with a mass resembling in shape a pear with its base upwards. ... An operation was decided on and an écraseur applied, but the chain broke. The operation was abandoned for the time and no unfavorable symptoms followed. Several days later removal was again attempted and was successful. There was virtually no hemorrhage. After the tumor was severed it could be rotated in the vagina but could not be removed in the ordinary way because of its size. Strong, straight hooked forceps in the grasp of a strong man failed to deliver the tumor. It was determined to produce expulsion by pressure superiorly and from within, in imitation of the powers of nature during labor. The sphincter ani having been forcibly dilated, Dr. Storer introduced his forearm into the rectum so far that the fingers entered the sigmoid flexure. The expulsive force thus applied, assisted by the vectis and forceps, was sufficient to deliver the tumor precisely as if it were a foetal head. The vagina was then plugged. The case recovered without a single unfavorable symptom.

Considerable discussion followed reading of the paper. Horatio's method of forcing out the tumor was criticized by Dr. W. Symington Brown as a "barbarous and unnecessary practice," since the tumor could have been cut up into pieces and removed. On the other hand, a Dr. Marsh indicated that he had introduced his arm into the rectum without producing injury.

Another paper presented to the Gynaecological Society of Boston, "The Ethics of Abortion, as a Method of Treatment in Legitimate Practice," probably caused mixed emotions in Horatio when he later read it, despite the author's well-articulated general condemnation of induced abortion.[19] The paper was by Dr. J.E. Kelly who had recently arrived in Boston from Ireland via New York. Kelly failed to mention Horatio's abortion-related efforts, but this may have reflected ignorance associated with his previous Ireland residence. One key sentence of Kelly's anti-abortion paper reads:[20]

> The prevalence of abortion as an established procedure in modern medicine, *the freedom with which it is practised and the enthusiasm with which it is advocated by gentlemen of great professional influence in this city,* some of whom I heard in public indignantly denounce other individuals, medical, lay, and clerical, because they conscientiously refused to assist or sanction the destruction of the embryo, are the circumstances which convince me that no existing enactment, either human or divine, can prevent many physicians from practising abortion in good faith, and consequently that some "new laws" are needed which shall tend to limit its application to the minimum, and to alleviate, in the juridical sense at least, the repugnant act of abortion into "justifiable foeticide."

No names of these influential Boston physicians who enthusiastically advocated abortion were given, but Dr. W. Symington Brown, the critic of Horatio's anal expulsion of the vaginal tumor, was reported in the published discussion of the paper to oppose Kelly's view that physicians had no right to take fetal life and Brown may have been in the camp of those physicians Kelly had cited as advocating abortion.

It is possible that hatred of Horatio produced advocacy of abortion by some of Horatio's Boston enemies. The opposition in Boston to gynecology (shown by the lag in its adequate teaching at the Harvard Medical School) and to the American Medical Association for decades following Horatio's departure from that city, both appear to have been largely anti-Horatio-Storer based. The "enthusiasm with which it [abortion] is advocated by gentlemen of great professional influence in this city," may have been another such reaction to Horatio, this time to something Horatio opposed rather than advocated.

During the discussion of Kelly's paper, Dr. A.P. Clarke stated "that criminal abortions are less frequent than formerly."[21] The physicians' crusade against abortion which Horatio started nearly thirty years earlier, may have been having the desired effect in Boston (as well as elsewhere), despite some influential physicians who were abortion advocates.

Although a Vice President of the International Medical Congress which commenced in Washington on September 5, 1887, Horatio was too ill to attend. He was, however, listed as having been in attendance in the *Transactions*, and Horatio subsequently wrote to Dr. Toner and chided him for this incorrect addition:[22]

> I notice that the worthy registrar entered upon the list a certain Dr.
> Storer of Newport, of whom I have heard. It was not my father,
> David Humphreys of Boston, nor myself, Horatio Robinson, nor my
> son Dr. Malcolm S., now an intern at the Mass. Gen. Hospital.
> However, with such an army to look after, the health of some of
> whom did not permit their personal registry at Washington, it is only
> a wonder that you did everything so well.

In his Presidential Address for the Section on Gynecology at the International Medical Congress, Dr. Henry Orlando Marcy paid special tribute to the late J. Marion Sims:[23]

> It seems so invidious, in this relation, to mention the name of Marion
> Sims, honored by the world, but doubly dear to America, with both
> pride and sorrow. With pride, since he conferred upon our country
> the great honor of being recognized as the birthplace of Gynaecology.
> With sorrow, since, in the fullness of a ripe manhood, he was all too
> soon taken from us, when we might have hoped his noble presence
> and eloquent speech would have welcomed you here, rather than poor
> words of mine. May the memory of his genial presence abide with
> us, and the earnest spirit in which he sought to know the truth preside
> over our councils.

One cannot help but think that Horatio also deserved "birthplace of Gynaecology" recognition for having started the first society and journal devoted to gynecology. On the other hand, we have heard Horatio's own high praise of Sims and Horatio no doubt was not displeased with Marcy for claiming Sims' advance in vesicovaginal fistula surgery (or his founding of the Bellevue women's hospital) as the evidence of gynecology's birth. Actually, an early death such as Sims' may do wonders for a reputation. Had Horatio not outlived most of his fans, he no doubt would have been given many more honors for his pioneering role in the development of gynecology.

A letter from Horatio to Dr. Toner on March 23, 1888[24] gives us the first indication that Newport was being considered as the site for the annual meeting of the American Medical Association in 1889 and that Horatio was the person being considered to head the Committee of Arrangements. The following paragraph discusses Horatio's now former partner, Dr. W. Thornton Parker, who was the "local Secretary" for the American Medical Association meeting: "My great anxiety in the matter I have already confided to you. The local Secretary has been appointed independently of any suggestions from myself. He is not upon speaking terms with one or more of those upon whose assistance I must mainly depend & I foresee for the year to come a task in comparison with which to try to combine oil & water without an emulsifying agent, would be but a trifle." In the same letter Horatio inquired: "Kindly inform me as to what is expected of the Committee of Arrangements other than engaging halls, attempting to reduce local RR fares, obtaining hotel accommodations, acting as missionaries upon the State Society, & upon strictly local sources of hospitality. Please also define the duties of the Secretary & to what extent he is independent of, or subject to, the aforesaid Committee."

Three additional letters to Toner[25] respectively describe a Horatio who will probably be away when the Association meets in Newport, one who wants to be kept wholly in the background as far as hosting the meeting, and one who accepts the reins of Chairman of the Committee of Arrangements. They also provide unique information on Horatio's experiences with the Newport Medical Society:[26]

> I myself though one of the founders of the local Society, resigned from it a couple of years ago, & it now consists of but four or five members. As a Society it was then out of sympathy with the Am. Med. Assoc. regarding the Internat. Med. Congress. I expressed my views very plainly, & when as Chairman of a Committee to prepare resolutions of regret at the death of a member (Samuel W. Francis) I had ended them with "May he rest in peace!", it was decided to expunge this sentence, I withdrew my name from the list.

Choice bits about Dr. Parker included:[27]

> As to the local Secretary. My own terms with the gentleman are still, as they have been, harmonious, but only through the exertion of constant self control. He was with me for a couple of years, till I became tired of the necessarily unremitting efforts to keep out of the hot water he himself was daily in. Do my best, however, I was more than once scalded & still tingle with the recollections. The difficulties I had anticipated upon his account have already commenced.

> His temperament is the one that insists that if a person is not absolutely *with* him, he must be as absolutely *against* him. This morning he asked me whether in case he did resign, I should not appoint X or Y, with whom he is still at variance, in his stead, both of these being persons whom I should not think of for a moment. I mention this matter only to show that my forebodings were not without foundation.

The Nominating Committee formed at the American Medical Association meeting in Cincinnati in 1888 "selected" Newport for the next Annual Meeting and "nominated" Horatio as Chairman of the Committee of Arrangements.[28]

Horatio's earlier letters to Toner show that both decisions were made months earlier, and it is obvious that key decisions in the Association were made by a few figures like Toner and Dr. Nathan Davis and were then rubber-stamped by the Nominating Committee.

Horatio's magnanimity toward his former Boston persecutors and his concern for the American Medical Association are shown by this paragraph from a June 28 letter to Toner:[29]

> I shall be greatly favored if you will send me a list of gentlemen in the NE states other than R. I. who would be most likely to assist ... There are of course two opposite classes to consider. In Massachusetts for instance, there are some, not always the most influential of its men, who have remained faithful to the Assoc^{tn} & its policy, attending its meetings & taking an active part therein. On the other hand, there are others, old & young, of whom H J Bigelow & J R Chadwick are typical, who would be of very great aid could they be brought back to allegiance. Unkindly as I have myself been treated by many of them, I would gladly forgive it all & for the sake of peace & harmony & the old historical names of the Assoc^{tn}, the sons of many of whom are now prominent upon the field, do all that I can to remove the unkindly feelings that have so long existed. As to this however I shall defer to the advice of yourself & Dr Davis, my seniors by a little, but who have done so infinitely more in establishing the Assoc^{tn} in the hearts of the profession. I am ready now to work. Do you but definitely tell me what to do.

Horatio concluded this letter by telling Toner that his papers on the medals of sanitation now numbered six and that he had also published several other medical medal comments. Dr. Toner wrote the following note to himself at the bottom of Horatio's letter: "Suggest to Dr Storer the project of making at Newport an exhibit of medical portraits, engrave [engravings], &c." This "suggestion" was carried out. Horatio described in a later paper presented before the Rhode Island Medical Society, how[30]

> The medals were shown *en masse* at the Newport meeting of the American Medical Association in 1889, but they then occupied six large cases at the hall of the Historical Society, and extensive accessions have since been made. Though I shall always be glad to have them inspected by medical gentlemen at my home, I have thought it preferable upon the present occasion to exhibit but a few, in a natural group by themselves, and to make such remarks concerning them as might seem suitable.

The Gynaecological Society of Boston continued in operation, although

Horatio apparently no longer attended its meetings. The tradition of a President's Annual Address at the first meeting of the year also continued in force. Dr. Horace C. White gave it on January 10, 1889 and, since it was the twentieth anniversary of the Society, he included the following tribute to the "founders" of the Society: "The Society was not only a pioneer, but it has done its share in causing Gynaecology to be recognized as an honorable science, and to reclaim it from opprobrium, and to place it upon a respected equality with other departments of medical science. Its founders were able, earnest, and conscientious men, who struggled with difficulties, which we of to-day, can hardly realize, and to them great credit is due for the honorable standing of the Society."[31]   This version, published in the *Journal of the American Medical Association* of March 30, 1889, did not mention Horatio Storer or any of the other "able, earnest, and conscientious founders" by name. Hopefully, it was not because Horatio's name now was unwelcome in the Society he had founded two decades earlier.

Horatio used an elaborate letterhead related to the next meeting of the American Medical Association for what ostensibly was a personal effort, the resignation of his Massachusetts Medical Society membership. However, his letter primarily was an attempt to ameliorate those Boston physicians long opposed to the American Medical Association and bring them back into the fold. His "resignation" letter included:[32]

> While writing, let me say that I shall be glad if you will take a personal interest in the approaching meeting of the Am. Med. Associat. The opportunity will be a favorable one for Massachusetts & Boston, to resume its former position of influence with regard to the general profession. Newport was formerly known as "The Isle of Peace," & this could be no better place for forgetting differences of opinion, & reuniting for the strengths & advantages of the whole country. It is especially desired that the present should be a scientific meeting, & contributions from yourself & colleagues will be very welcome. Whatever I can personally do for the interests of Boston, my birth place, will give me immense pleasure.

A February 28, 1889 letter to Dr. Toner dealt largely with medical medals, but also included the following information which indicated that the problem of Meeting Secretary and former partner, Dr. Thornton Parker, had resolved itself: "Association matters are running smoothly. The Local Secretary, about whom we had some correspondence, disturbed me by removing from the city and vacating the office to which the Association had appointed him, but the vacancy has now been filled, very acceptably to the profession here."[33]

As Chairman of the Committee of Arrangements, Horatio published an announcement of the Newport meeting in the *Journal of the American Medical Association* on March 9, 1889:[34]

ASSOCIATION NEWS.
American Medical Association. Fortieth Annual Meeting.
To be held at Newport, R. I., June 25, 26, 27, and 28, 1889
OFFICIAL NOTICE.

The Association having departed from its usual custom of convening in the chief cities, by deciding to meet the present year at a simple watering place that, despite its repute, is without certain of the resources hitherto relied upon, the Committee of Arrangements ask in advance for the kind consideration of the multitude of physicians whom they trust soon to welcome. A fact or two in this connection may perhaps be stated. Ordinarily a great many local medical men are appointed to aid the Arrangements' Committee, and thereby the duties of each are rendered less onerous. In the present instance, of the eighteen names fifteen comprise the sum total of the resident (regular) physicians of Newport, while the remaining three are dental practitioners. The Committee is therefore this time absolutely "of the whole." Of its number but a single one has ever been a member of the Association, or even attended a meeting. All who comprise it are, however, heartily in accord, and will do their best, trusting that their good will may make amends for their lack of previous experience.

This was followed by the list of members of the Arrangements Committee, an explanation of why Dr. Thornton wasn't included among the meeting organizers, and why the meeting was delayed until the end of June (main hotels did not open until then). The notice continued:

The meeting of the Association occurs nearly synchronously with the two hundred and fiftieth anniversary of the settlement of Newport. The City authorities will probably fittingly recognize the presence of the National Medical convention at such a moment, the more cordially since the virtual founder of the colony, certainly its principal leader, John Clark, was a physician. It will add to the interest of the occasion that the now Mayor of the City was one of the incorporators, in 1879, of the Newport Sanitary Protection Association, and is the parent of a rapidly rising physician, in New York.

The ancient name of Newport Island was "Aquidneck," or "the Isle of Peace." In view of this, it is to be hoped that the wisdom of the Association in turning away, the present year, from the mutual rivalries and the internal dissensions inseparable from the great centres of practice and of medical education, to what is virually [sic] neutral ground, may be made manifest, and that the coming Session may prove one of the largest, most harmonious, most scientific, and best contented meetings that has yet been held.

Horatio R. Storer, M.D.
Chairman Committee of Arrangements.
Newport, R. I., Feb. 25, 1889.

Horatio himself presented two papers at the AMA meeting in Newport. One, "The Medals of Benjamin Rush, Obstetrician,"[35] was read before the Section of Obstetrics and the Diseases of Women, and that Section recommended "that it be read in general session also as containing matter of interest to all practitioners of medicine." The other, "Volunteer Sanitary Organizations as an Aid to Official Boards of Health" was read only to the Section on State Medicine. The etiology of the paper on Rush's medals was described in a letter Horatio wrote Toner on April 3, 1889:[36] "In an evil hour, I have consented to try to give a lift to your Rush Monument Committee by reading a brief paper upon Rush as an Obstetrician, in the Section thereto devoted. You may recall his very remarkable statement regarding anaesthesia in Midwifery." Although the title of of Horatio's paper was "The medals of Benjamin Rush, Obstetrician," medals were really secondary in the paper to the statement Horatio found "very remarkable." In his research on medical medals, Horatio discovered that Benjamin Rush[37] had written his hope "that a medicine would be discovered that should suspend sensibility altogether, and leave irritability, or the power of motion, unimpaired, and thereby destroy labour pains altogether." Rush wrote this around 1800, nearly fifty years before anesthetics were used in surgery or obstetrics. Horatio told in his paper that he was greatly chagrined that he had not come across Rush's "hope" earlier, since it should have been mentioned in his *Eutokia*, which had claimed chloroform admirably reduced labor pains without impairing the labor process. On the other hand, Horatio indicated he was not alone in being derelict in his scholarship, since Horatio found only a very few references to the Rush "hope" and these were related to Walter Channing's mention of the Rush statement in his 1848 *Treatise on Etherization in Childbirth*. Horatio pointed out that even Simpson, meticulous as he was in searching out and granting credit to early researchers or practitioners whose contributions related to his own work, had failed to note Rush's prophetic "hope." Horatio even more pointedly noted that Jacob Bigelow had missed it in his "bitter letters" pertaining to Simpson, as did Jacob's son, Henry, in his "History of the Discovery of Modern Anaesthesia."[38] Although Horatio's references to the Bigelows seemed fairly mild, Henry Ingersoll Bowditch was to write the following to Horatio a few weeks after Horatio's paper on Dr. Rush was published: "I have just read your paper on Dr Rush. It is well done. You slap pretty hard the two Bigelows & perchance they deserve all you suggest."[39]

The Newport meeting evidently was a highly successful annual meeting of the Association. The following commenced the formal acknowledgement of this: "*Resolved,* That the thanks of the Association are tendered to Dr. H. R. Storer, Chairman, and the members of the Committee of Arrangements; to the

Profession of Newport and Rhode Island for the courtesies so liberally extended during the session; ..."[40] The following letter from Dr. Nathan Davis of Chicago to Henry Ingersoll Bowditch informally and, probably more validly, indicated the success of the Newport meeting:[41]

Chicago Ill. July 20th 1889
65 Randolph Street

Henry I. Bowditch M.D.

Dear Doctor: Your very kind and pleasant letter written on the 30th June and mailed the 18th inst. is received and read with much pleasure.

The Meeting of the Association in Newport was to me, a very pleasant one, and I trust a profitable one for all. After the very brief meeting we had on the platform, I looked for you several times until I learned you had returned home. I was glad to see so many of the younger members of the profession there from Massachusetts and other New England states.

You and I may not see many more of these national meetings, but I trust that the spirit of *unselfishness* and manly liberality will pervade the minds of those who may follow us. And if so, the Association will continue to exert its harmonizing and benign influence until the end of time.

Yours truly

N. S. Davis

However, no mention of Henry J. Bigelow or James Read Chadwick was made in the "Society Proceedings,"[42] and Horatio's hopes for bringing these men "back to allegiance" with the American Medical Association apparently were not fulfilled.

A paper on Dr. John Clarke was "written" and presented in conjunction with the Newport meeting by "the Chief R. I. lawyer now living," the "Hon. William P. Sheffield." Horatio submitted it to the *Journal of the American Medical Association* for publication and received a rejection letter from Dr. John H. Hollister, the *Journal*'s Supervising Editor, who related that: "Valuable as the paper is and much as we would desire its publicity, it does not fall within the line of medical literature to which the Journal is devoted."[43] This news was not well received in Newport, as the following letter to Dr. Toner indicates:[44]

Newport, R.I.
29 July 1889

Dear Doctor:

The enclosed letter from Dr. Hollister has placed us all here in a very unpleasant situation, & I am exceedingly anxious to have your aid in obtaining a reversal of the decision. After long consideration by the Committee of Arrangements, it was unanimously thought desirable to depart from the custom of merely furnishing drink &c, & to provide more refined & lasting, mental, food. It was thought that a notice of Rhode Island's greatest physician, John Clarke, till now almost unknown to the profession, would be appreciated, & especially so by those having the Association in charge. With great difficulty & almost against his will, Mr Sheffield was persuaded to write & deliver this necrological sketch. Had we not succeeded in effecting this, we should therefore probably have had no aid of any consequence from the City of Newport toward the success of the meeting, ... Dr. Hollister's letter was received this evening. The only one to whom I have yet shown it is Dr. Turner, & he takes it as a direct slight, not only to Mr. Sheffield, but to our Committee. It will be certain to be so considered by the rest of our men. ...

Sincerely yours,
H.R. Storer

Toner quickly straightened Hollister out, given Hollister's response to Toner, sent August 3, 1889: "Yours with Address of the Hon. Wm. P. Sheffield is to hand. I appreciate the feeling of Dr. Storer, and although other matters strictly medical are pressing for publication I will give it the first place in the issue of August 24th, and will so advise Dr. Storer to-day."[45] A testament to the speed of the U.S. Post Office is the following letter from Horatio, written three days later, thanking Toner for correcting the situation:[46]

Newport, R.I.
6 Aug. 1889

My Dear Dr. Toner,

  As St. Joseph is my patron, it is quite fitting that I should have to thank one of his name-children for intercessory aid. Dr. Hollister has written me a graceful letter, & you have extricated us all, Assoc^tn as well as Committee, from what would have been an awkward position.

  You have made a complete conquest of my daughter. Were she raising a temple to AEsculapius, I am quite sure that the statue of the Deity therein would be that of yourself.

Sincerely yours,
H.R. Storer

Dr. Toner.

The piece was indeed placed first in the August 24, 1889 number of the *Journal of the American Medical Association*,[47] showing Dr. Toner's large clout in the

American Medical Association. Sheffield's sketch of Clarke strongly resembles the sketches that Horatio wrote on Clarke around 1885, indicating that Horatio's efforts almost certainly were used by Sheffield in preparing his address, if, indeed, Horatio did not actually write it for him.

Horatio certainly highly valued his own American Medical Association paper on Dr. Benjamin Rush, given the following letter to Toner discussing reprints and foreign distribution:[48]

> Newport, R.I.
> 26 Aug. 1889
>
> Dear Doctor:
>
> I received today from Chicago the proof of my paper on Dr Rush & his medals. In it I acknowledged my obligation to you for very valuable assistance. I shall have a reprint of 500 copies for obstetricians & numismatists. Does the Smithsonian still distribute gratuitously such papers, not published by itself? If so, & you think the game worth the candle, please ascertain what number would be required for the list of medical societies, journals & libraries, & public libraries, abroad. Before hearing from you formally, I will direct a sufficiency to be forwarded to Washington, expressage paid.
>
> Sincerely yours,
> H.R. Storer
>
> Dr. Toner.

However, only a month later, Horatio told Dr. Toner that he ho longer had ambitions of "any kind" and that the Rush paper had been written solely to help along the Rush Monument Project.[49] Perhaps the dropped "ambitions" were related to the International Medical Congress scheduled for Berlin in 1890 to which foreign distribution of the Rush paper might produce a nomination of Vice President. However, it is probable the "ambitions" were related to an expectation of the next Presidency of the American Medical Association. Years later, Dr. Marcy was to write that he was approached in 1890 by the Nominating Committee and "declined in favor of my older friend, Dr. Horatio R. Storer."[50] However, Horatio was not nominated to the Presidency in 1890, which was conferred on Dr. William T. Briggs of Tennessee, and this decision about an 1890 President probably was made by Association insiders, such as Toner and Davis, as early as August 1889. Horatio's failure to be nominated may have been communicated by Toner to Horatio in Toner's letter of August 30 which Horatio mentioned in his letter of September 26. This letter has not been located among family papers or elsewhere.

Another event that must have greatly saddened Horatio was the death of his long-time friend and associate, Dr. Levi Farr Warner on October 12, 1889. Horatio provided a touching obituary of his friend which was published in the *Journal of the American Medical Association* a month after his death.[51]

Horatio described Warner as ever "successful in obtaining the full confidence of a patient," always worthy of this confidence, untiring, "restoring women to their full usefulness who had for many years apparently been hopeless invalids," "devoted in his friendship," etc. Horatio surely selected qualities and achievements of Dr. Warner for praise which Horatio himself highly valued and strove to achieve.

The year 1889 marked the painting by Frederic P. Vinton of a portrait of Horatio's father, David Humphreys Storer. It was commissioned by the Massachusetts Medical Society and the 182 physicians and ten non-physicians who contributed to have it painted.[52] At the time of this writing, this magnificent portrait is displayed on the fifth floor of the Countway Medical Library outside the Rare Book room. The year 1889 also was eventful because Horatio's son Malcolm graduated from the Harvard Medical School. Early the next year, he traveled to Vienna to continue his medical studies in gynecology; he would return from his European education at the end of June 1891.[53]

CHAPTER 20

LABRADOR II,
JENNER CENTENNIAL,
NEW ANTI-ABORTION ADDRESS

Horatio's correspondence relating to medical medals was enormous in 1889 and it continued in 1890.[1] He appeared to contact every medical school in the world to obtain information about medals that were given as prizes or for other reasons to their students. His papers on the medals relating to sanitation continued regularly in *The Sanitarian* and those on the medals illustrative of the science of medicine continued in the *American Journal of Numismatics*. Horatio's expertise in this area was employed for another purpose in 1890. A New York Training School for nurses sought and received his advice related to the design of a medal which they struck for presentation to their graduates.[2]

Horatio's daughter Agnes was sixteen in 1890. The first entries in the diary she maintained dealt with a trip by Horatio, Frances, and herself to New Brunswick and Nova Scotia in June.[3] Her diary also informs us that her brother Frank and his grandmother Gilmore had become Christian Scientists and the implication was that John Humphreys also was a Christian Scientist. She described how painful it was for Horatio to have his sons adopt such an irrational medical model. Agnes recounted numerous reunions of Horatio with his old physician friends on the trip. She also described a narrow escape from a fire in their hotel in New Brunswick and mentioned a number of walks with "Papa." Despite his disability and the need for crutches, Horatio could cover long distances. On the other hand, Horatio suffered at least one bad fall during the trip "bruising himself very badly," and Agnes noted several concerns when she and her mother feared that an overdue Horatio might have fallen.

The trip continued northward to Labrador and included stops at Red Bay and other locations that Horatio had visited in 1849. Unfortunately, an epidemic of diphtheria in that area kept them from several planned excursions. Years later, Horatio wrote about his two Labrador visits in a tribute to Dr. Wilfred T. Grenfell, who became the medical "savior" of that medically deprived region a few years after Horatio's second visit. His letter included:[4]

Many years later [after the 1849 trip], just before Dr. Grenfell's coming, I again visited Labrador and Newfoundland, with my wife and daughter, stopping at many of the tiny fishing hamlets along the coast unknown to the usual tourist. Everywhere, outside of St. John's itself, in Newfoundland, the pleasure of our summer holiday was sadly marred by the most pitiful sights of physical suffering unalleviated, of needless death fast approaching unchallenged, through the utter lack of doctors and nurses and all absolutely essential medical supplies. A single tragic incident from the many we witnessed will give some slight idea of the conditions along the Labrador as regards the dearth of all medical assistance "before Grenfell came."

After a perfect summer day, we dropped anchor in the glory of one of the most gorgeous Arctic nights I have ever beheld. The aurora spread over the entire heavens was a sight to marvel at, but our exclamations of delight and wonder quickly died in apprehension, so unusual was the number of small fishing boats that instantly made for the steamer, boats manned by men and boys who rowed as if for their very lives: Poor fellows! They rowed indeed in the desperate hope of saving lives—but lives dearer than their own. To this day I hear that first heartbreaking appeal. From the first boat that reached us there sprang erect the figure of a very old man. A patriarch among men, and evidently the little hamlet's leader and spokesman. With arms extended to heaven he cried out: "Captain! For the love of God, is there a doctor aboard? Our women and children are dying like flies. In God's name, man, help us, save us!"

Alone, unaided, just recovering as I was from severe illness, with nothing at hand but the ship's meagre medical supplies. I could do but pitifully little, nothing at all it seemed to me, as all that awful night I strove with death, and such anguish as in all my lifelong experience with mortal agony I had never witnessed. The old patriarch had told but the tragic truth. The people of that poverty-stricken hamlet were indeed dying "like flies," under an outbreak of the more virulent type of the dreaded "black diphtheria," and no possibility of help of any kind reaching them till we could send it from the mainland.

The family's return trip in September included a visit to Quebec City, and Agnes' diary indicates that, following a letter from Frank critical of Christian Science, Horatio was reported "very indignant about John's being such a believer in C.S."[5] Frank, at least, had apparently come to his senses.

Dr. Henry J. Bigelow died at age 82 on October 30, 1890. Horatio must have had mixed emotions at the death of the man who had so strongly opposed Horatio's efforts to advance the specialty and training of gynecology, reform Harvard medical education, return power to the Massachusetts Medical Society membership from the usurping Councillors, and advance the American Medical Association. An obituary of Horatio described how "He outlived all his antagonists and towards the end forgave them absolutely."[6] If any antagonist prolonged this amnesty process, however, it probably was Henry J. Bigelow.

Agnes collected autographs and several letters from her collection have been included in or referred to in this book. "Aunt Sarah," the wife of Robert Boyd Storer whom Horatio had visited so frequently when a student at Harvard, is indicated by the following to have provided Agnes with some treasures:[7]

> Cambridge,
> Jan 24, "91/

Dear Agnes,

I am very glad that you have enough confidence in your Aunt Sarah to ask a little favor of her. I have been looking over some of my letters and although I have many letters and papers, I have very few full autographs.

I send a poem of Mr. Emerson's which I suppose was the first draft of the poem, and will be very valuable in future years. I have appended a signature of a letter, the only one where there was more than "Waldo" or "R.W.E." And although I have much manuscript of Margaret Fuller, she also signs her letters "M." I think perhaps at Concord, I may find one signed by her whole name. Dr. Gray's you will value, I feel sure, and perhaps you will like to add Sophia Hawthorne's autograph to that of her husband. She was a distinguished person in her own way. As for "Uncle Robert," you will perhaps argue with my mother, who used to say that I must have been made on purpose for him, because I could always decipher his hand-writing. I am very sure that when it was deciphered it always expressed so much that was sweet and lovely that it was well worth doing.

I happen to have three letters of Edward Everett so I send one, thinking you may be able to exchange it with some other collector of autographs for some other that you have not. Have you read the Life & Letters of Arthur Hugh Clough—He was a poet and a friend of Emerson's.

I believe now I have explained my little enclosures and with love to your father and your Mamma and to yourself, from your Cousins and myself.

> I am
>> Most Affectionately
>> "Aunt Sarah."

Hopefully, these Emerson, Fuller, and Hawthorne materials have found their way to appropriate repositories.

Agnes' diary for early 1891 indicated much illness in Horatio. It was a theme to be repeated in the diary for thirty more years. Her diary also indicated that she and Horatio went to visit David Humphreys Storer on his eighty-seventh birthday which was March 26, 1891. This would be the last birthday he would celebrate. On September 10, 1891, David Humphreys died "surrounded by the children who had devoted their lives to his happiness and most tenderly cared for him he went to his eternal rest."[8] Agnes indicated in her diary that David Humphreys' will was read after the funeral by "Uncle Frank." She also wrote: "I can't write anything about it, but it was dreadful to be so disappointed in any one. To think that Grandfather could do anything so horribly unjust. Poor Papa! it was terribly hard for him and I don't wonder that he feels very badly about it."

This apparently was Horatio's first knowledge that his portion of his father's estate was to be held in trust with only the income paid him each quarter. Upon Horatio's death, his portion was to be divided among Horatio's children. This differed from his father's other legacies, which bequeathed equal portions to his brothers and sisters that went immediately and directly to them. David Humphreys Storer had changed his will shortly after Horatio's return from Europe, when he may have learned that Horatio was planning to become a Roman Catholic. It is only a guess, but he might have altered his will out of fear that Horatio would contribute his inheritance to the Catholic Church.

On January 20, there was a Memorial meeting for David Humphreys Storer at the Suffolk District Medical Society. Agnes' diary suggests that Horatio may have avoided the memorial meeting for his father, probably because he had been discriminated against in his father's will. "Aunt Abby hasn't asked me up for Paderewski or Miss Bush's Mass," Agnes wrote, "& I'm dreadfully afraid she's offended that I didn't go up for the memorial meeting—well I couldn't help it without making Pater feel badly."[9]

Horatio had frequently reflected that "history repeats itself" in his *Journal of the Gynaecological Society of Boston* "Editorial Notes" and other writing. The following letter from his old defender, Dr. Marcy, must have reinforced this belief in the repetition of history:[10]

> Henry O. Marcy, M.D. ...
> Boston, May 11 1891
>
> Dear Dr. Storer
>   I inclose you a slip cut form Dr Kelly's Bulletin for April of the Johns Hopkins Hospital. Is not this your method of "pocketing the pedicle" described and widely published years ago?
>   Sincerely
>   Henry O. Marcy

April 1892 was the date of publication of a paper by Horatio titled "The Medals Commemorative of Natural Scientists." Horatio's goals for the paper were set forth as follows: "In view of the rapid advance of the natural sciences, and the constantly progressing substitution of improved classification and methods of research, there is danger that the work and even the names of earlier naturalists may be forgotten. To remind workers of to-day of some of those who have preceded them, may therefore be of value."[11] He then called on other naturalists to assist him in the task of "extending and correcting the present list." This was followed by a unique perspective on medals which came down from ancient times:

> An ancient poetical saying, apposite in this connection, has been preserved by Bacon, to the effect that at the extremity of the thread representing the life of each person, there hangs a medal which bears his name. At the moment of death, Time detaches them all and casts them into the flood of oblivion, but upon the stream there are swans who collect the names that may rise to the surface, seize them, and bear them to immortality.

No doubt, Horatio viewed himself as one of the "swans," doing their work via his published descriptions of the medals and of the pioneers of sanitation, medicine, and natural science whom the medals honored.

Dr. Anita Tyng sent Horatio a long letter from Chicago in November 1893 which was primarily devoted to medical medals which she had seen, probably at the Hygienic Exposition of the World's Fair.[12] It was a response to a letter of Horatio's, since she declined Horatio's invitation to practice in Newport saying "too cold and too little business." At the time, she was living in Jacksonville, Florida. She later became a medical missionary to the Orient. Her last residence was Berkeley, California, where she died in 1913.[13]

Horatio proposed to Harvard President Eliot what might have been the first Professorship of Medical History in the world in the following:[14]

Newport, R. I.
20 Feb., 1894

My dear Mr. Eliot,

I have a valuable collection of medical medals, many of them portraits from life, which I have for several years been gathering through correspondents abroad, with the intention of eventually leaving them to Harvard University as a memorial of my father, who was so long a teacher in the Medical School. Of a large number of them, there are probably no other specimens in this country.

As my life is uncertain, I would transfer them at once to the College, and very likely continue to increase the collection, provided my son Dr. Malcolm Storer of Boston could have a chair of Medical and Surgical History, for illustration of which the medals would be of the greatest service. The department indicated would for obvious reasons be a useful one, as not one physician in a thousand has the slightest real knowledge of the subject. My son is learned in these matters, and would doubtless be contented with little compensation. He graduated in 1885, and in Medicine in 1889. ...

> Sincerely yrs
> H.R. Storer

Eliot's response read:[15]

> Harvard University,
> Cambridge, February 21st, 1894

Dear Dr. Storer,

I will talk with some of the leaders of the Medical Faculty about the very original and interesting suggestion contained in your note of February 20th. I am in pretty much your condition in regard to the Medical Faculty, except that I of course know personally all of its members; but there is only one person now in the Medical Faculty that was in it when I first joined that Faculty, and he had no vote in 1869. ...

Your son John has been of great service to us in connection with the coin collection in the College Library. The entire collection is now well catalogued and well mounted. It does not grow as fast as we could wish; but it is in a thoroughly creditable condition.

> Very truly yours,
> Charles W. Eliot

H.R. Storer, M.D.

This exchange between Horatio and Harvard President Eliot did not produce Horatio's hoped-for position for Malcolm, and Horatio's huge collection of medals later would be donated instead to the Boston Medical Library.

Illnesses of Horatio were described in Agnes' diary in the early 1890s, but so was his sailing and walking. Collection of medals and correspondence and articles pertaining to medals continued as major efforts. One frequent correspondent was Mr. William Speck of Haverstraw, New York, who was a scholar of Goethe and Schiller and a collector of medals and other materials honoring these men. Both Goethe and Schiller had been trained as physicians, and Horatio thus shared Speck's strong interest in their memorabilia. The following letter to Speck provides insights on Horatio's massive project.

> Newport R.I.
> 9 April. 1894

Dear Sir,

I am very glad if my Goethe list has been of any service to you.

It must be some time yet before we can reach Schiller in the serial that I am publishing in the Am Journal of Numismatics. Though I have had an installment in every quarterly number since Jan. 1889, we have only presented the medical medals of British, Central & South America, the United States, & a small portion of those of Great Britain. Holland, Belgium & France will precede Germany. I however have these all of them ready for the press in manuscript. But life is short, & Art is long. ...

Sincerely yrs
H.R. Storer

Mr. Speck.

Horatio received the "Diploma di Benemerenza" from the 11th International Medical Congress held from March 29 to April 5, 1894 in Rome, Italy.[16] This translates to "Diploma of Merit." However, there is no evidence that he attended this Congress. Agnes did go abroad in 1894 with some friends and reported home from many of the same locations in Scotland and England that she had lived in with Horatio and Frances in 1876 when she was two.[17] There was surprisingly little correspondence saved from 1894 and this was all related to medical medals. Illness probably was the reason, since at the end of the year, Agnes noted in her diary that her parents were "much better."[18] Their recovery allowed Agnes to visit her brother Frank in Deland, Florida.

The Harvard Class of 1850 published a directory of its members in 1895.[19] In February of that year, Horatio provided a long letter with much personal and professional data to the Class Secretary, Joseph Henry Thayer.[20] It included a number of events and activities on the part of Horatio in Newport which have not been mentioned elsewhere. For example: "Have been a Director of the Newport Co-operative Building Association; a Trustee of St. Joseph's Church, Newport; President of the St. Joseph's Total Abstinence Society (150 men); for a number of years a member of the Prohibition City Committee of Newport, and twice Prohibition Candidate for State Senator."

Agnes' entry for February 27, 1895 recorded that "Pater has decided to change the Hunter! I am deputed to lay his offer of it—for a private Hospital again before Mac. I know he'll have nothing to do with it—simply stay all his life in Boston & be contented with being one of a thousand others where he has this chance of making a name for himself." The "Hunter" was the large house next to Horatio's home. Horatio hoped that Malcolm would consent to be the attending physician or surgeon of a private women's hospital at the Hunter, probably with some consulting role for himself. "Came up yesterday—Mac refused of course," was Agnes' next entry.[21]

A June entry in Agnes' diary read:[22]

"Friday last Pater & I went over to Block Island & remained till yesterday. Mac joining us on Saturday. ... One day I went sword fishing with Pater in Capt. Edwin Dodge's little steamer & was most desperately unhappy & seasick. Another day he went out with Malcolm and by great good luck they captured *five* sword fish—a performance which so delighted my parent that he wants to go over to Block Island later for a week's fishing."

Block Island is about twenty-five miles southwest of Newport. Horatio seems to have enjoyed fishing at age sixty-five as much as he had as a youth in Concord and Labrador.

"When and where," Horatio wrote Dr. Toner, "are you to hold your Jenner Celebration?"[23] He was referring to a celebration of the 100th anniversary of Edward Jenner's discovery of the benefits of vaccination for small-pox. "I have prepared with care a list, with descriptions," he continued, "of the medals of Dr. Jenner, together with those illustrating Small Pox, Inoculation, and Vaccination generally." Horatio hoped his "list" might be of use to Toner's Jennerian Centennial. The answers to Horatio's initial questions were May 1896 and at Atlanta, Georgia in conjunction with the annual meeting of the American Medical Association. Dr. Toner obviously was interested in Horatio's paper and "The Memorials of Edward Jenner" was presented in Atlanta.[24] Horatio was too ill to attend the meeting and Dr. Henry Darwin Didama (or someone else) presented it for him.[25]

There was also a Jennerian Centennial at Newport, Rhode Island which was a joint effort of the Newport Historical, Medical, and Natural History Societies. Since Horatio was active in all three Societies, it is tempting to speculate that it was Horatio's effort. Horatio's contribution, "Edward Jenner as Naturalist," is certainly one of his finest historical papers.[26] Unfortunately, Horatio was too ill to present it on May 14, 1896, the day of the Centennial when several other tributes to Jenner were given. When Horatio recovered, they held a "second" Centennial on June 9, 1896. Horatio began his paper most prophetically:

> Ladies and Gentleman:—The festival which we have met this evening to close, marks an exceptional centennial. Ordinarily such a celebration commemorates a century, or even two centuries, or more, dating from a person's, a city's, or a nation's birth, and is comparatively of local interest. This, however, is in remembrance of an isolated act, or rather of an incalculably great discovery; for not only is vaccination in itself a priceless blessing, but we are only beginning to appreciate, and that but very faintly, to what it will eventually lead. The suppression of small pox is something wonderful, but upon it, and as a direct consequence has followed, the virtual control of hydrophobia and diphtheria, hitherto considered absolutely

incurable diseases, *and other similar victories are quite sure to ensue.*[27] The act, moreover, that we commemorate, did not affect a city, or a country, or a hemisphere merely, but the whole world.

Horatio then described the numerous tributes to Jenner around the country and around the world on the Centennial of Jenner's demonstration of the effectiveness of vaccination. He reminded the audience of what they had already heard from the Newport speakers on May 14 about the scourge that small-pox had been before widespread vaccination, how "not more than four persons in one hundred wholly escaped its ravages," and how it "frightfully disfigured when it did not kill." He continued:[28]

> My task upon this interesting occasion is to present to you glimpses into an entirely different portion of Dr. Jenner's life from those previously shown to you, and, if I can, to enable you to appreciate the influences which favorably influenced the moulding of his character, preparing him to become one of the most eminent physicians and one of the most pronounced benefactors of his race that have ever lived. ... It is for me to speak to you of Jenner from his ordinarily unappreciated standpoint of Naturalists, and to show you that had it not been for his innate bent in this direction, the very unusual opportunities that he had for observation and experiment, and as the exceptional mental training that he received from one of the most profound and philosophical natural historians that any age has ever produced, his great discovery had never, by him at least, been reached.

When Horatio spoke of "One of the most profound and philosophical natural historians that any age has ever produced," he was referring to John Hunter. Horatio provided a brief sketch of Hunter then followed it with this discussion of Hunter's key role in developing Jenner's abilities.

> Such was John Hunter, in many ways resembling Louis Agassiz. His mind, a veritable kingdom, was strewn everywhere with gems more precious than diamonds, and inlaid throughout with what was far more worth possessing than gold. Under such influences was Jenner placed, in most intimate relationship. Stimulated by this example, he became a skillful dissector of the most delicate tissues, and injected and otherwise prepared them with remarkable dexterity. A specimen bequeathed to his friend and biographer, Dr. John Baron, of Gloucester, well illustrates this. It represents the progress of the ovum of the domestic hen, from its first impregnation to its full and complete development when about to be discharged. ... It was undoubtedly in such embryological researches that he used to delight

when with Hunter.   Naturally quick to observe, his power of perception had been increased and strengthened. Prone to interpret, his faculties of induction, ... and of deduction .. had been greatly developed. ... His most salient traits as a naturalist were brought into even bolder relief. From what we know of Hunter's daily life and pursuits, we are made as certain of Jenner's constant occupations and mental development while in his long pupilage and comradeship. To Jenner's latest day he always called him "that dear man."

The Hunter-Jenner relationship described above so closely parallels the Agassiz-Horatio-Storer relationship that Horatio may be distorting the former. Horatio's own skill at dissection and Horatio's embryological investigations of the dogfish closely match Jenner's dissection and embryological work. No doubt Horatio was rightly convinced of his own powers of induction and deduction and rightly believed that these had been shaped by his interests in natural history and refined by Agassiz, just as Jenner's had been shaped by study of natural history and refined by Hunter. Horatio also discussed the intense resistance to Jenner's vaccination ideas and described Jenner's observations and paper on the cuckoo, its enthusiastic reception by most ornithologists, and its criticism by a jealous naturalist. The persecution of Jenner by people who were wrong would have been highly salient to Horatio who no doubt saw himself as persecuted by people who were wrong.

Horatio then described the critical event of May 14, 1796 which was the basis of all the centennials. On that date, Jenner successfully vaccinated a boy using matter from the hands of a milk-maid with cowpox contracted from cows. The boy's complete immunity to small-pox was demonstrated within a few weeks and eventually Jenner was able to convince others to be vaccinated. Despite numerous skeptics and enemies of vaccination, nearly worldwide acceptance of vaccination eventually followed. There were some areas which rejected vaccination, such as Gloucester, England. Horatio reported "as a direct consequence the city is now being decimated by small-pox in its very worst form." Horatio noted that carelessness in virus preparation or latent disease still produced illness and even fatalities after vaccination and this had led some to fiercely oppose vaccination. Horatio cautioned these opponents to recognize that their own cases or the cases of illness and fatalities of their relatives were highly atypical. If successful in their opposition to vaccination, their communities could be doomed to suffer Gloucester's fate. Horatio closed his paper on Jenner, saying:[29]

What more can one add to portray his beautiful character? I can but repeat the following tribute, long since paid him, and inscribed upon his tomb. It will grow more and more expressive with the recurring centuries:

"Within this tomb has found a resting place
The great physician of the human race—
Immortal Jenner! whose gigantic mind
Brought life and health to more than half mankind.
Let rescued infancy his worth proclaim,
And lisp out blessings on his honored name;
And radiant Beauty drop one grateful tear,
For Beauty's truest friend lies buried here."

The couplet beginning "Let rescued infancy" may well belong on another tomb marker—in Forest Hills.

A month later, Dr. Joseph Hunt of Brooklyn, New York wrote about their joint interests in medical numismatics.[30] His letter also included: "I suppose that you have received official notice that at the last meeting of our Kings Co. Society, we did ourselves the honor of electing you an honorary member, together with Drs. Pepper and Welch. That we are not in the habit of electing honorary members promiscuously will be understood when I tell you that you are the only ones now living. It is several years since one was elected."

On May 6, 1897, Horatio gave the Presidential Address before the Newport Natural History Society. It was entitled, "Commercial Products of the Sea in their Relations to Newport,"[31] and was highly reminiscent of the portion of his paper, "Aids in Treatment of Strumous Disease," of two decades earlier, which dealt with beneficial sea products obtained locally. He described the various unexploited sea resources of Newport: fish species discarded that are judged highly palatable in some quarters; cod and other fish livers discarded instead of being converted to valuable oil; fish swimming-bladders that were discarded instead of being turned into isinglass; and shark and other fish skins that could be converted to leather and to polishing cloths. There also were the sea weeds, the sea itself, and its salt. Horatio concluded: "There is much more that could be said of the sea as affecting Newport's business interests. In a word there is at Newport a great deal more money to be gathered from the sea than is as yet obtained. There are many people here who need it, and they have only to avail themselves of the opportunities that await a little good judgment, patience and not unpleasant labor."

Horatio returned to his campaign against criminal abortion in the Summer of 1897. He presented a paper, "Criminal Abortion: Its Prevalence, Its Prevention, and Its Relation to the Medical Examiner ...," at the Rhode Island Medico-Legal Society on August 12, 1897, and presented it again at the Newport Medical Society on August 18.[32] Horatio's paper is valuable in providing a history of the movement begun by Hodge in 1839; tied to women's disease by his father in 1855; advanced almost single-handedly by himself for three years, beginning in 1857; and which then became a national crusade by physicians and others after Horatio enlisted the AMA in the effort. Horatio began by discussing the stimuli that returned him to the fray:

> A recent failure to obtain conviction in a trial for criminal abortion in Rhode Island, the case having been thought a clear one, is said to have carried such discouragement to several of the members of this Society that they are unwilling to have even the general subject referred to. Upon the other hand, if we acknowledge the frequency of the crime, and of this there can be no question,[33] one would suppose that the time was peculiarly appropriate for attempting to ascertain the real cause of what may have been an exceptional instance of failure of justice and if possible, to find its remedy. Towards that a brief summary of the medical anti-abortion movement, comprised within the past half century, may perhaps be of aid.

Horatio began this history, not with his 1857 Suffolk District Medical Society commencement of the crusade, but with his American Academy of Arts and Sciences paper of December 1858, possibly because the Academy paper was his first effort *outside* the medical profession. Much of his long paragraph describing this 1858 paper was reproduced in an earlier chapter. Horatio followed this with a discussion of how "quickening," a "technical cloudiness of idea, of expression had crept into medical language and that of the law" and had made many believers that early abortion was not the destruction of an independent life. Hodge in 1839, Radford in 1848, and his father in 1855 were cited as controverting this notion and claiming "conception as the true beginning of foetal life." Horatio also noted that it was his father who had first pointed out the diseases associated with criminal abortion. Horatio then described what he viewed as his own original contribution:[34]

> None of these gentlemen, however, seem to have entered the at that time somewhat thorny path that connects induced abortion with political economy. I have always frankly acknowledged that it was from my father's recognition of the effect of abortion in producing pelvic disease that my attention was first drawn to the subject. Had it been otherwise I might never have pursued the inquiries which led me to appreciate the frequency of the crime.

Afterwards, Horatio discussed in detail his initial efforts as they began at the Suffolk District Medical Society in 1857 and then shifted to the American Medical Association:

> In 1857, at its meeting at Nashville, the subject was presented to the American Medical Association,[35] which I had joined in 1856, a committee was appointed, and its report was made at the meeting at Louisville in the ensuing year. My associates upon the committee

were: Drs. Blatchford, of New York; Hodge, of Pennsylvania; Pope, of Missouri; Barton, of South Carolina; Lopez, of Alabama; Semmes, of District of Columbia; and Brisbane of Wisconsin. Their standing in the profession was guarantee of their conservatism and their faithfulness in the inquiry. It interested them all, and they personally contributed towards the general decision.

Horatio went on to discuss the 1865 American Medical Association prize essay, its publication as *Why Not? A Book for Every Woman*, and the large distribution of this popular tract. "It was found, as the Association had anticipated," he observed, "that where religion and morality had failed, the fear of resulting physical lesions exerted a wonderfully deterrent influence, and hundreds of women acknowledged that they were thus induced to permit their pregnancy to accomplish its full period." He indicated that *Why Not?* went "virtually out of print" while he was abroad, but that he still continued to receive applications for it, with the most recent from the Board of Health of the Territory of Oklahoma only a month earlier.

Horatio decried that the abortion-inhibiting effect generated by the physicians' crusade was now overcome by a new generation who were no longer aware that abortion was morally wrong or physically destructive. Apathy of physicians and even complicity of some physicians were once more a problem. He stated that defects of the laws related to criminal abortion still existed, making convictions difficult or impossible. He then mimicked his efforts in the 1858 paper to the American Academy of Arts and Sciences, showing the current sharply lower birth rates in New England than those of foreign countries while marriage rates were similar. The implication was that New England married couples were not having children and Horatio indicated that prevention of conception was not the only reason. Illegitimacy was much higher in foreign countries than in New England, which he viewed as indicating that unmarried women were much more likely in New England to abort their pregnancies. His strongest statistics supporting a high rate of criminal abortion in New England in 1897 were the same he had used in 1858, namely the abnormally high rates of still births. Horatio concluded with the following recommendations:

> That these facts are true should be the greater reason for a Society like our own to exert itself anew, for surely such obstacles as we know exist can be overcome. All medico-legal societies and state organizations of examiners can combine towards improvement in the statutes regarding the crime. Offenders in our own profession can be discovered and pursued with greater rigor; and the measures towards enlightening the ignorance and awakening the conscience of the community, which have been pronounced legitimate by the American Medical Association, can be renewed. Now, as formerly, the well founded dread of the physical consequences of abortion can be

brought home to every pregnant woman. Such procedures cannot but
secure success. How perfect this may prove will depend upon the
persistence and earnestness of your movement. There can be
nothing, you may all be certain, that individually or collectively you
may undertake, that will more deserve the blessing of Almighty God.

The paper was well-received by his Medico-Legal Society audience. In the
subsequent discussion Horatio was asked "for suggestions as to what could be
done by this and similar societies." Horatio's answers paralleled his recommendations in 1859 to the American Medical Association. He recommended that the
Rhode Island Medico-Legal Society form a Committee to identify the problems
with abortion statutes and with the help of "friendly lawyers," identify solutions.
He also indicated the need to overcome the ignorance "of judges, juries and
advocates" regarding fetal development.

A stream cannot rise above its source. If the belief of these men,
who are but representatives of the community at large, rests upon
popular ignorance of the true character of the crime, and if prevention of abortion is better than attempts at conviction of foetal murder
after it has been committed, and if it can be prevented only through
awakening woman's consciences, arousing her maternal instinct, and
exciting her fear of physical peril to herself, then your course is
clear.

Another recommendation by Horatio was to bring "the subject directly to
the attention of the profession at large." He called for a "circular, judiciously
worded," to be sent to the American Medical Association, to "State Medical
Societies and, indeed, to all medical organizations in the country, of whatever
nature, with the request that they cordially endorse the movement." He noted
that there was evidence that "professedly reputable physicians" were performing
abortions. "It is the duty of every honorable practitioner," he continued, "for
the good name of our profession, and for humanity's sake and our national
prosperity, to assist in detecting, exposing and punishing these villains." Finally
he called on the smaller medical societies to bring to trial and expel any
abortionists in their midst.

When such is done by a minor organization, its State Society will take
up and similarly treat the case and so will the American Medical
Association, as a court of higher resort. This but accomplished,
public opinion will be quite sure to degrade the miscreant; while the
medical licensing bodies in each State will be as quick to withdraw
his right to practice. He then would become subject to the courts of
law upon another count, and if now pursued can easily be convicted
and fined or imprisoned, or both.

Although actions of the Rhode Island Medico-Legal Society as a result of Horatio's paper are not known, the following indicates that the Newport Medical Society was aroused to action after Horatio presented the paper to them.[36]

NEWPORT MEDICAL SOCIETY
Newport R.R.,
August 21, 1897.
Dear Sir:

At a regular meeting of the Newport Medical Society, held on August 18th, 1897, a paper previously communicated to the Rhode Island Medico-Legal Society, on August 12th, was, by request, read by Dr. H.R. Storer, Honorary President, in which it was shown that the induction of unnecessary abortion is probably now as prevalent in this country as when the subject was brought to the attention of the American Medical Association by him forty years ago in 1857.

The Society thereupon unanimously appointed the undersigned a Committee "to obtain through correspondence with medical societies and otherwise such action by the profession as may tend to lessen the occurrence of criminally induced abortion."

We accordingly ask you, through such measures as you may think most proper, to join in what should be an universal movement by physicians to check the present decrease of the rate of increase of our population.

We shall be glad to be informed of such action as you may find yourself able to take in this matter.

This letter, signed by five Newport Medical Society members other than Horatio, was printed and apparently mailed widely, since, in the next few months, several medical journals around the country made mention of this appeal to physicians in editorials condemning criminal abortion. Another tactic in Horatio's resumed crusade was to distribute a flyer advertising his books on the topic, including his 1897 paper. This indicated that *Why Not?* was still in print, as was *Is It I?* and Horatio's 1868 book with Franklin Fiske Heard. The flyer also included a number of favorable "medical press notices" for Horatio's 1897 address.[37]

Horatio or the Newport Medical Society apparently sent the pamphlet reprinted from the *Atlantic Weekly* to individual physicians. The following negative response came from surgeon and anthropologist, Daniel G. Brinton:[38]

Dr. Daniel G. Brinton,
Media, Penna.
Mch. 15 1898

Dear Dr. Storer:

Someone has had the kindness to send me a copy (reprint) of your article in the Atlantic Medical Weekly (Oct 2/97) on Criminal Abortion.

Although for some years I have not been active in medical questions, my interest in them continues especially where they touch sociology.

For this reason, I think you will not take it amiss if I send you some observations on your article, even if they are in the nature of objections to some of your statements.

My first objection is to the general statement on p. 25 (reprint) that the larger families of foreign parents "is to be explained by the watchful protection exercised by the Catholic church, etc."

This statement, which is a repetition of one previously made, (by you) assumes two premises, first that the "foreign parents" were Catholics; and second, that (as is stated by you elsewhere, p. 15) that "For religious reasons induced abortion practically never occurs among Catholics."

The census statistics of 1890 show that the large families of foreign parents are common among Protestants as well as Catholic immigrants; so your first premise is not applicable.

As to the second, how you can say it, when you well know that the country of all other where means are most employed to prevent conception and destroy foetal life,—France,—has a population 95% of whom are Catholics,—this I can only explain by an unwillingness to state the full facts of the case.[39]

Again you must know that the three causes of small families which you name on p. 31 are by no means exhaustive, and that it is superficial to consider them so. You must be acquainted with the studies of Dumong, Laponge & the other French students of this intricate & complex problem. Not to mention them in an essay intended for either scientific or popular reading is a sad oversight.

For these reasons, I regret the dissemination of the Essay, though I agree that the subject ought to be discussed & that no one could discuss it more ably than you, if you would approach it without prejudice. I remain

Very truly yours,

D. G. Brinton

The prejudice that Brinton saw no doubt was Horatio's Catholicism. On the other hand, Horatio had made the same mistake about Protestant immigrants when he wrote in 1859 while still a Unitarian. It should be noted that Brinton's criticisms were *not* of Horatio's anti-abortion stance.

CHAPTER 21

DONATION OF MEDALS, CANCER, A PROTEST AGAINST PREJUDICE, DEATH OF FRANCES

In the Summer of 1899, Horatio, Frances, Agnes and her friend Nelly traveled to Europe. Agnes' diary entry during the ocean crossing, "Pater has gained steadily,"[1] and other evidence indicate that a major purpose of the voyage and trip was to improve the sixty-nine-year-old Horatio's health. The party was in Scotland on July 10, 1899 when the Newport Natural History Society met, created the new office of Honorary Life President, and designated Horatio as such.[2] The following letter from the Newport Hospital Medical Board also suggests that being away produces honors and attention not bestowed while one is at home.[3]

Newport, R. I., July 22, 1899.

H.R. Storer, M.D.,

Dear Sir,

At the Annual Meeting of the Medical Board of the Newport Hospital, July 21, 1899, you were re-elected President of said Board, and on the motion of the Sec'y. it was voted to send you a copy of the resolution relative to your absence, which was passed at said meeting:-it is hereunto appended.

"To H.R. Storer, M.D., Pres. of the Medical Board of the Newport Hospital.

"The Medical Board of the Newport Hospital, assembled in Annual Meeting, send you their heartiest greeting: may your sojourn in Europe be fraught with advantage to your health, so that ere long you may return, to again aid us by your counsel, refreshed in both mind and body."

Respectfully Submitted,

H. G. MacKaye M.D.

Secy. Med. Board

While somewhere in Great Britain Horatio received the following letter from his old friend William Priestley:[4]

July 15/99
17 Hertford Street
Mayfair, _____

My dear Storer

I have give up the place I had in Scotland, and instead have bought a small property in Sussex near Horsham. Lady Priestley is however in Scotland just now, in the hope of getting good from the Strathpeffer waters. She is staying in a country house with a friend Mrs. Wilson, and the address is Brae House, Dingwall. If you are near there, she would I am sure be glad to see you. We shall be in Sussex in August and perhaps we might arrange a meeting there, if you propose to come South with your daughter. I am almost retired from Medical practice now, but represent the Universities of Edinburgh & St. Andrews in Parliament. This gives me complete employment. I was speaking on behalf of a poor ill used Doctor who lives in the Hebridies, last night.
With kind regards.
    Believe me
        Yours faithfully
        Wm O Priestley

Agnes' diary indicated that Lady Priestley was too ill to see Horatio and his family.[5] Agnes' entries in her diary became too sporadic to confirm or disconfirm a visit in Sussex, but "Westbrook Hall, Horsham" was written at the top of Priestley's letter by Horatio. This was Priestley's new Sussex country residence and this additional information obtained from or about Priestley suggests such a visit did take place.

At the age of sixty-nine, Horatio already had outlived many of his colleagues. Agnes made note of this in her diary for August 6, probably from Edinburgh: "We have spent much time in fruitless searches after Pater's old friends who alas seem nearly all to have moved away—that is of the few now left this side of Jordan. The great majority are dead."[6] Dr. Priestley also was to die less than a year later in London "after an illness of some months duration."

Horatio also visited the continent. A September 27, 1899 a letter to Horatio from John Ware,[7] a Harvard classmate living in Paris indicated that Horatio was traveling from Paris to Brussels. Horatio probably had returned from abroad by October 31, 1899 when his son, Malcolm, married Grace Ayrault.[8]

Horatio's address late in 1899 and early in 1900 was the Hotel Kensington in New York City. Later in 1900, he was still writing from New York, but from other hotels.[9] Perhaps renovations were being made at his Newport residence. Almost all of Horatio's correspondence at this time dealt with medical medals, indicating no let up in his massive effort to identify and describe all of the world's medals related to medicine.

Horatio donated his medal collection to the Boston Medical Library in October 1900. A key factor that influenced the timing and destination of his gift was that a new building of the Boston Medical Library was approaching completion and would be dedicated on January 12, 1901. The booklet published to honor this dedication[10] referred to Malcolm Storer as one of the Library Officers, specifically, "Curator of the Storer Collection of Medical Medals." It also mentioned that the collection would become a "unique object of interest" when the medals went on display in Holmes Hall, the reading room of the new library.[11] The following discussion of Horatio's unusual and valuable gift from Farlow's *History of the Boston Medical Library* shows that any anger against his father for his discriminatory will apparently had totally disappeared. Even more remarkable was the apparent total disappearance as well of the righteous anger against the "clique" of Boston physicians who Marcy and others indicated had so unjustly opposed him.[12]

At a meeting of the Executive Committee on October 11, 1900, a letter was read from Dr. Horatio R. Storer, of Newport, R.I., formerly of Boston, offering to the Library his Collection of Medals relating to medicine, in memory of his father, the late Dr. David Humphreys Storer, and to recall his own connection with the physicians of Boston; and it was Voted: That the Collection of Medals offered by Dr. Storer be gratefully accepted on the conditions proposed by him, viz:

"1. That the Collection shall be known as the Storer Memorial Collection of Medical Medals.

"2. That it shall be kept together, as far as may be possible, and in suitable cases.

"3. That its care shall be intrusted to my son, Dr. Malcolm Storer, during his willingness to serve. Thereafter, if either of my grandsons shall become a physician in Boston, I shall trust that he may have preference as Curator.

"4. That if at any time in the future, through now unforeseen circumstances, the Library shall cease to exist as such, or its control shall pass to persons according to the Code of Ethics of the American Medical Association in any way irregular, the Collection shall be transferred to the possession of Harvard University, from which my father received his medical degree in 1825, I my own in 1853, and my son his in 1889;"

That the thanks of the Library be transmitted to Dr. Storer, and that the desire expressed by him that his father's portrait, now the property of the Library, be hung in the vicinity of the Collection be acceded to.

The Medals, 2,139 in number when received, were arranged in

Holmes Hall in swinging leaves so that the both sides of each medal can be seen; others are kept in a cabinet and a few are framed and hang on the wall.

This was followed by a discussion of Horatio's collecting written by Malcolm. He indicated that Horatio's interest went back to 1878, and discussed the uniqueness of his father's gift which was only matched by European collections. Malcolm's strong involvement with his father's effort and no doubt a similar involvement by the other family numismatist, John Humphreys Storer, helps explain the incredible energy and effort, despite invalidism, that went into this unique documentation of medical history. On the other hand, incredible energy and effort appears to have characterized all of Horatio's endeavors. A month later, Horatio provided a letter to the President of Harvard describing his bequest of medals and requesting, on the one hand, that the Boston Medical Library become directly affiliated with Harvard University, and, on the other, repeating his 1852 request that Cambridge medical books be placed in that Library.[13] It took a few more decades, but Horatio's wish of 1852, repeated first in 1866 as a member of the Overseers Committee to Visit the Harvard Medical School,[14] and then in 1900, would finally be carried out.

Agnes' diary for 1901 begins with discussion of Horatio's coming down with the "grippe."[15] Illness also probably accounts for a sharp drop in Horatio's medal correspondence and a ten-month delay in answering a February request for an obituary of a colleague. On the other hand, Agnes referred frequently to walks she and her father took, including one only three days *after* "Pater had a terrible fall."[16] Agnes' diary also notes visits from and to Dr. James Joseph Walsh, a neurologist who was an instructor at the New York Poly-Clinic School of Medicine and who became the Dean of the Fordham University School of Medicine a few years later. Dr. Walsh was later to provide a series of biographies of physicians who had converted to Catholicism, including three versions dealing with Horatio. Walsh is credited in his *Dictionary of American Biography* sketch as teaching the first course of medical history in the country and Horatio's massive project to record the history of medicine through medical medals must have provided a strong bond between the two men. Given Horatio's earlier proposal for a Professorship of Medical History at Harvard, it is possible that Horatio influenced Walsh to develop his medical history course when Walsh moved to Fordham in 1907.

Agnes' diary also makes reference to the family apartment in New York at 230 Central Park South. This occurred in late October and suggests that the winter now was being spent away from the waterfront residence in Newport. It was at this time, and from New York, that Horatio provided Malcolm the long autobiographical letter that has frequently been referred to in this book.[17] Malcolm had requested information for a "history of gynaecological teaching" which he was preparing and which was published two years later.[18]

New York City was conducive to long walks by Agnes and her father, even though Horatio now was going on seventy-two, and certainly still on crutches. Horatio's practice of his adopted religion in New York suggests that his commitment to Catholicism could have been higher. Agnes' Sunday entries typically noted: "Low mass with Pater. High mass with Mama."

Horatio's correspondence on medals diminished sharply in 1902, although Mr. Speck still received three letters. Horatio was still regularly publishing articles on the medals of medicine in the *American Journal of Numismatics*, although the queue of such articles probably was long enough to not be eliminated by even a very long bout of "grippe." The year 1903 began well, but Agnes wrote in her diary, "Pater very ill," on August 8. Subsequent entries typically repeated this phrase, and by the end of the month Horatio was hospitalized and operated on, and Agnes' diary indicated "found cancer of the intestines."[19] Horatio is noted as suffering terribly in Agnes' diary. Her entry for September 1 reads: "At hospital. Still vomiting during night. Praying not to recover, poor darling." However, Horatio apparently improved quickly, and he is noted to have returned home on September 16. Another operation on November 4, was followed by Agnes' diary entry, "cancer entirely removed."[20] This surgery was not exploratory, but removed more cancer and several of Agnes' diary entries indicate that Horatio had some very bad days afterwards. Horatio returned from this hospital stay on November 28 and Agnes' entry for Christmas read: "A great happy day in the house."[21] Agnes reported she walked the several miles to Fort Greene with Horatio on January 24, 1904. However, February was filled with illness for Horatio, and it would be March 4, 1904 before Agnes again noted, "Walk with Pater."

On March 7, 1904 the new Secretary of the Class of 1850, John Noble, wrote Horatio to solicit a contribution for a portrait of President Charles Eliot. Horatio's note at the bottom indicates he sent $10 on March 8. The previous Class Secretary, Horatio's close friend and Hermann Warner's college roommate, Joseph Henry Thayer, had died in 1902. On July 1, Agnes tells us "Parent lectured at hospital," indicating Horatio was still involved in medical matters. A card printed in 1904 advertised the Newport Sanitary Protection Association and its house-inspection and water-analysis services. Only the Secretary and Treasurer were listed on the card and neither was Horatio. However, the presence of this card among family papers insures some involvement by Horatio in the Association he started twenty-six years earlier.

By the Fall of 1904, Horatio had fully recovered from his cancer and was again physically active, taking long walks with Agnes and making fishing excursions with Malcolm. Other references in Agnes' diary indicate Horatio went fishing on several days before and after his seventy-fifth birthday. Her entry on the birthday itself (February 27, 1905) makes only a brief reference to the event and to "calls." On April 9, Agnes wrote: "Pater went off fishing at 1.30 A.M this morning!" On July 5, her entry read: "P. caught 10. ft. shark

& has it in exhibition." At the end of July 1905, Agnes' diary entry included: "Pater assaulted by the City Pier Mob." No newspaper account of this assault or other reference to it was found, and this probably indicates that Horatio did not receive serious injury.

On January 23, 1906, the *Newport Daily News* published a letter of Horatio's condemning a pair of popular novels which praised the post-Civil-War activities of the Ku Klux Klan.[22] "There seems in Newport just now," Horatio began his letter, "a mild reawakening of a form of uncharitableness that in view of the history of the place it were well should be forgotten." He then praised a pamphlet by Kelly Miller, a Howard University professor, which also condemned Thomas Dixon's *The Leopard's Spots* and *The Clansman*. "The two novels now in question," Horatio continued, "are intentionally calculated to excite the fears and inflame the passions of the North, precisely as certain dime tales of the baser sort incite so many youths to acts of violence and crime." Horatio called for the banning of Dixon's works from public libraries because of the "mental and spiritual poison" they contained. He denied that there were any significant physiological or anatomical differences between the white and black races and noted that "labor anxieties" were a major factor in existing Northern prejudice against blacks. He indicated that Newport's sordid history as a slave port made it all the more important to prevent any exacerbation of racial prejudice in the city. He also described and praised key black leaders in Newport and their important contributions to the city in both earlier and modern times. The letter concluded:

> From what has been said, is it not evident that the extreme permissible limit of race prejudice has been reached, and that were it merely in justice alone, books and plays based upon them, which purport to show the absolute worth and necessity of the Ku Klux Khan [sic], and the more recent rapine and slaughterings, should be excluded from our public libraries and our theatres, as from our homes?

Horatio's condemnation of Dixon's books and his attempt to reduce racial animosities led to the following letter from Newport's black community:[23]

Dr. H. R. Storer:

Dear Sir: Since your communication in the Daily News January 23 you have been in our minds as never before. You had been known to us as one of our city physicians, but since the publishing of your "Race Prejudice" you have been recognized by us as a friend indeed. We had expected to see e'er now in public print expressions of gratitude for your timely words in our defense; you may have been officially written or called upon by representatives of some of the organizations of color of this city. As this we do not know, we have attempted to express our feelings of deepest esteem to you, who dares so nobly speak forth words of truth and encouragement concerning a people who for unavoidable conditions are constantly thrown down and trampled upon by many of those who pledge allegiance to our flag and the indivisible nation for which it is an emblem.

It must appear to those across the ocean that the statements made concerning the brutality and injuries along all lines inflicted upon the negroes of America are erroneous or the American nation is hypocrisy personified. There were times in the past when we were almost persuaded that the men of iron wills and sterling worth who were friends to the oppressed had died. We thought upon John Brown, Charles Sumner, Wendell Phillips, William Lloyd Garrison, Henry Ward Beecher, Harriet Beecher Stowe and others sleeping—aye, resting from their labors. When we were about to become discouraged we were led by divine prompting to look up and by looking we recognized a halo glowing fresh from God's eternal throne which bore testimony: "I am with thee." In all ages friends have been raised up who dared to speak, act and if need be die in the cause of right. Though apparently few, their worth cannot be told.

Dr. Storer, do not look upon these lines thinking them as coming from some who would feebly attempt to display their oratorical powers, but to the opposite they are the earnest of honest hearts, from women who have burdened upon them the interest and progress of the race, women who are hopeful notwithstanding the many obstacles placed in the way to hinder the progress of truth and right.

Please accept these as the sentiments of the Josephine Silone Yates Mothers' Club of Newport R. I.

In behalf of the J. S. Y. Mothers' Club.

I am yours.

Mrs. T. H. Jeter.

Several years later, Thomas Dixon's novels were the basis for the movie "The Birth of a Nation." As we will see, Horatio also publicly criticized the film, and was again to be thanked by Newport's blacks.

The year 1907 appears to have involved some illness, but nothing like the major cancer problem of 1903. We learn from Agnes' diary that Horatio was well enough to spend much of April and May in Washington D.C. and went for his first automobile ride there.[24] Horatio's college roommate, Dr. Gustavus Hay, died April 26, 1908 in Jamaica Plain, Massachusetts. Horatio probably was not at the funeral or memorial service, but he tried to provide information for Hay's obituary. This is shown in the following letter to classmate Frederick Dickinson Williams, who took over as Class Secretary from the ailing John

Noble:[25]

Newport, R. I.
4 July 1908

Dear Fred W.

It was a delight to see your familiar handwriting again.

Were I really able for the effort & the fatigue, it would make me very happy to meet you few who are still left, at C. I am still young in spirit, but my casing has begun to feel the inevitable, & I trust that when the break does come, it will be of the "altogether".

Dr. Ben Jeffries of Chestnut St. has written me that he is preparing a notice of his fellow eyeman, Gus Hay, for a medical journal. I have sent him some points, & referred him to Noble for others. In this matter, J. would be very glad to hear from yourself.

What ails Noble, beyond old age?

Give my love to all the men. You know that you have it already.

As ever, yrs sincerely H.R. Storer

Several months later, the obituary of Hay by Jeffries was published in the 1909 *Transactions of the American Ophthalmological Society*. It told that "He was prepared for college at the Boston Latin School, entered college when he was fifteen, and after completing the four years' course he petitioned the faculty to be allowed to remain another year, and so graduated with the class of 1850."[26] Horatio complained of this and other errors to Williams, in a November 12, 1908 letter:[27]

Astonished is a mild word to use regarding Jeffries. He has *not* sent me his memoir. He wrote me that he intended preparing it, but in a way that led me to think, although our relations together have always been pleasant, that he already had all the information concerning Hay that was desired. So that my reply was not a very lengthy one.

As H. was my room mate during the whole four years, I probably know as much about him as anyone else, & J. was doubtless aware of this. What you quote from J. is all new to me, & merely serves to confirm my [lack of] confidence in even current "history", as to that of the past, who chooses, may believe.

Hay was of course with us all the time, & an intimation to the contrary is simply *preposterous*.

Horatio's next letter to Williams indicated his regrets for the next class reunion at Cambridge and provided his "great secret of a happy old age":[28]

Newport, R. I.

12 May 1909

Dear Fred Dick[n],

It is always a great pleasure to hear from you, & your classmates. That you keep fairly well, you should feel grateful for. My own tolerable health despite all that I have gone through, I surely owe to my having solved the one great secret of a happy old age. For every joy, & they are numberless, that comes to me, I daily & devotedly thank Heaven,—& for every disappointment or physical pain, I as devoutly & very humbly rejoice that it is no worse.

Only last evening I was reading "Ugo Bassi's Sermon in the Hospital". B. was Chaplain to Garibaldi in 1849, & after capture by the Austrians was shot.

"And while we suffer, let us set our souls
To suffer perfectly, since this alone,
The suffering, which is this world's special grace,
May here be perfected and left behind".

I shall be with you at No. 5 in spirit,—would it could be in flesh also. To those who are left & come thither, my love.

Sincerely yrs

H.R. Storer

Soon there was another Secretary change. Horatio wrote:[29]

58 Washington St.

Newport, R. I.

11 Sept, 1909

My dear Hales Wallace [Suter],

Now that Noble has been "called to the bar" of the Supremest Court, I am glad that what remains of the class has been placed in your care, & trust, for the sake of us all, even including yourself, that in the race we are all of us now so swiftly running for Charon's skiff, you may be the last to reach it.

...

I have heard from Fred Williams that you are probably the best preserved of the remnants. It would be a great pleasure to know this through personal observation. Don't fail to recollect that should you come to Newport, a warm welcome awaits you at my house. I have not forgotten the pleasant years we passed together at C[ambridge]., & as time slips by, the memory of them becomes more vivid than ever.

Sincerely yrs

H.R. Storer

Henry Orlando Marcy was seventy-two when he presented a paper on "The Early History of Abdominal Surgery in America" before the Section on Obstetrics and Diseases of Women at the Sixtieth Annual Session of The American Medical Association held at Atlantic City in June 1909.[30] It is doubtful that Horatio was in Atlantic City to hear the following tributes to himself, although he surely read them when it was published a few months later. Horatio no doubt cringed at the errors Marcy made when discussing his life and work, particularly the claim of his "blind" "step in the direction of aseptic surgery," but must have been delighted to learn he had received such accolades in a speech before the Association he loved almost as much as Boston. The known errors that Marcy made in the following are footnoted or corrected in brackets:

> More than passing notice is due one of my first teachers, Dr. Horatio R. Storer of Boston. Personally I am under a debt of gratitude to Dr. Storer which can never be paid. We loved him despite, if not for, the enemies that he made. His equally distinguished father had carefully supervised his education. A graduate of Harvard, a student at law, in due course a doctor of medicine and for four[31] years a sharer in the home and training of the immortal Simpson of Edinburgh. ... Dr. Storer returned to Boston and was appointed an instructor on the diseases of women [Assistant Instructor in Obstetrics and Medical Jurisprudence] in the Harvard Medical School. He had a most enthusiastic following when, as an undergraduate, I first met him. He soon became one of the most popular practitioners in the city of Boston and was said to have had the largest income of any member of the profession in New England. He was indefatigable in his work. He founded the Gynecological Society of Boston, the first special society devoted to the diseases of women in the world; and for seven [three-and-one-half years, *seven* volumes] years he published the *Journal of the Gynecological Society of Boston.* The first successful case on record undertaken for the cure of umbilical hernia was one of his early operations.[32] In September, 1865, he successfully performed hysterectomy; and this was the twenty-fourth case of the operation placed on record and the fourth [sixth] successful case operated on in America. In 1866 Dr. Storer contributed an elaborate paper on the treatment of the pedicle of fibroid tumors and strongly advocated the use of the clamp. He devised an instrument capable of producing enormous compression and hinged on a pivot rotating so as to allow closure at any angle. I consider it the best, as well as last contribution for the external treatment of the pedicle by compression.
> Dr. Storer made a further contribution, and in my judgment a more valuable one, which he called "pocketing the pedicle." ... By it he was enabled, in the non-infected cases, to close off the abdominal wall and protect the peritoneal cavity. This was, of course, a step

in the direction of aseptic surgery, although taken blindly.[33]

Marcy concluded this tribute to Horatio with the paragraph beginning, "There is no doubt that Dr. Storer was the 'best-hated' member of the profession in Massachusetts," which was presented in Chapter 10.

A letter early in 1909 from fellow numismatist and friend, Howland Wood, of Brookline, Massachusetts, indicated that both were on the American Committee for the International Congress of Numismatics held in Belgium in 1910.[34] Horatio prepared a paper, "The Medals of Linnaeus,"[35] for that Congress, but there is no evidence that he actually traveled to Belgium. Horatio described fifty-seven medals that had been issued to honor the Swedish physician-naturalist who is celebrated for first bringing order to the classification of plants and animals and noted that most of these medals were extremely rare. Horatio stated in the paper that he was the first to describe thirty-two of these medals and that twenty-one were in his collection at the Boston Medical Library and these facts testify to the persistence of Horatio in his search for medallic history. Horatio also noted that nineteen of these medals had been part of "the recent celebration by the N. Y. Academy of Science, of the two hundredth anniversary of the birth of Linnaeus." Even without an interest in numismatics, one can appreciate the large contribution a collection of commemorative medals would provide to such a celebration.

Agnes' diary suggests that Christmas 1909 also provided Horatio one of the "numberless" joys for which Horatio did "devotedly thank Heaven": "Xmas—A wonderful night." She wrote, "P[ater]. M[ama]. & I going to midnight Mass at the C[enacle]."[36] Horatio's eightieth birthday on February 27, 1910 was reported in Agnes' diary to involve "Many callers, quantities of Hymns, and a congenial day here." Malcolm and "the cousins" were there for dinner. The following note and poem for the occasion from one of his neighbors survives among family papers and hints at Storer achievements otherwise unknown:[37]

> To Dr. Storer, on his 80th birthday, from his affectionate friend,
> Esther Morton Smith
> February 27th—1910
> H ere's to our neighbor and our friend
> O f thirty steadfast years;
> R eady with help in time of need,
> A lert with kindly word and deed
> T o meet our smiles and tears.
> I f ever we'd establish facts
> O n matters old or new,
> R ight drainage, lobsters, surgery,

S moke-nuisance, civic perjury,
T he Doctor'd see us through.
O ur dear old friend, well-tried and true,
R ich harvest, still we wish for you.
E ach year, each *day*, its blessing bring!
R ipe Autumn's fruit, to heart of Spring.

Horatio's first wife, Emily Elvira, was buried at Forest Hills Cemetery in Boston in a plot that included her parents. Horatio considered it important to eventually join her, given a May 19, 1910 letter from Agnes to Archbishop O'Connell at Boston which included: "I write to your Grace to ask for the desired permission for my father, my mother, & myself to receive Catholic burial in our family lot at Forest Hills. The details as to the officiating priest etc. I understand can be arranged when the need arises."[38]   Agnes' attention to a burial place was stimulated by the grave illness of Frances Sophia. Archbishop O'Connell quickly responded with permission for the Forest Hills Catholic burial.[39] Horatio added to Agnes' letter a note thanking the Archbishop for his kind reception of Agnes and added a postscript which read: "I am glad to notice your interest in the Guild of St. Luke."[40] The postscript indicates that Horatio probably was a member, perhaps even a founder, of this organization of Catholic physicians. Horatio had founded a similar "Medical Guild of St. Thomas Aquin"[41] in 1881, but it apparently was not successful, unless it evolved into the Guild of St. Luke.

Horatio was again called upon by the Class of 1850 Secretary to join the survivors at the annual Class dinner and declined with the following note:[42]

Newport, R. I.
26 May—1910

My dear Suter,

Were I as active as I hear you are, I should certainly try to join again our now octogenarian circle—you will have, however, to count me there in spirit, & when you call the roll, please answer in my behalf Adsuen.

It will do each of you old boys good to spend a day in Newport during the present summer, & whether you come alone or in each others' company, you will find a very hearty welcome at my home. I have chosen a most lovely spot, ... to die in, with the setting sun, across the water, just before me. When your turns come, may you each have such surrounding to cheer you, but may all your days still be long in the land.

The Class of Fifty, still here & gone, God bless us all.

Affy yrs
H.R. Storer

The death of Horatio's former student and assistant, Dr. Alexander Johnson Stone, occurred on July 16, 1910.[43] Stone was only sixty-four, and it must have caused Horatio to view his own survival to eighty as a particular blessing. Agnes' diary for September 2, 1910 told that "Pater had a great gathering of the Med[ical]. Fac[ulty]. to meet Dr Osler who was *charming.*" Agnes shared this view of Sir William Osler with many others in Canada, the United States, and Great Britain.

Secretary Suter called for a special class meeting later in 1910, related to financial support of Noble's widow. Horatio's reply gives one of his few references to his family's first tragedy and its profound effect on him:[44]

Newport, R. I.
24 Nov. 1910

My dear Suter,

I have been absent for the past month at Promfret, Ct. where my wife has been very dangerously ill. We brought her home last night by the hospital car of the N.Y., N. H., & H. RR, & I hasten to reply to your letters.

I remember Noble affectionately, & anything that can lend to the welfare of those who were dear to him has my cordial approval. I shall be glad if an opportunity shall occur for me to make Mrs. N.'s acquaintance.

Now that Quincy has gone, I am in doubt as to how many of us remain. Kindly mention to me their names.

Thanksgiving Day has for many years been for me one of the saddest in the year because upon it long ago my then only child lay dying. Today has been rendered especially happy, since Mrs S. has been spared to return to our home still living.

Sincerely yrs
H.R. Storer

Give my kindest wishes to all who may attend the meeting. Should any of them ever find their way to Newport, they will find a hearty welcome.

Agnes' diary for December 1, 1910 recounts the next Storer family tragedy:

My precious Madre died at dawn after ten hours agony beyond anything Dr Anderson (who stayed all night) & the others had ever seen. Thank God for her precious life & give me the grace to so live, I shall meet her in Heaven & hear the precious words that were her last on earth—Dearest Agnes!.

An obituary of Frances Sophia MacKenzie Storer from a Catholic periodical included this tribute:[45]

> Not only was she joint foundress with another devoted Franciscan tertiary long since gone to her reward, of a Home for Working Girls, which even in its struggling beginning did a great work in harboring the homeless and starting them in the right course for life, but this frail, often suffering woman, single-handed, without means or influence, and in the face of opposition and misunderstanding, became the sole foundress of a free hospital for women, and by her unswerving courage and faith and love made it the haven of hope and healing that it has been now for over forty years, under the wise guidance of a great religious order. To those who knew intimately the life history which has closed on earth amid great suffering met in such peace as this world cannot give, it seemed even as they prayed for her eternal rest that they could hear the Divine, ineffable welcome, "Come, ye blessed of My Father, possess the Kingdom prepared for you from the foundation of the world; for I was hungry and you gave Me to eat; I was thirsty and you gave Me to drink; I was a stranger and you took Me in; naked and you covered Me; sick and you visited Me; I was in prison, and you came to Me. ... As long as you did it unto one of these my least brethren, you did it unto Me."

Early in February 1911, Horatio and Agnes traveled to Deland, Florida to vacation at the home of Horatio's son, Frank Addison.[46] The Florida stay lasted until April and was followed by two weeks in Washington, D.C. and a stay in Atlantic City. It was in Atlantic City that Horatio wrote the long letter to Sir James Young Simpson's nephew, Sir Alexander R. Simpson, which described Horatio's 1854-1855 Edinburgh experience.

Horatio's friendship with Dr. James Joseph Walsh continued and the correspondence indicated their shared interest in medical history. Another friend of Horatio's was a New York neurologist, originally from Edinburgh, Dr. William J. Maloney. Horatio introduced Maloney to Walsh who was now Dean of the Fordham Medical School. Walsh wrote the following note of gratitude:[47]

JAS. J. WALSH, M. D.
110 West Seventy-Fourth Street

New York.
August 16, 1911.

My dear Dr. Storer,

    I have been meeting Dr. Maloney the Irish Scotchman several times of late as the result of your note of introduction. I am very glad indeed to know him. You did me a real favor in sending him.

We would like very much to keep him at Fordham however if that can be managed. We already have two Edinburgh men and I should like very much to have another. ...

I shall be glad to meet more of the stamp of Dr. Maloney, so whenever you can, send them on.

Yours very sincerely,

Jas J Walsh

Another convert to Catholicism whom Walsh was to honor biographically was Dr. Thomas Dwight who had succeeded Oliver Wendell Holmes as Professor of Physiology at the Harvard Medical School. Shortly before Dwight's death, Dwight responded to Horatio, indicating he was "glad that you like my little book" and giving the bad news that he was suffering from cancer.[48] Horatio's kind words about the "little book" were not Horatio's whole story as Horatio provided it to Dr. Walsh in a letter written September 12, 1911 after Dwight's death. The letter revealed that[49]

Holmes as a teacher of anatomy was unrivalled. The only man whom I could compare with him was Palmer, who was a colleague of mine in the old Berkshire School, & held Chair in several other colleges. H[olmes]. practically invented the stereoscope, made important improvements in the microscope, & when it came to dry bones, he clothed them with life. As with too many scientists he was, however, not always too generous,—as when his department was divided, & physiology for a short period transferred to Brown-Séquard, he violently & almost virulently resisted the change.

In reading Dwight's very recently published book, Thoughts of a Catholic Anatomist, 1911, you have doubtless been impressed by two very important characteristics. One of them is, that from beginning to end it might have been written by a dozen or even a hundred Protestant teachers, or even by those who are not Christians at all. ... One fails to find any reference to the divinity of our Lord, or indeed to any professedly R C tenet whatever, & this is what, & what only, unbelievers in the Faith will seek in the book.

Secondly, D. strongly defends not a new, but certainly not generally accepted theory, even by the most thoughtful or most biased anatomists, that the negro is not an undeveloped possibility of mental, and spiritual, & even physical development & betterment, but in every sense a degenerate from some unknown or mythical hyper excellent & exalted race in the past. Were this true, every effort in the present, even by the Holy Church itself, would be worse than thrown away, for it could only excite hopes, national, racial, & religious, that could never be fulfilled. ...

Your reference to myself was unexpected. I will think the matter

over. As for myself, I have no desire for notoriety. If you can make
me of any use, however, to others, is another thing. Of this you can
judge better than I.

Sincerely yrs

H.R. Storer

Dr. J.J. Walsh.

The danger of "notoriety" may have been a Walsh proposal of a Fordham
LL.D. for Horatio in conjunction with a Fordham Medical School post-graduate
program. The degree and program would occur almost exactly one year later.

Agnes' diary on a couple of occasions in 1911 makes reference to Horatio
as "in the depths," no doubt grieving for Frances Sophia. On the other hand,
"Walked with Pater" was still a frequent entry and twice she wrote "long walk
with Pater," which indicates that at eighty-one, Horatio was still just a "partial
invalid." Dr. Maloney's visits to their Newport home were frequent and Agnes'
diary comments indicate that he was a real favorite with her and Horatio.
However, Agnes' first reference to Horatio in her 1912 diary read: "Found I
should have to give up week-day Mass as Pater needs help dressing."[50] "Pater
wretchedly" is Agnes' entry for both the day before Horatio's eighty-second
birthday and on it. Fortunately, this was one of the few birthdays in Horatio's
old age which were not pleasant, even joyous, events.

CHAPTER 22

FORDHAM LL.D., THE STORER MEDALLION, CLASS SECRETARY

Agnes' entry in her diary for September 3, 1912 included: "Thrilling proposal of W.J.M's that P. go in to N.Y to receive an LL.D." "W.J.M." was their frequent guest, Dr. William J. Maloney, now Professor of Nervous and Mental Diseases at Fordham. Undoubtedly, his boss, Dean Walsh, was at least the co-"proposer" of this honor, and probably a year earlier. Horatio was awarded the LL.D. at Fordham on September 11, 1912. The following letter to Dr. Walsh indicated his hope of attending the ceremony, although the injury he mentions prevented him from going:[1]

Newport, R. I.

3 Sept. 1912

Dear Dr. Walsh,

It was very good of you to think of me amid all your cares attending the throes of Fordham's resurrection & I am duly thankful. I none the less feel, however, & very acutely, that the honor is entirely undeserved.

I shall endeavor to go on to NY on the date appointed, but am still quite incapacitated through a bad fall which has kept me most of the past month in bed.

Among the personal papers that I sent you, there was a little printed slip giving the details of the Boston post graduate scheme of 1867. As I have no other copy, please send me this at your first convenience, & much oblige

yours sincerely

H.R. Storer

The "slip" Horatio referred to is the one presented earlier which outlined the post-graduate offerings of Horatio and his eleven Boston colleagues planned for 1867.[2] The "extension course" of Horatio and his colleagues was relevant because Fordham was providing an extension course for physicians which began two days before the awarding of the honorary degrees to Horatio and four other physicians. The other four were experts in nervous and mental diseases and were the faculty for this polyclinic. The *Newport Daily News* write-up of the ceremony read:[3]

MADE A DOCTOR OF LAWS.

Dr. Horatio Robinson Storer of this city was given the honorary degree of doctor of laws by Fordham University, New York, Wednesday evening, on the occasion of the opening of a new clinic. He is the only American honored by a degree, the other recipients being Dr. Carl J. Jung, of Zurich, Switzerland; Dr. Henry Head, chief surgeon of the London Hospital, who were also made doctor of laws, and Dr. Nicholas Achucarro of the University of Madrid and Dr. Gordon Holmes of London, who received the degree of doctor of science. All these physicians are specialists in mental and nervous diseases and have an international reputation for their work and discoveries. Dr. Storer was one of the first physicians in this country to introduce the use of chloroform and was a specialist in gynaecology.

The following from the *Harvard Graduates' Magazine* for December 1912 expounded Horatio's pet peeve about the improper use of the caduceus of Mercury with its two serpents instead of the single-serpent staff of Aesculapius to represent medicine:[4]

VARIA.

The Boylston Society Bookplate.—Dr. H. R. Storer, '50, writes from Newport, R. I.: "In Mr. Prescott's article on Harvard Book Plates, in your September number, he speaks of one of the Boylston plates as showing the staff or AEsculapius. Upon examining the figure, however, you will see that this is not the case, and that the emblem given is the winged caduceus of Mercury, with its two serpents, illustrative of his attributes as the patron of thieves and liars. This error has been a common one with medical schools, libraries, and societies,—past and present,—at home and abroad,—and at my suggestion, in two or three instances, the proper changes have been made. The Boston Medical Library at first went thus astray, and so did the New York Academy of Medicine. Similar forgetfulness has occurred upon many medical medals, and certainly in its little way brings discredit upon the science of medicine. The staff of AEsculapius bears but a single serpent, suggesting the pursuit of Wisdom, pure and simple, first, last and all the time.

"*H. R. Storer*, '50."

Agnes' entry for May 25, 1913 included the news: "Dr R. Tait McKenzie (the sculptor) & [John] Humphreys [Storer, Jr.] came to supper & spent P.M." Agnes wrote on July 24th, "Dr McKenzie modelled P." She noted another "setting" occurred four days later in her journal. By Fall the medal was ready. What a great "joy" it must have been for Horatio, the foremost collector of medical medals in the country and probably in the world, to have a medical medal where he himself was depicted. Its struck (not engraved) inscription reads:

TO THE MASTER IN SVRGERY
MEDICAL NVMISMATIST
AND LOVER OF MAN AND NATVRE
HORATIO R. STORER, MD, LLD
FROM HIS FRIEND R. TAIT MCKENZIE MD 1913

The *Newport Daily News* gave this account of the new medal:[5]

MEDALLION OF DR. STORER.
Dr. McKenzie, Noted Surgeon,
Honors Friend of Many
Years.

Dr. R. Tait McKenzie, professor of physical education at the University of Pennsylvania and one of the best known surgeons in the country, has added an interesting medallion to his achievements. The medallion is that of Dr. Horatio R. Storer of this city. Dr. Storer is a friend of Dr. McKenzie of many years and the medallion is a token of that friendship.

For more than 10 years Dr. McKenzie has been recognized here and abroad as a sculptor of note. Some of his medallions, in which his knowledge of anatomy is exhibited, have been pronounced of unusual merit by the highest art critics in American and European galleries. He has been a consistent producer of works, and among the medallions made by him have been those of Francis Kinloch Huget, who attempted to rescue Lafayette from the fortress at Olmutz; Crawford W. Long, who is credited with having discovered the value of ether as an anaesthetic before its official discovery, and many prominent physicians and surgeons.

Agnes' diary for Saturday, November 22, 1913 read: "*The* Day Fine *Celestial*. Went with M[alcolm].S. & G[race]. & Dr. Draper to the great Yale-Harvard game at the Stadium, whereat Harvard under Robert's leadership won 15-5." "Robert" was John Humphreys Storer's second son, Robert Treat Paine Storer. He was an All-American right tackle and Captain of the Harvard team which was ranked number one in the nation. No doubt this athletic success of his grandson was another "joy" for which Horatio "devotedly thanked Heaven."

Horatio's brother Frank died on July 30, 1914. Agnes attended the funeral, but there is no indication in her diary that Horatio made the trip. Another death was Hales Wallace Suter. Suter's death prompted the following draft letter from Horatio to the remaining members of the Class of 1850, with its final paragraph omitted in the version actually sent:[6]

58 Washington St.
Newport R.I.
25 Aug. 1914

Dear Classmate,

You will have heard of the death of our Secretary, Suter. His official papers have been sent to me by his son, Rev. J.H.S., probably because his father sat next to me, alphabetically, during our four years at Cambridge. It has now become necessary for a successor to be chosen, and as it is improbable that we can ever again attend collectively, for this purpose, I suggest that each of you send me at your earliest leisure, the name of the one whom you would prefer to fill the vacant place. I will then inform you of the result.

Our survivors seem to be J.H. Cabot, Coolidge, Foster, Robinson, Storer, Warner, F.D. Williams, and Wyeth, with Gustavus Rudolphus Whitridge, Charleston, S.C. temporary member.

[The following paragraph was not sent—crossed out]

I often think of you all affectionately, and wish we might meet each other again to review happy memories. As our circle contracts, its bond should unite us the more closely together.

sincerely yours

H.R. Storer   seven copies

Robinson's[7] and Coolidge's[8] answers survive. Both thought Horatio the best choice to replace Suter as Class Secretary. All but Warner sent similar wishes and Horatio wrote the following to the editors of the Alumni publication:[9]

58 Washington St.
Newport, R. I.
25 Sept. 1914

Dear Sir,

To fill the Class Secretaryship of 1850, vacated by the recent death of Mr. H.W. Suter, a home vote has been taken by the remaining survivors: J.H. Cabot, Coolidge, Foster, Robinson, Storer, Warner, F.D. Williams, & Wyeth, all of whom are too old & infirm for another personal meeting, with the following results: Foster 1, Storer 6. The eighth member, Mr. H.J. Warner is probably marooned somewhere in Europe. He has been twice written, but as yet no reply.

Sincerely yrs.

Horatio R. Storer

M.D., LL.B.(Harvard); LL.D.(Fordham)

The Editors Quinquennial C.

If you wondered who voted for Foster, the following portion of the letter to Foster (similar to letters to all the others) gives the answer.[10]

Copy   Newport, R. I.
                                                  25 Sept. 1914

My dear Foster,

The poll for Class Secretary has resulted as follows: Foster 1 (H.R.S.), Storer 6. Warner is apparently marooned some where in Europe. I have written him twice, but as yet no reply. The others have answered most cordially, each of them expressing the utmost interest in those who remain. The script of Cabot, Coolidge, Robinson & yourself as yet shows no sign of debility. Williams, partially paralysed & with commencing mental failure, sends his love through his companion, Mrs. Esther von Nurscheim. Wyeth's pen betrays his feeble hand. I wrote twice to him at New Dorp, & finally reached him at the Florence Home through his townsman, Dr. Devlin. He closed his letter as several that were upon Suter's file, with this description appended to his signatures "John Noble, First Honor Man of the Class of 1850." I have told him that in this constant recollection of our Chief, we all join. ...

You will find an obituary of Suter in the Sept. Harvard Graduates' Magazine, which of course you take. It was probably furnished by his son, Secretary of the Class of 1889, from whom I requested, & now enclose, our classmate's latest photograph, which shows that he had evidently mellowed, & as plainly improved spiritually as his life advanced. If you will return it promptly, I will circulate it around the rest. Similarly, send me your own for it will give pleasure to *all* of us to again see you, & as you really are. I will endeavor to obtain the others also, & let me suggest that since our days are steadily growing fewer, you each send me upon the last day of every month a brief word of how completely you continue to hold your own. I will then notify the remainder & in this way we shall draw more *closely* towards each other & renew the dear memories of Auld Lang Syne. ...

                        yrs ever
                        HRS

Hermann Jackson Warner's reply to the first letter finally appeared on October 6 and it read:[11]

                        Grand Hotel Locarno
                        Lac Majeur—Suisse
                        Locarno, September 18, 1914

Dear Classmate:

In reply to your letter of date August 25,—received today,—I can only say that it is indifferent to me who may be chosen as Suter's successor. I leave the choice, as far as I am concerned, entirely to you, who are on the spot, as it were, and can judge better who would be most [sic] inconvenienced by the job.

Sincerely yours

H.J. Warner

'ἀποδημος

Warner's Greek translates to "One who is away on a journey." Horatio probably was ill when Warner's letter was "received 6 Oct. 1914", since a another note at the bottom indicated it was "Answered 4 Dec."

Class Secretary Horatio's first "News from the Classes" of the *Harvard Graduates' Magazine* appeared in December 1914. It read:[12]

News from the Classes. 1850. Dr. H. R. Storer, *Sec.*, Newport, R.I.

Since all the survivors of the class are invalided through old age, and another gathering at Cambridge therefore rendered very improbable, the filling of the secretaryship, vacated by the death of H. W. Suter, was effected by a home vote participated in by all who remain: J. H. Cabot, of Brookline; F. C. Foster, of Cambridge; J. H. Robinson, of Melrose; T. J. Coolidge and F. D. Williams, of Boston; H. J. Warner, N. J. Wyeth, and Storer. A temporary member, G. R. Whitridge, of Charleston, S.C., failed to be reached, and may be dead. Williams, the favorite N.E. landscape painter, is very feeble both in body and mind. Warner, long resident abroad, is in Switzerland, recognizing professionally that *inter arma silent leges*, ["Among weapons, laws are silent."] and Wyeth at the Florence Home, New Dorp, Staten Island. Recent photographs, showing the striking changes that all have undergone during the 64 years since graduation, are being circulated, and so warm have been the mutual expressions of affection accompanying the vote just taken, that frequent reports of the condition of each will probably now be interchanged until the Class has ceased to exist.—The Secretary has been elected a director of the ancient Redwood Library at Newport.

The number surviving dropped quickly and Horatio provided their obituaries in the *Harvard Graduates' Magazine*. June's "News from the Classes" read:[13]

Frederick Dickinson Williams, one of New England's most noted landscape artists, died after a long illness, at Brookline on Jan. 25, in his 87th year. ... Born in Boston, he was prepared for college at its Latin School, and even then gave constant evidence of the inspiration which was to decide his future profession. Upon graduating, he taught drawing in various Boston schools from 1850 until 1874. In 1870 he married Lucia M. Hunt, of Newburyport, whose tastes very fortunately so completely coincided with his own that in 1874 they opened a studio together in Paris, and there they remained until her death in 1888. He then returned to Boston. In 1904, his studio on Irvington St. was burned, and with it was destroyed the result of many years of patient woodland study and most fruitful reproduction. Such love's labor lost is always pathetic; doubly so in this case, for almost all that thus vanished had been so deeply identified with the companionship of his wife. Williams was a whole-souled, genial associate. Beloved at school and equally popular at college; while in after life these friendships were continuously prized. Pure in heart, clean in intercourse, upright and stainless, he has gone to his certain reward.

Horatio protested the showing of the movie "Birth of a Nation" in the following letter to the Newport mayor published in the *Newport Journal* on September 3, 1915.[14]

58 Washington Street, 27 August 1915.
His Honor, Mayor Burlingame:
My Dear Sir: Without having in any way been approached upon the subject, permit me to protest against allowing the much discussed and really very objectionable play, "The Birth of the Nation," to be exhibited in this city.

Shorn though it may be of its most demoralizing features, this has only been accomplished through the forcible insistence of the best of our white people, everywhere. The intent of the play, to make money and to fan the flame of race prejudice, which of late years has been rapidly lessening, still remains. That the setting is spectacularly gorgeous, and that it has been installed at great expense, has nothing to do with the main question. This outlay has been re-paid manyfold through the attendance of crowds of careless and ill advised persons, who would equally flock, were it permitted by the law, to a representation of even the Crucifixion itself.

The real author, a peculiar kind of clergyman, is through his reprehensible books. "The Clansman." "The Leopard's Spots." etc., said to have become a millionaire. Who can estimate the harm these have done to us all in a national way? Who can compute the mental suffering and the check to their enliftment they have caused to our colored brethren?

Years ago I publicly protested against the circulation of these books by the Redwood and People's libraries, and years ago I used my best efforts towards preventing license of the similar play that then was striven for. That it was refused by our authorities gained great credit for Newport throughout the country.

That our city was then true to its best sense of public duty was in slight reparation for its old inglorious and most regrettable history, of having been the creator and headquarters of the African slave trade. Think of the scores of distilleries here before the American Revolution, changing molasses from the West Indian sugar plantations into New England rum and then of this being exchanged in Guinea for nude men and women, of the countless poor creatures brought to our wharves, the best of these forced immigrants, the direct ancestors of many of the present attendants at our four colored churches, retained here for home labor, while the remainder were sold South, or were sent to the Caribbean in purchase of the main staple of that accursed rum, which from a Newport pulpit has been denounced as the chief cause, originally and continuously since, of our city's decadence from its old comparative supremacy.

Think of all this, dear sir, you who best represent the sober-minded, and then encourage, if you can, the entrance here even for a brief moment, of a virtual firebrand, inciting to dislike, personal affront, and even destruction, were this possible, of a large fraction of our people—no matter how it may be condoned as "now entirely unobjectionable, emasculated of its confessedly evil tendencies, and attractive even to the most refined." Every cent paid for admission would be to further encourage the worst negro hater in this country, and be a tribute to his prolonged defiance of all Christian precept. ...

Yours sincerely,

Horatio R. Storer,

(M.D., LL.D.)

As with Horatio's 1906 condemnation of the novels upon which "Birth of a Nation" was based, Horatio's criticism of the movie drew letters of praise from the black community in Newport. Three of these survive among family papers.

The September 1915 *Harvard Graduates' Magazine* "News from the Classes" gave the following obituary by Horatio:[15]

Joseph Hidden Robinson, counselor-at-law, was born Sept. 3, 1828, at Marblehead, and died Feb. 1, 1915, in his 87th year, at Melrose, where he had long resided. ... Mr. Robinson, though to the end a student, retained a good measure of physical ability, frequently walking to Boston after his 80th year, and still later taking long pedestrian strolls as his regular exercise. As was to be expected from one of his early training, he consistently proved himself a worthy representative of his Harvard class, and was an old-fashioned, refined, and ever courteous gentleman. The now remaining six will as such remember him.

Horatio's correspondence with his classmates began to outstrip his medal-related correspondence. This restoration of student bonds obviously was a great pleasure to these octogenarians. Horatio actually visited one of his remaining classmates. Francis Charles Foster wrote Horatio afterwards:[16]

> Woods Hole
> Massachusetts
> Sept 15, 1915
>
> My dear Storer—
> Your very welcome announcement (of 12th inst.) of your trip and return home was received yesterday and was pleasant news, as well as a relief. I am very glad it was such success and so enjoyable; if we are alive next summer I wish you repeat the trip with your Daughter and spend a night with us—instead of the Tabitha Inn and we will do our best for you and talk you deaf and dumb. ...
> My wife was greatly disappointed at missing you. Yes, Warner is the "missing link" and it seems strange he so enjoys expatriating himself.
> With warm regards and best wishes, I am
> Sincerely yours
> Francis C. Foster

When Francis Foster died only six weeks later, Horatio wrote to at least Coolidge, who responded:[17]

> Magnolia, Mass.
>
> My Dear Storer
> Much obliged for yours of the 25th.
> As I am not well enough to go to the funeral, I adopted your suggestion & wrote a word of sympathy to Mrs Foster.
> Sincerely yours
> T. Jefferson Coolidge
> Oct 26/15

Horatio's obituary of Foster appeared in the December 1915 *Harvard Graduates' Magazine*.[18]

Francis Charles Foster died at his home in Cambridge Oct. 24, 1915. ... To the above notes furnished by the family, the Secretary must add a word. Foster's personality, as a youth and even in old age, was peculiarly attractive. He was so unconscious of this, with no trace whatever of self-appreciation, that it added to the charm. He was very gracious, generous, wholehearted, and, while showing no desire of commendation therefor, a very public-spirited man. This is shown by his many affiliations with the cities of Boston and Cambridge, and with his church. His affection for his classmates was especially strong. In an interview at his beautiful summer home at Wood's Holl, after many years of separation and but a few days before his death, a brief hour was spent in recalling College days and the then intimates who had long and prematurely left us. Though his general strength was failing, he seemed then able to outlive us all, and it is hard to realize that he too has joined the dear absentees. To the five who remain, one of whom is now so feeble that it has not been thought wise to inform him of this death or that of Robinson who left but a little earlier, Foster's memory will be of a friend who lived and died as a Harvard graduate should, *devotus Christo et Ecclesica*.

The "so feeble" one of the five was probably Cabot who would be next to expire on February 5, 1916.

Coolidge who had served as minister to France and more recently on a high-level international commission on international boundaries and fisheries, was pessimistic about America's chances in a possible fight with Germany. He wrote Horatio:[19]

315 Dartmouth Street

Dear Storer

Peace at present is hopeless.

England & France are fighting for their existence, Germany has so far been successful and, if it ends in a victory for her, the next move will be an attack on the United States. She will rush us as she did Belgium & make us pay all of the expenses of the war. Nothing can save us but preparedness & I am afraid Wilson is not a great enough man to carry us thro' the struggle.

I should be sorry to live long enough to see my country lost.

Sincerely yours

T. Jefferson Coolidge

Dec. 20/15

Agnes' diary for this period has numerous "Took Pater to ..." entries. Horatio at eighty-five was still attending meetings of the Newport Medical

Society, Newport Improvement Society, church organizations, etc. There was no mention of any "Walks with Pater" in her diary, but the reason may be that Agnes now owned and drove a Ford.[20]

Hermann Jackson Warner wrote a second letter to Horatio from Europe:[21]

Hotel de Berguet: Geneva Switzerland
Tuesday Feb 1, 1916

My dear Storer:

I received a kind note from you a long time ago, in which you spoke of having paid a visit to our classmate Foster (I am sorry that I have not the note at hand: I cannot find it)—at his place somewhere in the country. Your report having found him enjoying serene days in a comfortable state of health.

Alas! Since then I have read in the *Weekly Transcript* that he too has passed beyond the Great Divide; and now there are few of us left: and in the name of those few I now elect you to be the Last Survivor.

Give us all good Obituaries, as [we] go one by one—and

Believe me as of old
Ever Most Sincerely Yours
H.J. Warner—

Horatio never saw Hermann's diary and could not have been aware of the depth of affection probably represented in Hermann's "Believe me as of old." Hermann added the following at the end of his letter:

I append a note of two books / the only ones which I have ever published/—to be placed—with this note—in the Archives of the Class,—which I take it for granted are in your possession!

European Years: The letters of an Idle Man: edited by George Edward Woodberry: Published by the Houghton Mifflin Company in 1911 in Boston By Hermann Jackson Warner

New Letters of an Idle Man: Edited by George E. Woodberry: Published by Constable & Co. in London in 1913

Note: It is possible that my *Last Letters of an Idle Man* may be published in New York in the course of this year,—1916

As Secretary, it was now Horatio's duty to notify class members of alumni meetings. Coolidge replied:[22]

March 23 1916

My Dear Storer

It would give me much pleasure to attend the Harvard Alumni

Association on April 10th but unfortunately I have lost my hearing and am not able to go anywhere. You are probably the only one of the class of 50 who is fit for any thing.

        Sincerely yours

                T. Jefferson Coolidge

As did Warner:[23]

> Grand Hotel Des Bergues Geneve
> Saturday April 1 1916
> Dear Storer,
>   Your kind letter of March 10 arrived here on March 27; and I was very sorry indeed to learn that you had been seriously ill; but I trust by this time you have recovered your strength and are ready once more to do all your useful work in the world.
>   I was much interested in the number and names of our surviving classmates, four only,—fancy! I remember Cabot as a quiet gentle youth, but I do not think I have ever seen him since we graduated.
>   It was pleasing to me to learn that your attention had been called to my Letters. ... I hope the two books will find a place in your Public Library, and any other Libraries which you might—influence them to obtain.
>   There will be, I hope, before the year is out another volume of "Last Letters", but my friend Professor Woodberry who edits them has been suffering from a long and wearisome attack of nervous prostration. He reports himself now however, as much improved in health, and hence I am hopeful that he may be able to undertake my work before very long.[24]
>   As in your case writing is to me also fatiguing and hence I am using the hand of my Secretary,—a much better hand than mine is now.
>   Again with many thanks for your kind letter, & earnest wishes for the recovery of health and strength
>   Believe me always
>   Sincerely yours
>   H. J. Warner, per A. Bloufield.

A most distressing Agnes diary entry for April 11, 1916 read: "Took Pater to the Murphys & he had a frightful sinking spell & almost died. Dr. M. Came." The next day Dr. Murphy again visited "Pater who is better."[25]

Horatio's "News from the Classes" in the June 1916 *Harvard Graduates' Magazine*, provided a pair of obituaries:[26]

John Higginson Cabot, of Brookline, died Feb. 5, 1916, aged 85. ... He lived in the present, keenly alive to the world's great movements. Toward the close of his life, failing health confined him for a year to his chamber, but he was surrounded by loving relatives, close association with whom proved very happy for all.—**Nathaniel Jarvis Wyeth**, ... soon followed Cabot, and was the sixth of the Class to succumb within less than two years. He died March 22, aged 85, was one of the oldest lawyers of New York City. ... Mr. Wyeth finally became entirely blind, but retained all his fondness for professional and literary work. His interest in his Class continued intense until the end. It had been said of him that he was a good man to have for a friend, for fidelity to friends was a prominent part of his religion. It was also said that no man ever carried within his bosom a kindlier or gentler heart, no man ever sought to live nearer the Golden Rule. Such an one surely deserves remembrance.—Three of the Class now remain; Coolidge, Warner, and the Secretary.

A polio outbreak in several American cities prompted Horatio to write a long letter in July 1916 to the *Newport Daily News* that gave the history of the Newport Sanitary Protection Association he founded nearly forty years earlier and which indicated that the Association was resuming its duties of house inspection and water analysis as one means of avoiding a polio epidemic in Newport.[27] At the end of the year, Coolidge wrote the following, perhaps providing Horatio his first awareness of Warner's death.[28]

Dec. 6/16
315 Dartmouth Street

Dear Storer

I see Warner is dead. Does that leave only you & me of the Class of 1850?

I hope you will [be] polite enough to outlive me. How are you?

I am deaf, & troubled with my kidneys & a bad foot. I hope you have escaped the ills of old age.

Sincerely yr classmate
T. Jefferson Coolidge

Horatio requested information for Hermann's obituary from the well-known literary critic, George Woodberry, who had edited Hermann Jackson Warner's two published books and was working on the third. Woodberry responded:[29]

Beverly, Dec. 15, 1916

Dear Dr. Storer:

I thank you for your note, and enclosure. The Warners had no children, so far as I know.

I enclose a brief note which might be added to the birth, college and nominal statistics of the *Transcripts* notice. I would write them out, but I do not know the usual form of the magazine's notices. You may consider my note simply as information, and compress it as much as you think best. It seems to me that any sketch of my old friend's character by me would be too personal for the occasion.

I found Mr. Warner was unusually sweet-tempered. Old experience, in him, had attained to a wonderfully mellow strain. His long journey through life had ripened an originally kindly nature. He retained great mental vigor in his old age, a sound mind, a good heart! I look on his friendship as one of the great goods of my life.

Doubtless I shall hear from his widow within a short time; and if there is anything of interest to you, I will communicate it. And let me say how pleased I am to have had this brief contact with a "classmate" of 1850.

Sincerely yours
G.E. Woodberry

Horatio's obituary of Warner appeared in the *Harvard Graduates' Magazine* of March 1917 and it read:[30]

Hermann Jackson Warner, the then third remaining member of the Class of 1850, in a recent affectionate letter to the Secretary, closed by the remark, "I do hereby solemnly appoint you the last survivor." And, now, in partial fulfillment of his wish, his own demise must be recorded. Mr. Warner was born in Boston on Feb. 15, 1831. His father, who died but shortly before his birth, was William Augustus Warner, the head of the Class of 1815, among it's graduates having been President Sparks, Profs. Convers Francis, J. G. Palfrey, Theophilus Parsons, and Wm. Sweetser of Bowdoin, T. W. Harris the entomologist and librarian of the College, John Jeffries (the elder), and John Amory Lowell. His mother was Sarah Inches Cobb. He graduated at the Law School, afterwards studying in the offices of Sohier and Welch, distinguished Boston advocates. He was of the Phi Beta Kappa Society. On June 13, 1883, he was married to Mary Poyntell, daughter of the late Andrew and Rebecca C. Staley, of Philadelphia, who survives him. For many years he had resided abroad, closing his life on Dec. 2, 1916, at Geneva, Switzerland in his 85th year. Mr. Warner will be chiefly recollected by the volumes of letters collected in his old age, and edited by George E. Woodberry, of the Class of '77, professor at Columbia University. The first of them, *European Years* (Houghton Mifflin, 1911, Boston), was followed by *New Letters of an Idle Man* (Constable, 1913, London, also separately with the Houghton Mifflin imprint), which were well received. The manuscript of a third series is now in Mr. Woodberry's hands. The ealiest of these books appeared anonymously, possibly that, like *Waverley*, it might the more pique its readers' interest. Another curious incident is that the house which was Scott's famous publisher was also that of Warner's second volume, in which his identity was revealed. There was a certain hilarity in this that must have amused the author. A quotation from the earliest book is germane to this trait in his character, and will bear reproduction. He is writing in 1903, from the Riviera, his description of the charms of which the Secretary the more fully appreciates from a winter of his own at Mentone, and two subsequent ones, farther south, at Sorrento and Naples. "By the way," he says, "did you ever come across Pope Leo XIII's poems? They are very curious. There is one on 'Frugality and Long Life: an Epistle addressed to Fabricius Rufus,' which you ought by all means to read and ponder; it contains a massive wisdom. Andrew Lang has made a version of it. You will enjoy especially the following passage:—

> "'And by thy vintage purest of the pure,
> To warm the heart and prove a pleasant lure,
> That shall both friends and wholesome mirth ensure;
> Be frugal here, however, nor decline
> To put a frequent water in your wine;
> And have in plenty all the goodly meat
> Of fowl and lamb and ox, but first be sure they're tender!'

"This strikes the right note: 'Be sure your meats are tender!' As a clever writer once put it, 'No heart is pure that is not passionate, no virtue is safe that is not enthusiastic!' Hence the Pope and I are safe. But no more: I must hasten into the sunlight, and sit by the shining sea. The Italians have a proverb, 'Praise the sea and keep to the land'; and yea, this will I do."

Quite Anacreontic. Prof. Woodberry has kindly furnished me with the following personal notes. As Warner's editor and probably most intimate friend, he says: "What I have found best (in his writings) and value most, is personality,—the salt of a strong mind, the flavor of humane studies, the tang of character, and of an earlier and more leisurely world that has gone. In his earlier life Mr. Warner was associated with the Boston committee in behalf of the Cretan revolutionists, and he was a writer for the *Boston Transcript*: but delicate health soon compelled him to live abroad, where, except for an occasional visit to this country, he remained, at first in Dresden, and later on the Italian Riviera. He traveled extensively, both over

Europe and in the Far East. He was a natural scholar, with a broad-ranging curiosity, indefatigable in mind, and gave his attention much to philosophical studies. He was one of the first American students of Shopenhauer, whose essays he had in part translated at an early date, but never published." ... As with the late richly deserved eulogies of Wyeth, the last till now to go, and of Fred. Williams, his immediate predecessor, it has been a pleasant, however sad duty thus to remember Warner. These three W.'s sat very closely together during the four years of College life. Each of them stood well the test of very advanced age, but that was to have been expected of the Class of 1850. C. and S. only remain.

Horatio in 1917 dutifully informed his single surviving classmate of upcoming Harvard Commencement activities. Coolidge replied:[31]

                    Magnolia Mass.
My Dear Storer
    I have read the circular you sent me. I am deaf & too feeble to go to Commencement.
    As you have already replied in your own name I will abide by any decision to which you have come.
    I am very sorry to hear that you have been ill in bed & hope that you are fully recovered.
    Are we the only two left of 1850?
    I hope we shall be spared the suffering which usually accompanies great age.
    Let me know every now & then how you get along & believe me
    Most sincerely your old classmate
            T. Jefferson Coolidge
My summer address is Magnolia Mass[ts]
May 29/ 17

Horatio's report on the Class of 1850 in the *Harvard Graduates' Magazine* of June 1917 was brief: "I am glad that thus far there is nothing for you from '50. Our reports have necessarily become but valedictorian, and therefore can hardly interest the majority of your readers."[32] Horatio was delinquent in the Secretarial duty of providing the annual report of his class to the Office of the Harvard President.[33] Horatio quickly made up the deficit with the following:

Sent 10 July-
    Class of 1850-
            Report for 1917.
        Death. H. J. Warner

Survivors-
>H. J. Warner [crossed out]
>
>T. J. Coolidge
>
>H. R. S.

Their physical condition—poor.
"   mental   "   —normal.
"   expectations of further longevity. nil.
"   feeling thereat—content.
"   affection for Harvard—undiminished.
>Respectfully submitted.
>
>Horatio Robinson Storer
>
>Secretary.[34]

Dr. James Joseph Walsh wrote an article published in *The Catholic Convert* entitled "American Physician Converts."[35]   It dealt with Thomas Dwight, Thomas Addis Emmet, and Horatio. Walsh's paragraphs related to Horatio included:

He [like Emmet] occupied himself more especially with the diseases of women and his successful work in the difficult pioneer days of that specialty which owes so much to American enterprise, has given him a place in medical history that is likely to endure. He came to be looked up to as an authority on questions relating to the health and disease of women and he used his prestige to excellent purpose in order to teach not alone the profession but all of his generation the ethical principles that underlie a great many of the problems that come up in obstetrics and gynaecology.

He was particularly noted for his thoroughgoing conservatism and recognition of high principles of morality with regard to the many questions where medicine touches morals, and he was the author of various popular manuals on these subjects which received wide attention and had an excellent influence. His little Book "Why Not? A Book for Every Woman" was the prize essay to which the American Medical Association awarded its gold medal for 1865 and it was published for general circulation by order of the American Medical Association. The companion volume "Is It I? A Book for Every Man" received scarcely less attention while the other number of this series written by him on "Nurses and Nursing" shows that some years before the introduction of the trained nurse into America from England, Dr. Storer had come to recognize the necessity for the training of nurses above all if the specialty of gynaecology was to develop properly. He pointed out very clearly the necessary details of their training and how valuable they would be, but besides this he organized a system of training nurses in connection with the Franciscan Hospital for Women in Boston in the later sixties.

His work for the medical profession in America was thoroughly appreciated by brother physicians and he was elected Vice-President of the American Medical Association and came to be looked up to as one of the leaders in American medicine. He is still alive as I write and there are occasional letters from him that are thoroughly indicative of his continuing interest in medical matters and especially in those concerned with history. He has made the best collection of medical medals, that is, of medals struck in honor of medical events and men, that has ever been made. I know that I am only echoing his own sentiments when I say that undoubtedly the most important event in his life as he looks back over his long years was his conversion.[36] It proved a source of consolation and happiness through many trials and has become the cornerstone of life itself in his later years.

Walsh did not specifically mention abortion, referring only to Horatio's "recognition of high principles of morality with regard to the many questions where medicine touches morals." A reader not familiar with Horatio's *Why Not?* and *Is It I?* would not recognize their subject was criminal abortion and one can only conclude that abortion was still such a taboo topic in 1917, that Walsh was reluctant to mention it, or, if Walsh did mention it, the editor of the *Convert* was unwilling to publish it.

Shortly after his article in *The Catholic Convert* was published, Dr. Walsh sought Horatio's views on the history of New York gynecology, including Horatio's role. Horatio responded:[37]

> Newport, R. I.
> 20 July, 1917
>
> Dear Dr. W.,
>
> I am very glad that you are to discourse upon NY gynaecology & shall look with great interest for the publication. Geo. Elliot, whose life was all too short, should be mentioned & also Peaslee, though he was at times unjust to me, & had a way of selecting his cases, so as to avoid all risk of failure where the chances did not promise well. I always try to do him justice, & while I endeavor to forget all unkind feeling towards any one still living, I do this even more regarding the dead. You might also refer to White, who when Flint & Hammilton came to N.Y. remained in Buffalo. All these five I knew intimately.
>
> You may be interested in the enclosed [list of publications], printed 39 years ago, which was compiled, almost without my knowledge, by Dr Toner of Washington, whom of course you recollect as President of the Am. Med. Association, & the most popular old

bachelor Catholic physician in the U. S. ... Since then I have kept no account of the quite a number of papers that I have published. I greatly appreciated the kind invitation I accepted from the N.Y. State Society & Academy of Medicine as indicated in the list. Of the Academy I was a non-resident Fellow, & one of the very few Bostonians who properly appreciated N.Y. The "circular enclosed" was not therein.

  Maloney & his wife are now visiting us.

Sincerely yours

H.R. Storer

Perhaps the honor that I have valued the most has been the Hon. Presidency of the Edinburgh University Club—Something like your St. Gregory.

Agnes' diary indicated a fairly fit Horatio at mid year with many visits to retired Navy Admiral Ensor Chadwick and others. However, December's entries suggest serious illness and on the 14th included, "A quiet day. Pater alas! Losing ground."[38] Fortunately, Horatio recovered and was well enough to enjoy his next birthday. Agnes wrote in her diary: "Feb 27 Pater's 88th birthday. Mass wh. Padre Higney said for Pater. John & Malcolm came down & many callers. Wonderful flowers, & many greetings, cards, telegrams, etc. A *very* happy day."[39]

Agnes' diary entry for May 12, 1918 simply reads: "Dr Grenfell came to lunch." Given the following letter of Horatio's published in the Newport paper the day before, it was undoubtedly a most grateful Dr. Grenfell who visited:[40]

From *The News* May 11-1918:

GRENFELL IN LABRADOR

Never Again Can the Fisher

Folk Suffer as of Old.

Dr. Storer Writes of the Transformation Wrought by the Medical Mission.

To the Editor of the Daily News:

  Dear Sir: It seems to me that the approaching visit to Newport of Dr. Grenfell of Labrador, of the man who to all that desolate land is at once its beloved physician, just judge, fearless leader and in all things truest friend, is an event which should interest your readers profoundly. I speak from deepest conviction, for, knowing the Labrador as I do, I know the transformation, nothing less, wrought throughout its entire length by the never failing faith and hope and love of my brother physician, whom I shall count it one of the honors of my life to greet when he comes to tell us Sunday of the pitiful needs of the people he has served for over a quarter of a century with abounding joy "in journeyings often, in perils of waters, in perils in the wilderness, in perils in the sea, in perils from false brethren, in labors and painfulness in much watchings, in hunger and thirst, in fastings often, in cold and nakedness."

Only the bare outline of Dr. Grenfell's history, both before and after his coming from England to the new world, is generally known. Despite all that has been published on the Labrador Medical Mission itself, we know but fragments of the life of its founder—of the happy boyhood and education in the noble profession of healing, in which he early distinguished himself as a surgeon of rare ability, and resourcefulness; of his experiences as a worker in London's most miserable slums, and subsequently among the great fleet of deep-sea fishermen in the North sea, and finally of his transfer to Newfoundland and Labrador, with the instant recognition that to this forbidding field he had indeed been called to a life work of sacrifice and consecration.

Four paragraphs followed which we presented previously where Horatio described his own frustrated attempts to deal with the "black diphtheria" that raged in Labrador. The letter concluded:

Thank God, now that "the doctor" has gone to them, never again can a situation so desperate arise for the brave people of Labrador, for a long chain of hospitals, as of schoolhouses and tiny social centres, now dot the coast, every one struggling doubly hard for existence in this terrific time, yet enduring, as they will, please God, to the end, preventing and assuaging every form of human ill. Nor have the wonders wrought been wholly material, but rather of the spirit which quickeneth. Thanks to Wilfred Grenfell's coming amongst them and far more to the example of his life than of his words—thanks to the little army of like-minded men and women who are working so valiantly with him, the fatherhood of God and the brotherhood of man are no longer seemingly empty words on the Labrador, but the very leaveness of life.

> Yours sincerely,
> Horatio R. Storer, M. D.

Newport, May 11, 1918.

Dr. Grenfell's thank-you note with a May 13 Boston postmark, read:[41]

The Muenchinger-King
Newport, Rhode Island
6.0 a. m. May 12, 18

Dear Doctor Storer

I enjoyed every minute of the pleasant interview you permitted me
on Sunday. To actually talk to a man who was a leading surgeon
before the day of anaesthetics[42] or antiseptics—a man who knew
Simpson, & Sims—Spencer Wells and all our Surgical Deities of that
day was an inspiration. I think, if there is any sacrifice at all in our
lives it is just that one—we lose the contact with the fine leaders of
men, which is such a joy at the time, and as a subsequent memory.
Men to me who serve so well their fellow men seem always to be the
men who best serve God & it must be a mighty solace to you facing
the future to look back on a life as a leader in that noblest of all arts
and professions which has to do with the healing of the bodies. ...

I am so glad to think that you should have these permanent joys-
for you certainly do much like the light of the rock we saw, spread
inspiration & ambition to do better, to your visitors. Long may you
live if not for your own sake, yet for the sake of those who come to
& fro to your prophet's chamber. Many thanks for your generous
gift for our work, & for the loan of your diary, which already I have
nearly read thro.

Wilfred L. Grenfell, M.D.

The loaned "diary" probably was Horatio's 100-page 1849 Labrador journal.

Agnes' diary for February 27 indicates: "Pater's 89th birthday Fr H[ig-
ney] brought Pater H[oly]. C[ommunion]. Many callers." However, Horatio
probably had mixed reactions to the following birthday wishes published in the
Boston Medical and Surgical Journal of April 3, 1919:[43]

It is always a pleasant duty to offer congratulations to a colleague
who has survived the vicissitude of a long professional career and is
entering in fair health and spirits upon another year of useful service.
But the opportunity to do so to one who is entering upon his ninth
[tenth] decade is so rare that we venture to call our readers' attention
to the fact that a notable anniversary occurred on February 27th last,
when Dr. Horatio Robinson Storer celebrated his eighty-ninth
birthday.

The name of Storer has been associated conspicuously with Boston
medicine for the better part of a century. The younger members of
the profession who frequent the halls of the Boston Medical Library
are familiar with that admirable portrait by Vinton of the father of
Dr. Storer. Dr. D. Humphreys Storer, Professor of Obstetrics in the

Harvard Medical School, was not only a prominent member of the faculty, and one of the groups of medical practitioners of his day who had the health of Boston families in his keeping, but enjoyed a well deserved reputation as one of the pioneer students of the natural history of his time.

At the period during which the son came into medical life great changes were about to take place in the advancement of science and the practice of medicine and surgery. The younger Storer was keenly alive to the situation and a conspicuous participator in the controversies that arose between his colleagues and the more conservative members of the profession.

Failing health prevented Dr. Storer from carrying on his strenuous exertions and forced an early retirement from active practice. His later years have not been passed, however, in unproductiveness. Most notable are his achievements in medical numismatics, the endeavor on his part to portray in this way medical history.

Many honors, both domestic and foreign, have come to Dr. Storer in his long life, and it is pleasant to be able to record evidence of his continued activities, for it is only quite recently that the American Social Sciences Association, a branch of the National Institute of Social Science, has awarded him its gold "Liberty Service" medal for his aid "in the control of pestilence among soldiers and sailors of the United States."

It is to be hoped that many more years of such usefulness are still to be his portion.

The near-total failure of this editorial to mention Horatio's large contributions to gynecology, abdominal surgery, medical ethics, and reform of medical education while living in Boston almost suggests that these actions were still regarded with disfavor by *Boston Medical and Surgical Journal* editors or by some of the other powerful Boston medical men who had been trained by the Bigelows or by Horatio's other long-dead and long-forgiven enemies.

The Liberty Service Medal mentioned in the article was awarded for Horatio's aid "in the control of pestilence among soldiers and sailors of the United States."[44] However, the only known publications on this topic were his papers shortly after moving to Newport which discussed relations between tuberculosis and syphilis and did not really discuss the control or treatment of the latter.

At the end of 1918, Horatio wrote a long letter to Dr. John Woodward Farlow, Curator of the Boston Medical Library, discussing his long-standing opposition to the widespread use of the two serpents of Mercury for a medical symbol in this country instead of the single serpent of Aesculapius.[45] Horatio cited the American Army Medical Corps as the chief villain, but other medical agencies were mentioned as following them in adopting the improper symbol as a further example of "Our Country—right or wrong." Horatio hoped that Farlow and his Library would undertake to have the rightful serpent of Aesculapius substituted for the obnoxious double-serpent caduceus. Horatio's crusade for caduceus replacement continued in 1919 with several letters to Fielding Hudson Garrison at the Army Medical Museum. One, dated June 7, also included the following reference to the Ether Controversy of Boston and to the related "stripes" he received in that city:[46]

> I came at once against my will into the midst of that terrible Ether Controversy, or rather most unseemly local broil, which was still, though nine years had passed since 1846, at the very height of its virulence. Being naturally a believer in chloroform, as I am still, I became the willing victim of many stripes, the smarting of which I yet remember, with a great deal of amusement, and much enjoyment.

One wonders whether anyone can recall the "smarting" from "many stripes" "with a great deal of amusement, and much enjoyment." Perhaps so, when one is almost ninety, and as committed as Horatio was to forgiving his enemies.

OLDEST LIVING HARVARD GRADUATE, FINAL CLASSMATE OBITUARY, LOVING CUP FROM THE CITY

The end of the year 1919 marked another period of serious illness for Horatio. Agnes' diary records:

Nov 21 Pater had a terribly alarming arterial haemorrhage.
Nov 26 Pater had another haem.
Nov 27 Fr Higney gave Pater H.C. & the Last Sacraments. Dr Stevenson in consultation with Dr M & M.S.
Dec 2 Another haemorrhage wh. Dr Stevenson with Dr Murphy cauterized again.

However, Horatio's health in the first part of 1920 appears to have been good. Agnes' diary made only a pair of references to illness and she wrote that Horatio greatly enjoyed his ninetieth birthday. The local paper provided an account of the occasion which included:[1]

A Daily News representative was fortunate enough to be invited to tea yesterday afternoon and have a chat with the doctor, who is a very optimistic man. Newspaper interviews are not new to Dr. Storer, himself a journalist of some note, and as he explained he usually enjoys turning the interview upon journalism rather than medicine.

...

Because one happens to begin his ninety-first year, does not mean that general subjects of the day are not debatable. With Dr. Storer they are, and politics proved an interesting subject of conversation. "I was once a mugwump," said the doctor, "and I feel today that we should be more independent in our choice of men to represent us in any form of government." He then went on to tell of some interesting episodes in his associations with Daniel Webster, of whom he was an ardent follower until their political ideas reached the cross roads, as it were.

Horatio's "interesting episodes in his associations with Daniel Webster" have their only known mention in this ninetieth birthday tribute. Webster did provide an unusual fish specimen to the Boston Society of Natural History in 1845[2] and a common interest in natural history may have been a factor. Webster's outspoken opposition to the war with Mexico no doubt contributed to Horatio's similar opposition as a Harvard student.

Unless it was his wise choice of the healthy Newport "Point" as a residence, Horatio's next achievement really was not of his own making. The March 1920 death of Charles French, a member of the Harvard Class of 1848, made Horatio the oldest living Harvard graduate. He was interviewed by the *Boston Post* and this was published on Sunday, April 4, 1920. The long interview reflects well on the reporter who asked questions that uniquely tapped Horatio's thinking about unusual subjects and also allowed Horatio to free-associate. Key portions are reproduced below:[3]

Post, Sunday, April 4, 1920

Owing to the death of Charles French, class of '48, Dr. Horatio Robinson Storer has become the oldest living graduate of Harvard.

Dr. Horatio Robinson Storer, dean of Harvard alumni, tells how in his 92 [90] years of life he has found happiness.

. . .

He speaks as familiarly of Lincoln and Garibaldi as we do of Wilson and Clemenceau.

His father, Dr. D. Humphreys Storer, was a professor of obstetrics at Harvard Medical School, and he himself became a famous specialist of women's diseases.

Although retired from active practice, he has a very active interest in people and likes to see new faces.

And out of his full and varied life he has extracted a secret—the secret of happiness.

A. Lawrence MacKenzie Jr.

I climbed the stairs of the old-fashioned Newport home built on the very edge of the sea. As I entered his room Dr. Horatio Storer stretched forth his hand to greet me and his mild blue eyes, but little dimmed by his many years, smiled in welcome up to mine. He was seated in a broad wicker armchair with a plaid steamer rug about his knees, facing the window. I turned to the window and a glorious scene caught my eye—a great expanse of clear blue sky, the green sun-flecked sea, laughing springtime, the beginning of life. Beside me was a man who had passed that springtime many years ago. Did this spell the beginning of life to him, too?

"I love the sea," he said, following my gaze and half reading my thoughts.

For a moment he sat there dreaming and I studied him. His broad, full forehead, aquiline nose and long flowing beard reminded me of the old patriarchs of ancient Greece.

"Out there is my promenade deck," he continued, pointing to a balcony just outside the window. "Every day when it is pleasant and

I am feeling well I go out there for an hour, walking up and down and looking at my ocean. From my chair here I can see the ocean in every one of her moods, and she is always magnificent. In the summer there is a continual stream of boats, all sort of boats, back and forth, and I never tire of watching them. It keeps my imagination alive and me interested in little things."

We talked of many things, watching the little government boats darting here and there, and the breast of the sea grow darker as the sun fell gradually lower. And then I asked him:

"In all your years what have you found to be true happiness?"

"That is a fine question," he answered, "and a hard one to answer. Many people have happiness without being able to define it, but I think I can tell you. In all the joys of life that I have had I have come to realize that they were real joys in our small way of understanding. In all my griefs and sorrows, and God has indeed give me my share of them, I know now that there are hundreds of others whose sorrows are so great that mine become very insignificant. Of course, it was no sudden decision on my part. Rather it came gradually, as an attitude of mind. My days for some time now have been days of reflection. Youth looks forward weighing nothing, age looks backward, weighing everything. With this judgment of things, for all its ups and downs, life proves to have been very good. This, this state of mind, has brought me contentment, and happiness is nothing else. Even now, in my physical pain, and always such age as mine has pain, I am comforted with the thought that it is no worse. Of such stuff is happiness built, and not so much that the sorrow we have might be far worse, as that even the smallest joy we find is from the bountifulness of God."

...

"After I had finished my studies at the Harvard Medical School I went to Edinboro to continue my studies there. The days spent there were perhaps some of the happiest of my life. Afterward when I was older I travelled extensively all through Europe, and during my illness I spent a period of six years mostly in Italy."

He paused a while, gazing dreamily out of the window on the sunlit sea, as though living all those days over again, and then back we came to America. He was speaking of Newport and the slave trade.

"Newport was the centre of the slave trade for a long time," he said, "and many of the present colored inhabitants are direct descendants of freed slaves. It is easy to picture the square-riggers coming up from Cuba loaded with molasses and going to Africa laden with New England rum. In those days the coastwise and foreign trade was very flourishing, and our ports were never empty.

"I have seen much, but there are not many things on this earth that are new. What to you in your youth is new, to me in my old age are only reoccurrences of what seemed new in my youth. The world's energy travels in waves, and each time they rise or fall it is only with a new coloring of something old. Each generation thinks that it has rediscovered the earth. Youth with its buoyancy feels that it may teach dull-eyed age, but it is only passing through the same lane that we walked with newly opened eyes."

"What do you think of spiritism?" I asked.

He laughed, his eyes seemed to be laughing all the time.

"Nor is that new to me," he answered. "I have seen at least three waves of it in my life time, and they were all just as fervent as this one seems to be.

"I have been a specialist in women's diseases, and I have treated many patients for insanity. Insanity in women, because of their highly emotional temperament, is far worse than in men. A number of the women I had to treat were mediums, dabblers in psychic phenomena, young hysterical girls playing with dangerous toys until the harm done was beyond repair. If this is the result, no matter whether there is anything in it or not, it is indeed best to leave it alone.

"Personally," he continued, "I believe that most of it is charlatanism, fakirs playing on the susceptibilities of those overwrought by sorrow or fear. Whether there is anything more than that in it I do not know. I do not believe that we were ever intended to know much about the other world while we are still on this earth. To me it is absurd that spirits who have gained the other world would be interested in any of the events of this world. I know that I wouldn't, and neither would I care to be bothered by the people of this world. When I have finished here I want my withdrawal complete."

I asked him if he thought it was the subconscious mind that influenced most of the spirit investigations.

"Undoubtedly," he replied, "the subconscious mind gives to the bulk of investigators what they choose to call their results. Here is an illustration of how clever some of the magicians and tricksters are. Some English officers whom I met in England told of the marvelous tricks that the magicians of India perform. One of them, the most startling was this: a Hindoo juggler threw a rope up into the air until the end seemed to disappear. His assistant then began to climb it, and he too disappeared; presently he reappeared and came down and then pulled the rope down. Of course it was all an illusion of some sort, but to them it appeared real. If some men are as clever as that we may be tricked into almost any belief. No, I do not believe that we will ever know what the other world is like, for I do not believe it was ever intended that we should know until the time comes for us to go there."

He sat there in his great wicker armchair that seemed a part of him, the fringed steamer rug giving a touch of color to the picture, gazing out on the flashing golden sea, when suddenly a little thrill of song filled the room. Looking up, I saw a little yellow canary hanging high in the streaming sunlight that came through the window. Dr. Storer's face lit up. I spoke to him of his bird. He had two of them, he told me, one in another room, and he took more pleasure in the song of a bird than in all the weighty discussions and investigations of the after-world. He would find out in time, he said, and he would not have long to wait.

On the writing board stretched across the arms of his chair, were many papers. He had been writing when I interrupted him by my entrance. Laying his hand on the pile of written sheets, he said:

"This is my hobby. Every man should have a hobby. For years I have been collecting medical medals; every medal that was ever stamped for any kind of medical work I have tried to find, and I collected many hundreds of them, 2500 of them altogether. They are now at the Boston Medical Library. This work that I am doing now is to be a catalogue of those medals, giving a brief description of each one and its history. My son, Dr. Malcolm Storer, a Boston surgeon, is making a collection of naval medals. Many men might say that my hobby was bringing water to a bottomless well, but it keeps my interest alive. If a man can keep up his interest in his friends and some small work to occupy his mind, he will not grow too tired of life."

In 1872 while performing an operation he became infected himself. For six years he sought health in Europe without success. The result of his infection made him a semi-invalid.

"One of my knees is stiff," he said, rapping the writing board in front of him, "as that board there."

Dr. Storer comes from a family of warriors. In the American Revolution his grandfather fought as a private and in the war of 1812 his uncle was a private. A grand-uncle afterward as General Boyd, distinguished himself in the East Indian warfare. In the Civil War, Mr. A. [R.] W. Storer, still living, long served his country on Southern battlefields while George Washington Storer, another relation also gave valuable service. In the late war Mr. John Humphreys Storer served here in Massachusetts as a member of the National Guard. Mr. and Mrs. Storer's sons, Major Robert Treat Paine Storer of the 305th Field Artillery, and Lieutenant Theodore Lyman Storer of the 101st Field Artillery, of our famous "Y. D.," while serving overseas were both cited for gallantry in action.

He went to live in Newport in 1877.

"I love my Newport home," he told me, "and I have always wanted to live and die close to the sea."

As I rose to take my leave I turned again to the window. The sea was no longer dancing, the laughing gold had turned to dusk, and the sky's blue was growing gray.

Agnes' entry in her diary for the day of the interview reads: "March 30 Pater ill. Reporter (McKenzie) from Boston Sunday Post comes down to interview Pater." What an interview Horatio might have given had he been well!

The Sunday paper interview prompted the following letter which surely was a joyful reminder of the Provincetown and Labrador adventures of his youth:[4]

> Treasury Department
> Unites States Customs Service
> Office of the Deputy Collector
> Provincetown. Mass
> April 5th. 1920

Horatio R. Storer, M. D.
Newport. R.I.
My dear Dr. Storer:

What was my surprise on reading the Sunday Post of April 4th, to find a portrait and interview of yourself by the Post Reporter, and it brought back to my memory many pleasant thoughts, and I determined to write you and offer my congratulations that you had reached the honorable distinction of being the oldest Harvard Graduate, and had spent so long and useful life of service to mankind.

Let me first introduce myself as the youngest son of your old friend Capt. Nathaniel E. Atwood, and say, that while I do not so much recall you, as other members of your family, and especially your honored father, Dr. D. Humphries [sic] Storer, whom it was always such a pleasure to meet, yet I do recall seeing you when a small boy, and I have heard my father tell so much about the trip in the old smack J. Sawyer, in 1849, to Labrador, with Prof. Wyman, your brother Frank. H. and yourself as passengers, that I have almost felt that I was on the voyage myself, although it was before I was born. Not long since, I came across a letter written by you to my father, dated about 1850, in which you ask, if it would be convenient for him to take you on one of his fishing trips in his vessel.[5]

I was born Aug. 16th. 1852, a day memorable in my family, not only for this fact, but that on that day my father received a call, which was the first, but by no means the last, visit from Prof. Agassiz who had not long before come to this country to remain. From this location on Long Point, we removed the family as well as the house in 1857 across the harbor. Being the youngest son, I was kept at home by father and worked with him until his death Nov. 7 1886, and as a small boy, went with him many years from 1860 to 1867 when he retired from the sealife; and carrying fish and lobsters from this place to Boston, brought us to the city often, and as a boy, I have many times attended the meetings of the Boston Society of Natural History with him, and made many pleasant calls at your father's house both while living on Tremont St. and Boylston, which calls were returned by your father by visiting us at Provincetown, and I remember well what a genial and kindly gentleman he was.

After reading your interview in the Boston Post, I turned to the old family album, and looked at your photo, and one of your son, who I judge may have been about ten years of age, when taken, also photos, of your honored father and mother, which must have been taken at least sixty years ago, and were always cherished by my father until his death, for the pleasant memories that they brought to him. ...

In closing, permit me to again offer my hearty congratulations and best wishes, and to express the hope, that you may yet have many more years of usefulness and happiness to come.

My wife joins me in these felicitations, and believe me;

Sincerely yours.
M.C. Atwood

M.C. Atwood
P.O. Box # 403
Provincetown. Mass

Later in 1920, Horatio appears to have had much illness. He provided a long letter late in April praising a solar treatment that was being implemented in Newport,[6] but no other letters *from* Horatio were found during the year. Horatio was judged so close to death on November 5, 1920 that he was given last rites, apparently the third time this had occurred. A week later, however, "Pater set up a little. Calls." was the entry in Agnes' diary.[7] Horatio was ill when his final surviving classmate, Thomas Jefferson Coolidge, died at Boston, November 17, 1920. It would be a few months before a somewhat recovered Horatio completed his obituary responsibilities as Class of 1850 Secretary. Horatio's touching, and also self-disclosing, obituary appeared in the March 1921 *Harvard Graduates' Magazine*:[8]

Thomas Jefferson Coolidge, LL.D., 1902, Harvard, the great-grandson of the third American president, and the last but one of his Class, died at Boston, November 17, 1920, in his 90th year. Of his classmates he was the most distinguished, and, *judging by men's standards the world over, his was the most useful life.*[9] Of his beneficence to Harvard, it is unnecessary here to speak. His record as a business and professedly public man has been well summarized in the preceding paper.

To the Secretary of his class, Coolidge was known otherwise. Both their lives were replete with interest, but of a wholly different character. The one a citizen of the world, of remarkably wide interests, saw most of his ambitions realized, though his later life was saddened by the untimely death of his son, who like himself was already a man of affairs. Coolidge did much for his country, as well as for his city, his associates, his family, and himself. The other, with equally high aspirations though doomed by persistent ill-health to early retirement from the usual activities of his profession, was yet privileged to outlive all those with whom he had unintentionally been forced into violent controversy, and to see the seeds of important movements, moral, educational, and spiritual, in the planting of which he had helped, develop and grow to abundant fruitage. Each life was probably, in its way, a very satisfactory one.

While still a child, Coolidge, with his three brothers, was placed at school in Switzerland, and there remained for the following eight years, long enough to have almost forgotten his native tongue. This reversion of type, which nearly made him an alien, was to serve him in peculiar and fortunate good stead on his return to Boston, a quite finished young Frenchman, or German, or both combined. The Secretary first met him at Cambridge in 1847, on his entering College in the Sophomore year. So complete had been his foreign training, that he took this advanced position without the slightest effort. He was with us in most of the ordinary studies, and in our advance in others. His advent was so unusual, like a stage play almost, that it is of interest still, and explains much of his quite wonderful progress after graduation.

The College, then but a higher school to us, was in its usual session. Suddenly there appeared upon the scene and outlandish-looking boy. As such we assumed him, for he proved a couple of years younger than most of us. He had not yet changed to the usual dress for young Americans, and there were features about his garb that to us seemed almost girlish. He faced us all in a partial semi-circle. We were largely Bostonians, and had shed the usual discrepancies and varieties of childish fashion, and were, so to speak, all of one adolescent manliness. Coolidge's pose was that of a dear little Lord Fauntleroy, accustomed to rule governess and tutors, and with an air of inborn superiority over his family and the world beside. Thus prepared, he came to us in study hours. The scene was quite unique. It bore a touch of both comedy and tragedy. He looked at us and we looked at him. The room was crowded, for additions were permitted to view the new arrival, so that the setting was quite abnormal. We were a group, cohesive, self-sufficient, wont to look with contempt upon the other city lads, ready to fight with them upon the slightest provocation, and indeed already sending belligerent challenges to the truckmen of Boston—and here was he, all alone, studying us with a certain air of seriousness, without the slightest trace of timidity or bewilderment. Exotics were far less frequent in those days, and at first we were inclined to resent his presence, he was so variant from us all. Had we been older, we should have thought of the co-educational experiment, anticipated pleasure from the companionship of a girlie boy—and then we began to appreciate that, girlie or boy, here was a chap who was contemplating ourselves with very similar convictions, querying at the same time as to our standing in the social scale, and watching us in our self-confidence, with apparently pluck enough to meet us all, either individually or combined, and with evident intention to come among us as our equal if not indeed as our superior. After what must have appeared to both sides a long period of mutual evaluation there seemed a very genuine decision that "he'll do."

...

Coolidge's early education served him in good stead when Minister to France, and stamped him as the equal in diplomacy of any court grandee. He proved fit successor of his distinguished ancestor, who held the same appointment, upon the foundation of the American Union.

Very shortly before Coolidge's death, the Secretary received from him an affectionate letter, towards the close of which he said. "All are gone save you and me. One of us must soon follow; it may be you and it may be myself, and the other will be expected to briefly discourse in the Harvard Graduates' Magazine. If this duty falls to you, do say something that is both civil and kind." As if any one who knew him could do otherwise!

As the Secretary, now in his ninety-second year, was seriously ill at the time of Coolidge's passing, and the then current number of the Magazine was already due, it was necessary that this slight tribute should be postponed. The daily press was filled with his praises. The men of the present day may be assured that could these desultory reminiscences be submitted to the dead classmates, every word would but express the affection of them all.

Some may wish to challenge Horatio's assessment on whose "was the most useful life" of the Class of 1850, "judging by men's standards the world over."

Horatio fully enjoyed the two days of celebration on his ninety-first birthday which Agnes' diary described as follows:

> Feb 27   Pater's 91st birthday.   great & glorious.   John & Malcolm
> Theodore & Muriel came down.   Pater presented with beautiful silver
> cup & girl scouts sang, etc. etc. etc.
> Feb 28   More callers & continuation of the birthday.

The *Newport Herald* report the next day gave a fuller description of the
event,[10] portions of which were published in the *Boston Transcript* and the *Boston Medical and Surgical Journal*:

LOVING CUP FOR DR. STORER
Pioneer Surgeon is Honored on His 91st Birthday
TESTIMONIAL FROM MANY FRIENDS
Dr. Storer observes Anniversary Quietly at Washington St. Home.

   Yesterday was Dr. Horatio Storer's 91st birthday.   During the
morning a committee consisting of Dr. Edward V. Murphy, Dr.
Norman M. McLeod and Chaplain E. S. Burke of the Training
Station, called upon him and presented him with a silver loving cup
as a testimonial of the esteem of his fellow physicians and citizens.
The cup was inscribed as follows:

"Horatio Robinson Storer

"the Physician

"Pioneer Surgeon, Philanthropist,

"Leader in Civic Administration

"and the

"Always Helpful Adviser,

"From His Admiring Fellow

"Citizens and Friends of

"Newport, Rhode Island.

"February 27th, 1921."

   The idea of the presentation originated among the physicians but
spread quickly to the numerous organizations in which Dr. Storer has
long been interested and to friends of Dr. Storer.   The following is
a list of the principle contributors: the physicians, the Redwood
Library, the Newport Historical Society, the Charity Organization,
the Advisory Council of the Newport Civic League, the Harvard
graduates of this city, all the Roman Catholic organizations and many
individual friends of the doctor.

   In presenting the loving cup which is large and of beautiful design
and superb workmanship, Dr. McLeod expressed the good wishes of
the subscribers.

   Dr. Storer was evidently deeply pleased and touched by this token
of esteem and responded briefly and feelingly.   He expressed his

appreciation of this honor which he felt as not so much a tribute to himself personally as to the joint efforts of himself, in the past and now in the present, of the many donors of the loving cup, to work all together and in all possible ways for the best interests of Newport.

Another feature of the day that especially delighted Dr. Storer and his family was an unexpected visit from a troop of Girl Scouts, accompanied by Mrs. William S. Sims, commissioner. The scouts presented the venerable physician with a basket of spring flowers and sang in his honor several spirited scout songs. The delightful occasion began with a congratulatory limerick, composed by the girls themselves.

Dr. Storer was fairly flooded throughout Saturday and Sunday with kind messages from all over the country and a constant succession of friends and acquaintances called to offer their congratulations and best wishes.

Dr. Malcolm Storer, with his daughter Miss Muriel Storer, Mr John H. Storer, with his son, Mr. Theodore Lyman Storer, came from Boston to spend yesterday with their father and grandfather.

Dr. Storer is enjoying better health at this time than he experienced at the outset of the winter, so that his enjoyment of the occasion and that of his family, was not impaired by any adverse effect thereto from the strain of such a large and popular demonstration of esteem and affection into which the quiet family reunion, at first contemplated, had ultimately grown.

Unfortunately, the girl scouts' "congratulatory limerick" does not seem to have survived.

Horatio's entry for the June 1921, *Harvard Graduate's Magazine*, read:[11]

T. J. Coolidge, LL.D., 1902, the most distinguished member of his Class, died at Boston, Nov. 17, 1920, in his 90th year. The Secretary's notice of this was published on page 408 of the March number of the Magazine. Through the death of Mr. Coolidge, the Class, as such, no longer exists. All save one are gone. The Secretary alone remains, divested of all his duties, even of the sad task of adding the final star to the names of his dear comrades. Of himself, too, he cannot say the parting word, which when his own time comes, and it must be now very soon, should rightfully be but the old quotation:
"He lived; he died.
"Behold the sum,—the abstract of
   "the Historian's page."

Agnes tells us on June 6, that she went to the Boston Medical Library and heard Malcolm give a "lecture on Pater's medals." A few weeks later she reported on July 16, "Over 20 Harvardians called on Pater here" and the next day more "Harvardians called including President Lowell & Dr Wright." As in so many of his later years, Horatio became "wretchedly" in the late months of the year and Agnes' diary mentioned a heart attack on November 3, 1921. No doubt Horatio had rallied somewhat by the first of February when he provided the following long letter to Dr. James Joseph Walsh, who was planning a new sketch of Horatio and had requested more biographical data:[12]

58 Washington Street
Newport, R.I.

Feb. first 1922

Dear Dr. Walsh:

I should have earlier acknowledged your kind letter, but before doing so I have been re-reading your eulogy of the 3 converts ... in the Convert League Journal of some six years ago. What can I add to what you then said? One does not like to have part in his own obituary. ...

I of course knew Dwight, and just before he died had a pathetic letter from him, regarding the progress of his disease. Emmet was among my intimates. Sims had been one of my correspondents before he came up from Montgomery, and while he and Bozeman, his then associate, never dreamed that they could quarrel. After reaching New York, he consulted me frequently about his Woman's Hospital, the progress of its bill through the New York Legislature, the first aid that he had in its financing through Mrs. Thompson of Springfield, etc. My acquaintance with Emmet probably began on or near the very day he came up from Virginia. Sims was interested by E's facility as a medical draughtsman, and doubtless many of the early records at the hospital, both of diagnosis and operative treatment, the majority of them "plastic," will be found to have been illustrated by him. At the close of 1855, after my long stay in Edinburgh as pupil and private assistant to Simpson, and although I at once received appointment to the staff of the Boston Lying-In Hospital, I gave two years to general practice, that I might prove to the profession that I was not a man of but one idea, and then came out as a pelvic specialist, pure and simple, refusing midwifery and even syphilis, which so many in those days somewhat justly considered among the "diseases of women." Of course it was impossible for Emmet, situated as he was in relation to Sims, to take such a step until some time afterwards. Emmet and I were for many years working in parallel lines. He in innumerable cases of partial prolapse from subinvolution, tried to lift up this organ by splints as it were, through lateral cicatrices, from "plastically" paring the vaginal walls. Whatever else the effect, the local constriction of the canal thus produced, went far to restore conjugal felicity. He thus obtained double gratitude, while his patients appreciated his faithful interest, from his standpoint, in their welfare.

Such was the famous "N.Y. Method," whatever its merits, it seemed to me better, however, to try to remove the cause of the procidentia, the undue uterine weight, than to treat merely its effect. The graduated Simpson's Sound kept me informed as to how much increased involution, or shrinkage in size, I was producing, and an occasional pregnancy in obstinate cases of sterility, gave evidence of the wisdom of my views. News of the "Boston Way" soon got about, and the N.Y. State Society once did me the honor to summon me to Albany, to tell them what I was about, & the why and wherefore. The Academy of Med., of which for some years I was a non-resident Fellow, once showed me a similar compliment, and called me in for a discussion of one of my procedures. I think it was "pocketing" the ovarian pedicula, which is now familiar both at home and abroad. Most of my work, however, from the beginning and whether for diagnosis, or for permanent results, was in abdominal surgery. I did not often hear of Emmet's essaying major operations.

Speaking of Sims, he was always my very dear friend. Very shortly before his death, he was here in Newport, and sitting in my study, weeping like a woman or a child. It was after the great break at the hospital came. As almost always happens at "institutions," jealousy got into the staff, and upon a comparatively trifling point of etiquette he was deserted by all the men he had virtually created, even Emmet and Gaillard Thomas. For several years subsequently I spent the winters in N.Y. Each time, I regularly made my first visit to Bryant Park, and no matter what the weather, stood for a while, hat in hand, before that bronze statue, in reverence. Sims was always good in trusting his friends as though they were his equals. I had been interested in vesico-vaginal. I had seen the elder Hayward operate several times, of course unsuccessfully, at the M.G.H., and also the quite famous Jobert de Lamballe in Paris. This gentlemen's cases would be reported in the Gazette des Hospitaux as guerisons, and next day the silk sutures would inevitably cut out. Sims' bent iron spoon, his duck bill speculum, or Levator perinei, was an inspiration. It at once solved the problem, but it was bulky and expensive. There was at or near the time in N.Y., a certain Dr. Augustus Gardner, now long dead, who was ambitious, but doing little practice. To evidence his erudition, he published prints of all the vaginal specula that it ever entered the brain of man to conceive. Simpson in Edinburgh had taught me for all purposes of diagnosis to throw all specula aside, as utterly deceptive and untrustworthy. I afterward owned a number, for exhibition to my pupils as unde-sirable. Several of us were examining Gardner's long array. I said that I thought that any valuable addition would be absolutely impossible, when one of the other men exclaimed "Well, I'll wager that Storer here, who has a way of inventing instruments as he goes along in his daily work, can get up something that will put these others clean out of sight." I laughed and begged to be spared. The next day I took my double bladed Cusco to Codman & Shurtleff, told them to alter slightly the position of a single screw, swung one of the blades back upon the other without removing it, and thus we had Sims' duckbill, as serviceable as the original, and more easy in manipulation.

I published a cut of it in the Journal of the Gynaecological Society of Boston, and asked that the new tool might be known as the Boston speculum, for in those days all my ambitions were for the future of Boston, and that it might become the great American Gynaecological centre. Partly, however, because of my loyalty to Simpson, and of my acceptance of his belief that chloroform in some respects, especially in obstetrics, was preferable to ether, my views were generally very naturally opposed. I lost my poor assistantship to my father's chair. I had been promised a full professorship of the diseases of women, of which he then practically recognized merely those of pregnancy, parturition and lactation, while he was to retain Obstetrics proper and Medical Jurisprudence. It is perhaps as well, however, though it cost me much grief before I could see this. Because if I had continued to have everything my own way, and each day had proved happier that the one before, I might never have become a Catholic.

...

But I might go on, thus disjointly and almost incoherently, through the garrulity of old age. I can only say do as you may think best. In your Emmet paper you seemed quite familiar with some of the things I have attempted. Let me know what papers of mine you have, I will see if I can add to them. You may perhaps find that apparently under the surface I have touched upon, perhaps influenced somewhat, some of the graver issues that at present seriously vex our portion of mankind.

Much may depend upon your reply to me.

Sincerely yours

H.R. Storer

My little typist & stenographer, she was a "Yeoman(F)," finds it difficult to interpret much of my writing, So do I, myself.

Horatio's "little typist & stenographer," is Gladys Bolhouse. At the time of this writing, Gladys is a robust ninety-plus example of the healthy climate of Newport. When she typed Horatio's letters she had just ended a stint with the U.S. Navy. "Yeoman(F)" stands for Yeoman female.

Walsh's response has not been saved, but it led to this letter of Horatio only eight days later and it too is filled with medical history:[13]

58 Washington Street
Newport, R.I.

February Ninth 1922.

Dear Dr. Walsh:

Again thanks. I return your MS. with slight suggestions. So long as you cannot use the notes I sent you please return them. The Converts' Journal was from March, 1917 and you spoke of D., E. and S.

The great change of sentiment in New England within the last few years has been owing in great measure to the American Medical Association and it was partly owing to the wide spread influence of my prize essay. The Association most emphatically placed its seal of condemnation upon what had really become the general custom, permitted and to a great extent encouraged by the members of our profession. When these gentlemen were convinced that in many respects they had been wrong, they yielded to the increasingly immense force of professional opinion, and what began in the local crusade against unbelieving and extremely refractory medical and domestic customs, similarly revolutionized the public mind and ended in so profound and general a revulsion of sentiment has produced a very general change in belief and practice. What commenced here spread like wildfire throughout New England, and as a matter of course had very great influence over the rest of the country. Think this over seriously, and then appreciate with me the character and universal extent of the change. Nothing that the Association has ever done has been more beneficent and universally effective than this.

As to your desire for the names of sympathizers in our work, I may frankly tell you that within the past century and in the locality referred to there have been almost none. ...

You of course know Dr. Marcy of Cambridge and Boston. I have not myself seen him for thirty years, but I have followed his course since its inception. He is probably a very wealthy man, purely from his profession, but I have probably not given him half the credit that was his due, because I have thought that a portion of his receipts must have been from the invention of the rubber glove, the Kangaroo suture, and a valuable improvement in tenning which came from his work upon the latter. Since, however, he has disclaimed all this, and

I can really give him the credit of having given all his attention to his strictly professional work, I can plainly say that I don't think there is another man in the country, not even the Mayos of Rochester, who has really done so much for American Surgery. He was Lister's first and chief American pupil and assistant, just as I was of Simpson, and our courses have been nearly parallel. I could say much upon this subject, but I can truly say that with your facile pen and your great gift of convincing your readers, I should be delighted if someday you would prepare a really truthful work about the history of modern general and particularly abdominal surgery. I don't know but I imagine that he must be a Methodist, for he has the LL.D. from the Wesleyan University. At any rate I have reason to believe that he is very fair and liberal in his views, and he is certainly very generous towards other people who might have been thought his rivals.

Sincerely yours

H.R. Storer

Upon the brink, eighteen days from now, if he lives so long, of his 93d year.

Less than a week later, the following was sent to Walsh, reiterating the preceding's emphasis on the key role of the American Medical Association and himself in condemning and successfully reducing criminal abortion:[14]

58 Washington Street
Newport, R.I.

14 Feb. 1922.

Dear Dr. W.

I have yours,

Since writing, I have been more than ever impressed by the great influence the Am. Med. Association has exerted, however unintentionally, & unwillingly even, had it but appreciate the result that would naturally follow, towards effecting what you & I are both praying for, the conversion of America. Fifty years ago it was believed, or assumed, by the mass of physicians, & by women, & by all that infantile life (O'Malley had not then laid down "the law" with a diagram to show birth controllers precisely how than can perform vasectomy) did not come until after quickening. The Association, by speech, the printed word, & by action, showed that life did initiate from the very beginning, & that "therapeutic abortion" was therefore very generally murder. Protestant pulpits were compelled to preach Catholic doctrines.

Will it then be too much, for you to insert in your Cyclopedia something like the following: Every single word helps in this crusade, & even a mouse may aid a lion like yourself.

Sincerely yrs
H.R. Storer

For nearly seventy years, Dr. Storer has written much upon the
real time of commencement of foetal life, & of its sanctity. He has
been supported, frequently and most authoritatively, by the concerted
aid of the American Medical Association, the great body of reputable
physicians, of which his father was a president and himself a vice-
president. That action of the Association has been the most beneficent of its existence, and for the fact that he was to a small extent
enabled to take a part, Dr. S. will be held in grateful remembrance,
rather than as a progressive and successful surgeon.

Horatio's admonition to Walsh in his previous letter was to:

Think this over seriously, and then appreciate with me the character
and universal extent of the change. Nothing that the Association has
ever done has been more beneficent and universally effective than
this.

This almost certainly indicates that Horatio appreciated in 1922, and probably
much earlier, that his and the AMA's opposition to abortion had and continued
to have a profound effect on who made up the population. Sharply increased
numbers of individuals had survived pregnancy and still were surviving pregnancy as a result of these anti-abortion efforts. These men and women
"survivors" were begetting children who would not have otherwise come into
existence. Even by 1922, many members of two and even three generations
could thank Horatio for at least one essential ancestor.[15] Although Horatio did
not spell this out, he probably recognized that the existence of a great many
human beings in 1922, was owed to the anti-abortion efforts he formally began
in 1857; which he continued at a high level through his books and editorials
until his illness of 1872; and which persisted after that, because of his widely-
circulated popular and professional books, and, probably of most importance,
because of the numerous state laws he helped initiate that were protecting the
fetus and forcing awareness of its value. There is no evidence that Horatio's
"obituary" of himself found its way into print, although as we will see, Walsh's
tribute in the *Ave Maria* a few months after Horatio's death, strongly emphasized Horatio's anti-abortion efforts.

As evidence of Horatio's high level of mental function during his last thirteen months, we have not only these cogent letters to Dr. Walsh, but the following from Dr. William R. White, a member of the Rhode Island Medical
Society published in the *Rhode Island Medical Journal* for February 1922:[16]

I have a message to communicate to you which I should have

communicated in September. A good many of us know that in August the Harvard Alumni of New England was invited to spend a week-end at the St. George's School at Newport. About 200 of us availed ourselves of that great privilege. We arrived Friday and were advised that Doctor Storer, oldest member of the association in the State, would be glad to see any of the alumni. The next morning we were told that 31 of the alumni went around and called on Doctor Storer. I, myself, reserved the privilege for Sunday and spent a half hour with Doctor Storer. He will be 92 in February. He is helpless; confined to his chair and table; unable to leave his chair without the assistance of a trained nurse but mentally just as clear as ever and it certainly was a very impressive half hour when he indulged me with reminiscences and spoke about scientific advancement.

Dr. Storer said, "Give my regards and best wishes to the R. I. Medical Society when you meet with them." He said he had always had a great regard for this Society. It is a privilege to communicate this message to you.

Agnes' diary for February 27 indicates that Horatio was well enough to enjoy his last birthday. Her entry reads: "Pater's 92nd birthday. Mass said by Fr H[igney] for Pater who had the happiest day imaginable with every conceivable letter, telegrams (incl Pres. Lowwell & Gen Edwards) callers & flowers galore." A beautifully printed note that was saved among family papers accompanied one of the bouquets. It reads:

Dear Dr. Storer:

We take great pleasure in presenting you this bouquet on the Ninety-second anniversary of your birth. Deeming it fitting that our sentiment should find expression in flowers that their beauty, and fragrance may convey to you better than words, the high esteem and respect in which you are held by the colored citizens of this city, and their deep appreciation of your many noble efforts in behalf of the race.

May peace and happiness be your reward.

On April 8, 1922, Agnes noted that "Pater ill." Almost every day after that it is "Pater very ill," and occasionally, "Pater desperately ill." Last rites were administered for the fourth or fifth time on May 15.[17] However, Agnes' references to his illness became less frequent and less "desperate," suggesting some improvement. On August 18, Dr. Henry Orlando Marcy, whom Horatio not seen for thirty years, visited Horatio.[18] Hopefully, Horatio was sufficiently well to appreciate his old defender and friend whom he had so heartily praised in his recent letter to Dr. Walsh. On September 7, Agnes reported the first of several angina attacks she was to mention in the next week. Agnes' entry for

September 18 reads: "Pater's last triumphant day. A second shock at 11 when Fr Higney anointed him for the 8th time. He slept in our Lord at 10 p.m."

Obituaries for Horatio were long and covered much of the same ground covered in newspaper stories about Horatio of the previous three years. However, this excerpt from the *Newport Mercury* for September 18 adds much:[19]

> Dr. Storer was a man of powerful intellect, highly trained, that would have made him a prominent figure in any assemblage of scientists, but after all it was his lovable personality that made him so generally esteemed. Strong in his opinions and unchangeable from any course that he had once adopted, he was yet very far from domineering and had the happy faculty of adhering to his arguments without a trace of hostility. Generous in the extreme, friendly to all, Dr. Storer had a heart that was bigger than his body and his many deeds of thoughtfulness will long remain in the minds of his friends.

The following from the September 19, 1922 *Newport Herald* obituary reminds us of Horatio's early schooling and the letters he sent to Boston:[20]

> Dr. Storer was early sent away to school. The school was situated at Sandwich Massachusetts, on the northern shores of Cape Cod. It was kept by an old Quaker, Captain Wing, or "Uncle Joseph" as he was more often called by his students. He was assisted in running the school by his wife, "Aunt Mercy." The influence of these two friends of the old school was never forgotten and Dr. Storer was sympathetically interested in the Society of Friends throughout his long and useful life, [including] the interest the doctor so actively displayed but a short time ago in the preservation of the Old Friends' Meeting House in this city.

This long obituary reflected a careful interview with Agnes or other family members, and perhaps earlier interviews with the living Horatio. The following paragraphs identify activities we would not otherwise know of:

> From the first moment of his residence here Dr. Storer was beneficently engaged in the life and progress of the community. The history of old time Newport fascinated him and his purchase of the old house adjoining his own residence served to interest him still further. This house has one of the best traditions of any in the city and it was in it that General Lafayette stayed during his residence here. The bay and its ever changing panorama interested him greatly, recalling the days when it was filled with shipping engaged in the slave and rum trades. He was not only interested, he investigated and he became

one of the authorities upon the Colonial life of Newport.

While Dr. Storer had abandoned his active practice before he came here, he never forgot his duty to the community as a member of the medical profession. He worked unceasingly for the betterment of civic health. He was perhaps the most prominent member of the Sanitary Protective Association which many years ago was responsible for securing to this city a proper sewerage system. The results of this undertaking were immeasurable. Without such a system Newport would never have been able to become the beautiful and attractive city that it is. "When judging a city and its citizens," said Victor Hugo. "I look not to their public edifices erected to impress and bewilder the beholder; I look to its drains." It is largely due to Dr. Storer that by this test Newport is not entirely to be condemned.

It has been said that the nineteenth century was the age of the glorification of science. In a sense this is true. Certainly all the men who achieved any prominence during that era were ardent, if not always profound, students of nature and her laws. Dr. Storer was no exception. He was a member of the Newport Natural History Society, a society which numbered among its members many of the best intellects of the time. The great Agassiz was himself a member though never an active one. Mr. Storer's wide experience and travels, his large fund of general information and his deep interest in every branch of knowledge, made him a member whose advice was always respected and desired in the many discussions upon natural history that his society gave rise to.

By far the greatest part of what the doctor did for the community can never be known. His was a generous heart and he gave freely. His charity knew no bounds and it sprung from a genuine love of his fellow-man. He was prominent in the Newport Charity organization and not a little of its success is attributable to him. Only a few years ago he offered his home on Washington street as a home for convalescents. His generous offer was not taken advantage of and he turned the property over to St. Joseph's church for use as a convent. There was no more genial friend or more public spirited citizen than the late Dr. Storer.

Dr. Storer was not one of those who believed that they can serve the community and not connect themselves in any way with politics. He was one of the fathers of the present city charter, which is unique among municipal charters. It is one of the nearest approaches to government by the whole people that has been devised. When the Newport Civic League was founded, Dr. Storer was made a member of the advisory council and his knowledge of conditions and advice as to remedies contributed not a little to the initial successes of the league.

Horatio was buried in Boston's Forest Hills cemetery on Thursday afternoon after a morning service at St. Joseph's Church.[21]

Horatio's numismatist friend, Howland Wood, provided the following tribute to Horatio published in the *Newport Herald* on the day of his funeral:[22]

TRIBUTE TO DR. STORER
His Zeal in Civic Reforms Commended by Mr. H. B. Wood
BROUGHT OUT STATE's TRUE RECORD
Initiated Many Undertakings That Greatly Benefitted Newport
To the Editor of the Herald:—

Notable have been the tributes in the Newport and Boston papers to Newport's grand man, Dr. Storer. It would not be right to speak of him as our "grand old man," for he was ever young, optimistic, active in some good cause, with never a moment to worry or repine. I feel totally unqualified to try to add anything to the able words already said of him and yet I wish I could add a word of appreciation—not to say affection—for one who richly deserves it from Newport as a community, and from many an individual. As I look back to the days of my young manhood, it seems as if it was the genial, friendly doctor, and indefatigable treasurer of the Newport Historical Society, who (why I never could see, unless it was his kindly nature) took the trouble to get me busy as recording secretary of that grand organization and to take an interest in public matters. Many benefits have followed it, and a cordial welcome and real sympathy were always found in his hospitable home.

I have not noticed any reference to the pioneer work he did in bringing out the true record of Rhode Island, and the part John Clarke had in it. It seems to me, in fact, that Dr. Storer and John Clarke were not dissimilar, both being regular graduates in medicine, having studied in Great Britain, and both being noticeably able, far-sighted and untiring in public spirited work for the common good. It seems as if Dr. Storer, in connection with the tablet to John Clarke, in the Historical rooms was the instigator of the discoveries about Newport's leading founder.

Another department of Dr. Storer's activity in advance of many of his fellow citizens was his determined battle for temperance. As I remember it, it was he more than any other man who rid the first ward of its last saloon and kept that district one of the quietest and most desirable parts of the city. He was a friend to all temperance work and workers, and while some of those of today have never seen him, they should all do him honor.

His home was permeated with a religious calm, and anybody feeling overburdened with any public problem was welcomed and went away relieved and refreshed. There religion and public good met, and it is not generally known that there, in that spirit, great benefits to Newport, including the Washington street boulevard and the Tammany Hill Memorial Park were considered and the work planned. It was a great grief to him that the whole drive to and around Coddington Point, once in Newport's grasp, was put off and lost. He was ready to make a telling move for it, I doubt not at his own expense, but a hurry-up sale, unbeknown to him, blocked it. I believe the first start towards the Tammany Hill Park was made in Dr. Storer's house, out of which came the possibility to buy the hill at a reachable figure before most people had heard of the idea. These are but a few of many great benefits to Newport connected with the man we all should always remember with grateful admiration.

H. B. Wood.

Newport, September 20, 1922.

Norman Thomas had been a visitor at Horatio's. His sympathy note read:[23]

The Nation
20 Vesey Street
New York

Sept. 25, 1922

My dear Miss Storer:

Violet and I only heard through Aunt Isa of your father's death. You have access to the source of all comfort; I can only send you our love and sympathy and congratulate you even in your sorrow in the noble heritage your father left, not only to his family but to mankind.

Sincerely yours
Norman Thomas

The sympathy note of R. Tait McKenzie, who struck the medal of Horatio, included:[24]

I have just received a notice of your father's death and hasten to write you my sympathy for what must always be a great loss even if he has long outlived the allotted span.

It was one of the greatest inspirations I have ever had to meet him and to talk about the wonderful experiences of his long life.

I have never met anyone who maintained his boyish enthusiasm as he did. Surely he had the secret of long life in his constant and active interest in the hobbies that meant so much to him.

Agnes wrote to Dr. Walsh, related to Walsh's plan to write something "for publication" about Horatio. The following excerpts from her letter include references to unfortunate family conflicts and other trials of Horatio, which, unless new sources of data should be located, may remain mostly mysteries:[25]

> If you do propose anything for publication—as I gathered from your very kind letter to Malcolm you were considering doing, I wonder if you would be so *very* gracious & considerate as to allow me to look over the manuscript? There were diverse episodes in my father's life which have not always been quite correctly related,—though entirely unintentionally I am certain. You might feel my physician brother is the one who should be asking this favor, but naturally your wish "to bring out his connection with the Catholic Church" would not meet with his sympathetic interest.
>
> The last weeks of the dear father's long warfare were weeks of such unspeakable physical anguish that I could not sadden my brothers whole after lives by letting them share my memories. And yet in all the heartbreak at sight of each fiery trial & I so powerless to aid I was & am uplifted & upborne at sight of what ins[piration] Faith divine can give & can *be* to her children in lifes supreme years & months & moments—that "last of life for which the first was made." ... here he was after a long life of intense disappointments—the treachery of one he counted as a brother who defrauded him of great wealth by means so foul & cowardly it is *all* I can do to forgive even now! Lifelong illness—having to give up his beloved profession & all it held of accomplishment & promise of great usefulness & help to his brother men. Domestic trials, whose vanity & intensity would astonish you. The giving up literally father & mother brothers & sisters position & influence his "place in the world."—at his Lord's clear call & then, & then, this other long lifetime spent so quietly in Newport—not simply undaunted by the deepening physical suffering but growing steadily in grace through the way he accepted them. Of course there were times when he longed for death—but there was never *impatient* longing, it was a steadfast "waiting for the Lord" and meanwhile no anguish could really dampen his ardor to try "the fair admonition of the morrow." Even though it held nothing beyond several hours propped up in bed in great discomfort, working away zealously at the beloved medals (we children are to publish that life work you will be glad to hear)—Other hours studying the world wide problems and questions which interested him as intensely as did the little civic affairs of his beloved little Newport, and from his quiet nook urging on, encouraging, heartening every one of us who came to him—relations, priests, friends, strangers, city fathers—to do each one his or her little bit for the public good.

Another letter from Agnes to Walsh quickly followed:[26]

"DRIFTWOOD"
Newport, R. I.

October 17, 1922.

Dear Dr. Walsh:

As I was only at Intervale for a few days your letter has been returned to me here.

Of course I was very much thrilled at the possibility of an article in "The Dublin." In this connection, it may be of interest to you to know that my father for many years was singularly honored, being listed in the British Medical Register as one of their "Practitioners resident abroad, registered under the Medical Act of Great Britain and Ireland 1858." ...

He often spoke with pleasure of how he came to be so honored, several British medical friends arranged the matter entirely without his knowledge or consent. The chief conspirators, if I remember aright, being Sir Robert Christison and T. Spencer Wells. When we meet, remind me to tell you the rather amusing conversation my father had with the Registrar apropos of that pleasant happening.

I suppose you have talked with Dr. Maloney apropos both of the Ave Maria article and this other possibility. Pater so keenly delighted in going over the Edinburgh days with his sympathetic self that he will, I am sure, recall all sorts of medical tales which would be of interest.

Do you expect to be in New York all of next month? I should be sorry indeed to find that I had happened on a time, quite needlessly, when you were far away.

believe me with best wishes to you all
very sincerely yours
Agnes C. Storer

I am sending to the Ave Maria for copies.

No "article in the Dublin" has been located, but the *Ave Maria* obituary appeared on November 11, 1922. It began:[27]

With the death of Horatio R. Storer on September 18, 1922, there passed from American life, well on in his ninety-third year, a man who had deeply influenced medicine in this country from the scientific as well as from the professional, and, above all, the ethical standpoint. He had been for some years the oldest living graduate of Harvard University, the only survivor of the class of 1850, which contained a number of men who had attained prominence. He retired from the active practice of his profession on account of ill health in his early forties, but not until he had deeply impressed himself upon American surgery; and after that he devoted himself to many different phases of special work relating to medicine which have redounded to his reputation. His work as a physician and its significance has passed almost completely out of the memory of even his professional colleagues, the physicians of the present generation; but those who are familiar with the course of medical history and professional ethics in the United States have continued to appreciate how much Dr. Storer accomplished for the solution of some very thorny problems in professional life in his middle years.

Walsh then recounted Horatio's career and life as depicted in the sketch of Horatio written by Toner in 1878, in Horatio's series of three letters to Walsh written in the month of February 1922 (reproduced earlier), and from the long, accurate, and comprehensive *Newport Herald* obituary Agnes had provided Walsh and which we have largely reproduced above. In addition, Walsh described Horatio's claims, no doubt made in personal discussions, as well as in the letter of February 1, of the importance to Horatio of his Catholic faith.

Walsh's *Ave Maria* sketch is generally accurate, and does appropriately emphasize Horatio's anti-abortion efforts, unlike his piece on Horatio in the March 1918 *Catholic Convert* which only spoke of contributions "where medicine touches morals" without actually mentioning abortion. The following are the *Ave Maria* paragraphs pertaining to Horatio's anti-abortion crusade:

What brought Dr. Storer into great medical prominence, however, was not so much his work in his specialty, though this gave him an important position in his profession, as his taking up a crusade for the protection of unborn children. Many sad abuses had crept into the practice of physicians, the rights of the unborn child to life being sometimes utterly unrecognized. Medical ethics had lapsed in this matter, and Professor Storer took up the task of setting the house in order. It was not an easy thing to do; above all, it was not a popular thing to do. He himself has told how many misgivings he had in the matter. It seemed as though he might appear to be setting himself up as better than the rest of his colleagues. There were other considerations, too. His devotion to this cause even threatened to interfere with his consultant practice, for it inevitably would lead many patients, present and prospective, to conclude that he was more conscientious—perhaps they would think him over-conscientious, or even too scrupulous,—than the rest of his colleagues; and, with issues of life and death for matters hanging in the balance, they would be tempted to avoid employing him.

While Dr. Storer seemed, then, to be risking the success of his whole career, the outcome proved altogether different from any of these unfavorable anticipations. He saw a good work to be done; and though there were many possible selfish considerations against it, these carried no weight with him. There were certain serious evils to be corrected; there were certain still more serious developments, which were quite inevitable, if some one did not take up the unpopular work; and so he turned to it whole-heartedly. The result was that he won the admiration and regard of his colleagues among the regular physicians of the country, so that, when he was still under forty years of age, he was chosen vice-President of the American Medical Association, the representative organization of the scientifically trained physicians of the country. Before this, a special prize had been awarded him by the Association for his monograph relating to the right of the unborn child to life; and he received, besides, the tribute of a widespread distribution of his pamphlets among the leading physicians and lawyers. His work in this regard came at a time when it was sadly needed, as he showed very clearly by statistics, and when conditions were rapidly growing worse. It awakened a genuine sense of honor among the better class of physicians, and accomplished an immense amount of good. His election as vice-President of the American Medical Association gave him position and prestige which furthered the magnificent moral purposes that he had set himself to promote.

At an unknown late date, Horatio's tiny longhand recorded the following autobiographical note on the back of a ballot for voting for or against liquor licensing. It tells:[28]

> During his whole life Dr. S. has given thought to matters of the highest social importance. While in Paris and London in the fifties he studied the questions of foundlings & the subjugation of public women & his very first appointment upon returning to this country was to the Boston Lying-in Hospital. There applicants were at that time compelled to show their "marriage license." He insisted that this should not be required in first pregnancies. As early as 1856[8], he published the first of his long series of papers upon Criminal Abortion, this being a paper sent to the American Academy of Arts and Sciences of which he was perhaps then the youngest Fellow. Another was a prize essay of the American Medical Association entitled the Physical Evils of Forced Abortions, published in its Transactions, & subsequently, by special vote of the Association, issued by Messrs Lee & Shepard of Boston under the title of "Why Not? A Book for every Woman." Many thousands of this were circulated.
>
> With regard to the social evil [venereal disease], Dr. S. was one

of the first to act towards the present crusade, which is becoming so much better than that against tuberculosis. In a presidential address at Chicago, before the Rocky Mountain Medical Association upon "The Extirpation of Syphilis" which was published in the journal of the American Medical Association he initiated much that is now of universal belief. As a graduate of the Harvard Law School as well as that of Medicine, he published with Dr. F.H. Heard a Boston lawyer, through Messrs, Little, Brown & Co. the famous law firm, a manual of procedures in criminal abortion cases.

In the medical education of nurses he was previously the leader in this country. As Chief of Staff of St. Elizabeth's Hospital in Boston, a Franciscan institution he established regular and systematic training, both religious and lay. This was in the sixties.

Upon being forced by illness to relinquish active practice, & as a student of the University of Edinburgh being greatly interested in emanations from that city he introduced at Newport the then new system of Sanitary Protection that revolutionized conditions in that city and established a precedent which has been very largely followed.

Upon ceasing relations as a teacher, in Harvard University, he established a course of instruction in gynaecology for graduated physicians, receiving no applicants save members of the American Medical Association & those courses were attended by physicians from all over the country. He thus anticipated by several years all post graduate institutions, as at the NY Post Graduate Hospital & College.

By the now celebrated collection of medical medals that he founded at the Boston Medical Library in memory of his father, who had been president of the American Medical Association, while he himself had reached the Vice-presidency, he furnished an additional great aid in medical solution.

Agnes, copied most of these autobiographical paragraphs with minor modifications into an undated letter to Dr. Walsh sent probably at about the end of 1922 or early 1923.[29] She also included a draft of an obituary that Malcolm had written for the *Harvard Graduates' Magazine* and it is among Dr. Walsh's papers. Agnes had penciled a few corrections on Malcolm's draft. Dr. Walsh made several additions to the draft, including much from Agnes' version of the above handwritten paragraphs by Horatio.

Malcolm's obituary of his father as slightly modified by Agnes and added to by Dr. Walsh was published in March 1923.[30] Unfortunately, it contains a large number of minor errors such as claiming Horatio visited Archangel in 1846 instead of St. Petersburgh in 1847, plus the more serious error of claiming that Horatio did not know why he was using carbolic acid in his operating room when Horatio was well aware of Lister and antisepsis. Malcolm's description of Horatio's later life is accurate and the following closing paragraphs describe events in Horatio's later life, including those of his very last days:[31]

But while movements for the public good were an absorbing interest to him, I think his chief sympathy was with the lowly when he thought they were being put upon, and treated unfairly. Thus at one time legislation was being pushed to curtail the activities of the hard-working Greek and Portuguese fishermen of Newport—unjustly, as Dr. Storer thought. He took active and successful steps to block this legislation, and so one evening his house was swamped by these picturesque foreigners coming to thank him in person. At another time he helped the colored citizens of Newport when they were under stress, and he was much touched when a delegation of sisters came to present him with a magnificent basket of roses in token of their gratitude.

With such occupations, barely mentioning his favorite fishing, in which he and his sons spent many happy days pursuing the elusive finny inhabitants of Narragansett Bay and surrounding waters, often going as far as Block Island and No Man's Land, he warded off any "rusting away." The last fifteen years of his life were rendered very trying by two serious operations and their results, and much illness, as attested by the fact that on eight different occasions he was given the last consolations of the Church, yet he always managed to fight off the grim spectre—often to the great amazement of his physicians. He was indomitable to the end. Once last summer the writer went down to Newport expecting to find him *in extremis*, if alive at all, but as a matter of fact found him resting easily after dictating a long address to a visiting medical convention. On the very morning of the day he died, between heartrending attacks of angina, he tried to correct some numismatic proof of the writer's. He certainly did not rust out. After a long and honored life, well worthy of the title of Newport's Grand Old Man, as his fellow citizens sometimes lovingly called him, he welcomed rest at the last. On his last afternoon, recognizing that the end was near he expressed a natural curiosity as to that the morrow would bring forth, and then after intimate messages to the members of his family who were not present he sent his love to "the dear Harvard men" and gave especial directions that his "Salve" be given to Mr. Peabody, his successor as Senior Alumnus.

Horatio's 1,146-page book, *Medicina in nummis*, was completed by Malcolm and published in 1931.[32] Malcolm was to die suddenly less than four years later at the age of seventy-two.

AFTERWORD

It is perhaps rare for so much documentation of a long life to exist as exists for Dr. Horatio Robinson Storer. Despite this, there are huge gaps. These included his engagement to Emily Elvira; his marriage with her in health and during her progressing sickness; the half-year Texas trip; his sometimes stormy relations with his father, brothers, and sisters; his courtship and brief marriage with Augusta Caroline; and the long relationship with Frances Sophia from its onset sometime in the mid-1860s until her death. We have some fine pictures of Horatio at different ages, but we cannot be sure how Horatio presented himself before a gallery of American Medical Association physicians, although we know he sometimes wrapped them around his finger and even warned his Association of Medical Editors in 1871 about the dangers of following such a leader. And how did he appear when confronting those powerful Massachusetts Medical Society Councillors whose negativity toward him was so great it prevented or delayed their acceptance of his beloved medical specialty and warped their views of his beloved American Medical Association?

Hermann Jackson Warner provided us adjectives like "bombastic," "egotistic," and "conceited" to describe Horatio and we have learned how Warner loved Horatio, with only brief respites of hate, despite such appellations. Horatio, himself, however is the greatest source of the words used by others to refer to him such as "egotistic," "arrogant," "plucky," "cranky," and "too self-assertive," the latter apparently used by his father when Horatio took the unusual step of acquiring an associate in his gynecological practice. However, Bowditch's "improvident" may be the best characterization.

Horatio certainly was no "wall-flower" as the active social life described in his student diaries shows and his medical convention persuasiveness proves. His fellow members of the Gynaecological Society of Boston typically skipped Society meetings when Horatio was out of town or ill. Some of these Society members at times appeared, as described in the Proceedings of the Society, to be Horatio's sycophants as much as they were prone to attribute this trait to the followers of Henry J. Bigelow.

We have some indications of his intense devotion to the key women in his life. Hermann provided second- and third-hand descriptions of this for his fiance and wife, Emily Elvira. And what a tragedy it is that none of the "long letters to the girl" have survived, given Horatio's superb near love letter to Hermann when he thanked Hermann for the gift of the microscope. Agnes in her diaries and letters described Horatio's devotion as it was manifested for herself and for Frances Sophia MacKenzie Storer. We have Horatio's own tribute to Augusta Caroline in the dedication of his book on Italy and his description of the infatuation of a young father for Jessie Simpson Storer in his letter to his sister. We know this devotion was reciprocated from explicit statements of Agnes and from the behavior of Aunt Carrie and Sister Frances during Horatio's family and health crises in the 1870s when Augusta Caroline followed him across a continent and both followed him across an ocean.

As to his sons, Frank Addison, the oldest is somewhat of a mystery. No Harvard degree, no marriage, apparent lifelong poor health, and living his whole adult life more than a thousand miles to the south of his family, although regularly visiting Newport in the summers. John Humphreys and Malcolm did graduate from Horatio's beloved Harvard with Malcolm even following his father in medicine and the specialty of gynecology. Their graduation dates find their way into a dozen surviving letters of the proud Horatio to his *alma mater* and to its alumni. These boys fished and collected coins with their father and continued these pursuits with him as adults. John Humphreys and Malcolm and their families visited the sick and the well Horatio with a regularity that indicated immense devotion.

Of Horatio's many accomplishments in natural science, medicine, surgery, medical ethics, medical journalism, medical history, "non-medical" history, philanthropy, civil rights, ..., what should he be remembered for? Horatio's own wishes on this may suit as an answer. We repeat the self sketch he provided near the end of his long life for Dr. Walsh's *Cyclopedia*:

> For nearly seventy years, Dr. Storer has written much upon the real time of commencement of foetal life, & of its sanctity. He has been supported, frequently and most authoritatively, by the concerted aid of the American Medical Association, the great body of reputable physicians, of which his father was a president and himself a vice-president. That action of the Association has been the most benefi-cent of its existence, and for the fact that he was to a small extent enabled to take a part, Dr. S. will be held in grateful remembrance, rather than as a progressive and successful surgeon.

Horatio was aware when he wrote these words, that he, and the American Medical Association had initiated a crusade that saved many thousands from an unnecessary uterine death. His instruction to Dr. Walsh: "Think this over seriously, and then appreciate with me the character and universal extent of the change," suggests that Horatio recognized the ramifications of this on the offspring of these survivors, and the offspring of offspring for the three generations he monitored from 1857 to 1922. He no doubt also saw the expand-ing ramifications on every succeeding generation as well.

It is not farfetched to indicate that the reader can thank his or her existence to this man, since the effects of even a small increase in surviving pregnancies exponentially increase on succeeding generations, and there is evidence that this increase in surviving pregnancies was not small. Even if each ancestor of the reader would have been in place without Horatio, some key teachers, coaches, mentors, friends, would not have been around to make their contribution to that existence. Is Dr. Horatio Robinson Storer thus the most important figure in America in the 19th Century? Only decades of reluctance to discuss the taboo topic of criminal abortion may have prevented recognition of this long ago.

NOTES

Abbreviations used:

CEB=Charles Edward Buckingham
DHS=David Humphreys Storer
GSB=Gynaecological Society of Boston
HJW=Hermann Jackson Warner
HRS=Horatio Robinson Storer
MHS=Massachusetts Historical Society
SFP=Storer Family Papers

AJMS=American Journal of the Medical Sciences
BMSJ=Boston Medical and Surgical Journal
JAMA=Journal of the American Medical Association
JGSB=Journal of the Gynaecological Society of Boston
TAMA=Transactions of the American Medical Association

Foreword

1. HRS to Malcolm Storer, October 30, 1901, SFP and In Press (July or October 1999) *Journal of the History of Medicine and Allied Sciences.*
2. James C. Mohr, *Abortion in America: The Origins and Evolution of National Policy, 1800-1900* (New York, Oxford University Press, 1978).

Chapter 1

1. Margaret Susannah Storer to Abby Jane Brewer Storer, undated, but probably written in August or September 1835, SFP.
2. Abigail Brewer to HRS, January 10, 1836, SFP.
3. DHS (translator), *General Species and Iconography of Recent Shells Comprising the Massena Museum, the Collection of Lamarck, the Collection of the Museum of Natural History, and the recent discoveries of travellers. By L. C. Kiener ..., No. 1* (Boston, William D. Ticknor, 1837). DHS was born in Portland Maine in 1804, graduated from Bowdoin College in 1822, and graduated from the Harvard Medical School in 1825. He also studied medicine in the office of John Collins Warren. He married Abby Jane Brewer in 1829 and practiced medicine in Boston. Although he became a Harvard Medical School professor and Dean, he may be better remembered for his work in natural history, particularly ichthyology.
4. Francis Humphreys Storer to Samuel H. Scudder, June 28, 1892, SFP.
5. HRS, "Observations on the Fishes of Nova Scotia and Labrador, with Descriptions of New Species," *Boston Journal of Natural History* 6, no. 32 (1850): 246-270. Horatio's dedication is on p. 253.
6. Oology is the study of bird's eggs.

7. Brewer was trained as a physician, but never practiced medicine. His natural history contributions were primarily in the area of ornithology. One questionable contribution was Brewer's introduction of the English Sparrow into America.

8. HRS to the Editor of the *Newport Daily News*, May 11, 1918. Published in the paper on the same date.

9. Robert Buchanan, editor, *The Life and Adventures of John James Audubon the Naturalist* (New York, G.P. Putnam & Son, 1869), 322.

10. Francis Humphreys Storer to Samuel H. Scudder, June 28, 1892.

11. Chauncy-Hall School report card for HRS, April 1837, SFP.

12. HRS to Abby Jane Brewer Storer, July 14, 1838, SFP. The letter includes a note added by Mercy K. Wing, Headmistress of the Sandwich School.

13. G.F. Thayer to Abby Jane Brewer Storer, January 6, 1840, SFP.

14. HRS to Abby Jane Brewer Storer, May 24, 1840, SFP.

15. HRS to Abby Jane Brewer Storer, April 20, 1840, SFP.

16. HRS to Abby Jane Brewer Storer, May 15, 1840, SFP.

17. HRS to Abby Jane Brewer Storer, May 31, 1840, SFP.

18. HRS to David Humphreys and Abby Jane Brewer Storer, June 12, 1839, SFP.

19. HRS to Abby Jane Brewer Storer, May 24, 1840.

20. HRS to Elizabeth H. Brewer, April 19, 1840, SFP.

21. HJW, "Diary," v. 12 (January 22, 1851-July 4, 1851), May 3, 1851 and v. 15 (December 11, 1851-November 24, 1852), April 12, 1852. The 42 volumes that make up HJW's "Diary" are located at the MHS.

22. "Medical School of Harvard University" (A list of new Harvard Medical School M.D.s with dissertation titles), *BMSJ* 48, no. 26 (July 27, 1853): 527. The actual dissertation has not been located at Harvard repositories or among SFP, and apparently has not been preserved.

23. DHS to Jeffries Wyman, May 15, 1842, Countway Library.

24. Jerome Van Crowningshield Smith, "Catalogue of the Marine and Fresh Water Fishes of Massachusetts." In Edward Hitchcock, *Report on the Geology, Mineralogy, Botany and Zoology of Massachusetts* (Amherst, J.S. & C. Adams, 1833).

25. DHS, "An Examination of the 'Catalogue of the Marine and Fresh Water Fishes of Massachusetts,'" *Boston Journal of Natural History* 1, no. 3 (March 1836): 347-356, 356.

26. DHS, "A Report on the Fishes of Massachusetts," *Boston Journal of Natural History* 2, no. 3-4 (August 1839): 289-570.

27. DHS, *A Synopsis of the Fishes of North America* (Cambridge, Metcalf, 1846).

28. John Parker Boyd Storer to HRS, April 24, 1841, SFP.

29. HRS to David Humphreys and Abby Jane Brewer Storer, August 21, 1844, SFP.

30. Malcolm Storer, "David Humphreys Storer." In Howard A. Kelly and Walter L. Burrage, *Dictionary of American Medical Biography* (New York, Appleton, 1928), 1175.

31. HRS to Malcolm Storer, October 30, 1901.

32. HJW, "Diary," v. 1 (November 27, 1844-November 8, 1845), October 17, 1845.

33. HJW, "Diary," v. 2 (May 8, 1845-May 31, 1846), January 8, 1846. One classic diary entry by Herman, afterwards Herman*n*, is the following from v. 1 (November 27, 1844-November 8, 1845), April 25, 1845:

> Today I have come to the conclusion of writing my name with 2 ns instead of one as e.g. Hermann instead of Herman, & continue to write it so till I make mention in this journal which I shall write it as it originally was.

Hermann never was to "write it as it originally was."

34. Ibid., February 9, 1846.

35. Ibid., March 24, 1846.

36. Ibid., April 7, 1846.

37. Gustavus Hay, like Horatio, obtained the Harvard M.D. By specializing in ophthalmology, he somewhat combined a love of mathematics with his profession.

38. HRS to DHS, undated, but the Sunday after Exhibition was May 24, 1846, SFP.

39. "Autobiography of Capt. Nathaniel E. Atwood, of Provincetown, Mass.: Section IV. The Fishermen of the United States," in *The Fisheries and Fishery Industries of the United States* (Washington, Government Printing Office, 1887), 149-168, 162.

40. HRS to David Humphreys and Abby Jane Brewer Storer, May 27, 1846, SFP.

41. A longhand version of this dissertation is among the SFP, probably the manuscript that was submitted for the prize. A brief attempt to locate the published version in newspapers was not successful.

42. Abby Jane Brewer Storer to HRS with note from DHS, undated, but content indicates May 27, 1846, SFP.

43. Boston Society of Natural History. Minutes, meeting of August 19, 1846, *Proceedings of the Boston Society of Natural History* 2, no. 16 (September 1846): 170.

44. HJW, "Diary," v. 3 (June 1, 1846-December 1, 1846), August 19, 1846.

45. John Parker Boyd Storer to HRS, April 24, 1841.

Chapter 2

1. HRS, handwritten note, about September 1846, SFP.

2. HRS to Francis Humphreys Storer, September 13, 1846, SFP.

3. HJW, "Diary," v. 3 (June 1, 1846-December 1, 1846), December 1, 1846.

4. HJW, "Diary," v. 3 (June 1, 1846-December 1, 1846), October 18, 1846; v. 4 (December 5, 1846-February 2, 1848), January 30 and March 30, 1847.

5. HJW, "Diary," v. 4 (December 5, 1846-February 2, 1848), May 5, 1847.

6. Passport issued by Commonwealth of Massachusetts to HRS, May 11, 1847, SFP.

7. HRS, "Russia/Harvard Journal," May 18, 1847-January 19, 1849, SFP.

8. Ibid., June 13, 1847.

9. Helsingør.

10. HRS, "Russia/Harvard Journal," June 27, 1847.

11. Ibid., July 24, 1847. HRS provided an interesting detailed description of the steam bath.

12. Ibid., September 1, 1847.

13. Ibid., September 24, 1847.

14. *Harvard Faculty Records*, v. 13, 142, Courtesy of the Harvard University Archives.

15. HRS, "Russia/Harvard Journal," October 9, 1847.

16. HJW, "Diary," v. 4 (December 5, 1846-February 2, 1848), October 9, 1847.

17. See Edward Lurie, *Louis Agassiz: A Life in Science* (Chicago, University of Chicago Press, 1960).

18. Francis Humphreys Storer to Samuel H. Scudder, June 28, 1892.

19. Edward Lurie, *Louis Agassiz: A Life in Science*, 158.

20. Francis Humphreys Storer to Samuel H. Scudder, June 28, 1892.

21. HJW, "Diary," v. 6 (August 28, 1848-July 26, 1849), May 2, 1849.

22. HJW, "Diary," v. 6 (August 28, 1848-July 26, 1849), April 27, 1849.

23. HRS, "Russia/Harvard Journal," November 4, 1847.

24. HJW, "Diary," v. 4 (December 5, 1846-February 2, 1848), November 15, 1847.

25. Edgar Allen Poe, *The Conchologists first book: ...* (Philadelphia, Published for the author, by Haswell, Barrington, and Haswell, 1839).

26. HRS, "Russia/Harvard Journal," November 19, 1847.

27. Frederick Ozni Vaille, *The Harvard Book* (Cambridge, Welch, Bigelow, and Company, 1875), 385.

28. C.F. Simmons to DHS, April 4, 1840, requests Storer to deliver the annual address to the Harvard Natural Society. Harvard Natural History Society to DHS, May 29, 1840, tells Storer of his election as an honorary member. Summaries only of both letters are with Boston Society of Natural History papers at the Boston Science Museum.

29. HRS, "Russia/Harvard Journal," December 17, 1847.

30. Ibid., dates as noted.

31. Ibid., March 2, 1848. "Translate" in the following did not involve any change of language. The passage is from Samuel Taylor Coleridge's "Fears in Solitude" written in 1798.

2d [March] Today feels no more like Spring than yesterday; cold, raw and disagreeable. Took a walk with Gus in the evening to the 'Port. Saw an effusion relating to War, which pleased me, and I therefore "translated" it.
"Boys and girls,
And women, that would groan to see a child
Pull off an insect's leg, all read of war,
The best amusement for a morning meal!
The poor wretch who has learnt his only prayers
From curses, who knows scarcely words enough
To ask a blessing from his Heavenly Father,
Becomes a fluent phraseman, absolute
And technical in victories and defeats,
And all our dainty terms for fratricide;
Terms which we trundle smoothly o'er our tongue,
Like mere abstractions, empty sounds to which
We join no feeling and attach no form!
As if the soldier died without a wound;

As if the fibres of their godlike frames
Were gored without a pang; as if the wretch
Who fell in battle doing bloody deeds,
Passed off to Heaven, translated, and not killed—
As though he had no wife to pine for him,
No God to judge him!"

I call this very good but do not know who wrote it. If some of our "heroes" would only accede to its doctrine. This bloody war would be ended and much expense and many lives spared.

32. Ibid., March 11, 1848.

33. "John Hunter," *Encyclopedia Americana* 14, 1967, 514.

34. HRS, "Edward Jenner as Naturalist," *The Sanitarian* 37 (July 1896), 110-134.

35. HRS, "Russia/Harvard Journal," March 12, 1848.

36. Miles Farmer (Plaintiff), *Report of a trial: Miles Farmer, versus Dr. David Humphreys Storer, commenced in the Court of Common Pleas, April term, 1830 ...* (Boston, Printed for the plaintiff, 1831).

37. Horatio's Uncle Thomas Mayo Brewer was a Washington correspondent of the *Boston Atlas*, "a leading Whig newspaper," and his editorials were read by Horatio when he was only ten (HRS to Abby Jane Brewer Storer, May 31, 1840.). Horatio no doubt continued to follow his Uncles's writing until Brewer left the *Atlas* in 1857.

38. "John Quincy Adams," *The National Cyclopaedia of American Biography* (New York, James T. White, 1907), 73-76, 75-76.

39. An attack of the Harvard students on the police who were preventing their entry to the overcrowded hall is described in the journal of John Mead, another Harvard student. John N. Mead, "Harvard Journal," 1847-1850, Harvard Archives: HUD 848.54.6.

40. Horatio reported in his "Russia/Harvard Journal" for November 27, 1848 that he learned "to my great sorrow" of Everett's resignation from the Harvard Presidency.

41. HRS, "Russia/Harvard Journal," April 22, 1848.

42. Ibid., May 31, 1848.

43. See Victor Robinson, *Pathfinders in Medicine* (New York, Medical Life Press, 1929), 542-545.

44. Simpson's *Encyclopaedia Britannica* article appeared in the eighth edition edited by T.S. Trail. There were twenty-two volumes published in Edinburgh by A. and C. Black and in Boston by Little, Brown and Company between 1853 and 1860.

45. HRS, "Russia/Harvard Journal," June 30, 1848.

46. HJW, "Diary," v. 5 (February 3, 1848-August 27, 1848), July 1, 1848.

47. HRS, "Russia/Harvard Journal," excerpts from July 17 to August 17, 1848.

48. HRS to DHS, July 26, 1848, SFP.

49. HRS, "Russia/Harvard Journal," November 1, 1848.

50. Ibid., November 2, 1848.

51. Ibid., October 20, 1848.

52. Ibid., November 3, 1848.

53. "Report of the Curator of Ornithology," Courtesy of the Harvard Archives: HUD 3599.510, Harvard Natural History Society Minutes and Correspondence.

54. HRS, "Russia/Harvard Journal," December 8, 1848.

55. Ibid., as noted during December 1848.

56. HJW, "Diary," v. 6 (August 28, 1848-July 26, 1849), March 13, 1849.

57. Ibid., April 9, 1849.

58. Ibid., April 14, 1849. Italics are not in the original.

59. Ibid., May 25, 1849.

60. Ibid., June 16, 1849.

61. Ibid., June 29, 1849.

62. Ibid., July 2, 1849.

63. DHS to Harvard President, undated, but during the week of July 8, 1849, Courtesy of the Harvard University Archives: *Harvard Corporation Records*, v. 17.

64. HRS, "Labrador Journal," July 7-September 8, 1849, SFP.

65. "Autobiography of Capt. Nathaniel E. Atwood, of Provincetown, Mass.: Section IV. The Fishermen of the United States," 165.

66. These and the following events are described in HRS's "Labrador Journal," July-September 1849.

67. Dr. Horatio Robinson (1803-1849) was DHS's close friend in medical school and after. DHS named Horatio after him. There was a strong precedent for naming Storer males after family friends. David Humphreys (1752-1818), a prominent "soldier, statesman, poet" and aide-de-camp to George Washington during the Revolutionary War [*Dictionary of American Biography* (New York, Scribner's, 1933/1961, v. 5, 373-375, 373.], was a friend of DHS's father, Woodbury Storer. Almost no information about Horatio Robinson was located. He never achieved the status of David Humphreys, DHS, or HRS.

68. Woodbury Storer to HRS, December 20, 1849, SFP.

69. HJW, "Diary," v. 8 (July 27, 1849-February 18, 1850), September 14, 1849.

70. Ibid., September 28, 1849.

71. Charles Hale to Edward Everett Hale, October 11, 1849, Smith's College: Sophia Smith Collection.

72. HJW, "Diary," v. 8 (July 27, 1849-February 18, 1850), December 14, 1849.

73. Ibid., January 9, 1850.

74. Ibid., January 26, 1850.

75. Ibid., February 18, 1850.

76. HJW, "Diary," v. 9 (February 19, 1850-July 1, 1850), February 21, 1850.

77. Ibid., March 2, 1850.

78. Ibid., April 12, 1850.

79. Ibid., May 1, 1850.

80. Horatio's dissertation was a review of Humboldt's *Cosmos*. It is on file at the Harvard Archives: HWC 6849.38, and Hermann's assessment appears accurate.

81. HJW, "Diary," v. 9 (February 19, 1850-July 1, 1850), May 7, 1850.

82. Ibid., May 16, 1850.

83. Ibid., June 4, 1850.

84. Ibid., June 6, 1850.

85. Ibid., June 9, 1850.

86. HRS, "The History and Resources of the Valley of the Mississippi," Courtesy of the Harvard University Archives: HU 89.165.221.

87. HJW, "Diary," v. 9 (February 19, 1850-July 1, 1850), June 14, 1850. Stress added.

88. HJW, "Diary," v. 10 (July 2, 1850-September 11, 1850), July 9, 1850.

89. HRS, "Medical School Journal," September 2, 1850-June 9, 1851, September 4, 1850, SFP.

90. HRS, "Observations on the Fishes of Nova Scotia and Labrador, with Descriptions of New Species," *Boston Journal of Natural History* 6, no. 32 (October 1850): 246-270.

Chapter 3

1. HRS, "Medical School Journal," September 2, 1850.

2. Ibid., September 27, 28, and 30, 1850; October 1-4 and 7-11, 1850.

3. Ibid., September 7, 1850.

4. Ibid., September 22, 1850.

5. Ibid., October 2, 1850.

6. HJW, "Diary," v. 10 (July 2, 1850-September 11, 1850), July 6, 1850.

7. HJW, "Diary," v. 11 (September 11, 1850-January 21, 1851), September 29, 1850.

8. Ibid., November 18, 1850.

9. Ibid., December 3, 1850.

10. HRS, "Medical School Journal," November 6, 1850.

11. It read: "Resolved, That we have no objection to the education and evaluation of blacks, but do decidedly remonstrate against their presence in College with us," according to Edwin P. Hoyt, *The Improper Bostonian: Dr. Oliver Wendell Holmes* (New York, Morrow, 1979), 148.

12. Harvard Medical School Records, Countway Library.

13. HRS, "Medical School Journal," December 9, 10, and 11, 1850.

14. Ibid., December 14, 1850.

15. Ibid., December 26, 1850.

16. Louis Rodolphe Agassiz, "The Diversity of Origin of the Human Races," *Christian Examiner* 49 (July 1850), 110-145, 143.

17. Ibid., 144-145.

18. HRS, "Medical School Journal," December 27 and 28, 1850. Stress added.

19. Ibid., January 7, 1851.

20. Ibid., February 11, 1851.

21. Horatio's ancestors on both sides were very early settlers of New England. See Malcolm Storer, *Annals of the Storer Family Together with Notes on the Ayrault Family* (Boston, Published for the Author by Wright and Potter, 1927).

22. HRS, "Medical School Journal," February 15 and 17, 1851.

23. Ibid., January 10, 1851.

24. HJW, "Diary," v. 12 (January 22, 1851-July 4, 1851), January 25, 1851.

25. Ibid., January 28, 1851.

26. Boston Society of Natural History, Minutes, meeting of February 19, 1851, *Proceedings of the Boston Society of Natural History* 4, no 1 (June 1851); 29.

27. HRS, "Medical School Journal," February 21, 1851.

28. Described in HJW's "Diary," v. 12 (January 22, 1851-July 4, 1851) during February 1851.

29. James Melville Gilliss, *The U.S. Naval Astronomical Expedition to the Southern Hemisphere, During the Years 1849-'50-'51-'52* (Washington, A.O.P. Nicholson, 1855).

30. HJW, "Diary," v. 12 (January 22, 1851-July 4, 1851), March 1, 1851.

31. Ibid., March 3, 1851.

32. *Catalogue of the Past and Present Officers and Members of the Boylston Medical Society of Harvard University* (Boston, David Clapp, 1858).

33. Boylston Medical Society. Minutes, meeting of March 3, 1851, Countway Library.

34. HJW, "Diary," v. 12 (January 22, 1851-July 4, 1851), March 7, 1851.

35. Ibid., March 8, 1851.

36. Zabdiel B. Adams, "Interesting Reminiscences of a long Professional Life," Countway Library (H MS c 49.4), 2.

37. Charles Newton Peabody, *ZAB* (Boston, The Francis A. Countway Library of Medicine, 1984), 30.

38. HJW, "Diary," v. 12 (January 22, 1851-July 4, 1851), March 15, 1851.

39. Ibid., March 16, 1851.

40. Ibid., March 22, 1851.

41. HRS, "Medical School Journal," April 5, 1851.

42. HJW, "Diary," v. 12 (January 22, 1851-July 4, 1851), April 6, 1851.

43. HRS, "Medical School Journal," April 6-19, 1851.

44. Ibid., April 29, 1851.

45. DHS, "Report of the Committee on Obstetrics," *TAMA* 4 (1851): 404-407.

46. Had the same sequence been followed, HRS would have been elected President in 1890 after bringing the American Medical Association to his home city of Newport, Rhode Island in 1889. This did not happen, but, as will be seen, it almost happened.

47. HRS, "Medical School Journal," May 24, 1851.

48. HRS to Malcolm Storer, October 30, 1901.

49. HJW, "Diary," v. 12 (January 22, 1851-July 4, 1851), May 19, 1851.

50. HRS, "Medical School Journal," May 19, 1851.

51. HJW to HRS, May 27, 1851, Warner's copy of letter in Warner's letter book covering May 1851 (v. 49, p. 77), MHS.

52. HJW, "Diary," v. 12 (January 22, 1851-July 4, 1851), May 27, 1851. Stress in the original.

53. Ibid., May 28, 1851. Stress added.

54. Boston Society of Natural History. Minutes, Annual Meeting, May 5, 1852, *Proceedings of the Boston Society of Natural History* 4, no. 14 (October 1852): 216-221, 217-218.

55. Unidentified newspaper clipping, SFP.

56. HRS to HJW, July 11, 1851, from Warner's copy of letter, "Received in Lenox, Massachusetts in July 1851," in Warner's letter book covering July 1851 (v. 49, pp. 104-109), MHS.

57. HJW, "Diary," v. 14 (September 13, 1851-December 10, 1851), September 28, 1851.

58. Ibid., October 11, 1851.

59. Ibid., November 24, 1851.

60. Ibid., November 28, 1851.

61. "In Memoriam. David Humphreys Storer," *BMSJ* 76, no. 12 (March 24, 1892): 291-294.

62. Boylston Medical Society. Minutes, meeting of December 1, 1851.

63. Ibid., meeting of December 12, 1851.

64. HRS to the Harvard University Corporation, January 3, 1852, Countway Library.

65. President and Fellows of Harvard College. Minutes, Stated Meeting in Boston, March 27, 1852, *Harvard Corporation Records* 9, 205, Harvard Archives.

Chapter 4

1. Boylston Medical Society. Minutes, meeting of December 12, 1851.

2. Ibid., meeting of January 2, 1852.

3. Ibid., meeting of January 9, 1852.

4. HJW, "Diary," v. 14 (September 13, 1851-December 10, 1851), December 2, 1851.

5. Ibid., December 3, 1851.

6. HJW, "Diary," v. 15 (December 11, 1851-November 24, 1852), December 21, 1851.

7. A conversation between Joseph Henry Thayer and Horatio's father [reported in HJW's "Diary," v. 17 (November 25, 1852-July 30, 1853), June 18, 1853] indicated that Horatio had done little studying "Ever since his falling in with his girl" a year-and-a-half earlier.

8. HJW, "Diary," v. 15 (December 11, 1851-November 24, 1852), January 10, 1852.

9. Boylston Medical Society. Minutes, meeting of February 6, 1852.

10. Boston Society of Natural History. Minutes, meeting of February 4, 1852, *Proceedings of the Boston Society of Natural History* 4, no. 12 (May 1852): 185-189, 188.

11. HJW, "Diary," v. 15 (December 11, 1851-November 24, 1852), April 12, 1852.

12. Jacob Bigelow, "1852-3 Lectures on Materia Medica, Bound by His Student, Horatio R. Storer," Countway Library.

13. "Medical School of Harvard University," *BMSJ* 48, no. 26 (July 27, 1853): 527. This article lists the new Harvard Medical School M.D.s with their dissertation titles.

14. Boylston Medical Society. Minutes, meeting of February 13, 1852.

15. HJW, "Diary," v. 12 (January 22, 1851-July 4, 1851), March 1, 1851.

16. Boylston Medical Society. Minutes, meeting of February 13, 1852.

17. HJW, "Diary," v. 15 (December 11, 1851-November 24, 1852), March 18, 1852 and March 20, 1852.

18. Malcolm Storer, *Annals of the Storer Family Together with Notes on the Ayrault Family*, 64.

19. Addison Gilmore of Watertown in the County of Middlesex (died 1851), Last Will and Testament, Massachusetts Supreme Judicial Court Archives.

20. HRS to Nathaniel E. Atwood, April 10, 1852, SFP.

21. HJW, "Diary," v. 15 (December 11, 1851-November 24, 1852), April 12, 1852.

22. Ibid., April 17, 1852.

23. "Autobiography of Capt. Nathaniel E. Atwood, of Provincetown, Mass.: Section IV. The Fishermen of the United States," 166.

24. Boston Society of Natural History. Minutes, meeting of April 21, 1852, *Proceedings of the Boston Society of Natural History* 4, no. 14 (October 1852): 209-215, 215.

25. HJW, "Diary," v. 15 (December 11, 1851-November 24, 1852), May 9, 1852.

26. Ibid., July 15, 1852.

27. HJW, "Travel Journal," v. 16, Summer 1852.

28. HJW, "Diary," v. 15 (December 11, 1851-November 24, 1852), September 3, 1852.

29. "Dr. Brown-Séquard's Lectures," *BMSJ* 47, no. 21 (December 22, 1852): 452-453. The article included a series of resolutions by established physicians who attended the lectures and a letter from three medical students thanking Brown-Séquard.

30. Boston Society of Natural History. Minutes, meeting of December 15, 1852. *Proceedings of the Boston Society of Natural History* 4, no. 19 (May 1853): 286-290, 288-290. Memorializing state legislatures was to become a hallmark of Horatio's various crusades.

31. Ibid., 290.

32. Boylston Medical Society. Minutes, meeting of December 3, 1852.

33. Ibid., meeting of December 31, 1852.

34. HJW, "Diary," v. 17 (November 25, 1852-July 30, 1853), March 27, 1853.

35. Ibid., May 21, 1853.

36. Ibid., May 30, 1853.

37. "The Railroad Accident," *Boston Daily Evening Traveller* (May 7, 1853), p. 1.

38. HJW, "Diary," v. 17 (November 25, 1852-July 30, 1853), June 18, 1853.

39. HRS and Emily E. Gilmore, Marriage Certificate, July 12, 1853, Massachusetts State Archives.

40. HJW, "Diary," v. 17 (November 25, 1852-July 30, 1853), July 6, 1853.

41. HRS to Edward Hitchcock, November 16, 1853, Amherst College Archives.

42. HRS to John Collins Warren, December 19, 1853, Boston Science Museum: Boston Society of Natural History Correspondence.

43. U.S. Passport issued to HRS, December 15, 1853, SFP.

44. "List of Passengers," *Boston Daily Advertiser*, December 24, 1853.

45. "Sailed," *Boston Daily Advertiser*, December 26, 1853.

46. HJW, "Diary," v. 18 (July 31, 1853-February 18, 1854), December 23, 1853.

47. HRS, "Artificial Dilatation of the Os and Cervix Uteri, by Fluid Pressure from Above," *BMSJ* 68, no. 22 (July 2, 1863): 431-439, 431.

48. Horatio errs in mentioning October and appears to have it confused with his October departure for his next trip abroad in 1872.

49. HRS to Malcolm Storer, October 30, 1901.

50. U.S. Passport issued to HRS.

51. HRS to Malcolm Storer, October 30, 1901.

52. HRS to John Collins Warren, May 24, 1854, MHS: Warren Papers.

53. HJW, "Diary," v. 19 (February 19, 1855-July 5, 1855), June 17, 1854.

54. HRS, "Reminiscences of J. Y. Simpson," *Edinburgh Medical Journal* 7, no. 1 (July 1911) 12-17.

55. HRS to Malcolm Storer, October 30, 1901.

56. The "sound" upon which Simpson urged reliance was a graduated probe which was used to measure the uterine cavity and to detect fibroids or other abnormal material. This uterine sound would be discussed repeatedly in Horatio's writing on gynecology and abortion where he praised the instrument, but cautioned physicians against its use if there were even the slightest possibility of pregnancy.

57. HRS, "The So-Called Chronic Metritis, and Its Rational Treatment," *Transactions of the Medical Society of the State of New York* (1867): 212-229, 213.

58. HRS to Mary Goddard Storer, October 20, 1854, SFP.

59. Thomas Mayo Brewer's first child, Lucy Stone Brewer, and John Reed Brewer's second child, Helen Reed Brewer, also were born in 1854.

60. "The Works of Professor J. Y. Simpson," *BMSJ* 52, no. 8 (March 29, 1855): 165.

61. William Overend Priestley and HRS, editors, *The Obstetric Memoirs and Contributions of Sir James Y. Simpson, Professor of Midwifery in the University of Edinburgh, 1* (Philadelphia, J.B. Lippincott & Co., 1855); *2* (Philadelphia, J.B. Lippincott & Co., 1856). The Edinburgh edition was published by Adam and Charles Black.

62. HRS, "Preface to the American Edition," *The Obstetric Memoirs ...*, *1* (Philadelphia, J.B. Lippincott & Co., 1855), xv-xix.

63. "Prof. Simpson's Obstetric Memoirs and Contributions," *BMSJ* 52, no. 21 (June 28, 1855): 426.

64. Bennett Dowler, "Prof. Simpson's *Obstetric Memoirs*," *New Orleans Medical and Surgical Journal* 12, no. 5 (March 1856): 653-665, 655.

65. Karlem Riess, "The Rebel Physiologist—Bennet Dowler," *Journal of the History of Medicine and Allied Sciences* 16, no. 1 (January 1961): 39-48.

66. Bennet Dowler, "Prof. Simpson's *Obstetric Memoirs*," 663.

67. HRS, "New Form of Intra-uterine Pessary," *BMSJ* 55, no. 14 (November 6, 1856): 289-290, 289.

68. Editorial comment: "Caries of Elbow-Joint," *Edinburgh Medical and Surgical Journal* 83, no. 1 (January 1855): 154.

69. This letter and a response from Gillespie in the same *London Medical Times and Gazette* were republished in the *AJMS* 30, no. 60 (October 1855): 543-546. A final comment was appended to these by Horatio (pp. 546-548).

70. "Extracts from the Records of the Boston Society for Medical Improvement—April 9th, 1855," *BMSJ* 52, no. 23 (July 12, 1855): 461-463.

71. HJW, "Diary," v. 19 (February 19, 1855-July 5, 1855), June 8, 1855.

72. Frederick C. Irving. *Safe Deliverance* (Boston, Houghton Mifflin Co, 1942), 121. The other two attending physicians were Dr. William Read and Dr. Horace Dupee.

73. HRS to Charles Hale, June 26, 1851 and July 13, 1855, Harvard Archives: HUD 250.505, Class of 1850 Secretary's File, Class Meetings Folder.

74. "Report of the Boston Society for Medical Improvement," *BMSJ* 54, no. 17 (May 29, 1856): 339.

75. HRS, "Preface to the American Edition," xvi.

76. HRS, "Elm Tents for the Dilatation of the Cervix Uteri," *BMSJ* 53, no. 15 (November 8, 1855): 297-302, 297.

77. Ibid., 297-302.

Chapter 5

1. "Medical Lectures of Harvard University," *BMSJ* 53, no. 14 (November 1, 1855): 295.

2. DHS, *An Introductory Lecture before the Medical Class of 1855-56 of Harvard University* (Boston, David Clapp Printer, 1855).

3. DHS, "Two Frequent Causes of Uterine Disease," *JGSB* 6, no. 3 (March 1872): 194-203.

4. DHS, *An Introductory Lecture before the Medical Class of 1855-56 of Harvard University*, 6.

5. Ibid., 8.

6. Hugh L. Hodge, *Introductory Lecture* (Philadelphia, T.K. and P.G. Collins, 1854). Available on Microfiche—LAC 40061. This and the previous quote came from a brief Introduction on page 4.

7. HRS, "Self Abuse in Women: Its Causation and Rational Treatment," *Western Journal of Medicine* 1, no. 2 (August, 1867): 449-457, 451.

8. DHS, "Two Frequent Causes of Uterine Disease," 195.

9. Ibid., 197.

10. Ibid., 198-199.

11. Ibid., 200-201.

12. Harvard Medical School Student Committee to DHS, November 10, 1855, Countway Library (B MS c 8.2).

13. "An Introductory Lecture ...," *BMSJ* 53, no. 20 (December 13, 1855): 409-411, 410-411.

14. Ibid., 411.

15. "Criminal Abortion," *New-Hampshire Journal of Medicine* 7, no. 7 (July 1857): 208-216, 208.

16. HRS, "The Mutual Relations of the Medical Profession, Its Press, and the Community," *JGSB (Supplement)* 4, no. 6 (June 1871): 4-5. In this address Horatio claimed: "If the medical colleges are content to underbid each other, and year after year to pursue the suicidal warfare, they should not grieve that their students, [once] become practitioners, so often are starvelings and so frequently do them discredit."

17. DHS, "Two Frequent Causes of Uterine Disease," 194.

18. "Editorial Notes," *JGSB* 6, no. 5 (May 1872): 393-394. The footnote read: "March, 1872, p. 194."

19. HRS and Franklin Fiske Heard, *Criminal Abortion: Its Nature, Its, Evidence, and Its Laws* (Boston, Little, Brown, and Company, 1868), 2.

20. HRS to Malcolm Storer, October 30, 1901.

21. "Boston Lying-in Hospital," *BMSJ* 52, no. 21 (June 28, 1855): 423-425.

22. "The Boston Lying-in Hospital," *BMSJ* 54, no. 2 (February 14, 1856): 46-47, 47.

23. For example, the *Proceedings* for October 17, 1855 indicate "Dr. H. R. Storer presented, in the name of Dr. D. H. Storer, some specimens of very large Oyster Shells, probably *Ostrea Virginica*, taken from the milldam by Samuel Nicholson, Esq."

24. Boston Society for Medical Observation. Minutes, meeting of November 19, 1855, Countway Library.

25. Ibid., meeting of December 3, 1855.

26. Ibid., meeting of December 17, 1855.

27. Jessie S. Storer Death Certificate (died December 2, 1855), Massachusetts State Archives.

28. HRS to Hales Wallace Suter, November 24, 1910, Harvard Archives: HUD 250.505, Class of 1850 Secretary's File.

29. HRS, "Protracted First Stage of Labor.—Rigidity of Os Uteri," *BMSJ* 54, no. 2 (February 14, 1856): 38-39.

30. Ibid., 38.

31. "Death from Inhalation of Chloroform in Edinburgh," *BMSJ* 53, no. 24 (January 10, 1856): 494.

32. "Death from Chloroform," *BMSJ* 53, no. 25 (January 17, 1856): 512-513.

33. "Student" (CEB), "Letter from Boston—Medical Societies," *The Medical and Surgical Reporter* 10, no. 2 (February 1857): 66-67, 66.

34. Boston Society for Medical Observation. Minutes, meeting of February 4, 1856.

35. HRS, "Retained Placenta," *BMSJ* 54, no. 5 (March 13, 1856): 119-121.

36. Ibid., 120. As will be seen, years later, Horatio strongly criticized Charles Buckingham's failure to use ice to stem puerperal hemorrhage.

37. "*" (HRS), "Female Physicians," *BMSJ* 54, no. 9 (April 3, 1856): 169-174.

38. Ibid., 169. Italics are in the original.

39. Samuel Gregory, *Man-Midwifery Exposed* ... (New York, Fowlers and Wells, 1848).

40. "*" (HRS), "Female Physicians," 173. Gregory's "grossly indelicate works" included a pair of treatises on masturbation: *Facts and Important Information for Young Women, on the Subject of Masturbation* ... (Boston, Gregory, 1850) and *Facts and Important Information for Young Men, on the Subject of Masturbation* ... (Boston, Gregory, 1857). Horatio would make no mention of Gregory's "works" in his own writing on male and female masturbation.

41. HJW, "Diary," v. 22 (March 19, 1856-December 23, 1856), April 2, 1856.

42. Boston Society of Natural History. Minutes, meeting of April 2, 1856, *Proceedings of the Boston Society of Natural History* 5, no. 23 (July 1856): 346-355, 353-354.

43. HRS, "Puerperal Mania. Recovery," *BMSJ* 55, no. 1 (August 7, 1856): 20-22.

44. HRS, "Operation for Intra-Mural Fibrous Tumor," *BMSJ* 55, no. 5 (September 4, 1856): 101-103.

45. HRS, "Review of Charles Clay's *The Complete Handbook of Obstetric Surgery*," *BMSJ* 55, no. 14 (November 6, 1856): 281-285, 284.

46. Suffolk District Medical Society. Minutes, meeting of May 31, 1856, *BMSJ* 54, no. 25 (July 24, 1856): 500-501.

47. HRS, "Elm Tents for the Dilatation of the Cervix Uteri," 299. Additional evidence that Parks was being referred to is Parks' mention of Horatio's paper on elm tents in Parks' review of Horatio's *Is it I?* (discussed in Chapter 11).

48. Suffolk District Medical Society. Minutes, meeting of July 26, 1856, *BMSJ* 55, no. 9 (October 2, 1856): 186.

49. James Clarke White, *Sketches from my Life* (Cambridge, Massachusetts, Riverside Press, 1913), 197.

50. HRS, "Operation for Intra-Mural Fibrous Tumor," 103.

51. Minutes, 1856 Annual Meeting, *TAMA* 9 (1856), 10.

52. Rhoda Truax, *The Doctors Warren of Boston: First Family of Surgery* (Boston, Houghton Mifflin Co., 1968).

53. HRS, "Russia/Harvard" Journal, September 25, 1847; October 20, 1847; November 30, 1847; and March 4, 1848.

54. HJW, "Diary," v. 22 (March 19, 1856 to December 23, 1856), May 7, 1856.

55. HRS, "Cases of Nymphomania," *AJMS* 32, no. 64 (October 1856): 378-387.

56. Ibid., 384.

57. Ibid., 385-386.

58. HJW, "Diary," v. 22 (March 19, 1856-December 23, 1856), July 23, 1856.

59. "Student" (CEB), "Letter from Boston—Medical Societies," 66.

60. Suffolk District Medical Society. Minutes, meeting of August 30, 1856, *BMSJ* 55. no. 14 (November 6, 1856): 286-291.

61. Ibid., 290. Years later Horatio would mention a pair of cases he had earlier reported to the Suffolk District Medical Society where he himself had accidentally induced abortion. It is possible that he was the "most respectable practitioner" who inserted the pessary.

62. Boston Society for Medical Observation. Minutes, meeting of September 1, 1856.

63. Walter L. Burrage, "Charles Edward Buckingham." In Howard A. Kelly and Walter L. Burrage, *Dictionary of American Medical Biography*, 166.

64. HRS, "Review of Charles Clay's *The Complete Handbook of Obstetric Surgery*," 281-285.

65. Frederick C. Irving, *Safe Deliverance*, 123.

66. "Student" (CEB), "Letter from Boston—Hospitals," *The Medical and Surgical Reporter* 10, no. 2 (February 1857): 65.

67. "Bishop's Journal," IV (1849-1861), November 30, 1856, Archdiocese of Boston Archives.

68. Frederick C. Irving, *Safe Deliverance*, 123.

69. HRS to Malcolm Storer, October 30, 1901.

70. "The Boston Lying-in Hospital," *BMSJ* 54, no. 2 (February 14, 1856): 47.

71. Boston Society of Natural History, "Donations to the Museum," *Proceedings of the Boston Society of Natural History* 6, no. 6 (February 1857): 92-93, 93. Henry David Thoreau speculated in his *Journal* (v. 10. p. 356) that this came from Flint's Pond and was collected by the "Hoars or Emersons."

72. Boston Society for Medical Observation. Minutes, meeting of December 15, 1856.

73. Suffolk District Medical Society. Minutes, meeting of December 27, 1856, *BMSJ* 56, no. 6 (March 12, 1857): 121-122.

74. "Dr. Brown-Séquard," *BMSJ* 55, no. 15 (November 13, 1856): 314.

75. HRS, *Why Not? A Book for Every Woman (2nd Edition)* (Boston, Lee and Shepard, 1868), iii.

76. HRS, "Review of Charles Clay's *The Complete Handbook of Obstetric Surgery*," 283.

77. Jesse Boring, "Foeticide," *Atlanta Medical and Surgical Journal* 2, no. 5 (January 1857): 257-267.

Chapter 6

1. John Keith to HRS, February 17, 1857, Countway Library: Storer Abortion File.

2. Suffolk District Medical Society. Minutes, meeting of February 28, 1857, *BMSJ* 56, no. 14 (May 7, 1857): 282-284, 283.

3. Ibid., 283-284.

4. As Horatio wrote about his father's capitulation in his 1901 letter to Malcolm.

5. Suffolk District Medical Society. Minutes, meeting of February 28, 1857, 282-283.

6. HRS, "Criminal Abortion: Its Prevalence, Its Prevention, and Its Relation to the Medical Examiner ...," Microfiche #AN 0320 in the Adelaide Nutting Historical Nursing Microfilm Collection which is a microfiche of an offprint of the article in *Atlantic Medical Weekly* (Providence, R.I.) 8, no. 14 (October 2, 1897): 209-218. Page numbers of the offprint are 1-34.

7. HRS to Malcolm Storer, October 30, 1901.

8. HRS to Edward Jarvis, March 7, 1857, Countway Library: Jarvis Papers.

9. Mrs Apollonio (City Registrar's Office) to HRS, March 26, 1857, Countway Library: Storer Abortion File.

10. Countway Library: Storer Abortion File.

11. James W. Hoyte to HRS, March 20, 1857, Countway Library: Storer Abortion File.

12. "Student" (CEB), "Letter from Boston: Criminal Abortion," *The Medical and Surgical Reporter* 10, no. 4 (April 1857): 207.

13. C.E.B. (Charles E. Buckingham), "Letter from Boston," *The Medical and Surgical Reporter* 10, no. 9 (September 1857): 472.

14. See Note 12.

15. Henry Ingersoll Bowditch to HRS, April 20, 1857, Countway Library: Storer Abortion File.

16. HRS, Henry Ingersoll Bowditch, and Calvin Ellis, "Suffolk District Medical Society Report of the Committee on Criminal Abortion," April 25, 1857. The only known original copy of the Report is located at the Countway Library. Records indicate its availability at the National Library of Medicine, however, they were unable to locate it. It is reproduced in large part in the *American Medical Gazette* 8, no. 7 (July 1857): 390-397.

17. The cover letter for the Report indicates it was read at the April meeting. Suffolk District Medical Society meetings were held the last Saturday of each month.

18. This letter from Secretary Charles D. Homans to Society members precedes and is part of the printed Report.

19. HRS, Henry Ingersoll Bowditch, and Calvin Ellis, "Suffolk District Medical Society Report of the Committee on Criminal Abortion," 2.

20. Ibid., 4.

21. Ibid., 2.

22. Ibid., 8.

23. Ibid., 9-10.

24. Ibid., 11.

25. Ibid., 12-13.

26. Suffolk District Medical Society. Minutes, Special Meeting of May 9, 1857, Countway Library.

27. Ibid. The Minutes of the Regular Meetings of the Suffolk District Medical Society, unlike those of the Special Meetings, apparently have not been preserved.

28. See the discussion of a brief submitted to the Supreme Court on behalf of over 400 professional historians for *Webster* v. *Reproductive Health Services* (1989) in "Aborting History," *National Review* 47, no. 20 (October 23, 1995): 29-32.

29. Stephen Tracy to HRS, May 7, 1857, Countway Library.

30. Thomas W. Blatchford to HRS, May 13, 1857, Countway Library: Storer Abortion File.

31. Stephen Tracy, *The Mother and Her Offspring* (New York, Harper & Brothers, 1853).

32. Ibid., 109.

33. "B." (CEB), "The Report upon Criminal Abortions," *BMSJ* 56, no. 17 (May 28, 1857): 346-347.

34. The May 7 *BMSJ* issue prompted Tracy's letter to Horatio on May 7 and Tracy lived in Andover.

35. "B." (CEB), "The Report upon Criminal Abortions," 346. These italics were not in the original. This sentence would become the focus of numerous discussions.

36. "Criminal Abortion," *New-Hampshire Journal of Medicine* 7, no. 7 (July 1857): 213.

37. "Medicus," "Communications—Suffolk District Medical Society," *The Medical World* 2, no. 11 (1857): 211-212.

38. "Criminal Abortion," *New-Hampshire Journal of Medicine* 7, no. 7 (July 1857): 214.

39. "The Report of the Committee upon Criminal Abortion," *BMSJ* 56, no. 19 (June 11, 1857): 386-387.

40. James C. Mohr, *Abortion in America: The Origins and Evolution of National Policy, 1800-1900.*

41. "Criminal Abortion," *New-Hampshire Journal of Medicine* 7, no. 7 (July 1857): 208.

42. Massachusetts Medical Society. Minutes, meeting of June 3, 1857, Countway Library.

43. "Criminal Abortion," *New-Hampshire Journal of Medicine* 7, no. 7 (July 1857): 213-214.

44. Ibid., 216.

45. "Student" (CEB), "Criminal Abortions," *Medical and Surgical Reporter* 10, no. 8 (August 1857): 414-415.

46. J. Berrien Lindsley to HRS, July 4, 1857, Countway Library: Storer Abortion File.

47. "The Report upon Criminal Abortions—Comments of the *New Hampshire Journal of Medicine*," *BMSJ* 56 no. 25 (July 23, 1857): 503-504.

48. "Criminal Abortion; The Boston Medical and Surgical Journal and its Attempts at Bullying," *New-Hampshire Journal of Medicine* 7, no. 8 (August 1857): 248-251.

49. "B." (CEB), "Criminal Abortion," *BMSJ* 57, no. 2 (August 13, 1857): 45-46. Stress added.

50. "Suffolk," "The Report upon Criminal Abortions," *BMSJ* 57. no. 3 (August 20, 1857): 67.

51. "Abortionism, Pro et Contra," *American Medical Gazette* 8, no. 7 (July 1857): 390-397, 390.

52. Ibid., Stress added.

53. HRS, "Review of *An Exposition of the Signs and Symptoms of Pregnancy*," *North-American Medico-Chirurgical Review* 1, no. 2 (March 1857): 249-254.

54. Ibid., 254. Horatio wrote: "[The book] has freshened our recollections of the cheery, genial face, the thoughtful mind, and, better than all, the kind heart of whose existence we have had abundant proof."

55. Ibid, 251. A few years later, Horatio mentioned that "shortly previous to his death, however, Dr. Montgomery wrote me that he both accepted and indorsed the limitation I had made" [HRS, "Surgical Treatment of Amenorrhoea," *AJMS* 47, no. 93 (January 1864): 88.].

56. Ibid., 253.

57. HRS, "Removal of the Cervix Uteri for Non-Malignant Hypertrophy," *New-Hampshire Journal of Medicine* 7, no. 4 (April 1857): 97-101. Interactions with the New-York-based Editor of the *New-Hampshire Journal of Medicine* on this April article

no doubt facilitated Horatio's "use" of that journal three months later in his campaign to counter "B." and to criticize the *BMSJ.*

58. "Student" (CEB), "Letter from Boston—Medical Societies," 67.

59. Boston Society for Medical Observation. Minutes, meeting of May 18, 1857.

60. Ibid., meeting of June 1, 1857.

61. Ibid., meeting of July 20, 1857.

62. Ibid., meeting of October 19, 1857.

63. HRS, "The Treatment of Vaginal Fistula," *AJMS* 34, no. 68 (October 1857): 387-394.

64. Horatio's mention of "ill health, abundant worldly means, or ambition" as the things which enable or compel this specialization probably described his own three reasons for specializing in "Obstetric Surgery."

65. HRS, "The Treatment of Vaginal Fistula," 387.

66. Ibid., 394.

67. HRS, "Adaptation of the Clamp and Button Sutures to Prolapse of the Vagina," *North-American Medico-Chirurgical Review* 2, no. 1 (January 1858): 64-70.

68. HRS, "The Treatment of Vaginal Fistula," 389.

69. Ibid., 394.

70. HJW, "Diary," v. 23 (December 24, 1856-April 15, 1858), November 18, 1857.

71. Ibid., January 4, 1858.

72. Ibid., January 5, 1858.

73. HRS to Spencer F. Baird, December 15, 1857 and January 5, 1858, Smithsonian Archives: RU 52: Box 10.

74. HJW, "Diary," v. 24 (April 16, 1858-December 31, 1858), May 30, 1858.

75. Councillors of the Massachusetts Medical Society. Minutes, meeting of February 3, 1858, pp. 201-202, Countway Library.

76. "Massachusetts Medical Society Report on Abortion," Countway Library (B MS c 75.2).

77. American Academy of Arts and Sciences. Minutes, meeting of May 11, 1858, Boston Athenaeum.

Chapter 7

1. "Execution of McGee," Newspaper clipping attached to page 51 (June 25, 1858) of Jonathan Mason Warren's "Journal," MHS: Warren Papers (Vol. 111).

2. Jonathan Mason Warren, "Journal," June 25, 1858.

3. "Execution of Magee: Post-mortem Appearances," *BMSJ* 58, no. 24 (July 15, 1858): 480-482.

4. "The Case of Magee, the Murderer—the Post-Mortem Examination," *Boston Evening Traveler* (August 2, 1858), 1.

5. "Case of James Magee," *BMSJ* 59, no. 2 (August 12, 1858): 45-47.

6. The original article in the *BMSJ* indicated the autopsy began forty minutes after the body was lowered and *twenty-five* minutes after the rope was loosened instead of "thirty-five minutes."

7. HJW, "Diary," v. 24 (April 16, 1858-December 31, 1858), July 22, 1858.

8. "An Execution in the House," *London Lancet (New York)* (October 1858): 307.

9. The "President's" Second Annual Address to the Gynaecological Society of Boston [*JGSB* 4, no. 2 (February 1871): 84-106, 105.] made reference to Brown-Séquard having indicated that McGee "was not at the time of his dissection 'as yet a cadaver.'" It is possible that this was a reference to the *Lancet* editorial.

10. Elin L. Wolfe, "Calvin Ellis—The Forgotten Dean," *Harvard Medical Alumni Bulletin* 56, no. 2 (Spring 1982): 27-31, 28.

11. HRS, "The Use and Abuse of Uterine Tents," *AJMS* 37, no. 73 (January 1859): 57-62.

12. Ibid., 61.

13. The paper here included as part of a footnote: "N.A. Med.-Chir. Rev., Jan 1858." "1858" was a misprint and should have read "1859."

14. American Academy of Arts and Sciences. Minutes, meeting of December 14, 1858.

15. HRS, "Criminal Abortion: Its Prevalence, Its Prevention, and Its Relation to the Medical Examiner."

16. Ibid., 4-5.

17. HRS to Richard Bliss, December 12, 1909, Archives of the Redwood Library and Athenaeum, Newport, Rhode Island.

18. HRS, "On the Decrease of the Rate of Increase of Population now Obtaining in Europe and America," *American Journal of Science and Art (Silliman's)* 43, no. 128 (March 1867): 141-155.

19. Ibid., 155. A footnote indicated the final quote was from Thomas Percival, *Medical Ethics* (1803), 72.

20. "Contributions to Obstetric Jurisprudence," *North-American Medico-Chirurgical Review* 2, no. 6 (December 1858): 1149-1150.

21. HRS, "Contributions to Obstetric Jurisprudence: No. I.—Criminal Abortion," *North-American Medico-Chirurgical Review* 3, no. 1 (January 1859): 64-72, 66.

22. Ibid., 64.

23. This expectation of losing practice by opposing abortion, indicates that the crusade against abortion was not initiated as a means to increase the practice of regular physicians by eliminating competition from the "irregulars" who were more apt to perform abortions.

24. HRS, "Contributions to Obstetric Jurisprudence: No. I.—Criminal Abortion," 65.

25. Ibid., 68-69.

26. Ibid., 72. The "Burke and Hare" reference refers to William Burke and William Hare who were indicted in 1828 for sixteen murders they carried out in Edinburgh, Scotland within a single year. The Burke and Hare murders no doubt were highly salient to Horatio because of his year in medical training at the same Edinburgh University Medical School which had innocently bought the bodies of the murder victims so they could be dissected by medical students.

27. HRS to the Councillors of the Massachusetts Medical Society, January 37, 1859, Countway Library: Massachusetts Medical Society Collection.

28. Massachusetts Medical Society. Minutes, Councillors meeting of February 2, 1859, Countway Library.

29. HRS, "Two Cases illustrative of Criminal Abortion," *AJMS* 37, no. 74 (April 1859): 314-318.

30. Ibid., 316-318.

31. HRS, "Contributions to Obstetric Jurisprudence—Criminal Abortion II: Its Frequency, and the Causes Thereof," *North-American Medico-Chirurgical Review* 3, no. 2 (March 1859): 260-282.

32. Ibid., 278. Horatio's footnote read: "*Report to Suffolk Dist. Med. Society, May, 1857; New York ["American"] Med. Gazette, July, 1857, p. 390; N. H. Journal of Medicine, July, 1857, p. 211." Both journals contained long excerpts of the Suffolk District Medical Society Report on Criminal Abortion *beginning on these pages*. Horatio may have incorrectly referred to the *American Medical Gazette* as the *New York Medical Gazette*, because the journal was based in New York.

33. HRS, "Its Frequency, and the Causes Thereof," 278.

34. Ibid., 280.

35. Ibid., 281.

36. Alexander J. Semmes to HRS, March 16, 1859, Countway Library: Storer Abortion File.

37. Charles A. Pope to HRS, March 18, 1859, Countway Library: Storer Abortion File.

38. William Henry Brisbane to HRS, March 19, 1859, Countway Library: Storer Abortion File.

39. Samuel D. Gross to HRS, March 19, 1859, Countway Library: Storer Abortion File.

40. Edward H. Barton to HRS, April 3, 1859, Countway Library: Storer Abortion File.

41. Alexander J. Semmes to HRS, March 26, 1859, Countway Library: Storer Abortion File.

42. Hugh L. Hodge to HRS, March 30, 1859, Countway Library: Storer Abortion File.

43. A. Lopez to HRS, April 2, 1859, Countway Library: Storer Abortion File.

44. William Henry Brisbane to HRS, April 6, 1859, Countway Library: Storer Abortion File.

45. Thomas Blatchford to HRS, May 3, 1859, Countway Library: Storer Abortion File.

46. Edward H. Barton to HRS, April 12, 1859, Countway Library: Storer Abortion File.

47. "Report on Criminal Abortion," *TAMA* 12 (1859): 75-78, 75.

48. Ibid., 77. Horatio's quote came from *Man Transformed* (Oxford, 1653).

49. Minutes, 1859 Annual Meeting, *TAMA* 12 (1859): 27-28.

50. Thomas W. Blatchford to HRS, May 3, 1859, Countway Library: Storer Abortion File.

51. Thomas W. Blatchford to HRS, May 5, 1859, Countway Library: Storer Abortion File.

52. HRS, "Contributions to Obstetric Jurisprudence—Criminal Abortion III: Its Victims," *North-American Medico-Chirurgical Review* 3, no. 3 (May 1859): 446-455.

53. Ibid., 449.

54. Ibid., 455.

55. HRS, "Contributions to Obstetric Jurisprudence—Criminal Abortion IV: Its Proofs," *North-American Medico-Chirurgical Review* 3, no. 3 (May 1859): 455-465.

56. Ibid., 460.

57. Ibid., 463.

58. Ibid., 465.

59. HRS, "Contributions to Obstetric Jurisprudence—Criminal Abortion V: Its Perpetrators," *North-American Medico-Chirurgical Review* 3, no. 3 (May 1859): 465-470.

60. Ibid., 466-467.

61. Horatio would claim otherwise a few years later in his *Is It I? A Book for Every Man.*

62. HRS, "Its Perpetrators," 468-469.

63. William Overend Priestley to HRS, June 3, 1859, National Library of Medicine.

64. HRS, "Contributions to Obstetric Jurisprudence—Criminal Abortion VI: Its Innocent Abettors," *North-American Medico-Chirurgical Review* 3 no. 4 (July 1859): 643-657.

65. Ibid., 650-651.

66. HRS, "Contributions to Obstetric Jurisprudence—Criminal Abortion VII: Its Obstacles to Conviction," *North-American Medico-Chirurgical Review* 3 no. 5 (September 1859): 833-854.

67. Ibid., 834.

68. Ibid., 849.

69. "Leading Articles," *British Medical Journal* no. 147 (October 22, 1859): 857.

70. HRS, "Contributions to Obstetric Jurisprudence—Criminal Abortion VIII: Can It be at all Controlled by Law?" *North-American Medico-Chirurgical Review* 3, no. 6 (November 1859): 1033-1038.

71. Ibid., 1034. Eight years later, Horatio was to be a principal in the establishment of such a hospital in Boston.

72. HRS, "Contributions to Obstetric Jurisprudence—Criminal Abortion IX: The Duty of the Profession," *North-American Medico-Chirurgical Review* 3, no. 6 (November 1859): 1039-1046, 1039.

73. Ibid., 1046.

74. "Memorial. To the Governor and Legislature, ..." "To the President and Councilors of the State Medical Society." Both documents are among SFP and the Indiana State Archives also has a copy of the "Memorial" sent to them sometime in 1860.

75. HRS to Mr. Collins, 17 Dec. 1859, College of Physicians of Philadelphia: Joseph Carson Collection (v. 2 [Z10c/10]).

76. "The New York State Medical Society," BMSJ 62, no. 3 (February 16, 1860): 67.

77. Massachusetts Medical Society. Minutes, Stated Meeting of the Councillors, October 3, 1860, Countway Library.

78. HRS, *On Criminal Abortion in America* (Philadelphia, Lippincott & Co., 1860).

79. "Criminal Abortion," *BMSJ* 62, no. 3 (February 16, 1860): 65-67.

80. Ibid., 67.

Chapter 8

1. "Address of Henry Miller, M.D., President of the Association," *TAMA* 13 (1860): 56.

2. Ibid., 57-58.

3. Minutes, 1860 Annual Meeting, *TAMA* 13 (1860): 41-42.

4. James C. Mohr, *Abortion in America*, 202.

5. Massachusetts Medical Society. Minutes, Stated Meeting of the Councillors, May 30, 1860, Countway Library.

6. Massachusetts Medical Society. Minutes, Stated Meeting of the Councillors, October 3, 1860, Countway Library.

7. Johnathon Mason Warren, "Journal," September 22, 1860, MHS: Warren Papers.

8. Announcement of new medical practice, October 1, 1860, Card among Storer papers at Countway Library.

9. HJW, "Diary," v. 30 (August 17, 1860-November 3, 1862), January 26, 1862.

10. HRS to Charles Sumner, May 26, 1862, Houghton Library: Sumner Collection (shelfmark bMS Am1). Publication is "by permission of the Houghton Library, Harvard University."

11. Charles Sumner to Abraham Lincoln, May 28, 1862, MHS: Agnes Storer Autograph Collection.

12. HRS to Charles Sumner, June 1, 1862, Houghton Library: Sumner Collection (shelfmark bMS Am1). Publication is "by permission of the Houghton Library, Harvard University."

13. HRS to Joseph Toner, November 26, 1890, Library of Congress: Toner Folio 21044-21045.

14. American Academy of Arts and Sciences. Minutes, meeting of May 27, 1862, Boston Athenaeum.

15. Loose copies of the *BMSJ* with covers intact for this period are at the Countway Library.

16. HRS, "Studies of Abortion," *BMSJ* 68, no. 1 (February 5, 1863): 15-20.

17. Ibid., 20.

18. Malcolm Storer, "The Teaching of Obstetrics and Gynecology at Harvard," *Harvard Medical Alumni Association* 8 (1903): 427-445, 439.

19. Agnes C. Vietor, *A Woman's Quest: The Life of Marie E. Zakrzewska, M.D.* (New York/London, D. Appleton and Co., 1924), 310.

20. "Report of The New England Hospital for Women and Children," April 3, 1863, Smith's College: Sophia Smith Collection.

21. HRS, "On Artificial Dilatation of the Os and Cervix Uteri by Fluid Pressure from Above: A Reply to Drs. Keiller of Edinburgh and Arnott and Barnes of London," *BMSJ* 68, no. 22 (July 2, 1863): 431-439.

22. HRS, "The Uterine Dilator," *AJMS* 38, no. 75 (July, 1859): 107-113.

23. HRS, "On Artificial Dilatation of the Os and Cervix Uteri by Fluid Pressure from Above: A Reply to Drs. Keiller of Edinburgh and Arnott and Barnes of London," 438. This ended with the footnote: "American Journal of the Medical Sciences, April, 1829, p. 285."

24. HRS, "On the Employment of Anaesthetics in Obstetric Medicine and Surgery," *BMSJ* 69, no. 13 (October 29, 1863): 249-258, 250.

25. Ibid., 255-256.

26. Which at least was not Horatio's idea, but a theory which he credited to "Andral and Gavarret."

27. HRS, "An Outline History of American Gynaecology, Article II," *JGSB* 1, no. 5 (November 1869): 292-309, 309.

28. HRS, "On the Employment of Anaesthetics in Obstetric Medicine and Surgery," 249.

29. Robert Johns, "Practical Observations on the Injurious Effects of Chloroform Inhalation During Labor," *BMSJ* 69, no. 1 (August 6, 1863): 12-23.

30. HRS, "On Chloroform Inhalation during Labor; With Especial Reference to the Paper by Dr. Johns, of Dublin, Lately Admitted into This Journal," *BMSJ* 69, no. 3 (August 20, 1863): 49-54, 49.

31. Ibid., 52.

32. "The criticism of Dr. H. R. Storer ...," *BMSJ* 69, no. 3 (August 20, 1863): 62-64.

33. HRS, "On the Employment of Anaesthetics in Obstetric Medicine and Surgery," 249.

34. "Dr. H. R. Storer on Chloroform in Midwifery," *BMSJ* 69, no. 14 (November 5, 1863): 284-286, 284.

35. HRS, *Eutokia: A Word to Physicians and to Women upon the Employment of Anaesthetics in Childbirth* (Boston, A. Williams & Co., 1863). Dr. Oliver Wendell Holmes coined the name "anaesthesia" a few days after its first Boston demonstrations. Horatio may have expected "eutokia" to become a similarly commonplace name for anesthesia during childbirth.

36. Ibid., 5-6.

37. Harvard Law School Archives give dates of attendance and of degree.

38. James J. Walsh, "A Great Convert Physician," *Ave Maria* (November 11, 1922): 619-624, 622.

39. Frederick C. Irving, *Safe Deliverance*, 117.

40. HRS to Malcolm Storer, October 30, 1901.

41. Neither Horatio's or William Read's expectations were to be fulfilled.

42. HRS to Edward Jarvis, August 28, 1863, Countway Library: Jarvis Papers.

43. Josiah Quincy, Jr., Alfred Hitchcock, and HRS, "Report of the Commission on Insanity," *Massachusetts Legislative Document (Senate 72)* (February 1864), 1-20, 2.

44. HRS, "Cases Illustrative of Obstetric Disease," *BMSJ* 70, no. 4 (February 25, 1864): 69-74.

45. HRS, "Cases Illustrative of Obstetric Disease—Deductions Concerning Insanity in Women," *BMSJ* 70, no. 10 (April 7, 1864): 189-200.

46. This translation was given in M.L. Holbrook, editor, *Parturition Without Pain* (New York, M.L. Holbrook, Publisher, 1889), 14.

47. HRS, "Cases Illustrative of Obstetric Disease—Deductions Concerning Insanity in Women," 200.

48. Josiah Quincy, Jr., Alfred Hitchcock, and HRS, "Report of the Commission on Insanity."

49. This was from HRS's 1901 letter to Malcolm. "Too timid coitus" meant prevention of impregnation, presumably by withdrawal of the penis prior to ejaculation or other means. DHS had described physical changes (uterine hypertrophy, induration, and organic disease) which he believed were produced by this in his Introductory Lecture of November 1855.

50. HRS, "Cases Illustrative of Obstetric Disease—Deductions Concerning Insanity in Women," 193.

51. HRS, "The Relations of Female Patients to Hospitals for the Insane: The Necessity on Their Account of a Board of Consulting Physicians to Every Hospital," *TAMA* 15 (1864): 125-133.

52. HRS, "Advisory Medical Boards Requisite at Asylums," *BMSJ* 71, no. 11 (October 13, 1864): 209-218.

53. "*," "Advisory Medical Boards for Insane Asylums," *BMSJ* 71, no. 15 (November 10, 1864): 289-291.

54. HRS to Edward Jarvis, November 5, 1864, Countway Library: Jarvis Papers.

55. HRS, "Confirmation by an Ex-Superintendent ... of the Views Already Advanced," *BMSJ* 71, no. 17 (November 24, 1864): 329-337, 331.

56. Ibid., 337. Horatio would indicate in his 1901 letter to Malcolm: "When I commenced, gynaecology, in the English language and as confined to medicine, was apparently unnamed. Holmes has had the credit of Anglicizing and specializing the Greek term, just as in the similar 'anaesthesia.'"

57. "*," "Advisory Medical Boards for Insane Asylums," *BMSJ* 71, no. 23 (January 5, 1865): 451-453.

58. Ibid., 452. Stress added.

59. HRS, "Cases Illustrative of the Diseases of Women," *BMSJ* 71, no. 24 (January 12, 1865): 469-479, 474-475.

60. James Clarke White to HRS, February 15, 1865, Countway Library: Storer Collection.

Chapter 9

1. Minutes, 1864 Annual Meeting, *TAMA* 15 (1864): 1-53.

2. Ibid., 50.

3. Ibid., 52. The other members were Drs. Homberger and Brinsmade of New York, Jewell, of Pennsylvania, and Hooker, of Connecticut.

4. HRS, "The Causation, Course, and Treatment of Insanity in Women: A Gynaecist's Idea Thereof; Being the Report of the Standing Committee on Insanity for 1864-5," *TAMA* 16 (1865): 121-255. This was later published with little change as the book, *The Causation, Course, and Treatment of Insanity in Women* (Boston, Lee and Shepard, 1870).

5. HRS, "The Criminality and Physical Evils of Forced Abortions," *TAMA* 16 (1865): 709-745.

6. "Salutatory by the Publisher," *JGSB* 1, no.1 (July 1869): 9.

7. "Editorial Notes," *JGSB* 3, no. 1 (July 1870): 55 (footnote).

8. "Editorial Notes," *JGSB* 4, no. 5 (May 1871): 316.

9. "The American Medical Association," *BMSJ* 73, no. 15 (May 11, 1865): 303.

10. Jonathan Mason Warren, "Journal," February 1, 1865.

11. See Note 6.

12. HRS to Joseph Toner, October 2, 1877, Library of Congress: Toner Folio 20979-20980.

13. HRS, "The Causation, Course, and Treatment of Insanity in Women."

14. Ibid., 124 (footnote).

15. Minutes, 1865 Annual Meeting, *TAMA* 16 (1865): 38.

16. HRS, "The Criminality and Physical Evils of Forced Abortions," 717.

17. Hugh L. Hodge was earlier, but was from Philadelphia, not New England.

18. "Philadelphia Friend" to HRS, February 10, 1866, *Why Not? A Book for every Woman* (Boston, Lee and Shepard, 1867), 88-89.

19. HRS, "The Criminality and Physical Evils of Forced Abortions," 714-715.

20. Ibid., 727.

21. "Report of the Section on Practical Medicine and Obstetrics," *TAMA* 16 (1865): 91.

22. Minutes, 1865 Annual Meeting, *TAMA* 16 (1865): 47. Being "laid on the table," neither Homberger's nor Horatio's 1865 reports were published in that year's *Transactions*. Horatio later published his as "Specialism and Especialism: Their Respective Relations to the Profession," *JGSB* 2, no. 1 (January 1870): 39-51.

23. "The Late Meeting of the American Medical Association," *BMSJ* 74, no. 18 (May 31, 1866): 366.

24. HRS, "Specialism and Especialism: Their Respective Relations to the Profession."

25. The other was Thomas Addis Emmet.

26. HRS, "Specialism and Especialism: Their Respective Relations to the Profession," 42.

27. HRS, "The so-called Chronic Metritis, and its Rational Treatment," 213-214.

28. HRS, "Specialism and Especialism: Their Respective Relations to the Profession," 49-50.

29. As will be seen, Horatio was in the midst of the controversy that had labeled Calvin Ellis' autopsy of the hanged criminal Magee, "vivisection."

30. "Proceedings of the Association of Medical Superintendents," *American Journal of Insanity* 41, no. 3 (January 1884): 247-325, 283.

31. Agnes C. Vietor, *A Woman's Quest: The Life of Marie E. Zakrzewska, M.D.*, 337-338.

32. Sullivan became Horatio's assistant and his collaborator in medical politics opposing unethical Massachusetts Medical Society practices. Horatio later dismissed his assistant when Sullivan pretended to be the Dr. Horatio Storer a patient was seeking.

33. HRS, "Successful Removal of the Uterus and Both Ovaries by Abdominal Section," *AJMS* 51, no. 101 (January 1866): 110-139.

34. Horatio published an article in French on Miss Colcord's unusual menstruation [HRS, "De la Menstruation Sans Ovaires," *Archives de Physiologie Normale et Pathologique* 1 (1868): 376-378.]. This was a new journal edited by Brown-Séquard, Charcot, and Vulpian. Publication probably was at Brown-Séquard's request. I am grateful to Dr. Micheline M. Mathews-Roth for kindly providing a translation of this article.

35. GSB. Proceedings, meeting of February 16, 1869, *JGSB* 1, no. 2 (August 1869): 73-82, 79.

36. William Mayo to HRS, March 14, 1866, David Karpeles Manuscript Library, Santa Barbara, California.

37. Caroline Dall, "Diary when in Rhode Island," unspecified date between May 16 and June 14, 1870, MHS: Dall Papers (Box 22, Folder 4).

38. HRS, "A Medico-legal Study of Rape," *New York Medical Journal* 2, no. 8 (November 1865): 81-116.

39. Peter D. Gibbons, "The Berkshire Medical Institution," *Bulletin of the History of Medicine* 38, no. 1 (January-February 1964): 45-64.

40. HRS to Malcolm Storer, October 30, 1901.

41. Dr. Holmes was Dr. Oliver Wendell Holmes, Sr., who was one of the founders of the Tremont Street Medical School with Horatio's father and shortly thereafter Professor of Anatomy and Physiology at the Harvard Medical School. Holmes is better remembered for his poetry, essays, novels, and Supreme-Court-Justice son, than for his substantial medical achievements.

42. HRS, "Medico-Numismatic Queries—No. II.: The Dr. Alden March Medal of Albany, N. Y. Was it Ever Struck?" *The Numismatist* 30, no. 4 (April 1917): 168-170.

43. HRS, "A Medico-legal Study of Rape," 83.

44. HRS, "The Law of Rape," *Quarterly Journal of Psychological Medicine and Medical Jurisprudence* 2, no. 1 (January 1868): 47-67.

45. Ibid., 50.

Chapter 10

1. HRS, "A New Operation for Umbilical Hernia," *Medical Record* 1, no. 3 (April 2, 1866): 73-76.

2. Ibid., 73.

3. Ibid., 74. Stress added.

4. Ibid., 76. Stress added.

5. "Professional Criticism," *BMSJ* 74, no. 13 (April 26, 1866): 263-264, 264.

6. Jonathan Mason Warren, "Journal," April 28, 1866.

7. HRS, "Letter from Dr. Storer, of Boston," *Medical Record* 1, no. 3 (July 16, 1866): 244-245, 244.

8. "Editorial Notes," *JGSB* 3, no. 4 (October 1870): 253-272, 261.

9. HRS, "Letter from Dr. Storer, of Boston," 244.

10. Suffolk District Medical Society. Minutes, Special Meeting of May 31, 1866, Countway Library.

11. HRS, "Letter from Dr. Storer, of Boston," 244.

12. Ibid., 245.

13. HRS to Malcolm Storer, October 30, 1901.

14. "Horatio R. Storer," *Photographs of the Medical & Surgical Staff of the Carney Hospital* (1863), Carney Hospital (Boston) Archives.

15. "Editorial Notes," *JGSB* 3, no. 2 (August 1870): 106-119, 110-111.

16. George Frisbee Hoar, *Autobiography of Seventy Years* (New York, Charles Scribner's and Sons, 1903), 103.

17. "Address of D. Humphreys Storer, M.D., President of the Association," *TAMA* 17 (1866): 55-65.

18. HRS, "The Clamp Shield: An Instrument Designed to Lessen Certain Surgical Dangers, More Particularly those of Excision of the Uterus by Abdominal Section." *TAMA* 16 (1866): 207-227.

19. Ibid., 221.

20. HRS, "The Clamp Shield: An Instrument Designed to Lessen Certain Surgical Dangers, More Particularly those of Excision of the Uterus by Abdominal Section." *Medical Record* 1, no. 16 (October 15, 1866): 385-387, 386.

21. HRS, "Report of the Delegate to the Association of Superintendents of Asylums for the Insane, for 1865-66," *TAMA* 17 (1866): 395-406.

22. Minutes, 1866 Annual Meeting, *TAMA* 17 (1866): 41.

23. Agnes Vietor, *A Woman's Quest: The Life of Marie E. Zakrzewska, M.D.*, 339-340.

24. Ibid., 339.

25. Ednah Dow Cheney to HRS, August 13, 1866, Countway Library.

26. HRS, "Female Physicians," *BMSJ* 75, no. 9 (September 27, 1866): 191-192.

27. "Women as Physicians," *New York Medical Journal* 4, no. 2 (November 1866): 156-158.

28. HRS, "Female Physicians," 191.

29. Some additional evidence that the Hospital was not as charitable as it could have been, comes from a note in Caroline Dall's diary, March 9, 1869, which indicated that Dr. Z had "no interest in the poor unless she *chooses* them."

30. Anita Tyng to HRS, November 3, 1893, Countway Library. This letter makes reference to other letters.

31. The date following the "Prefatory Remarks" was April 1866 and this would be the earliest that this first edition was published.

32. HRS, *Why Not? A Book for every Woman*, 10 and 87-91.

33. "Review of *Why Not? A Book for every Woman*," *Medical and Surgical Reporter* 15, no. 3 (July 21, 1866): 74.

34. "Review of *Why Not? A Book for every Woman*," *BMSJ* 75, no. 5 (August 30, 1866): 104.

35. "Review of *Why Not? A Book for every Woman*," *New Orleans Medical & Surgical Journal* 20, no. 1 (July 1867): 111-115, 112.

36. HRS, "On Self Abuse in Women, its Causation and Rational Treatment," *The Western Journal of Medicine* 2, no. 8 (August 1867): 449-457, 452.

37. Caroline Dall to HRS, June 5, 1866, *Is It I? A Book for Every Man* (Boston, Lee and Shepard, 1867), 139.

38. HRS to Caroline Dall, June 18, 1866, MHS: Dall Papers.

39. "'Why Not? A Book for Every Woman.' A Woman's View," *BMSJ* 75, no. 14 (November 1, 1866): 273-276.

40. "'A Woman's View' of 'Why Not?'" *BMSJ* 75, no. 24 (January 10, 1867): 490.

41. Henry Orlando Marcy, "The Early History of Abdominal Surgery in America," *JAMA* 54, no. 8 (February 19, 1910): 600-605, 602.

42. HRS, "The Abetment of Criminal Abortion by Medical Men," *New York Medical Journal* 3, no. 18 (September 1866): 422-433.

43. Ibid., 426.

44. Ibid., 433.

45. Massachusetts Medical Society.   Minutes, Annual Meeting, May 30, 1866, Countway Library.

46. HRS, "Letter to the Editors," *BMSJ* 75, no. 22 (December 27, 1866): 448.

47. Massachusetts Infant Asylum for Foundlings.   Minutes, meeting of January 11, 1867, MHS: Massachusetts Infant Asylum Records, 1867-1912.

48. Morse Stewart, "Criminal Abortion," *Detroit Review of Medicine and Pharmacy* 2, no. 1 (January 1867): 1-11.

49. HRS, "Appendix." In Albert Day, *Methomania* (Boston, James Campbell, 1867), 55-67.

50. Ibid., 63-64.

51. HRS, "The So-called Chronic Metritis, and its Rational Treatment."

Chapter 11

1. HRS, *Is It I? A Book for Every Man.*

2. HRS to Thomas Addis Emmet, June 3, 1867, *Is It I? A Book for Every Man*, iv.

3. F. Donaldson to HRS, May 21, 1867, *Is It I? A Book for Every Man*, 15-16.

4. "Publishers' Note," *Is It I? A Book for Every Man*, vii.

5. Ibid., viii-ix.

6. Asa Millet to Mssrs. Editors, June 8, 1867, *BMSJ* 76, no. 23 (June 20, 1867): 420.

7. "Publishers' Note," *Is It I? A Book for Every Man*, ix.

8. Horatio's universal "kindly notice" statement no doubt was written before he became aware of the "unkindly" notice of the *New Orleans Medical and Surgical Journal* published in July 1867.

9. HRS, *Is It I? A Book for Every Man*, 57.

10. Ibid., 61-62.

11. Ibid., 89-90.

12. Ibid., 92

13. Ibid., 94-95. The footnote following the asterisk read "Percival. Medical Ethics, p. 79."

14. Ibid., 111.

15. Ibid., 125.

16. Ibid., 147,

17. Ibid., iii.

18. Thomas Addis Emmet to HRS, June 5, 1867, Countway Library.

19. Horatio dedicated his second edition of *Why Not?* to Charles Brown-Séquard.

20. "P.," "Review of *Is It I? A Book for Every Man*," *BMSJ* 1 (New Series), no. 2 (February 13, 1868): 27-28.

21. It is not too hard for this experimental psychologist to understand how a twenty-five-year-old medical scientist might have his first medical publication reprinted as a pamphlet and show it off in "social circles." P's mention of Horatio's 1855 paper on uterine tents in this review of *Is It I?*, which almost certainly was by Luther Parks, Jr., is additional evidence that Horatio's criticism in that pamphlet of a physician who "unaccountably" rejected uterine tents was criticism of Dr. Parks.

22. Ibid., 28.

23. HRS, "Self Abuse in Women: Its Causation and Rational Treatment."

24. Ibid., 454.

25. Ibid., 457.

26. Ibid., 449-450.

27. "Editorial and Medical News," *Western Journal of Medicine* 2, no. 8 (August 1867): 511-512.

28. John Todd, *Serpents in the Dove's Nest* (Boston, Lee and Shepard, 1867), 1-28, 5.

29. J.E. Todd, *John Todd: The Story of His Life, Told Mainly by Himself* (New York, Harper & Brothers, 1876), 468-469.

30. "Editorial Notes," *JGSB* 2, no. 3 (March 1870): 188.

31. Massachusetts Medical Society. Minutes, meeting of Councillors, September 23, 1867, Countway Library.

32. GSB. Proceedings, meeting of October 18, 1870, *JGSB* 4, no. 5 (May 1871): 257-269, 260.

33. Massachusetts Medical Society. Minutes, meeting of Councillors, September 23, 1867.

34. HRS, "Pocketing the Pedicle," *AJMS* 55, no. 109 (January 1868): 77-86, 78.

35. Henry Orlando Marcy to HRS, May 11, 1891, Countway Library.

36. Henry Orlando Marcy, "The Early History of Abdominal Surgery in America," 602.

37. "Prof. H. R. Storer's Course of Lectures," *BMSJ* 77, no. 20 (December 19, 1867): 426.

38. J. Eckman, "Alexander J. Stone, M.D., LL.D.: Founder of Minnesota's First Medical Journal," *Annals of Medical History* 3rd Series, no. 4 (1941): 306-325.

39. It is possible that Stone was upset that Horatio was dropped from the Harvard Medical School and followed Horatio to Pittsfield.

40. HRS to Malcolm Storer, October 30, 1901.

41. "Special Instruction in Medical Science," Flyer advertising post-graduate medical instruction, November 1, 1867, SFP.

42. HRS, "The Present Problems in Abdominal Section: Illustrated by a Successful Case of Double Ovariotomy," *Canada Medical Journal* 4 (May 5, 1868): 337-348.

43. Ibid., 347-348.

44. HRS to Oliver Wendell Holmes, December 28, 1867, Houghton Library: Holmes Collection (shelfmark bMS Am 1241.1). Publication is "by permission of the Houghton Library, Harvard University."

45. Oliver Wendell Holmes to HRS, December 30, 1867, MHS: Agnes Storer Autograph Collection.

46. HRS, *On Nurses and Nursing; with Especial Reference to the Management of Sick Women* (Boston, Lee and Shepard, 1868).

47. Horatio included St. Vincent De Paul's "picture:"

> "Her only convent shall be the house of sickness; her only cell, a hired lodging; her chapel, the parish church; her cloister, the streets of the city, or the wards of the hospital; her only wall, obedience; her veil, her modesty; her grate, the fear of God."

48. HRS, *On Nurses and Nursing*, 9-10.

49. Ibid., 22.

50. Ibid., 53-54.

51. Ibid., 80.

52. HRS, "The Rectum in its Relations to Uterine Disease," *American Journal of Obstetrics* 1, no. 1 (May 1868): 66-75.

53. Ibid., 71-72. Horatio still had located no other originator of the procedure when he described it in a publication for the fifth time in a British journal in 1873. In 1882, he noted that it "is practised now by every surgeon," and the implication was that their knowledge of it could be traced to himself.

54. Ibid., 74-75.

55. HRS, "Removal of a Large Horse-shoe Pessary (Hodge's Open Lever) from within the Cavity of the Bladder without Incision." *Medical Record* 3, no 9 (July 1, 1868) 220-222.

56. Ibid., 221-222.

57. DHS to Oliver Wendell Holmes, July 6, 1868, Houghton Library: Holmes Collection (shelfmark bMS Am 1241.1). Publication is "by permission of the Houghton Library, Harvard University."

58. Authors as noted to DHS, July 8, 1868, Countway Library.

59. CEB to DHS, July 8, 1868, Countway Library.

60. J.B.S. Jackson to DHS, July 4, 1868, Countway Library.

61. HRS and Franklin Fiske Heard, *Criminal Abortion: Its Nature, Its Evidence, and Its Law* (Boston, Little, Brown, and Co., 1868).

62. Ibid., 2. The italics in both of the previous sentences were not in the originals.

63. Ibid., 3.

64. Ibid., 60.

65. Ibid., 74.

66. Ibid., 78.

67. Ibid., 90.

68. "Proceedings of the Association of Medical Superintendents," *American Journal of Insanity* 41, no. 3 (January 1884): 281-283.

69. HRS and Franklin Fiske Heard, *Criminal Abortion: Its Nature, Its Evidence, and Its Law*, 100-101.

70. Ibid., 115.

71. Ibid., 121.

72. Ibid., 147.

73. Caroline Dall to HRS, September 9, 1868, MHS: Dall Papers. Copied in Mrs. Dall's list of her correspondence. Subsequent Dall correspondence from Dr. Tyng indicated that she remained in Providence and did not come to Boston.

74. HRS, "A Modification of Cusco's Speculum, by which it Becomes also a Retractor," *BMSJ* 2 (New Series), no. 14 (November 5, 1868): 214-215.

Chapter 12

1. "Carney Hospital," *BMSJ* 1 (New Series), no. 26 (July 30, 1868): 414.

2. "Horatio R. Storer," *Photographs of the Medical & Surgical Staff of the Carney Hospital.*

3. HRS to Malcolm Storer, October 30, 1901.

4. GSB. Proceedings, meeting of January 22, 1869, *JGSB* 1, no. 1 (July 1869): 11-22.

5. "The Hospitals of St. Elizabeth and St. Francis for the Diseases Peculiar to Women," Advertising flyer, November 1, 1869, SFP and Archives of St. Elizabeth's Hospital.

6. GSB. Proceedings, meeting of January 22, 1869, 11-13.

7. GSB. Proceedings, meeting of January 25, 1869, *JGSB* 1, no. 1 (July 1869): 22-30.

8. GSB. Proceedings, meeting of February 2, 1869, *JGSB* 1, no. 2 (August 1869): 67-73, 67.

9. GSB. Proceedings, meeting of February 16, 1869, *JGSB* 1, no. 2 (August 1869): 73-82, 73-74.

10. HRS, "Upon Pocketing the Pedicle in Ovariotomy: A Reply to Certain Strictures by Dr. Kimball, of Lowell," *JGSB* 1, no. 3 (September 1869): 147-154.

11. Gilman Kimball, "Ovariotomy," *BMSJ* 2, no. 7 (September 17, 1868): 97-101.

12. HRS, "Upon Pocketing the Pedicle in Ovariotomy: A Reply to Certain Strictures by Dr. Kimball, of Lowell," 148-149.

13. Ibid., 151.

14. Ibid., 152.

15. J. Ford Prioleau, "Ovariotomy, in which 'Pocketing the Pedicle' was Performed: Recovery," *AJMS* 58, no. 115 (July 1869): 80-83, 83.

16. GSB. Proceedings, meeting of February 16, 1869, 81-82.

17. HRS, "Golden Rules for the Treatment of Ovarian Diseases," *JGSB* 1, no. 6 (December 1869): 338-341.

18. GSB. Proceedings, meeting of March 2, 1869, *JGSB* 1, no. 3 (September 1869): 131-141, 141.

19. GSB. Proceedings, meeting of August 2, 1870, *JGSB* 4, no. 2 (February 1871): 65-73, 69.

20. GSB. Proceedings, meeting of March 16, 1869, *JGSB* 1, no. 3 (September 1869): 142-147, 142.

21. HRS, "Physicians in their Relations to Invalid Women," *JGSB* 1, no. 5 (November 1869: 284-288.

22. Caroline H. Dall to the Editor of *The New England Medical Gazette*, February 1, 1869, *The New England Medical Gazette* 4, no. 3 (March 1869): 87-90.

23. HRS, "Physicians in their Relations to Invalid Women," 287.

24. "*" (HRS), "Female Physicians."

25. HRS, "Physicians in their Relations to Invalid Women," 288.

26. GSB. Proceedings, meeting of March 16, 1869, 147.

27. GSB. Proceedings, meeting of April 6, 1869, *JGSB* 1, no. 4 (October 1869): 195-208, 208.

28. Ibid., 203.

29. GSB. Proceedings, First Special Meeting on April 9, 1869, *JGSB* 1, no. 4 (October 1869): 208-210.

30. Like the Connecticut statute which Horatio probably influenced either directly or through his father, the New York statute which Horatio helped draft was a model for the new legislation on criminal abortion which protected the fetus and would spread to almost every state by 1890.

31. GSB. Proceedings, meeting of April 20, 1869, *JGSB* 1, no. 4 (October 1869): 210-223, 221.

32. GSB. Proceedings, meeting of May 4, 1869, *JGSB* 1, no. 5 (November 1869): 259-266.

33. HRS, "The Frequency and Causation of Uterine Disease in America," *JGSB* 1, no. 1 (July 1869): 39-48.

34. Ibid., 40.

35. GSB. Proceedings, meeting of June 1, 1869, *JGSB* 1, no. 6 (December 1869): 323-328.

36. GSB. Proceedings, Second Special Meeting on June 1, 1869, *JGSB* 1, no. 6 (December 1869): 333-338, 337.

37. GSB. Proceedings, Third Special Meeting on June 2, 1869, *JGSB* 2, no. 1 (January 1870): 18-34.

38. Ibid., 33-34.

39. GSB. Proceedings, meeting of July 6, 1869, *JGSB* 2, no. 1 (January 1870): 1-12.

40. GSB. Proceedings, meeting of July 20, 1869, *JGSB* 2, no. 1 (January 1870): 12-18, 18.

41. "Salutatory by the Editors," *JGSB* 1, no. 1 (July 1869): 3-5, 3.

42. "Salutatory by the Publisher," *JGSB* 1, no. 1 (July 1869): 5-11.

43. Ibid., 11.

44. "Editorial Notes," *JGSB* 1, no. 1 (July 1869): 53-65.

45. HRS to Malcolm Storer, October 30, 1901.

46. Stress added.

47. Efforts have been unsuccessful to identify "Croker" and the break in silence "yesterday" (October 27, 28, or 29, 1901—The date of the letter, 28 was written over with 30 probably indicating that he began it on October 28, and ended it on October 30).

48. Stress added.

49. George H. Bixby, "Extirpation of the Puerperal Uterus by Abdominal Section," *JGSB* 1, no. 4 (October 1869): 223-232.

50. GSB. Proceedings, meeting of August 10, 1869, *JGSB* 2, no. 2 (February 1870): 65-69.

51. "Editorial Notes," *JGSB* 1, no. 2 (August 1869): 119-128, 120-121.

52. "Editorial Notes," *JGSB* 1, no. 3 (September 1869): 180-192, 184-185. Italics were not in the original.

53. "Editorial Notes," *JGSB* 1, no. 4 (October 1869): 247-258.

54. Ibid., 253. Horatio must have been somewhat uncomfortable defending Bixby, who if excited and confused by an examination, might not be expected to handle an emergency medical situation appropriately either. But defend Bixby he did, and, unlike most segments of the "Editorial Notes," this defense is initialed "H.R.S." to indicate that the subject, co-editor Bixby, was not an author.

55. HRS to the Fellows of the Massachusetts Medical Society, October 1, 1869, letter commencing the pamphlet, "Fiat Justitia Ruat Coelum," a reprint of pp. 247-257 of the "Editorial Notes" for October 1869, Countway Library.

56. GSB. Proceedings, meeting of October 5, 1869, *JGSB* 2, no. 4 (April 1870): 193-207, 197. The patient's rapid progress was mentioned at the next meeting on October 19. The attending physician had even notified Horatio that "she will soon be married."

57. "Editorial Notes," *JGSB* 1, no. 5 (November 1869): 310-321, 315-316. The "Jackson's four years' silence" reference was to Charles T. Jackson, the Boston physician-dentist, who claimed to have discovered the analgesic effect of ether in 1842, when using it to lessen his own poisoning by chlorine gas, and over the next four years attempted to induce dentists to employ it for deadening the pain of dental surgery, finally succeeding with W.T.G. Morton in late 1846.

58. GSB. Proceedings, meeting of November 2, 1869, *JGSB* 2, no. 5 (May 1870): 257-289.

59. "Editorial Notes," November 1869, 311.

60. "Editorial Notes," *JGSB* 1, no. 6 (December 1869): 370-386.

61. HRS to "Dear Miss Minnie," December 27, 1869, SFP.

Chapter 13

1. "Editorial Notes," *JGSB* 2, no. 1 (January 1870): 51-64, 53.

2. GSB. Proceedings, First Annual Meeting on January 4, 1870, *JGSB* 3, no. 1 (July 1870): 1-5, 1.

3. Winslow Lewis (HRS), "The Demands upon Every Thoughtful Physician to Give Closer and More Intelligent Heed to the Diseases Peculiar to Women: The Annual Address for 1870," *JGSB* 2, no. 2 (February 1870): 77-88.

4. Stress added.

5. GSB. Proceedings, First Annual Meeting on January 4, 1870, 5.

6. GSB. Proceedings, meeting of January 18, 1870, *JGSB* 3, no. 1 (July 1870): 5-26, 17.

7. HRS, "Lacing the breast: A New Operation for Removal of the Mamma," *JGSB* 3, no. 5 (November 1870): 291-293.

8. GSB. Proceedings, meeting of January 18, 1870, 26.

9. William Lloyd Garrison, "Fair Play for Woman in the Medical Profession," *The Independent* (December 23, 1869): 1.

10. Israel T. Talbot to Caroline Dall, October 25, 1869, MHS: Dall papers.

11. William Lloyd Garrison, "Fair Play for Woman in the Medical Profession," 1.

12. HRS, "The Gynaecological Society of Boston and Women Physicians; A Reply to Mr. Wm. Lloyd Garrison," *JGSB* 2, no. 2 (February 1870): 95-99.

13. HRS, "The Gynaecological Society of Boston," *The Independent* (January 13, 1870): 2.

14. "The Gynaecologists Again," *New England Medical Gazette* 5, no. 2 (February 1870): 93.

15. GSB. Proceedings, meeting of July 20, 1869, 16.

16. "The Journal of the Gynaecological Society, Boston," *Northwestern Medical & Surgical Journal* 1, no. 1 (June 1870): 24.

17. "Editorial Notes," *JGSB* 2, no. 2 (February 1870): 108-128, 108-109.

18. The *Journal* or its Harvard Medical School controllers (Bigelow's "suborned claqueurs") had provided Bigelow's criticism of Simpson to the Boston newspapers.

19. "Anaesthetic Inhalation," *BMSJ* 4, nos. 20-21 (November 25, 1869): 295.

20. "Editorial Notes," February 1870, 110-111.

21. "Edinburgh's Part in the History of Anaesthesia. An Answer to Dr. Jacob Bigelow, of Boston," *JGSB* 2, no. 2 (February 1870): 88-94.

22. "Editorial Notes," February 1870, 112.

23. "Editorial Notes," *JGSB* 2, no. 3 (March 1870): 167-190.

24. This refers to the fact that Editor Parks acknowledged the London *Medical Times* as its source of Simpson's "Reply."

25. Ibid., 188-189.

26. CEB, *Correspondence Concerning a Fatal Case of Placenta Proevia* (Boston, Alfred Mudge & Son, 1870).

27. CEB, *Correspondence Concerning a Fatal Case of Placenta Proevia (Republished with an Appendix by D. Barnard)* (Boston, Nation Press, 1870).

28. "Editorial Notes," March 1870, 189.

29. GSB. Proceedings, meeting of March 1, 1870, *JGSB* 3, no. 3 (September 1870): 145-153, 148.

30. HRS, "The Surgical Treatment of Hemorrhoids and Fistula in Ano, with Their Result," *JGSB* 3, no. 4 (April, 1870): 221-249.

31. Ibid., 221-222.

32. The other was David Humphreys Storer.

33. Ibid., 223-224.

34. Ibid., 249.

35. "Editorial Notes," *JGSB* 2, no. 5 (May 1870): 307-320, 312-313.

36. "Professor Bigelow's Final Reply to Professor Gunn," *BMSJ* 5, no. 8 (February 24, 1870): 150-151.

37. "Ether and Chloroform—Boston and Edinburgh: Correspondence of Sir James Y. Simpson and Dr. Jacob Bigelow," *BMSJ* 5, no. 10 (March 10, 1870): 187-190.

38. "Editorial Notes," *JGSB* 2, no. 4 (April 1870): 250-256, 250.

39. GSB. Proceedings, meeting of April 19, 1870, *JGSB* 3, no. 4 (October 1870): 224-237.

40. "Editorial Notes," *JGSB* 2, no. 5 (May 1870): 307-320, 307.

41. CEB, *Correspondence Concerning a Fatal Case of Placenta Proevia*, 29.

42. CEB, *Correspondence Concerning a Fatal Case of Placenta Proevia (Republished with an Appendix by D. Barnard)*, 34.

43. Dr. George Parkman was killed on November 23, 1849 with the murder occurring at the Harvard Medical School. Shortly thereafter, Dr. John White Webster, Professor of Chemistry and Mineralogy at Harvard, was indicted for the crime, and after a long and highly publicized trial, was found guilty and hanged. This was an immense scandal which was to produce strong local public reactions against the Harvard Medical School, already suspect because of the grave-robbing that provided some of the cadavers for dissection.

44. "Editorial Notes," May 1870, 311.

45. Ibid., 314.

46. H.B. Storer to Clara Barton, October 28, 1875, Smith College: Sophia Smith Barton Collection.

47. Clairvoyant Examination of Miss C. Barton (Dr. H.B. Storer: Diagnosis), November 8, 1875, Smith College: Sophia Smith Barton Collection.

48. GSB. Proceedings, meeting of May 3, 1870, *JGSB* 3, no. 5 (November 1870): 273-281. Horatio was away at the meeting of the AMA in Washington.

49. "Draft letter of protest," May 1870, MHS: Warren Papers, John Collins Warren Collection, v. 36 (1867-1871).

50. "190?" probably should read 1906. This was when the new buildings of the Harvard Medical School were dedicated and the American Medical Association held their annual meeting in Boston that year.

51. This was not included in Collins' draft. The *TAMA* (vol. 21, page 29) describe a "partial report" signed by Dr. Stillé, which read:

Whereas, The charge of tolerating in the Massachusetts Medical Society, men acknowledged to have become Homeopaths and Eclectics, is fully proved, and is plainly in violation of the Code of Ethics;

But inasmuch as it also appears that the parties making the charges here, being themselves members of the same Society, have not previously made, or caused to be made, any specific charges against such irregular practitioners in the proper form, before the Massachusetts Medical Society or its counsellors [sic], it is the opinion of this Committee that such steps should have been taken and their results obtained before appealing to this Association; and it is therefore recommend that the Committee of Registration should register all regularly accredited delegates from that Society to the present meeting. This Committee further recommends that unless said Society takes the necessary steps to purge itself of irregular practitioners, it ought not to be entitled to future representation in this Association.

52. Minutes, 1870 Annual Meeting, *TAMA* 21 (1870): 1-67, 39-40.

53. Ibid., 63.

54. "Report of the Section on the Practice of Medicine and Obstetrics," *TAMA* 21 (1870): 367-368.

55. "The American Medical Association: C. C. P. Clark to Mr. Editor," *BMSJ* 5, no. 26 (June 30, 1870): 498-499.

56. "Minutes," 1870 Annual Meeting, 66-67.

57. "Editorial Notes," *JGSB* 2, no. 6 (June 1870): 364-392, 366.

58. Ibid., 375.

59. GSB. Proceedings, meeting of May 17, 1870, *JGSB* 2, no. 6 (June 1870): 380-392.

60. Ibid., 385-387.

61. The asterisk denoted this footnote: "*Tom Brown's School Days, p. 104."

62. "Editorial Notes," June 1870, 364-366.

Chapter 14

1. GSB. Proceedings, meeting of June 7, 1870, *JGSB* 3, no. 6 (December 1870): 337-357, 337.

2. Ibid., 353-355.

3. GSB. Proceedings, meeting of June 21, 1870, *JGSB* 3, no. 6 (December 1870): 357-373, 373.

4. Ibid., 369.

5. Ibid., 373.

6. "B." (CEB), "The Report upon Criminal Abortions," 346.

7. "Editorial Notes," *JGSB* 3, no. 1 (July 1870): 47-64, 47-48.

8. Ibid., 48.

9. Ibid., 52.

10. Ibid., 54.

11. Ibid., 62.

12. GSB. Proceedings, meeting of July 5, 1870, *JGSB* 4, no. 1 (January 1871): 1-9, 8-9.

13. "Editorial Notes," *JGSB* 3, no. 2 (August 1870): 106-119.

14. This was followed by the footnote: "*A book as amusing to old as to little people. Published by Lee & Shepard. No one should fail to see the illustration to which we have referred."

15. "Editorial Notes," August 1870, 109.

16. "We have received a pamphlet ...," *BMSJ* (April 21, 1870): 302-304, 303-304.

17. "Editorial Notes," August 1870, 109.

18. Ibid., 112.

19. Ibid., 113. It is likely this date should have read 1865 and Sinclair had helped Horatio keep the scheduled American Medical Association meeting in Boston.

20. Ibid., 115.

21. Ibid., 116-118. Horatio's footnote after the first asterisk read: "*Boston Medical and Surgical Journal*, May 26, 1870."

22. This footnote read: "When the votes vindicating the authority of the American Medical Association over the College and the Society were passed, a few moments after the above remarks were made, Dr. ____ [Almost certainly, Calvin Ellis], of this city, apparently forgetting his own past history, turned to the senior editor of this Journal, and exclaimed in great heat, that he wished 'S____ was hung, and' (to give greater point to the remark we suppose) 'thrown out of the window.'"

23. GSB. Proceedings, meeting of August 2, 1870, *JGSB* 4, no. 2 (February 1871): 65-73, 73.

24. GSB. Proceedings, meeting of August 16, 1870 , *JGSB* 4, no. 2 (February 1871): 74-84, 75.

25. GSB. Proceedings, meeting of September 20, 1870, *JGSB* 4, no. 3 (March 1871): 134-148, 148.

26. "Editorial Notes," *JGSB* 3, no. 4 (October 1870): 253-272.

27. Ibid., 257-263.

28. Horatio's footnote read: "*New York Medical Journal*, August, 1870, p. 101 [actually p. 102]."

The comments of the journal's editor, Dr. Edward S. Dunster on page 102, included:

"We have taken occasion previously to refer to this publication, and now have only to add that it is growing in favor, and is a most essential adjunct to the library of those engaged in the study or practice of diseases of women. It has been charged upon American medical periodicals that they have no positive or well-settled opinions, or at all events that they never express them. Let those who entertain this view only read Dr. Storer's editorials—sparkling, almost startling at times, and brimful of life and earnestness—and they will find at least one brilliant exception to this accusation. We wish the *Journal* most hearty success."

29. It is possible that the 1867 venture of a dozen physicians that "was frustrated by the treachery of Buckingham" was to be the faculty of the new school, and that it was Buckingham who was confided with "against our better reason," perhaps as a potential

obstetrics lecturer.

30. Ibid., 265.

31. Ibid., 267.

32. Ibid., 269-270. The Massachusetts Medical Society Councillors expelled the abortionist at their meeting of October 5, 1870. The Minutes indicate: "Dr. Asa T. Newhall, of Lynn, had been expelled by a Board of Trial, for alleged criminal abortion."

33. GSB. Proceedings, meeting of October 4, 1871, *JGSB* 4, no. 4 (April 1871): 193-207, 200.

34. Ibid., 201, 203-205.

35. GSB. Proceedings, Fourteenth Special Meeting on October 8, 1870, *JGSB* 4, no. 4 (April 1871): 207-217.

36. "Meeting of the Councillors of the Massachusetts Medical Society," *BMSJ* 6, no. 17 (October 27, 1870): 266-267, 266.

37. GSB. Proceedings, Fourteenth Special Meeting, 208.

38. "Editorial Notes," *JGSB* 3, no. 5 (November 1870): 314-336, 324-325.

39. GSB. Proceedings, meeting of October 18, 1870, *JGSB* 4, no. 5 (May 1871): 257-269, 258-259.

40. "Editorial Notes," November 1870, 314-336.

41. Ibid., 318-319.

42. Ibid., 320-321.

43. Ibid., 329-330.

44. Ibid., 327.

Chapter 15

1. "Proceedings of the Association of Medical Superintendents," *American Journal of Insanity* 41, no. 3 (January 1884): 281-283.

2. A review of the log of admissions to the Worcester asylum did not show the name, Emily Elvira Storer.

3. HRS, *The Causation, Course, and Treatment of Reflex Insanity in Women* (Boston, Lee and Shepard, 1871).

4. GSB. Proceedings, meeting of November 1, 1870, *JGSB* 4, no. 5 (May 1871): 270-292.

5. Henry Orlando Marcy, "The Early History of Abdominal Surgery in America," 603.

6. Ibid. Henry Orlando Marcy, "The Semi-Centennial of the Introduction of Antiseptic Surgery in America," *Transactions of the Southern Surgical Association* 33 (1920): 25-46.

7. GSB. Proceedings, meeting of November 1, 1870, 290-291.

8. Ibid., 291-292.

9. Ibid., 333-334.

10. "Editorial Notes," *JGSB* 3, no. 6 (December 1870): 378-400.

11. Ibid., 384.

12. Ibid., 387.

13. Ibid., 390-391.

14. Ibid., 400. A footnote following "examination" read: "*Boston Medical and Surgical Journal, November 24, 1870, p. 351."

15. GSB. Proceedings, meeting of December 6, 1870, *JGSB* 4, no. 6 (June 1871): 334-354, 338.

16. GSB. Proceedings, meeting of December 20, 1870, *JGSB* 5, no. 1 (July 1871): 1-17.

17. Ibid., 13.

18. "Editorial Notes," *JGSB* 4, no. 1 (January 1871): 38-64, 39-40.

19. Ibid., 41-42.

20. Ibid., 51-52. The footnote after "pressure" read: "See this Journal for November, 1870, p. 320." Horatio was apparently referring to the passage in the "Editorial Notes" calling for President Eliot to sweep "professional spiders from their lurking places."

21. Start date of the *JGSB*.

22. Ibid., 55. Horatio was so pleased with the Introductory Address that he indicated in the "Editorial Notes" that Professor White was worthy of membership in the Gynaecological Society. "That, however, must be a question of the future," he continued, "for as yet he might not appreciate the honor, were it conferred."

23. James Clarke White, *Sketches from My Life*, 274-275.

24. GSB. Proceedings, meeting of January 3, 1871, *JGSB* 5, no. 1 (July 1871): 17-21.

25. Winslow Lewis (HRS), "The Gynaecological Society, and its Work During 1870: The Annual Address for 1871," *JGSB* 4, no. 2 (February 1871): 84-106, 86.

26. Ibid., 102.

27. Ibid., 104-105.

28. GSB. Proceedings, meeting of January 17, 1871, *JGSB* 5, no. 2 (August 1871): 65-76.

29. Ibid., 72.

30. "Editorial Notes," *JGSB* 4, no. 2 (February 1871): 110-128.

31. Ibid., 113.

32. HRS to Malcolm Storer, October 30, 1901.

33. HRS to John Humphreys Storer, February 2, 1871, SFP.

34. HRS to Malcolm Storer, October 30, 1901.

35. GSB. Proceedings, meeting of February 7, 1871, *JGSB* 5, no. 2 (August 1871): 76-87.

36. Ibid., 84.

37. Senders included Isaac Hays, William Peppers, and William A. Hammond. The letters are at the Countway Library.

38. GSB. Proceedings, meeting of February 21, 1871, *JGSB* 5, no. 3 (September 1871): 129-143, 136.

39. Ibid., 137-138.

40. "Editorial Notes," *JGSB* 4, no. 3 (March 1871): 178-192, 183.

41. Ibid., 187.

42. Ibid., 187-188.

43. Ibid., 192.

44. GSB. Proceedings, meeting of March 7, 1871, *JGSB* 5, no. 3 (September 1871): 143-158, 145.

45. Ibid., 147.

46. Ibid., 151-153, 152.

47. Morrill Wyman to Francis Humphreys Storer, February 15, 1883, Countway Library (incorrectly labled as to HRS).

48. HRS to John Humphreys Storer, March 28, 1871, SFP.

49. David Donald, *Charles Sumner and the Coming of the Civil War* (New York, Alfred Knoph, 1960), 338.

50. "Editorial Notes," *JGSB* 4, no. 4 (April 1871): 240-256.

51. Ibid., 251.

52. GSB. Proceedings, meeting of April 4, 1871, *JGSB* 5, no. 4 (October 1871): 212-228, 222-224.

53. "Editorial Notes," *JGSB* 4, no. 5 (May 1871): 313-320.

54. "Editorial Notes," *JGSB* 4, no. 6 (June 1871): 375-383.

55. Ibid., 380.

Chapter 16

1. Robert Lowell (John's schoolmaster) to John Humphreys Storer, July 20, 1871, SFP. The letter closed by "sending love to Father and Frank and respect to Miss Gilmore."

2. HRS, "The Mutual Relations of the Medical Profession, Its Press, and the Community," *JGSB (Supplement)* 4, no. 6 (June 1871): 1-20.

3. HRS, "Female Hygiene," *JGSB (Appendix)* 6, no. 6 (June 1872): 1-20.

4. HRS, "The Propriety of Operating for Malignant Ovarian Disease," *JGSB* 5, no. 3 (September 1871): 158-167.

5. HRS, "Female Hygiene," 1.

6. Ibid., 18.

7. Ibid., 20.

8. HRS, "The Mutual Relations of the Medical Profession, Its Press, and the Community," 1-2.

9. Ibid., 4.

10. Ibid., 6-8.

11. Ibid., 12.

12. Ibid., 14-15.

13. Ibid., 18.

14. Minutes, 1871 Annual Meeting, *TAMA* 22 (1871): 41.

15. Ibid., 30-31.

16. "The Discussion on the Female Physician Question in the American Medical Association," *BMSJ* 7, no. 22 (June 2, 1871): 371-372.

17. Washington Atlee and D.A. O'Donnell, "Report on Criminal Abortion," *TAMA* 22 (1871): 239-258.

18. "Editorial Notes," *JGSB* 5, no. 1 (July 1871): 48-64, 48-49.

19. "Editorial Notes," *JGSB* 5, no. 2 (August 1871): 123-128.

20. E.D. Churchill, editor, *To Work in the Vineyard of Surgery: The Reminiscences of J. Collins Warren* (Cambridge, Harvard University Press, 1958), 179.

21. According to Horatio's paper, it begins on page 76.

22. HRS, "The Propriety of Operating for Malignant Ovarian Disease," 159-163.

23. Ibid., 165-166.

24. "Editorial Notes," *JGSB* 5, no. 3 (September 1871): 188-192.

25. "Editorial Notes," *JGSB* 5, no. 4 (October 1871): 251-256.

26. Ibid., 256.

27. GSB. Proceedings, meeting of September 26, 1871, *JGSB* 6, no. 1 (January 1872): 2-8.

28. Ibid., 6.

29. GSB. Proceedings, meeting of October 3, 1871, *JGSB* 6, no. 2 (February 1872): 81-93.

30. GSB. Proceedings, meeting of October 17, 1871, *JGSB* 6, no. 3 (March 1872): 161-175, 173.

31. Ibid., 174.

32. "Editorial Notes," *JGSB* 5, no. 5 (November 1871): 306-320.

33. Ibid., 307-308. The footnote read: "*See this Journal, August, 1871, p. 124." Page 124 marked the start of Dr. Eliot's address to the Fellows of the Massachusetts Medical Society describing the changes at the Medical School.

34. Ibid., 310-311.

35. Ibid., 316-317.

36. "Editorial Notes," *JGSB* 5, no. 6 (December 1871): 370-384, 371.

37. Ibid., 380-381.

38. Ibid., 382-383.

39. GSB. Proceedings, meeting of December 5, 1871, *JGSB* 6, no. 6 (June 1872): 401-426, 412-414.

40. Ibid., 415-416.

41. GSB. Proceedings, meeting of December 19, 1871, *JGSB* 7, no. 1 (July 1872): 1-10, 6-9.

42. "Editorial Notes," *JGSB* 6, no. 1 (January 1872): 63-80, 70.

43. Ibid., 72.

44. Winslow Lewis (HRS), "The History and Progress of Gynaecology in New England," *JGSB* 6, no. 2 (February 1872): 94-114.

45. Published in three segments in the *JGSB* 1, no. 2 (August 1869): 103-118; 1, no. 5 (November 1869): 292-309; and 5, no. 6 (December 1871): 334-347.

46. Winslow Lewis (HRS), "The History and Progress of Gynaecology in New England," 107.

47. Ibid., 108.

48. Ibid., 112-113.

49. GSB. Proceedings, meeting of January 16, 1872, *JGSB* 7, no. 2 (August 1872): 81-96, 94-95.

50. "Editorial Notes," *JGSB* 6, no. 2 (February 1872): 141-160, 143-148.

51. The institution described in "Retreat for Intemperate Women," *BMSJ* 69, 14 (November 5, 1863): 286-287, never came to fruition for reasons Horatio described in his Appendix to *Methomania*.

52. "Editorial Notes," February 1872, 148-153.

53. GSB. Proceedings, meeting of February 6, 1872, *JGSB* 7, no. 2 (August 1872): 97-113, 103.

54. GSB. Proceedings, meeting of February 20, 1872, *JGSB* 7, no. 3 (September 1872): 161-176, 163.

55. Ibid., 164.

56. "This fact" probably referred to his father's origination of these ideas, not to other's taking or being given "unwarranted credit" for them.

57. "Editorial Notes," *JGSB* 6, no. 3 (March 1872): 226-240, 232-233.

58. GSB. Proceedings, meeting of March 5, 1872, *JGSB* 7, no. 3 (September 1872): 176-192, 182-183.

59. GSB. Proceedings, meeting of March 19, 1872, *JGSB* 7, no. 4 (October 1872): 241-245.

60. "Editorial Notes," *JGSB* 6, no. 4 (April 1872): 310-320, 310-313.

61. GSB. Proceedings, meeting of April 2, 1872, *JGSB* 7, no. 4 (October 1872): 246-261.

62. GSB. Proceedings, meeting of April 16, 1872, *JGSB* 7, nos. 5 and 6 (November and December 1872): 321-323.

63. GSB. Proceedings, meeting of May 7, 1872, *JGSB* 7, nos. 5 and 6 (November and December 1872): 324-330.

64. "Editorial Notes," *JGSB* 6, no. 5 (May 1872): 393-400.

65. Ibid., 400.

Chapter 17

1. Alexander Stone to Joseph Toner, May 25, 1872, Library of Congress: Toner Collection—Volume 91, 20940-20941.

2. Augusta Caroline Gilmore to John Humphreys Storer, undated (Spring or Summer 1872), SFP.

3. "Editorial Note," *JGSB* 7, no. 1 (July 1872): 80.

4. Augusta Caroline Gilmore to John Humphreys Storer, undated (Summer 1872), SFP.

5. Abby Matilda Storer to John Humphreys Storer, July 15, 1872, SFP.

6. Augusta Caroline Gilmore to John Humphreys Storer, undated (c. July 1872), SFP.

7. "Editorial Note," *JGSB* 7, no. 4 (October 1872): 290.

8. List of Cabin Passengers, North German-Lloyd Steamship *Main*, Sailing for Bremen via Southampton, Saturday, October, 5th, 1872, SFP.

9. Rent receipt, Menton, January 4, 1873, SFP.

10. HRS, "An Improved Method of Examining and Surgically Treating the Female Rectum," *The Lancet* 1 (May 31, 1873): 766-767.

11. Minutes, 1873 Annual Meeting, *TAMA* 24 (1873): 47-48, 55.

12. This date was given by Horatio as part of his input for an 1895 Harvard Alumni document. A newspaper clipping from a Boston newspaper among SFP gave the date as July 21, 1873 and somehow the *Dictionary of American Biography* came up with September 1872.

13. "John Humphreys Storer," *National Cyclopaedia of American Biography* 14 (New York, James T. White, 1917), 344.

14. HRS, *Southern Italy as a Health Station for Invalids* (Naples, R. Marghieri, 1875), 3.

15. Phillips Brooks to HRS, May 16, 1874, SFP.

16. Margaret Susannah Storer to Mrs. Hobart Williams, June 9, 1874, SFP.

17. Minutes, 1875 Annual Meeting, *TAMA* 26 (1875): 49.

18. "Obstetrics Review: H. Debauge, 'The Utero-Ovarian Amputation as Complementary to the Caesarian Operation,'" *Chicago Medical Journal* 38 (March 1879): 324-327, 327.

19. "Report of the Section on Practical Medicine," *TAMA* 26 (1875): 110.

20. HRS, *Southern Italy as a Health Station for Invalids*, Dedication.

21. Ibid., 6.

22. Ibid., 25.

23. Ibid., 37.

24. Ibid., 63-70.

25. J.A. Menzies to HRS, July 24, 1876, SFP.

26. "Forty-fourth Annual Meeting of the British Medical Association: The Dinner," *The British Medical Journal* 2 (August 19, 1876): 238-241, 241.

27. HRS, "The Importance of the Uterine Ebb as a Factor in Pelvic Surgery," *Edinburgh Medical Journal* 22, no. 7 (January 1877): 577-584, 577.

28. HRS to Malcolm Storer, October 30, 1901.

29. "Founders," *Transactions of the American Gynaecological Society* 1 (1877): 15-18, 17.

30. Thanks in part to the GSB, the climate was much more hospitable for gynecology in 1876 than in 1869. There no longer was the large stigma on the specialty of the diseases of women which might have made DHS unwilling to join Horatio in founding the Boston society in 1869.

31. "Proceedings of the First Annual Meeting," *Transactions of the American Gynaecological Society* 1 (1877): 18-28, 19.

32. HRS, "The Importance of the Uterine Ebb as a Factor in Pelvic Surgery," 577.

33. J. Matthews Duncan to HRS, August 14, 1876, SFP.

34. J. Marion Sims to HRS, August 30. 1876, SFP.

35. Charles Brown-Séquard to HRS, September 13, 1876, Jeremy Norman & Co., Inc., San Francisco.

36. J. Marion Sims to HRS, July 16, 1876, reproduced by permission of Philip J. DiSaia, M.D.

37. Marriage of HRS and Frances Sophia MacKenzie, No. 314, September 20, 1876, Register of Marriages for the District of St. Andrew in the Burgh of Edinburgh.

38. Frank Hawkins (Registrar) to HRS, December 7, 1876, SFP.

39. T. Spencer Wells to HRS, October 7, 1876, Countway Library.

40. Niam E. Emmet to HRS, November 10, 1876, SFP.

41. Dr. Mann to HRS, November 20, 1876, SFP.

42. Margaret Susannah Storer to Frances Sophia Storer, December 8, 1876, SFP.

43. "Out" suggests a Cambridge school, possibly Harvard, but unlike for sons, John Humphreys and Malcolm, Horatio never in his later writing proudly provided the date of a Harvard degree for Frank Addison Storer.

44. HRS, "As to the Practically Absolute Safety of Profoundly Induced Anaesthesia in Childbirth, as Compared with its Employment in General Surgery," *Edinburgh Medical Journal* 12, no. 8 (February, 1877): 741-743.

45. Ibid., 742-743.

46. John Codman Ropes to HRS, February 21, 1877, SFP.

47. HRS, "Newport, R.I., as a Winter Resort for Consumptives," *The Sanitarian* 1 (New Series), no. 4 (January 25, 1883): 49-52, 50.

Chapter 18

1. HRS to Joseph M. Toner, September 1, 1877, Library of Congress—Toner Folio 20977-20978.

2. HRS to Joseph M. Toner, October 2, 1877, Library of Congress—Toner Folio 20979-20980.

3. Joseph M. Toner, "A Sketch of the Life of Horatio Robinson Storer, M.D.," Reprint from *The Memorial Volume of the Rocky Mountain Medical Association*, 5. The reprint is available at the Countway Library and numerous other repositories.

4. HRS to Malcolm Storer, October 30, 1901.

5. John Codman Ropes to James Read Chadwick (with copy of Storer letter), September 3, 1877, Countway Library.

6. HRS to James Read Chadwick, September 4, 1877, Countway Library.

7. HRS to James Read Chadwick, November 2, 1877, Countway Library.

8. Levi Farr Warner to HRS, December 13, 1877, Countway Library.

9. HRS to John Codman Ropes, January 2, 1877 [1878], Countway Library.

10. GSB. Transactions, meeting of January 1, 1878, *American Journal of Obstetrics* 12, no. 4 (October 1879): 795.

11. The 78th meeting, October 8, 1872, was the last reported in the *JGSB*.

12. John L. Sullivan to James Read Chadwick, January 14, 1878, Countway Library.

13. "H.R.S. L.F.W." referred to Horatio and Dr. Levi Farr Warner.

14. HRS to Malcolm Storer, October 30, 1901.

15. Charles Brown-Séquard to HRS, February 19, 1878, Countway Library.

16. Fordyce Barker to HRS, February 25, 1878, Countway Library.

17. HRS to Joseph M. Toner, March 12, 1878, Library of Congress—Toner Folio 20984-20985.

18. HRS, "Upon the Arsenical Atmosphere and Arsenical Hot Spring of the Solfatara at Pozzuoli (Near Naples) in the Treatment of Consumptives," *The Lancet* (September 29, 1877): 456-458. Horatio also presented this paper at the second meeting of the resumed Gynaecological Society of Boston and it was published as "Upon the Treatment of Strumous Disease by What May be called the Solfatara Method," *BMSJ* 94, no. 26 (June 27, 1878): 831-838.

19. December 17, 1877 Codicil to Last Will and Testament, DHS (March 26, 1804-September 10, 1891), Massachusetts Supreme Judicial Court Archives.

20. B.F. Beardsley to HRS, May 6, 1878, Countway Library.

21. B.F. Beardsley to HRS. H. McGrew to HRS, November 6, 1877, Countway Library.

22. HRS, "The Frequently Gynaecological Origin of Inherited Forms of Strumous Disease (Especially Phthisis), and the Consequent Indications for Treatment," *TAMA* 29 (1878): 421-432.

23. Minutes of the Section on Obstetrics and Diseases of Women and Children, *TAMA* 29 (1878): 365-371, 370.

24. HRS to Joseph M. Toner, June 15, 1878, Library of Congress—Toner Folio 20987-20988.

25. Henry Ingersoll Bowditch, "Letter from Buffalo," *BMSJ* 98, no. 24 (June 13, 1878): 788-789.

26. Henry Ingersoll Bowditch to HRS, July 17, 1878, Countway Library.

27. HRS, "New or Unappreciated Aids in the Treatment of Strumous Disease," *Virginia Medical Monthly* 6, no. 1 (April 1879): 1-7.

28. Ibid., 7.

29. Spencer F. Baird to HRS, March 6, 1878, Countway Library.

30. Spencer F. Baird to HRS, April 9, 1878, Dickinson College Library.

31. Overseers of Harvard University to HRS (Copy), undated with "Answered 13 Nov, 1878." written at bottom, SFP.

32. GSB. Transactions, meeting of January 2, 1879, *American Journal of Obstetrics* 12, no. 4 (October 1879): 795-796.

33. HRS, "The New 'Protective' Principle in Public Sanitation," *The Sanitarian* 7, no. 72 (March 1879): 97-106.

34. Ibid., 97-98. The footnote following "foreign journal" read: "*Edinburgh Medical Journal*, April, 1878, p. 865."

35. Ibid., 105.

36. GSB. Transactions, meeting of March 6, 1879, *American Journal of Obstetrics* 12, no. 4 (October 1879): 803.

37. GSB. Transactions, meeting of May 1, 1879, *American Journal of Obstetrics* 13, no. 1 (January 1880): 177-182.

38. GSB. Transactions, meeting of June 5, 1879, *American Journal of Obstetrics* 13, no. 1 (January 1880): 185-186.

39. HRS, "The New Principle of 'Protective' (Private) Sanitation in Its Relations to Public Hygiene," *TAMA* 30 (1879): 357-381.

40. E.S. Lewis, "Address in Obstetrics and Diseases of Women and Children," *TAMA* 30 (1879): 227-240, 231.

41. "Newport," *Providence Daily Journal*, June 10, 1879.

42. GSB. Transactions, meeting of July 1879, *American Journal of Obstetrics* 13, no. 1 (January 1880): 191-194.

43. Ibid., 193.

44. GSB. Transactions, meeting of August 5, 1879, *American Journal of Obstetrics* 13, no. 2 (April 1880): 404-408.

45. Spencer F. Baird to HRS, October 8, 1880, MHS: Agnes Storer Autograph Collection.

46. HRS to Spencer F. Baird, December 8, 1880, Smithsonian Institution Archives, Record Unit 7002, S.F. Baird Collection, Box 34.

47. HRS to Spencer F. Baird, December 17 1880, Smithsonian Institution Archives, Record Unit 7002, S.F. Baird Collection, Box 34.

48. HRS, "Sanitary Protection in Newport," *American Public Health Association: Public Health Papers and Reports* 6, (1880): 209-216, 215-216.

49. It is now known as the Hunter House.

50. Fortuna Menella to HRS, April 19, 1881, SFP. An attached note indicates that Horatio contributed 150 lira.

51. William Turner to HRS, June 28, 1880 [1881 postmark], SFP.

52. HRS, "Sanitary Protection at Newport, R. I.," *The Sanitarian* 9, no. 98 (May 1881): 193-200, 200.

53. HRS, "Anticipatory Treatment of Local Epidemics," An address to the Rhode Island Medical Society sometime after March 11, 1886 (the date of the last case discussed) and published as a pamphlet that is included in the SFP.

54. Notice, December 1, 1881, Countway Library.

55. HRS to Samuel D. Gross, September 20, 1882, College of Physicians of Philadelphia—Gross Library MS Collection.

56. Joseph M. Toner, "A Sketch of the Life of Horatio Robinson Storer, M.D."

57. Samuel D. Gross to HRS, September 24, 1882, Jeremy Norman & Co., Inc., San Francisco.

58. "The American Surgical Association," *BMSJ* 108, no. 24 (June 14, 1883): 561.

59. HRS to Agnes Storer, December 24, 1882, SFP.

60. HRS, "Newport, R.I., as a Winter Resort for Consumptives," *The Sanitarian* 11, nos. 119-121 (January 11, 18, and 25, 1883): 17-19; 37-39; 49-52.

61. J. Hilgard Tyndale, "Concerning Newport, R. I., As a Resort for Consumptives," *BMSJ* 108, no. 8 (February 22, 1883): 188-189.

62. HRS, "Concerning Newport, R. I., As a Resort for Consumptives," *BMSJ* 108, no. 12 (March 22, 1883): 282-284.

63. J. Hilgard Tyndale, "Concerning Newport, R. I., As a Resort for Consumptives," *BMSJ* 108, no. 14 (April 5, 1883): 331-332.

64. HRS, "A Few Questions for Dr. Tyndale Concerning Newport, R. I., As a Resort for Consumptives," *BMSJ* 108, no. 17 (April 26, 1883): 404-405.

65. "Proceedings of the Association of Medical Superintendents," *American Journal of Insanity* 41, no. 3 (January 1884): 247-325.

66. W. B. Goldsmith, "A Case of Moral Insanity," *American Journal of Insanity* 40, no. 2 (October 1883): 162-177.

67. "Proceedings of the Association of Medical Superintendents," 281-284.

68. Thaddeus A. Reamy, "Battey, Robert (1828-1895)," Howard A. Kelly and Walter L. Burrage, *Dictionary of American Medical Biography* (New York, Appleton, 1928), 74.

69. "Proceedings of the Association of Medical Superintendents," 324.

70. HRS to Joseph M. Toner, April 9, 1888, Library of Congress—Toner Folio 21013-21014.

71. Msgr. Cleary to HRS, July 10, 1883, John J. Burns Library, Boston College.

72. HRS, "The Mild Winter Climate of Newport, R.I., As the Effect of the Gulf Stream," *Medical Record* 24, no. 25 (December 22, 1883): 679-681.

73. Richard Manning Hodges to DHS, April 6, 1884, Countway Library.

74. "Necrology: David Humphreys Storer, M.D., LL.D. and Ex-President," *JAMA* 17, no. 14 (October 3, 1891): 533-534, 534.

75. Richard Manning Hodges to DHS, April 6, 1884.

Chapter 19

1. HRS, "Address," *First Annual Report of the Newport Historical Society* (Newport, John P. Sanborn, Printer, 1886), 28-37.

2. Ibid., 28-30.

3. Ibid., 34. His footnote read: "*Since the above was written, the Prohibitory Amendment to the Constitution has been adopted by Rhode Island, in part through Newport influence."

4. Longhand drafts of both Clarke histories exist in the SFP. They may have been the basis for a brief paper on Clarke presented to the American Medical Association in Newport by a prominent lawyer which will be discussed.

5. John P. Reynolds to HRS, September 12, 1885, Countway Library.

6. HRS, "A Sea Change," *Philadelphia Medical Times* 16, no. 2 (October 1885) 51-52.

7. HRS to Robert Treat Paine, November 9, 1885, MHS: R.T. Paine II Collection.

8. HRS to Joseph M. Toner, April 5, 1886, Library of Congress—Toner Folio 21000-21001.

9. HRS, "The Medals, Jetons and Tokens Illustrative of Midwifery and the Diseases of Women," *New England Medical Monthly* 6 (1886-1887): 78-102.

10. "Officers and Council," *Proceedings of the Newport Natural History Society 1888-1891* (April 1892).

11. "Autobiography of Capt. Nathaniel E. Atwood, of Provincetown, Mass.: Section IV. The Fishermen of the United States," 168.

12. Simeon L. Deyo, "Nathaniel E. Atwood," *History of Barnstable County* (New York, H.W. Blake & Co., 1890), 995-997, 996.

13. Nathan S. Davis to HRS, June 17, 1886, Countway Library.

14. "Section V-Gynaecology: Officers," *Transactions of the Ninth International Medical Congress* (1888): 509.

15. HRS, "The Importance and Eradication of Syphilis," *JAMA* 10, no. 8 (February 25, 1888): 221-224.

16. HRS, "The Medals, Jetons, and Tokens Illustrative of Sanitation," *The Sanitarian* 18, no. 210 (May 1887): 428-450.

17. HRS, "The Medals, Jetons, and Tokens Illustrative of the Science of Medicine," *American Journal of Numismatics* 23, no. 3 (January 1889): 59-61.

18. GSB. Transactions, meeting of November 9, 1886, *JAMA* 8, no. 10 (March 5, 1887): 278-279.

19. J.E. Kelly, "The Ethics of Abortion, As a Method of Treatment in Legitimate Practice," *JAMA* 7, no. 19 (November 6, 1886): 505-509. Horatio was not mentioned as being one of the discussants and surely was not present when it was read.

20. Ibid., 509. Stress added.

21. GSB. Transactions, meeting of September 9, 1886, *JAMA* 7, no. 19 (November 6, 1886): 529-531, 529.

22. HRS to Joseph M. Toner, September 5, 1887, Library of Congress—Toner Folio 21023b; January 8, 1889.

23. Henry Orlando Marcy, "Presidential Address," *Transactions of the Ninth International Medical Congress* (1888), 510.

24. HRS to Joseph M. Toner, March 23, 1888, Library of Congress—Toner Folio 21011-21012.

25. HRS to Joseph M. Toner, April 9, 1888; May 14, 1888; June 5, 1888, Library of Congress—Toner Folios 21013-21014, 21015-21016, and 21017-21018.

26. HRS to Joseph M. Toner, April 9, 1888.

27. HRS to Joseph M. Toner, June 5, 1888.

28. "Society Proceedings: Thirty-ninth Annual Meeting," *JAMA* 10, no. 22 (June 2, 1888): 671-700, 695, .

29. HRS to Joseph M. Toner, June 28, 1888, Library of Congress—Toner Folio 21021.

30. HRS, "The Medallic Medical History of the United States," *Transactions of the Rhode Island Medical Society* 4, part 3, (1891): 1-4 (of journal reprint), 1.

31. GSB. Transactions, meeting of "second Thursday of October, 1883," *JAMA* 12, no. 13 (March 30, 1889): 462-465, 463.

32. HRS to Dr. Draper, January 11, 1889, Countway Library.

33. HRS to Joseph M. Toner, February 28, 1889, Library of Congress—Toner Folio 21026.

34. "Association News," *JAMA* 12, no. 10 (March 9, 1889): 348-349.

35. HRS, "The Medals of Benjamin Rush, Obstetrician," *JAMA* 13, no. 10 (September 7, 1889): 330-335.

36. HRS to Joseph M. Toner, April 3, 1889, Library of Congress—Toner Folio 21027-21029.

37. Rush was America's most famous physician in the early years of the nation and was a signer of the Declaration of Independence.

38. Henry J. Bigelow, "History of the Discovery of Modern Anaesthesia," Edward H. Clarke, editor, *A Century of American Medicine* (Philadelphia, H.C. Lea, 1876), 73-112.

39. Henry Ingersoll Bowditch to HRS, October 11, 1889, Countway Library.

40. "Official Report of the Fortieth Annual Meeting," *JAMA* 13, no. 3 (July 20, 1889): 97-104, 104.

41. N.S. Davis to Henry Ingersoll Bowditch, July 20, 1889, Countway Library—Uncatalogued Bowditch File.

42. "Official Report of the Fortieth Annual Meeting," *JAMA* 13, no. 2 (July 13, 1889): 60-68; *JAMA* 13, no. 3 (July 20, 1889): 97-104.

43. John H. Hollister to HRS, July 23, 1889, Library of Congress—Toner Folio Vol. 80-16903.

44. HRS to Joseph M. Toner, July 29, 1889, Library of Congress—Toner Folio 21034.

45. John H. Hollister to Joseph M. Toner, August 3, 1889, Library of Congress—Toner Folio Vol. 80-16907.

46. HRS to Joseph M. Toner, August 6, 1889, Library of Congress—Toner Folio 21035-21036.

47. William P. Sheffield, "John Clarke, Physician, Philanthropist, Preacher and Patriot," *JAMA* 13, no. 8 (August 24, 1889): 253-257.

48. HRS to Joseph M. Toner, August 26, 1889, Library of Congress—Toner Folio 21037.

49. HRS to Joseph M. Toner, September 26 1889, Library of Congress—Toner Folio 21038.

50. Henry Orlando Marcy, notes in the possession of Henry Orlando Marcy, IV. Dr. Marcy was to get the honor a year later.

51. "Necrology: Dr. L. F. Warner," *JAMA* 13, no. 20 (November 16, 1889): 720-721.

52. "Handwritten list of contributors," Countway Library.

53. Malcolm Storer, "Malcolm Storer," *Annals of the Storer Family*, 67.

Chapter 20

1. The bulk of the letters to Horatio are at the Countway Library and others are among the SFP.

2. L.S. Pilcher to HRS, March 10, 1890, Countway Library.

3. Agnes Storer, "Diary," June 11, 1890 to September 14, 1890, SFP. The diaries consist of three notebooks covering 1890 to 1900 and annual volumes from 1900 to 1941.

4. HRS to the Editor of the *Newport Daily News*, May 11, 1918. Published in the paper on the same date.

5. Agnes Storer, "Diary," August 28, 1890.

6. Malcolm Storer, "Horatio Robinson Storer, '50," *Harvard Graduates' Magazine* 31, no. 123 (March 1923): 361-367, 363.

7. Sarah Hoar Storer to Agnes Storer, Jan 24, 1891, SFP.

8. James Clarke White, "Commemorative Sketch of Dr. Storer," *Proceedings of the Boston Society of Natural History* 25, no. 23 (May 1892): 347-353, 353.

9. Agnes Storer, "Diary," February 8, 1892.

10. Henry Orlando Marcy to HRS, May 11, 1891, Countway Library.

11. HRS, "The Medals Commemorative of Natural Scientists," *Proceedings of the Newport Natural History Society* (1888-1891): 3-5.

12. Anita Tyng to HRS, November 3, 1893, Countway Library.

13. "Deaths: Anita E. Tyng," *JAMA* 61, no. 25 (December 20, 1913): 2256.

14. HRS to Charles W. Eliot, February 20, 1894, Harvard Archives: Eliot Collection.

15. Charles W. Eliot to HRS, February 21, 1894, SFP.

16. "News from the Classes," *Harvard Graduates' Magazine* 3, no. 12 (June 1895): 568.

17. Agnes Storer, "Diary," June 1894 to August 1894.

18. Agnes Storer, "Diary," December 31, 1894.

19. *Class of 1850* (Cambridge, Privately printed for the use of the Class, 1895).

20. HRS to Joseph Henry Thayer, February 21, 1895, Harvard Archives: HUD 250.505, Class of 1850 Secretary's File.

21. Agnes Storer, "Diary," February 28, 1895.

22. Ibid., June 19, 1895.

23. HRS to Joseph M. Toner, April 5, 1896, Library of Congress—Toner Folio 21054.

24. HRS, "The Memorials of Edward Jenner," *JAMA* 27, no. 6 (August 8, 1896): 312-317.

25. Horatio wrote Toner on April 18, 1896 [Library of Congress-Toner Folio 21055] that he was too ill to attend and he had been advised to have Dr. Didama read the paper. Presumably, that happened.

26. HRS, "Edward Jenner as Naturalist," *The Sanitarian* 37 (July, 1896): 110-134. This publication incorrectly lists Horatio as President of the Newport Historical Society instead of the Newport Natural History Society.

27. Stress added.

28. Ibid., 113.

29. Ibid., 134.

30. Joseph H. Hunt to HRS, July 24, 1896, Countway Library.

31. HRS, "Commercial Products of the Sea in their Relations to Newport," *Proceedings of the Newport Natural History Society* (1899): 72-78.

32. HRS, "Criminal Abortion: Its Prevalence, Its Prevention, and Its Relation to the Medical Examiner—Based on the 'Summary of the Vital Statistics of the New England States for the Year 1892' By the Six Secretaries of the New England State Boards of Health."

33. Ibid., 1. James Mohr in *Abortion in America* reported a large drop in criminal abortion by the end of the century. New England may have been atypical, however.

34. Ibid., 6-7.

35. This passage about the Nashville American Medical Association meeting where Horatio was selected to lead the Committee on Criminal Abortion, apparently led James Mohr to incorrectly report that Horatio was in attendance at that meeting. Mohr wrote, "at the AMA meeting in 1857, when Storer called for action, ...," *Abortion in America*, 155.

36. Newport Medical Society to "medical societies and otherwise," August 21, 1897, SFP.

37. The advertising flyer included "Medical Press Notices" for Horatio's 1897 pamphlet, quoting praising passages from the *Texas Medical News*, "*Medical Council, Philadelphia,*" *JAMA*, and *New England Medical Gazette*. The flyer is in the SFP.

38. Daniel G. Brinton to HRS, March 15, 1898, Countway Library.

39. Horatio in his earlier writing had noted the French exception to Catholic reluctance to abort their children.

Chapter 21

1. Agnes Storer, "Diary," entry with date June 23-July 4, 1899.

2. Newport Natural History Society, undated printed notice, SFP.

3. Medical Board of the Newport Hospital to HRS, July 22, 1899, Countway Library.

4. William Overend Priestley to HRS, July 15, 1899, Countway Library.

5. Agnes Storer, "Diary," July 24, 1899.

6. Ibid., August 6, 1899.

7. John Ware to HRS, September 27, 1899, Harvard Archives: HUD 250.505, Class of 1850 Secretary's File, Ware Folder.

8. Malcolm Storer, "Malcolm Storer," *Annals of the Storer Family*, 67.

9. Several letters to William Speck about medical medals track this New York stay, Beinecke Library (Yale): Speck Collection.

10. *Dedication of the New Building of the Boston Medical Library* (Boston, S.J. Parkhill & Co. 1901), SFP and the Countway Library.

11. Ibid., 41.

12. John W. Farlow, *History of the Boston Medical Library* (Norwood, Massachusetts, Plimpton Press, 1918):141-142.

13. HRS to Charles W. Eliot, November 16, 1900. Harvard Archives: Eliot Collection.

14. A brief version of the Committee's report is provided in the *BMSJ* 76, no. 6 (March 14, 1867): 109-114.

15. Agnes Storer, "Diary," January 2, 1901.

16. Ibid., December 24, 1901.

17. HRS to Malcolm Storer, October 30, 1901.

18. Malcolm Storer, "The Teaching of Obstetrics and Gynecology at Harvard."

19. Agnes Storer, "Diary," August 28, 1903.

20. Ibid., November 4, 1903.

21. Ibid., December 25, 1903.

22. HRS, "Race Prejudice," *Newport Daily News* (January 23, 1906).

23. Josephine Silone Yates Mothers' Club to HRS, *Newport Daily News* (February 17, 1906).

24. Agnes Storer, "Diary," April 19, 1907.

25. HRS to Frederick Dickinson Williams, July 4, 1908, Harvard Archives: HUD 250.505, Class of 1850 Secretary's File.

26. "Necrology: Dr. Gustavus Hay," *Transactions of the American Ophthalmological Society* 12, part 1, (1909): 10-13, 11.

27. HRS to Frederick Dickinson Williams, November 12, 1908, Harvard Archives: HUD 250.505, Class of 1850 Secretary's File.

28. HRS to Frederick Dickinson Williams, May 12, 1909, Harvard Archives: HUD 250.505, Class of 1850 Secretary's File.

29. HRS to Hales Wallace Suter, September 11, 1909, Harvard Archives: HUD 250.505, Class of 1850 Secretary's File.

30. Henry Orlando Marcy, "The Early History of Abdominal Surgery in America."

31. A marked up copy of the Marcy paper in the family papers has *four* crossed out and *two* written in. *One* would have been more correct.

32. Presumably, the controversial one that led to the argument with Ellis. The patient rallied but died a day-and-a-half later of a "fright."

33. Henry Orlando Marcy, "The Early History of Abdominal Surgery in America," 601-602. Horatio no doubt rightly shook his head "no" when he read "blindly."

34. Howland Wood to HRS, January 9, 1909, SFP.

35. HRS, "The Medals of Linnaeus," *Proceedings of the International Congress of Numismatics* (Brussels, 1910), 405-425.

36. Agnes Storer, "Diary," December 25, 1909.

37. Esther Morton Smith to HRS, February 27, 1910, SFP.

38. Agnes Storer to Archbishop J.W.H. O'Connell, May 19, 1910, Archives, Archdiocese of Boston (O'Connell Papers, 10:9).

39. Archbishop J.W.H. O'Connell to Agnes Storer, May 20, 1910 (Copy), Archives, Archdiocese of Boston (O'Connell Papers, 10:9).

40. Agnes Storer to Archbishop J.W.H. O'Connell, May 19, 1910.

41. The Constitution and By-Laws of the Medical Guild of St. Thomas Aquin are included among SFP.

42. HRS to Hales Wallace Suter, May 26, 1910, Harvard Archives: HUD 250.505, Class of 1850 Secretary's File.

43. "Deaths: Alexander Johnson Stone, M.D.," *JAMA* 55, no. 5 (July 30, 1910): 417.

44. HRS to Hales Wallace Suter, November 24, 1910, Harvard Archives: HUD 250.505, Class of 1850 Secretary's File.

45. Clipping among SFP.

46. Agnes Storer, "Diary," dates as described.

47. James Joseph Walsh to HRS, August 16, 1911, Countway Library.

48. Thomas Dwight to HRS, July 15, 1911, Countway Library.

49. HRS to James Joseph Walsh, September 12, 1911, Walsh Family Papers. Letter on stationary with black border.

50. Agnes Storer, "Diary," January 9, 1912.

Chapter 22

1. HRS to James Joseph Walsh, September 3, 1912, Walsh Family Papers.

2. "Special Instruction in Medical Science," SFP.

3. *Newport Daily News*, September 12, 1912.

4. HRS, "The Boylston Society Bookplate," *Harvard Graduates Magazine* 21, no. 82 (December 1912): 386.

5. *Newport Daily News*, October 20, 1913.

6. HRS to Classmates, August 25, 1914, Harvard Archives: HUD 250, Class of 1850 Secretary's Record Book. Note from Horatio at bottom of letter says: "notification sent 25 Aug 1914."

7. Joseph Hidden Robinson to HRS, August 26, 1914, Harvard Archives: HUD 250.505, Class of 1850 Secretary's File, Robinson Folder.

8. Thomas Jefferson Coolidge to HRS, August 26, 1914, Harvard Archives: HUD 250.505, Class of 1850 Secretary's File, Coolidge Folder.

9. HRS to the editors of the Quinquennial Catalogue, September 25, 1914, Harvard Archives: HUD 250.505, Class of 1850 Secretary's File.

10. HRS to Francis Charles Foster, September 25, 1914, Harvard Archives: HUD 250.505, Class of 1850 Secretary's File.

11. HJW to HRS, September 18, 1914, Harvard Archives: HUD 250.505, Class of 1850 Secretary's File, Warner Folder.

12. HRS, "News from the Classes," *Harvard Graduates' Magazine* 23, no. 90 (December 1914): 294.

13. HRS, "News from the Classes," *Harvard Graduates' Magazine* 23, no. 92 (June 1915): 676.

14. HRS to Mayor Burlingame, August 27, 1915, *Newport Journal* (September 3, 1915).

15. HRS, "News from the Classes," *Harvard Graduates' Magazine* 24, no. 93 (September 1915): 153.

16. Francis Charles Foster to HRS, September 15, 1915, Harvard Archives: HUD 250.505, Class of 1850 Secretary's File, Foster Folder.

17. Thomas Jefferson Coolidge to HRS, October 26, 1915, MHS: Agnes Storer Autograph Collection.

18. HRS, "News from the Classes," *Harvard Graduates' Magazine* 24, no. 94 (December 1915): 327-328.

19. Thomas Jefferson Coolidge to HRS, December 20, 1915, MHS: Agnes Storer Autograph Collection.

20. Agnes Storer, "Diary," June 13, 1915.

21. HJW to HRS, February 1, 1916, Harvard Archives: HUD 250.505, Class of 1850 Secretary's File, Warner Folder.

22. Thomas Jefferson Coolidge to HRS, March 23, 1916, Harvard Archives: HUD 250.505, Class of 1850 Secretary's File, Coolidge Folder.

23. HJW to HRS, April 1, 1916, Harvard Archives: HUD 250.505, Class of 1850 Secretary's File, Warner Folder.

24. Hermann's *Last Letters* does not appear to have been published. However, a manuscript at the Library of Congress donated by Hermann's grand nephew, Hermann Warner Williams, Jr., probably is this unpublished book.

25. Agnes Storer, "Diary," April 12, 1916.

26. HRS, "News from the Classes," *Harvard Graduates' Magazine* 24, no. 96 (June 1916): 692.

27. *Newport Daily News*, July 16, 1916.

28. Thomas Jefferson Coolidge to HRS, December 6, 1916, MHS: Agnes Storer Autograph Collection.

29. George Woodberry to HRS, December 15, 1916, Harvard Archives: HUD 250.505, Class of 1850 Secretary's File.

30. HRS, "News from the Classes," *Harvard Graduates' Magazine* 25, no. 99 (March 1917): 396-397.

31. Thomas Jefferson Coolidge to HRS, May 29, 1917, Harvard Archives: HUD 250.505, Class of 1850 Secretary's File, Coolidge Folder.

32. HRS, "News from the Classes," *Harvard Graduates' Magazine* 25, no. 100 (June 1917): 554.

33. Office of the President at Harvard to HRS, July 7, 1917, Harvard Archives: Office of the President Correspondence.

34. HRS to Office of the President at Harvard, July 10, 1817, Harvard Archives: HUD 250.505, Class of 1850 Secretary's File.

35. James Joseph Walsh, "American Physician Converts," *Catholic Convert* 4, no. 1 (March 1917): 1-2, & 17, 17.

36. Although Horatio did describe some things as "most important in his life," particularly his time with Simpson, no written statement of his has been located which mentioned this to be his conversion to Catholicism. However, this would only be the first of a number of times that Walsh made this point, and the later claims were that it was from Horatio's lips.

37. HRS to James Joseph Walsh, July 20, 1917, Walsh Family Papers.

38. Agnes Storer, "Diary," December 14, 1917.

39. Ibid., February 27, 1918.

40. HRS to the Editor of the *Newport Daily News*, May 11, 1918. Published in the paper on the same date.

41. Wilfred L. Grenfell to HRS, May 12, 1918, SFP.

42. Horatio must have really felt old as he read this erroneous dating of Horatio's surgical achievements to before the first use of anesthesia.

43. "A Distinguished Nonagerian," *BMSJ* 180, no. 14 (April 3, 1919): 397-398.

44. "Awarded a Medal," *Newport Daily News* (February 18, 1920).

45. HRS to John Woodward Farlow, December 8, 1918, Countway Library.

46. HRS to Fielding Hudson Garrison, June 7, 1919, National Library of Medicine Archives.

Chapter 23

1. "Begins Ninety-first Year," *Newport Daily News* (February 27, 1920).

2. Boston Society of Natural History. Minutes, meeting of July 16, 1845, *Proceedings of the Boston Society of Natural History* 2, no. 7 (July 1845): 51-52, 51.

3. "Harvard's Oldest Graduate," *Boston Post* (April 4, 1920), pp. 45 and 53.

4. Myrick C. Atwood to HRS, April 5, 1920, SFP.

5. Either with Myrick C. Atwood's letter, or later, the letter was returned to Horatio and is with the SFP. It was printed in full in Chapter 4.

6. HRS, "Sun Treatment Endorsed," *Newport Daily News* (April 27, 1920).

7. Agnes Storer, "Diary," November 5 and 12, 1920.

8. HRS, "News from the Classes," *Harvard Graduates' Magazine* 29, no. 115 (March 1921): 408-414.

9. Stress added.

10. "Loving Cup for Dr. Storer," *Newport Herald* (February 28, 1921).

11. HRS, "News from the Classes," *Harvard Graduates' Magazine* 29, no. 116 (June 1921): 619.

12. HRS to James Joseph Walsh, February 1, 1922, Walsh Family Papers.

13. HRS to James Joseph Walsh, February 9, 1922, Walsh Family Papers.

14. HRS to James Joseph Walsh, February 14, 1922, Walsh Family Papers.

15. If only one generation showed an increase in surviving pregnancies amounting to three percent of children this would provide a parent (or two) for 5.9 percent of the next generation, for 11.5 percent of the second generation, for 21.6 percent of the third generation, etc.

16. William R. White, *Rhode Island Medical Journal* 5, no. 2 (whole no. 149) (February 1922): 204.

17. Agnes Storer, "Diary," May 15, 1922.

18. Agnes Storer, "Diary," August 18, 1922.

19. "Dr. Horatio R. Storer," *Newport Mercury* (September 18, 1922).

20. "Dr. H. R. Storer Died Last Night," *Newport Herald* (September 19, 1922).

21. St. Joseph's has a beautiful wooden pulpit dedicated to Horatio which was a gift of his daughter, Agnes.

22. Howland Wood, "Tribute to Dr. Storer," *Newport Herald* (September 21, 1922).

23. Norman Thomas to Agnes Storer, September 25, 1922, SFP.

24. R. Tait McKenzie to Agnes Storer, September 25, 1922. SFP.

25. Agnes Storer to James Joseph Walsh, indecipherable, but probably October 1922, Walsh Family Papers.

26. Agnes Storer to James Joseph Walsh, October 17, 1922, Walsh Family Papers.

27. James Joseph Walsh, "A Great Convert Physician," *Ave Maria* 16 (New Series), no. 20 (November 11, 1922): 619-624, 619-620.

28. HRS, Handwritten note, undated, but probably 1921 or 1922, SFP.

29. Located in Walsh Family Papers.

30. Malcolm Storer, "Horatio Robinson Storer, '50," *Harvard Graduates' Magazine* 31, no. 123 (March 1923): 361-367.

31. Ibid., 366.

32. HRS, *Medicina in nummis* (Boston, Wright & Potter Printing Co., 1931).

INDEX

5/01